A PEOPLE AND A NATION

A PEOPLE

A

AND A NATION
History of the United States

Second Edition   Volume I: To 1877

MARY BETH NORTON
Cornell University

DAVID M. KATZMAN
University of Kansas

PAUL D. ESCOTT
University of North Carolina, Charlotte

HOWARD P. CHUDACOFF
Brown University

THOMAS G. PATERSON
University of Connecticut

WILLIAM M. TUTTLE, JR.
University of Kansas

HOUGHTON MIFFLIN COMPANY · BOSTON
Dallas   Geneva, Illinois   Lawrenceville, New Jersey   Palo Alto

Mary Beth Norton

Now a professor of history at Cornell University, Mary Beth Norton was born in Ann Arbor, Michigan, and received her B.A. from the University of Michigan (1964). Harvard University awarded her the Ph.D. in 1969, the year her dissertation won the Allan Nevins Prize. Her writing includes *The British-Americans: The Loyalist Exiles in England, 1774–1789* (1972) and *Liberty's Daughters: The Revolutionary Experience of American Women, 1750–1800* (1980). With Carol Berkin she has edited a book of original essays, *Women of America: A History* (1979). Her many articles have appeared in such journals as the *William and Mary Quarterly*, *Signs*, and the *American Historical Review*. Mary Beth has served on the National Council on the Humanities. From 1983 to 1985 she was president of the Berkshire Conference of Women Historians, and in 1984 she was elected vice president for research of the American Historical Association. Besides holding honorary degrees from Siena College and Marymount Manhattan College, she has received research assistance from the Shelby Cullom Davis Center, Charles Warren Center, National Endowment for the Humanities, and the American Antiquarian Society.

David M. Katzman

A graduate of Queens College (B.A., 1963) and the University of Michigan (Ph.D., 1969), David M. Katzman is now a professor of history at the University of Kansas. Born in New York City, David is known for his work in labor, social and black history. His book *Seven Days a Week: Women and Domestic Service in Industrializing America* (1978) won the Philip Taft Labor History Prize. He has also written *Before the Ghetto: Black Detroit in the Nineteenth Century* (1973) and contributed to *Three Generations in Twentieth-Century America: Family, Community and the Nation* (Second Edition, 1981). With William M. Tuttle, Jr., David has edited *Plain Folk: The Life Stories of Undistinguished Americans* (1981). The Guggenheim Foundation, National Endowment for the Humanities, and Ford Foundation have awarded him research assistance. He has written articles for the *Dictionary of American Biography* and has served as the associate editor of the journal *American Studies*. For 1984–1985 he was Visiting Professor of Economic and Social History, University of Birmingham, England.

Paul D. Escott

Born and reared in the Midwest (St. Louis, Missouri), Paul D. Escott studied in New England and the South. His interest in southern history and the Civil War era probably began with southern parents, but it became conscious at Harvard College (B.A., 1969) and matured at Duke University (Ph.D., 1974). Now a professor of history at the University of North Carolina, Charlotte, Paul has written *After Secession: Jefferson Davis and the Failure of Confederate Nationalism* (1978), *Slavery Remembered: A Record of Twentieth-Century Slave Narratives* (1979), and *Many Excellent People: Power and Privilege in North Carolina, 1850–1900* (1985). Paul's articles have appeared in such journals as *Civil War History*, *Georgia Historical Quarterly*, and *Journal of Southern History*. Active in the profession, he has served on committees of the Southern Historical Association. Fellowships from the Whitney M. Young, Jr., Memorial Foundation, the American Philosophical Society, and the Rockefeller Foundation have aided his research.

Howard P. Chudacoff

A professor of history at Brown University, Howard P. Chudacoff was born in Omaha, Nebraska, and received his degrees from the University of Chicago (A.B., 1965; Ph.D., 1969). At Brown he has co-chaired the American Civilization Program. His books include *Mobile Americans: Residential and Social Mobility in Omaha, 1880–1920* (1972) and the *Evolution of American Urban Society* (Third Edition, 1986). His many articles on topics in urban and social history have appeared in such journals as the *Journal of Family History, Reviews in American History,* and the *Journal of American History.* Howard has lectured and presented papers at many universities and historical meetings, and has received research awards from the Rockefeller Foundation, National Endowment for the Humanities, and the Population Studies and Research Center of Brown University.

Thomas G. Paterson

Thomas G. Paterson was born in Oregon City, Oregon. He graduated from the University of New Hampshire (B.A., 1963) before earning his doctorate from the University of California, Berkeley in 1968. He is now a professor of history at the University of Connecticut. His books include *Soviet-American Confrontation* (1973), *On Every Front* (1979), and *American Foreign Policy: A History* (Second Edition, 1983). Among his edited scholarship is *Major Problems in American Foreign Policy* (Second Edition, 1984). The author of over thirty articles, Tom's work has appeared in the *American Historical Review* and the *Journal of American History.* He has served on the editorial boards of the *Journal of American History* and *Diplomatic History,* on committees of the Organization of American Historians and Society for Historians of American Foreign Relations, and on the Board of Trustees of Stonehill College. Tom has also directed National Endowment for the Humanities Summer Seminars for College Teachers. His research has been assisted by the American Philosophical Society, Institute for the Study of World Politics, National Endowment for the Humanities, and others.

William M. Tuttle, Jr.

A native of Detroit, Michigan, who graduated from Denison University (1959) and the University of Wisconsin, Madison (Ph.D., 1967), William M. Tuttle, Jr. is now a professor of history at the University of Kansas. Bill has written the award-winning *Race Riot: Chicago in the Red Summer of 1919* (1970) and has edited *W. E. B. Du Bois* (1973) and, with David M. Katzman, *Plain Folk* (1982). As an historical consultant, he has helped prepare several public television documentaries and docudramas. Bill's numerous articles have appeared in the *Journal of Negro History, Labor History, Agricultural History, Technology and Culture,* and the *Journal of American History.* The Guggenheim Foundation, National Endowment for the Humanities, and American Council of Learned Societies have provided him with research assistance. He has also been awarded fellowships from the Institute of Southern History at Johns Hopkins University, Charles Warren Center at Harvard, and Stanford Humanities Center. He was elected to the Nominating Board of the Organization of American Historians.

ABOUT THE COVER

The Little Navigator.   This shipmaster sighting the sun was carved about 1810 for use as a trade sign. It hung over the shop of James Fales, a maker of navigational instruments, in Newport, Rhode Island. In the 1820s, the sign was moved by Fales's son to hang over his watch and clock shop in New Bedford, Massachusetts. It can now be seen at the Old Dartmouth Historical Society Whaling Museum, New Bedford.

Printed in the U.S.A.
Library of Congress Catalog Card Number: 85-60315
ISBN: 0-395-37936-9
  BCDEFGHIJ-D-89876

CONTENTS

Chapter 1

THE MEETING OF OLD WORLD AND NEW, 1492–1650

Chapter 2

AMERICAN SOCIETY TAKES SHAPE, 1650–1720

Chapter 3

GROWTH AND DIVERSITY, 1720–1770

Chapter 4

SEVERING THE BONDS OF EMPIRE, 1754–1774

Chapter 5

A REVOLUTION, INDEED, 1775–1783

Chapter 6

FORGING A NATIONAL REPUBLIC, 1776–1789

Chapter 7

POLITICS AND SOCIETY IN THE EARLY REPUBLIC, 1790–1800

Chapter 12

REFORM, POLITICS, AND EXPANSION, 1824–1844

Chapter 13

TERRITORIAL EXPANSION AND SLAVERY: THE ROAD TO WAR, 1845–1861

Chapter 14

TRANSFORMING FIRE: THE CIVIL WAR, 1861–1865

RECONSTRUCTION BY TRIAL AND ERROR, 1865–1877

APPENDIX

MAPS/CHARTS

PREFACE

The generous reception given to the first edition of this volume by our colleagues in history, the encouragement and suggestions of the many instructors who used the book in their classrooms, and the appearance of new scholarship in the last few years have afforded us the opportunity to improve and update *A People and a Nation*. In this second edition we have retained and strengthened those characteristics of the first edition that students and faculty found attractive. As teachers and students we are always recreating our past, rediscovering the personalities and events that have shaped us, inspired us, and bedeviled us. This book is our rediscovery of America's past—its people and the nation they founded and sustained. Sometimes we find this history comforting, sometimes disturbing. As with our own personal experience, it is both triumphant and tragic, filled with injury as well as healing. As a mirror on our lives, it is always significant.

We draw on recent research as well as on seasoned, authoritative works to offer a comprehensive book that tells the whole story of American history. Presidential and party politics, congressional legislation, Supreme Court decisions, diplomacy and treaties, wars and foreign interventions, economic patterns, and state and local government have been the stuff of American history for generations. Into this traditional fabric we weave social history, broadly defined. We investigate the history of the majority of Americans—women—and of minorities. We study the history of social classes, and we illuminate the private, everyday life of the American people.

Characteristics of the Book

From the ordinary to the exceptional—the factory worker, the slave, the office secretary, the local merchant, the small farmer, the plantation owner, the ward politician, the president's wife, the film star, the scientist, the army general—Americans have had personal stories that have intersected with the public policies of their government. Whether victors or victims, all have been actors in their own right, with feelings, ideas, and aspirations that have fortified them in good times and bad. All are part of the American story; all speak here through excerpts from their letters, diaries, and other writings, and oral histories.

Several questions guided our telling of this narrative. On the official, or public, side of American history, we emphasize Americans' expectations of their governments and the everyday practice of those local, state, and federal institutions. We identify the mood and mentality of an era, in which Americans reveal what they think about themselves and their public officials. And in our discussion of foreign policy we particularly probe its domestic sources.

Major Themes

In the social and economic spheres, we emphasize patterns of change in the population, geographic mobility, and people's adaptation to new environments. We study the interactions of people of different races, ethnic backgrounds, religions, and genders, the social divisions that emerged, and the efforts made, often in reform movements, to heal them. As well, we focus on the effects of technological development on the economy, the worker and workplace, and lifestyles.

In the private, everyday life of the family and the home, we pay particular attention to sex roles, childbearing and childrearing, and diet and dress. We ask how Americans have chosen to entertain themselves, as participants or spectators, with sports, music, the graphic arts, reading, theater, film, and television. Throughout American history, of course, this private part of American life and public policy have interacted and influenced one another.

Students and instructors have liked our use of clear, concrete language, and have commented on how enjoyable the book is to read. They have also told us that we challenged them to think about the meaning of American history, not just to memorize it; to confront our own interpretations and at the same time to understand and respect the views of others; and to show how an historian's mind works to ask questions and to tease conclusions out of a mass of information.

For this revised edition, the authors met to discuss at length the themes and questions of the book. We reviewed numerous reports from instructors and worked to incorporate their suggestions. We also researched the most recent scholarship, alert to new evidence and new interpretations. As well, we examined every line of the text with an eye to conciseness, clarity, and readability. In the course of writing, the six of us read and reread one another's drafts and debated one another with a friendly spririt and mutual respect that strengthened us as scholars.

Several changes in this second edition stand out. First, that part of the book devoted to the post-1941 years has been substantially reorganized to match the way most instructors teach that **Changes in the** period. All of the material on the **Second Edition** Second World War—domestic and foreign—is now in Chapter 28. The Truman years are covered in Chapter 29 and the Eisenhower years in 30. They are followed by a chapter (31) on the social history of the postwar period. Chapter 32, a foreign policy segment, has been recast to emphasize the origins, experience, and aftermath of the Vietnam War. Chapter 33 then treats the domestic effects of the war and political and economic events for 1961–1973, whereas Chapter 34 does so for 1973–1981. Finally, an altogether new Chapter 35 studies the Reagan years and the interaction among social, political, economic, and diplomatic currents in the 1980s.

Second, Chapter 1 has been significantly reworked to provide the stories of the three divergent cultures— Native American, African, and European—that intersected in the New World to mold the early history of the United States. Third, we have expanded our coverage of Asians and Hispanics, constitutional history, and the nuclear arms race. Fourth, throughout the book we have explained the significance of gender in employment—the sexual division of labor. Fifth, we have set out more prominently the themes of each chapter, following the opening vignette. And, finally, *A People and a Nation* has a new look. Not only have new illustrations and maps been added— they have also been improved through the use of full color. Full color makes the maps (all ninety of them) easier to read and understand and the illustrations (all historically accurate because they are contemporaneous with a chapter's period) truer prints of their originals.

As in the first edition, each chapter opens with the story of an American, ordinary or exceptional, whose experience was representative of the times or whose commentary facilitates our understanding of the chapter themes, which immediately follow this vignette. To help students study and **Study Aids** review, we use bold-typed notes— like the one here—to highlight key personalities, events, concepts, and trends. Significant concepts and words are defined and italicized; important events are listed in a chart near the end of most chapters; and suggested readings for further study close each chapter. The Appendix, updated and expanded, is a unique compendium providing a historical overview of the American people and their nation.

To make the book as useful as possible for students and instructors, several learning and teaching ancillaries are available, including a *Study Guide* and *Computerized Study Guide*, an *In-* **Ancillaries** *structor's Manual*, a *Test Items* file, a *Computerized Test Items* file, and *Map Transparencies*. The *Study Guide*, which was prepared by George Warren and Cynthia Ricketson of Central Piedmont Community College, includes an introductory chapter on study techniques for history students, as well as learning objectives and a thematic guide for each chapter in the text and exercises on evaluating and using information and on finding the main idea in passages from the text, as well as test questions on the content of each chapter. The *Study Guide* is also available in a computerized version that provides the student with tutorial instruction. The *Instructor's Manual*, by Richard Rowe of Golden West College, contains chapter outlines, suggestions for lectures and discussion, and lists of audio-visual resources. The accompanying *Test Items* file, also by Professor Rowe, offers more than 1,500 multiple-choice and essay questions and more than 700 identification terms. The test items are available to adoptors on computer tape and disk. In addition, there is a set of forty full-color map transparencies available on adoption.

Though each of us feels answerable for the whole, we take primary responsibility for particular chapters: Mary Beth Norton, Chapters 1–7, David M. Katzman, Chapters 8–10, 12; Paul D. Escott, Chapters 11, 13–15; Howard P. Chudacoff, Chapters 16–21, 24; Thomas G. Paterson, Chapters 22–23, 25, 27, 30, 32, and part of 35; William M. Tuttle, Jr., Chapters 26, 28–29, 31, 33–34, and part of 35. Thomas G. Paterson also served as the coordinating author and prepared the Appendix.

Many instructors have read and criticized the successive drafts of our manuscript.

Acknowledgments

Their constructive suggestions have informed and improved this second edition. We heartily thank:

John K. Alexander, *University of Cincinnati*
Roberta Alexander, *University of Dayton*
John Borden Armstrong, *Boston University*
James Barrett, *University of Illinois*
John Britton, *Francis Marion College*
Richard Burns, *California State University, Los Angeles*
Ballard Campbell, *Northeastern University*
Ron Carden, *South Plains College*
Patricia Cohen, *University of California, Santa Barbara*
Frank Costigliola, *University of Rhode Island*
Jay Coughtry, *University of Nevada, Las Vegas*
William Fleming, *Pan American University*
James Gormly, *Pan American University*
Maurine Greenwald, *University of Pittsburgh*
Linda Guerrero, *Palomar College*
James Hijiya, *Southeastern Massachusetts University*
Richard J. Hopkins, *Ohio State University*

George Juergens, *Indiana University*
Harry Lupold, *Lakeland Community College*
Bart McCash, *Middle Tennessee State University*
John Muldowny, *University of Tennessee*
Leonard Murphy, *San Antonio College*
Paul L. Murphy, *University of Minnesota*
Philip Nicholson, *Nassau Community College*
Lawrence Powell, *Tulane University*
Howard Rabinowitz, *University of New Mexico*
Roy Rosenzweig, *George Mason University*
James H. Sasser, *Central Piedmont Community College*
Constance Schulz, *University of South Carolina*
Peter Shattuck, *California State University, Sacramento*
Rebecca Shoemaker, *Indiana State University*
Harvard Sitkoff, *University of New Hampshire*
William R. Swagerty, *University of Idaho*
Emory Thomas, *University of Georgia*
James Walter, *Sinclair Community College*
Nelson Woodard, *California State University, Fullerton*

We acknowledge with thanks as well the contributions of Ruth Alexander, Nancy Fisher Chudacoff, J. Garry Clifford, Christopher Collier, Mary Ellen Erickson, Elizabeth French, William Gienapp, James L. Gormly, Frederick Hoxie, Nathan Huggins, Jacqueline Jones, Sharyn A. Katzman, Freeman Meyer, William H. Moore, Holly Izard Paterson, Shirley Rice, Barney J. Rickman, III, Janice Riley, Daniel Usner, Deborah White, David Wyllie, and Thomas Zoumaras. We also appreciate the continued guidance and generous assistance of the staff of the Houghton Mifflin Company.

T.G.P.

A PEOPLE AND A NATION

THE MEETING OF OLD WORLD AND NEW
1492–1650

CHAPTER 1

"*It spread over* the people as great destruction," the old man told the priest. "Some it quite covered [with pustules] on all parts—their faces, their heads, their breasts. . . . There was great havoc. Very many died of it. They could not stir; they could not change position, nor lie on one side, nor face down, nor on their backs. And if they stirred, much did they cry out. Great was its destruction. Covered, mantled with pustules, very many people died of them. And very many starved; there was death from hunger, [for] none could take care of [the sick]; nothing could be done for them."

It was, by European reckoning, September 1520. Spanish troops led by Hernando Cortés had abandoned the Aztec capital of Tenochtitlan after failing in their first attempt to gain control of the city. But they had unknowingly left behind the smallpox germs that would ensure their eventual triumph. By the time the Spaniards returned three months later, the great epidemic described above had fatally weakened Tenochtitlan's inhabitants. Even so, the city held out for months against the Spanish siege. But in the Aztec year Three House, on the day One Serpent (August 1521), Tenochtitlan finally surrendered. The Spaniards had conquered Mexico, and on the site of the Aztec capital they built what is now Mexico City.

After many millennia of separation, inhabitants of the Eastern Hemisphere—the so-called Old World—had encountered the residents of the Americas, with catastrophic results for the latter and untold benefits for the former. By the time Spanish troops occupied Tenochtitlan, the age of European expansion and colonization was already well under way. Over the next three hundred and fifty years, Europeans would spread their civilization across the globe. They would come to dominate native peoples in Asia and Africa as well as in the New World of the Western Hemisphere. The history of the thirteen tiny English colonies in North America that eventually became the United States must be seen in this broader context of worldwide exploration and exploitation.

That context is complex. After 1400, European nations sought to improve their positions relative to neighboring countries not only by fighting wars on their own continent but also by acquiring valuable colonies elsewhere in the world. Simultaneously, the warring tribes and nations of Asia, Africa, and the Americas attempted to use the alien intruders to their own advantage or, failing that, to adapt successfully to the Europeans' presence in their midst. All the participants in the resulting interaction of divergent cultures were indelibly affected by the process. The contest among Europeans for control of the Americas and Africa changed the course of history in all four continents. Strategies selected by American and African tribes influenced the outcome of the Europeans' contest as well as determining the fate of their own societies. Although Europeans emerged politically dominant at the end of the long process of interaction among divergent cultures, they by no means controlled every aspect of it.

Nowhere is that lack of European control shown more clearly than in the early history of the English settlements in North America. England's first attempts to establish colonies on the mainland failed completely. Its second tries—in the early seventeenth century—succeeded only because neighboring Indians assisted the newcomers. The English colonists prospered by learning to grow such unfamiliar American crops as corn and tobacco and by developing extensive trading relationships with Native Americans. Eventually, as shall be seen in Chapter 2, they discovered a third source of prosperity—importing enslaved African laborers to work in their fields.

Only in this last case were the English able to exert more than partial control over the success of their efforts. To achieve the first goal of providing food, they had to adopt agricultural techniques suited both to the new crops and to an alien environment. As for the second goal, maintaining the trade networks essential to their survival required them to deal regularly on a more or less equal basis with people who seemed very different from themselves and who were far more familiar with America than they were. The early history of the United States, in short, can best be understood as a series of complex interactions among different peoples and environments rather than as the simple story of a triumph by only one of those groups—the English colonists.

SOCIETIES OF THE AMERICAS
AND AFRICA

In the Christian world, it was the year 1400; by the Muslim calendar, 802; by Chinese count, 2896, the year of the hare; and to the Maya, who had the most accurate calendar of all, the era started with the date 1 Ahau 18 Ceh. Regardless of the name or the reckoning system, the two-hundred-year period that followed changed the course of world history. For thousands of years, human societies had developed largely in isolation from each other. The era that began in the Christian fifteenth century brought that long-standing isolation to an end. As European explorers and colonizers sought to exploit the resources of the rest of the globe, peoples from different races and cultural traditions came into regular contact for the first time.

The civilizations that had developed separately had several basic characteristics in common. All had political structures governing their secular affairs, kinship systems regulating their social life, and one or more sets of indigenous religious beliefs. In addition, they all organized their work assignments on the basis of the sexual division of labor. Throughout the world, men and women performed different tasks, although the specific definitions of those tasks varied. Many, but not all, of the societies shared yet another characteristic: they relied on agriculture for their essential food supply. (Some of the world's societies were nomadic, surviving by moving continually in search of wild animals and edible plants.) Agricultural civilizations, assured of steady supplies of meat, grains, and vegetables, did not have to devote all their energies to mere subsistence. They accumulated wealth, produced ornamental objects, and created elaborate rituals and ceremonies. In brief, they developed distinctive cultural traditions.

These cultural distinctions became the focal point for the interactions that occurred in the fifteenth century and thereafter among the various human societies. The basic similarities were obscured by the shock of discovering that not all people were the same color as oneself, that other folk worshipped other gods, or that some people defined the separate roles of men and women differently from the way one's own society did. Because three major human groups—Native Americans, Africans, and Europeans—met and mingled on the soil of the Western Hemisphere during the age of European colonization, their relationships can be examined in that context.

Since the earliest known humanlike remains, about 3 million years old, have been found in what is now Ethiopia, it is likely that human beings originated on the continent of Africa. During many millennia, the growing human population slowly dispersed to the other continents. Some of the peoples participating in this vast migration crossed a now-submerged stretch of land that joined the Asian and North American continents at the site of the Bering Strait. These forerunners of the Native American population,

Paleo-Indians known as Paleo-Indians, probably arrived in the Americas more than thirty thousand years ago—about the same time that parts of present-day China and the Soviet Union were also being settled. The Paleo-Indians were nomadic hunters of game and gatherers of wild plants. Over many centuries, they spread through North and South America, probably moving as extended families, or "bands." ("Tribes" were composed of groups of allied bands.)

By approximately 5,500 years ago (or B.P., the archeologists' term for before the present), Indians living in central Mexico had begun to cultivate food crops. Their most important products were maize (corn), squash, beans, gourds, and chili peppers. As knowledge of agricultural techniques spread, most Indian groups started to live a more stationary existence. Some established permanent settlements; others moved two or three times a year among fixed sites. Over the centuries, groups of North American Indians adapted their once-similar ways of life to specific and very different geographical settings, thus creating the diversity of cultures that Europeans encountered when they first arrived (see map, page 6).

Indian Cultures of North America

The French artist Jacques Le Moyne, who visited northern Florida in 1564–1565, showed one aspect of the sexual division of labor as practiced by the Indians of the region. At planting time, the men break up the ground with hoes made from fish bones while the women dig holes into which they drop the seeds. Library of Congress.

Those Indian bands that lived in environments not well suited to agriculture—because of a lack of adequate rainfall, for example—continued the nomadic lifestyle of their ancestors. Within the area of the present-day United States, these tribes included the Paiute and Shoshoni, who inhabited the Great Basin (now Nevada and Utah). Bands of such hunter-gatherers were small, because of the difficulties of finding sufficient food for more than a few people. They were usually composed of one or more related families, with men hunting small animals and women gathering seeds and berries. Where large game was more plentiful and food supplies therefore more certain, as in present-day Canada or the Great Plains, bands of hunters could be somewhat larger.

In more favorable environments, Indians combined agriculture in varying degrees with gathering, hunting, and fishing. The more heavily a tribe relied on agriculture, the less likely it was to be highly mobile, since fields required attention. The cultivation of crops also tended to increase the size of Indian communities, because of the greater availability of food. Those tribes that lived near the sea coasts, like the Chinook of present-day Washington and Oregon, consumed large quantities of fish and shellfish, in addition to growing crops and gathering seeds and berries. Tribes of the interior (for example, the Arikara of the Missouri River valley) hunted large game animals while also cultivating fields of corn, squash, and beans. That was true, too, of the Algonkian tribes that inhabited much of what is now eastern Canada and the northeastern United States. (Indians are often described by linguistic groups, since large numbers of tribes spoke related languages and shared similar cultures. For example, the most important linguistic groups east of the Mississippi River were the Algonkians and the Iroquoians, found primarily in the north, and the Muskogeans of the south.)

Agricultural Indians differed in how they assigned the task of cultivating crops to the sexes. In the Southwest, the Pueblo peoples, who began raising squash and beans by 3000 B.P., defined agricultural labor as "men's work." In the East, by contrast, Algonkian, Iroquoian, and Muskogean peoples allocated agricultural chores to women. Among these eastern tribes, men's major assignments were hunting large animals and clearing the land. In all the cultures, women gathered wild foods, prepared the food for consumption or storage, and cared for the children.

Sexual Division of Labor in America

The southwestern and eastern agricultural Indians had similar social organizations. They lived in villages, sometimes sizable ones with a thousand or more inhabitants. Pueblo villages were large multistoried buildings, constructed on terraces along the sides of cliffs or other easily defended sites. Northern Iroquois villages were composed of large, rectangular, bark-covered structures (long houses), and Muskogeans and southern Algonkians lived in similarly large houses made of thatch. Most of the eastern villages were also laid out defensively, often being surrounded by wood palisades and ditches. In these cultures, each dwelling housed an extended family defined *matrilineally* (that is, through the female line). The families in such dwellings were linked together into clans, again defined by matrilineal kinship ties.

In both southwestern and eastern cultures, the most important political structures were those of the village. Indeed, among Pueblo and Muskogean peoples the village council, composed of ten to thirty men, was the highest political authority; there was no government at the tribal level. The Iroquois, by contrast, had an elaborate political hierarchy linking villages into tribes, and tribes into a widespread confederation. (The Iroquois Confederacy will be discussed in detail in Chapter 2.) In all the cultures, political power was divided between civil and war chiefs, who had authority only so long as they retained the confidence of the people.

Indian Politics and Religion

The political position of women varied from tribe to tribe. Women were more likely to assume leadership roles among the agricultural peoples (especially where females were the chief cultivators) than among nomadic hunters. For example, women could become chiefs of certain Algonkian bands, but they never held that position in the hunting tribes of the Great Plains. Iroquois women did not become chiefs, yet tribal matrons nevertheless exercised political power, as will be seen in Chapter 2. Probably the most powerful female chiefs were found in what is now the southeastern United States. In the mid-sixteenth century a female ruler known as the Lady of Cofitachique governed a large group of villages in present-day western South Carolina.

Indian religious beliefs varied even more than did their political systems. One common thread was that they were all *polytheistic*; that is, they all involved a multitude of gods. Another was the relationship of the most important rituals to the tribe's chief means of subsistence. That is, the major deities of agricultural Indians like Pueblos and Muskogeans were associated with cultivation, and their chief festivals centered on planting and harvest. The most important gods of hunting tribes (like the Siouan-speakers of the Great Plains), by contrast, were associated with animals, and their major festivals were related to hunting. The tribe's main source of food and women's role (or lack of role) in its production helped to determine women's potential as religious leaders. Women held the most prominent positions in those agricultural societies (like the Iroquois) in which they were also the chief food producers.

The most advanced Indian civilizations on the North American continent were located in present-day Mexico and Guatemala (Mesoamerica). The major Indian societies encountered by the Spanish in the sixteenth century— the Aztec and the Maya—were the heirs of earlier civilizations (such as the Olmec), which had also built great empires. Characteristic of these Mesoamerican cultures were large cities, ceremonial sites featuring massive pyramid-shaped temples, rule by an hereditary elite of warrior-priests, primary dependence on agriculture for food, and religious practices that included human sacrifice. The Aztec, who entered central Mexico in the fourteenth century, were a warlike people who had consolidated their control over the entire region by the

Aztec and Maya

John White, an artist who accompanied the exploratory mission Raleigh sent to America in 1585, sketched Pomeioc, a typical Algonkian village composed of houses made from woven mats stretched over poles, and surrounded by a defensive wooden palisade. *Library of Congress.*

time of Cortés's arrival. The Maya, whose civilization was already in decline when the Spaniards came, were the intellectual leaders of Mesoamerica. They invented systems of writing and mathematics, and their calendar was the most accurate then known.

In the fifteenth century, then, a wide variety of Indian cultures, comprising perhaps 4 to 6 million people, inhabited North America. In modern Mexico, hereditary rulers presided over vast agricultural empires. Along the Atlantic coast of the present-day United States, Indians likewise cultivated crops, but their political systems differed greatly from those of Mesoamerica. To the north and west, in what is now Canada and the Great Plains, lived nomadic and seminomadic societies primarily dependent on hunting large animals. Still farther west were the hunter-gatherer bands of the Great Basin and the agricultural Indians of the Southwest. Finally, on the Pacific coast lived tribes that based their subsistence chiefly on fish. All told, these diverse groups spoke well over one thousand different languages. For obvious reasons, they did not consider themselves as one people, nor did they—for the most part—think of uniting to repel the European invaders. Instead, each tribe or band continued to pursue the same goal it always had: bettering its own circumstances relative to its neighbors, regardless of who those neighbors were.

Fifteenth-century Africa, like fifteenth-century America, housed a variety of cultures adapted to different geographical settings (see map, page 10).

Africa: Its Peoples

Many of these cultures were of great antiquity. In the north, along the Mediterranean Sea, lived the Berbers, a Muslim people of Middle Eastern origin. (Muslims are adherents of the Islamic religion founded by the prophet Mohammed in the seventh century.) On the east coast of Africa, city-states dominated by Muslim merchants engaged in extensive trade with India, the Moluccas (part of

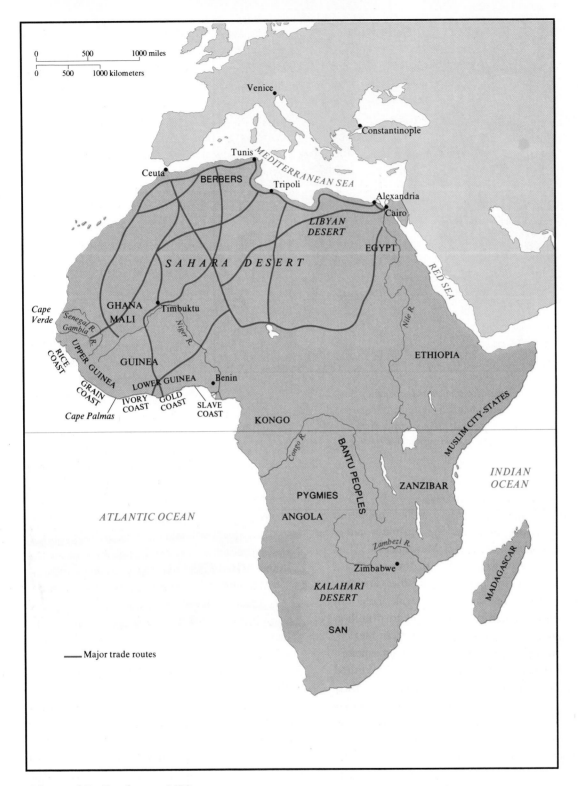

Africa and Its Peoples, ca. 1400

modern Indonesia), and China. Through these ports passed a considerable share of the trade between the eastern Mediterranean and Far East; the rest followed the long land route across Central Asia known as the Silk Road.

In the African interior, south of the Mediterranean coast, lie the great Sahara and Libyan deserts, huge expanses of nearly waterless terrain that pose a formidable barrier to travel. Below the deserts, much of the continent is divided between tropical rain forests and grassy plains. Over the centuries, this fertile landscape came to be dominated by Bantu peoples, who left their homeland in modern Nigeria about two thousand years ago and slowly migrated southward across the continent, assimilating and conquering other ethnic groups (like the Pygmies and the San) as they went. The capital of their empire was the great city whose ruins are now known as Zimbabwe, the "stone houses."

Most of the unwilling black migrants to the Americas came from West Africa, or Guinea, a land of tropical forests and small-scale agriculture that had been inhabited for at least ten thousand years before Europeans set foot there in the fifteenth century.

West Africa (Guinea)

The northern region, or Upper Guinea, was heavily influenced by Islamic culture. As early as the eleventh century, many of its inhabitants had become Muslims; more important, the trans-Saharan trade between Upper Guinea and the Muslim Mediterranean was black Africa's major connection to Europe and the Middle East. In return for salt, dates, and such manufactured goods as silk and cotton cloth, Africans exchanged ivory, gold, and slaves with the northern merchants. (Slaves, who were mostly captives of war, were in great demand as household servants in the homes of the Muslim Mediterranean elite.) This commerce was controlled first by the great kingdom of Ghana (ca. 900–1100), then by its successor, the empire of Mali, which flourished in the fourteenth and fifteenth centuries. Black Africa and Islam intersected at the city that was the intellectual and commercial heart of the trade, the near-legendary Timbuktu. A cosmopolitan center, Timbuktu attracted merchants and scholars from all parts of North Africa and the Mediterranean.

Along the coast of West Africa and in the south, or Lower Guinea, Islam had less influence. There, most Africans continued to practice their indigenous religions, which—like those of the agricultural Indians of the Americas—revolved around rituals designed to ensure good harvests. The vast interior kingdoms of Mali and Ghana had no counterparts on the coast. Throughout Lower Guinea, individual villages composed of groups of kin were linked into small, often rigidly hierarchical kingdoms. At the time of initial contact with Europeans, the region was characterized by fragmented political and social authority.

Just as the political structures varied, so too did the means of subsistence pursued by the different peoples of Guinea. Upper Guinea runs roughly north-south from Cape Verde to Cape Palmas. Its northernmost region was the so-called Rice Coast, lying just south of the Gambia River (present-day Gambia, Senegal, and Guinea). The people who lived there fished and cultivated rice in coastal swamplands. The Grain Coast, the next region to the south, was thinly populated and not readily accessible from the sea because it had only one good harbor (modern Freetown, Sierra Leone). Its people concentrated on farming and animal husbandry.

South of the Grain Coast, at Cape Palmas, the coastline turns east, and Lower Guinea begins. The Ivory Coast and the Gold Coast were each named by Europeans for the major trade goods they obtained there. The Gold Coast, comprising thirty little kingdoms known as the Akan States, later formed the basis of the great Asante kingdom. Initially many of the slaves destined for sale in the Americas came from the Akan States. By the eighteenth century, though, it was the next section of Lower Guinea, the modern nations of Togo and Benin, that supplied most of the slaves sold in the English colonies. The Adja kings of the region, which became known as the Slave Coast, encouraged the founding of slave trading posts and served as middlemen in the trade.

The ancient kingdom of Benin (modern Nigeria), which lay east of the Slave Coast and west of the Niger River, was the strongest and most centralized coastal state in Guinea. Long before Europeans arrived it was, like Mali, a center of trade for West and North Africa. Like the peoples of the Rice Coast, those who lived in Benin along the delta of the Niger made much of their living from the water. They fished, made salt, and used skillfully constructed dugout canoes to carry on a wide-ranging commerce.

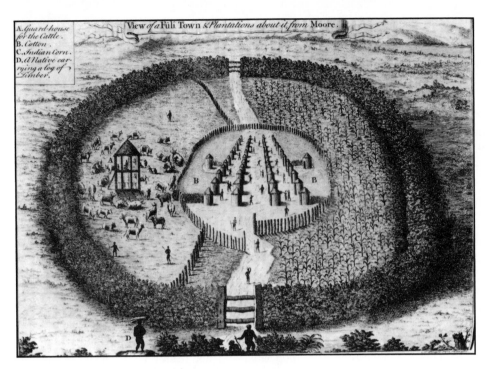

A West African village as drawn by a European observer. A wooden defensive palisade surrounds the circular houses made of woven plant materials. In this the African village resembles Pomeioc, the Indian village pictured on page 9. But note a major difference—a herd of livestock enclosed in a larger fence. Note also that the Africans are growing Indian corn, thus illustrating the exchange of plants between America and Africa (see page 19). *Library of Congress.*

The societies of West Africa, like those of the Americas, assigned different tasks to men and women. In general, the sexes shared agricultural duties, but in some Guinean cultures women bore the primary responsibility for growing crops, whereas in others men assumed that chore. In addition, men hunted, managed livestock, and did most of the fishing. Women were responsible for childcare, food preparation, and cloth manufacture. Everywhere in West Africa women were the primary local traders. They had charge of the extensive local and regional networks through which goods were exchanged among the various families, villages, and small kingdoms.

Sexual Division of Labor in West Africa

Despite their different modes of subsistence and deep political divisions, the peoples of West Africa had largely similar social systems organized on the basis of what anthropologists have called the dual-sex principle. In the societies of West Africa, each sex handled its own affairs: just as male political and religious leaders governed the men, so females ruled the women. In the Dahomean kingdom, every male official had his female counterpart; in the Akan States, chiefs inherited their status through the female line and each chief had a female assistant who supervised women's affairs.

Indigenous religious beliefs likewise stressed the complementary nature of male and female roles. Both women and men served as heads of the cults and secret societies that directed the spiritual life of the villages. Although African women rarely held formal power over men (unlike some of their Native American contemporaries), they did govern other females.

The West Africans brought to the Americas, then, were agricultural peoples, skilled at tending livestock, hunting, fishing, and manufacturing cloth from plant fibers and animal skins. Both men and women were accustomed to working communally, alongside other members of their own sex. They were also accustomed to a relatively egalitarian relationship between the sexes. In the New World, they entered societies that used their labor but had little respect for their cultural traditions. Of the three peoples whose experience intersected in the Americas, their lives were the most disrupted.

EUROPE AND
ITS EXPLORATIONS

After 1400, Europe had begun to recover from centuries of decline. Northern Europe—England and France in particular—had long been an intellectual and economic backwater, far outstripped in importance by the states of the Mediterranean, especially the great Italian city-states like Venice and Florence. The cultural flowering known as the Renaissance began in those city-states in the fourteenth century and spread northward, awakening Europeans' intellectual curiosity. At the same time, the pace of economic activity quickened. Near-constant warfare (for example, the Hundred Years' War between England and France, which ended in a French victory in 1453), promoted feelings of nationalism within the combatant countries. All these developments helped to set the stage for extraordinary political and technological change after the middle of the fifteenth century.

Yet in the midst of that change the life of Europe's common people remained basically untouched for at least another century. European societies were hierarchical, with a few wealthy aristocratic families wielding arbitrary power over the majority of the people. Europe's kingdoms accordingly resembled those of Africa or Mesoamerica, but differed greatly from the more egalitarian, consensus-based societies found in America north of Mexico. Most Europeans, like most Africans or Native Americans, lived in small agricultural villages. But because the Roman Catholic church—to which almost all Europeans belonged—insisted on *exogamy* (marriage to nonrelatives), villages were not based solely, or even primarily, on kinship groups, as they were in Africa or the Americas. On those continents, the kin groups that constituted a village together controlled the surrounding land. Europe had no comparable coresident extended families; perhaps that was why European land tended to be held by individual farmers rather than by villages as a whole.

Even though European farmers, or peasants, had separate landholdings, they nevertheless worked their fields communally, like most Africans and Native Americans. That was because fields had to lie fallow every second or third year to regain their fertility after having been planted with wheat or rye, the most common European food grains. A family could not have ensured its own food supply in alternate years had not the work and the crop been shared annually by all the villagers.

In European cultures, men did most of the field work, with women helping out chiefly at planting and harvest. At other times, women's duties consisted primarily of childcare and household **Sexual** tasks (including food preservation, **Division of** milking cows, and caring for poul- **Labor in** try). If a woman's husband was an **Europe** artisan or storekeeper, she might assist him in business. Since Europeans usually kept domesticated animals (especially pigs, sheep, and cattle) to use for meat, hunting had little economic importance in their cultures. Rather, hunting was viewed mainly as a sport for male aristocrats.

Whereas in African or Native American societies women often played major roles in politics and religion, in Europe men were dominant in all areas of life. A few women from noble families—for example, Queen Elizabeth I of England—achieved status or power, but the vast majority of European women were excluded from positions of political authority. In the Catholic church, leadership roles were reserved for men, who alone could become priests and bishops. At the familial level, husbands and fathers expected to control the lives of their wives, children, and servants (a *patriarchal* system of family governance). In short, European women held inferior positions in both public and private realms.

The husband man doth choose his sowing graine
And makes it cleane before it go to ground
He knowes at length then encrease will quit ÿ paine
the cleaner corne lesse darnell shalbe founde

October
scorpio

the plowman

A 1622 English manuscript illustrated the seasonal cycle of work for ordinary farmers. In October, the month shown here, the wise husbandman (farmer) plowed his fields and sowed a crop of winter wheat (which the English called corn). Note that these scenes contain only men, showing that the sexual division of labor in European agriculture was quite different from that of the Indians illustrated on page 7. Folger Shakespeare Library.

The traditional hierarchical social structure of Europe changed little in the fifteenth century, but the opposite was true of politics. The century witnessed rapid and dynamic political change, as ruthless monarchs expanded their territories through conquest and marriage and centralized previously diffuse political power in their own hands. In England, Henry VII in 1485 founded the Tudor dynasty and began uniting a previously divided land. In France, the successors of Charles VII unified the kingdom and established new, more secure sources of revenue. Most successful of all, at least in the short run, were Ferdinand of Aragon and Isabella of Castile. In 1469 they married and combined their kingdoms, thus creating the foundation of a strongly Catholic Spain. In 1492, they defeated the Muslims (who had lived on the Iberian peninsula for centuries) and expelled all Jews from their domain.

Political and Technological Change

The fifteenth century also brought significant technological change to Europe. Movable type and the printing press, invented in Germany in the 1450s, made information more widely and more readily accessible than ever before. Other discoveries led to the development of navigational instruments like the astrolabe, which allowed oceanic sailors to estimate their position by measuring the relationship of sun, moon, or stars to the horizon. Such inventions simultaneously stimulated Europeans' curiosity about fabled lands across the seas and enabled them to think about reaching exotic places by ship. For example, Marco Polo's *Travels*, which described a Venetian merchant's adventures in thirteenth-century China and reported that that nation was bordered on the east by an ocean, circulated widely among Europe's educated elites after it was printed in 1477. This book led many Europeans to believe that they could trade directly with China via ocean-going vessels, instead of relying on the Silk Road or the trade route through East Africa. That would also allow them to circumvent the Muslim merchants who had hitherto controlled their access to Asian goods.

Thus the European explorations of the fifteenth and sixteenth centuries were made possible by technological advances and by the financial might of newly powerful national rulers. But **Motives for Exploration** the primary motivation for the exploratory voyages was a desire for direct access to the wealth of the East. That motive was supported by a secondary concern to spread Christianity around the world. The linking of materialist and spiritual goals might seem contradictory today, but fifteenth-century Europeans saw no necessary conflict between the two. Explorers and colonizers could honestly wish to convert heathen peoples to Christianity. At the same time they could also hope to increase their nation's wealth by establishing direct trade with China, India, and the Moluccas, the sources of spices like pepper, cloves, cinnamon, and nutmeg (needed to season the bland European diet), silk, dyes, perfumes, jewels, and gold.

The seafaring Portuguese people, whose land was located on the southwestern corner of the continent of Europe, began the age of European expansion in 1415 when they seized control of Ceuta, a Muslim city in North Africa (see map, page 10). Prince Henry the Navigator, son of King John I, realized that vast wealth awaited the first European nation to tap the riches of Africa and Asia directly. Each year he dispatched ships southward along the coast of Africa, attempting to discover a passage to the East. Not until after Prince Henry's death did Bartholomew Dias round the southern tip of Africa (1488) and Vasco da Gama finally reach India (1498). Long before that, the Portuguese had established trading posts in Guinea, so that they no longer needed to use the long trans-Saharan trade route through Timbuktu. They earned immense profits by transporting African goods swiftly to Europe. Among their most valuable cargoes were slaves; when they carried African Muslim prisoners of war back to the Iberian peninsula, the Portuguese introduced the custom of black slavery into Europe.

Spain, with its reinvigorated monarchy, was the next country to sponsor exploratory voyages, chiefly those of Christopher Columbus, a Genoese sea captain.

Christopher Columbus Like other experienced sailors, Columbus believed the world to be round. (Only ignorant folk still thought it was flat.) Where he differed from his contemporaries was in his estimate of its size. He believed that Japan lay only 3,000 miles from the southern European coast—the distance is actually 12,000 miles—and therefore that it would be easier to reach the East by sailing west than by making the difficult voyage around the southern tip of Africa.

After being rejected as a crackpot by the monarchs of France, Portugal, and England, Columbus sought and received financial backing from Queen Isabella. Envious of Portuguese successes, she hoped to gain a foothold in Asia for her nation. On August 3, 1492, with three ships under his command—the *Pinta*, the *Niña*, and the *Santa Maria*—Columbus sailed west from the port of Palos in Spain. On October 12, he landed on an island in the Bahamas, which he named San Salvador and claimed for the king and queen of Spain. Because he thought he had reached the Indies, he called the inhabitants of the region Indians.

Columbus made three more voyages to the west, during which he explored most of the major Caribbean islands and sailed along the coasts of Central and South America. Until the day he died in 1506, Columbus continued to believe that he had reached Asia. Even before his death, others knew better. Because the Florentine Amerigo Vespucci (who explored the South American coast in 1499) was the first to publish the idea that a new continent had been discovered, a mapmaker in 1507 labeled the land *America*.

More than five hundred years earlier, Norse explorers had briefly colonized present-day Newfoundland, but it was the voyages of Columbus and his successors that finally brought the Old and New Worlds together. John Cabot (1497), Giovanni da Verrazano (1524), Jacques Cartier (1534), and Henry Hudson (1609 and 1610) all explored the North American coast (see map, page 17). They were primarily searching for the legendary, nonexistent "Northwest Passage" through the Americas, hoping to find an easy route to the riches of the East. Although they did not attempt to plant colonies in the Western Hemisphere, their discoveries interested European nations in the New World for its own sake.

Only Spain immediately moved to take advantage of the discoveries. On his first voyage, Columbus had established a base on the island of Hispaniola. From there, Spanish explorers fanned out **Conquistadores** around the Caribbean basin: in 1513, Juan Ponce de León reached Florida and Vasco Nuñez de Balboa crossed the Isthmus of Panama and found the Pacific Ocean. Less than ten years later, the Spaniards' dreams of wealth were realized when Cortés conquered the Aztec empire, killing its ruler, Moctezuma, and seizing a fabulous treasure of gold and silver. Venturing northward, conquistadores like Juan Rodriguez Cabrillo (who sailed along the California coast), Hernando de Soto (who discovered the Mississippi River), and Francisco Vásquez de Coronado (who explored the southwestern portion of what is now the United States) found little of value. By contrast, Francisco Pizarro, who explored the western coast of South America, conquered and enslaved the Inca in 1535, thus acquiring the richest silver mines in the world. Just half a century after Columbus's first voyage, the Spanish monarchs—who treated the American territories as their personal possessions—controlled the richest, most extensive empire Europe had known since ancient Rome.

Spain established the model of colonization that other countries later attempted to imitate, a model with three major elements. First, the crown maintained tight control over the colonies, establishing a rigidly hierarchical government that allowed little autonomy to New World jurisdictions. (That control included, for example, allowing only selected persons to migrate to America and insisting that the colonies import all their manufactured goods from Spain.) Second, the colonies' wealth was based on the exploitation of both the native population and slaves imported from Africa. A Spanish law adopted in 1542 forbade the enslavement of Indians, but the conquerors, accustomed to African slavery in their homeland, had no similar scruples about blacks. And many Indians, though technically not enslaved, labored in mines and fields in a status resembling peonage (perpetual service for debt). Third, the colonists sent from Spain were almost wholly male. They married Indian—and later black—women, thereby creating the racially mixed population that characterizes Latin America to the present day.

The New World's gold and silver, though a boon at first, ultimately brought about the decline of Spain as a major power. The influx of hitherto undreamed-of wealth led to rapid inflation, which (among other adverse effects) caused Spanish products to be overpriced in international markets and imported goods to become cheaper in Spain. The once-profitable Spanish textile manufacturing industry collapsed, as did scores of other businesses. The seemingly endless income from New World colonies also emboldened successive Spanish monarchs to spend lavishly on wars against the Dutch and the English. Several times in the late sixteenth and early seventeenth centuries the monarchs repudiated the state debt, thus wreaking havoc with the nation's finances. When the South American mines started to give out in the mid-seventeenth century, Spain's economy crumbled and the nation lost its political pre-eminence.

American civilizations suffered even more. The Spaniards deliberately leveled Indian cities, building cathedrals and monasteries on sites once occupied by Aztec, Incan, and Mayan temples. Despite the protests of some priests, they sought to erase all vestiges of the great Indian cultures by burning whatever written records they found. As a result, present-day knowledge of the Aztec, Maya, and Inca civilizations rests almost entirely on architectural remains, pottery artifacts, and a few records left by priests who sympathized with the Indians.

The native peoples to the north initially fared somewhat better because the English, French, and Dutch, unlike the Spanish, did not immediately start **Northern** to colonize the coast their sailors **Traders** had explored. Instead, they left the region to European mariners, who came to fish in the rich waters off Newfoundland. Eventually, these fishermen learned that they could supplement their profits by exchanging cloth and metal goods (like pots and knives) for the Indians' beaver pelts, which Europeans used to make fashionable felt hats. At first the Europeans conducted their trading from ships sailing along the coast, but later they established permanent outposts on the mainland to centralize and control the traffic in furs. Among the most successful of these were the French trading posts at Quebec (1608) and Montreal (1642), on the St. Lawrence River; the Swedish settlement at Fort Christina (1638) on the Delaware River; and

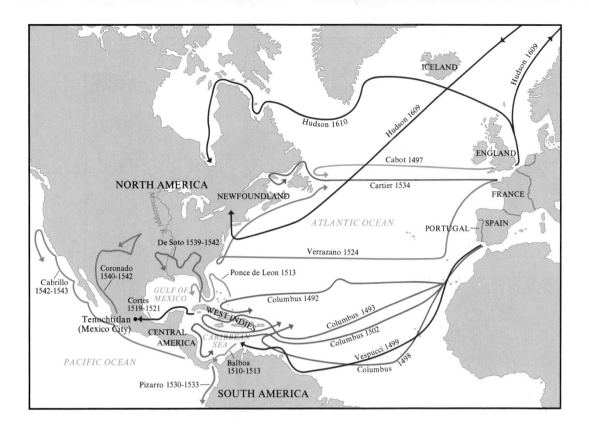

European Explorations in America

the Dutch forts of New Amsterdam and Fort Orange on the Hudson River, both founded in 1624. All were inhabited chiefly by male adventurers, whose sole aim was to send as many pelts as possible home to Europe.

Even though the northern Europeans did not conquer the Indians, as the Spanish had, their trading activities had a significant effect on the native societies. The Europeans' insatiable demand for furs, especially beaver, was matched by the Indians' desire for European goods that could make their lives easier and establish their superiority over neighboring tribes. Some tribes concentrated so completely on trapping for the European market that they abandoned their traditional modes of subsistence. The Abenaki of Maine, for example, became partially dependent on food supplied by their neighbors to the south, the Massachusett tribe, because they devoted most of their energies to catching beaver to sell to French traders. The Massachusett, in turn, intensified their production of foodstuffs, which they traded to the Abenaki in exchange for the European metal tools

that they preferred to their own handmade stone implements. The northeastern tribes, in other words, began to change their traditional ways of life: some specialized in producing pelts for the market, others in supplying foodstuffs to the fur hunters, who became the agriculturalists' major source of European trade goods, rather than the Europeans themselves.

The Europeans' greatest impact on the Americas was, however, unintended. Diseases carried from the Old World to the New by the alien invaders killed hundreds of thousands, even millions, of Native Americans, who had no immunity to germs that had infested Europe, Asia, and Africa for centuries. The greatest killer was smallpox, which was spread by direct human contact. The epidemic that hit Tenochtitlan in 1520 had begun in Hispaniola two years earlier. Pizarro easily conquered the Inca partly because their society had been devastated by the epidemic shortly before his arrival. Smallpox was not the only villain; influenza, measles, and other diseases added to the destruction.

Killer Diseases

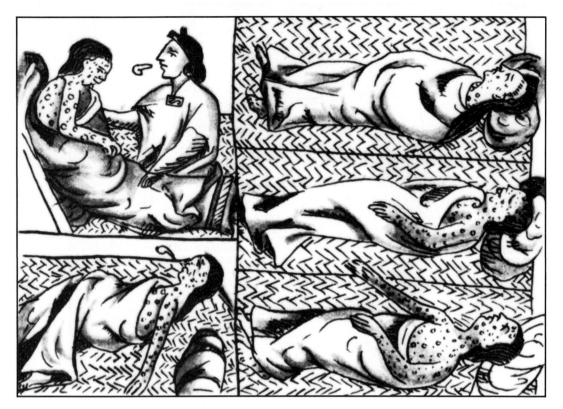

Aztec Indians suffering from smallpox during the Cortes invasion. From Fray Bernardo de Sahagun's General History of the Things of New Spain (Historia de las Cosas de Nueva Espana), *published in the sixteenth century.* Library of Congress.

The statistics are staggering. When Columbus landed on Hispaniola in 1492, more than 3 million Indians resided there. Fifty years later, only five hundred were still alive.

Even in the north, where smaller Indian populations encountered only a few European explorers, traders, and fishermen, disease ravaged the countryside. A great epidemic, most likely chicken pox, swept through the Indian villages along the coast north of Cape Cod in 1616–1618. The mortality rate may have been as high as 90 percent. An English traveler several years later commented that the Indians had "died on heapes, as they lay in their houses," and that bones and skulls covered the remains of their villages. Because of this dramatic depopulation of the area, just a few years later English colonists were able to establish settlements virtually unopposed by native peoples. As one historian has observed, America was more a widowed land than a virgin one when the English arrived there.

The Americans, though, took a revenge of sorts. They gave the Europeans a virulent form of syphilis. The first recorded case of the new disease in Europe occurred in Barcelona, Spain, in 1493, shortly after Columbus's return from the Caribbean. Although less deadly than smallpox, syphilis was extremely dangerous and debilitating. It spread quickly through Europe and Asia, carried by soldiers, sailors, and prostitutes, even reaching China by 1505.

The exchange of diseases was only part of a broader mutual transfer of plants and animals that resulted directly from Columbus's voyages. The two hemispheres had evolved separately over millions of years, developing widely different forms of life. Many large

Exchange of Plants and Animals

mammals were native to the connected continents of Europe, Asia, and Africa, but the Americas contained no domesticated beasts larger than dogs and llamas. On the other hand, the vegetable crops of the New World—particularly corn, beans, squash, manioc, and potatoes—were more nutritious and produced higher yields than those of the Old, like wheat and rye. In time Indians learned to raise and consume European domestic animals, and Europeans and Africans became accustomed to planting and eating American crops. As a result, the diets of all three peoples were vastly enriched. One consequence was the doubling of the world's population over the next three hundred years, after centuries of stability.

The exchange of two other commodities significantly influenced European and American civilizations. In America, Europeans discovered tobacco, which was at first believed to have beneficial medicinal effects. Smoking and chewing the "Indian weed" became a fad in the Old World. Tobacco cultivation was later to form the basis for the prosperity of the first successful English colonies in North America. Despite the efforts of such skeptics as King James I of England, who in 1604 pronounced smoking to be "loathsome to the eye, hatefull to the Nose, harmfull to the brain, [and] dangerous to the Lungs," tobacco's popularity has continued to the present day.

More important was the impact of the horse on some Indian cultures. Spaniards brought the first horses to America; inevitably, some fell into the hands of the Native Americans. They were traded northward among the tribes and eventually became essential to the life of the nomadic buffalo hunters of the Great Plains. The Apache, Comanche, and Blackfeet, among others, used horses for transportation and hunting, calculated their wealth in the number of horses owned, and waged wars primarily from horseback. Because their horses continually needed fresh pastures, they had to move their camps frequently. Some tribes that had previously cultivated crops abandoned agriculture altogether. As a result of the acquisition of horses, then, a mode of subsistence that had been based on hunting several different animals, combined with some gathering and agriculture, became one focused almost wholly on hunting buffalo.

ENGLAND COLONIZES THE NEW WORLD

When Englishmen began to think about planting colonies in the Western Hemisphere, they took Spain's possessions in the New World as both a model and a challenge. New Spain's existence posed a threat to England, Spain's greatest rival, not only because of the wealth Spain derived from the colonies, but also because of their strategic importance. Even remote outposts could be of use to warring countries. By establishing its own settlements, England could prevent Spain from dominating the Western Hemisphere and could also gain direct access to valuable American commodities.

England's first colonial planners thus hoped to reproduce Spanish successes by dispatching to America men who would exploit the native peoples for their own and their nation's benefit. In the 1580s, a group that included Sir Humphrey Gilbert and his younger half-brother Sir Walter Raleigh promoted a scheme to establish outposts that could trade with the Indians and provide bases for attacks on New Spain. Approving the idea, Queen Elizabeth I authorized Raleigh and Gilbert to colonize North America. Gilbert failed to plant a colony in Newfoundland, dying in the attempt, and Raleigh was only briefly more successful. In 1587 he sent 117 colonists to the territory he named Virginia (for Elizabeth, the "Virgin Queen"). They established a settlement on Roanoke Island, in what is now North Carolina, but in 1590 a supply ship could not find them. The colonists had vanished, leaving only the word "Croatoan" (the name of a nearby island) carved on a tree.

Raleigh's Roanoke Colony

The failure of Raleigh's attempt to colonize Virginia ended English efforts at settlement in North America for nearly two decades. When, in 1606, Englishmen decided to try once more, they again planned colonies that imitated the Spanish model. Success came only when they abandoned that model and founded settlements very different from those of other European

TUDOR AND STUART MONARCHS OF ENGLAND
1509–1649

Monarch	Years of Reign	Relation to Predecessor
Henry VIII	1509–1547	son
Edward VI	1547–1553	son
Mary I	1553–1558	half-sister
Elizabeth I	1558–1603	half-sister
James I	1603–1625	cousin
Charles I	1625–1649	son

powers. Unlike Spain, France, or the Netherlands, England eventually sent large numbers of men *and women* to set up *agriculturally based* colonies in the New World. Before the history of those colonies is discussed, it is important to examine the two major developments that prompted approximately two hundred thousand ordinary English men and women to move to North America in the seventeenth century and that led their government to encourage them.

The first development was a significant change in English religious practice, a transformation that eventually led large numbers of English dissenters to leave their homeland. In 1533, **English Reformation** Henry VIII, wanting a male heir and infatuated with Anne Boleyn, sought to annul his marriage to his Spanish-born queen, Catherine of Aragon, despite nearly twenty years of marriage. When the pope refused to approve the annulment, Henry left the Roman Catholic church, founded the Church of England, and—with Parliament's concurrence—proclaimed himself its head. The English people welcomed the schism, because they had little respect for the English Catholic church, which was at the time filled with corrupt bishops and ignorant, drunken priests. At first the reformed Church of England differed little from Catholicism in its practices, but under Henry's daughter Elizabeth I (child of his marriage to Anne Boleyn), new currents of religious belief that had originated on the European continent early in the

sixteenth century dramatically affected the English church.

The leaders of the continental Protestant Reformation were Martin Luther, a German monk, and John Calvin, a French cleric and lawyer. Combating the Catholic doctrine that priests had to serve as intermediaries between lay people and God, they both insisted that each person could interpret the Bible for him or herself. (One result of that notion was the spread of literacy: to understand and interpret the Bible, people obviously had to learn how to read it for themselves.) Both Luther and Calvin rejected Catholic rituals and denied the need for an elaborate church hierarchy. They also asserted that salvation came through faith alone, rather than—as Catholic teaching had it—through a combination of faith and good works. Calvin, though, went further than Luther in stressing God's absolute omnipotence and emphasizing the need for people to submit totally to His will.

Elizabeth I tolerated religious diversity among her subjects as long as they generally acknowledged her authority as head of the Church of England. Accordingly, during her long reign **Puritans** (1558–1603) Calvin's ideas gained influence within the English church. By the early seventeenth century, many English Calvinists believed that the Reformation had not gone far enough. Henry had simplified the church hierarchy; they wanted to abolish it altogether. Henry had subordinated the church to the interests of the state; they wanted a church free from political interference. And the Church of England, like the Catholic church, continued to define its membership as including everyone in the state. Some Calvinists preferred a more restricted definition; they wanted to confine church membership to persons believed to be "saved." Because these seventeenth-century English Calvinists said they wanted to *purify* the church, they became known as Puritans.

Elizabeth I's Stuart successors, her cousin James I (1603–1625) and his son Charles I (1625–1649) were less tolerant of Puritans than she. As Scots, they also had little respect for the traditions of representative government that had developed in England under the Tudors and their predecessors. The wealthy, taxpaying landowners who sat in Parliament had grown accustomed to having considerable influence on government policies, especially taxation. But James I, taking a position later endorsed by his son, publicly declared his adherence to the theory of the divine right of kings. The Stuarts insisted that a monarch's power came directly from God and that his subjects had no alternative but to obey him. A king's authority, they argued, was absolute, just like the authority of a father over his children. Both James I and Charles I believed that their authority included the power to enforce religious conformity among their subjects and so they authorized the persecution of Puritans, who were challenging many of the most important precepts of the English church. Consequently, in the 1620s and 1630s a number of English Puritans decided to move to America, where they hoped to put their religious beliefs into practice unmolested by the Stuarts or the church hierarchy.

The second major development that led English folk to move to North America was the onset of dramatic social and economic change caused by the doubling of the English population in the 150-year period after 1530. All those additional people needed food, clothing, and other goods. The competition for goods led to high inflation, coupled with a fall in real wages as the number of workers increased. In these new economic and demographic circumstances, some English people—especially those with sizable landholdings that could produce food and clothing fibers for the growing population—sub-

Social Change in England

Puritan doctrines aroused so much controversy in sixteenth- and seventeenth-century England that clergymen with Puritan beliefs were occasionally physically attacked while they were preaching. Such an incident is illustrated in this English cartoon of the period. Library of Congress.

stantially improved their lot. Others, particularly landless laborers or those with very small amounts of land, fell into unremitting poverty. When landowners raised rents or decided to enclose and combine small holdings into large units, they forced tenant farmers off the land. Consequently, geographical as well as social mobility increased, and the population of the cities (especially London) swelled.

Well-to-do English people reacted with alarm to what they saw as the disappearance of traditional ways of life. The streets and highways were filled with steady streams of the landless and the homeless. Officials became obsessed with the problem of maintaining order and came to believe that England was overcrowded. They concluded that colonies established in the New World could siphon off England's "surplus population," thus easing the social strains at home. For similar reasons, many English people decided that they could improve their circumstances by migrating from a small, land-scarce, apparently overpopulated island to a large, land-rich continent. Such economic considerations affected English people's decisions to migrate to the colonies as much as, if not more than, a desire for escape from religious persecution.

The initial impetus for the establishment of what was to become England's first permanent colony in

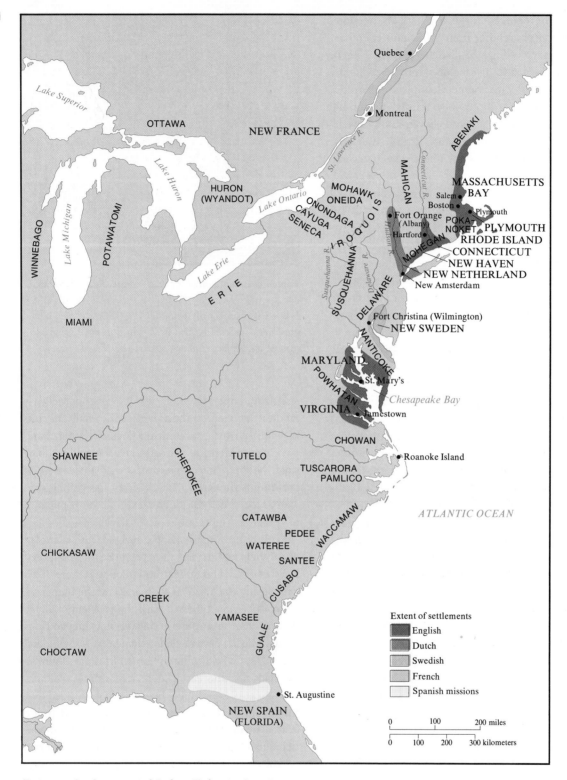

Extent of settlements
■ English
■ Dutch
■ Swedish
■ French
□ Spanish missions

| 0 | 100 | 200 miles |
| 0 | 100 | 200 | 300 kilometers |

European Settlements and Indian Tribes in America,
1650

the Western Hemisphere came from a group of merchants and wealthy gentry. In 1606, envisioning the possibility of earning great profits from a New World settlement, they set up a joint-stock company, the Virginia Company, to plant colonies in America.

Joint-stock companies had been developed in England during the sixteenth century as a mechanism for pooling the resources of a large number of small

Joint-Stock Companies

investors. These forerunners of modern corporations were funded through the sale of stock. Until the founding of the Virginia Company, they had been used primarily to finance trading voyages; for that purpose they worked well. No one person risked too much money, and investors usually received quick returns. But joint-stock companies turned out to be a poor way to finance colonies, because the early settlements required enormous amounts of capital and with rare exceptions failed to return much immediate profit. The colonies founded by joint-stock companies accordingly suffered from a chronic lack of capital—for investors did not want to send good money after bad—and from constant tension between stockholders and colonists (who claimed they were not being adequately supported).

The Virginia Company was no exception to this rule. Chartered by King James I in 1606, the company tried but failed to start a colony in Maine, and barely

Founding of Virginia

succeeded in planting one in Virginia. In 1607 it dispatched 144 men and boys to North America. Ominously, only 104 of them survived the voyage. In May of that year, they established the settlement called Jamestown on a swampy peninsula in a river they also named for their monarch. The colonists were ill equipped for survival in the unfamiliar environment, and the settlement was afflicted by dissension and disease.

By January 1608, only 38 of the original colonists were still alive. Many of the first migrants were gentlemen unaccustomed to working with their hands and artisans with irrelevant skills like glassmaking. Having come to Virginia expecting to make easy fortunes, most could not adjust to the conditions they encountered. They resisted living "like savages," retaining English dress and casual work habits despite their desperate circumstances. Such attitudes, combined with the effects of chronic malnutrition and

epidemic disease, took a terrible toll. Only when Captain John Smith, one of the colony's founders, imposed military discipline on the colonists in 1608 was Jamestown saved from collapse. Still, after Smith's departure, some colonists resorted to cannibalism during the notorious "starving time," the winter of 1609 to 1610. Although conditions later improved somewhat, as late as 1624 only 1,300 of approximately 8,000 English migrants to Virginia remained alive.

That the colony survived at all was a tribute not to the English but rather to the Indians within whose territories they settled (see map). The Powhatan

Powhatan Confederacy

Confederacy—a group of six Algonkian tribes—is known by the name of its leader. Powhatan, a powerful figure, was consolidating his authority over some twenty-five other small tribes in the area at the time the Europeans arrived. Fortunately for the Englishmen, Powhatan viewed them as potential allies instead of threats to his control of the region. And, indeed, Powhatan found the English colony a reliable source of such items as steel knives and guns, which gave him a technological advantage over his Indian neighbors. In return, Powhatan's tribes traded their excess corn and other foodstuffs to the starving colonists. In 1614, Powhatan signed a formal treaty with the settlers and sealed the deal in traditional fashion by marrying his daughter Pocahontas to John Rolfe, one of the English colony's most prominent residents.

Yet the relationship between the Jamestown colony and the coastal tribes was an uneasy one, like later relationships between other colonies and their neighboring tribes. English and Algonkian peoples had much in common (deep religious beliefs, a lifestyle oriented around agriculture, clear political and social hierarchies, and sharply defined sex roles). Yet the English and Indians themselves usually focused on their cultural differences, not their similarities. English men thought that Indian men were lazy because they hunted (a sport in English eyes) and did not work in the fields, whereas Indian men thought English men effeminate because they did "women's work" of cultivation. In the same vein, the whites believed that Indian women were oppressed since they did heavy field labor.

Other differences between the two cultures caused serious misunderstandings. Although both societies

Pocahontas (1595/96?–1617), here called Matoaka alias Rebecka, portrayed in Elizabethan dress. During her visit to England with her husband John Rolfe in 1616, the Indian princess became the toast of London society. She died the following year, just as she was leaving England to return to her homeland, and was buried in the parish church at Gravesend. National Portrait Gallery, Smithsonian Institution, Washington, D.C.

were hierarchical, the nature of the hierarchies differed considerably. Among the east-coast

Algonkian and English Cultural Differences

Algonkian tribes, people were not born to automatic positions of leadership, nor were political power and social status necessarily inherited through the male line. The English gentry did inherit their position from their fathers, and English political and military leaders tended to rule autocratically. By contrast, the authority of Indian leaders rested largely on the consent of their fellow tribesmen. Accustomed to the European concept of powerful kings, the English sought such figures within the tribes. Often (for example, when negotiating treaties) they willfully overestimated the ability of chiefs to make independent decisions for their people.

Furthermore, the Indians and the English had very different notions of property ownership. In most eastern tribes, land was held communally by the entire group. It could not be bought or sold absolutely, although certain rights to use the land (for example, for hunting or fishing) could be transferred. The English, on the other hand, were accustomed to individual farms and to buying and selling land. In addition, the English refused to accept the validity of Indian claims to traditional hunting territories, insisting that only land intensively cultivated could be regarded as owned or occupied by a tribe.

An aspect of the cultural clash that needs particular emphasis is the English settlers' unwavering belief in the superiority of their civilization. Although in the early years of colonization they often harbored thoughts of living peacefully alongside the Indians, they always assumed that they themselves would dictate the terms of such coexistence. They expected the Indians to adopt English customs and to convert to Christianity. They showed little respect for traditional Indian ways of life, especially when they believed their own interests were at stake. That attitude was clearly revealed in the Virginia colony's treatment of the Powhatan Confederacy in the years following the treaty of 1614.

What upset the previous balance between the English and the Indians was the spread of tobacco cultivation. In tobacco the settlers and the Virginia

Tobacco: The Basis of Virginia's Success

Company found the salable commodity for which they had been searching. John Rolfe planted the first crop in 1611. In 1620 Virginians exported 40,000 pounds of cured leaves, and by the end of that decade shipments had jumped dramatically to 1.5 million pounds. The great tobacco boom had begun, fueled by high prices and substantial profits for planters. The price later fell almost as sharply as it had risen, and it fluctuated wildly from year to year in response to increasing supply and international competition. Nevertheless, tobacco became the foundation of Virginia's prosperity.

Successful tobacco cultivation required abundant land, since the crop quickly drained soil of nutrients. Planters soon learned that a field could produce only about three satisfactory crops before it had to lie fallow for several years to regain its fertility. Thus the once small English settlements began to expand rapidly: eager planters applied to the Virginia Company for large land grants on both sides of the James River and its tributary streams. Lulled into a false sense of security by years of peace, the planters established farms at some distance from one another along the river banks—a settlement pattern convenient for tobacco cultivation but poorly designed for defense.

Opechancanough, Powhatan's brother and successor, watched the English colonists steadily encroaching on Indian lands and attempting to convert members of the tribes to Christianity. He recognized the danger his brother had overlooked. On March 22 (Good Friday), 1622, under his leadership, the confederacy launched coordinated attacks all along the river. By the end of the day 347 colonists (about one-quarter of the total) lay dead, and only a timely warning from two Christianized Indians saved Jamestown itself from destruction.

The Virginia colony reeled from the blow but did not collapse. Reinforced by new shipments of men and arms from England, the settlers launched a series of attacks on Opechancanough's villages. In April 1644 Opechancanough tried one last time to repel the invaders, but he failed, dying in the war that ensued. In 1646, survivors of the Powhatan Confederacy accepted a treaty formally subordinating them to English authority. Although they continued to live in the region, their alliance crumbled and their efforts to resist the spread of white settlement ended.

LIFE IN THE CHESAPEAKE: VIRGINIA AND MARYLAND

The 1622 Indian uprising that failed to destroy the Virginia colony did succeed in killing its parent company, which had never made any profits from the enterprise. (The heavy costs had offset all the company's earnings.) In 1624 James I revoked the charter and made Virginia a royal colony, ruled by the king through appointed officials. At the same time, though, he continued an important policy designed to attract settlers, which the company had first adopted in 1617. Under the "headright" system, every new arrival was promised a land grant of fifty

acres; those who financed the passage of others received headrights for each. To ordinary English farmers, many of whom had owned little or no land, the headright system offered a real incentive to migrate to Virginia. To wealthy gentry, it promised even more: the possibility of establishing vast agricultural enterprises worked by large numbers of laborers.

In 1619, the company had introduced a second policy that James was more reluctant to retain: it had authorized the landowning men of the major Virginia settlements to elect representatives to a legislature called the House of Burgesses. Although England was a monarchy, English landholders had long been accustomed to electing members of Parliament and controlling their own local governments. In accordance with his belief in the absolute power of the monarchy and his distrust of legislative bodies, James at first abolished the Virginia assembly. But the settlers protested so vigorously that by 1629 the House of Burgesses was functioning once again. Only two decades after the first permanent English settlement was planted in the New World, the colonists were insisting on governing themselves at the local level. They thus ensured that the political structure of England's American possessions would differ from that of New Spain, which was ruled autocratically by the Spanish monarchs.

By the 1630s, tobacco was firmly established in Virginia as the staple crop and chief source of revenue. It quickly became just as important in the second English colony planted on Chesapeake Bay: the proprietorship of Maryland, chartered by the king in 1632. (Because Virginia and Maryland both bordered Chesapeake Bay—see map, page 22—they are often referred to collectively as "the Chesapeake.") The Calvert family, who founded Maryland, intended the colony to serve as a haven for their fellow Roman Catholics, who were being persecuted in England. Cecilius Calvert, second Lord Baltimore, became the first colonizer to offer prospective settlers freedom of religion, as long as they were practicing Christians. He did so because he realized that his Catholic coreligionists would likely compose a minority of the colony's population. Only in that respect did Maryland differ from Virginia, where the Church of England was the sole officially recognized religion.

Founding of Maryland

In other ways the two Chesapeake colonies resembled each other. In Maryland as in Virginia, tobacco planters spread out along the river banks, establishing isolated farms instead of towns. The region's deep, wide rivers offered dependable water transportation in an age of few and inadequate roads. Each farm or group of farms had its own wharf, where oceangoing vessels could take on or discharge cargo. As a result, Virginia and Maryland had few towns, for these colonies did not need commercial centers in order to buy and sell goods.

The planting, cultivation, and harvesting of tobacco had to be done by hand; these tasks did not take much skill, but they were repetitious and time-consuming. When the headright system was adopted in Maryland in 1640, a prospective tobacco planter anywhere in the Chesapeake could simultaneously obtain both land and the labor to work it. Good management could make the process self-perpetuating: a planter could use his profits to pay for the passage of more workers, and thus gain title to more land.

There were two possible sources of laborers for the growing tobacco farms of the Chesapeake: Africa and England. In 1619, a Dutch privateer brought more than twenty blacks to Virginia; they were the first known black inhabitants of the English colonies in North America. Over the next few decades small numbers of blacks were carried to the Chesapeake, but even as late as 1670 the black population of Virginia was at most 2,000 and probably no more than 1,500, making up less than 5 percent of the inhabitants. Rather than relying on Africa or the West Indies, then, Chesapeake tobacco planters first looked to England to supply their labor needs. Because men did the agricultural work in European societies, planters and workers alike assumed that field laborers should be males, preferably young, strong ones. Such laborers migrated to America as indentured servants; that is, in return for their passage they contracted to work for planters for periods ranging from four to seven years.

Indentured servants accounted for 75 to 85 percent of the approximately 130,000 English migrants to Virginia and Maryland during the seventeenth century. Roughly three-quarters of them were **Migrants to the Chesapeake** men between the ages of fifteen and twenty-four. Most had been farmers and laborers; some had additional skills. They were what their contemporaries called the "common" or "middling" sort. Judging by their youth, though, most had probably not yet established themselves in England.

Many of the servants came from areas of England that were experiencing especially severe societal disruption during that era of economic change. Some had already moved several times within England before they decided to migrate to America. For such people the Chesapeake appeared to offer good prospects. Once they had fulfilled the terms of their indentures, servants were promised "freedom dues" consisting of clothes, tools, livestock, casks of corn and tobacco, and sometimes even land. From a distance at least, America seemed to hold out chances for advancement unavailable in England.

Still, their lives as servants were difficult. They typically worked six days a week, ten to fourteen hours a day, in a climate much warmer than they were accustomed to. Their masters **Conditions of** could discipline or sell them, and **Servitude** they faced severe penalties for running away. Even so, the laws did offer them some protection. For example, their masters had to supply them with sufficient food, clothing, and shelter, and they could not be beaten excessively.

On occasion, servants turned to the courts with complaints of mistreatment, although many incidents must have gone unreported. Judges clearly favored masters, yet tried to prevent the worst atrocities. In early Maryland, for example, the courts carefully investigated cases in which servants died under mysterious circumstances, in order to assure themselves that a master was not responsible for the death in question. A 1655 case illustrated the way the Maryland courts balanced the financial interests of masters against the physical well-being of servants. A runaway maidservant, who complained of "Extream Usage" and was known to have been beaten by her mistress for "two hours by the clock," was ordered freed from her indenture. Yet the court insisted that she compensate her master for the loss of her time. Sympathetic planters attending court that day contributed the amount she needed.

Servants and planters alike had to contend with epidemic disease; death rates in the Chesapeake were

THE INCONVENIENCIES
THAT HAVE HAPPENED TO SOME PER-
SONS WHICH HAVE TRANSPORTED THEMSELVES
from *England* to *Virginia*, without prouisions necessary to sustaine themselues, hath
greatly hindred the *Progresse* of that noble *Plantation*: For preuention of the like disorders
heereafter, that no man suffer, either through ignorance or misinformation; it is thought requisite to publish this short declaration: wherein is contained a particular of such necessaries, as either priuate families or single persons shall haue cause to furnish themselues with, for their better
support at their first landing in *Virginia*; whereby also greater numbers may receiue in part,
directions how to prouide themselues.

Apparell.	li. s. d.	Tooles.	li. s. d.
One Monmouth Cap	00 01 10	Fiue broad howes at 2 s. a piece	10 00
Three falling bands	01 03	Fiue narrow howes at 16 d. a piece	06 08
Three shirts	07 06	Two broad Axes at 3 s. 8 d. a piece	07 04
One waste-coate	02 02	Fiue felling Axes at 18 d. a piece	07 06
One suite of Canuase	07 06	Two steele hand sawes at 16 d. a piece	02 08
One suite of Frize	10 00	Two two-hand-sawes at 5 s. a piece	10 00
One suite of Cloth	15 00	One whip-saw, set and filed with box, file, and wrest	10 00
Three paire of Irish stockins	04	Two hammers 12 d. a piece	02 00
Foure paire of shooes	08 08	Three shouels 18 d. a piece	04 06
One paire of garters	00 10	Two spades at 18 d. a piece	03 00
One dozen of points	00 03	Two augers 6 d. a piece	01 00
One paire of Canuase sheets	08 00	Sixe chissels 6 d. a piece	03 00
Seuen ells of Canuase, to make a bed and boulster, to be filled in Virginia 8 s.	08 00	Two percers stocked 4 d. a piece	00 08
One Rug for a bed 8 s. which with the bed seruing for two men, halfe is	05 00	Three gimlets 2 d. a piece	00 06
Fiue ells coorse Canuase, to make a bed at Sea for two men, to be filled with straw, iiij. s.	05 00	Two hatchets 21 d. a piece	03 06
One coorse Rug at Sea for two men, will cost vj. s. is for one	03 00	Two froues to cleaue pale 18 d.	03 00
		Two hand bills 20 d. a piece	03 04
		One grindlestone 4 s.	04 00
		Nailes of all sorts to the value of	02 00
		Two Pickaxes	03 00

Victuall.	li. s. d.	Houshold Implements.	li. s. d.
Eight bushels of Meale	02 00	One Iron Pot	07
Two bushels of pease at 3 s.	06 00	One kettle	06
Two bushels of Oatemeale 4 s. 6 d.	09 00	One large frying pan	02 06
One gallon of Aquauitæ	02 06	One gridiron	01 06
One gallon of Oyle	03 06	Two skillets	05
Two gallons of Vineger 1 s.	02 00	One spit	02
		Platters, dishes, spoones of wood	04

Armes.	li. s. d.
One Armour compleat, light	17 00
One long Peece, fiue foot or fiue and a halfe, neere Musket bore	01 02 00
One sword	05 00
One belt	01 00
One bandaleere	01 06
Twenty pound of powder	18 00
Sixty pound of shot or lead, Pistoll and Goose shot	05 00

For Sugar, Spice, and fruit, and at Sea for 6 men.

So the full charge of Apparell, Victuall, Armes, Tooles, and houshold stuffe, and after this rate for each person, will amount vnto about the summe of

The passage of each man is

The fraight of these prouisions for a man, will bee about halfe a Tun, which is

So the whole charge will amount to about — 20 00 00

Nets, hookes, lines, and a tent must be added, if the number of people be greater, as also some kine.

And this is the vsuall proportion that the Virginia Company doe bestow vpon their Tenants which they send.

Whosoeuer transports himselfe or any other at his owne charge vnto *Virginia*, shall for each person so transported before Midsummer 1625, haue to him and his heires for euer fifty Acres of Land vpon a first, and fifty Acres vpon a second diuision.

Imprinted at London by FELIX KYNGSTON. 1622.

The difficulties of the early settlers in Virginia prompted the printing of this broadside in 1622. It advised prospective emigrants to take adequate supplies of food, clothing, weapons, tools, and household goods with them to America, offering specific suggestions aimed at individuals and at families of six persons. Courtesy of the John Carter Brown Library at Brown University.

higher than in England. Migrants first had to survive the process the colonists called seasoning—a bout with disease (probably malaria) that usually occurred during their first summer in the Chesapeake. They then had to endure recurrences of malaria, along with dysentery, influenza, typhoid fever, and other diseases. As a result, approximately 40 percent of male servants did not survive long enough to become freedmen. Even young men of twenty-two who had successfully weathered their "seasoning" could expect to live only another twenty years at best.

For those who survived the term of their indentures, however, the opportunities for advancement were real. Until the last decades of the century, former servants were usually able to become independent planters ("freeholders") and to live a modest but comfortable existence. Some even assumed such positions of political prominence as justice of the peace or militia officer. But in the 1670s tobacco prices entered a fifty-year period of stagnation and decline. At the same time, good land grew increasingly scarce and expensive. In 1681 Maryland dropped its legal requirement that servants receive land as part of their freedom dues, forcing large numbers of freed servants to live as wage laborers or tenant farmers instead of acquiring freeholder status. By 1700 the Chesapeake was no longer the land of opportunity it had once been.

Life in the seventeenth-century Chesapeake was hard for everyone, regardless of sex or status. Farmers (and sometimes their wives) toiled in the fields alongside the servants, laboriously clearing

Family Life in the Chesapeake

the land of trees, then planting and harvesting not only tobacco but also corn, wheat, and vegetables. Chesapeake households subsisted mainly on pork and corn, a filling but monotonous and not particularly nutritious diet. Thus the health problems caused by epidemic disease were magnified by diet deficiencies and the near-impossibility of preserving food for safe winter consumption. (Salting, drying, and smoking, the only methods the colonists knew, did not always prevent spoilage.) Few households had many material possessions other than farm implements, beds, and basic cooking and eating utensils. Even their houses were little more than shacks. Planters devoted their income to improving their farms, buying livestock, and purchasing more laborers rather than to improving their lifestyle. Instead of making such items as clothing and tools, planter families concentrated their energies solely on growing tobacco, importing necessary manufactured goods from England.

The predominance of males, the incidence of servitude, and the high mortality rates combined to produce unusual patterns of family life. Female servants normally were not allowed to marry during their terms of indenture, since masters did not want pregnancies to deprive them of workers. Many male ex-servants could not marry at all, because there were so few women. On the other hand, nearly every adult free woman in the Chesapeake married, and the many widows commonly remarried within a few months of a husband's death. Yet because their marriages were delayed by servitude or broken by death, Chesapeake women bore only one to three children, in contrast to English women, who normally had at least five.

Thus seventeenth-century Chesapeake families were relatively few, small, and short-lived. The migrants could not reproduce the English patriarchal system, even if they wanted to, for they came to America as individuals free of paternal control and they tended to die while their own children were still quite young. (In one Virginia county, for example, more than three-quarters of the children had lost at least one parent by the time they either married or reached twenty-one.)

As a result of the demographic patterns that led to a low rate of natural increase, migrants made up a majority of the Chesapeake population throughout the seventeenth century. That fact had important implications for politics in Maryland and Virginia. Since migrants dominated the population, they also composed the vast majority of the membership of both Virginia's House of Burgesses and Maryland's House of Delegates (established in 1635). So too they dominated the governors' councils in both colonies. (The council acted in three important capacities: as part of the legislature, as the colony's highest court, and as executive advisor to the governor.)

Chesapeake Politics

English-born colonists naturally tended to look to England for solutions to their problems, and migrants frequently relied on English allies to advance their cause. The seventeenth-century leaders of the Chesapeake colonies engaged in bitter and prolonged struggles for power and personal economic advantage; these struggles then crossed the Atlantic, and decisions made in America were laid open to reversal in London. The incessant quarreling and convoluted political tangles thwarted the Virginia and Maryland governments' ability to function effectively.

Representative institutions based on the consent of the governed, it is often argued, are a major source of political stability. In the seventeenth-century Chesapeake, most property-owning white males could vote, and such freeholders chose as their legislators the local elites who seemed to be the natural leaders of their respective areas. But because of the nature of the population, the existence of the assemblies did not lead to political stability. Indeed, the contrary may well have been true. Virginia and Maryland paid a high political price for their unusual demographic patterns.

THE FOUNDING OF NEW ENGLAND

The economic motives that prompted English people to move to the Chesapeake colonies also drew men and women to New England, as the area north and east of the Hudson River soon came to be called (see map). But because Puritans organized the New England colonies, and also because of environmental differences between the two regions, the northern settlements turned out very differently from those in the South. Except for the Catholics who moved to Maryland (where they made up a minority of the population), migrants to the Chesapeake seem to have been little affected by religious motives. Yet religion was a primary motivating factor in the minds of many, though certainly not all, of the people who colonized New England. The Puritan church quickly became one of the most important institutions in colonial New England; in the Chesapeake, neither the Church of England nor Roman Catholicism had much impact on the settlers. In addition, the northern landscape and climate were not suitable for staple-crop production, and so diversified small farms became the dominant economic units.

Religion was a constant presence in the lives of pious Puritans. As followers of John Calvin, they believed that an omnipotent God predestined souls to heaven or hell before birth, and that Christians could do nothing to change their ultimate fate. One of their primary duties as Christians, though, was to assess the state of their own souls. They thus devoted themselves to self-examination and Bible study, and families prayed together each day under the guidance of the husband and father. Yet even the most pious

Puritan Beliefs

could never be absolutely certain that they were numbered among the saved. Consequently, devout Puritans were filled with anxiety about their spiritual state. Many kept diaries in which they minutely examined their everyday feelings for signs of their status.

Some Puritans (called Congregationalists) wanted to reform the Church of England rather than abandon it. Another group, known as Separatists, believed that church to be so corrupt it could not be salvaged. The only way to purify it, they believed, was to start anew, establishing their own religious bodies, with membership restricted to the saved (as nearly as they could be identified).

Separatists were the first to move to New England. In 1609 a group of Separatists migrated to Holland, where they found the freedom of worship denied them in Stuart England. But they were nevertheless troubled by the Netherlands' too-tolerant atmosphere; the nation that tolerated them also tolerated other religions and behaviors they abhorred. Hoping to isolate themselves and their children from the corrupting influence of worldly temptations, they received permission from a branch of the Virginia Company to colonize the northern part of its territory.

In September 1620, more than one hundred people, only thirty of them Separatists, set sail from Plymouth, England, on the old and crowded *Mayflower*. Two

Founding of Plymouth

months later they landed in America, but farther north than they had intended to be. Still, given the lateness of the season—winter was closing in—they decided to stay where they were. They established their colony on a fine harbor that had been occupied by an Indian village destroyed in the great epidemic of 1616–1618. Their settlement was named after the city from which they had sailed.

Even before they landed, the Pilgrims had to surmount their first challenge—from the "strangers," or non-Puritans, who had sailed with them to America. Because they landed outside the jurisdiction of the Virginia Company, some of the strangers questioned the authority of the colony's leaders. In response, the Mayflower Compact, signed in November 1620 while everyone was still on board the ship, established a "Civil Body Politic" and a rudimentary legal authority for the colony. The settlers elected a governor and

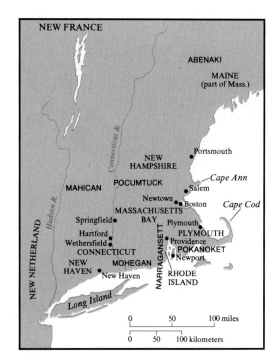

New England Colonies, 1650

at first made all decisions for the colony at town meetings. Later, after more towns had been founded and the population had increased, Plymouth, like Virginia and Maryland, created an assembly to which the landowning male settlers elected representatives.

A second challenge facing the Pilgrims in 1620 and 1621 was, quite simply, survival. Like the Jamestown settlers before them, they were poorly prepared to survive in the new environment. Their difficulties were compounded by the season of their arrival, for they barely had time to build shelters before winter descended on them. Only half of the *Mayflower's* passengers were still alive by spring. But, again like the Virginians, the Pilgrims benefited from the political circumstances of their Indian neighbors.

The Pokanoket (also known as the Wampanoag) controlled the area in which the Pilgrims had settled, yet their villages had suffered terrible losses in the epidemic of 1616–1618. In order to protect themselves from the powerful Narragansett Indians of the southern New England coast (who had been spared the ravages of the disease), the Pokanoket decided to ally themselves with the newcomers. In the spring of 1621,

Algonkian men of the northeastern tribes carved wooden utensils of great beauty. This bowl, dating from before 1630, was probably made by a young Pokanoket or Massachusett man for his bride. The heads of two mythic animals serve as handles.   Private Collection, New York City. Photo: Robert and Aida Mates.

their leader, Massasoit, signed a treaty with the Pilgrims, and during the colony's first difficult years the Pokanoket supplied the English with essential foodstuffs. The settlers were also assisted by Squanto, an Indian whose village had been wiped out by the epidemic. Squanto spoke English—he had been captured by traders and held prisoner in England for several years—and so he served as the Pilgrims' interpreter, as well as their major source of information about the unfamiliar environment.

Before the 1620s had ended, another group of Puritans—this time Congregationalists, not Separatists—launched the colonial enterprise that would

Founding of Massachusetts Bay

come to dominate New England and would absorb Plymouth in 1691. When Charles I, who was more hostile to Puritan beliefs than his father James I, became king in 1625, some non-Separatists began to think about settling in America. A group of Congregationalist merchants sent out a body of settlers to Cape Ann, north of Cape Cod, in 1628. The following year the merchants obtained a royal charter, constituting themselves as the Massachusetts Bay Company.

The new company quickly attracted the attention of Puritans of the "middling sort" who were becoming increasingly convinced that they would no longer be able to practice their religion freely in England. They remained committed to the goal of reforming the Church of England, but came to believe they should pursue that aim in America rather than at home. In a dramatic move, the Congregationalist merchants boldly decided to transfer the headquarters of the Massachusetts Bay Company to New England. The settlers would then be answerable to no one in the mother country and would be able to handle their affairs, secular and religious, as they pleased.

The most important recruit to the new venture was John Winthrop, a pious but practical landed gentleman from Suffolk and a justice of the peace.

Governor John Winthrop

In October 1629, the members of the Massachusetts Bay Company elected the forty-one-year-old Winthrop as their governor. With the exception of isolated years in the mid-1630s and early 1640s, he served in that post until his death in 1649. It thus fell to Winthrop to organize the initial segment of the great Puritan migration to America. In 1630 more than one thousand English men and women came to Massachusetts—most of them to Boston, which soon became the largest town in North America. By 1643 nearly twenty thousand compatriots had followed them.

On board the *Arbella*, en route to New England in 1630, John Winthrop preached a sermon, "A Modell of Christian Charity," laying out his expectations for the new colony. Above all, he stressed the communal nature of the endeavor on which he and his fellow settlers had embarked. God, he explained, "hath so disposed of the condition of mankind as in all times some must be rich, some poor, some high and eminent in power and dignity, others mean and in subjection." But differences in status did not imply differences in worth. On the contrary: God had planned the world so that "every man might have need of other, and from hence they might be all knit more nearly together in the bond of brotherly affection." In America, Winthrop asserted, "we shall be as a city upon a hill, the eyes of all people are upon us." If the Puritans failed to carry out their "special commission" from God, "the Lord will surely break out in wrath against us."

Winthrop's was a transcendent vision. The society he foresaw in Puritan America was a true commonwealth, a community in which each person put the good of the whole ahead of his or her private concerns. It was, furthermore, to be a society whose members all lived according to the precepts of Christian charity, loving and aiding friends and enemies alike. Of course, such an ideal was beyond human reach. Early New England had its share of bitter quarrels and unchristian behavior. What is remarkable is how long the ideal prevailed as a goal to be sought, if seldom or never attained.

The Puritans' communal ideal was expressed chiefly in the doctrine of the covenant. They believed God had made a covenant—that is, an agreement or contract—with them when He chose **Ideal of the** them for the special mission to **Covenant** America. In turn they covenanted with each other, promising to work together toward their goals. The founders of churches and towns in the new land often drafted formal documents setting forth the principles on which such institutions would be based. The same was true of the colonial governments of New England. The Pilgrims' Mayflower Compact was a covenant; so too was the Fundamental Orders of Connecticut (1639), which laid down the basic law for the settlements established along the Connecticut River valley in 1636 and thereafter.

The leaders of Massachusetts Bay likewise transformed their original joint-stock company charter into the basis for a covenanted community based on mutual consent. Under pressure from the settlers, they gradually changed the General Court, officially merely the company's governing body, into a colonial legislature and opened the status of freeman, or voting member of the company, to all adult male church members resident in Massachusetts. Less than two decades after the first large group of Puritans had arrived in Massachusetts Bay, the colony had a functioning system of self-government composed of a governor and a two-house legislature. The General Court also established a judicial system modeled on England's and in 1641 adopted a legal code, *The Laws and Liberties of Massachusetts*, spelling out crimes and their proper punishments.

The colony's method of distributing land helped to further the communal ideal. Unlike Virginia and Maryland, where individual applicants sought headrights for themselves and their servants, in Massachusetts groups of families—often from the same region of England—applied together to the General Court for grants of land on which to establish towns. The men who received the original town grant had the sole authority to determine how the land would be distributed. Understandably, they copied the villages from which they came. First they **New England** laid out town lots for houses and a **Towns** church. Then they gave each family parcels of land scattered around the town center: pasture here, a woodlot there, an arable field elsewhere. They also reserved the best and largest plots for the most distinguished among them (usually including the minister); people who had been low on the social scale in England were given much smaller and less desirable allotments. Even when migrants began to move beyond the territorial limits of the Bay Colony into Connecticut (1636), New Haven (1638), and New Hampshire (1638), the same pattern of town land grants was maintained.

Thus New England settlements initially tended to be more compact than those of the Chesapeake. Town centers grew up quickly, developing in three distinctly different ways. Some, chiefly isolated agricultural settlements in the interior, tried to sustain Winthrop's vision of harmonious community life based on diversified family farms. A second group, the coastal towns like Boston and Salem, became bustling seaports, serving as the places of entry for thousands of new migrants and as focal points for trade. The third category, commercialized agricultural towns, grew up in the Connecticut River valley. There the easy water transportation made it possible for farmers to sell surplus goods readily. In Springfield, Massachusetts, for example, the merchant-entrepreneur William Pynchon and his son John began as fur traders and ended as large landowners with thousands of acres on which tenant farmers produced grain for export. Even in Puritan New England, in other words, the acquisitive, individualistic spirit characteristic of the Chesapeake found some room for expression.

The migration to the Connecticut valley ended the Puritans' relative freedom from clashes with neighboring Indians. The first English settlers in the valley moved there from Newtown (Cambridge), under the direction of their minister, Thomas Hooker. Connecticut was fertile, though remote from the other English towns, and the wide river promised ready access to the ocean. The site had just one problem: it fell within the territory controlled by the Pequot Indians.

John Eliot, painted in 1659 by an unknown artist. Determined to convert the New England Indians to Christianity, Eliot translated the Bible into their language. His Up-Biblum was published in 1663, the first Bible printed in the English colonies. Huntington Library.

many of them women and children. The few surviving Pequots were captured and enslaved.

Just five years later the Narragansett leader Miantonomi realized that the Pequot had been correct in assessing the danger posed by the Puritan settlements. He in turn attempted to forge a pan-Indian alliance, telling other bands that "so are we all Indians as the English are . . . so must we be one as they are, otherwise we shall all be gone shortly." But his words fell on deaf ears, and he was killed in 1643 by other Indians acting at the English colonists' behest.

For the next thirty years, the New England Indians tried to accommodate themselves to the spread of white settlement. They traded with the whites and sometimes worked for them, but for the most part they resisted acculturation or incorporation into English society. Indeed, most whites showed little interest in the Indians except as laborers or producers of valuable trade goods. Only a few Puritan clerics (most notably John Eliot) seriously attempted to convert the Massachusetts Bay Indians to Christianity. Since most of them insisted that converts give up their traditional seminomadic lifestyle to reside in English-style houses and towns, they met with relatively little success. At the peak of Eliot's efforts, only 1,100 Indians lived in the fourteen "Praying Towns" he had established, and just 10 percent of those town residents had been formally baptized.

LIFE IN NEW ENGLAND

Two sets of comparisons will help to illuminate the lives of early New Englanders: first, with the Indians of the region, and second, with the Chesapeake colonists.

The major contrast between the lifestyles of Indian and white residents of New England was the mobility of the former and the stability of the latter. The

Indian and English Lifestyles Compared agricultural Algonkians of New England commonly moved four or five times during the course of a year to take full advantage of their environment. In the spring, women

Pequot dominance was based on their role as primary middlemen in the trade between New England Indians and the Dutch in New Netherland. The arrival of English settlers signaled the end of

Pequot War Pequot power over the regional trading networks, for their tributary bands could now trade directly with Europeans. Clashes between the Pequot and the English began even before the Connecticut valley settlements were established, but their founding tipped the balance toward war. After trying without success to enlist other Indians to resist English expansion into the interior, the Pequot (after an English raid on their villages) attacked the new town of Wethersfield in April 1637, killing nine and capturing two of the colonists. In retaliation, a Massachusetts Bay expedition the following month attacked and burned the main Pequot town on the Mystic River. The Englishmen and their Narragansett Indian allies slaughtered at least four hundred people,

Fairbanks House, Dedham, Massachusetts, built ca. 1637 (as photographed in 1880). Unlike their Indian neighbors or the English residents of the Chesapeake, the migrants to New England constructed dwellings designed to last for many years. Later additions (like those shown on the right of this picture) expanded the size of the original small and simple houses. Society for the Preservation of New England Antiquities.

would plant the fields, but once the crops were well established they would not need regular attention for several months. Accordingly, villages then broke into small mobile bands; women occupied themselves with gathering, men with hunting and fishing. The village would reassemble for harvest, then once again disperse for the fall hunting season. Finally, the people would spend the harsh winter months together, probably in some protected valley, before returning to their fields again in the spring. And every few years they would alter the site of those fields, thus avoiding any need to use fertilizer.

The English settlers, by contrast, lived year-round in the same location. Unlike the Indians or the Chesapeake colonists, New Englanders constructed sturdy, permanent dwellings intended to last for many years. (Indeed, some survive to this day.) They used

the same fields again and again, believing it was less arduous to employ fertilizer than to clear new fields every few years. Although they hunted and fished, their chief source of meat was the livestock they bred on their farms. Hogs in particular reproduced so rapidly that they caused major problems for the settlers. Farmers had to fence their croplands to keep hogs, sheep, and cattle from eating the growing plants; many disputes between neighbors or even entire towns had their origins in one side's livestock having invaded the other side's fields. When New Englanders began to spread out over the countryside, the reason was not so much human crowding as it was animal crowding. All the livestock constantly needed more grazing land on which to survive.

In their heavy reliance on cattle and hogs, white New Englanders resembled their Chesapeake counterparts. But in other ways they differed sharply from them. The contrast between Chesapeake and New England settlement patterns has already been made clear; in addition, the regions varied in their family organization and behavior and with respect to the importance of religion in the settlers' daily lives.

Unlike migrants to the Chesapeake, Puritans commonly moved to America in family groups. Thus, the age range of New Englanders was wide and the sexes more balanced numerically, so that the population could immediately begin to reproduce itself. Moreover, New England's climate was much healthier than that of the Chesapeake. Once Puritan settlements had survived the difficult first two or three years and established self-sufficiency in foodstuffs, New England proved to be even healthier than the mother country. Though adult male migrants to the Chesapeake lost about ten years from their English life expectancy of fifty to fifty-five years, their Massachusetts counterparts gained about ten years.

Consequently, although Chesapeake population patterns made for families that were few in number, small in size, and transitory, the demographic characteristics of New England made **Family Life in** families there numerous, large, and **New England** long-lived. In New England most men were able to marry; migrant women married young (at twenty, on the average); and marriages lasted longer and produced more children, who were more likely to live to maturity. If seventeenth-century Chesapeake women could expect to rear one to three healthy children, New England women could anticipate raising five to seven.

The nature of the population had other major implications for family life. New England in effect created grandparents, since in England people rarely lived long enough to know their children's children. And whereas seventeenth-century southern parents normally died before their children married, northern parents exercised a good deal of control over their adult children. Young men could not marry without acreage to cultivate, and because of the communal land-grant system they were dependent on their fathers to supply them with that land. Daughters, too, needed the dowry of household goods their parents would give them when they married. Yet parents needed their children's labor and were often reluctant to see them marry and start their own households. That at times led to considerable conflict between the generations. On the whole, though, children seem to have obeyed their parents' wishes, for they had few alternatives.

Another important difference lay in the influence of religion on New Englanders' lives. The governments of Massachusetts Bay, Plymouth, Connecticut, and the other early northern colonies were all controlled by Puritans. Congregationalism was the only officially recognized religion; members of other sects had no freedom of worship except in Rhode Island. Only male church members could legally vote in colony elections, although some non-Puritans appear to have voted in town meetings. All households were taxed to build meetinghouses and pay ministers' salaries. Massachusetts' *Body of Laws and Liberties* incorporated regulations drawn from Old Testament scriptures into the legal code of the colony. Moreover, penalties were prescribed for expressing contempt for ministers or their preaching, and for failing to attend church services regularly.

In the New England colonies, church and state were intertwined. Puritans objected to secular interference in religious affairs, but at the same time expected the church to influence the conduct of politics. They also believed that the state had an obligation to support and protect the one true church—theirs. As a result, though they came to America seeking freedom to worship as they wished, they saw no contradiction in their refusal to grant that freedom to others. Indeed, the two most significant divisions in early Massachusetts were caused by religious disputes and by Massachusetts Bay's unwillingness to tolerate dissent.

Roger Williams, a Separatist, migrated to Massachusetts Bay in 1631 and became assistant pastor at Salem. Williams soon began to express the eccentric ideas that the king of England had **Roger** no right to give away land belonging **Williams** to the Indians, that church and state should be kept entirely separate, and that Puritans should not impose their religious beliefs on others. Banished from Massachusetts in 1635, Williams founded the town of Providence on Narragansett Bay. Because of his beliefs, Providence and other towns in what became the colony of Rhode Island adopted a policy of tolerating all religions, including Judaism.

IMPORTANT EVENTS

1492	Christopher Columbus reaches Bahama Islands	1611	First Virginia tobacco crop
1513	Ponce de Leon reaches Florida	1619	First blacks arrive in Virginia
1518–30	Smallpox pandemic decimates Indian population of Central and South America	1620	Plymouth Colony founded
		1622	Powhatan Confederacy attacks Virginia colony
1521	Tenochtitlan surrenders to Cortés; Aztec empire falls to Spaniards	1624	Dutch settle on Manhattan Island
		1625	Charles I becomes king
1533	Henry VIII divorces Catherine of Aragon; English reformation begins	1630	Massachusetts Bay Colony founded
1539–42	Hernando de Soto explores southeastern United States	1634	Maryland founded
		1635	Roger Williams expelled from Massachusetts Bay; founds Providence, Rhode Island
1540–42	Francisco Vásquez de Coronado explores southwestern United States		
		1636	Connecticut founded
1558	Elizabeth I becomes queen	1637	Pequot War
1587–90	Sir Walter Raleigh's Roanoke colony fails		Anne Hutchinson expelled from Massachusetts Bay
1603	James I becomes king	1646	Treaty ends hostilities between Virginia and Powhatan Confederacy
1607	Jamestown founded		

The other dissenter, and an even greater challenge to Massachusetts Bay orthodoxy, was Anne Marbury Hutchinson. A skilled midwife popular with the women of Boston, she was a follower of John Cotton, a minister who stressed the covenant of grace, or God's free gift of salvation to unworthy, utterly helpless human beings. (By contrast, most Massachusetts clerics emphasized the need for Puritans to engage in good works, study, and reflection in preparation for receiving God's grace.) In 1636 Hutchinson began holding women's meetings in her home to discuss Cotton's sermons. Soon men also started to attend. Hutchinson emphasized the covenant of grace more than did Cotton himself and she even

Anne Hutchinson

adopted the belief that the elect could communicate directly with God and be assured of salvation. Such ideas had an immense appeal for Puritans. Anne Hutchinson offered them certainty of salvation instead of a state of constant tension. Her approach also made the institutional church less important.

Hutchinson's ideas were a dangerous threat to Puritan orthodoxy, so in November 1637 she was brought before the General Court of Massachusetts. She was charged with claiming that the colony's ministers preached salvation through works. For two days she defended herself cleverly against her accusers, matching scriptural references and wits with John Winthrop himself. Finally, in an unguarded moment late in the second day, Hutchinson declared that God had spoken to her "by an immediate revelation." That heretical assertion assured her banishment; she and her family, along with some faithful followers, were exiled to Rhode Island.

The authorities in Massachusetts Bay perceived Anne Hutchinson as doubly dangerous to the existing order: she threatened not only religious orthodoxy but also traditional gender roles. Puritans believed in the equality before God of all souls, including women, but they also considered women inferior to men, forever tainted by Eve's guilt. Christians had long followed St. Paul's dictum that women should keep silent in church and be submissive to their husbands. Anne Hutchinson did neither. The magistrates' comments during her trial reveal that they were almost as outraged by her "masculine" behavior as by her religious beliefs. Winthrop charged her with having set wife against husband, since so many of her followers were women. Another judge told her bluntly: "You have stept out of your place, you have rather bine a Husband than a Wife and a preacher than a Hearer; and a Magistrate than a Subject."

The New England authorities' reaction to Anne Hutchinson reveals the depth of their adherence to European gender-role concepts. To them, an orderly society required the submission of wives to husbands as well as the obedience of subjects to rulers. Indeed, one reason why they perceived Indian societies as disorderly was because Indian women seemed to be largely independent of male authority. English people intended to change many aspects of their lives by colonizing North America, but not the sexual division of labor or the assumption of male superiority.

In 1630 John Winthrop wrote to his wife Margaret, who was still in England, "my deare wife, we are heer in a paradise." He was, of course, exaggerating. Yet even though America was not a paradise, it was a place where English men and women could free themselves from Stuart persecution or attempt to better their economic circumstances. Many died, but those who lived laid the foundation for subsequent colonial prosperity. That they did so by dispossessing the Indians bothered few besides Roger Williams. By the middle of the seventeenth century, English people had unquestionably.come to North America to stay.

The permanent presence of Europeans on the soil of the Americas signaled major changes for the peoples of both Old and New Worlds. European political rivalries, once confined to their own continent, now spread around the globe, as the competing nations of England, Spain, Portugal, France, and the Netherlands vied for control of the peoples and resources of Asia, Africa, and the Americas. Because of the varying nature of Indian societies, France and the Netherlands earned their profits from Indian trade rather than imitating the Spanish example and engaging in wars of conquest. Although they too at first relied on trade, the English colonies soon took another form altogether when so many English people of the "common sort" decided to migrate to North America. In the years to come, the European rivalries would grow even fiercer, and residents of the Americas—whites, Indians, and blacks alike—would inevitably be drawn into them. Not until after France and England in the mid-eighteenth century had fought the greatest war yet known, and until the thirteen American colonies had won their independence, would those rivalries cease to affect Americans of all races.

SUGGESTIONS FOR FURTHER READING

General

Charles M. Andrews, *The Colonial Period of American History: The Settlements*, 3 vols. (1934–1937); Gary B. Nash, *Red, White, and Black: The Peoples of Early America*, 2nd ed. (1982); John E. Pomfret, *Founding the American Colonies, 1583–1660* (1970); Robert V. Wells, *Revolutions in Americans' Lives: A Demographic Perspective on the History of Americans, Their Families, and Their Society* (1982).

Indians

Harold E. Driver, *Indians of North America*, 2nd ed. (1969); Alvin Josephy, Jr., *The Indian Heritage of America* (1968); Alice B. Kehoe, *North American Indians: A Comprehensive Account* (1981); Eleanor B. Leacock and Nancy O. Lurie, eds., *North American Indians in Historical Perspective* (1971); Smithsonian Institution, *Handbook of North American Indians*, 6: *Subarctic* (1981), 8: *California* (1978), 9, 10: *The Southwest* (1979, 1983), 15: *The Northeast* (1978); Robert F. Spencer, Jesse D. Jennings, *et al.*, *The Native Americans: Ethnology and Backgrounds of the North American Indians*, 2nd ed. (1977).

Africa

Robin Hallett, *Africa to 1875* (1970); George P. Murdock, *Africa: Its Peoples and Their Culture History* (1959); Richard Olaniyan, *African History and Culture* (1982); Roland Oliver, ed., *The Cambridge History of Africa*, vol. 3: *c. 1050–c. 1600* (1977); Roland Oliver and J. D. Fage, *A Short History of Africa* (1975).

England

Carl Bridenbaugh, *Vexed and Troubled Englishmen, 1590–1642*, rev. ed. (1976); Mildred Campbell, *The English Yeoman under Elizabeth and the Early Stuarts* (1942); Peter Laslett, *The World We Have Lost* (1965); Wallace Notestein, *The English People on the Eve of Colonization 1603–1630* (1954); Lawrence Stone, *The Crisis of the Aristocracy, 1558–1641* (1965); Michael Walzer, *The Revolution of the Saints* (1965); Keith Wrightson, *English Society 1580–1680* (1982).

Exploration and Discovery

Fredi Chiappelli, *et al.*, eds., *First Images of America: The Impact of the New World on the Old*, 2 vols. (1976); Alfred W. Crosby, Jr., *The Columbian Exchange: Biological and Cultural Consequences of 1492* (1972); J. H. Elliott, *The Old World and the New, 1492–1650* (1970); Charles Gibson, *Spain in America* (1966); Samuel Eliot Morison, *The European Discovery of America: The Northern Voyages, A.D. 1500–1600* (1971), *The Southern Voyages, A.D. 1492–1616* (1974); J. H. Parry, *The Age of Reconnaissance* (1963); David B. Quinn, *North America from Earliest Discovery to First Settlements* (1977).

Early Contact Between Whites and Indians

James Axtell, *The European and the Indian: Essays in the Ethnohistory of Colonial North America* (1981); William Cronon, *Changes in the Land: Indians, Colonists, and the Ecology of New England* (1983); Francis Jennings, *The Invasion of America: Indians, Colonialism, and the Cant of Conquest* (1975); Karen O. Kupperman, *Roanoke, The Abandoned Colony* (1984); Karen O. Kupperman, *Settling with the Indians: The Meeting of English and Indian Cultures in America, 1580–1640* (1980); Kenneth Morrison, *The Embattled Northeast: The Elusive Ideal of Alliance in Abenaki-Euroamerican Relations* (1984); Neal Salisbury, *Manitou and Providence: Indians, Europeans, and the Making of New England, 1500–1643* (1982); Bernard Sheehan, *Savagism and Civility: Indians and Englishmen in Colonial Virginia* (1980); Alden T. Vaughan, *American Genesis: Captain John Smith and the Founding of Virginia* (1975); Alden T. Vaughan, *The New England Frontier: Puritans and Indians 1620–1675*, rev. ed. (1979).

New England

David Grayson Allen, *In English Ways: The Movement of Societies and the Transferal of English Law and Custom to Massachusetts Bay in the Seventeenth Century* (1981); Ben Barker-Benfield, "Anne Hutchinson and the Puritan Attitude Toward Women," *Feminist Studies*, I (1972), 65–96; Charles E. Clark, *The Eastern Frontier: The Settlement of Northern New England, 1610–1763* (1970); John Demos, *A Little Commonwealth: Family Life in Plymouth Colony* (1970); Philip J. Greven, Jr., *Four Generations: Population, Land, and Family in Colonial Andover, Massachusetts* (1970); Stephen Innes, *Labor in a New Land: Economy and Society in Seventeenth-Century Springfield* (1983); Sydney V. James, *Colonial Rhode Island* (1975); Lyle Koehler, *A Search for Power: The 'Weaker Sex' in Seventeenth-Century New England* (1980); George Langdon, *Pilgrim Colony: A History of New Plymouth, 1620–1691* (1966); Kenneth A. Lockridge, *A New England Town: The First Hundred Years (Dedham, Massachusetts, 1636–1736)* (1970); Edmund S. Morgan, *The Puritan Dilemma: The Story of John Winthrop* (1958); Edmund S. Morgan, *The Puritan Family: Religion and Domestic Relations in Seventeeth-Century New England*, rev. ed. (1966); Sumner Chilton Powell, *Puritan Village: The Formation of a New England Town* (1963); Darrett Rutman, *Winthrop's Boston: A Portrait of a Puritan Town, 1630–1649* (1965); Darrett Rutman, *American Puritanism: Faith and Practice* (1970); Alan Simpson, *Puritanism in Old and New England* (1955).

Chesapeake

Lois Green Carr and Lorena Walsh, "The Planter's Wife: The Experience of White Women in Seventeenth-Century Maryland," *William and Mary Quarterly*, 3rd ser., 34 (1977), 542–571; Wesley Frank Craven, *The Southern Colonies in the Seventeenth Century, 1607–1689* (1949); Wesley Frank Craven, *White, Red, and Black: The Seventeenth Century Virginian* (1971); David Galenson, *White Servitude in Colonial America: An Economic Analysis* (1981); Ivor Noel Hume, *Martin's Hundred: The Discovery of a Lost Colonial Virginia Settlement* (1979); Karen O. Kupperman, "Apathy and Death in Early Jamestown," *Journal of American History*, 66 (1979), 24–40; Gloria L. Main, *Tobacco Colony: Life in Early Maryland, 1650–1720* (1983); Edmund S. Morgan, *American Slavery, American Freedom: The Ordeal of Colonial Virginia* (1975); Darrett Rutman and Anita Rutman, *A Place in Time: Middlesex County, Virginia, 1650–1750* (1984); Abbot E. Smith, *Colonists in Bondage: White Servitude and Convict Labor in America, 1607–1776* (1947); Thad W. Tate and David L. Ammerman, eds., *The Chesapeake in the Seventeenth Century: Essays on Anglo-American Society & Politics* (1979); *William and Mary Quarterly*, 3rd ser., 30, No. 1 (Jan. 1973): *Chesapeake Society*.

AMERICAN SOCIETY TAKES SHAPE

1650–1720

CHAPTER 2

Olaudah Equiano was eleven years old in 1756 when black raiders seeking slaves for white traders kidnapped him and his younger sister from their village in what is now Nigeria. Until then, he had lived peacefully with his father and mother, his father's other wives, and his seven siblings and half-siblings in a mud-walled compound resembling a small village. Equiano and other members of the Ibo tribe were, he later observed, "habituated to labour from our earliest years." Men, women, and children worked together to cultivate corn, yams, beans, cotton, tobacco, and plantains (a type of banana). Men also herded cattle and goats, and the women spun and wove cotton into clothing. Equiano's family, like others in the region, held prisoners of war as slaves. With what may have been idealizing hindsight, he later recalled that the slaves did "no more work than other members of the community, even their master; their food, clothing, and lodging were nearly the same."

Equiano's experiences as a captive differed sharply from the life he had led as a child in his father's house. For months he was passed from master to master, finally arriving at the coast, where an English slave ship lay at anchor. Terrified by the light complexions, long hair, and strange language of the sailors, he was afraid that "I had gotten into a world of bad spirits and that they were going to kill me." Equiano was placed below decks, where "with the loathsomeness of the stench and crying together, I became so sick and low that I was not able to eat, nor had I the least desire to taste anything." The whites flogged him to make him eat, and he thought about jumping overboard but he was too closely watched. At last some other Ibos told him that they were being taken to the whites' country to work. "I then was a little revived," Equiano remembered, "and thought if it were no worse than working, my situation was not so desperate."

After a long voyage during which many of the Africans died of disease caused by the cramped, unsanitary conditions and poor food, the ship arrived at Barbados, a British island in the West Indies. (In the 1620s and 1630s, English people settled on a number of Caribbean islands where they soon began to rely on slave labor to raise a lucrative crop—sugar cane.) Equiano and his shipmates feared that "these ugly men" were cannibals, but experienced slaves were brought on board to assure them that they would not be eaten and that many blacks like themselves lived on the islands. "This report eased us much," Equiano recalled, "and sure enough soon after we landed there came to us Africans of all languages." Everything in Barbados was new and surprising, but Equiano later remarked particularly on two-storied buildings and horses, neither of which he had ever seen.

Equiano was not purchased in the West Indies because planters there preferred older, stronger slaves. Instead, he was carried to Virginia along with the other less-valuable Africans. There, on the plantation of his new owner, he was separated from the other Africans and put to work weeding and clearing rocks from the fields. "I was now exceedingly miserable and thought myself worse off than any of the rest of my companions," Equiano reported, "for they could talk to each other, but I had no person to speak to that I could understand. In this state I was constantly grieving and pining and wishing for death rather than anything else."

But Equiano did not remain in Virginia for long. Bought by a sea captain, Olaudah Equiano eventually became an experienced sailor. He learned to read and write English, purchased his freedom at the age of twenty-one, and later actively supported the English antislavery movement. In 1789 Equiano published *The Interesting Narrative of the Life of Olaudah Equiano . . . Written by Himself*, from which this account of his captivity is drawn. Until he was purchased by the sailor, Equiano's experiences differed very little from those of other Africans who were forced into slavery in the English colonies of the New World. Like him, many were sold by black slavers and taken first to the West Indies, then to North America. His *Interesting Narrative*, one of a number of memoirs by former slaves, depicts the captives' terror powerfully and convincingly.

Chapter 2: AMERICAN SOCIETY TAKES SHAPE, 1650–1720

Charles II, who returned from exile to become king in 1660, consolidated England's hold over eastern North America by chartering six new colonies. Moreover, his commercial policies ensured that the economies of the American settlements would be closely linked to that of England. National Portrait Gallery, London.

Equiano's life story illustrates one of the major developments in colonial life during the century after 1650: the importation of more than two hundred thousand unwilling, captive Africans into North America. The introduction of the institution of slavery and the arrival of large numbers of West African peoples dramatically reshaped colonial society. Indeed, the geographic patterns of that migration continue to influence the United States to the present day.

The other important trends in colonial life between 1650 and 1720 were external rather than internal. That is, they pertained to the English colonists' relationships with others: first, with England itself, and second, with their neighbors in America. Although in the early years of settlement events in England had little direct impact on North America, that situation changed when civil war broke out in the colonists' homeland in 1642. First the Puritan victory in the war, then the restoration of the Stuart monarchy, and finally the Glorious Revolution of 1688 and 1689 indelibly affected the residents of England's American possessions. By the end of the seventeenth century, the New World colonies were no longer isolated outposts but an integral part of a far-flung mercantile empire. As such, policies made in distant London became constant reminders that they were tied, willingly or not, to the world of Europe.

The English colonists likewise interacted regularly with their neighbors on the American continent—their Indian trading partners and other transplanted Europeans, with whom they increasingly competed for control of North America. As the English settlements expanded, they came into violent conflict not only with the powerful Indian tribes of the interior but also with the Dutch, the Spanish, and especially the French. By 1720, war—between Europeans and Indians, among Europeans, and among Indians allied with different colonial powers—had become an all-too-frequent feature of American life.

THE ENGLISH CIVIL WAR, THE STUART RESTORATION, AND THE AMERICAN COLONIES

By the time Charles I became king in 1625, members of the Puritan sect dominated Parliament. For eleven years (1629–1640) Charles, who wanted to suppress Puritanism, refused to call Parliament into session, ruling the nation arbitrarily. When Parliament finally met, it passed laws limiting the monarch's authority. In 1642 civil war broke out between supporters of the king and those who favored Parliament. Four years later, Parliament triumphed; Charles I was executed in 1649.

Oliver Cromwell, the leader of the parliamentary army, assumed control of the government, taking the title of Lord Protector in 1653. After Cromwell's death in 1658, Parliament decided to restore the

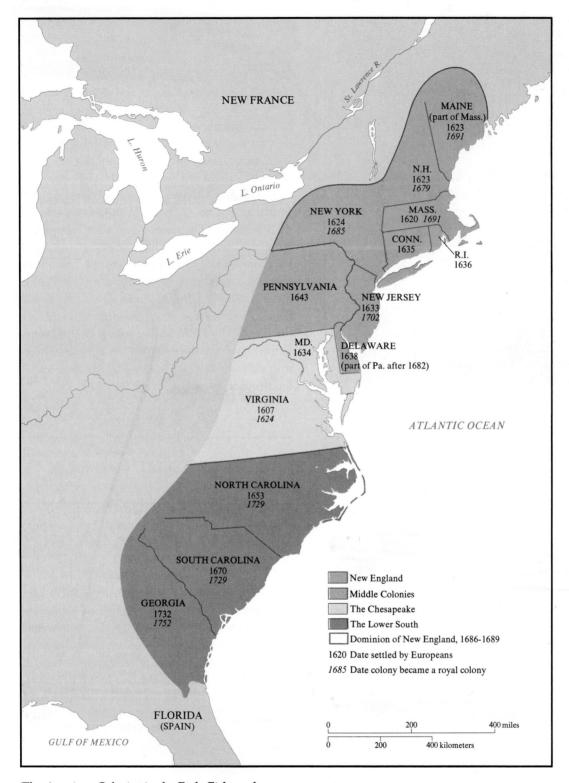

NEW FRANCE

St. Lawrence R.

L. Huron

L. Ontario

L. Erie

MAINE
(part of Mass.)
1623
1691

N.H.
1623
1679

NEW YORK
1624
1685

MASS.
1620 *1691*

CONN.
1635

R.I.
1636

PENNSYLVANIA
1643

NEW JERSEY
1633
1702

MD.
1634

DELAWARE
1638
(part of Pa. after 1682)

VIRGINIA
1607
1624

ATLANTIC OCEAN

NORTH CAROLINA
1653
1729

SOUTH CAROLINA
1670
1729

GEORGIA
1732
1752

FLORIDA
(SPAIN)

GULF OF MEXICO

New England
Middle Colonies
The Chesapeake
The Lower South
Dominion of New England, 1686-1689
1620 Date settled by Europeans
1685 Date colony became a royal colony

0   200   400 miles

0   200   400 kilometers

**The American Colonies in the Early Eighteenth
Century**

monarchy if Charles I's son and heir would agree to certain restrictions on his authority. In 1660, Charles II assumed the throne, having promised to seek Parliament's consent for any new taxes and to support the Church of England. Thus ended the tumultuous chapter in English history known as the Interregnum (Latin for "between reigns").

The Civil War and Interregnum had both short-term and long-term consequences for England's American colonies. Political disruption in the mother country fostered similar disruption in America, especially in the Chesapeake. Both Virginia and Maryland were wracked by disputes over the structure of political and religious authority. In Maryland, for example, the provincial court could not meet from 1644 to 1647 because of a Protestant uprising. During those years, no debts could be collected, no crimes prosecuted, and no wills probated.

The effects on New England were long-term and quite different. Puritan New Englanders welcomed the victory of their compatriots across the Atlantic, and some of them even packed up and returned home to the mother country. More important, because the Puritan triumph in England removed dissenters' major incentive for moving to America, migration to Massachusetts Bay largely ceased after 1640. This had a profound impact on the colony's economy and on its subsequent development. The Stuart Restoration, which again placed Anglicans (members of the Church of England) in power, effectively isolated the New England Puritans within the empire. Stuart monarchs proved to be highly suspicious of New Englanders, whose coreligionists had executed Charles I, and the Puritans thereafter found it difficult to deal with English officials. By the last quarter of the century, friction between the northern colonies and the mother country had increased substantially. These developments will be considered in detail later in this chapter (see pages 57–62).

The reign of Charles II (1660–1685) had enormous significance for the future United States. Six of the thirteen colonies that eventually would form the nation were either founded or came under English rule during that period: New York, New Jersey, Pennsylvania (including Delaware), and North and South Carolina (see map). All were proprietorships; that is, like Maryland they were granted in their entirety to one man or a group of men, who both held title to the soil and controlled the government. Charles II gave these vast American holdings as rewards to the men who had supported him during his years of exile. Several of his favorites even shared in more than one grant.

One of the first to benefit was Charles's younger brother James, the Duke of York. In March 1664, acting as though the Dutch colony of New Netherland did not exist, Charles II gave James the region between the Connecticut and Delaware rivers, including the Hudson Valley and Long Island. James immediately organized an invasion fleet. In late August the vessels anchored off Manhattan Island and demanded New Netherland's surrender. The Dutch complied without firing a shot. Although the Netherlands briefly regained control of the colony in 1672 during one of the Anglo-Dutch wars, it permanently ceded the province in 1674.

Thus England acquired a tiny but heterogeneous possession. New Netherland had been founded in 1624, but had remained small in comparison to its English neighbors. As a trading outpost of the Dutch West India Company, whose chief economic interests lay elsewhere (in Africa, Brazil, and modern-day Indonesia), New Netherland was neglected. And because the Dutch were not afflicted by the economic and religious pressures that caused English people to move to the New World, migration was sparse. Even a company policy of 1629 that offered a large land grant, or patroonship, to anyone who would bring fifty settlers to the province failed to attract takers. (Only one such tract—Rensselaerswyck, near modern Albany—was ever fully developed.) In the mid-1660s, when the Duke of York assumed control, New Netherland had only about five thousand inhabitants.

New Netherland Becomes New York

Logically enough, the Dutch made up the largest proportion of the population. There was also an appreciable minority of English people in the colony, for Puritan New Englanders had begun to settle on Long Island as early as the 1640s. New York, as it was now called, also included sizable numbers of Germans, French-speaking Walloons, Scandinavians (New Netherland had swallowed up Swedish settlements on the Delaware River in 1655), and Africans, as well as an additional smattering of other European peoples. Because the Dutch West India Company

t' Fort nieuw Amsterdam op de Manhatans

New Amsterdam in 1651. Appropriately, given their importance to the survival of the colony, fur-trading Indians and vessels of the Dutch West India Company figure prominently in the earliest known view of the Dutch outpost on Manhattan Island. Library of Congress.

actively imported slaves into the colony after its efforts to attract white settlers had failed, almost one-fifth of New York City's approximately 1,500 inhabitants were black. Slaves thus constituted a higher proportion of New York's urban population than of the Chesapeake's at the same time. One observer commented that eighteen different languages could be heard in the colony.

Recognizing the diversity of the population, the Duke of York's representatives moved cautiously in their efforts to establish English authority. The Duke's Laws, a legal code proclaimed in March 1665, at first applied only to the Puritan settlements on Long Island; they were later extended to the rest of the colony. Dutch forms of local government were maintained and Dutch land titles confirmed. Religious toleration was guaranteed through a sort of multiple establishment: each town was permitted to decide which church to support with its tax revenues. Furthermore, the Dutch were allowed to maintain their customary legal practices. Until the 1690s, for example, many Dutch couples wrote joint wills, which were

enforced in New York courts even though under English law married women could not draft wills. Much to the chagrin of English residents of the colony, the Duke's Laws made no provision for a representative assembly. Like other Stuarts, James was suspicious of legislative bodies, and so not until 1683 did he agree to the colonists' requests for an elected legislature. Before then, New York was ruled by an autocratic governor, as it had been under the Dutch.

The English takeover thus had little immediate effect on the colony. Its population grew slowly, barely reaching eighteen thousand by the time of the first English census in 1698. Until the second decade of the eighteenth century, New York City remained a commercial backwater within the orbit of Boston.

One of the chief reasons why the English conquest brought so little change to New York was that the Duke of York quickly regranted the land between the Hudson and Delaware rivers—New Jersey—to

Founding of New Jersey his friends Sir George Carteret and John Lord Berkeley. That left his own colony confined between Connecticut to the east and New Jersey to the west, depriving it of much fertile land and hindering its economic growth. He also failed to promote migration. Meanwhile the New Jersey proprietors acted rapidly to attract settlers, promising generous land grants, freedom of religion, and—without authorization from the crown—a representative assembly. In response, large numbers of Puritan New Englanders migrated southward to New Jersey, along with some Dutch New Yorkers and a contingent of families from Barbados.

Within twenty years, Berkeley and Carteret sold their interests in New Jersey to separate groups of investors. Because of the resulting large number of individual proprietary shares, and because the governor of New York had granted lands in New Jersey before learning that the duke had given it away, land titles in northern New Jersey were clouded for many years to come. Nevertheless, New Jersey grew quickly; at the time of its first census in 1726, it had 32,500 inhabitants, only 8,000 fewer than New York.

The purchasers of all of Carteret's share (West Jersey) and portions of Berkeley's East Jersey were Quakers seeking a refuge from persecution in England. The Quakers, formally known as the Society of Friends, denied the need for an intermediary between the individual and God. Anyone, they believed, could receive the "inner light" and be saved, and all were equal in God's sight. They had no formally trained clergy; any Quaker, male or female, who felt the call could become a "public Friend" and travel from meeting to meeting to discuss God's word. Moreover, any member of the Society could speak in meetings if he or she desired. In short, the Quakers were true religious radicals in the mold of Anne Hutchinson. (Indeed, Mary Dyer, who followed Hutchinson into exile, became a Quaker, returned to Boston as a missionary, and was hanged for preaching Quaker doctrines).

The Quakers obtained a colony of their own in 1681, when Charles II granted the region between Maryland and New York to William Penn, one of the sect's most prominent members.

Pennsylvania, a Quaker Haven The pious yet fun-loving Penn was then thirty-seven years old. Penn's father, Admiral William Penn, had originally served Oliver Cromwell, but later joined forces with Charles II and even loaned the monarch a substantial sum of money. The younger Penn became a Quaker in the mid-1660s, much to his father's dismay. But despite Penn's radical political and religious beliefs, he and Charles II were close personal friends. Were it not for their friendship (and the desire of Charles's advisors to rid England of religious dissenters), the despised Quakers would never have won a charter for an American settlement. As it was, the publicly stated reason for the grant—repayment of the loan from Penn's father—was just that, a public rationalization for a private act.

William Penn held the colony as a personal proprietorship, and the vast property holdings earned profits for his descendants until the American Revolution. Even so, Penn, like the Roman Catholic Calverts of Maryland before him, saw the province not merely as a source of revenue but also as a haven for his persecuted coreligionists. Penn offered land to all comers on liberal terms, promised toleration for all religions (though only Christians were given the right to vote), guaranteed such English liberties as the right to bail and trial by jury, and pledged to establish a representative assembly. He also publicized the ready availability of land in Pennsylvania through promotional tracts printed in German, French, and Dutch.

Penn's activities and the natural attraction of his lands for Quakers gave rise to a migration whose magnitude was equaled only by the Puritan exodus to New England in the 1630s. By mid-1683, over three thousand people—among them Welsh, Irish, Dutch, and Germans—had already moved to Pennsylvania, and within five years the population had reached twelve thousand. (By contrast, it took Virginia more than thirty years to achieve a comparable population.) Philadelphia, carefully planned to be the major city in the province, drew merchants and artisans from throughout the English-speaking world. From mainland and West Indian colonies alike came Quakers seeking religious freedom; they brought with them years of experience on American soil and well-established trading connections. Pennsylvania's lands were both plentiful and fertile, and the colony soon began exporting flour and other foodstuffs to the West Indies. Practically overnight Philadelphia acquired more than two thousand citizens and began to challenge Boston's commercial pre-eminence.

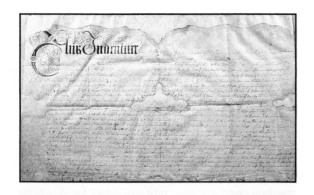

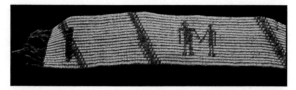

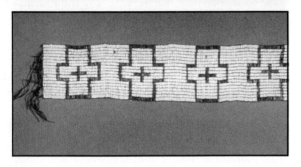

When the Delaware Indians sold land to William Penn, each side recorded the deed in its own way. The English drew up a written document, signed and sealed by all concerned; the Delawares prepared wampum belts portraying the four tribal groups participating in the sale and the peaceful agreement between Indians and whites (shown standing hand in hand). Deed and top belt: Historical Society of Pennsylvania; bottom belt: Courtesy Museum of the American Indian.

A pacifist with egalitarian principles, Penn was determined to treat the Indians of Pennsylvania fairly. He carefully purchased tracts of land from the Delaware (or Lenni Lenape), the dominant tribe in the region, before selling them to settlers. Penn also established strict regulations for the Indian trade and forbade the sale of alcohol to tribesmen. In 1682 he visited a number of Lenni Lenape villages, after taking pains to learn the language. "I must say," Penn commented, "that I know not a language spoken in Europe that hath words of more sweetness in Accent and Emphasis, than theirs."

Penn's Indian policy provides a sterling example of the complexity of the interaction among whites and Indians, because it prompted several tribes to move to Pennsylvania. Indians from western Maryland, Virginia, and North Carolina came northward near the end of the seventeenth century to escape repeated clashes with white settlers. The most important of these tribes was the Tuscarora, whose experiences will be described later in this chapter. Likewise, the Shawnee and Miami chose to move eastward from the Ohio valley. By a supreme irony, however, the same toleration that attracted Indians to Penn's domains also brought non-Quaker Europeans who showed little respect for Indian claims to the soil. In effect, Penn's policy was so successful that it caused its own downfall. The Scotch-Irish, Palatine Germans, and Swiss who settled in Pennsylvania in the first half of the eighteenth century clashed repeatedly over land with tribes that had also recently migrated to the colony.

The other proprietary colony, granted by Charles II in 1663, encompassed a huge tract of land stretching from the southern boundary of Virginia to Spanish Florida. The area had great strategic importance; a successful English settlement there would prevent the Spanish from pushing further north. The semitropical land was also extremely fertile, holding forth the promise of producing such exotic and valuable commodities as figs, olives, wines, and silk. The proprietors named their new province Carolina in Charles's honor (in Latin his name was Carolus). The "Fundamental Constitutions of Carolina," which they asked

Founding of Carolina

the political philosopher John Locke to draft for them, set forth an elaborate plan for a colony governed by a hierarchy of landholding aristocrats and characterized by a carefully structured distribution of political and economic power. But Carolina failed to follow the course the proprietors laid out. Instead it quickly developed two distinct population centers, which in 1729 permanently split into two separate colonies.

The Albemarle region that became North Carolina was settled by Virginians. They established a society much like their own, with an economy based on tobacco cultivation and the export of such forest products as pitch, tar, and timber. Because North Carolina lacked a satisfactory harbor, its planters continued to rely on Virginia's ports and merchants to conduct their trade, and the two colonies remained tightly linked.

South Carolina developed quite differently. Its first settlers, who founded Charleston in 1670, came from Barbados. That tiny island had been colonized by the English in 1627 and was already overcrowded less than fifty years later. When white planters from Barbados moved to the mainland of North America, they brought with them the slaves who had worked on their sugar plantations. By so doing they irrevocably shaped the future of South Carolina and the subsequent history of the United States.

THE FORCED MIGRATION OF AFRICANS

During the first six decades of English settlement in America few blacks were imported into the mainland colonies. After 1670 that pattern changed dramatically. Why did the change occur, in the Chesapeake as well as in South Carolina? And, more important, since England itself had no tradition of slavery, why did English settlers in the New World begin to enslave Africans at all? The answers to both questions lie in the combined effects of economics and racial attitudes.

The English were an ethnocentric people. As was seen in Chapter 1, they believed firmly in the superiority of their values and civilization, especially when compared with the native cultures of Africa and North America. Furthermore, they believed that fair-skinned peoples like themselves were superior to the darker-skinned races. Those beliefs alone did not cause them to enslave Indians and Africans, but the idea that other races were inferior to whites helped to justify slavery.

Although the English had not previously practiced slavery, other Europeans had. The Spanish and Portuguese, for example, had long enslaved African Muslims and other "heathen" peoples. Further, Christian doctrine could even be interpreted as allowing enslavement as a means of converting such people to the true faith. European colonizers needed a large labor force to exploit the riches of the New World, and few free people were willing to work as wage laborers in the difficult and dangerous conditions of South American mines or Caribbean sugar plantations. Needing bound laborers, then, Europeans sought them chiefly in the ranks of dark-skinned non-Christians.

The most obvious source of workers would have been the Indians native to the Americas. But, for a variety of reasons, although some Indians were indeed enslaved (see page 54), they could not supply all the Europeans' labor needs. As was noted in Chapter 1, alien diseases had taken a terrible toll of the Native Americans; in addition, in the Spanish colonies Indian slavery was not only illegal but also actively discouraged by the Catholic Church. No such religious motive worked against Indian slavery in the English settlements, but they also had good reason not to enslave too many Indians. For one thing, the native peoples' familiarity with the environment enabled them to escape easily from their white masters. For another, the presence of Indian slaves in a white settlement might provoke retaliatory raids from their fellow tribesmen. Colonial authorities also feared that if they enslaved Indian captives, the tribes might treat captured whites in a similar fashion.

Africans were a different story. Transported far from home and set down in alien surroundings, like Olaudah Equiano they were frequently unable to communicate with their fellow workers. They were also the darkest (and thus, to European eyes, the most inferior) of all peoples. Black Africans therefore seemed to be ideal candidates for perpetual servitude. By the time the English established settlements in the Caribbean and North America, Spanish colonists had already held Africans in slavery for over a century. The English newcomers to the New World, in other words, had a ready-made model to copy.

Nevertheless, a fully developed system of lifelong slavery did not emerge immediately in the English colonies. Lack of historical evidence makes it difficult

Slavery Established to determine the legal status of blacks during the first two or three decades of English settlement, but many of them seem to have been indentured, like whites, which meant that they eventually became free. (Massachusetts, in 1641, was the first to mention slavery in its legal code.) After 1640, some blacks were being permanently enslaved in each of the English colonies. By the end of the century, the blacks' status was fixed. Barbados adopted a comprehensive slave code as early as 1661, and the mainland provinces soon did the same. In short, even before the expansion of slavery in North America, the English settlements there had established the legal basis for a slave system.

But why did Chesapeake tobacco planters, who had long relied on indentured English servants, begin to purchase blacks in ever-increasing numbers near the end of the seventeenth century? The answer was simple: After about 1675 they could no longer obtain an adequate supply of white workers. A falling birth rate and improved economic conditions in England decreased the number of possible migrants to the colonies. At the same time new English settlements in North America had started to compete with the Chesapeake for settlers, both indentured and free. As a result, the number of servant migrants to the Chesapeake leveled off after 1665 and fell in the 1680s. After 1674, when the shortage of servants became acute, imports of Africans increased dramatically. As early as 1690, the Chesapeake colonies contained more black slaves than white indentured servants, and by 1710 one-fifth of the region's population was black. Slaves usually cost about two-and-a-half times as much as servants, but they repaid the greater investment by their lifetime of service.

Yet not all white planters could afford to devote so much money to purchasing workers. Accordingly, the transition from indentured to enslaved labor increased the social and economic distance between richer and poorer planters. Whites with enough money could acquire slaves and accumulate greater wealth, while less affluent whites could not even buy indentured servants, whose price had been driven up by scarcity. In addition, the transition to slave labor ended what had become a common way for poorer white planters to earn essential income: renting parts of their property to newly freed servants. Deprived of that source of capital—since there were far fewer ex-servants—many marginal planters sank into landless status. As time passed, white Chesapeake society thus became more and more stratified; that is, the gap between rich and poor steadily widened. The introduction of large numbers of Africans into the Chesapeake, in other words, had a significant impact on white society, in addition to reshaping the population as a whole.

In South Carolina, as has been seen, the first slaves arrived with the first white settlers. Indeed, one-quarter to one-third of South Carolina's early population was black. The Barbados whites quickly discovered that Africans had a variety of skills well suited to the semitropical environment of South Carolina. African-style dugout canoes became the chief means of transportation in the colony, which was crisscrossed by rivers. Fishing nets copied from African models proved to be more efficient than those of English origin. The baskets slaves wove and the gourds they hollowed out came into general use as containers for food and drink. Africans' skill at killing crocodiles equipped them to handle alligators as well. And, finally, slaves adapted African techniques of cattleherding for use in the American context. Since meat and hides, not the exotic products originally envisioned, were the colony's chief exports in its earliest years, blacks obviously contributed significantly to South Carolina's prosperity.

Blacks in South Carolina

The similarity of South Carolina's environment to West Africa, coupled with the large number of blacks in the population, ensured that more aspects of West African culture survived in that colony than elsewhere on the mainland of North America. Only in South Carolina did black parents continue to give their children African names; only there did a dialect develop that combined English words with African terms. (Known as Gullah, it was used in certain areas until the twentieth century.) African skills remained useful, and so techniques that in other regions were lost when the migrant generation died were instead passed down to their children. And in South Carolina, as in West Africa, black women were the primary traders, dominating the markets of Charleston as they did those of Gambia or Benin. One white observer commented that "these women have such a connection with and influence on the country negroes who come to that market, that they generally find means to obtain whatever they choose, in preference to any white person; thus they forestall and engross many articles, which some hours afterwards you must buy back from them at 100 or 150 per cent advance."

Blacks' central position in the colony's economy was firmly established near the end of the seventeenth

Mulberry Plantation, South Carolina, in the late eighteenth century. The mansion house on this indigo and rice plantation (built 1708) is surrounded by slave quarters—African-style huts constructed by Africans and their Afro-American children. Some of the tiny houses survived into the twentieth century. Painting by Thomas Coram. Carolina Art Association/Gibbes Art Gallery.

century, when South Carolinians began to cultivate a new staple crop: rice. English people knew little about the techniques of growing and processing rice, and their first attempts to raise it were unsuccessful. But slaves from Africa's Rice Coast (see page 11) had spent their lives working with the crop. Significantly, the importation of large numbers of Africans coincided with the successful introduction of rice as a staple crop in South Carolina. Although the evidence is circumstantial, it seems likely that the Africans' expertise enabled their English masters to cultivate the crop profitably. In the mid-eighteenth century a South Carolina merchant commented that "the Slaves from the River Gambia are preferr'd to all others with us save the Gold Coast." After rice had become South Carolina's major export, 43 percent of the Africans imported into the colony came from rice-producing regions.

South Carolina later developed a second staple crop, and it too made use of blacks' special skills. The crop was indigo, much prized in Europe as a blue dye for clothing. In the early 1740s, Eliza Lucas, a young white West Indian woman who was managing her father's South Carolina plantations, began to experiment with indigo cultivation. Drawing on the knowledge of white and black West Indians, she developed the planting and processing techniques later adopted throughout the colony. Indigo was grown on high ground, and rice was planted in low-lying swampy areas; rice and indigo also had opposite growing seasons. Thus the two crops complemented each other perfectly. Although South Carolina indigo never matched the quality of that raised in the West Indies, the indigo industry flourished because Parliament offered Carolinians a bounty on every pound they exported to Great Britian.

After 1700 white southerners were irrevocably committed to black slavery as their chief source of

In the early eighteenth century, the king of Dahomey formed a women's brigade to help him conquer neighboring kingdoms. This contemporary print, which shows him leading his armed female troops to war, both illustrates the continuing importance in West Africa of dual-sex social organization and shows the significant political changes caused by the slave trade, as rulers sought to extend their power over wider areas. (The women's brigade was not disbanded until 1892.) The New York Public Library, Astor, Lenox, and Tilden Foundations.

labor. The same was not true of white northerners.

Slavery in the North

Only a small proportion of the slaves brought to the English colonies in America went to the northern mainland provinces, and most of those who did worked as domestic servants. Lacking large-scale agricultural enterprises, the rural North did not demand many enslaved laborers. In northern urban areas, though, white domestic servants were hard to find and harder to keep (because higher wages were paid for other jobs in the labor-scarce economy), and blacks there filled an identifiable need. In some northern colonial cities (notably Newport, Rhode Island, and New York City), black slaves accounted for more than 10 percent of the population.

The introduction of large-scale slavery in the South, coupled with its near-absence in the North, accentuated regional differences that had already begun to develop in England's American colonies. To the distinction between diversified agriculture and staple-crop production was now added a difference in the race and status of most laborers. That difference was one of degree, but it was nonetheless crucial. In the latter years of the seventeenth century, white southern planters chose a course of action that nearly two centuries later took the future United States into civil war.

Between 1492 and 1770 more Africans than Europeans came to the New World. But just 4.5 percent of them (345,000 persons by 1861, or 275,000 during the eighteenth century) were imported into the region that later became the United States. By contrast, 42 percent of the approximately 9.5 million enslaved blacks were carried to the Caribbean, and 49 percent went to South America, mainly to the Portuguese colony of Brazil. The magnitude of this trade in slaves raises three important and related questions. First, what was its impact on West Africa, the source of most of the slaves taken to North America? Second, how was the trade organized and conducted? Third, what was its effect on the blacks it carried?

The West African coast was one of the most fertile

Cape Coast Castle in 1692. Built by the Royal African Company, this fort on the Gold Coast was one of the most important English slave-trading posts in West Africa. After Greenhill.

and densely inhabited regions of the continent. Despite the extent of forced migration to the Western Hemisphere, the area was not noticeably

West Africa and the Slave Trade

depopulated by the trade in human beings. (Further south, though, Angola—which was the chief source of slaves carried by the Portuguese to Brazil—did suffer severe depopulation.) In Guinea, the primary consequences of the trade were political. The coastal kings who served as middlemen in the trade used it as a vehicle to consolidate their power and extend their rule over larger territories. They controlled European traders' access to slaves and at the same time controlled inland peoples' access to desirable European trade goods like cloth, beads, alcohol, tobacco, firearms, and iron bars that could be made into knives and other tools. The centralizing tendencies of the trade thus helped in the formation of such powerful eighteenth-century kingdoms as Dahomey and Asante (created from the Akan States; see page 11).

These West African kings played a crucial role in the functioning of the slave trade. Europeans set up permanent slave-trading posts in Lower Guinea under the protection of local rulers, who then supplied the resident Europeans with slaves to fill the ships that stopped regularly at the coastal forts. In Upper Guinea, the lack of good harbors caused a somewhat different trading pattern: Europeans would sail along the coast, stopping to pick up cargoes when signaled from the shore. Most persons thereby sold into American slavery were wartime captives (including leaders of high status), criminals sentenced to enslavement, or persons seized for nonpayment of debts. A smaller proportion had been kidnapped, like Olaudah Equiano.

The Portuguese, who initially controlled most of the slave trade, were supplanted by the Dutch in the middle of the seventeenth century. The Dutch in turn lost out to the English, who came to dominate the trade through the efforts of the Royal African Company, a joint-stock company chartered by Charles II in 1672. Holding a monopoly on all English trade

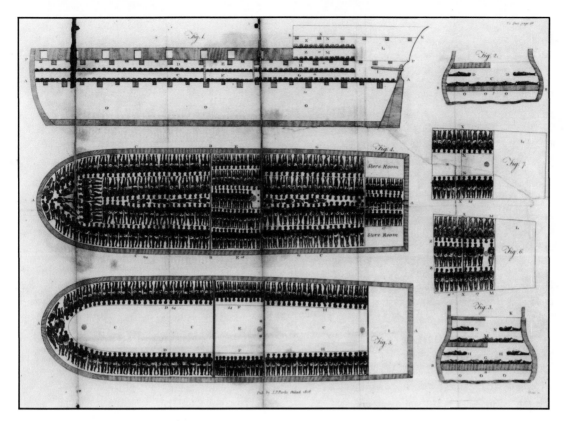

Eighteenth-century diagram of a slave ship, with its human cargo stowed according to British regulations. Many captains did not give slaves even this much room. On the assumption that a large number of Africans would die en route, shipmasters packed as many slaves as possible into the hold to increase their profit. Library of Congress.

with black Africa, the company built and maintained eight forts, dispatched to West Africa hundreds of ships carrying English manufactured goods, and transported more than 120,000 slaves to England's American colonies. Yet even before the company's monopoly expired in 1712 many individual English traders had illegally entered the market for slaves. By the early eighteenth century, such independent traders were carrying most of the Africans imported into the colonies, making slaves more readily available in Anglo-America than they had been previously.

At first, most of the slaves imported into the English colonies went to the Caribbean islands. As mainland planters began to purchase slaves in greater numbers, some blacks were re-exported from the West Indies to meet the demand. Even before the end of the seventeenth century, though, most blacks brought to the future United States came directly from Africa. And although Chesapeake and South Carolina planters initially bought approximately equal numbers of slaves, by the middle of the eighteenth century Carolinians were purchasing three times as many blacks each year as Virginians and Marylanders combined. One result was that blacks made up a majority of the population of South Carolina even before midcentury.

The experience of the Middle Passage (thus named because it was the middle section of the so-called triangular trade among England, Africa, and the Americas; see pages 58–59) was always traumatic and sometimes fatal for the Africans who made up the ship's cargo. An average of 10 to 20 percent of the slaves died en route, but on voyages that were particularly long or were hard hit by epi-

The Middle Passage

demic diseases, the mortality rates were much higher. In addition, some slaves usually died either before the ships left Africa or shortly after their arrival in the New World. Their white captors died at the same, if not higher, rates, chiefly through exposure to alien African germs. Just 10 percent of the men sent to run the Royal African Company's forts in Lower Guinea lived to return home to England, and one in every four or five white sailors died on the Middle Passage. Once again, the exchange of diseases that accompanied the interaction of alien peoples caused unanticipated death and destruction.

On shipboard, men were usually kept shackled in pairs, while women and children were released from any bonds once the ship was well out at sea. The slaves were fed a vegetable diet of beans, rice, yams, or corn, cooked together in various combinations to create a warm mush. In good weather, they were normally allowed on deck for fresh air, because only healthy slaves commanded high prices. Many ships also carried a doctor whose primary role was to treat the slaves' illnesses. The average size of a cargo was about 250 slaves, although since the size of ships varied greatly, so too did the number of slaves carried.

Records of slave traders reveal numerous instances of Africans' resistance to captivity. Recall that Olaudah Equiano contemplated suicide; many of his fellow captives took that means of avoiding servitude. Others participated in shipboard revolts; more than 150 occurred during the three-hundred-year history of the Middle Passage. Yet most of the Africans who embarked on the slave vessels arrived in the Americas alive and still in captivity; the whites saw to that, for only thus could they make a profit. The kind of life those Africans found in their new homes will be discussed in Chapter 3.

RELATIONS BETWEEN WHITES AND INDIANS

Everywhere in North America, European colonizers depended heavily on the labor of native peoples. But their reliance on the Indians took varying forms in different parts of the continent. In the Northeast, France, England, and the Netherlands competed for the pelts supplied by Indian hunters. In the Southeast, England, Spain, and later France each tried to control a thriving trade with the tribes in deerskins and Indian slaves. Finally, in the Southwest, Spain attempted to exploit the agricultural and artisan skills of the Pueblo peoples (see page 8).

Spanish colonizers first settled in the present-day United States during the last half of the sixteenth century. In 1565, Pedro Menendez de Aviles, a Spanish noble, along with a group of soldiers, settlers, and priests, established the first permanent settlement in the United States: St. Augustine, Florida. Just over thirty years later (1598) a similar group led by Juan de Oñate, a Mexican-born adventurer, colonized New Mexico. The Spaniards had three goals: to gain wealth for themselves, preferably through finding precious metals; to claim new territories for their monarch; and to convert the Indians to Christianity. They located few precious metals, although some of the westerners did become wealthy by other means. They were more successful in achieving their other aims. In both Florida and the Southwest, Franciscans set up long chains of missions, and by the late eighteenth century Spain claimed a vast territory that stretched from California (initially colonized in 1769) through Texas (chiefly settled after 1700) to the Gulf Coast.

But Spain's ability to control such an immense area was questionable, to say the least. Nowhere was that more clear than in New Mexico, the heartland of northern New Spain. During the seventeenth century, Spanish settlers and missionaries based at Santa Fé (founded 1610) ruthlessly forced Indian laborers—slaves in all but name—to work their fields and care for their livestock. The Franciscans also adopted brutal and violent tactics as they tried to wipe out all vestiges of the native religion. Finally, in 1680 the Pueblos revolted under the leadership of Popé, a respected medicine man, and successfully drove the Spaniards out of New Mexico. Although Spanish authority was nominally restored in 1692, Spain had learned its lesson. From that time on Spanish governors stressed cooperation, rather than confrontation, with the Pueblos and no longer attempted to reduce them to bondage or to violate

Popé and the Pueblo Revolt

their cultural integrity. The Pueblo revolt was the most successful and longest sustained Indian resistance movement in colonial North America.

Along the eastern seaboard Europeans valued the Indians as hunters rather than as agricultural workers, but they were no less dependent on Indian labor than were the Spanish in the west. The Dutch and French settlements in North America were little more than trading posts. Although the English colonies eventually began to market their own products, in the earliest phase of each colony's history its primary exports were furs and skins obtained from neighboring Indians.

South Carolina provides a case in point. The Barbadians who colonized the region moved quickly to establish a vigorous trade in deerskins with nearby tribes. During the first decade of the eighteenth century, South Carolina exported to Europe an average of 54,000 skins annually, a number that later climbed to a peak of 160,000. The trade gave rise to other exchanges that reveal the complexity of the economic relationships among Indians and Europeans. For example, the horses white Carolinians needed to carry the deerskins came from the Creek Indians, who had in turn obtained them from the Spaniards through trade and capture.

Another important component of the Carolina trade was traffic in Indian slaves. The warring tribes of South Carolina (especially the Creek) profited from selling their captive enemies **Indian Slave Trade** to the whites, who then either kept them in the colony as slaves or exported them to the West Indies or other mainland settlements. There are no reliable statistics on the extent of the trade in Indian slaves, but in 1708 they made up 14 percent of the population of South Carolina. Many were Christians converted by the Spanish missions in northern Florida, then captured by Englishmen and their Indian allies.

A major conflict between white Carolinians and neighboring tribes also added to the supply of Indian slaves. In 1711, the Tuscarora, an Iroquoian people who had migrated southward many years earlier, attacked the Swiss-German settlement of New Bern, which had expropriated their lands without payment. The Tuscarora had been avid slavers and had sold many captives from weaker Algonkian tribes to the whites. Those tribes seized the opportunity to settle old scores, joining with the English colonists to defeat their enemy in a bloody two-year war. In the end, more than a thousand Tuscarora were themselves sold into slavery, and the remnants of the tribe drifted northward, returning to their ancient homeland in northern Pennsylvania and southern New York.

The abuses of the slave trade led to the most destructive Indian war in Carolina. White traders regularly engaged in corrupt, brutal, and fraudulent practices. They were notorious for cheating the Indians, physically abusing them (including raping the women), and selling friendly tribesmen into slavery when no enemy captives came readily to hand. In the spring of 1715 the Yamasee, aided by the Creek and a number of other tribes, retaliated by attacking the English colonists. As the raids continued through the summer, white refugees streamed into Charleston by the hundreds. At times the Creek-Yamasee offensive, often guided by information from Indian slaves held by the whites, came close to driving the intruders from the mainland altogether. But then colonial reinforcements arrived from the north, and the Cherokee joined the whites against their ancient enemies, the Creek. Their cause lost, the Yamasee moved south to seek Spanish protection, and the Creek retreated to their villages in the west. Still, it was years before South Carolina fully recovered from the effects of the Yamasee War.

That the Yamasee could escape by migrating southward exposed the one remaining gap in the line of English coastal settlements, the area between the southern border of South Carolina **Founding of Georgia** and Spanish Florida. The gap was plugged in 1732 with the chartering of Georgia, the last of the colonies that would become part of the United States. Intended as a haven for debtors by its founder James Oglethorpe, Georgia was specifically designed as a garrison province. Since all its landholders were expected to serve as militiamen to defend English settlements, the charter prohibited women from inheriting or purchasing land in the colony. The charter also prohibited the use of alcoholic beverages and forbade the introduction of slavery. Such provisions reveal the founders' intention that Georgia should be peopled by sturdy, sober yeoman farmers who could take up their weapons against the Indians or Spaniards at a moment's notice. None of the conditions could be enforced, however, and all had been abandoned by 1752, when Georgia became a royal colony.

In the Northeast, relationships were complicated by the number of European nations and Indian tribes involved in the fur trade. Before the large-scale migration of English people, the Dutch at Fort Orange (Albany) on the upper Hudson River competed for control of the fur trade with the French on the St. Lawrence. In the 1640s, the Iroquois, who traded chiefly with the Dutch, went to war against the Huron, who traded primarily with the French. The Iroquois' object was to become the major supplier of pelts to the Europeans, and they achieved that goal by practically exterminating the Huron tribe through the use of guns obtained from their Dutch allies. The Iroquois thus established themselves as a major force in the region, one that Europeans could ignore only at their peril.

The Iroquois nation was not one tribe, but five: the Mohawk, Oneida, Onondaga, Cayuga, and Seneca. (In 1722 the Tuscarora became the sixth.) Under the terms of a defensive alliance forged early in the sixteenth century, key decisions of war and peace for the entire Iroquois Confederacy were made by a council composed of tribal representatives. Each tribe retained some autonomy, and no tribe could be forced to comply with a council directive against its will. The Iroquois were unique among Indians not only because of the strength and persistence of their alliance but also because of the role played by their tribal matrons. The older women of each village chose its chief and could either start wars (by calling for the capture of prisoners to replace dead relatives) or stop them (by refusing to supply warriors with necessary foodstuffs).

Iroquois Confederacy

Before the arrival of the Europeans, the Iroquois had waged wars primarily for the purpose of acquiring captives to replenish their population. Contact with white traders brought ravaging disease as early as 1633 and thus intensified the need for captives. At the same time the arrival of whites created an economic motive for warfare: the desire to control the fur trade and gain unimpeded access to European goods. The war with the Huron was but the first of a series of

A French settler in Canada made this drawing of an Iroquois about 1700. The artist's fascination with his subject's mode of dress and patterned tattoos is evident. Such pictorial representations of "otherness" help to suggest the cultural gulf that divided the European and Indian residents of North America. Library of Congress.

conflicts with other tribes known as the Beaver Wars, in which the Iroquois fought desperately to maintain a pre-eminent position in the trade. In the mid-1670s, just when it appeared they would be successful, the French stepped in to prevent an Iroquois triumph (which would have destroyed France's plans to trade directly with the Indians of the Great Lakes and Mississippi Valley regions). Over the next twenty years the French launched repeated attacks on Iroquois villages. The English, who replaced the Dutch at Albany after 1664, offered little assistance other than weapons to their trading partners and nominal allies. Their people and resources depleted by constant warfare, the Iroquois in 1701 negotiated neutrality treaties with France, England, and their tribal neighbors. For the next half-century they maintained their power through diplomacy and trade.

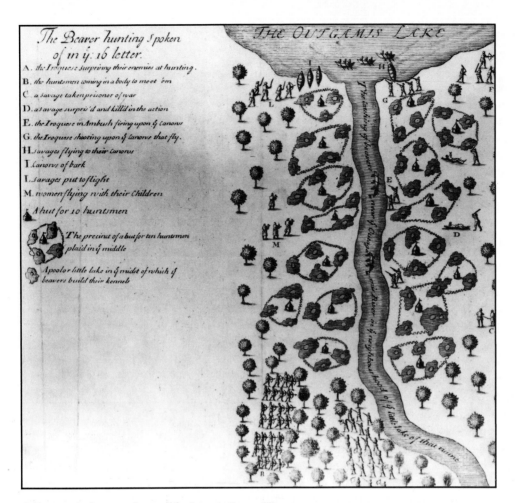

The Beaver hunting spoken
of in y. 16 letter.

A. the Iroquese surprising their enemies at hunting.
B. the huntsmen coming in a body to meet 'em
C. a savage taken prisoner of war
D. a savage surpris'd and kill'd in the action
E. the Iroquese in Ambush firing upon y Canons
G. the Iroquese shooting upon y Canons that fly.
H. savages flying to their Canons
I. Canons of bark
L. savages put to flight
M. women flying with their Children

A hut for 10 huntsmen

The precinct of a hut for ten huntsmen plac'd in y middle

A pool or little lake in y midst of which y beavers build their kennels

THE OUTGAMIS LAKE

A European's diagram of one of the Iroquois Beaver Wars.
At the bottom of the picture, the main body of the Iroquois
attacks a group of beaver hunters (note that the Iroquois
have guns and their opponents only bows and arrows); in
the center are the beaver pools and hunting camps. At letter
M, women are fleeing from the fighting, carrying their
children to safety. At the top, groups of hunters paddle off
in their canoes.   Library of Congress.

In the Carolinas and the middle colonies, then,
it was friction arising from trade relationships that
produced the major conflicts between whites and
Indians. But in Virginia, the cause of a renewed
outbreak of violence was the white colonists' hunger
for land on which to grow still more tobacco.

By the early 1670s, some Virginians were eagerly
eyeing the rich lands north of the York River that
had been reserved for Indians under earlier treaties.
Using as a pretext the July 1675 killing of a white
servant by some Doeg Indians, they attacked not

only the Doeg but also the Susquehannock, a powerful
tribe that had recently occupied the region. In retaliation, Susquehannock bands began to raid frontier
plantations in the winter of 1676. The land-hungry
whites rallied behind the leadership of Nathaniel
Bacon, a planter who had arrived in the colony only
two years before. Bacon and his followers wanted,
in his words, "to ruine and extirpate all Indians in
generall." Governor William Berkeley, however,
hoped to avoid setting off a major war.

Berkeley and Bacon soon clashed. After Bacon

forced the House of Burgesses to authorize him to attack the Indians, Berkeley declared Bacon and his men to be in rebellion. As the cha-

Bacon's Rebellion

otic summer of 1676 wore on, Bacon alternately pursued Indians and battled with the governor's supporters. In September he marched on Jamestown itself and burned the capital to the ground. But after Bacon died of dysentery the following month, the rebellion collapsed. A new Indian treaty signed in 1677 opened much of the disputed territory to whites.

It was more than coincidence that New England, which had also been settled more than fifty years earlier, was wracked by conflict with Indians at precisely the same time. In both areas the whites' original accommodation with the tribes—reached after the defeat of the Pequot in the North and the Powhatan Confederacy in the South—no longer satisfied both parties. In New England, though, it was the Indians, rather than the whites, who felt aggrieved.

In the half-century since the founding of New England, white settlement had spread far into the interior of Massachusetts and Connecticut. In the

King Philip's War

process the whites had completely surrounded the ancestral lands of the Pokanoket (Wampanoag) on Narragansett Bay. Their chief, Metacomet (known to the whites as King Philip), was the son of Massassoit, who had signed the treaty with the Pilgrims in 1621. Troubled by white encroachments on Pokanoket lands and equally concerned about the impact European culture and Christianity were having on his people, Metacomet in late June 1675 led his warriors in attacks on nearby white communities.

By the end of the year, two other local tribes, the Nipmuck and the Narragansett, had joined Metacomet's forces. In the fall, the three tribes jointly attacked settlements in the northern Connecticut River valley; in the winter and spring of 1676, they devastated well-established villages and even attacked Plymouth and Providence. Altogether, the alliance totally destroyed twelve of the ninety Puritan towns and attacked forty others. A tenth of the able-bodied adult males in Massachusetts were captured or killed; proportional to population, it was the most costly war in American history. New England's very survival seemed to be at stake.

But the tide turned in the summer of 1676. The Indian coalition ran short of food and ammunition, and whites began to use "praying Indians" as guides and scouts. After Metacomet was killed in an ambush in August, the alliance crumbled. Many surviving Pokanokets, Nipmucks, and Narragansetts, including Metacomet's wife and son, were captured and sold into slavery in the West Indies. The power of New England's coastal tribes was broken. Thereafter they lived in small clusters, subordinated to the whites and often working as servants or sailors. Only on the isolated island of Martha's Vineyard were some surviving Pokanokets able to preserve their tribal identity intact.

NEW ENGLAND AND THE WEB OF IMPERIAL TRADE

The New England settlements that Metacomet attacked had changed in three major ways since the early years of colonization. The population had grown dramatically; the nature of the residents' religious commitment had altered; and the economy had developed in unanticipated ways.

The expansion of the population was the result not of continued migration from England (for that had largely ceased after 1640), but rather of natural increase. The original settlers' many

Population Pressures

children also produced many children, and subsequent generations followed suit. By 1700, New England's population had quadrupled to reach approximately 100,000. That placed great pressure on the available land, and many members of the third and fourth generations of New Englanders had to migrate—north to New Hampshire or Maine, south to New York, west beyond the Connecticut River—to find sufficient farm land for themselves and their children. Others abandoned agriculture and learned skills like blacksmithing or carpentry so that they could support themselves in the growing number of towns that dotted the countryside in that area.

In addition, American-born Puritans did not display

the same religious fervor that had prompted their ancestors to cross the Atlantic. Many of them had

Halfway Covenant

not experienced the gift of God's grace, or "saving faith," which was required for full membership in the Congregational church. Yet they had been baptized as children, attended church services regularly, and wanted their own infants to be baptized, even though that sacrament was supposed to be available only to the children of church members. A synod of Massachusetts ministers, convened in 1662 to consider the problem, responded by establishing a category of "halfway" membership in the church. In a statement that has become known as the Halfway Covenant, the clergymen declared that adults who had been baptized as children but were not full church members could have their children baptized. In return, such parents had to acknowledge the authority of the church and live according to moral precepts. They were not allowed to vote in church affairs or take communion.

The Halfway Covenant attempted to deal with one problem of changing religious mores, but it did not touch another: a newly noticeable difference between the experiences of the two sexes. By the end of the seventeenth century, women were more likely than men to experience "saving faith" and so they made up a majority in many New England congregations. Searching for the cause of this phenomenon, Cotton Mather—the most prominent member of a family of distinguished ministers—speculated that the fear of dying in childbirth made women especially sensitive to their spiritual state. Modern historians have also argued that women were attracted to religion because the church offered them a spritual equality that offset their secular inferiority. Whatever the explanation, Mather's increasingly female audiences prompted him to deliver sermons outlining women's proper role in church and society—the first formal examination of that theme in American history. Mather was the first of many men to urge American women to be submissive to their husbands, watchful of their children, and attentive to religious duty.

The differential rate of church membership in late-seventeenth-century New England suggests a growing division between pious women and their more worldly husbands. That split reflected significant economic changes, which constitute the third major way in which the Puritan colonies were being transformed.

New England's first economic system had been based on two pillars: the fur trade and the constant flow of migrants. Together those had allowed New Englanders to acquire the manufactured goods they needed: the fur trade gave them valuable pelts to sell in England, and the migrants were always willing to exchange clothing and other items for the earlier settlers' surplus seed grains and livestock. But New England's supply of furs was limited, because the region lacked rivers giving ready access to the interior of the continent, and the migrants stopped coming with the outbreak of civil war in England. Thus in 1640 that first economic system collapsed.

The Puritans then began a search for new salable crops and markets. They found such crops in the waters off the coast—fish—and on their own land—grain and wood products. By 1643

New England's Trading System

they had also found the necessary markets: first the Wine Islands (the Azores and Canaries) in the Atlantic, and then the new English colonies in the Caribbean, which were beginning to cultivate sugar intensively and to invest heavily in slaves. The islands lacked precisely the goods New England could produce in abundance: cheap food (corn and salted fish) to feed the slaves, and wood for barrels to transport wine (from the Atlantic islands) and molasses (from the Caribbean colonies).

Thus developed the series of transactions that has become known, inaccurately, as the triangular trade. Since New England's products duplicated England's, the northern colonists sold their goods in the West Indies and elsewhere to earn the money with which to purchase English products. (Southerners did not have the same problem. Their crops—tobacco, rice, and indigo—could be sold directly to England.) There soon grew up in New England's ports a cadre of merchants who acquired—usually through barter—cargoes of timber and foodstuffs, which they then dispatched to the West Indies for sale. In the Caribbean the ships sailed from island to island, exchanging fish, barrel staves, and grains for molasses, fruit, spices, and slaves.

Once they had a full load, the ships returned to Boston, Newport, or New Haven to dispose of their

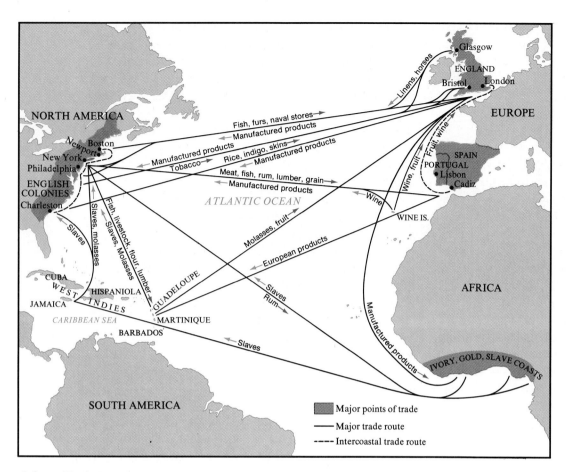

Atlantic Trade Routes

cargoes. New Englanders then traded those items they did not consume to other colonies or to England. Most important, they distilled West Indian molasses into the more valuable rum, a widely used alcoholic beverage. Rum was a key component of the only part of the trade that could be termed triangular: Rhode Islanders took rum to Africa and traded it for slaves, whom they carried to the West Indies to exchange for more molasses to produce still more rum. With that exception, the trading pattern was not a triangle but a shifting set of shuttle voyages (see map). Its sole constant was uncertainty, due to the weather, rapid changes of supply and demand in the small island markets, and the delicate system of credit on which the entire structure depended.

The network of seventeenth-century trade, which had achieved mature form by the 1660s, was fueled

not by cash (no one had much of that) but by credit in the form of bills of exchange. These were, in effect, promissory notes in which one merchant pledged to pay another a certain sum on demand. Bills of exchange passed from hand to hand, circulating much as currency does today. Ultimately, though, their value rested on trust and the credit standing of the first merchant in the chain. That was one of the major reasons why the seventeenth-century mercantile community was composed chiefly of men related to each other by blood or marriage. A Bostonian who needed a reliable representative in Barbados would send his brother-in-law, son, or cousin to handle his interests; a London merchant might dispatch a relative to Boston for the same reason.

The Puritan New Englanders who ventured into commerce were soon differentiated from their rural

Sea Captains Carousing in Surinam, *a scene that could have occurred in any tavern in any Caribbean port. Several recognizable Rhode Island merchants are included among the merrymakers. Painted by John Greenwood (1758), a Bostonian who lived in Surinam (Dutch Guiana), on the northern coast of South America. The St. Louis Art Museum.*

Puritans and Anglicans

counterparts by their ties to a wider transatlantic world and by their preoccupation with material endeavors. Moreover, as time passed, increasing numbers of Puritans became involved in trade. Small investors who owned shares of voyages soon dominated the field numerically if not monetarily. The gulf between commercial and farming interests widened after 1660, when—with the end of the Interregnum and the restoration of the Stuarts to the English throne—Anglican merchants began to migrate to New England. Such men had little stake in the survival of Massachusetts Bay and Connecticut in their original form, and some were openly antagonistic to Puritan traditions. As non-Congregationalists they were denied the vote and they could not practice their religion freely. They resented their exclusion from the governing elite, believing that their wealth and social status entitled them to political power. Congregationalist clergymen returned their hostility in full measure and preached sermons called jeremiads lamenting New England's new commercial orientation. The Reverend Increase Mather (Cotton Mather's

father) reminded his congregation in 1676 that "*Religion and not the World* was that which our Fathers came hither for."

But Mather spoke for the past, not the future or even for his own contemporaries. By the 1670s, New England and the other American colonies were deeply enmeshed in an intricate international trading network. The seventeenth-century colonies should not be seen as primitive, isolated, self-sufficient communities. Indeed, the early colonies were, if anything, more dependent on overseas markets and imported goods than was eighteenth-century America. During the 1600s, the colonies lacked sufficient population to support an elaborate internal economy. (For example, all attempts to establish ironworks or glass factories in the first decades of settlement failed because there simply were not enough colonial customers for their products.) Furthermore, the colonies' economic fortunes largely depended on the sale of their exports in foreign markets: furs, deerskins, tobacco, rice, indigo, fish, and timber products together formed the basis for Anglo-America's prosperity.

At mid-century, this valuable American commerce

attracted the attention of English officials seeking a new source of revenue after the disruptions of the Civil War. They realized that the colonies could make important contributions to England's economic well-being. Tobacco from the Chesapeake and sugar from the West Indies had obvious value, but other colonial products also had profitable potential. The king needed tax revenues, and English merchants wanted to ensure that they—not their Dutch rivals—reaped the benefits of trading with the English colonies. Parliament and the restored Stuart monarchs accordingly began to design a system of laws that would, they hoped, confine the profits of colonial trade primarily to the mother country.

They based their commercial policy on a series of assumptions about the operations of the world's economic system. Collectively, these assumptions are usually called *mercantilism,* though neither the term itself nor a unified mercantilist theory was formulated until a century later. The economic world was seen as a collection of national states, each competing for shares of a finite amount of wealth. What one nation gained was automatically another nation's loss. Each nation's goal was to become as economically self-sufficient as possible while maintaining a favorable balance of trade with other countries (that is, exporting more than it imported). Colonies had an important role to play in such a scheme. They could supply the mother country with valuable raw materials to be consumed at home or sent abroad, and they could serve as a market for the mother country's manufactured goods.

Parliament applied that mercantilist theory to the American colonies in a series of laws known as the Navigation Acts. The major acts—passed in 1651, 1660, 1663, and 1673—established three main principles. First, only English or colonial merchants and ships could engage in trade in the colonies. Second, certain valuable American products could be sold only in the mother country. At first these "enumerated" goods were wool, sugar, tobacco, indigo, ginger, and dyes; later acts added rice, naval stores (masts, spars, pitch, tar, and turpentine), copper, and furs to the list. Third, all foreign goods destined for sale in the colonies had to be shipped via England and pay English import duties. Some years later, a new series of laws declared a fourth principle: the

Navigation Acts

colonies could not make or export items that competed with English products (such as wool clothing, hats, and iron).

The intention of the Navigation Acts was clear: American trade was to center on England. The mother country was to benefit from both colonial imports and exports. England had first claim on the most valuable colonial exports, and all foreign imports into the colonies had to pass through England first, enriching its customs revenues in the process. Moreover, English and colonial shippers were given a monopoly of the American trade. However, the American provinces, especially those in the north, did produce many goods that were not enumerated—such as fish, flour, and barrel staves. These products could be traded directly to foreign purchasers as long as they were carried in English or American ships.

The English authorities soon learned that it was easier to write mercantilist legislation than to enforce it. The many harbors of the American coast provided ready havens for smugglers, and colonial officials often looked the other way when illegally imported goods were offered for sale. In ports such as Curaçao in the Dutch West Indies, American merchants could easily dispose of enumerated goods and purchase foreign items on which duty had not been paid. Consequently, Parliament in 1696 enacted another Navigation Act designed to strengthen enforcement of the first four. This law established in America a number of vice-admiralty courts, which operated without juries. In England such courts dealt only with cases involving piracy, vessels taken as wartime prizes, and the like. But since American juries had already demonstrated a tendency to favor local smugglers over customs officers (a colonial customs service was started in 1671), Parliament decided to remove Navigation Act cases from the regular colonial courts.

England took another major step in colonial administration in 1696 by creating the Board of Trade and Plantations to replace the loosely structured standing committee of the Privy Council that had handled colonial affairs since 1675. The fifteen-member Board of Trade thereafter served as the chief organ of government concerned with the American colonies. It gathered information, reviewed Crown appointments in America, scrutinized legislation passed by colonial assemblies, supervised trade policies, and

Board of Trade

advised successive ministries on colonial issues. Still, the Board of Trade did not have any direct powers of enforcement. Furthermore, it shared jurisdiction over American affairs not only with the customs service and the navy but also with the secretary of state for the southern department (the member of the ministry responsible for the colonies). In short, although the Stuart monarchs' reforms considerably improved the quality of colonial administration, supervision of the American provinces remained decentralized and haphazard.

Even inefficient enforcement of the Navigation Acts was too much for many colonists, and they resisted the laws in various ways—not only by attempting to circumvent them but also by formally protesting to the government in London. Governor William Berkeley of Virginia was among the most vocal critics of the new laws. Tobacco prices declined significantly after 1660, causing serious economic problems in both Virginia and Maryland. Thus when English officials asked Berkeley about the state of trade in Virginia, he responded unhesitatingly that great hardship had resulted from "that severe act of Parliament which excludes us from having any commerce with any nation in Europe but our own," thereby preventing the development of new markets for tobacco. But such protests had little effect, chiefly because policymakers in England were more concerned about preserving the revenues obtained from colonial trade than about any adverse impact the acts might have on the colonies.

COLONIAL POLITICAL DEVELOPMENT AND IMPERIAL REORGANIZATION

English officials who dealt with colonial administration in the 1670s and 1680s were confronted not only by resistance to the Navigation Acts but also by a bewildering array of colonial governments. Massachusetts Bay still functioned under its original corporate charter, and its New England neighbors

Connecticut and Rhode Island had been granted similar corporate status by Charles II in 1662 and 1663, respectively. Virginia was a royal colony, and New York became one when its proprietor ascended the throne in 1685 as James II, but all the other mainland settlements were proprietorships. Further, the latter had varying political structures, for the royal charters gave the proprietors a great deal of leeway in governing their possessions.

Still, the political structures of the colonies shared certain characteristics. Most were ruled by a governor and a two-house legislature. In New England, the governors were elected by the people or the legislature; in the Chesapeake, they were appointed by the king or the proprietor. A council, elected in some colonies and appointed in others, advised the governor on matters of policy and sometimes served as the province's highest court. The council also had a legislative function: initially its members met jointly with representatives elected by their districts to debate and vote on laws affecting the colony. But as time passed, the fundamental differences between the two legislative groups' purposes and constituencies led them to separate into two distinct houses. In Virginia, that important event occurred in 1663; in Massachusetts Bay it had happened earlier, in 1644. Thus developed the two-house legislature still used in almost all of the United States.

Colonial Political Structures

While provincial governments were taking shape, so too were local political institutions. In New England, elected selectmen governed the towns at first, but by the end of the century the town meeting, held at least annually and attended by most adult white townsmen, handled most matters of local concern. In the Chesapeake the same function was performed by the judges of the county court and by the parish vestry, a group of laymen charged with overseeing church affairs, whose power also encompassed secular concerns.

By late in the seventeenth century, therefore, the American colonists were accustomed to exercising a considerable degree of local political autonomy. The tradition of consent was especially firmly established in New England. Massachusetts, Connecticut, and Rhode Island were, in effect, independent entities, subject neither to the direct authority of the king nor to a proprietor. Everywhere in the English colonies, white males owning more property than a stated minimum (which varied from province to province) expected to have an influential voice in how they were governed, and especially how they were taxed.

After James II became king, these expectations clashed with those of their monarch. The new king and his successors sought to bring order to the apparently chaotic state of colonial administration by tightening the reins of government and reducing the colonies' political autonomy. (Simultaneously, of course, they used the Navigation Acts to reduce the colonies' economic autonomy.) They began to chip away at the privileges granted in colonial charters and to reclaim proprietorships for the Crown. New Hampshire (1679), its parent colony Massachusetts (1691), New Jersey (1702), and the Carolinas (1729) all became royal colonies. The charters of Rhode Island, Connecticut, Maryland, and Pennsylvania were temporarily suspended as well, but were ultimately restored to their original status.

Dominion of New England

The most drastic reordering of colonial administration was attempted in 1686 through 1689, and its chief target was Puritan New England. Reports from America had convinced English officials that New England was a hotbed of smuggling. Moreover, the Puritans refused to allow freedom of religion and insisted on maintaining laws that often ran counter to English practice. New England thus seemed an appropriate place to exert English authority with greater vigor. The charters of all the colonies from New Jersey to Maine (then part of Massachusetts) were revoked and a Dominion of New England was established in 1686 (see map, page 42). Sir Edmund Andros, the governor, was given immense power: all the assemblies were dissolved, and he needed only the consent of an appointed council to make laws and levy taxes.

New Englanders endured Andros's autocratic rule for more than two years. Then came the dramatic news that James II had been overthrown in a bloodless rebellion (known as the Glorious Revolution) and had been replaced on the throne by his daughter Mary and her husband, the Dutch prince William of Orange. Seizing the opportunity to rid themselves of the hated Dominion, New Englanders jailed Andros and his associates, proclaimed their loyalty to William and Mary, and wrote to England for instructions as to the form of government they should adopt. Most of Massachusetts Bay's political leadership hoped that the new monarchs would renew their original charter, which had been revoked in 1684 prior to the establishment of the Dominion.

Glorious Revolution in America

In other American colonies too, the Glorious Revolution proved to be a signal for revolt. In Maryland the Protestant Association overturned the government of the Catholic proprietor, and in New York Jacob Leisler, a militia officer of German origin, assumed control of the government. Like the New Englanders, the Maryland and New

LATE

Memorable Providences

Relating to

Witchcrafts and *Possessions,*

Clearly Manifesting,

Not only that there are Witches, but that Good Men (as well as others) may possibly have their Lives shortned by such evil Instruments of Satan.

Written by *Cotton Mather* Minister of the Gospel at *Boston* in *New-England.*

𝕿𝖍𝖊 𝕾𝖊𝖈𝖔𝖓𝖉 𝕴𝖒𝖕𝖗𝖊𝖘𝖘𝖎𝖔𝖓.

Recommended by the Reverend Mr. *Richard Baxter* in *London*, and by the Ministers of *Boston* and *Charlestown* in *New-England.*

LONDON,

Printed for *Tho. Parkhurst* at the *Bible* and *Three Crowns* in *Cheapside* near *Mercers-* Chapel. 1691.

Shortly before the hysteria at Salem Village, the prominent New England minister Cotton Mather published this treatise on witchcraft. The incidents in Salem Village were not isolated but rather reflected the New Englanders' everyday view of the world. They often used witchcraft to explain otherwise inexplicable events. Folger Shakespeare Library.

York rebels allied themselves with the supporters of William and Mary. They saw themselves as carrying out the colonial phase of the English revolt against Stuart absolutism. The problem was that the new monarchs and their colonial administrators did not view American events in the same light.

The Glorious Revolution occurred in the mother country because members of Parliament feared that once again, just as in Charles I's reign, a Stuart king was attempting to seize absolute power. James II, like his father, had levied taxes without parliamentary approval. He had also announced his conversion to Roman Catholicism. The Glorious Revolution affirmed the supremacy of Parliament and of Protestantism when Parliament offered the throne to the Protestants William and Mary. But—and this was the difficulty for the colonists—it did not directly affect English policies toward America. William and Mary, like James II, believed that the colonies were too independent and that England should exercise tighter control over its unruly American possessions.

Consequently, the only American rebellion that received royal sanction was that in Maryland, which was approved primarily because of its anti-Catholic thrust. In New York, Jacob Leisler was hanged for treason, and Massachusetts, to the dismay of its Puritan leaders, became a royal colony, complete with an appointed governor. The province was allowed to retain its town meeting system of local government and to elect its council, but the new charter issued in 1691 removed the traditional Puritan religious test for voting. An Anglican parish was even established in the heart of Boston. The "city upon a hill," at least as envisioned by John Winthrop, was no more.

Compounding New England's difficulties in a time of political uncertainty and economic change was a war with the French and their Indian allies. King Louis XIV of France allied himself with the deposed James II, and England therefore declared war on France in the summer of 1689. In Europe, the conflict, which lasted until 1697, was known as the War of the League of Augsburg, but the colonists called it King William's War. The American phase of the war was fought chiefly on the northern frontiers of New England and New York; among the English settlements devastated by enemy attacks in 1690 were Schenectady, New York, and Casco (Falmouth), Maine. Expeditions organized by the colonies against Montreal and Quebec that same year both failed miserably, and throughout the rest of the war New England found itself on the defensive.

In this period of extreme stress there occurred the famous outbreak of witchcraft accusations in Salem Village (now Danvers), Massachusetts, a rural community adjoining the bustling port of Salem Town. Like their contemporaries elsewhere, seventeenth-century New Englanders believed in the existence of witches, whose evil powers came from the devil. If people could not find rational

Witchcraft in Salem Village

IMPORTANT EVENTS

1642–46	English Civil War
1649	Charles I executed
1660	Stuarts restored to throne; Charles II becomes king
1662	Halfway Covenant drafted
1663	Carolina chartered
1664	English conquer New Netherland; New York founded; New Jersey established
1675–76	King Philip's (Metacomet's) War (New England)
1676	Bacon's Rebellion (Virginia)
1680–92	Pueblo revolt (New Mexico)
1681	Pennsylvania chartered
1685	James II becomes king
1686–89	Dominion of New England
1688–89	James II deposed in Glorious Revolution; William and Mary ascend throne
1689–97	King William's War
1692	Witchcraft outbreak in Salem Village
1696	Board of Trade and Plantations established
1701	Iroquois adopt neutrality policy
1702–13	Queen Anne's War
1711–13	Tuscarora War (North Carolina)
1715	Yamasee War (South Carolina)
1732	Georgia chartered

explanations for their troubles, they tended to suspect they were bewitched. Before 1689, 103 New Englanders, most of them middle-aged women, had been accused of practicing witchcraft, chiefly by neighbors who had suffered misfortunes that they attributed to the suspected witch (with whom they usually had an ongoing dispute). Although most such accusations occurred singly, on occasion a witchcraft panic could result when one charge set off a chain reaction of similar charges (that happened in Hartford, Connecticut, in 1662 and 1663, for example). But nothing else in New England's history ever came close to matching the Salem Village cataclysm.

The crisis began in early 1692 when a group of adolescent girls accused some older women of having bewitched them. Before the hysteria spent itself ten months later, nineteen people (including several men, most of them related to accused female witches) had been hanged, another pressed to death by heavy stones, and more than one hundred persons jailed. Historians have proposed various explanations for

this puzzling episode, but to be understood it must be seen in its proper context—one of political and legal disorder, of Indian war, and of religious and economic change. It must have seemed to Puritan New Englanders as though their entire world was collapsing. At the very least they could have had no sense of security about their future.

Nowhere was that more true than in Salem Village, a farming town torn between old and new styles of life because of its position on the edge of a commercial center. And for no residents of the village was a feeling of insecurity sharper than it was for the girls who issued the initial accusations. Many of them had been orphaned in the recent Indian attacks on Maine; they were living in Salem Village as domestic servants. Their involvement with witchcraft began when they experimented with fortunetelling as a means of foreseeing their futures, in particular the identity of their eventual husbands. As the most powerless people in a town apparently powerless to affect its fate, they offered their fellow New Englanders a compelling explanation for the seemingly endless chain of troubles afflicting them: their province was under direct attack from the devil and his legion of witches. Interpreted thus, it is not the number of witchcraft accusations that seems surprising but rather their abrupt cessation in the fall of 1692.

There were two reasons for the rapid end to the crisis. First, the accusers had grown too bold. When they started to charge some of the colony's most distinguished and respected residents with being in league with the devil, members of the ruling elite began to doubt their veracity. Second, the new royal charter was fully implemented in late 1692, ending the worst period of political uncertainty and removing a major source of psychological stress. The war continued, and the Puritans were not entirely pleased with the charter, but at least order had formally been restored.

Over the course of the next three decades, Massachusetts and the rest of the English colonies in America accommodated themselves to the new imperial order. Most colonists did not like the class of alien officials who arrived in America determined to implement the policies of king and Parliament, but they adjusted to their demands and to the trade restrictions imposed by the Navigation Acts. They fought another imperial war—the War of the Spanish Succession, or Queen Anne's War—from 1702 to 1713, without enduring the psychological stress of the first, despite the heavy economic burdens the conflict imposed. Colonists who allied themselves with royal governors received patronage in the form of offices and land grants and composed "court parties" that supported English officials. Others, who were perhaps less fortunate in their friends, or more principled in defense of colonial autonomy (opinions differ), made up the opposition, or "country" interest. By the end of the first quarter of the eighteenth century, most men in both groups were native-born Americans, members of elite families whose wealth derived from staple-crop production in the south and commerce in the north.

During the seventy years from 1650 to 1720, then, the English colonies in America had changed dramatically. In 1650, there were just two isolated centers of population, New England and the Chesapeake; in 1720, nearly the entire eastern coast of mainland North America was in English hands. What had been

a migrant population was now mostly American-born; economies originally based on the fur trade had become far more complex and more closely linked with the mother country; and a wide variety of political structures had been reshaped into a more uniform pattern. Yet at the same time the introduction of large-scale slavery into the Chesapeake and the Carolinas had irrevocably differentiated their societies from those of the colonies to the north. Staple-crop production for the market was not the key distinguishing feature of the southern regional economies; rather, their uniqueness lay in their reliance on a racially based system of perpetual servitude.

By 1720, the essential elements of the imperial structure that would govern the colonies until 1775 were in place. And the regional economic systems originating in the late seventeenth and early eighteenth centuries continued to dominate American life for another century—until after independence had been won. This period, in other words, established the basic economic and political patterns that were to structure all subsequent changes in colonial American society.

SUGGESTIONS FOR FURTHER READING

General

Charles M. Andrews, *The Colonial Period of American History*, vol. 4 (1938); George Louis Beer, *The Old Colonial System, 1660–1754*, 2 vols. (1912); Carl Bridenbaugh, *Cities in the Wilderness: The First Century of Urban Life in America, 1625–1742* (1938); Wesley Frank Craven, *The Colonies in Transition, 1660–1713* (1968); Jack P. Greene and J. R. Pole, eds., *Colonial British America: Essays in the New History of the Early Modern Era* (1984); Gary Walton and James Shepherd, *The Economic Rise of Early America* (1979).

Africa and the Slave Trade

Jay Coughtry, *The Notorious Triangle: Rhode Island and the African Slave Trade 1700–1807* (1981); Philip D. Curtin, *The Atlantic Slave Trade: A Census* (1969); Basil Davidson, *Black Mother* (1969); David B. Davis, *The Problem of Slavery in Western Culture* (1966); Henry Gemery and Jan Hogendorn, eds., *The Uncommon Market: Essays in the Economic History of the Atlantic Slave Trade* (1979); Herbert Klein, *The Middle Passage* (1978); Daniel C. Littlefield, *Rice and Slaves: Ethnicity and the Slave Trade in Colonial South Carolina* (1981); James Rawley, *The Transatlantic Slave Trade: A History* (1981).

Blacks in Anglo-America

T. H. Breen and Stephen Innes, "*Myne Own Ground*": *Race and Freedom on Virginia's Eastern Shore, 1640–1676* (1980); Richard S. Dunn, *Sugar and Slaves: The Rise of the Planter Class in the English West Indies, 1624–1713* (1972); Lorenzo Johnson Green, *The Negro in Colonial New England* (1942); Edgar J. McManus, *Black Bondage in the North* (1973); Russell Menard, "From Servants to Slaves: The Transformation of the Chesapeake Labor System," *Southern Studies*, 16 (1977), 355–390; Edmund S. Morgan, *American Slavery, American Freedom: The Ordeal of Colonial Virginia* (1975); Peter H. Wood, *Black Majority: Negroes in Colonial South Carolina from 1670 Through the Stono Rebellion* (1974).

Indian-White Relations

Henry Bowden, *American Indians and Christian Missions: Studies in Cultural Conflict* (1981); Judith K. Brown, "Economic Organization and the Position of Women among the Iroquois," *Ethnohistory*, 17 (1970), 151–167; David H. Corkran, *The Creek Frontier, 1540–1783* (1967); Verner W. Crane, *The Southern Frontier, 1670–1732* (1929); Francis Jennings, *The Ambiguous Iroquois Empire* (1984); Elizabeth A. H. John, *Storms Brewed in Other Men's Worlds: The Confrontation of Indians, Spanish, and French in the Southwest, 1540–1795* (1975); Douglas Leach, *Flintlock and Tomahawk: New England in King Philip's War* (1958); Daniel K. Richter, "War and Culture: The Iroquois Experience," *William and Mary Quarterly*, 3rd ser., 40 (1983), 528–559; Allen W. Trelease, *Indian Affairs in Colonial New York: The Seventeenth Century* (1960); C. A. Weslager, *The Delaware Indians: A History* (1972); J. Leitch Wright, Jr., *The Only Land They Knew: The Tragic Story of the American Indians in the Old South* (1981).

New England

Bernard Bailyn, *The New England Merchants in the Seventeenth Century* (1955); Paul Boyer and Stephen Nissenbaum, *Salem Possessed: The Social Origins of Witchcraft* (1974); Richard Bushman, *From Puritan to Yankee: Character and the Social Order in Connecticut, 1690–1765* (1967); John Demos, *Entertaining Satan: Witchcraft and the Culture of Early New England* (1982); Mary Maples Dunn, "Saints and Sisters:

Congregational and Quaker Women in the Early Colonial Period," *American Quarterly*, 30 (1978), 582–601; Perry Miller, *The New England Mind: From Colony to Province* (1953); Richard Pares, *Yankees and Creoles: The Trade Between North America and the West Indies Before the American Revolution* (1956); Robert G. Pope, *The Half-Way Covenant: Church Membership in Puritan New England* (1969); Laurel Thatcher Ulrich, *Good Wives: Image and Reality in the Lives of Women in Northern New England 1650–1750* (1982).

New Netherland and the Restoration Colonies

Edwin B. Bronner, *William Penn's "Holy Experiment": The Founding of Pennsylvania 1681–1701* (1962); Thomas J. Condon, *New York Beginnings: The Commercial Origins of New Netherland* (1968); Wesley Frank Craven, *New Jersey and the English Colonization of North America* (1964); Mary Maples Dunn, *William Penn: Politics and Conscience* (1967); Michael Kammen, *Colonial New York: A History* (1975); Robert C. Ritchie, *The Duke's Province: A Study of Politics and Society in Colonial New York, 1660–1691* (1977); Robert M. Weir, *Colonial South Carolina: A History* (1983).

Colonial Politics

Bernard Bailyn, "Politics and Social Structure in Virginia," in *Seventeenth-Century America: Essays in Colonial History*, ed. James M. Smith (1959), 90–115; Lois Green Carr and David W. Jordan, *Maryland's Revolution of Government 1689–1692* (1974); Richard R. Johnson, *Adjustment to Empire: The New England Colonies, 1675–1715* (1981); Kenneth A. Lockridge and Alan Kreider, "The Evolution of Massachusetts Town Government, 1640–1740," *William and Mary Quarterly*, 3rd ser., 23 (1966), 549–574; David S. Lovejoy, *The Glorious Revolution in America* (1972); Jack M. Sosin, *English America and the Restoration Monarchy of Charles II: Transatlantic Politics, Commerce, and Kinship* (1980).

Imperial Administration

Viola F. Barnes, *The Dominion of New England: A Study in British Colonial Policy* (1923); Thomas C. Barrow, *Trade and Empire: The British Customs Service in Colonial America 1660–1775* (1967); Lawrence A. Harper, *The English Navigation Laws: A Seventeenth-Century Experiment in Social Engineering* (1939); Michael Kammen, *Empire and Interest: The American Colonies and the Politics of Mercantilism* (1970); I. K. Steele, *Politics of Colonial Policy: The Board of Trade in Colonial Administration* (1968); Stephen Saunders Webb, *The Governors-General: The English Army and the Definition of the Empire, 1569–1681* (1979); Stephen Saunders Webb, *1676: The End of American Independence* (1984).

GROWTH AND DIVERSITY
1720–1770

CHAPTER 3

In June 1744, Dr. Alexander Hamilton, a thirty-four-year-old Scottish-born physician living in Annapolis, Maryland, paid his first visit to Philadelphia. There he encountered two quite different worlds. One consisted of men of his own status, the merchants and professionals he called "the better sort." Hamilton mingled with them at the Governor's Club, "a society of gentlemen that met at a taveren every night and converse on various subjects." The night Hamilton attended, the "entertaining" discussion focused on Cervantes and some English poets.

Hamilton reacted differently to the other world of Philadelphia, that composed of people he variously termed "rabble," "a strange medley," or "comicall, grotesque phizzes." Most spoke, he thought, "ignorantly," regardless of the subject. One evening he dined at a tavern with "a very mixed company" of twenty-five men. "There were Scots, English, Dutch, Germans, and Irish; there were Roman Catholicks, Church men, Presbyterians, Quakers, Newlightmen, Methodists, Seventh day men, Moravians, Anabaptists, and one Jew." Some discussed business, and a few argued about religion, but the "prevailing topick" was politics and the threat of war with France. Hamilton refused to be drawn into any of the conversations. As a gentleman, he consciously set himself apart from ordinary folk, commenting on their behavior but not participating in their exchanges.

And what of the women in Philadelphia? Hamilton met few of them, other than his landlady and one of her friends. "The ladies," he explained, "for the most part, keep att home and seldom appear in the streets, never in publick assemblies except att the churches or meetings." Hamilton was referring, of course, to women of "the better sort." He could hardly have walked the streets of the city without seeing many female domestic servants, market women, and wives of ordinary laborers going about their daily chores.

Despite his obvious biases, Dr. Hamilton was an astute observer of mid-eighteenth-century Philadelphia. The residents' chief employment, he wrote, "is traffick and mercantile business"; and the richest merchants of all were the Quakers. Members of that sect also controlled the government of Pennsylvania,

but, Hamilton noted, "the standing or falling of the Quakers in the House of Assembly depends upon their making sure the interest of the Palatines [Germans] in this province, who of late have turned so numerous that they can sway the votes which way they please." And Hamilton deplored the impact on the city of the Great Awakening, a religious revival that was then sweeping the colonies. "I never was in a place so populous where the gout [taste] for publick gay diversions prevailed so little," he remarked. "There is no such thing as assemblys of the gentry among them, either for dancing or musick; these they have an utter aversion to ever since Whitefield preached among them."

Hamilton's comments provide an excellent introduction to mid-eighteenth-century American life, for the patterns he observed in Philadelphia were not unique to that city. Although ethnic diversity was especially pronounced in urban areas, by midcentury non-English migrants were settling in many regions of the mainland colonies. Their arrival not only added noticeably to the total population, it also altered political balances worked out before 1720 and affected the religious climate by increasing the number of different sects. The diverse group of men Hamilton encountered in that tavern could have been duplicated in other cities and even in some rural areas.

Hamilton correctly recognized that the Quakers maintained control of Pennsylvania politics because they had managed to win the support of recent German immigrants. The ruling elites in other provinces handled immigrants in a way that eventually was to backfire on them: they ignored the newcomers, refusing to allow them adequate representation and government services. Through these tactics such elites, now primarily native-born, established stable political regimes in each of the colonies. They contended with English-born governors and councillors for control of their colonies' governmental machinery, and in some cases they won. These victories were to serve them well when they began battling for independence later in the century.

In addition, Hamilton accurately assessed the importance of commerce in Americans' lives. The web of imperial trade woven before 1720 became even more complex and all-encompassing during the next fifty years. Americans of all descriptions were tied to an international commercial system that fluctuated wildly for reasons having little to do with the colonies, but whose effects were nonetheless inescapable. As the colonies would learn when they attempted to break their trade ties with Great Britain at the time of the Revolution, they were heavily dependent on England for both imported manufactured goods and markets for their exports.

As a well-educated man, Dr. Hamilton was heavily influenced by the Enlightenment, the major European intellectual movement of the day. The Enlightenment stressed reason and empirical knowledge, deliberately discarding superstition and instinct as guides to human behavior. Hamilton, like other enlightened thinkers, believed above all in rationality. To him, God was a distant presence who had ordered the world, setting forth natural laws that humans could discover through careful investigation and logical thought. From this perspective came Hamilton's distaste for the Great Awakening, since that revival drew primarily on the Calvinistic concept of a God that people could never fully comprehend. Moreover, the hallmark of the Great Awakening was emotion, expressed in a single identifiable moment of conversion. To a believer in the primacy of reason, the passions of the newly converted were more than foolish—they were idiotic.

The Enlightenment affected Dr. Hamilton in another way as well, for it helped to create the elite world of which he was a part, a world that seemed so different from that of ordinary folk. Wealthy, well-read Americans participated in a transatlantic intellectual community, whereas most colonists of "the lesser sort" could neither read nor write. Hamilton and his peers lived in comfortable houses and entertained at lavish parties; most colonists struggled just to make ends meet. Hamilton could take a leisurely four-month journey for his health (for his visit to Philadelphia was but one stop on a long trip), but most Americans had to work daily from dawn to dark. The eighteenth century, then, brought an increasing gap between rich and poor. The colonies had always been composed of people of different ranks, but by the last half of the century the social and economic distance between those ranks had widened noticeably.

Above all, the eighteenth-century colonies present a picture of growth and diversity. Population increased dramatically, and the area settled by whites and blacks expanded until it filled almost all of the region between the Appalachian mountains and the Atlantic Ocean. At the same time, the colonies became more diverse; the two original regional economies (the Chesapeake and New England) became four (those two plus the middle colonies and the Lower South). By midcentury, many of the colonies, not just New York, were home to a variety of ethnic groups and religious sects. The urban population, though still tiny by today's standards, grew larger; and in the cities were found the greatest extremes of wealth and poverty. Such changes transformed the character of England's North American possessions. The colonies that revolted in unison against British rule after 1765 were very different from the colonies that revolted separately against Stuart absolutism in 1689.

Population Growth and Ethnic Diversity

One of the most striking characteristics of the mainland colonies in the eighteenth century was their rapid population growth. Only about 250,000 Euro- and Afro-Americans resided in the colonies in 1700; thirty years later that number had more than doubled, and by 1775 it had become 2.5 million. Although migration accounted for a considerable share of the growth, most of it resulted from natural increase. Once the difficult early decades had passed, the American population doubled approximately every twenty-five years. Such a rate of growth is essentially unparalleled in human history. It had a variety of causes, the chief one being the youthful marriage age of women (early twenties for whites, late teens for blacks); since married women became pregnant every two or three years, this meant that women normally bore five to eight children. Because the eighteenth-century colonies, especially those north of Virginia, were very healthful places to live, a large proportion of the children born reached maturity and

This portrait of an eighteenth-century family shows the typical colonial childbearing pattern in the large number of "stairstep" children, born at approximately two-year intervals. National Gallery of Art, Washington, D.C., Gift of Edgar William and Bernice Chrysler Garbisch.

began families of their own. As a result, in 1775 about half the American population, white and black, was under sixteen years of age. (In 1980, by contrast, only about one-third of the American population was under sixteen.)

Such a dramatic phenomenon did not escape the attention of contemporaries. As early as the 1720s, Americans began to point with pride to their fertility, citing population growth as evidence of the advantages of living in the colonies. In 1755 Benjamin Franklin published his *Observations Concerning the Increase of Mankind*, which predicted that in another century "the greatest Number of Englishmen will be on this Side the Water. What an Accession of Power to the British Empire by Sea as well as Land!" he rhapsodized. "What Increase of Trade and Navigation!"

Interestingly enough, Franklin's purpose in writing his *Observations* was to argue that Britain should

prevent Germans from migrating to Pennsylvania. Since the English population in America was increasing so rapidly, he asked, "why should the Palatine Boors be suffered to swarm into our Settlements? . . . Why should Pennsylvania, founded by the English, become a Colony of *Aliens,* who will shortly be so numerous as to Germanize us instead of our Anglifying them, and will never adopt our Language or Customs?"

Whether Franklin's fears were shared by a majority of his American-born contemporaries is not known. But the eighteenth-century migration to the English colonies was massive; it comprised approximately 375,000 whites and 275,000 blacks (see map). Because some of the whites (for example, convicts sentenced to exile by English courts) and all the blacks did not choose freely to come to the colonies, nearly half the eighteenth-century migrants moved to America against their will. That contrasts sharply with the

Chapter 3: GROWTH AND DIVERSITY, 1720–1770

nineteenth-century pattern of voluntary migration from Europe that is discussed in Chapter 10.

Africans made up the largest single racial or ethnic group that came to the colonies during the eighteenth century. More important than the number of black migrants, however, is the fact that in the first half of the century the black population of the mainland colonies began to grow faster through natural increase than through importation. In the slaveholding societies of South America and the Caribbean, a surplus of males over females and appallingly high mortality rates together produced very different slave population patterns. There, only massive and continuing importations from Africa were able to maintain the enslaved work force at adequate levels. South Carolina, where rice cultivation was difficult and unhealthy work (chiefly because malaria-carrying mosquitoes bred in the rice swamps) and where planters preferred to purchase males, bore some resemblance to such colonies in that it too required a constant influx of Africans. But in the Chesapeake the black population grew primarily through natural increase after 1740. As shall be seen later in this chapter, that increase had significant implications for the society and economy of the region.

The German migrants who so worried Franklin numbered about 100,000. Most of them emigrated from the Rhineland between 1730 and 1755, usually landing in Philadelphia. They be-

German Immigration

came known locally as the Pennsylvania Dutch (a corruption of *Deutsch*); late in the century they and their descendants made up one-third of the colony's residents. But many other Germans moved west and then south along the eastern slope of the Appalachian mountains, eventually finding homes in western Maryland and Virginia. Others sailed first to Charleston or Savannah and settled in the interior of South Carolina or Georgia. A smaller number found land along the Mohawk River Valley in northern New York. The German immigrants belonged to a wide variety of Protestant sects—primarily Lutheran, German Reformed, and Moravian—and therefore added to the already substantial religious diversity of the middle colonies.

Many Germans arrived in America as redemptioners. Under that variant form of indentured servitude, migrants paid as much as possible of the cost of their

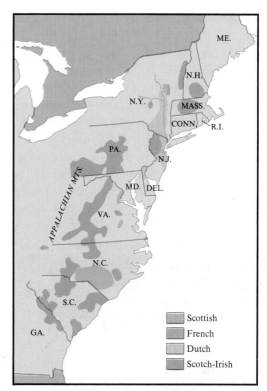

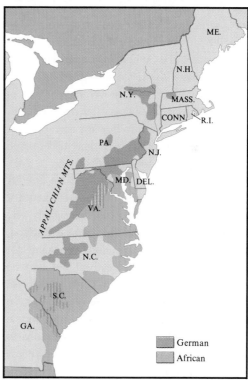

Non-English Ethnic Groups in the British Colonies, ca. 1775

passage before sailing from Europe. After they landed in the colonies, the rest of the fare had to be "redeemed." If poor folk had no friends or relatives in America willing to take on the burden of payment, they were indentured for a term of service proportional to the amount they still owed. That term could be as brief as a year or two, but was more likely to be four. In contrast to the unmarried English indentured servants who had migrated to the Chesapeake in the seventeenth century, German redemptioners often traveled in family groups. In America, the family was sometimes divided among different purchasers, or one member (often a son or daughter) was indentured to pay for the others' passages.

The largest group of white non-English immigrants to America was the Scotch-Irish, chiefly descended from Presbyterian Scots who had settled in Protestant

Scotch-Irish and Scottish Immigration

portions of Ireland during the seventeenth century. Perhaps as many as 250,000 Scotch-Irish people moved to the colonies. Fleeing economic distress and religious discrimination at home—Irish law favored Anglicans over Presbyterians and other dissenters—they were lured as well by hopes of obtaining land in America. Like the Germans, the Scotch-Irish often landed in Philadelphia. They also moved west and south from that city, settling chiefly in the western portions of Pennsylvania, Maryland, Virginia, and the Carolinas. Frequently unable to afford to buy any acreage, they squatted on land belonging to Indian tribes, land speculators, or colonial governments.

The more than 25,000 Scots who came directly to America from Scotland should not be confused with the Scotch-Irish. Many Scottish immigrants were supporters of Stuart claimants to the throne of England, or Jacobites (so called because the Latin name for James was Jacobus). After the death of William and Mary's successor Queen Anne in 1714, the British throne passed to the German house of Hanover, in the person of King George I. In 1715 and again in 1745, Jacobite rebels attempted unsuccessfully to capture the crown for the Stuart pretender, and many were exiled to America as punishment for their treason. Most of the Jacobites settled in North Carolina. Ironically, they tended to become loyalists during the Revolutionary War because of their strong commitment to monarchy. Another wave of Scottish immigration

began in the 1760s and flowed mainly into northern New York; most of these new arrivals settled as tenants on large tracts of land in the Mohawk River valley.

Because of these migration patterns and the concentration of slaveholding in the South, half the colonial population south of New England was of non-English origin by 1775. Whether the migrants assimilated readily into Anglo-American culture depended largely on the patterns of settlement, the size of the group, and the strength of the migrants' ties to their common culture. The Huguenots, for instance, were French Protestants who fled religious persecution in their homeland after 1685. They settled in tiny enclaves in American cities like Charleston and New York, but were unable to sustain either their language or their distinctive religious practices. Within two generations they had been almost wholly absorbed into the dominant culture. The equally small group of colonial Jews, by contrast, largely maintained a separate identity. The Jews in early America were Sephardic in origin, most of them descended from persons who had originally migrated first to the Netherlands to escape persecution in Spain and Portugal, and from there to the Dutch colonies in the New World. In a few cities—most notably New York and Newport, Rhode Island—they established synagogues and worked actively to preserve their culture (for example, by opposing intermarriage with Christians).

Members of the larger groups of migrants (the Germans, Scotch-Irish, and Scots) found it easier to sustain Old World ways if they wished. Countless local areas of the colonies were settled almost exclusively by one group or another. Near Frederick, Maryland, a visitor would have heard more German than English; in Anson and Cumberland Counties, North Carolina, that same visitor might have thought she was in Scotland. Where migrants from different countries settled in the same region, ethnic antagonisms often surfaced. One German clergyman, for example, explained his efforts to stop German young people from marrying persons of different ethnic origins by asserting that the Scotch-Irish were "lazy, dissipated and poor" and that "it is very seldom that German and English blood is happily united in wedlock."

Recognizing that it was to their benefit to keep other racial and ethnic groups divided, the dominant whites on occasion deliberately fostered such antagonisms. When the targets of their policies were Eu-

Spencer Hall shipyard, Gray's Inn Creek, Kent County, Maryland, about 1760. The earliest known view of a Chesapeake Bay shipyard, this oil painting on a wooden panel shows the wide variety of ships that sailed on the bay, as well as (in the background) lumbermen preparing a supply of timber. Maryland Historical Society.

ropean migrants, the goal was the maintenance of political and economic power. When the targets were Indians and blacks, as they were in South Carolina, the stakes were considerably higher. In 1758 one official remarked, "it has been allways the policy of this government to create an aversion in them [Indians] to Negroes." The reason? South Carolina whites, who composed a minority of the population of the colony, wanted to prevent Indians and blacks from making common cause against them. So that slaves would not try to run away to join the Indians, whites hired Indians as slave catchers. So that Indians would not trust blacks, whites used blacks as soldiers in Indian wars.

Although the dominant elites probably would have preferred to ignore the colonies' growing racial and ethnic diversity, they could not do so for long and still maintain their power. When such men decided to lead a revolution in the 1770s, they recognized that they needed the support of non-English Americans. Not by chance, then, did they begin to speak of "the rights of man," rather than "English liberties," when they sought recruits for their cause.

ECONOMIC GROWTH AND DEVELOPMENT

The eighteenth-century American economy was characterized more by sharp fluctuations than by a consistent long-term trend. There were two primary causes of the fluctuations: the impact of European wars and variations in the overseas demand for American products. The dramatic increase in colonial population was the only source of stability in the shifting economic climate.

Each year the rising population generated ever-greater demands for goods and services, which led to the development of small-scale colonial manufacturing and to the creation of a complex network of internal trade. As the area of settlement expanded, new roads, bridges, mills, and stores were built to serve the new communities. A lively coastal trade developed; by the late 1760s more than half (54 percent) of the vessels leaving Boston harbor were sailing to other mainland colonies rather than to foreign ports. Such ships were not only collecting goods for export and distributing imports, but also selling items made in America. In the middle decades of the eighteenth century, the colonies finally began to move away from their earlier pattern of near-total dependence on Europe for manufactured goods. For the first time, the American population sustained sufficient demand to encourage home-grown manufacturing enterprises.

The major energizing—yet destabilizing—influence on the colonial economy was foreign trade. Colonial prosperity still depended heavily on overseas demand for American products like tobacco, rice, indigo, fish, and barrel staves, for it was through the sale of such items that the colonists earned the credit they needed to purchase English and European imports. If the demand for American exports slowed, the colonists' income dropped and so did their demand for imported goods. Accordingly, even small merchants could be affected by sudden economic downswings they had not anticipated. In 1754, a woman who ran a small dry-goods store in Boston reported to her brother (her chief financial backer) that another female merchant had been "obliged to sell all her goods this week," to pay her creditors. "Such things make me double my diligence," she commented, "and endeavor to keep my self as clear [from debt] as is possible."

Despite fluctuations, there was a slow growth in the economy over the course of the eighteenth century, which resulted in higher standards of living for all property-owning Americans. Estate

Rising Standard of Living

inventories show that in the first two decades of the century households began to acquire amenities like crude earthenware dishes (for eating, food storage, and dairying), chairs, and knives and forks. (Seventeenth-century colonists had used only spoons.) Diet also improved; inventories reveal larger quantities and wider varieties of stored foods. After 1750, luxury items like silver plate appeared in the homes of the wealthy, and the "middling sort" started to purchase imported English ceramics and teapots. Even the poorest property owners showed some improvement in the number and type of their household possessions. Probably this was caused by the falling price of British manufactures relative to the income Americans earned from their exports.

Yet the benefits of economic growth were not evenly distributed: wealthy Americans improved their position relative to other colonists. The native-born elite families who dominated American political, economic, and social life by 1750 were those who had begun the century with sufficient capital to take advantage of the changes caused by population growth. They were the urban merchants who exported raw materials and imported luxury goods, the large landowners who rented small farms to German or Scotch-Irish tenants, the slave traders who supplied white planters with their bondspeople, and the owners of rum distilleries. The rise of this group of monied families helped to make the social and economic structure of mid-eighteenth-century America more rigid than it had been previously. The new non-English immigrants did not have the opportunities for advancement that had greeted their English predecessors.

At the very bottom of the social scale, poverty increased in colonial cities, particularly Boston. Families of urban laborers lived on the edge of destitution.

Urban Poverty

In Philadelphia, for instance, a male laborer's average annual earnings fell short of the amount needed to supply his family with the bare necessities. Even in a good year, then, other members of the family (wife or children) had to do wage work; in a bad year, the family could be reduced to beggary. By the 1760s, urban poor-relief systems were overwhelmed with applicants for assistance, and some cities began to build workhouses or almshouses to shelter the growing number of poor people. How could that have happened at a time when the lot of the average American family was improving?

A possible answer is that, although the living standard of property owners was rising, some colonists were being deprived of any access to property. Such

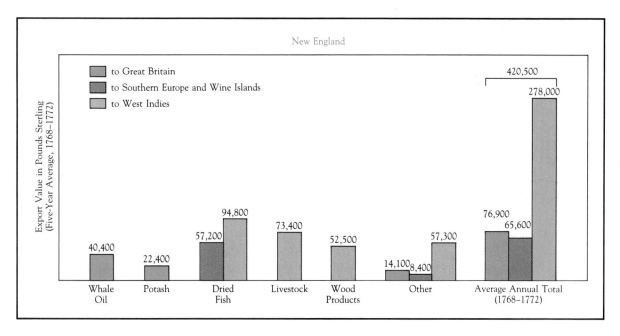

New England

Export Value in Pounds Sterling (Five-Year Average, 1768–1772)

Legend:
- to Great Britain
- to Southern Europe and Wine Islands
- to West Indies

Whale Oil	40,400
Potash	22,400
Dried Fish (to Great Britain)	57,200
Dried Fish (to West Indies)	94,800
Livestock	73,400
Wood Products	52,500
Other (to Great Britain)	14,100
Other (to Southern Europe)	8,400
Other (to West Indies)	57,300
Average Annual Total to Great Britain	76,900
Average Annual Total to Southern Europe	65,600
Average Annual Total to West Indies	278,000
Average Annual Total (combined)	420,500

Regional Trading Patterns: New England *Source: James F. Shepherd and Gary M. Walton, Shipping, Maritime Trade, and the Economic Development of Colonial America (1972), Tables 2–5, pp. 211–226.*

people clustered in the cities where they could more easily find work. Another explanation might be that poverty was a stage people passed through at particular points in their lives rather than a constant condition. That is, a laborer's family afflicted by disease, a youth not yet established in a trade, a recent immigrant, or an elderly or infirm person might be among the poor at one time but not at another. Again, such people were more likely to be found in a city than in the countryside. A third answer points to the preponderance of women, mostly widows, among the urban poor. Since women in the eighteenth century, like women today, were paid about half the wages men earned for the same or comparable work, it may well be that urban poverty was primarily a sex-typed phenomenon, with poor *men* being the aberration rather than the rule. In any event, it is not clear whether poverty was rising in rural areas, and that was where more than 90 percent of the American population lived.

Within this overall picture, it is important to distinguish among the various regions: New England, the middle colonies, the Chesapeake, and the Lower South (the Carolinas and Georgia). In New England, three elements combined to exert a major influence on economic development: the nature of the landscape, New England's leadership in colonial shipping, and the impact of the imperial wars. New England's soil was rocky and thin, and farmers did not normally produce large surpluses of grains or other crops to sell abroad. Farms were worked primarily by family members; the region had relatively few hired laborers. It also had the lowest average wealth per freeholder in the colonies. New England had its share of wealthy men, though; they were the merchants and professionals whose income was drawn from overseas trade, primarily with the West Indies.

Boston's central position in the New England economy and its role as a shipbuilding center ensured that it would be directly affected by any resumption of warfare. Thus when England declared war on Spain in 1739, setting off the conflict that was known in Europe as the War of the Austrian Succession and in America as King George's War, the first impact on Boston's economy

New England and King George's War

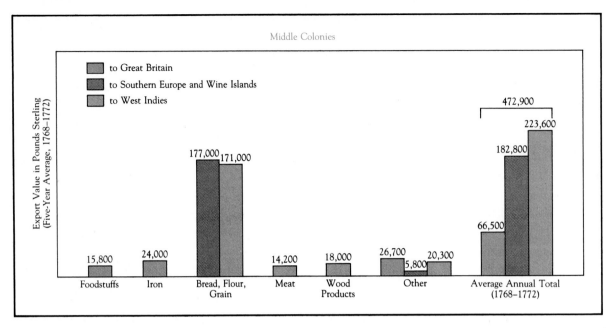

Export Value in Pounds Sterling (Five-Year Average, 1768–1772)

■ to Great Britain
■ to Southern Europe and Wine Islands
■ to West Indies

	Foodstuffs	Iron	Bread, Flour, Grain	Meat	Wood Products	Other	Average Annual Total (1768–1772)
to Great Britain	15,800	24,000	177,000	14,200	18,000	26,700	66,500
to Southern Europe						5,800	182,800
to West Indies			171,000			20,300	223,600

472,900

Regional Trading Patterns: Middle Colonies *Source: James F. Shepherd and Gary M. Walton,* Shipping, Maritime Trade, and the Economic Development of Colonial America *(1972), Tables 2–5, pp. 211–226.*

was positive. Ships—and sailors—were in great demand to serve as privateers (privately owned vessels authorized by the British to capture the enemy's commercial shipping). Wealthy merchants like Thomas Hancock became even wealthier by profiting from contracts to supply military expeditions.

But Boston suffered heavy losses of manpower both in several Caribbean battles and in forays against the French in Canada after 1744, when France became Spain's ally. The most successful expedition was also the most costly. In 1745 a Massachusetts force captured the French fortress of Louisbourg, which guarded the mouth of the St. Lawrence River, but the colony had to levy extremely heavy taxes on its residents to pay for the expensive effort. For decades Boston's economy felt the continuing effects of King George's War. The town was left with unprecedented numbers of widows and children on its relief rolls, the boom in shipbuilding ended when the war did, and taxes remained high. As a final blow, Britain gave Louisbourg back to France in the treaty of Aix-la-Chapelle (1748).

Because of one key difference between the northernmost and the middle colonies, the latter were more positively affected by King George's War and

its aftermath. That difference was the greater fertility of the soil in New York and Pennsylvania, where commercial farming was already the norm. (An average Pennsylvania farm family consumed only 40 percent of what it produced, selling the rest.) New York and New Jersey both had many tenant farmers, who rented acreage from large landowners and often paid their rental fees by sharing crops with their landlords. Prosperous middle-colony property holders were thus in an ideal position to profit from the wartime demand for foodstuffs, especially in the West Indies. After the war a series of poor grain harvests in Europe caused flour prices to rise even more rapidly. Philadelphia and New York, which could draw on large, fertile grain- and livestock-producing areas, took the lead in the foodstuffs trade while Boston, which had no such fertile hinterland, found its economy stagnating.

Prosperity of the Middle Colonies

The increased European demand for grain (and consequent higher prices) in the mid-eighteenth century also had a significant impact on the Chesapeake. After 1745, some Chesapeake planters began to convert tobacco fields to wheat and corn, because the

Chapter 3: GROWTH AND DIVERSITY, 1720–1770

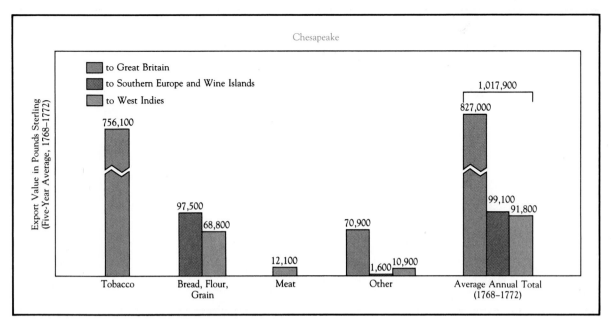

Chesapeake

Export Value in Pounds Sterling (Five-Year Average, 1768–1772)

Legend:
- to Great Britain
- to Southern Europe and Wine Islands
- to West Indies

Tobacco: 756,100

Bread, Flour, Grain: 97,500; 68,800

Meat: 12,100

Other: 70,900; 1,600; 10,900

Average Annual Total (1768–1772): 1,017,900; 827,000; 99,100; 91,800

Regional Trading Patterns: The Chesapeake Source: *James F. Shepherd and Gary M. Walton,* Shipping, Maritime Trade, and the Economic Development of Colonial America *(1972), Tables 2–5, pp. 211–226.*

price of grain was rising faster than that of tobacco. They saw the benefit of diversifying their crops, so they would not be so dependent on one product for their income. But tobacco still ruled the region, and it was the largest single export from the mainland colonies as a whole. (The value of tobacco exports was nearly double that of grain products, the next contender.) Thus it is useful to focus briefly on tobacco's continuing impact on the Chesapeake.

Two major results of the region's concentration on tobacco growing can be discerned in the mid-eighteenth century. The first derived from the substitution of enslaved for indentured **Natural** labor. The offspring of slaves were **Increase** also slaves, whereas the children of **of Black** servants were free. The conse-**Population** quences of that fact were not clear until the black population of the Chesapeake began to grow through natural increase, which occurred between 1720 and 1740. It then became evident that a planter who began with only a few slave families could watch the size of his labor force increase steadily over the years without making additional major investments in workers. Not co-

incidentally, the first truly large Chesapeake plantations appeared in the 1740s. Some years later, the slaveholder Thomas Jefferson indicated that he fully understood the connections when he declared, "I consider a woman who brings a child every two years more profitable than the best man of the farm. What she produces is an addition to the capital, while his labors disappear in mere consumption."

The second effect of tobacco cultivation on the Chesapeake related to patterns of trade. In the first half of the eighteenth century, wealthy planters served as middlemen in the tobacco trade. They collected and shipped tobacco grown by their less prosperous neighbors, extended credit to them, and ordered the English imports they wanted. Indeed, they often profited more from fulfilling these functions than from selling their own crops. In the process, though, they went heavily into debt to English merchants, because the entire system operated on credit.

Beginning in the 1740s, a major change in the system of marketing tobacco affected all Chesapeake planters, though in varying ways. That change was **Scots Factors** the entry into the tobacco trade of Scottish merchants, who organized

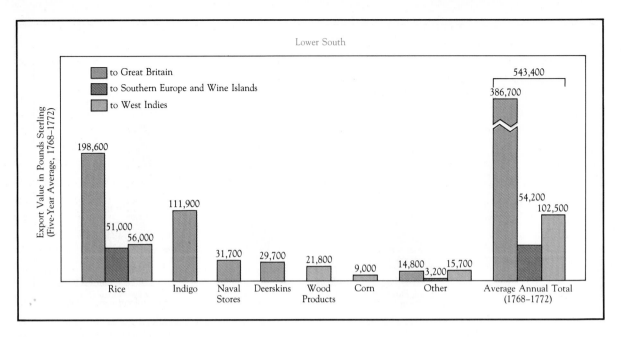

Lower South

Export Value in Pounds Sterling (Five-Year Average, 1768–1772)

- to Great Britain
- to Southern Europe and Wine Islands
- to West Indies

	to Great Britain	to Southern Europe and Wine Islands	to West Indies
Rice	198,600	51,000	56,000
Indigo	111,900		
Naval Stores	31,700		
Deerskins	29,700		
Wood Products	21,800		
Corn	9,000		
Other	14,800	3,200	15,700
Average Annual Total (1768–1772)	386,700	54,200	102,500

543,400

Regional Trading Patterns: The Lower South Source: *James F. Shepherd and Gary M. Walton,* Shipping, Maritime Trade, and the Economic Development of Colonial America *(1972), Tables 2–5, pp. 211–226.*

their efforts differently from their London-based competitors. They stationed representatives (called factors) in the Chesapeake to purchase tobacco, arrange for shipments, and sell imports. The arrival of the Scots factors created genuine competition for the first time and thus pushed up tobacco prices. The Scots provided planters with an alternative system for marketing their crops. Large planters could avoid going into debt, and smaller planters could decrease their economic dependence on their wealthier neighbors. When the Chesapeake finally began to develop port towns later in the century, they grew up in centers of Scots mercantile activity (like Norfolk, Virginia) or in regions that had largely converted to grain production (like Baltimore, Maryland).

Lower South Trade Patterns The Lower South, like the Chesapeake, depended on staple crops and an enslaved labor force for its prosperity, but its pattern of economic growth was distinctive. In contrast to tobacco prices, which rose slowly through the middle decades of the century, rice prices climbed steeply, doubling by the late 1730s. The sharp rise was caused primarily by a heavy demand for rice in southern Europe.

Because Parliament removed rice from the list of enumerated products in 1730, South Carolinians were able to do what colonial tobacco planters never could: trade directly with continental Europe. But dependence on European sales had its drawbacks, as rice growers discovered at the outbreak of King George's War in 1739. Trade with the continent was completely disrupted, rice prices plummeted, and South Carolina entered a depression from which it did not emerge until the following decade. Still, by the 1760s prosperity had returned; indeed, in that period the Lower South experienced more rapid economic growth than the other regions of the colonies. Partly as a result, it had the highest average wealth per freeholder in Anglo-America by the time of the Revolution.

Each region of the colonies, then, had its own economic rhythm derived from the nature of its export trade. King George's War initially helped New England and hurt the Lower South, but in the long run those effects were reversed. In the Chesapeake and the middle colonies, the war initiated a long period of prosperity. The variety of these economic experiences points up a crucial fact about the eighteenth-century mainland colonies: they did not compose a unified whole. They were linked economically into regions, but they had few political or social ties beyond or even within those regions.

Despite the growing coastal trade, the individual colonies' economic fortunes depended not on their neighbors in America but rather on the shifting markets of Europe and the West Indies. Had it not been for an unprecedented crisis in the British imperial system (which will be discussed in Chapter 4), it is hard to see how they could have been persuaded to join in a common endeavor. Even with that impetus, as will become evident, they found unity difficult to maintain.

DAILY LIFE

The basic unit of colonial society was the household. Headed by a white male (or perhaps his widow), the household was the chief mechanism of production and consumption in the colonial economy. Its members—bound by ties of blood or servitude—worked together to produce goods for consumption or sale. The white male head of the household represented it to the outside world, serving in the militia or political posts, casting the household's sole vote in elections. He managed the finances and held legal authority over the rest of the family—his wife, his children, and his servants or slaves. (Eighteenth-century Americans used the word *family* for people who lived together in one house, whether or not they were blood kin.) Such households were considerably larger than American families today; in 1790, the average home contained 5.7 whites. And most of those large families were nuclear—that is, they did not include extended kin like aunts, uncles, or grandparents.

The vast majority of eighteenth-century American families—more than 90 percent of them—lived in rural areas. Therefore nearly all adult white men were farmers and all adult white women farm wives. Though men might work as millers, blacksmiths, or carpenters, and women might sell surplus farm produce to neighbors, they typically did so in addition to their primary agricultural tasks. In colonial America, as in the societies discussed in Chapter 1, household tasks were allocated by gender. The master, his sons, and his male servants or slaves performed one set of chores; the mistress, her daughters, and her female servants or slaves, an entirely different set. So rigid were the gender classifications that when households for some reason lacked a master or mistress the appropriate jobs were often not done. For example, a foreign traveler visiting a Pennsylvania farm remarked that its owner, a bachelor, did not keep poultry or make cheese or clothing because "these domestic farm industries . . . can be carried on well only by women." Only in emergencies and for brief periods of time would women do "men's work" or men do women's.

The mistress of the rural household was responsible for what were termed indoor affairs. She and her female helpers prepared the food, kept the house clean and neat, did the laundry, and often made the clothing. In eighteenth-century America, these basic chores were enormously complex and time-consuming. Preparing food involved planting and cultivating a garden, harvesting and preserving vegetables, salting and smoking meat, drying apples and pressing cider, milking cows and making butter and cheese, not to mention cooking and baking. Making clothing (the chief job of daughters) meant processing raw wool and flax fibers, spinning thread, weaving cloth, dyeing and softening the cloth, and finally cutting out and sewing garments by hand. Nor was keeping one's clothes and home clean an easy job, since the soap had to be made in the household—from ashes, rendered fat, and lye—and water had to be carried by hand from a well or stream. No wonder one harried Long Island housewife filled her diary in 1768 and 1769 with such entries as these: "It has been a tiresome day it is now Bed time and I have not had won minutts rest"; "full of freting discontent dirty and miserabel both yesterday and today."

The head of the household and his male helpers, responsible for outdoor affairs, also had heavy work loads. They had to plant and cultivate fields, build fences, chop wood for the fireplaces, harvest and market crops, and butcher cattle and hogs to provide the household with meat. Only in the plantation South and in northern cities could even a few adult white males lead lives free from arduous physical

Sexual Division of Labor among White Americans

In 1775, a Connecticut woman, Prudence Punderson, created this needlework picture, which she entitled The First, Second, and Last Scene of Mortality. At right she depicted a baby tended by a black servant; at center a mature woman doing needlework; and at left a coffin. Thus she summed up a woman's life from birth to the grave, with traditionally female work—like her picture itself—at its core. Connecticut Historical Society, Hartford.

labor. Indeed, so extensive was the work involved in maintaining an eighteenth-century farm household that a married couple could not do it alone. They had to have help—if not children, then servants or slaves.

Farm households were governed by the seasons and by the hours of daylight. (Candles too had to be manufactured at home; they were too precious to be wasted, so most people rose and went to bed with the sun.) Men and boys had the most leisure in the winter, when there were no crops that needed care. Women and girls were freest in the summer, before embarking on autumn food preservation and winter spinning and weaving. Other activities, including education, had to be subordinated

Rhythms of Rural Life

to seasonal work. Thus farm boys attended school in the winter, and their sisters went to classes in the summer. The seasons also affected travel plans. Because the roads were muddy in spring and fall, most visiting took place in summer and, in the North, in winter, when sleighs could be used.

Because most farm families were relatively isolated from their neighbors and had these heavy seasonal work obligations, rural folk took advantage of every possible opportunity for socializing. Men taking grain to be milled would stop at a crossroads tavern for a drink and conversation with friends. Women gathering to assist at childbirth would drink tea and exchange news. Barbecues and week-long house parties were popular among southern planter families. The Reverend Charles Woodmason, an Anglican missionary, found to his consternation that residents of the Carolina backcountry regarded his church services as social events. "No making of them sit still during Service—but they will be in and out—forward and backward the whole Time (Women especially) as Bees to and fro to their Hives," he wrote of one congregation in 1768. And work itself provided opportunities for visiting. Harvest frolics, corn-husking bees, barn raisings, quilting parties, spinning bees, and other communal endeavors brought together neighbors from miles around, often for several days of work followed by feasting, dancing, and singing in the evenings.

The few eighteenth-century colonial cities were nothing but large towns by today's standards. (The largest, Boston and Philadelphia, had just seventeen thousand and thirteen thousand inhabitants, respectively.) Still, city life differed considerably from rural life. A young Massachusetts man who had moved to Providence described one difference to his farmer father: the city, he remarked, was filled with "Noise and Confusion and Disturbance. I must confess, the jolts of Waggons, the Ratlings of Coaches, the crying of Meat for the Market, the Hollowing of Negros and the ten thousand jinggles and Noises, that continually Surround us in every Part almost of the Town, Confuse my thinking." In the cities, lives were governed by clocks instead of the sun and by work schedules that did not depend so wholly on the seasons. True, a city wife might preserve a ham in the fall, and a merchant's business might vary according to the weather (which determined sailing schedules), but city dwellers were not inextricably tied to the seasons. Year-round, they could purchase foodstuffs and wood at city markets and cloth at dry-goods stores. They could see friends any time they wished. Wealthy urbanites had plenty of leisure time to read, take walks around town or rides in the countryside, play cards, or attend dances, plays, and concerts, for by midcentury most colonial cities had theaters and assembly halls.

Rhythms of Urban Life

City people also had much more contact with the world beyond their own homes than did their rural compatriots. By the middle of the century, every major city had at least one weekly newspaper, and most had two or three. Newspapers printed the latest "advices from London" (usually two to three months

In eighteenth-century colonial cities, where most of the buildings were constructed of wood, fire was an ever-present danger. Thus the young men of the towns formed volunteer fire companies, which not only served a useful purpose but also provided their members with convivial companionship. New York Public Library.

old) and news of events in other English colonies, as well as reports on matters of local interest. The local newspaper was available at taverns and inns, so people who could not afford to buy it could nevertheless read it. (Even illiterates could acquaint themselves with the latest news, since the paper was often read aloud by literate customers.) However, contact with the outside world also had drawbacks. Sailors sometimes brought exotic and deadly diseases into port with them. Cities like Boston, New York, and Philadelphia endured terrible epidemics of smallpox and yellow fever, which the countryside largely escaped.

Cities attracted many migrants from rural areas. Young men came to learn a skill through an apprenticeship, for cities housed the artisans who printed books and newspapers, crafted fine furniture, made shoes, or created expensive gold or silver items. Ordinary laborers too came seeking work, and widows came looking for a means of supporting their families. Without an adult man in the household, a woman had a difficult time running a farm. Consequently, widows tended to congregate in port cities, where they could sell their services as nurses, teachers, seamstresses, servants, or prostitutes, or (if they had some capital) open shops, inns, or boardinghouses. In rural areas, where the economy was based largely on subsistence agriculture and most families produced nearly all their own necessities, there was little demand for the services that landless women and men could perform. In the cities, though, someone always needed another servant, blacksmith, or laundress.

Only widows and the very few never-married women could legally run independent businesses. An unmarried colonial woman had the same legal rights as a man (with the exception of voting), but an Anglo-American wife was subordinate to her husband in law as well as custom. Under the common-law doctrine of coverture, a married woman became one person with her husband. She could not sue or be sued, make contracts, buy or sell property, or draft a will. Any property she owned prior to marriage became her husband's after the wedding; any wages she earned were legally his; and all children of the marriage fell under his absolute control. Moreover, since divorces were practically impossible to obtain, men and women had little chance to escape from a bad marriage.

Status of Women

Anglo-American men expected their wives to defer to their judgment. Most wives seem to have accepted secondary status without murmuring. When girls married, they were commonly advised to devote themselves to their husbands' interests. "Let your Dress your Conversation & the whole Business of your life be to please your Husband & to make him happy & you need not fail of being so your self," a New Yorker told his daughter in the 1730s. That women followed such advice is evident in their diaries. A Virginia woman remarked, for example, that "one of my first resolutions I made after marriage, was never to hold disputes with my husband." It was wives' responsibility, she declared, "to give up to their husbands" whenever differences of opinion arose between them. Not until very late in the eighteenth century, during and after the American Revolution, would such women as Abigail Adams begin to question these traditional notions.

The man's legal and customary authority extended to his children as well. Indeed, childrearing was the one task regularly undertaken by both men and women in colonial America; all their other chores were divided by sex. Women cared for infants and toddlers, but thereafter both parents disciplined the children. The father set the general standards by which they were raised and usually had the final word on such matters as their education or vocational training. White parents normally insisted on unquestioning obedience from their offspring, and many freely used physical punishment to break a child's will. In the homes of America's elite families, though, more nurturant childrearing practices seem to have prevailed. In such households, the most burdensome chores were performed by white or black servants, freeing parents to spend more time with their offspring and reducing the need for strict disciplinary measures. The relaxed upbringing of these wealthy youngsters foreshadowed nineteenth-century white Americans' greater indulgence of their children.

Not all families in the English colonies, of course, were white. And more than 95 percent of black families were held in perpetual bondage. In South Carolina, a majority of the population was black; in Georgia, about half; and in the Chesapeake, 40 percent. Although the populations of some backcountry areas of Virginia, Maryland, and the Carolinas were less than one-fifth black, some parts of the Carolina lowcountry were nearly 90 percent black by 1790. A trend toward consolidation of landholding and slave ownership after 1740 had a profound effect on the lives of Afro-Americans. In areas with high proportions of blacks in the population, most slaves resided on plantations with at least nine other bondspeople. Although many southern blacks lived on farms with only one or two other slaves, the majority had the experience of living and working in a largely black setting.

The size of such plantation households allowed for the specialization of labor. Encouraged by planters whose goal was to create as self-sufficient a household as possible, Afro-American men and women became highly skilled at tasks whites believed appropriate to their sex. Each large plantation had its own male

Sexual Division of Labor among Black Americans

blacksmiths, carpenters, valets, shoemakers, and gardeners, and female dairymaids, seamstresses, cooks, and at least one midwife, who attended pregnant white and black women alike. These skilled slaves—between 10 and 20 percent of the black population—were as essential to the smooth functioning of the plantation as the ordinary field hands who labored "in the crop." But whites assigned most male and female slaves to work in the fields. Since West African women were accustomed to agricultural labor (see page 12), that task must have coincided with their own cultural expectations. But whites had a different concept of sexual division of labor. To them black women's work in the fields connoted inferior status.

The typical Chesapeake tobacco plantation was divided into small "quarters" located at some distance from one another. White overseers supervised work on the distant quarters, while the planter personally took charge of the "home" quarter (which included the planter's house). In the Carolina lowcountry, where planters usually spent months in Charleston in the hope of avoiding the malaria and yellow fever seasons, blacks often supervised their fellow slaves. Planters commonly assigned "outlandish" (African-born) slaves to do field labor in order to accustom them to plantation work routines and to enable them to learn some English. Artisans, on the other hand, were usually drawn from among the plantation's American-born blacks. In such families skills like carpentry and midwifery were passed down from father to son and from mother to daughter; such knowledge often constituted a slave family's most valuable possession.

Plantation Life

Eighteenth-century planters were considerably less worried that their slaves might run away than were their counterparts seventy-five years later, and with good reason. All the English colonies legally permitted slavery, so blacks had few places to go to escape bondage. Sometimes recently arrived Africans tried to steal boats to return home or ran off in groups to the frontier, where they attempted to establish traditional villages. Occasionally slaves from South Carolina tried to reach Spanish Florida. But Afro-Americans usually recognized that they had few long-term alternatives to remaining on their plantations.

About 1784, slave artisans on the plantation of Joel Lane, near Raleigh, North Carolina, fashioned this beautiful china cabinet. Every plantation had its share of skilled slaves. Planters reserved traditionally male jobs like cabinet-making for their male slaves, assigning skilled women to "feminine" tasks like spinning, dairying, and cooking. Index of American Design, National Gallery of Art, Washington, D.C.

This is not to say that Afro-American slaves never ran away. They did, in large numbers. But they did so to visit friends or relatives, or simply to escape their normal work routines for a few days or months; they could have had little hope of remaining permanently at large. In a society in which blackness automatically connoted perpetual servitude, no black person anywhere could claim free status without being challenged. And, from the blacks' perspective, violent resistance had even less to recommend it than running away. Whites may have been in the minority in some areas, but they controlled the guns and ammunition. Even if a revolt succeeded for a time, whites could easily muster the armed force necessary to put it down. Only in very unusual circumstances, therefore—as will be seen in the last section of this chapter—did colonial blacks attempt to rebel against their white oppressors.

An Overseer Doing His Duty, *by Benjamin H. Latrobe. Most slave women were field hands like these, sketched in 1798 near Fredericksburg, Virginia. White women were believed to be unsuited for heavy outdoor labor. Maryland Historical Society.*

Afro-Americans did try to improve the conditions of their bondage and gain some measure of control over their lives. Their chief vehicle for doing so was the family. Planters' records reveal how members of extended kin groups provided support, assistance, and comfort to each other. They asked to live on the same quarters, protested excessive punishment administered to relatives, and often requested special treatment for children or siblings. On one Virginia plantation, for instance, a mother arranged for her daughter to be treated by a particular black doctor, and a father successfully convinced his master that his daughter should be allowed to live with her stepmother. The extended-kin ties that developed among Afro-American families who had lived on the same plantation for several generations served as insurance against the uncertainties of existence under slavery. If a nuclear family was broken up by sale, there were always relatives around to help with

Black Families

childrearing and other tasks. Among colonial blacks, in other words, the extended family probably served a more important function than it did among whites.

Yet blacks were always subject to white intrusions into their lives. Black house servants had to serve the white family rather than their own, and even field hands were constantly at the whites' beck and call. Still, most black families managed to carve out a small measure of autonomy. On many plantations, slaves were allowed to plant their own gardens, hunt, or fish in order to supplement the standard diet of corn and salt pork. Some Chesapeake mistresses permitted their female slaves to raise chickens, which they could then sell or exchange for such items as extra clothing or blankets.

In South Carolina, slaves were often able to accumulate personal property, because most rice and indigo plantations operated on a task system. Once slaves had completed their assigned tasks for the day, they were free to work for themselves. (Occasionally they could even cultivate rice or indigo crops of their own.) In Maryland and Virginia, where by the end of the century some whites had begun to hire out their slaves to others, blacks were sometimes allowed to keep a small part of the wages they earned. Such advances were slight, but against the bleak backdrop of slavery they deserve to be highlighted.

Relations between blacks and whites varied considerably from household to household. In some, masters and mistresses enforced their will chiefly through physical coercion. Thus one **Black-White** woman's diary noted matter-of-**Relations** factly: "December 1: Lucy whippt for getting key of Celler door & stealing apples. December 2: Plato Anthoney & Abraham Pegg's housband whipt for Hog stealing." On other plantations, masters were more lenient and respectful of slaves' property and their desire to live with other members of their families. But even in households where whites and blacks displayed genuine affection for one another, there were inescapable tensions. Such tensions were caused not only by the whites' uneasiness about the slave system in general but also by the dynamics of day-to-day relationships when a small number of whites wielded absolute legal power over the lives of many blacks.

Thomas Jefferson was deeply concerned about that issue. In 1780 he observed, "The whole commerce between master and slave is a perpetual exercise of the most boisterous passions, the most unremitting despotism on the one part, and degrading submission on the other. Our children see this, and learn to imitate it. . . . The man must be a prodigy who can retain his manners and morals undepraved by such circumstances." Thus, what troubled him most was the impact of the system on whites, not on the people they held in bondage. Before the Revolution, only a tiny number of Quakers (most notably John Woolman in his *Some Considerations on the Keeping of Negroes*, published in 1754) took a different approach, criticizing slavery out of sympathy for blacks. The other white colonists who questioned slavery took Jefferson's approach, stressing the institution's adverse effect on whites, and they were extremely few in number. A labor system so essential to the functioning of the colonial economy met with little open challenge.

In the third quarter of the eighteenth century, the daily work routines of most Americans had changed little from those of their Old World ancestors. Ordinary white folk lived in farm households, their lives governed by the sexual division of labor. Most Afro-Americans were held in perpetual bondage, but their work was performed as it had been in West Africa, communally in the fields. Even in colonial cities life differed little from European cities in previous centuries. Yet if the routines of daily life seemed fixed and unchanging, the wider context in which those routines occurred did not. In both Europe and America the eighteenth century was a time of great cultural and intellectual ferment. The movement known as the Enlightenment at first primarily influenced the educated elites. Ordinary people seemed little touched by it. But since enlightened thinking played a major part in the ideology of the American Revolution, it was eventually to have an important impact on the lives of all Americans.

COLONIAL CULTURE

The older, traditional form of colonial culture was oral, communal, and—for at least the first half of the eighteenth century—intensely localized. The newer culture of the elite was print-oriented, more individualized, and self-consciously cosmopolitan. The two will be discussed separately but they also mingled in a variety of ways, since people of both descriptions lived side by side in small communities.

A majority of the residents of British America (almost all the blacks, half the white women, and at least one-fifth of the white men) could neither read nor write. That had important **Oral Culture** consequences for the transmission and development of American culture. In the absence of literacy, the primary means of communication was face-to-face conversation. Information tended to travel slowly and within relatively confined regions. Different locales developed divergent cultural traditions, and those differences were heightened by racial or ethnic variations.

When Europeans or Africans migrated to the colonies, they left familiar environments behind but brought with them sets of cultural assumptions about how society should work and how their own lives fitted into the broader social context. In North America, those assumptions influenced the way they organized their lives. Yet Old World customs usually could not be recreated intact in the New World, because people from different origins now resided in the same communities. Accordingly, the colonists had to forge new cultural identities for themselves.

In New England, communal culture centered on the church and on religious observances in the civic sphere. Colonial governments proclaimed official days of thanksgiving (for good harvests, victories in war, and so forth) or days of fasting and prayer (when the colony was experiencing difficulties). Everyone in the community was expected to participate in the public rituals held on such occasions. Militia musters (known as training days), normally scheduled once a month, were similar moments that brought the community together, since all able-bodied men between the ages of sixteen and sixty were members of the militia.

Attendance at church was perhaps the most important public ritual in New England. Church services publicly affirmed one's standing in the community.

Religious Rituals In Congregational (Puritan) churches, seating was assigned by church leaders: each family had its own pew, whose location at the front, back, or sides of the church depended on the family's wealth and social prominence. A similar statement about the local status hierarchy was conveyed at Anglican parishes in Virginia. There too families purchased their own pews, and in some parishes the landed gentlemen customarily strode into church as a group just before the service was to begin, deliberately drawing attention to their exalted position. Quite a different message came from the entirely egalitarian, but sex-segregated, seating system used in Quaker meetinghouses. Where one sat in colonial churches, in other words, symbolized one's place in society and the values of the local community.

Other aspects of the service also reflected communal values. In most colonial churches, trained clergymen delivered formal sermons, but in Quaker services members of the meeting spoke informally to each other. Communal singing in Congregational churches added an egalitarian element to an otherwise status-conscious experience. Not by accident was the first

book printed in the colonies *The Bay Psalm Book* (1640), consisting of Old Testament psalms recast in short, rhyming, metrical lines so they could be easily learned, remembered, and sung even by people who could not read. Communal singing helped to reduce the ritual significance of hierarchical seating arrangements, bringing a kind of crude democracy into the church. Everyone participated in the singing on an equal basis and all had an equal voice in deciding which version of the psalms to use and whether instruments should accompany the singing.

In the Chesapeake, some of the most important cultural rituals were civic in nature, in particular court and election days. When the county court was in session, men would come from miles around to sue one another for debt, appear as witnesses, serve as jurors, or simply observe the goings-on. Attendance at court functioned as a method of civic education; from watching the proceedings men learned what behavior their neighbors expected of them. Elections served the same purpose, for freeholders voted in public. An election official, often flanked by the candidates for the office in question, would call each man forward in turn to declare his preference. The voter would then be thanked politely by the gentleman for whom he had cast his oral ballot. Traditionally, the candidates also treated their supporters to rum at nearby taverns. (Note, in this context, that public rituals in the Chesapeake region were more male-centered than those in New England, where rituals focused on religion, in which women participated fully, rather than politics.)

In such settings as church and courthouse, then, elite and ordinary folk alike participated in the oral, communal culture that served as the cement holding their communities together. But the genteel residents of the colonies also took part in a newer kind of culture, one organized through the world of print and the message conveyed by reading as well as by observing one's neighbors.

Literacy was certainly less essential in eighteenth-century America than it is today. People—especially women—could live their entire lives without ever being called upon to read a book or write a letter. Thus education beyond the bare rudiments of reading, writing, and "figuring" was

Civic Rituals

Attitudes Toward Education

Chapter 3: GROWTH AND DIVERSITY, 1720–1770

usually regarded as a frill for either sex. Men might have to know how to read a contract or keep rough accounts, and women might need or want to read the Bible, but beyond that little learning appeared to be necessary. Education accordingly was an accomplishment, a sign of status. Only parents who wanted their children to be distinguished from less fortunate peers (perhaps for reasons of piety, or a desire for upward mobility or maintenance of status) were willing to forgo their children's valuable labor to allow them to attend school. And when parents did so, the education they gave their sons differed from that given their daughters. Girls ordinarily received little intellectual training beyond the rudiments, though they might learn music, dancing, or fancy needlework (since those skills all connoted genteel status). Elite boys, on the other hand, studied with tutors or attended grammar schools that prepared them to enter college at age fourteen or fifteen.

Not surprisingly, therefore, the colonial system of higher education for males was more fully developed than was basic instruction for either sex. The first American colleges were chiefly designed to train young men for the ministry. Following the earlier examples of Harvard (1636), William and Mary (chartered 1693, but not a functioning entity until 1726), and Yale (1701), the colleges founded in the mid-eighteenth century—those now known as Princeton (1747), Columbia (1754), Brown (1765), and Rutgers (1766)—were intended to supply clergymen to fill the pulpits of Presbyterian, Anglican, Baptist, and Dutch Reformed churches, respectively. (Dartmouth College, founded 1769, though not explicitly aimed at educating clerics, also had a religious purpose, that of Christianizing the Indians.) But during the eighteenth century the curriculum and character of all these colleges changed considerably. Their students, the sons of the colonial elite, were now interested in careers in medicine, law, and business instead of the ministry. And the learned men who headed the colleges, though ministers themselves, were deeply affected by the Enlightenment.

In the seventeenth century, some European thinkers had begun to analyze nature in an effort to determine the laws that govern the universe. They and their successors in subsequent centuries employed experimentation and abstract reasoning to discover general

The Enlightenment

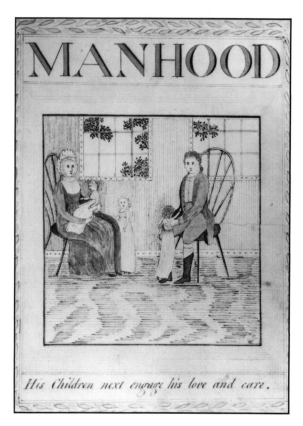

A colonial boy's education included not just reading and writing but instruction in the duties of the patriarchal role. The unpublished picture book, The Ages of Man, prepared about 1760, taught its young male readers that a mature man should demonstrate "love and care" for his children. Free Library of Philadelphia, Rosenbach Collection.

principles behind such everyday phenomena as the motions of the planets and stars, the behavior of falling objects, and the characteristics of light and sound. Above all, the Enlightenment philosophers emphasized acquiring knowledge through reason, rather than through intuition and revelation. They took a particular delight in challenging previously unquestioned assumptions; for example, John Locke's *Essay Concerning Human Understanding* (1690) disputed the notion that human beings were born already imprinted with innate ideas. All knowledge, Locke asserted, came rather from one's observations of the external world.

The Enlightenment had an enormous impact on well-to-do, educated people in Europe and America. It supplied them with a common vocabulary and a unified view of the world, one that insisted that the enlightened eighteenth century was better than all previous ages. It joined them in a common endeavor, the effort to make sense of God's orderly creation. Thus American naturalists like John and William Bartram supplied European scientists with information about New World plants and animals, so that they could be fitted into newly formulated universal classification systems. So too Americans interested in astronomy took part in 1769 in an international effort to learn about the workings of the solar system by studying a rare occurrence, the transit of Venus across the face of the sun.

These intellectual currents had a dramatic effect on the curriculum of the colonial colleges. Whereas in the seventeenth century Harvard courses focused on the study of the ancient languages and theology, after the 1720s colleges began to introduce courses in mathematics (including algebra, geometry, and calculus), the natural sciences, law, and medicine (including anatomy and physiology). The young men educated in such colleges—and their sisters at home, with whom they occasionally shared their books and ideas—developed a rational outlook on life that differentiated them from their fellow colonists. This was the world of Dr. Alexander Hamilton and his associates. When he left Annapolis in 1744, he carried letters of introduction to "the better sort" in all the places he intended to visit. Such people had learned the value of reading, of regular correspondence with like-minded friends, of convivial gatherings at which the conversation focused on the books most recently imported from Europe (especially the daring novels by Samuel Richardson).

Well-to-do graduates of American colleges, along with others who like Hamilton had obtained their education in Great Britain, formed the core of genteel culture in the colonies. Men and **Elite Culture** women from these families wanted to set themselves apart from ordinary folk. Beginning in the 1720s they constructed grandiose residences for themselves, substantial houses furnished with imported carpets, silver plate, and furniture. They entertained their friends at elaborate dinner parties and balls, at which all present dressed in the height of fashion. They cultivated polite manners and saw themselves as part of a transatlantic and intercolonial network.

In what ways, if at all, did this genteel, enlightened culture affect the lives of the majority of colonists? Certainly no resident of the colonies could have avoided some contact with members of the elite, even if it was only an occasional glimpse of them. Some groups were more directly affected; for example, the elite's demand for consumer goods of all kinds led to the growth of artisan industries (like silversmithing or fine furniture-making) in the colonies. But the Enlightenment's most immediate impact on all Americans was in the realm of medicine.

The key figure in the drama was the Reverend Cotton Mather, the Puritan clergyman, who was a member of England's Royal Society, an organization of the intellectual elite. In a Royal **Smallpox** Society publication Mather read **Inoculations** about the benefits of inoculation (deliberately infecting a person with a mild case of a disease) as a protection against the dreaded smallpox. In 1720 and 1721, when Boston suffered a major smallpox epidemic, Mather and a doctor ally urged people to be inoculated; there was fervent opposition, including that of Boston's leading physician. When the epidemic had ended, the statistics bore out Mather's opinion: of those inoculated, fewer than 3 percent died; of those who became ill without inoculation, nearly 15 percent perished. Though it was midcentury before inoculation was generally accepted as a preventive procedure, enlightened methods had provided colonial Americans with protection from the greatest killer disease of all.

If the lives of genteel and ordinary folk in the eighteenth-century colonies seemed to follow different patterns, there was one man who in his person appeared to combine their traits; ap- **Benjamin** propriately enough, he later became **Franklin,** for Europeans the symbolic Amer- **the Symbolic** ican. That man was Benjamin **American** Franklin. Born in Boston in 1706, he was the perfect example of a self-made, self-educated man. Apprenticed at an early age to his older brother James, a Boston printer and newspaper publisher, Franklin ran away to Philadelphia in 1723. There he worked as a printer and eventually started his own publishing business, printing the *Pennsylvania Gazette* and *Poor Richard's Almanack* among other books. The business was so successful that Franklin was able to retire from active control in 1748, at forty-two. He thereafter devoted himself to intellectual endeavors and public service (as deputy postmaster general for the colonies, as an agent representing colonial interests in London, and finally as a diplomat during the Revolution). Franklin's *Experiments and Observations on Electricity* (1751) was the most important scientific work by a colonial American; it established the terminology and basic theory of electricity still in use today.

In 1749 and 1751 Franklin published pamphlets proposing the establishment of a new educational institution in Pennsylvania. The purpose of Franklin's "English School" was not to produce clerics or scholars but to prepare young men "for learning any business, calling or profession, except such wherein languages are required." He wanted to enable them "to pass through and execute the several offices of civil life, with advantage and reputation to themselves and country." The College of Philadelphia, which he founded in 1755, was intended to graduate youths who would resemble Franklin himself—talented, practical men of affairs competent in a number of different fields.

Franklin and the student he envisioned thus fused the conflicting tendencies of colonial culture. Free of the Old World's traditions, the ideal American would achieve distinction through hard work and the application of common-sense principles. Like Franklin, he would rise from an ordinary family into the ranks of the genteel, thereby transcending the cultural boundaries that divided the colonists. He would be unpretentious but not unlearned, simple but not ignorant, virtuous but not priggish. The American would be a true child of the Enlightenment, knowledgeable about European culture yet not bound by its fetters, advancing through reason and talent alone. To him all things would be possible, all doors open.

The contrast with the original communal ideals of the early New England settlements could not have been sharper. Franklin's American was an individual, free to make choices about his future, able to contemplate a variety of possible careers. John Winthrop's American, outlined in his "Modell of Christian Charity" (see pages 30–31), had been a component of a greater whole that required his unhesitating, unquestioning submission. But the two visions had one point in common: both described only white males. Neither blacks nor females played any part in them.

Benjamin Franklin (1706–1789), painted by the itinerant artist Robert Feke in 1746, when Franklin was forty. The portrait shows Franklin at the height of his business career, a prosperous Philadelphian. Harvard University Portrait Collection, Bequest, Dr. John C. Warren in 1856.

Not until many years later would America formally recognize what had been true all along: that females and nonwhites had participated in the creation of the nation's cultural traditions.

POLITICS AND RELIGION: STABILITY AND CRISIS AT MIDCENTURY

In the first decades of the eighteenth century, colonial political life developed a new stability. Despite the large migration from overseas, a majority of the residents of the mainland colonies were now native-born. Men from genteel families dominated the political structures in each province, for voters (white men who met property-holding requirements) tended to defer to their well-educated "betters" on election days. (Whether that deference was voluntary or forced is disputed among historians, but the result was the same.) The most noticeable consequence of such deferential behavior was a declining rate of turnover among elected officials in most of the colonies.

Logically enough, colonial political leaders sought to increase the powers of the elected assemblies relative to those of the governors and other appointed officials.

Rise of the Assemblies Colonial assemblies began to claim privileges associated with the British House of Commons, such as the right to initiate all tax legislation and to control the militia. The assemblies also developed effective ways of influencing British appointees, especially by threatening to withhold their salaries. In some colonies (like Virginia and South Carolina), the elite members of the assemblies most often presented a united front to royal officials, but in others (like New York), they fought with each other long and bitterly. It was in the latter province that the first steps on the road to modern American democracy were taken. In their attempts to win hotly contested elections, New York's genteel leaders began to appeal to "the people," competing openly for the votes of ordinary freeholders.

Yet eighteenth-century assemblies bore little resemblance to twentieth-century state legislatures. In the first place, much of their business was what today would be termed administrative; only on rare occasions did they formulate new policies or pass laws of major importance. Second, members of the assemblies conceived of their role differently from modern legislators. Instead of believing that they should act *positively* to improve the lives of their constituents, eighteenth-century assemblymen saw themselves as acting *negatively* to prevent encroachments on the people's rights. That is, in their minds their primary function was to stop the governors or councils from enacting (for example) oppressive taxes; it was not to pass laws that would actively benefit their constituents.

By the middle of the century, politically aware colonists commonly drew analogies between their governments and the balance between king, lords, and commons found in Great Britain—a combination that was thought to produce a stable polity. Although the analogy was not exact, the colonists equated their governors with the monarch, their councils with the aristocracy, and their assemblies with the House of Commons. All three were thought essential to good government, but Americans did not regard them with the same degrees of approval. They saw the governors and appointed councils as aliens who posed a potential threat to colonial freedoms and customary ways of life. As representatives of England rather than America, the governors and councils were to be feared rather than trusted. Colonists saw the assemblies, on the other hand, as the people's protectors. And for their part, the assemblies regarded themselves as representatives of the people.

But again, such beliefs should not be equated with modern practice. The assemblies, firmly controlled by dominant families whose members were re-elected year after year, rarely responded to the concerns of their poorer constituents. Although settlement continually spread westward, assemblies failed to re-apportion themselves to provide adequate representation for newer communities—a lack of action that led to serious grievances among frontier dwellers, especially those from non-English ethnic groups. Moreover, the assemblies occasionally acted in a manner that appears oppressive to modern eyes. For example, in 1735 the New York assembly jailed the printer John Peter Zenger for publicly criticizing its actions in his newspaper. Thus it is important to distinguish between the colonial *ideal,* which placed the assembly to the forefront in the protection of people's liberties, and the *reality,* in which the people protected tended chiefly to be the wealthy and well-born and the assembly members themselves.

At midcentury, the political structures that had stabilized in a period of relative calm confronted a series of crises. None affected all the mainland provinces, but on the other hand no colony escaped wholly untouched by at least one. The crises were of various sorts—ethnic, racial, economic, religious—and they exposed the internal tensions building in the pluralistic American society. They foreshadowed the greater disorder of the revolutionary era. Most important, they demonstrated that the political accommodations arrived at in the aftermath of the Glorious Revolution were no longer adequate to govern Britain's American empire. Once again, changes appeared necessary.

In 1748, the colony of Massachusetts constructed its impressive State House in Boston. Here met the Assembly and the Council. The solidity and imposing nature of the building must have symbolized for its users the increasing consolidation of power in the hands of the Massachusetts legislature. Library of Congress.

One of the first—and greatest—of the crises occurred in South Carolina. Early one morning in September 1739, about twenty South Carolina slaves gathered near the Stono River south of Charleston. After seizing guns and ammunition from a store, they killed the storekeepers and some nearby planter families. Then, joined by other slaves from the area, they headed south toward Florida in hopes of finding refuge in that Spanish colony. By midday, however, the alarm had been sounded among whites in the district. In the late afternoon a troop of militia caught up with the fugitives, then numbering about a hundred, and attacked them, killing some and dispersing the rest. More than a week later, the whites finally captured most of the remaining con-

Stono Rebellion

spirators. Those not killed on the spot were later executed, but for more than two years afterward renegades were rumored to be still at large.

The Stono Rebellion shocked white South Carolinians and residents of other colonies as well. Laws governing the behavior of blacks were stiffened throughout British America. But the most immediate response came in New York, which itself had suffered a slave revolt in 1712. There the news from the South, coupled with fears of Spain generated by the outbreak of King George's War, set off a reign of terror in the summer of 1741. Hysterical whites transformed a biracial gang of thieves and arsonists into malevolent conspirators who wanted to foment a slave uprising under the guidance of a supposed priest in the pay of Spain. By summer's end, thirty-one blacks and four whites had been executed for participating in the "plot." Not only did the Stono Rebellion and the New York Conspiracy expose and confirm whites' deepest fears about the dangers of slaveholding, they also revealed the assemblies' inability to prevent serious internal disorder. Events of the next two decades confirmed that pattern.

By midcentury, most of the fertile land east of the Appalachians had been purchased or occupied. As a result, conflicts over land titles and conditions of landholding grew in number and

Land Riots frequency as colonists competed for control of land good for farming. In 1746, for example, New Jersey farmers holding land under grants from the governor of New York (dating from the brief period when both provinces were owned by the Duke of York) clashed violently with agents of the East Jersey proprietors. The proprietors claimed the land as theirs and demanded annual payments, called quitrents, for the use of the property. Similar violence occurred in the 1760s in the region that later became Vermont. There, farmers (many of them migrants from eastern New England) holding land grants issued by New Hampshire battled with speculators claiming title to the area through grants from New York authorities.

The most serious land riots of the period took place along the Hudson River in 1765 and 1766. Late in the seventeenth century, Governor Benjamin Fletcher of New York had granted several huge tracts in the lower Hudson valley to prominent colonial families. The proprietors in turn divided these estates into small farms, which they rented chiefly to poor Dutch and German migrants, who evidently regarded tenancy as a step on the road to independent freeholder status. By the 1750s, some proprietors were earning as much as £1,000 to £2,000 annually from quitrents and other fees.

After 1740, though, increasing migration from New England brought conflict to the great New York estates. The mobile New Englanders, who had moved in search of land, did not want to become tenants. Many squatted on vacant portions of the manors and resisted all attempts to evict them. In the mid-1760s, the Philipse family brought suit against the New Englanders, some of whom had lived on Philipse land for twenty or thirty years. New York courts upheld the Philipse claim and ordered the squatters to make

way for tenants with valid leases. Instead of complying, the farmers organized a rebellion against the proprietors. For nearly a year the insurgent farmers controlled much of the Hudson valley. They terrorized proprietors and loyal tenants, freed their friends from jail, and on one occasion battled a county sheriff and his posse. The rebellion was put down only after British troops dispatched from New York City captured its most important leaders.

Violent conflicts of a different sort erupted just a few years later in the Carolinas. The "Regulator" movements of the late 1760s (South Carolina) and early 1770s (North Carolina) pitted

The Regulators backcountry farmers against the eastern planters who controlled their provinces' governments. The frontier dwellers, most of whom were Scotch-Irish, protested their lack of an adequate voice in colonial political affairs. The South Carolinians for months policed the countryside in vigilante bands, contending that law enforcement in the region was too lax. The North Carolinians, many of whose grievances had their origin in heavy taxation, fought a battle with eastern militiamen at Alamance in 1771. Regional, ethnic, and economic tensions thus combined to create these disturbances, which ultimately arose from frontiersmen's dissatisfaction with the Carolina governments.

The most widespread of all midcentury crises occurred not in politics but in religion. From the late 1730s through the 1760s, waves of religious revivalism—known collectively as the

First Great Awakening Great Awakening—swept over various parts of the colonies, primarily New England (1735–1745) and Virginia (1750s and 1760s). Eighteenth-century America was ripe for religious renewal, because orthodox Calvinists were troubled by the influence on religion of Enlightenment rationalism (which denied innate human depravity). The Great Awakening was also related to the colonies' new population patterns. Because many of the recent immigrants and residents of the backcountry had no religious affiliation, they offered evangelists a likely source of converts.

The first indications of what was to become the Great Awakening occurred in western Massachusetts, in the Northampton congregation of the Reverend Jonathan Edwards, a noted preacher and theologian. During 1734 and 1735, Edwards noticed a remarkable response in his flock (and especially its more youthful members) to a message based squarely on Calvinist principles. Individuals, Edwards argued, could attain salvation only through recognition of their own depraved natures and the need to surrender completely to God's will. Such surrender, when it came, brought release from worry and sin; it was an intensely emotional experience. Indeed, people in Edwards's congregation began to experience that surrender as a single identifiable moment of conversion.

The effects of such conversions remained isolated until 1739, when George Whitefield, an English adherent of the Methodist branch of Anglicanism, arrived in America. For fifteen months **George Whitefield** Whitefield toured the colonies, preaching to large audiences from Georgia to New England and concentrating his efforts in the major cities: Boston, New York, Philadelphia, and Charleston. An effective orator, Whitefield was the chief generating force behind the Great Awakening. Everywhere he traveled, his fame preceded him; thousands turned out to listen—and to experience conversion. At first, regular clerics welcomed Whitefield and the native itinerant evangelist preachers who sprang up to imitate him. Soon, however, many clergymen began to realize that "revived" religion, though it filled their churches, ran counter to a more rational approach to matters of faith. Furthermore, they disliked the emotional style of the revivalists, whose itinerancy also disrupted normal patterns of church attendance.

Opposition to the Awakening heightened rapidly, and large numbers of churches splintered in its wake. "Old Lights"—traditional clerics and their followers—engaged in bitter disputes with the "New Light" evangelicals. American religion, already characterized by numerous sects, became further divided as the major denominations split into Old Light and New Light factions, and as new evangelical sects—Methodists and Baptists—quickly gained adherents. Paradoxically, the angry fights and the rapid rise in the number of distinct denominations eventually led to an American willingness to tolerate religious diversity. No one sect could make an unequivocal claim to orthodoxy and so they all had to coexist if they were to exist at all.

The most important effect of the Awakening was its impact on American modes of thought. Common

George Whitefield (1714–1770), an English evangelist who made frequent tours of the American colonies. This portrait, painted in England, shows the effects his powerful preaching had on his listeners. National Portrait Gallery, London.

folk had long been expected to accept unhesitatingly the authority of their "betters," whether wealthy gentry, government officials, or educated clergymen. The message of the Great Awakening directly challenged that tradition of deference. The revivalists, many of whom were not ordained clergymen, claimed they understood the word of God far better than orthodox clerics. The Awakening's emphasis on emotion rather than learning as the road to salvation further undermined the validity of received wisdom. Supported by the belief that God was with them, New Lights began to question not only religious but also social and political orthodoxy.

Nowhere was this trend more evident than in Virginia, where the plantation gentry and their ostentatious lifestyle dominated society. By the 1760s, Baptists had gained a major foothold in Virginia, and their beliefs and behavior were openly at odds with the way most gentry families lived. They rejected as sinful the horse racing, gambling, and dancing that occupied much of the gentry's leisure time. Like the Quakers before them, they dressed plainly and simply, in contrast to the fashionable opulence of the gentry. Most strikingly of all, they addressed each other as "brother" and "sister" and organized their congregations on the basis of equality. And at least some Baptist congregations included blacks as well as whites, which was truly revolutionary.

At midcentury the Great Awakening injected an egalitarian strain into American life. Although primarily a religious movement, the Awakening also had important social and political consequences, calling into question habitual modes of behavior in the secular as well as the religious realm. In combination with the other changes occurring in the colonies—the increasing ethnic and racial diversity, the expanding economy, the introduction of new lifestyles and forms of thought—the Great Awakening helped to break Americans' ties to their limited seventeenth-century origins. A century and a half

after English people had first settled in North America, the colonies were only nominally English. Rather, they mixed diverse European, American, and African traditions into a novel cultural blend. That culture owed much to the Old World, but just as much, if not more, to the New. In the 1760s Americans began to recognize that fact. They realized that their interests were not necessarily those of Great Britain, or of its rulers; for the first time they offered a frontal challenge to British authority.

SUGGESTIONS FOR FURTHER READING

General

Jack P. Greene and J. R. Pole, eds, *Colonial British America: Essays in the New History of the Early Modern Era* (1984); James A. Henretta, *The Evolution of American Society, 1700–1815* (1973); Richard Hofstadter, *America at 1750: A Social Portrait* (1971); Robert V. Wells, *The Population of the British Colonies in America before 1776: A Survey of Census Data* (1975).

Rural Society

Carl Bridenbaugh, *Myths and Realities: Societies of the Colonial South* (1963); Rhys Isaac, *The Transformation of Virginia 1740–1790* (1982); Christopher Jedrey, *The World of John Cleaveland: Family and Community in Eighteenth-Century New England* (1979); Sung Bok Kim, *Landlord and Tenant in Colonial New York: Manorial Society, 1664–1775* (1978); James T. Lemon, *The Best Poor Man's Country: A Geographical Study of Early Southeastern Pennsylvania* (1972); Michael Zuckerman, *Peaceable Kingdoms: New England Towns in the Eighteenth Century* (1970).

Urban Society

Carl Bridenbaugh, *Cities in Revolt: Urban Life in America, 1743–1776* (1955); Gary B. Nash, *The Urban Crucible: Social Change, Political Consciousness, and the Origins of the American Revolution* (1979); Frederick B. Tolles, *Meeting House and Counting House: The Quaker Merchants of Colonial Philadelphia 1682–1763* (1948); Stephanie Grauman Wolf, *Urban Village: Population, Community, and Family Structure in Germantown, Pennsylvania, 1683–1800* (1976).

Economic Development

Paul G. E. Clemens, *The Atlantic Economy and Colonial Maryland's Eastern Shore: From Tobacco to Grain* (1980); Marc Egnal, "The Economic Development of the Thirteen Continental Colonies, 1720–1775," *William and Mary Quarterly*, 3rd ser., 32 (1975), 191–222; Alice Hanson Jones, *Wealth of a Nation To Be: The American Colonies on the Eve of the Revolution* (1980); Edwin J. Perkins, *The Economy of Colonial America* (1980); Jacob M. Price, "Economic Function and the Growth of American Port Towns in the Eighteenth Century," *Perspectives in American History*, 8 (1974), 123–186; James F. Shepherd and Gary M. Walton, *Shipping, Maritime Trade and the Economic Devlopment of Colonial North America* (1972); Gary M. Walton and James F. Shepherd, *The Economic Rise of Early America* (1979).

Politics

Bernard Bailyn, *The Origins of American Politics* (1968); Patricia U. Bonomi, *A Factious People: Politics and Society in Colonial New York* (1971); Edward M. Cook, Jr., *The Fathers of the Towns: Leadership and Community Structure in Eighteenth-Century New England* (1976); Jack P. Greene, *The Quest for Power: The Lower Houses of Assembly in the Southern Royal Colonies 1689–1776* (1963).

Immigration

Jon Butler, *The Huguenots in America: A Refugee People in New World Society* (1983); R. J. Dickson, *Ulster Immigration to Colonial America, 1718–1775* (1966); Albert B. Faust, *The German Element in the United States*, 2 vols. (1909); Ian C. C. Graham, *Colonists from Scotland: Emigration to North America 1707–1783* (1956); James G. Leyburn, *The Scotch-Irish: A Social History* (1962).

Blacks

Ira Berlin, "Time, Space, and the Evolution of Afro-American Society in British Mainland America," *American Historical Review*, 85 (1980), 44–78; Herbert Gutman, *The Black Family in Slavery and Freedom 1750–1925* (1976); Allan Kulikoff, "The Origins of Afro-American Society in Tidewater Maryland and Virginia, 1700 to 1790," *William and Mary Quarterly*, 3rd ser., 35 (1978), 228–259; Gerald W. Mullin, *Flight and Rebellion: Slave Resistance in Eighteenth-Century Virginia* (1972).

Women and Family

J. William Frost, *The Quaker Family in Colonial America* (1972); Philip J. Greven, *The Protestant Temperament: Pat-*terns of Child-Rearing, Religious Experience, and the Self in Early America* (1977); Mary Beth Norton, *Liberty's Daughters: The Revolutionary Experience of American Women, 1750–1800* (1980); Daniel Blake Smith, *Inside the Great House: Planter Family Life in Eighteenth-Century Chesapeake Society* (1980); Daniel Scott Smith, "Parental Power and Marriage Patterns: An Analysis of Historical Trends in Hingham, Massachusetts," *Journal of Marriage and the Family*, 35 (1973), 419–428.

Colonial Culture and the Enlightenment

Daniel J. Boorstin, *The Americans: The Colonial Experience* (1958); Richard Beale Davis, *Intellectual Life in the Colonial South, 1585–1763*, 2 vols. (1978); Howard Mumford Jones, *O Strange New World. American Culture: The Formative Years* (1964); Henry F. May, *The Enlightenment in America* (1976); Louis B. Wright, *The Cultural Life of the American Colonies, 1607–1763* (1957).

Education

James Axtell, *The School upon a Hill: Education and Society in Colonial New England* (1974); Bernard Bailyn, *Education in the Forming of American Society* (1960); Patricia Cline Cohen, *A Calculating People: The Spread of Numeracy in Early America* (1982); Lawrence A. Cremin, *American Education: The Colonial Experience 1607–1783* (1970); Kenneth A. Lockridge, *Literacy in Colonial New England: An Inquiry into the Social Context of Literacy in the Early Modern West* (1974).

Science and Medicine

Jane Donegan, *Women and Men Midwives: Medicine, Morality, and Misogyny in Early America* (1978); John Duffy, *Epidemics in Colonial America* (1953); Brooke Hindle, *The Pursuit of Science in Revolutionary America* (1956); Raymond P. Stearns, *Science in the British Colonies of America* (1970).

Religion and the Great Awakening

Carl Bridenbaugh, *Mitre and Sceptre: Transatlantic Faiths, Ideas, Personalities, and Politics, 1689–1775* (1962); J. M. Bumsted and John E. Van de Wetering, *What Must I Do To Be Saved? The Great Awakening in Colonial America* (1976); Edwin S. Gaustad, *The Great Awakening in New England* (1957); Alan E. Heimert, *Religion and the American Mind: From the Great Awakening to the Revolution* (1966); William McLoughlin, *Isaac Backus and the American Pietistic Tradition* (1967); Patricia Tracy, *Jonathan Edwards, Pastor* (1980).

Severing the Bonds of Empire

of Empire

1754–1774

Chapter 4

In late October 1769, the young Boston shopkeeper Betsy Cuming was visiting a sick friend when outside the house she heard "a voilint Skreeming Kill him Kill him." Betsy ran to the window and saw John Mein, a bookseller and newspaper publisher, being chased by "a larg Croud of those who Call themselves Gentelman, but," she added, "in reality they ware no other then Murderers for there disigne was certinly on his life." Later that evening a crowd of at least a thousand men and boys passed the door, "& on a Kart a Man was Exibited as we thought in a Gore of Blod." Betsy concluded that the mob had caught Mein, but she was mistaken. She learned the next day that the victim was a customs informer seized by the crowd after Mein had taken shelter in a British army guardhouse. That same night, Mein fled to a vessel anchored in the harbor. He later sailed to England and never returned to the city.

What had John Mein done to arouse the antagonism of the "gentlemen" of Boston? He published a newspaper, the *Boston Chronicle*, which generally supported the British side in the current disputes with the colonies. The offense that led to the mobbing, though, was more specific: he had printed several lists of names of local merchants who had recently cleared imports through the Boston customs house. The Mein incident thus involved one of the first recorded examples in American history of a carefully orchestrated political "leak" from official sources. Some administrator had given the printer access to the supposedly private customs records. But why was the information Mein revealed so explosive? Because in the fall of 1769 many American merchants had signed an agreement not to import goods from Great Britain; Mein's lists indicated that some of the most vocal supporters of nonimportation (including the patriot leader John Hancock) had been violating the agreement. That was why the "gentlemen" of Boston had to silence the outspoken publisher.

John Mein was not the first, and he would be far from the last, resident of the colonies who found his life wholly disrupted by the growing political antagonism between England and her American possessions. Indeed, even Betsy Cuming herself was eventually forced into exile in Nova Scotia because she opposed the trend of American resistance to Great Britain. Long afterwards, John Adams identified the years between 1760 and 1775 as the period in which the true American Revolution had occurred. The Revolution, Adams declared, was completed before the fighting started, for it was "in the Minds of the people," involving not the actual winning of independence but rather a shift of allegiance from England to America. Today, not all historians would agree with Adams's assertion that that shift constituted the Revolution. But none would deny the importance of the events of those crucial years, which led to the division of the American population along political lines and started the colonies on the road to independence.

The story of the 1760s and early 1770s is one of an ever-widening split between England and America, and among their respective supporters in the colonies. In the long history of British settlement in the Western Hemisphere, there had at times been considerable tension in the relationship between individual provinces and mother country. Still, that tension had rarely been sustained for long, nor had it been widespread, except in 1688 and 1689. The primary divisions affecting the colonies had been internal rather than external. In the 1750s, however, a series of events began to change all that, shifting the colonists' attention from domestic matters to their relations with Great Britain. It all started with the French and Indian War (1754–1763).

Britain's overwhelming victory in that war forever altered the balance of power in North America. France was ousted from the continent, an event with major consequences for both the Indian tribes of the interior and the residents of the British colonies. Northern Indians could no longer play European powers off against one another, and so they lost one of their major diplomatic tools. Anglo-Americans, for their part, no longer had to fear a French threat on their borders. Some historians have argued that if the colonies had had to worry about the continuing presence of France on the North American mainland, the Revolution could never have occurred. The British

Chapter 4: Severing the Bonds of Empire, 1754–1774

A LIST of the Names of *thofe* who AUDACIOUSLY continue to counteract the UNITED SENTIMENTS of the BODY of Merchants thro'out NORTH-AMERICA ; by importing British Goods contrary to the Agreement.

John Bernard,
(In King-Street, almoſt oppofite Vernon'sHead.

James McMaſters,
(On Treat's Wharf.

Patrick McMaſters,
(Oppofite the Sign of the Lamb.

John Mein,
(Oppofite the White-Horfe, and in King-Street.

Nathaniel Rogers,
(Oppofite Mr. Henderfon Inches Store lower End King-Street.

William Jackfon,
At the BrazenHead, Cornhill, near theTown-Houfe.

Theophilus Lillie,
(Near Mr.Pemberton'sMeeting-Houfe,North-End.

John Taylor,
(Nearly oppofite the Heart andCrown inCornhill.

Ame & Elizabeth Cummings,
(Oppofite the Old Brick Meeting Houfe, all of Bofton.

Ifrael Williams, Efq; & Son,
(Traders in the Town of Hatfield.

And, **Henry Barnes,**
(Trader in the Town of Marlboro'.

The following Names ſhould have been inſerted in the Liſt of Juſtices.

County of Middleſex.	County of Lincoln.
Samuel Hendley	
John Borland	John Kingſbury
Henry Barnes	
Richard Cary	County of Berkſhire.
County of Briſtol.	Mark Hopkins
George Brightman	Elijah Dwight
County of Worceſter.	Ifrael Stoddard
Daniel Blifs	

A blacklist printed in the North American Almanac *for 1770 identified those Boston merchants who had ignored the nonimportation agreement. Among their number were both John Mein, the object of the mob's wrath the previous October, and Betsy (Elizabeth) Cuming, the narrator of the story, who—with her sister Anne—ran a small dry-goods store. Library of Congress.*

colonies would never have dared to break with their mother country, it is said, if an enemy nation and its Indian allies had controlled the interior of the continent.

The British victory in 1763, then, constituted a major turning point in American history because of its direct effect on white and Indian residents of North America. It also had a significant impact on Great Britain, one that soon affected the colonies as well. To win the war, Britain had gone heavily into debt. To reduce the debt, Parliament for the first time laid revenue-raising taxes on the colonies. That decision exposed differences in the political thinking of Americans and Britons—differences that had until then been obscured by the use of a common political vocabulary.

During the 1760s, a broad coalition of white Americans, men and women alike, resisted new tax levies and attempts by British officials to tighten controls over the provincial governments. America's elected leaders became ever more suspicious of Britain's motives as the years passed. They laid aside traditional intercolonial antagonisms to coordinate their response to the new measures, and they slowly began to reorient their political thinking. As late as the summer of 1774, though, most were still seeking a solution within the framework of the empire; few harbored thoughts of independence. When independence, as opposed to loyal resistance, did become the issue, the coalition of the 1760s broke down. That, however, did not happen until after the battles of Lexington and Concord in April 1775. Before then, only a few Americans, most of them closely connected to colonial administration or the Church of England, opposed the trend of resistance.

RENEWED WARFARE AMONG EUROPEANS AND INDIANS

While the English colonists had been consolidating control of the Atlantic seaboard, the French and Spanish had been extending their influence into the interior of North America around the edges of English settlement. The Spanish outposts in Florida and along the coast of the Gulf of Mexico posed little threat to the English, for Spain's days as a major power had passed. The French, though, were another matter. In the late seventeenth and early eighteenth centuries France had explored the Great Lakes and Mississippi valley regions, establishing a long chain of forts and settlements stretching from New Orleans at the mouth of the Mississippi to Michilimackinac at the junction of Lakes Huron and Michigan. From

European Settlements and Indian Tribes, 1750

Labels on map:

Quebec
Montreal
NEW FRANCE
Lake Superior
CHIPPEWA
Lake Huron
Lake Michigan
CHIPPEWA
OTTAWA
Ft. Detroit
POTAWATOMI
MIAMI
WYANDOT
ILLINOIS CONFEDERATION
WEA
OHIO COUNTRY
SHAWNEE
Lake Erie
Lake Ontario
Ft. Niagara
St. Lawrence R.
MOHAWK
ONEIDA
TUSCARORA
ONONDAGA
CAYUGA
SENECA
Ft. Stanwix
Albany
NEW YORK
Allegheny R.
1720-1760
Ft. Western (Augusta)
MAINE (Part of Mass.)
Falmouth (Portland)
N.H.
Portsmouth
Boston
MASS.
Hartford
CONN.
Providence R.I.
New York
N.J.
PENNSYLVANIA
DELAWARE
Ft. Duquesne (Pitt)
Philadelphia
New Castle
Monongahela R.
Ft. Necessity
Tuscarora Migration,
Baltimore
MD.
DEL.
Mississippi R.
Ohio R.
Line of 1763
Proclamation
Richmond
VIRGINIA
Williamsburg
ATLANTIC OCEAN
CHEROKEE
Salem
Hillsboro
NORTH CAROLINA
New Bern
CATAWBA
Camden
Wilmington
CHICKASAW
SOUTH CAROLINA
Ft. Augusta (Augusta)
GEORGIA
Charleston
CREEK
Savannah
CHOCTAW
NEW SPAIN
St. Augustine

Total population of
English colonies: c.1.5 million
Extent of settlement

0   100   200 miles
0   100   200   300 kilometers

these posts they traded for furs with the tribes whose territories lay west of the Appalachian mountains. In none of the three wars fought between 1689 and 1748 was England able to shake France's domination of the North American interior, which rested on control of the inland system of rivers and lakes. Under the Peace of Utrecht, which ended Queen Anne's War in 1713, the English won control of such peripheral northern areas as Newfoundland, Hudson's Bay, and Nova Scotia (Acadia). But Britain made no additional territorial gains in King George's War (see map).

During both Queen Anne's War and King George's War, the Iroquois Confederacy adhered to the policy of neutrality it first developed in 1701 (see page 55).

Iroquois Neutrality While English and French forces fought for nominal control of the North American continent, the confederacy that actually dominated a large portion of that continent took no formal role. Instead, the Iroquois council skillfully played the Europeans off against one another, refusing to commit its warriors fully to either side despite being showered with presents by both. When the Iroquois went to war in those years, it was against a traditional southern enemy, the Catawba. Since the French repeatedly urged them to attack the Catawba (a tribe allied with the English), the Iroquois thereby achieved two desirable goals. They kept the French happy and simultaneously consolidated their control over the entire interior region north of Virginia. In addition, these southern wars (by identifying a common enemy) enabled the confederacy to cement its alliance with its weaker tributaries, the Shawnee and Delaware, and to ensure the continued subordination of those tribes.

But even the careful Iroquois diplomats could not prevent the region inhabited by the Shawnee and Delaware (now western Pennsylvania and eastern Ohio) from providing the spark that set off a major war. That conflict spread from America to Europe (a significant reversal of previous patterns) and proved decisive in the contest for North America. Trouble began in 1752 when English fur traders ventured into the area, known as the Ohio country. The French could not permit their English rivals to dominate the region, for it contained the source of the Ohio River, which offered direct access by water to their posts

In 1754 Benjamin Franklin produced his famous cartoon calling for unity among the English colonies in the face of the threat from the French and Indians. Later, during the Revolution, it was widely used as a symbol of the colonies' need to unite against Great Britain. *Library of Congress.*

on the Mississippi. A permanent English presence in the Ohio country could challenge France's control of the western fur trade and even threaten its prominence in the Mississippi valley. Accordingly, in 1753 the French pushed southward from Lake Erie, building fortified outposts at strategic points along the rivers of the Ohio country.

In response to the threat posed by the French to their western frontiers, delegates from seven northern and middle colonies gathered in Albany, New York, in June 1754. With the backing of

Albany Congress administrators in London, they sought two goals: to persuade the Iroquois to abandon their traditional neutrality, and to coordinate the defenses of the colonies. In neither aim were they successful. The Iroquois, while listening politely to the colonists' arguments, saw no reason to change a policy that had served them well for half a century. And although the Albany Congress delegates adopted a Plan of Union (which would have established an elected intercolonial legislature with the power to tax), the plan was uniformly rejected by their provincial governments—primarily because those governments feared a loss of autonomy.

The delegates to the Congress did not know that, while they deliberated, the war they sought to prepare for was already beginning. Governor Robert Dinwiddie

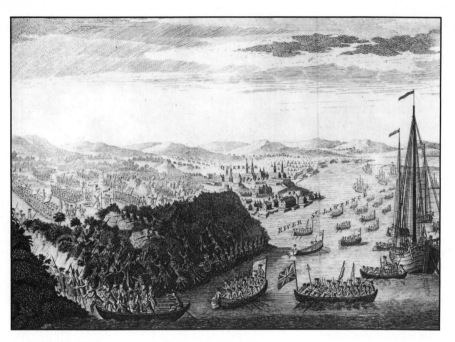

On the night of September 13, 1759, British forces under General James Wolfe scaled the heights of Quebec and defeated the French army led by General Louis Joseph Montcalm. Both generals died on the battlefield. Library of Congress.

of Virginia had sent a small militia force westward to counter the French moves. Virginia claimed ownership of the Ohio country, and Dinwiddie was eager to prevent the French from establishing a permanent post there. But the Virginia militiamen arrived too late. The French had already taken possession of the strategic point—now Pittsburgh—where the Allegheny and Monongahela rivers meet to form the Ohio, and they were busily engaged in constructing Fort Duquesne. The foolhardy and inexperienced young colonel who commanded the Virginians attacked a French detachment, then allowed himself to be trapped by the French in his crudely built Fort Necessity at Great Meadows, Pennsylvania. After a day-long battle (on July 3, 1754), during which more than one-third of his men were killed or wounded, the twenty-two-year-old George Washington surrendered. He signed a document of capitulation, and he and his men were allowed to return to Virginia.

Beginning of the French and Indian War

Washington had blundered grievously. He had started a war that would eventually encompass nearly the entire world. He had also ensured that the tribes of the Ohio valley, many of whom had moved west to escape Iroquois domination and to trade directly with the French, would for the most part support France in the coming conflict. The Indians took Washington's mistakes as an indication of Britain's inability to win the war, and nothing that occurred in the next four years made them change their minds. In July 1755 a combined force of French and Indians ambushed General Edward Braddock, two regiments of British regulars, and some colonial troops a few miles south of Fort Duquesne. Braddock was killed and his men demoralized by their complete defeat.

For three more years one disaster followed another for Great Britain. The war went so badly that Britain began to fear that France would attempt to retake Newfoundland and Nova Scotia. Trying to consolidate their control of the region, the British administrators of Nova Scotia forced its French residents to leave

Chapter 4: SEVERING THE BONDS OF EMPIRE, 1754–1774

the homes they had occupied for generations. After years of wandering, many of these Acadian exiles made their way to Louisiana, where they became known as Cajuns.

At last, under the leadership of William Pitt, who was named secretary of state in 1757, the British mounted the effort that won them the war in North America. In July 1758 they recaptured the fortress at Louisbourg; in a surprise night attack in September 1759 they broke down the defenses of Quebec. Sensing a British victory, the Iroquois abandoned their policy of neutrality and allied themselves with the British, hoping to gain some diplomatic leverage by that decision. A year later the British took Montreal, the last French stronghold. The war in America thus ended in 1760, though fighting continued for three more years in the Caribbean, India, and Europe.

When the Treaty of Paris was signed in 1763, France ceded its major North American holdings to Britain. Spain, an ally of France toward the end of the war, gave Florida to the victorious English. And since Britain feared the presence of France in Louisiana, it forced the French to cede that region to Spain, a weaker power. No longer would the English seacoast colonies have to worry about the threat to their existence posed by France's extensive North American territories (see maps).

Pitt achieved this stunning victory by encouraging cooperation between the colonists and Great Britain. In the early years of the war—the years of England's many defeats—British army and navy officers had adopted coercive recruiting techniques. They arbitrarily commandeered supplies from American farmers and merchants and ordered the quartering of royal troops in private homes. All these actions aroused the colonists' ire. Pitt, by contrast, agreed to reimburse the colonies for their military expenditures and placed troop recruitment wholly in local hands. Consequently, Americans (especially New Englanders) began to support the war effort more fully. As many as one-third of all Massachusetts men between the ages of sixteen and twenty-nine served for a time in the provincial army.

Yet British commanders denigrated the American contributions to the winning campaigns. For one thing, most of the actual fighting was carried on by British regulars, with colonial troops being relegated

BEFORE 1754
English   New Spain
New France   Russian

AFTER 1763
English   New Spain
New France   Russian

European Claims in North America

to support roles (a practice the Americans resented). For another, the British army leaders alleged that American merchants were prolonging the conflict by continuing to trade with the French West Indies. (The Americans responded that their economies would collapse without the West Indian trade, and that in any event the French islands were contributing little to the mainland war.) And, finally, redcoat officers and enlisted men alike looked down on their American counterparts as undisciplined and ignorant of military procedures. As one arrogant colonel declared, "The Provincials [are] sufficient to work our Boats, drive our Waggons, and fell our Trees, and do the Work that in inhabited Countrys are performed by Peasants."

Over the decade and a half following the close of the American phase of the war in 1760, as the colonies and Great Britain moved slowly toward a confrontation, each drew on impressions of the other gained during the French and Indian War. The British dismissed any suggestion of American military prowess with a laugh. The Americans, meanwhile, remembered the threat of arbitrary military power, the British officers' arrogance, and their own wounded pride. In other words, the victorious alliance of colonies and mother country had done nothing to dispel—and possibly much to promote—the gathering clouds of disagreement.

1763: A TURNING POINT

The overwhelming British victory over France had an irreversible impact on North America. Its effects were felt first by the Indian tribes that had used the competition among European powers to maintain their autonomy. With France excluded from the continent altogether and Spanish territory now confined to the area west of the Mississippi, the diplomatic strategy that had served the tribes well for so long could no longer be employed. The consequences were immediate and devastating.

Even before the Treaty of Paris, southern Indians had to adjust to the new circumstances. After the British gained the upper hand in the American war in 1758, the Creek and Cherokee lost their ability to force concessions from the British by threatening to turn instead to the French or the Spanish. In desperation and in retaliation for British atrocities, the Cherokee attacked the Carolina and Virginia frontiers in 1760. Although initially victorious, the tribesmen were defeated the following year by a force of British regulars and colonial militia. Late in 1761 the two sides concluded a treaty under which the Cherokee allowed the construction of English forts in tribal territories and also opened a large tract of land to white settlement.

The fate of the Cherokee in the South was a portent of things to come in the Northwest. There, the western tribes—the Ottawa, Chippewa, and Potawatomi—became angry when Great Britain, no longer facing French competition, raised the price of trade goods and ended the practice of paying rent for forts. In addition, the British allowed settlers to move into the Monongahela and Susquehanna valleys, onto Delaware and Iroquois lands.

Pontiac, the war chief of an Ottawa village near Detroit, understood the implications of such British actions. Only unity among the western tribes, he realized, could possibly prevent total **Pontiac's** dependence on and subordination **Uprising** to the victorious British. Using his considerable powers of persuasion, in the spring of 1763 he forged an unprecedented alliance among the Huron, Chippewa, Potawatomi, Delaware, and Shawnee tribes, even gaining the participation of some Mingoes (Pennsylvania Iroquois). Pontiac then laid seige to the fort at Detroit while his war parties attacked the other British outposts in the Great Lakes region. Detroit withstood the siege, but by the end of June all the other forts west of Niagara and north of Fort Pitt (old Fort Duquesne) had fallen to the Indian alliance.

That was the high point of the uprising. The tribes raided the Virginia and Pennsylvania frontiers at will throughout the summer, killing at least two thousand whites. But they could not take the strongholds of Niagara, Fort Pitt, or Detroit. In early August, a combined force of Delawares, Shawnees, Hurons, and Mingoes was soundly defeated at Bushy Run, Pennsylvania, by troops sent from the coast. Conflict ceased when Pontiac broke off the siege of Detroit

In 1764, Colonel Henry Bouquet, the victor the preceding year at the battle of Bushy Run, negotiated with representatives of the Seneca, Shawnee, and Delaware at a council held on the Muskingum River in the Ohio country. The agreement reached there opened part of the region to white settlement.   Library of Congress.

in late October, after most of his warriors had returned to their villages. A formal treaty ending the war was finally negotiated in 1766.

In the aftermath of the bloody summer of 1763, Scotch-Irish frontiersmen from Paxton Township, Pennsylvania, sought revenge on the only Indians within reach, a peaceful band of Christian converts living at Conestoga. In December the whites raided the Indian village twice, killing twenty people. Two months later hundreds of frontier dwellers known to history as the Paxton Boys marched on Philadelphia to demand military protection against future Indian attacks. City officials feared violence and mustered the militia to repel the westerners, but the protesters presented their request in an orderly fashion and returned home.

Pontiac's uprising and the march of the Paxton Boys showed that Great Britain would not find it easy to govern the huge territory it had just acquired from France. The central administration in London

Proclamation of 1763

had had no prior experience in managing such a vast tract of land, particularly one inhabited by two hostile peoples—the remaining French settlers along the St. Lawrence and the many Indian tribes. In October, in a futile attempt to assert control over the interior, the ministry issued the Proclamation of 1763, which declared the headwaters of rivers flowing into the Atlantic from the Appalachian Mountains to be the temporary western boundary for colonial settlement. The proclamation was intended to prevent future clashes between Indians and colonists by forbidding whites to move onto Indian lands until the tribes had given up their land by treaty. But many whites had already established farms west of the proclamation line, and the policy was doomed to failure from its outset.

The proclamation directly affected only frontier families; other decisions made in London in 1763 and thereafter had a much broader impact in British

King George III in his coronation robes, 1760, painted by Allan Ramsay. Colonial Williamsburg photograph.

North America. The victory in the French and Indian War both posed problems for and offered opportunities to the British government. The most pressing problem was Britain's immense war debt. The men who had to solve that problem were King George III and his new prime minister, George Grenville.

In 1760 George III, then twenty-two years old, succeeded his grandfather, George II, on the English throne. The young king, a man of mediocre intellect and even more mediocre education,

George III was unfortunately a poor—or, more accurately, an erratic—judge of character. During the crucial years between 1763 and 1770, when the rift between England and the colonies was growing ever wider, he replaced ministries with bewildering rapidity. The king, though determined to assert the power of the monarchy, was immature and unsure of himself. He often substituted stubbornness for intelligence, and he regarded adherence to the status quo as the hallmark of true patriotism.

The man he selected as prime minister in 1763,

George Grenville, believed that the American colonies should be more tightly administered than in the past. Grenville confronted a financial crisis: England's burden of indebtedness had nearly doubled since 1754, from £73 million to £137 million. Annual expenditures before the war had amounted to no more than £8 million; now the yearly interest on the debt alone came to £5 million. Obviously, Grenville's ministry had to find new sources of funds, and the English people themselves were already heavily taxed. Since the colonists had been major beneficiaries of the wartime expenditures, Grenville concluded that the Americans should be asked to pay a greater share of the cost of running the empire.

It did not occur to Grenville to question Great Britain's right to levy taxes on the colonies. Like all his countrymen, he believed that the government's legitimacy derived ultimately from the consent of the people, but he

Theories of Representation defined consent far more loosely than did the colonists. Americans had come to believe that they could be represented only by men for whom they or their property-holding neighbors had actually voted; otherwise they could not count on legislators to protect them from oppression. To Grenville and his English contemporaries, Parliament—king, lords, and commons acting together—by definition represented all English subjects, wherever they resided (even overseas) and whether or not they could vote. According to this theory of government, called *virtual representation*, the colonists were said to be virtually, if not actually, represented in Parliament. Thus their consent to acts of Parliament could be presumed.

In other words, the Americans and the English began at the same theoretical starting point but arrived at different conclusions in practice. In England, members of Parliament saw themselves as *collectively* representing the entire nation, composed of nobility and common folk. Only members of the House of Commons were elected, and the particular constituency that chose a member had no special claim on his vote. In the colonies, by contrast, members of the lower houses of the assemblies were viewed as *individually* representing the voters who had elected them. Before Grenville proposed to tax the colonists, the two notions existed side by side without apparent contradiction. But the events of the 1760s pointed up the difference between the English and colonial definitions of representation.

The same events threw into sharp relief Americans' attitudes toward political power. The colonists had become accustomed to a government that wielded only limited authority over them and affected their daily lives very little. In consequence, they believed that a good government was one that largely left them alone, a view in keeping with the theories of a group of British writers known as the Real Whigs. Drawing on a tradition of English dissenting thought that reached back to the days of the Civil War, the Real Whigs stressed the dangers inherent in a powerful government, particularly one headed by a monarch. They warned that the people had to guard constantly against the government's attempts to encroach on their liberties. Political power was always to be feared, wrote John Trenchard and Thomas Gordon in their essay series *Cato's Letters* (originally published in England in 1720–1723 and reprinted many times thereafter in the colonies). Rulers would try to corrupt and oppress the people. Only the perpetual vigilance of the people and their elected representatives could preserve their fragile yet precious freedoms.

Britain's attempts to tighten the reins of government and raise revenues from the colonies in the 1760s and early 1770s convinced many Americans that the Real Whigs' reasoning applied to their circumstances. They began to interpret British measures in light of the Real Whigs' warnings and to see evil designs behind the actions of Grenville and his successors. Historians disagree over the extent to which those perceptions were correct, but by 1775 a large number of colonists unquestionably believed they were. In the mid-1760s, colonial leaders did not, however, immediately accuse Grenville of an intent to oppress them. They at first simply questioned the wisdom of the laws Grenville proposed.

The first such measures, the Sugar and Currency Acts, were passed by Parliament in 1764. The Sugar Act revised the existing system of customs regulations; laid new duties on certain foreign **Sugar and** imports into the colonies; established **Currency Acts** a vice-admiralty court at Halifax, Nova Scotia; and included special provisions aimed at stopping the widespread smuggling of molasses, one of the chief commodities in American trade. Although the Sugar Act appeared to resemble the Navigation Acts (see page 64), it broke with tradition because it was explicitly designed to raise revenue, not to channel American trade through Britain. The Currency Act in effect outlawed colonial issues of paper money. (For years, the colonies had printed their own money to supplement the private bills of exchange that circulated chiefly among merchants.) Americans could accumulate little hard cash, since they imported more than they exported; thus the act seemed to the colonists to deprive them of a useful medium of exchange.

The Sugar and Currency Acts were visited upon an economy already in the midst of depression. A business boom had accompanied the French and Indian War, but the brief spell of prosperity ended abruptly in 1760, when the war shifted overseas. Urban merchants could not sell all their imported goods to colonial customers alone, and without the military's demand for foodstuffs, American farmers found fewer buyers for their products. The bottom dropped out of the European tobacco market, threatening the livelihood of Chesapeake planters. Sailors were thrown out of work, and artisans found few employers to hire them. In such circumstances, the prospect of increased customs duties and inadequate supplies of currency naturally aroused merchants' hostility.

It is not surprising that both individual colonists and colonial governments decided to protest the new policies. But, lacking any precedent for a united campaign against acts of Parliament, Americans in 1764 took only hesitant and uncoordinated steps. Eight colonial legislatures sent separate petitions to Parliament requesting repeal of the Sugar Act. They argued that the act placed severe restrictions on their commerce (and would therefore hurt Britain as well), and that they had not consented to its passage. The protests had no effect. The law remained in force and Grenville proceeded with another revenue plan.

THE STAMP ACT CRISIS

The Stamp Act, Grenville's most important proposal, was modeled on a law that had been in effect in England for nearly a century. It touched nearly every colonist by requiring tax stamps on most printed materials, but placed the heaviest burden on merchants and other members of the colonial elite, who used printed matter more frequently than ordinary folk. Anyone who purchased a newspaper or pamphlet, made a will, transferred land, bought dice or playing cards, needed a liquor license, accepted a government appointment, or borrowed money would have to pay the tax. Never before had a revenue measure of such scope been proposed for the colonies. The act would also require that tax stamps be paid for with hard money and that violators be tried in vice-admiralty courts, without juries. Finally, such a law would break decisively with the colonial tradition of self-imposed taxation.

The most important colonial pamphlet protesting the Sugar Act and the proposed Stamp Act was *The Rights of the British Colonies Asserted and Proved*, by James Otis, Jr., a brilliant young Massachusetts attorney. Otis starkly exposed the ideological dilemma that was to confound the colonists for the next decade. How could they justify their opposition to certain acts of Parliament without questioning Parliament's authority over them? On the one hand, Otis asserted that Americans were "entitled to all the natural, essential, inherent, and inseparable rights" of Britons, including the right not to be taxed without their consent. "No man or body of men, not excepting the parliament . . . can take [those rights] away," he declared. On the other hand, Otis was forced to admit that, under the British system established after the Glorious Revolution of 1688 and 1689, "the power of parliament is uncontroulable, but by themselves, and we must obey. . . . Let the parliament lay what burthens they please on us, we must, it is our duty to submit and patiently bear them, till they will be pleased to relieve us."

Otis's Rights of the British Colonies

Otis's first contention, drawing on colonial notions of representation, implied that Parliament could not constitutionally tax the colonies because Americans were not represented in its ranks. Yet his second point both acknowledged political reality and accepted the prevailing theory of British government—that Parliament was the sole, supreme authority in the empire. Even unconstitutional laws enacted by Parliament had to be obeyed until Parliament decided to repeal them. According to orthodox British political theory, there could be no middle ground between absolute submission to Parliament and a frontal challenge to its authority. Otis tried to find such a middle ground by proposing colonial representation in Parliament, but his idea was never taken seriously on either side of the Atlantic. The British believed that the colonists were already virtually represented in Parliament, and the Americans quickly realized that a handful of colonial delegates to London would simply be outvoted.

Otis wrote his pamphlet before the Stamp Act was passed. When Americans learned of its adoption in the spring of 1765, they did not at first know how to react. Few colonists publicly favored the law; opposition to it was nearly universal, even among appointed government officials. But colonial petitions had already failed to prevent its adoption, and further lobbying appeared futile. Perhaps Otis was right, and the only course open to the Americans was to pay the stamp tax, reluctantly but loyally. Acting on that assumption, colonial agents in London sought the appointment of their American friends as stamp distributors, so that the law would at least be enforced equitably.

Not all the colonists were resigned to paying the new tax without a fight. Just such a man was a twenty-nine-year-old lawyer serving his first term as a member of the Virginia House of Burgesses. Patrick Henry later recalled that he was at the time "young, inexperienced, unacquainted with the forms of the House and the members that composed it," and appalled by his fellow legislators' unwillingness to oppose the Stamp Act openly. Henry decided to act. "Alone, unadvised, and unassisted, on a blank leaf of an old law book," he wrote the Virginia Stamp Act Resolves.

Patrick Henry and the Virginia Stamp Act Resolves

Little in Henry's earlier life foreshadowed his success in the political arena he entered so dramatically. The son of a prosperous Scottish immigrant to western Virginia, Henry had had little formal education. After marrying at eighteen, he failed at both farming and storekeeping before turning to the law as a means of supporting his wife and their six children. Henry lacked legal training, but his oratorical skills made him an effective advocate, first for his clients and

Chapter 4: SEVERING THE BONDS OF EMPIRE, 1754–1774

later for his political beliefs. As a prominent Virginia lawyer said of him, "He is by far the most powerful speaker I ever heard. Every word he says not only engages, but commands the attention; and your passions are no longer your own when he addresses them."

Patrick Henry introduced his proposals in late May, near the end of the legislative session; many members of the House of Burgesses had already departed for home. Henry's fiery speech in support of his resolutions led the Speaker of the House to accuse him of treason. (Henry quickly denied the charge, contrary to the nineteenth-century myth that had him exclaiming in reply, "If this be treason, make the most of it!") The small number of burgesses remaining in Williamsburg adopted five of Henry's resolutions by a bare majority. Though they repealed the most radical resolution the next day, their action had far-reaching effects. Some colonial newspapers printed Henry's seven original resolutions as if they had been uniformly passed by the House, even though one had been rescinded and two others were evidently never debated or voted on at all.

The four propositions adopted by the burgesses repeated the arguments James Otis had already advanced. The colonists had never forfeited the rights of British subjects, they declared, and consent to taxation was one of the most important of those rights. The other three resolutions went much further. The one that was repealed claimed for the burgesses "the only exclusive right" to tax Virginians. The final two asserted that residents of the colony did not have to obey tax laws passed by other legislative bodies (namely Parliament) and termed any opponent of that opinion "an Enemy to this his Majesty's Colony."

The burgesses' decision to accept only the first four of Henry's resolutions accurately predicted the position most Americans would adopt throughout the following decade. Though willing to contend for their rights, the colonists did not seek independence. They merely wanted some measure of self-government. Accordingly, they backed away from the assertions that they owed Parliament no obedience and that their own assemblies alone could tax them. Indeed, declared the Maryland lawyer Daniel Dulany, whose *Considerations on the Propriety of Imposing Taxes on the British Colonies* was the most widely read pamphlet of 1765, "The colonies are dependent upon Great Britain, and the supreme authority vested in the king, lords, and commons, may justly be exercised to secure, or preserve their dependence." But, warned Dulany, a superior did not have the right "to seize the property of his inferior when he pleases"; there was a crucial distinction between a condition of "dependence and *inferiority*" and one of "absolute *vassalage* and *slavery*."

Over the course of the next ten years, America's political leaders searched for a formula that would enable them to control their internal affairs, especially taxation, but remain within the British Empire. The chief difficulty lay in British officials' inability to compromise on the issue of parliamentary power. The notion that Parliament could exercise absolute authority over all colonial possessions was basic to the British theory of government. Even the harshest British critics of the ministries of the 1760s and 1770s questioned only the wisdom of specific policies, not the principles on which they were based. In effect, the Americans wanted British leaders to revise their fundamental understanding of the workings of their government. That was simply too much to expect, given the circumstances.

The ultimate effectiveness of Americans' opposition to the Stamp Act did not rest on ideological arguments over parliamentary power. What gave the resistance its primary force were the decisive and inventive actions of some colonists during the late summer and fall of 1765.

In August the Loyal Nine, a Boston social club of printers, distillers, and other artisans, organized a demonstration against the Stamp Act. Hoping to show that people of all social and economic ranks opposed the act, they approached the leaders of the city's rival laborers' associations, one based in the North End and one in the South End. The two gangs, composed of unskilled workers and poor tradesmen, often battled with each other, but the Loyal Nine convinced them to lay aside their differences and participate in the demonstration. After all, the stamp taxes would have to be paid by all colonists, not just affluent ones.

Early in the morning of August 14, the demonstrators hung an effigy of Andrew Oliver, the province's stamp distributor, from a tree on Boston Common. That night a large crowd led by a group of about

Loyal Nine

This woodcut, produced half a century after the event, shows a crowd parading the effigy of the New Hampshire stamp distributor through the streets of Portsmouth in 1765. The procession is led by men carrying a coffin to symbolize the death and burial of the Stamp Act. The Metropolitian Museum of Art, Bequest of Charles Allen Munn.

fifty well-dressed tradesmen paraded the effigy around the city. The crowd tore down a small building they thought was intended as the stamp office and built a bonfire with the wood near Oliver's house. They then beheaded the effigy and added it to the flames. Members of the crowd broke most of Oliver's windows and threw stones at officials who tried to disperse them. In the midst of the melee, the North End and South End leaders drank a toast to their successful union. The Loyal Nine's demonstration achieved its objective when Oliver publicly promised not to fulfill the duties of his office. One Bostonian jubilantly told a relative, "I believe people never was more Universally pleased not so much as one could I hear say he was sorry, but a smile sat on almost every ones countinance."

But another crowd action twelve days later, aimed this time at Oliver's brother-in-law Lieutenant Governor Thomas Hutchinson, drew no praise from the respectable citizens of Boston. On the night of August 26, a mob reportedly led by the South End leader, Ebenezer MacIntosh, attacked the homes of several customs officers. The crowd then completely destroyed Hutchinson's elaborately furnished townhouse in one of Boston's most fashionable districts. The lieutenant governor reported that by the next morning "one of the best finished houses in the Province had nothing remaining but the bare walls and floors." His trees and garden were ruined as well, and the mob had "emptied the house of every thing whatsoever except a part of the kitchen furniture." But Hutchinson took some comfort in the fact that "the encouragers of the first mob never intended matters should go this length and the people in general express the utmost detestation of this unparalleled outrage."

The differences between the two Boston mobs of August 1765 exposed divisions that would continue to characterize colonial protests in the years that followed. Although few residents of the colonies sided with Great Britain during these early years of protest,

Chapter 4: SEVERING THE BONDS OF EMPIRE, 1754–1774

**Americans'
Divergent
Interests**
the various colonial interest groups often had divergent goals that caused splits in their ranks. The skilled craftsmen who composed the Loyal Nine and members of the educated elite like merchants and lawyers preferred orderly demonstrations confined to political issues. For the city's laborers, by contrast, economic grievances may well have been paramount; certainly, their "hellish Fury" as they wrecked Hutchinson's house suggests a resentment against his ostentatious display of wealth.

The colonies, like the mother country, had a long tradition of crowd action, in which disfranchised people took to the streets to redress deeply felt local grievances (such as the high cost of food during a depression or the operation of a house of prostitution in a residential neighborhood). But the Stamp Act controversy drew ordinary urban folk into the vortex of imperial politics for the first time. Matters that had previously been of concern only to genteel folk, or to members of colonial legislatures, were now discussed on every street corner. Sally Franklin observed as much when she wrote to her father, Benjamin, who was then serving as a colonial agent in London, that "nothing else is talked of, the Dutch [Germans] talk of the stompt act the Negroes of the tamp, in short every body has something to say."

The entry of lower-class whites, blacks, and women into the realm of imperial politics both threatened and afforded an opportunity to the well-to-do white men who wanted to mount effective opposition to British measures. On the one hand, crowd action could have a stunning impact (see map). Anti–Stamp Act demonstrations occurred in cities and towns stretching from Halifax, Nova Scotia, in the north, to the Caribbean island of Antigua. They were so successful that by November 1, when the law was scheduled to take effect, not a single stamp distributor was willing to carry out the duties of his office. As a result, the act could not be enforced. But at the same time, since the goals of the crowd were not always identical to the goals of its nominal leaders (as the Boston experience so clearly showed), members of the elite recognized that mobs composed of the formerly powerless could potentially endanger their own dominant position in society. What would happen, they wondered, if the "hellish Fury" of the crowd were turned against them?

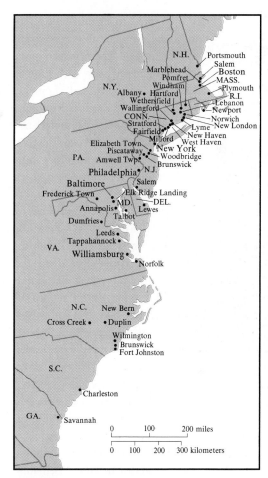

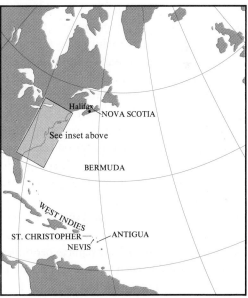

Sites of Major Demonstrations Against the Stamp Act

Therefore, they attempted to channel resistance into acceptable forms by creating an intercolonial association, the Sons of Liberty. The first such group was created in New York City in early November, and branches spread rapidly through the colonies. Largely composed of merchants, lawyers, prosperous tradesmen, and the like, the Sons of Liberty linked resistance leaders in cities from Charleston, South Carolina, to Portsmouth, New Hampshire, by early 1766.

Sons of Liberty

But the Sons of Liberty could not control all reactions in the new climate of protest. In Charleston in late October 1765 an organized crowd shouting "Liberty Liberty and stamp'd paper" forced the resignation of the South Carolina stamp distributor. The event was celebrated a few days later in the largest demonstration the city had ever known, at which was displayed a British flag with the word LIBERTY written across it. But white resistance leaders were horrified when in January 1766 local slaves paraded through the streets similarly crying "Liberty." The local militia was mustered, messengers were sent to outlying areas with warnings of a possible plot, and one black was banished from the colony.

In Philadelphia, resistance leaders were dismayed when an angry mob threatened to attack Benjamin Franklin's house. The city's laborers believed Franklin to be partly responsible for the Stamp Act, since he had obtained the post of stamp distributor for a close friend. But Philadelphia's artisans—the backbone of the opposition movement there and elsewhere—were fiercely loyal to Franklin, one of their own who had made good. They gathered to protect his home and family from the crowd. The house was saved, but the resulting split between the better-off tradesmen and the common laborers prevented Philadelphians from establishing a successful workingmen's alliance like that of Boston.

During the fall and winter of 1765 and 1766, opposition to the Stamp Act proceeded on three separate fronts. The colonial legislatures petitioned Parliament to repeal the hated law and sent delegates to an intercolonial congress, the first since 1754. In October the Stamp Act Congress met in New York to draft a unified but relatively conservative statement of protest. At the same time, the Sons of Liberty held mass meetings in an effort to win public support for the resistance movement. Finally, American merchants organized nonimportation associations to put economic pressure on British exporters. By the 1760s one-quarter of all British exports were being sent to the colonies, and American merchants reasoned that London merchants whose sales had suffered severely would lobby for repeal. Since times were bad and American merchants were finding few customers for imported goods in any case, a general moratorium on future purchases would also help to reduce their bloated inventories.

In March 1766, Parliament repealed the Stamp Act. The nonimportation agreements had had the anticipated effect, creating allies for the colonies among wealthy London merchants. But boycotts, formal protests, and crowd actions were less important in winning repeal than was Grenville's replacement as prime minister in summer 1765. Lord Rockingham, the new minister, had opposed the Stamp Act, not because he believed Parliament lacked power to tax the colonies but because he thought the law unwise and divisive. Thus, although Rockingham proposed repeal, he linked it to passage of the Declaratory Act, which asserted Parliament's ability to tax and legislate for Britain's American possessions "in all cases whatsoever."

Repeal of the Stamp Act

News of the repeal arrived in Newport, Rhode Island, in May, and the Sons of Liberty quickly transmitted the welcome tidings to all parts of the colonies. They also organized many celebrations commemorating the glorious event, all of which stressed the Americans' unwavering loyalty to Great Britain. Their goal achieved, the Sons of Liberty dissolved. Few colonists saw the ominous implications of the Declaratory Act.

RESISTANCE TO
THE TOWNSHEND ACTS

The colonists had accomplished their immediate aim, but the long-term prospects were unclear. Another change in the ministry, in the summer of 1766, revealed how fragile their victory had been.

BRITISH MINISTRIES AND THEIR AMERICAN POLICIES

Head of Ministry	Major Acts
George Grenville	Sugar Act (1764)
	Currency Act (1764)
	Stamp Act (1765)
Lord Rockingham	Stamp Act repeal (1766)
	Declaratory Act (1766)
William Pitt/Charles Townshend	Townshend Acts (1767)
Lord North	Townshend duties repealed (all but tea tax) (1770)
	Coercive Acts (1774)
	Quebec Act (1774)

Charles Townshend, a Grenvillite, was named chancellor of the exchequer in a new administration headed by the ailing William Pitt. Pitt was ill much of the time, and Townshend became the dominant force in the ministry. He decided to renew the attempt to obtain additional funds from the colonies.

The taxes Townshend proposed in 1767 were to be levied on trade goods like paper, glass, and tea, and thus seemed on the surface to be nothing more than extensions of the existing Navigation Acts. But the Townshend duties differed from previous customs taxes in two ways. First, they were levied on items imported into the colonies from Britain, not from foreign countries. Thus they were at odds with mercantilist theory (see page 61). Second, they were designed, like the Sugar Act, to raise money. The receipts, moreover, would pay the salaries of royal officials in the colonies. That posed a direct challenge to the colonial assemblies, which derived considerable power from threatening to withhold officials' salaries. In addition, Townshend's scheme provided for the establishment of an American Board of Customs Commissioners and for the creation of vice-admiralty courts at Boston, Philadelphia, and Charleston. Both moves angered merchants, whose profits would be threatened by more vigorous enforcement of the Navigation Acts. Lastly, Townshend proposed the appointment of a secretary of state for American affairs and the suspension of the New York legislature for refusal to comply with an act requiring colonial governments to supply certain items (like firewood and candles) to British troops stationed permanently in America.

Unlike 1765, when months passed before the colonists began to protest the Stamp Act, the passage of the Townshend Acts drew a quick response. One series of essays in particular, *Letters from a Farmer in Pennsylvania* by the prominent lawyer John Dickinson, expressed a broad consensus. Eventually all but four colonial newspapers printed Dickinson's essays; in pamphlet form they went through at least seven American editions. Dickinson contended that Parliament could regulate colonial trade, but could not exercise that power for the purpose of raising revenues. By drawing a distinction between the acceptable regulation of trade and unacceptable commercial taxation, Dickinson entirely avoided the sticky issue of consent and how it affected the extent of colonial subordination to Parliament. But his argument created a different, and equally knotty, problem. In effect it forced the colonies to assess Parliament's motives in passing any law pertaining to imperial trade before deciding whether to obey it. That was clearly an unworkable position.

The Massachusetts assembly responded to the Townshend Acts by drafting a circular letter to the

John Dickinson, as painted by Charles Willson Peale in 1770. Dickinson was then at the height of his popularity as a spokesman for the colonial cause; this portrait was commissioned by an English admirer of his work. *The Historical Society of Pennsylvania.*

other colonial legislatures, calling for unity and suggesting a joint petition of protest.

Massachusetts Assembly Dissolved

It was less the letter itself than the ministry's reaction to it that united the colonies. When Lord Hillsborough, the first secretary of state for America, learned of the circular letter, he ordered Governor Francis Bernard of Massachusetts to insist that the assembly recall it. He also directed other governors to prevent their assemblies from discussing the letter. Hillsborough's order gave the colonial assemblies the incentive they needed to forget their differences and join forces to meet the new threat to their prerogatives. In late 1768 the Massachusetts legislature met, debated, and resoundingly rejected recall by a vote of 92 to 17. Bernard immediately dissolved the assembly, and other governors followed suit when their legislatures debated the circular letter.

The figure 45 became a symbol of resistance to Great Britain when John Wilkes, a radical Englishman sympathetic to the American cause, was jailed for libel because of his publication of the essay *The North Briton No. 45*. After the events in Massachusetts, 92, the number of votes cast against recalling the circular letter, assumed ritual significance as well. In Boston, for example, the silversmith Paul Revere made a punchbowl weighing 45 ounces, which held 45 gills (half-cups) and was engraved with the names of the 92 legislators; James Otis, John Adams, and others publicly drank 45 toasts from it.

Pleasant social occasions though they were, such public rituals served important educational functions. Just as the pamphlets by Otis, Dulany, Dickinson, and others acquainted literate colonists with the issues raised by British actions, so the public rituals taught illiterate Americans about the reasons for resistance and familiarized them with the terms of the argument. When Boston's revived Sons of Liberty invited hundreds of the city's residents to dine with them each August 14 to commemorate the first Stamp Act uprising, and the Charleston Sons of Liberty held their meetings in public, crowds gathered to watch and listen. The participants in such events were openly expressing their commitment to the cause of resistance and encouraging others to join them.

Rituals of Resistance

During the two-year campaign against the Townshend duties, the Sons of Liberty and other American leaders made a deliberate effort to involve ordinary folk in the formal resistance movement, not just in occasional crowd actions. In a June 1769 Maryland nonimportation agreement, for instance, the signers (who were identified as "Merchants, Tradesmen, Freeholders, Mechanics [artisans], and other Inhabitants") agreed not to import or consume items of British origin. Such tactics helped to increase the number of colonists who were publicly aligned with the protest movement.

Women, who had previously regarded politics as outside their proper sphere, now took a part in resisting British policy. In towns throughout America, young women calling themselves Daughters of Liberty met to spin in public, in an effort to spur other women to make homespun and end the colonies' depen-

Daughters of Liberty

Chapter 4: Severing the Bonds of Empire, 1754–1774

dence on English cloth. These symbolic displays of patriotism served the same purpose as the male rituals involving the numbers 45 and 92. When young ladies from well-to-do families sat publicly at spinning wheels all day, eating only American food and drinking local herbal tea, and afterwards listening to patriotic sermons, they were serving as political instructors. Many women took great satisfaction in their new-found role. When a New England satirist hinted that women discussed only "such triffling subjects as Dress, Scandal and Detraction" during their spinning bees, three Boston women replied angrily: "Inferior in abusive sarcasm, in personal invective, in low wit, we glory to be, but inferior in veracity, sincerity, love of virtue, of liberty and of our country, we would not willingly be to any."

Women also took the lead in promoting nonconsumption of tea. In Boston more than three hundred matrons publicly promised not to drink tea, "Sickness excepted." The women of Wilmington, North Carolina, burned their tea after walking through town in a solemn procession. Housewives throughout the colonies exchanged recipes for tea substitutes or drank coffee instead. The best known of the protests (because it was satirized by a British cartoonist), the so-called Edenton Ladies Tea Party, actually had little to do with tea; it was a meeting of prominent North Carolina women who pledged formally to work for the public good and to support resistance to British measures.

But the colonists were by no means united in support of nonimportation. If the Stamp Act protests had occasionally (as in Boston and Philadelphia) revealed a division between artisans and merchants, on the one hand, and common laborers, on the other, resistance to the Townshend Acts exposed new splits in the American ranks. The most important divided the former allies of 1765 and 1766, the urban artisans and merchants, and it arose from a change in economic circumstances. The Stamp Act boycotts had helped to revive a depressed economy. In 1768 and 1769, by contrast, merchants were enjoying boom times and had no financial incentive to support a boycott. As a result, merchants signed the agreements only reluctantly. And, as John Mein revealed, they often secretly violated those agreements. Artisans, on the other hand, supported nonimportation enthusiastically, re-

Divided Opinion over Boycotts

MADE at the Subscriber's Glass-Works, and now on Hand, to be sold at his House in Market-Street. opposite the Meal-Market, either wholesale or retail between Three and Four Hundred BOXES of WINDOW GLASS, consisting of the common Sizes, 10 by 12, 9 by 11, 8 by 10, 7 by 9, 6 by 8, &c. Lamp Glass, or any uncommon Sizes, under 16 by 18, are cut upon a short Notice. Where also may be had, most Sorts of Bottles, Gallon, Half Gallon, and Quart, full Measure Half Gallon Case Bottles, Snuff and Mustard, Receivers and Retorts of various Sizes; also electrifying Globes and Tubes, &c. As the abovementioned Glass is of American Manufactory, it is consequently clear of the Duties the Americans so justly complain of, and at present it seems peculiarly the Interest of America to encourage her own Manufactories, more especially those upon which Duties have been imposed, for the sole Purpose of raising a Revenue.

N B. He also continues to make the Philadelphia Brass Buttons, well noted for their Strength, such as were made by his deceased Father, and are warranted for seven Years.

Philadelphia, August 10. RICHARD WISTAR.

At the peak of the nonimportation movement in the summer of 1769, the Philadelphia glassmaker Richard Wistar placed this advertisement in the New York Journal. *In addition to listing his wares, he appealed for customers by arguing that Americans should patronize local glassmakers instead of paying the hated Townshend duties on imported glass. Thus could patriotic pleas serve to increase an artisan's business at the expense of merchants dealing in imported goods. The Historical Society of Pennsylvania.*

cognizing that the absence of British goods would create a ready market for their own manufactures. Thus tradesmen formed the core of the crowds that coerced both importers and their customers by picketing stores, publicizing offenders' names, and sometimes destroying property.

Such tactics were effective: colonial imports from England dropped dramatically in 1769, especially in New York, New England, and Pennsylvania. But they also aroused significant opposition, creating a second major division among the colonists. Some Americans who supported resistance to British measures began to question the use of violence to force others to join the boycott. In addition, wealthier and more conservative colonists were frightened by the threat to private property inherent in the campaign. Moreover, political activism on the part of ordinary colonists challenged the ruling elite's domination, just as they had feared in 1765. Thus a Charleston essayist warned in 1769 that "the industrious mechanic [is] a useful and essential part of society . . . in his own sphere," but "when he steps out of it, and sets up for a statesman! believe me he is in a fair way

A Society of Patriotic Ladies, *painted by Philip Dawes (?) in 1775. A disapproving Briton produced this grotesque caricature of female patriots. At left the women empty their tea cannisters into a chamber pot. The cartoon bears no resemblance to the actual event, the signing of an anti-British petition by female residents of Edenton, North Carolina.* Library of Congress.

to expose himself to ridicule, and his family to distress, by neglecting his private business." Pretending concern for tradesmen's welfare, the author obviously feared for his own position in society.

Americans were relieved when the news arrived in April 1770 that a new prime minister, Lord North, had persuaded Parliament to repeal the Townshend

Repeal of the Townshend Duties

duties, except the tea tax, on the grounds that duties on trade within the empire were bad policy. Although some political leaders argued that nonimportation should be continued until the tea tax was repealed, merchants quickly resumed importing. The rest of the Townshend Acts remained in force, but repeal of the taxes made the other laws appear less objectionable. In addition, John Mein's widely circulated disclosure that leading patriots like John Hancock were themselves violating

the nonimportation agreement caused dissension in the ranks of the boycotting merchants. That too hastened the end of nonimportation.

GROWING RIFTS

At first the new ministry did nothing to antagonize the colonists. Yet on the very day Lord North proposed repeal of the Townshend duties, a clash between civilians and soldiers in Boston led to the death of five Americans. The origins of the event patriots called the Boston Massacre lay in repeated clashes between customs officers and the people of Massachusetts. The Townshend Acts' creation of an American Board of Customs Commissioners had been error enough, but a decision to base it in Boston severely compounded the mistake.

From the day of their arrival in November 1767, the customs commissioners were frequent targets of mob action. In June 1768, their seizure of the patriot leader John Hancock's sloop *Liberty* on suspicion of smuggling caused a riot in which prominent customs officers' property was destroyed. The riot in turn helped to convince the ministry in London that troops were needed to maintain order in the unruly port. The assignment of two regiments of regulars to their city confirmed Bostonians' worst fears; the redcoats were a constant reminder of the oppressive potential of British power.

Bostonians, accustomed to leading their lives with a minimum of interference from government, now found themselves hemmed in at every turn. Guards on Boston Neck, the entrance to the city, checked all travelers and their goods. Redcoat patrols roamed the city day and night, questioning and sometimes harassing passers-by. Military parades were held on Boston Common, accompanied by loud martial music and often the brutal public whipping of deserters and other violators of army rules. Parents began to fear for the safety of their daughters, who were subjected to the soldiers' coarse sexual insults when they ventured out on the streets. But the greatest potential for violence lay in the uneasy relationship between the soldiers and Boston laborers. Many redcoats sought

Chapter 4: SEVERING THE BONDS OF EMPIRE, 1754–1774

The Bloody Massacre perpetrated in King Street Boston on March 5th 1770 by a party of the 29th Regt.

Paul Revere's engraving of the Boston Massacre, a masterful piece of propaganda. At right the British officer seems to be ordering the soldiers to fire on a peaceful, unresisting crowd. The Customs House has been labeled Butcher's Hall, and smoke drifts up from a gun barrel sticking out of the window. Library of Congress.

employment in their off-duty hours, competing for unskilled jobs with the city's ordinary workingmen, and members of the two groups brawled repeatedly in taverns and on the streets.

On March 2, 1770, workers at a ropewalk (a ship-rigging factory) attacked some redcoats seeking jobs; a pitched battle resulted when both groups acquired reinforcements. Three days later, the tension exploded. Early on the evening of March 5, a crowd began throwing hard-packed snowballs at sentries guarding the Customs House. Goaded beyond endurance, the sentries fired on the crowd against express orders to the contrary, killing four and

Boston Massacre

wounding eight, one of whom died a few days later. Resistance leaders idealized the dead rioters as martyrs for the cause of liberty, holding a solemn funeral three days later and commemorating March 5 annually with patriotic orations. The best-known engraving of the massacre, by Paul Revere, was itself a part of the propaganda campaign. It depicts a peaceful crowd, an officer ordering the soldiers to fire, and shots coming from the window of the Customs House.

The leading patriots wanted to make certain the soldiers did not become martyrs as well. Furthermore, despite the political benefits the patriots derived from the massacre, it is unlikely that they approved of the crowd action that provoked it. Ever since August

1765 the men allied with the Sons of Liberty had supported orderly demonstrations and expressed distaste for uncontrolled riots, of which the Boston Massacre was a prime example. Thus when the soldiers were tried for the killings in November, they were defended by John Adams and Josiah Quincy, Jr., both unwavering patriots. All but two of the accused men were acquitted, and those convicted were released after having been branded on the thumb. Undoubtedly the favorable outcome of the trials prevented London officials from taking further steps against the city.

For more than two years after the Boston Massacre and the repeal of the Townshend duties, a superficial calm descended on the colonies. Local incidents, like the burning of the customs vessel *Gaspée* in 1772 by Rhode Islanders, marred the relationship of individual colonies and the mother country, but nothing caused Americans to join in a unified protest. Even so, the resistance movement continued to gather momentum. The most outspoken colonial newspapers, such as the *Boston Gazette*, the *Pennsylvania Journal*, and the *South Carolina Gazette*, published essays drawing on Real Whig ideology and accusing Great Britain of a deliberate plan to oppress America. After repeal of the Stamp Act, the patriots had praised Parliament; following repeal of the Townshend duties, they warned of impending tyranny. What had seemed to be an isolated mistake, a single ill-chosen stamp tax, now appeared to be part of a plot against American liberties. Among other things, essayists pointed to Parliament's persecution of the English radical John Wilkes, the stationing of troops in Boston, and the growing number of vice-admiralty courts as evidence of a plan to enslave the colonists. Indeed, patriot writers played repeatedly on the word *enslavement*. Most white colonists had direct knowledge of slavery (either being slaveholders themselves or having slave-owning neighbors), and the threat of enslavement by Britain must have hit them with peculiar force.

Still, no one yet advocated complete independence from the mother country. Though the patriots were becoming increasingly convinced that they should seek freedom from parliamentary authority, they continued to acknowledge their British identity and to pledge their allegiance to George III. They began, therefore, to try to envision a system that would enable them to be ruled largely by their own elected legislatures while remaining loyal to the king. But any such scheme was totally alien to Britons' conception of the nature of their government, which was that Parliament held sole undivided sovereignty over the empire. Furthermore, in the British mind, Parliament encompassed the king as well as the House of Lords and the Commons, and so separating the monarch from the legislature was impossible. Conservative colonists recognized the dangers inherent in the patriots' new mode of thinking. The former stamp distributor Andrew Oliver, for example, predicted in 1771 that "serious consequences" would follow from the fact that "the leaders of the people were never [before] so open in asserting our independence of the British Legislature," even though "there is an intermission of Acts of violence at present."

Oliver's prediction proved correct when, in the fall of 1772, the North ministry began to implement the portion of the Townshend Acts that provided for governors and judges to be paid from customs revenues. In early November, voters at a Boston town meeting established a Committee of Correspondence to publicize the decision by exchanging letters with other Massachusetts towns. Heading the committee was the man who had proposed its formation, Samuel Adams. A year earlier, Adams had described the benefits of organizing an official communications network within and among the separate colonies. "If conducted with a proper spirit," Adams had asked, "would it not afford reason for the Enemies of our common Liberty, to tremble?"

Committees of Correspondence

Samuel Adams was fifty-one years old in 1772, thirteen years the senior of his distant cousin John and a decade older than most other leaders of American resistance. He had been a Boston tax collector, a member and clerk of the Massachusetts assembly, and an ally of the Loyal Nine (though evidently not a member). Unswerving in his devotion to the American cause, Adams drew a sharp contrast between a corrupt Britain and the virtuous colonies. His primary forum was the Boston town meeting. An experienced political organizer, Adams continually stressed the necessity of prudent collective action. His Committee of Correspondence thus undertook to create an informed consensus among all the citizens of Massachusetts.

Such committees, which were soon established

throughout the colonies, represented the next logical step in the organization of American resistance. Until 1772, the protest movement was largely confined to the seacoast, and primarily to major cities and towns (see map, page 113). Adams realized that the time had now come to widen the movement's geographic scope, to attempt to involve the residents of the interior in the struggle that had hitherto enlisted chiefly the residents of urban areas. Accordingly, the Boston town meeting directed the Committee of Correspondence "to state the Rights of the Colonists and of this Province in particular," to list "the Infringements and Violations thereof that have been, or from time to time may be made," and to send copies to the other towns in the province. In return, Boston requested "a free communication of their Sentiments on this Subject."

Samuel Adams, James Otis, Jr., and Josiah Quincy, Jr., prepared the statement of the colonists' rights. Declaring that Americans had absolute rights to life, liberty, and property, the committee asserted that the idea that "a British house of commons, should have a right, at pleasure, to give and grant the property of the colonists" was "irreconcileable" with "the first principles of natural law and Justice . . . and of the British Constitution in particular." The list of grievances, drafted by another group of prominent patriots, was similarly sweeping. It complained of taxation without representation, the presence of unnecessary troops and customs officers on American soil, the use of imperial revenues to pay colonial officials, the expanded jurisdiction of vice-admiralty courts, and even the nature of the instructions given to American governors by their superiors in London.

The entire document, which was printed as a pamphlet for distribution to the towns, exhibited none of the hesitation that had characterized colonial claims against Parliament in the 1760s. No longer were patriots—at least in Boston—concerned about defining the precise limits of parliamentary authority. No longer did they mention the necessity of obedience to Parliament. They were committed to a course that placed American rights first, loyalty to Great Britain a distant second.

The response of the Massachusetts towns to the committee's pamphlet must have caused Samuel Adams to rejoice. Some towns disagreed with Boston's assessment of the state of affairs, but most aligned

themselves with the city. From Braintree came the assertion that "all civil officers are or ought to be Servants to the people and dependent upon them for their official Support, and every instance to the Contrary from the Governor downwards tends to crush and destroy civil liberty." The town of Holden declared that "the People of New England have never given the People of Britain any Right of Jurisdiction over us." The citizens of Petersham commented that resistance to tyranny was "the first and highest social Duty of this people." And Pownallborough warned, "allegiance is a relative Term and like Kingdoms and commonwealths is local and has its bounds." It was beliefs like these that made the next crisis in Anglo-American affairs the final one.

THE BOSTON TEA PARTY

The only one of the Townshend duties still in effect by 1773 was the tax on tea. In the years since 1770 some Americans had continued to boycott English tea, while others had resumed drinking it either openly or in secret. Tea had long been an important component of the Anglo-American diet, and the possession of tea-drinking equipment (teapots and matched sets of cups) indicated high status (see page 76). Well-to-do Americans, women and men alike, socialized frequently at private tea parties, so that observing the tea boycott required colonial elites not only to change the beverage they habitually drank but also to alter their lifestyles. Tea thus retained an explosively symbolic character even though the boycott was less than fully effective after 1770.

In May 1773, Parliament passed an act designed to save the East India Company from bankruptcy by changing the way British tea was sold in the colonies. Resistance leaders were immediately **Tea Act** suspicious. Under the Tea Act, certain duties paid on tea were to be returned to the company. Furthermore, tea was to be sold only by designated agents, which would enable the East India Company to avoid colonial middlemen and undersell any competitors, even smugglers. The

The Able Doctor, or America Swallowing the Bitter Draught. Paul Revere engraved this cartoon for the Royal American Magazine *of June 1774. Lord North, a copy of the Boston Port Act in his pocket, is forcing tea down the throat of America, represented as an Indian woman. While Britannia weeps, a Frenchman and a Spaniard comment on the proceedings. In the background, the British fleet bombards Boston.   Library of Congress.*

net result would be cheaper tea for American consumers. But many colonists interpreted the new measure as a pernicious device to make them admit Parliament's right to tax them, since the less expensive tea would still be taxed under the Townshend law. Others saw the Tea Act as the first step in the establishment of an East India Company monopoly of all colonial trade. Residents of the four cities singled out to receive the first shipments of tea accordingly prepared to respond to what they perceived as a new threat to their freedom.

In New York City, the tea ships failed to arrive on schedule. In Philadelphia, the captain was persuaded to turn around and sail back to England. In Charleston, the tea was unloaded, stored under the direction of local tradesmen, and later destroyed. The only confrontation occurred in Boston, where both sides—the town meeting, joined by participants from nearby towns, and Governor Thomas Hutchinson, two of whose sons were tea agents—rejected compromise.

The first of three tea ships, the *Dartmouth,* entered Boston harbor on November 28. Under the customs laws, a cargo had to be landed and the appropriate duty paid within twenty days of a ship's arrival. If that was not done, the cargo would be seized by customs officers. After a series of mass meetings, Bostonians voted to prevent the tea from being unloaded and to post guards on the wharf. Hutchinson, for his part, refused to permit the vessels to leave the harbor.

On December 16, 1773, one day before the cargo would have to be confiscated, more than five thousand people (nearly a third of the city's population) crowded into Old South Church. The meeting, chaired by Samuel Adams, made a final attempt to persuade Hutchinson to send the tea back to England. But Hutchinson remained adamant. At about 6 p.m., Adams reportedly announced "that he could think of nothing further to be done—that they had now done all they could for the Salvation of their Country." As if his statement were a signal, cries rang out from the back of the crowd: "Boston harbor a tea-pot night! The Mohawks are come!" Small groups pushed their way out of the meeting. Within a few minutes, about sixty men crudely disguised as Indians assembled at the wharf, boarded the three ships, and dumped the cargo into the harbor. By 9 p.m. their work was done: 342 chests of tea worth approximately £10,000 floated in splinters on the ebbing tide.

Among the "Indians" were many representatives of Boston's artisans. Five masons, eleven carpenters and builders, three leatherworkers, a blacksmith, a hatter, three coopers, two barbers, a coachmaker, a silversmith, and twelve apprentices have been identified as participants. Their ranks also included four farmers from outside Boston, ten merchants, two doctors, a teacher, and a bookseller. The next day John Adams exulted in his diary that the Tea Party was "so bold, so daring, so firm, intrepid and inflexible" that "I can't but consider it as an epocha in history."

The North administration reacted with considerably less enthusiasm when it learned of the Tea Party. In March 1774, after failing in an attempt to charge the Boston resistance leaders with high treason, the ministry proposed the first of the four laws that became known as the Coercive, or Intolerable, Acts. It called for closing the port of Boston until the tea was paid for and prohibiting all but coastal trade in food and firewood. Colonial sympathizers in Parliament were easily outvoted by those who wished to punish the city that had been the center of opposition to British policies. Later in the spring, Parliament passed three further punitive mea-

Coercive and Quebec Acts

sures. The Massachusetts Government Act altered the province's charter, substituting an appointed council for an elected one, increasing the powers of the governor, and forbidding special town meetings. The Justice Act provided that a person accused of committing murder in the course of suppressing a riot or enforcing the laws could be tried outside the colony where the incident had occurred. Finally, the Quartering Act gave broad authority to military commanders seeking to house their troops in private dwellings.

After passing the last of the Coercive Acts in early

IMPORTANT EVENTS	
1754	Albany Congress French and Indian War begins
1760	American phase of war ends George III becomes king
1763	Treaty of Paris Pontiac's uprising Proclamation of 1763
1764	Sugar Act
1765	Stamp Act Sons of Liberty formed
1766	Repeal of Stamp Act Declaratory Act
1767	Townshend Acts
1770	Lord North becomes prime minister Repeal of Townshend duties except tea tax Boston Massacre
1772	Boston Committee of Correspondence formed
1773	Tea Act Boston Tea Party
1774	Coercive Acts

June, Parliament turned its attention to much-needed reforms in the government of Quebec. The Quebec Act, though unrelated to the Coercive Acts, thus became linked with them in the minds of the patriots. Intended to ease the strains that had arisen since the British conquest of the formerly French colony, the Quebec Act granted greater religious freedom to Catholics—alarming the Protestant colonists, who regarded Roman Catholicism as a mainstay of religious and political despotism. It also reinstated French civil law, which had been replaced by British procedures in 1763, and established an appointed council (rather than an elected legislature) as the governing body of the colony. Finally, in an attempt to provide the northern Indian tribes some protection against white settlement, the act annexed to Quebec the area east of the Mississippi River and north of the Ohio River. Thus that region, parts of which were claimed by individual seacoast colonies, was removed from their jurisdiction.

Members of Parliament who voted for the punitive legislation believed that the acts would be obeyed, that at long last they had solved the problem posed by the troublesome Americans. But the patriots showed little inclination to bow to the wishes of Parliament. In their eyes, the Coercive Acts and the Quebec Act proved what they had feared since 1768: that Great Britain had embarked on a deliberate plan to oppress them. If the port of Boston could be closed, why not those of Philadelphia or New York? If the royal charter of Massachusetts could be changed, why not that of South Carolina? If certain people could be removed from their home colonies for trial, why not all violators of all laws? If troops could be forcibly quartered in private houses, did not that pave the way for the occupation of all of America? If the Roman Catholic church could receive favored status in Quebec, why not everywhere? It seemed as though the full dimensions of the plot against American rights and liberties had at last been revealed.

The Boston Committee of Correspondence urged all the colonies to join in an immediate boycott of British goods. But the other provinces were not yet ready to take such a drastic step. Instead, they suggested that another intercolonial congress be convened to consider an appropriate response to the Coercive Acts. Few people wanted to take hasty action; even the most ardent patriots still hoped for reconciliation with Great Britain. Despite their objections to British policy, they continued to see themselves as part of the empire. Americans were approaching the brink of confrontation, but they had not committed themselves to an irrevocable break. And so the colonies agreed to send delegates to Philadelphia in September.

Over the preceding decade, momentous changes had occurred in the ways politically aware colonists thought about themselves and their allegiance. Once linked unquestioningly to Great Britain, they had begun to develop a sense of their own identity as Americans. They had started to realize that their concept of the political process differed from that held by people in the mother country. They also had come to understand that their economic interests did not necessarily coincide with those of Great Britain. In the late summer of 1774, they were committed to resistance, but not to independence. Even so, they had started to sever the bonds of empire. During the next decade, they would forge the bonds of a new American nationality to replace those rejected Anglo-American ties.

SUGGESTIONS FOR FURTHER READING

General

Ian R. Christie, *Crisis of Empire: Great Britain and the American Colonies 1754–1783* (1966); Ian R. Christie and Benjamin W. Labaree, *Empire or Independence, 1760–1776: A British-American Dialogue on the Coming of the American Revolution* (1976); Lawrence Henry Gipson, *The Coming of the Revolution 1763–1775* (1954); Merrill Jensen, *The Founding of a Nation: A History of the American Revolution, 1763–1776* (1968); Robert Middlekauff, *The Glorious Cause: The American Revolution, 1763–1783* (1982); Edmund S. Morgan, *The Birth of the Republic, 1763–1789* (1956).

Colonial Warfare and the British Empire

Lawrence Henry Gipson, *The British Empire Before the American Revolution*, 15 vols. (1936–1970); Robert C. Newbold, *The Albany Congress and Plan of Union of 1754*

(1955); Howard H. Peckham, *The Colonial Wars, 1689–1762* (1963); William Pencak, *War, Politics, and Revolution in Provincial Massachusetts* (1981); Alan Rogers, *Empire and Liberty: American Resistance to British Authority, 1755–1763* (1974); John Shy, *Toward Lexington: The Role of the British Army in the Coming of the American Revolution* (1965).

British Politics and Policy

George L. Beer, *British Colonial Policy 1754–1765* (1907); John Brewer, *Party Ideology and Popular Politics at the Accession of George III* (1976); John Brooke, *King George III* (1972); John L. Bullion, *A Great and Necessary Measure: George Grenville and the Genesis of the Stamp Act, 1763–1765* (1981); Bernard Donoughue, *British Politics and the American Revolution: The Path to War, 1773–1775* (1965); Michael Kammen, *A Rope of Sand: The Colonial Agents, British Politics, and the American Revolution* (1968); Lewis B. Namier, *England in the Age of the American Revolution*, 2nd ed. (1961); P. D. G. Thomas, *British Politics and the Stamp Act Crisis* (1975); Carl Ubbelohde, *The Vice-Admiralty Courts and the American Revolution* (1960).

Indians and the West

Thomas P. Abernethy, *Western Lands and the American Revolution* (1959); John R. Alden, *John Stuart and the Southern Colonial Frontier: A Study of Indian Relations, War, Trade, and Land Problems in the Southern Wilderness, 1754–1775* (1944); Richard Aquila, *The Iroquois Restoration: Iroquois Diplomacy on the Colonial Frontier 1701–1754* (1983); David H. Corkran, *The Cherokee Frontier: Conflict and Survival, 1740–1762* (1962); David H. Corkran, *The Creek Frontier, 1540–1783* (1967); Georgiana C. Nammack, *Fraud, Politics, and the Dispossession of the Indians: The Iroquois Land Frontier in the Colonial Period* (1969); Howard H. Peckham, *Pontiac and the Indian Uprising* (1947); Jack M. Sosin, *Whitehall and the Wilderness: The Middle West in British Colonial Policy, 1760–1775* (1961).

Political Thought

Bernard Bailyn, *The Ideological Origins of the American Revolution* (1967); Edwin G. Burrows and Michael Wallace, "The American Revolution: The Ideology and Psychology of National Liberation," *Perspectives in American History*, 6 (1972), 167–302; Jay Fliegelman, *Prodigals & Pilgrims: The American Revolution Against Patriarchal Authority 1750–1800* (1982); J. G. A. Pocock, "Machiavelli, Harrington, and English Political Ideologies in the Eighteenth Century," *William and Mary Quarterly*, 3rd ser., 22 (1965), 547–583; Caroline Robbins, *The Eighteenth-Century Commonwealthman: Studies in the Transmission, Development, and Circumstance of English Liberal Thought from the Restoration of Charles II until the War with the Thirteen Colonies* (1959); Clinton Rossiter, *Seedtime of the Republic: The Origin of the American Tradition of Political Liberty* (1953).

American Resistance

David Ammerman, *In the Common Cause: American Response to the Coercive Acts of 1774* (1974); Richard Beeman, *Patrick Henry: A Biography* (1974); Richard D. Brown, *Revolutionary Politics in Massachusetts: The Boston Committee of Correspondence and the Towns, 1772–1774* (1970); Joseph Albert Ernst, *Money and Politics in America, 1755–1775: A Study in the Currency Act of 1764 and the Political Economy of Revolution* (1973); Dirk Hoerder, *Crowd Action in Revolutionary Massachusetts, 1765–1780* (1977); Rhys Isaac, *The Transformation of Virginia, 1740–1790* (1982); Benjamin W. Labaree, *The Boston Tea Party* (1964); Pauline R. Maier, *From Resistance to Revolution: Colonial Radicals and the Development of American Opposition to Britain, 1765–1776* (1972); Pauline R. Maier, *The Old Revolutionaries: Political Lives in the Age of Samuel Adams* (1980); Edmund S. Morgan and Helen M. Morgan, *The Stamp Act Crisis: Prologue to Revolution* (1953); Gary B. Nash, *The Urban Crucible: Social Change, Political Consciousness, and the Origins of the American Revolution* (1979); Richard Ryerson, *The Revolution Is Now Begun: The Radical Committees of Philadelphia, 1765–1776* (1978); Arthur M. Schlesinger, *The Colonial Merchants and the American Revolution 1763–1776* (1918); Peter Shaw, *American Patriots and the Rituals of Revolution* (1981); Richard Walsh, *Charleston's Sons of Liberty: A Study of the Artisans, 1763–1789* (1959); John J. Waters, Jr., *The Otis Family in Provincial and Revolutionary Massachusetts* (1968); Alfred H. Young, ed., *The American Revolution: Explorations in the History of American Radicalism* (1976); Hiller B. Zobel, *The Boston Massacre* (1970).

A Revolution, Indeed

1775–1783

Chapter 5

One April morning in 1775, Hannah Winthrop awoke with a start to drumbeats, bells, and the continuous clang of the Cambridge fire alarm. She and her husband, a professor at Harvard, soon learned that redcoat troops had left Boston late the evening before, bound for Concord. A few hours later they watched British soldiers march through Cambridge to reinforce the first group. The Winthrops quickly decided to leave home and seek shelter elsewhere. Along with seventy or eighty other refugees, mostly wives and children of patriot militiamen, they made their way to an isolated farmhouse near Fresh Pond. But it was no secure haven. They were, Mrs. Winthrop later wrote, "for some time in sight of the Battle, the glistening instruments of death proclaiming by an incessant fire that much blood must be shed, that many widowd and orphand ones be left as monuments of that persecuting Barbarity of British Tyranny."

Afraid to abandon their refuge even after the sounds of battle ceased, the Winthrops and their companions remained in the farmhouse overnight, sleeping in chairs and on the floor. The next morning, warned that Cambridge was still unsafe, the couple headed north toward Andover. The roads were filled with other frightened families, some carrying all their belongings. Their route took them through Menotomy (now Arlington), scene of some of the bloodiest fighting the day before. The battlefield, Mrs. Winthrop recorded, was "strewd with the mangled bodies." Along the way they encountered a farmer gathering the corpses of his neighbors and searching for the body of his son, who had reportedly been killed in battle. As she walked toward Andover, Hannah Winthrop mentally compared herself with Eve expelled from the Garden of Eden; lines from John Milton's *Paradise Lost*, she later told a friend, had echoed repeatedly in her mind. She was convinced that nothing would be the same again.

In that expectation, Hannah Winthrop was wrong. She and her husband soon returned to their Cambridge home and resumed their normal lives. But their experience in 1775 was typical of that of thousands of other Americans over the next eight years. The Revolution, one of only two major conflicts ever fought on American soil—the other was the Civil War—was more than just a series of clashes between British and patriot armies. It also uprooted thousands of civilian families, disrupted the economy, reshaped society by forcing many colonists into permanent exile, and led Americans to develop new conceptions of politics. Indeed, even before the shooting began the patriots had established functioning revolutionary governments throughout the colonies.

The struggle for independence required revolutionary leaders to accomplish three separate but closely related tasks. The first was political and ideological. They had to transform the 1760s consensus favoring loyal resistance into a coalition supporting independence: a different goal entirely. They took a variety of steps ranging from persuasion to coercion to enlist all whites in the patriot cause. In the case of blacks and Indians, America's elected leaders hoped for cooperation at best, neutrality at worst. Still, they had good reason to fear that Indians, blacks, and the English would unite against them.

The second task was diplomatic. To win their independence, the patriot leaders knew they needed international recognition and aid, particularly assistance from France. Thus they dispatched to Paris Benjamin Franklin, the most experienced American diplomat (he had served for years as a colonial agent in London). Franklin skillfully negotiated the Franco-American alliance of 1778, which was to prove crucial to the winning of independence.

Only the third task directly involved the British. George Washington, commander-in-chief of the American army, quickly realized that his primary goal should be not to win battles but rather to avoid losing them decisively. He understood that, as long as his army survived to fight another day, the outcome of any individual battle was more or less irrelevant (although at times victories were necessary, if only to bolster morale). Accordingly, the story of the Revolutionary War reveals British action and American reaction, British attacks and American defenses. The American war effort was aided by British military planners' failure to analyze accurately the problem confronting them. Until it was too late, they treated the war against the colonists as they did wars against other Europeans; that is, they concentrated on winning battles and did not consider the difficulties inherent in achieving their main goal, retaining the colonies' allegiance. In the end, the Americans' triumph owed more to their own endurance and to Britain's mistakes than to their military prowess.

GOVERNMENT BY CONGRESS
AND COMMITTEE

W hen the fifty-five delegates to the First Continental Congress convened in Philadelphia in September 1774, they knew that any measures they adopted were likely to enjoy support among many of their fellow countrymen and women. During the summer of 1774, open meetings held in towns, cities, and counties throughout the colonies had endorsed the idea of another nonimportation pact. Participants in such meetings had promised (in the words of the freeholders of Johnston County, North Carolina) to "strictly adhere to, and abide by, such Regulations and Restrictions as the Members of the said General Congress shall agree to, and judge most convenient." The committees of correspondence that had been established in many communities publicized these popular meetings so effectively that Americans everywhere knew about them. Most of the congressional delegates were selected by extralegal provincial conventions whose members were chosen at such local gatherings, since the royal governors had forbidden the regular assemblies to conduct formal elections. Thus the very act of designating delegates to attend the congress involved Americans in open defiance of British authority.

First Continental Congress

The colonies' leading political figures—most of them lawyers, merchants, or planters—were sent to the Philadelphia congress. The Massachusetts delegation included both Samuel Adams, the experienced organizer of the Boston resistance, and his younger cousin John, an ambitious lawyer. Among others

New York sent John Jay, a talented young attorney. From Pennsylvania came the conservative Joseph Galloway, speaker of the assembly, and his long-time rival John Dickinson. Virginia elected Richard Henry Lee and Patrick Henry, both noted for their patriotic zeal, as well as the stolid and reserved George Washington. Most of these men had never met, but in the weeks, months, and years that followed they were to become the chief architects of the new nation.

The congressmen faced three tasks when they convened at Carpenters Hall on September 5, 1774. The first two were explicit: defining American grievances and developing a plan for resistance. The third was implicit—outlining a theory of their constitutional relationship with England—and proved troublesome. The delegates readily agreed on a list of the laws they wanted repealed (notably the Coercive Acts) and chose as their method of resistance an economic boycott coupled with petitions for relief. But they could not reach a consensus on the constitutional issue. Their discussion of this crucial question was rendered all the more intense by events in Massachusetts.

On the second day of the meeting, word arrived that the British had attacked the Massachusetts countryside and were bombarding Boston from land and sea. This rumor was proven false two days later, but it nevertheless lent a sense of urgency to the congressmen's discussions. That thousands of militiamen had gathered in Cambridge to repel the rumored attack demonstrated how close to the brink of war Great Britain and the colonies had already come. The congressmen accordingly set about their work with particular fervor and commitment.

Since the colonists' resistance was based on the claim that their constitutional rights had been violated, it seemed necessary to define what the colonies' constitutional relationship with England was. But the delegates held widely differing views on that subject. The most radical congressmen, like Lee of Virginia and Roger Sherman of Connecticut, agreed with the position published a few weeks earlier by Thomas Jefferson—who was not a delegate—in his *Summary View of the Rights of British America*. Jefferson argued that the colonists owed allegiance only to George III, and that Parliament was nothing more than "the legislature of one part of the empire." As such, he declared, it could not exercise legitimate authority

EXTRACTS

From the

VOTES and PROCEEDINGS

Of the AMERICAN CONTINENTAL

CONGRESS,

Held at Philadelphia on the

5th of *September* 1774.

CONTAINING

The Bill of Rights, a Lift of Grievances, Occafional Refolves, the
Affociation, an *Addrefs* to the People
of Great-Britain, and a *Memorial*
to the Inhabitants of the British
American Colonies.

Publifhed by order of the Congress.

PHILADELPHIA:

Printed by William and Thomas Bradford,
October 27th, M,DCC,LXXIV.

The First Continental Congress publicized its actions in this pamphlet, which was widely reprinted in the colonies. It informed Americans of the various steps their representatives had taken to protest the Coercive Acts. Library of Congress.

over the American provinces, which had historically been governed by their own assemblies.

Meanwhile the conservative Joseph Galloway and his ally James Duane of New York insisted that the congress should acknowledge Parliament's supremacy over the empire and its right to regulate American trade. Galloway embodied these ideas in a formal plan of union. His plan proposed the establishment of an American legislature, its members chosen by individual colonial assemblies, which would have to consent to laws pertaining to America. After a heated debate, the delegates rejected Galloway's proposal. But they were not prepared to go as far as Jefferson had.

Finally, they accepted a compromise position worked out by John Adams. The crucial clause Adams drafted in the congress's Declaration of Rights and Grievances read in part: "From the necessity of

Declaration of Rights and Grievances the case, and a regard to the mutual interest of both countries, we cheerfully consent to the operation of such acts of the British parliament, as are bona fide, restrained to the regulation of our external commerce." Note the key phrases. "From the necessity of the case" indicated Americans' abandonment, once and for all, of the unquestioning loyalty to the mother country that had so bedeviled James Otis, Jr., just a decade earlier. The colonists were now declaring that they owed obedience to Parliament only because they had decided it was in the best interest of both countries. "Bona fide, restrained to the regulation of our external commerce" resonated with overtones of the Stamp Act controversy and Dickinson's arguments in his *Farmer's Letters*. The delegates intended to make clear to Lord North that they would continue to resist taxes in disguise, like the Townshend duties. Most striking of all was that such language, which only a few years before would have been regarded as irredeemably radical, could be presented and accepted as a compromise in the fall of 1774. The Americans had come a long way since their first hesitant protests against the Sugar Act (see page 109).

Once the delegates had resolved the constitutional issue, they discussed the tactics by which to force another British retreat. They adopted an agreement known as the Continental Association, which called for nonimportation of all goods from Great Britain and Ireland, as well as tea and molasses from other British possessions and slaves from any ource, effective December 1. An end to the consumption of British products was also readily accepted, to become effective on March 1, 1775. Nonexportation, on the other hand, generated considerable debate. The Virginia delegation adamantly refused to accept a ban on exports to England until after its planters had had a chance to market their 1774 tobacco crop, which needed to be dried and cured before it could be sold. As a result, the congress provided that nonexportation would not begin until September 10, 1775.

More influential than the details of the Continental Association was the method the congress recommended for its enforcement: the election of committees

Committees of Observation

of observation and inspection in every county, city, and town in America. Such committees were officially charged only with overseeing enforcement of the association, but over the next six months they became de facto governments. Since the congress specified that committee members be chosen by all persons qualified to vote for members of the lower house of the colonial legislatures, the committees were guaranteed a broad popular base. Furthermore, their numbers ensured that many new men would be incorporated into the resistance movement. In some places the committeemen were former local officeholders; in other places they were obscure men who had never before held office. Everywhere, however, these committeemen—perhaps seven to eight thousand of them in the colonies as a whole—found themselves increasingly linked to the cause of American resistance.

At first the committees confined themselves to enforcing the nonimportation clause—examining merchants' records and publishing the names of those who continued to import or sell British goods. But the Continental Association also promoted home manufactures and encouraged Americans to adopt simple modes of dress and behavior. Wearing homespun garments became a sign of patriotism, just as it had been in the late 1760s. Since expensive leisure-time activities were symbols of vice and corruption, the congress urged Americans to forgo dancing, gambling, horse racing, cock fighting, and other forms of "extravagance and dissipation." In enforcing these injunctions, sometimes even by jailing offenders, the committees gradually extended their authority over nearly all aspects of American life.

Some committees forbade public and private dancing, extracted apologies from people caught gambling or racing, prohibited the slaughter of lambs (because of the need for wool), and offered prizes for the best locally made cloth. The Baltimore County committee even advised citizens not to attend the upcoming town fair, which they described as nothing more than an occasion for "riots, drunkenness, gaming, and the vilest immoralities."

The committees also attempted to identify opponents of American resistance. Although seeking to protect American rights—which presumably included freedom of speech and thought—the patriots saw no reason to grant those rights to people who disagreed with them. They viewed the resistance movement as a collective endeavor that would succeed only if all colonists supported it. Consequently, the committees developed elaborate spy networks, circulated copies of the association for signatures, and investigated reports of dissident remarks and activities. Suspected dissenters were first urged to convert to the colonial cause; if that failed, the committees had them watched or restricted their movements. Sometimes people engaging in casual political exchanges with friends one day found themselves charged with "treasonable conversation" the next. Committees cooperated with each other, too. In 1775, for example, the Northampton, Massachusetts, committee told its counterpart in nearby Hadley that a townsman had been heard to call the congress "a Pack or Parcell of Fools" that was "as tyrannical as Lord North and ought to be opposed & resisted." The Hadley committee examined the accused man, who admitted his statements and refused to recant. The committee thereafter had him watched.

While the committees were expanding their power during the winter and early spring of 1775, the established governments of the colonies were collapsing.

Provincial Conventions

Only in Connecticut, Rhode Island, Delaware, and Pennsylvania did regular assemblies continue to meet without encountering patriot challenges to their authority. In every other colony, popularly elected provincial conventions took over the task of running the government, sometimes entirely replacing the legislatures and at other times holding concurrent sessions. In late 1774 and early 1775, these conventions approved the Continental Association, elected delegates to the Second Continental Congress (scheduled for May), organized militia units, and gathered arms and ammunition. The British-appointed governors and councils, unable to stem the tide of resistance, watched helplessly as their authority crumbled.

The frustrating experience of Governor Josiah Martin of North Carolina is a case in point. When a provincial convention was called to meet at New Bern on April 4, 1775—the same day the legislature was to convene—Martin proclaimed that "the Assembly of this province duly elected is the only true and lawful representation of the people." He asked all citizens to "renounce disclaim and discourage all such meetings cabals and illegal proceedings . . . which can only tend to introduce disorder and anarchy." Martin's proclamation had no visible effect, and when the convention met at New Bern its membership proved to be virtually identical to that of the colonial legislature. The delegates proceeded to act alternately in both capacities and even passed some joint resolves. Continuing the farce, the exasperated Martin delivered a speech to the assembly denouncing the election of the convention. On April 7, Martin admitted to Lord Dartmouth, the American Secretary in North's ministry, that his government was "absolutely prostrate, impotent, and that nothing but the shadow of it is left."

Royal officials in the other colonies suffered the same frustrations. Courts were prevented from holding sessions; taxes were paid to agents of the conventions rather than provincial tax collectors; sheriffs' powers were questioned; and militiamen refused to muster except by order of the local committees. In short, during the six months preceding the battles at Lexington and Concord, independence was being won at the local level, but without formal acknowledgment and for the most part without shooting or bloodshed. Not many Americans fully realized what was happening. The vast majority of colonists still proclaimed their loyalty to Great Britain and denied that they sought to leave the empire. Among the few Americans who did recognize the trend toward independence were those who opposed it.

CHOOSING SIDES: LOYALISTS, BLACKS, AND INDIANS

The first protests against British measures, in the mid-1760s, had won the support of most colonists. Only in the late 1760s and early 1770s did a significant number of Americans begin to question

both the aims and the tactics of the resistance movement. In 1774 and 1775 such people found themselves in a difficult position. Like their more radical counterparts, most of them objected to parliamentary policies and wanted some kind of constitutional reform. (Joseph Galloway, for instance, was a conservative by American standards, but his plan for restructuring the empire was too novel for Britain to accept.) Nevertheless, if forced to a choice, these colonists sympathized with Great Britain rather than with an independent America. The events of the crucial year between the passage of the Coercive Acts and the outbreak of fighting in Massachusetts crystallized their thinking. Their doubts about violent protest, their desire to uphold the legally constituted colonial governments, and their fears of anarchy combined to make them especially sensitive to the dangers of resistance.

In 1774 and 1775 some conservatives began to publish essays and pamphlets critical of the congress and its allied committees. In New York City, a group of Anglican clergymen jointly wrote pamphlets and essays arguing the importance of maintaining a cordial connection between England and America. In Pennsylvania, Joseph Galloway published *A Candid Examination of the Mutual Claims of Great Britain and the Colonies*, attacking the Continental Congress for rejecting his plan of union. In Massachusetts, the young attorney Daniel Leonard, writing under the pseudonym Massachusettensis, engaged in a prolonged newspaper debate with Novanglus (John Adams). All the conservative authors stressed the point that Leonard put so well in his sixth essay in January 1775: "There is no possible medium between absolute independence and subjection to the authority of parliament." Leonard and his fellows realized that what had begun as a dispute over the extent of American subordination within the empire had now raised the question of whether the colonies would remain linked to Great Britain at all. "Rouse up at last from your slumber!" the Reverend Thomas Bradbury Chandler of New Jersey cried out to Americans. "There is a set of people among us . . . who have formed a scheme for establishing an independent government or empire in America."

Some colonists heeded the conservative pamphleteers' warnings. About one-fifth of the white American population remained loyal to Great Britain, actively

Loyalists, Patriots, and Neutrals opposing independence. Unlike their fellow countrymen and women, loyalists remained true to the colonial self-conception once held by most eighteenth-century white Americans. In other words, it was the patriots who changed their allegiance, not the loyalists. What is therefore surprising is that there were so few active loyalists, not that there were so many.

With notable exceptions, most people of the following types remained loyal to the crown: British-appointed government officials; merchants whose trade depended on imperial connections; Anglican clergy everywhere and lay Anglicans in the North—where their denomination was in the minority—since the king was the head of their church as well as the state; former officers and enlisted men from the British army, many of whom had settled in America after 1763; non-English ethnic minorities, especially Scots; tenant farmers, particularly those whose landlords sided with the patriots; members of persecuted religious sects; and many of the backcountry southerners who had rebelled against eastern rule in the 1760s and early 1770s. All these people had one thing in common: the patriot leaders were their long-standing enemies, though for different reasons. Local and provincial disputes thus helped to determine which side a person chose in the imperial conflict.

The active patriots, who accounted for about two-fifths of the population, came chiefly from the groups that had dominated colonial society, either numerically or politically. Among them were yeoman farmers, members of dominant Protestant sects (both Old and New Lights), Chesapeake gentry, merchants dealing mainly in American commodities, city artisans, elected officeholders, and people of English descent. Wives usually but not always adopted their husbands' political beliefs. Although all these patriots supported the Revolution, many pursued different goals within the broader coalition, as they had done in the 1760s. Some sought limited political reform, others extensive political change, and still others social and economic reforms. (The ways in which their concerns interacted will be discussed in Chapter 6.)

There remained in the middle perhaps two-fifths of the white population. Some of those who tried to avoid taking sides were sincere pacifists, such as Pennsylvania Quakers. Others opportunistically shifted

Connecticut imprisoned many of its loyalists in notorious Newgate prison, a converted copper mine. The offenders were housed in caverns below the large structure left of center. Some prominent loyalists (like Benjamin Franklin's son William, the last royal governor of New Jersey) were held in private homes. The Connecticut Historical Society.

their allegiance depending on which side happened to be winning at the time. Still others simply wanted to be left alone to lead their lives; they cared little about politics and normally obeyed whichever side controlled their area. But such colonists also resisted the British and the Americans alike when the demands made on them seemed too heavy—when taxes became too high, for example, or when calls for militia service came too often. Their attitude might best be summed up in the phrase "a plague on both your houses." Such persons made up an especially large proportion of the population in the southern backcountry, where the Scotch-Irish settlers had little love for either the patriot gentry or the English authorities.

To American patriots, that sort of apathy or neutrality was a crime as heinous as loyalism. Those who were not for them were against them; in their minds, there could be no conscientious objectors. By the winter of 1775 and 1776, less than a year after Lexington and Concord, the Continental Congress was recommending to the states that all "disaffected" persons be disarmed and arrested. The state legislatures quickly passed laws prescribing severe penalties for suspected loyalists. Many began to require all voters (or, in some cases, all free adult males) to take oaths of allegiance; the punishment for refusal was usually banishment or extra taxes. In 1778 and thereafter, many states formally confiscated the property of banished loyalists.

During the war, loyalists tended to congregate in cities held by the British army. When those posts were evacuated at the end of the war, the loyalists scattered to different parts of the British Empire— England, the West Indies, and especially Canada. In the provinces of Nova Scotia, New Brunswick, and Ontario they recreated their lives as colonists, laying the foundations of British Canada. All told, perhaps as many as 100,000 white Americans preferred to leave their homeland rather than to live in a nation independent of British rule. That fact speaks volumes about the depth of their loyalty to an Anglo-American definition of their identity.

The patriots' policies helped to ensure that the weak, scattered, and persecuted loyalists could not band together to threaten the Revolutionary cause. But loyalists were not the patriots' only worry. They had reason to believe that Indians and enslaved blacks might join the forces arrayed against them.

Afro-American slaves faced a dilemma at the beginning of the Revolution: how could they best achieve their goal of escaping perpetual servitude? Should they fight with or against their white masters? The correct choice was not immediately apparent, and so blacks made different decisions. Some joined the revolutionaries, others the British. In the early days of the war, those who decided to join the American side were primarily free blacks from New England, men to whom the issue of slavery or freedom did not apply. They were already free men, even if few of them owned property and none of them could vote. They made choices about their allegiance in the same way as their white neighbors.

The Blacks' Dilemma

For blacks who were still enslaved, alliance with the British held out more promise. Not surprisingly, therefore, news of slave conspiracies surfaced in different parts of the colonies in late 1774 and early 1775. All shared a common element: a plan to assist the British in return for freedom. A group of blacks petitioned General Thomas Gage, the commander-in-chief of the British army in Boston, promising to fight for the redcoats if he would liberate them. The governor of Maryland authorized the issuance of extra guns to militiamen in four counties where slave uprisings were expected. The most serious incident occurred during the summer of 1775 in Charleston, where Thomas Jeremiah, a free black harbor pilot, was brutally executed after being convicted of attempting to foment a slave revolt.

A fear of acts such as these made white residents of the British West Indian colonies far more cautious in their opposition to parliamentary policies than their counterparts on the mainland. On most of the Caribbean islands, blacks outnumbered whites by six or seven to one. The planters simply could not afford to risk opposing Britain, their chief protector, with the ever-present threat of black revolt hanging over their heads. The Jamaica assembly agreed with the mainland colonial legislatures that citizens should not be bound by laws to which they had not consented. Nevertheless its members assured the king in 1774 that "it cannot be supposed, that we now intend, or ever could have intended Resistance to Great Britain." They cited as reasons Jamaica's "weak and feeble" condition, "its very small number of white inhabitants, and . . . the incumbrance of more than Two hundred thousand Slaves."

Racial composition affected politics in the continental colonies as well. In the North, where whites greatly outnumbered blacks, revolutionary fervor was at its height. In Virginia and Maryland, where whites constituted a safe majority of the population, there was occasional alarm over potential slave revolts but no disabling fear. But in South Carolina, which was over 60 percent black, and Georgia, where the racial balance was nearly even, whites were noticeably less enthusiastic about resistance. Georgia, in fact, sent no delegates to the First Continental Congress, and reminded its representatives at the Second Continental Congress to consider its circumstances, "with our blacks and tories within us," when voting on the question of independence.

Racial Composition and Patriotic Fervor

The whites' worst fears were realized in November 1775, when Lord Dunmore, the governor of Virginia, offered to free any slaves and indentured servants who would leave their patriot masters to join the British forces. Dunmore hoped to use blacks in his fight against the revolutionaries, and to disrupt the

RUN away from *Hampton*, on *Sunday* laſt, a luſty Mulatto Fellow named ARGYLE, well known about the Country, has a Scar on one of his Wriſts, and has loſt one or more of his fore Teeth; he is a very handy Fellow by Water, or about the Houſe, &c. loves Drink, and is very bold in his Cups, but daſtardly when ſober. Whether he will go for a Man of War's Man, or not, I cannot ſay; but I will give 40 s. to have him brought to me. He can read and write.

NOVEMBER 2, 1775. JACOB WRAY.

An advertisement for a runaway slave suspected of joining Lord Dunmore—a common sight in Virginia and Maryland newspapers during the fall and winter of 1775 and 1776. Virginia State Library.

economy by depriving white Americans of their labor force. But fewer blacks than expected rallied to the British standard in 1775 and 1776 (there were at most two thousand). Many of those who did perished in a smallpox epidemic that raged through the naval vessels housing them in Norfolk harbor. Even so, Dunmore's proclamation led Congress in January 1776 to modify its previous policy prohibiting the enlistment of blacks in the Continental Army (the first New England black patriots served only in local militias).

Though black Americans did not pose a serious threat to the revolutionary cause in its early years, the patriots managed to turn rumors of slave uprisings to their own advantage. In South Carolina in particular, they won adherents by promoting white unity under the revolutionary banner. The Continental Association was needed, they argued, to protect whites from blacks at a time when the royal government was unable to muster adequate defense forces. Undoubtedly many wavering Carolinians were drawn into the revolutionary camp by fear that an overt division among the colony's whites would encourage a slave revolt.

A similar factor—the threat of Indian attacks—helped to persuade some reluctant westerners to support the struggle against Great Britain. In the years since the Proclamation of 1763, British officials had won the trust and respect of the interior tribes by attempting to protect them from land-hungry whites. The British-appointed superintendents

Indian Neutrality

of Indian affairs, John Stuart in the South and Sir William Johnson in the North, lived among and sympathized with the Indians. In 1768, Stuart and Johnson negotiated separate agreements modifying the proclamation line and attempting to draw realistic defensible boundaries between tribal holdings and white settlements. The two treaties—signed respectively at Hard Labor Creek, South Carolina, in October and at Fort Stanwix, New York, in November—supposedly established permanent borders for the colonies. But just a few years later, in the treaties of Lochaber (1770) and Augusta (1773), the British pushed the southern boundary even farther west to accommodate the demands of whites in western Georgia and Kentucky.

By the time of the Revolution, the Indians were impatient with white Americans' aggressive pressure on their lands. The relationship of the tribes and frontier whites was filled with acrimony, misunderstanding, and occasional bloody encounters. In combination with the tribes' confidence in Stuart and Johnson, such grievances predisposed most Indians toward an alliance with the British. Even so, the latter hesitated to make full and immediate use of their potential Indian allies. The superintendents were well aware that the tribes might prove a liability, since their aims and style of fighting were not necessarily compatible with those of the British. Accordingly, John Stuart and Guy Johnson (who became northern superintendent following his uncle's death) sought nothing more from the tribes than a promise of neutrality. The superintendents even helped to prevent a general Indian uprising in the summer of 1774. Through clever maneuvering they ensured that the Shawnee attracted few Indian allies for an attack on frontier villages in Kentucky. Lord Dunmore's War, between the Shawnee and the Virginia militia, ended with Kentucky being opened to white settlement but with hunting and fishing rights still being reserved to the Shawnee.

The patriots, recognizing that their standing with the tribes was poor, also sought the Indians' neutrality. In 1775 the Second Continental Congress sent a general message to the tribes describing the war as "a family quarrel between us and Old England" and requesting that they "not join on either side," since "you Indians are not concerned in it." A branch of the Cherokee tribe, led by Chief Dragging Canoe, nevertheless decided that the whites' "family quarrel" would allow them to settle some old scores. They attacked white settlements along the western borders of the Carolinas and Virginia in the summer of 1776. But a coordinated campaign by Carolina and Virginia militia destroyed many Cherokee towns, along with crops and large quantities of supplies. Dragging Canoe and his diehard followers fled west to the Tennessee River, where they established new outposts, while the rest of the Cherokee agreed to a treaty that ceded more of their land to the whites.

The fate of the Shawnee and Cherokee—each forced to fight alone without other Indian allies, and more easily defeated as a result—foreshadowed much of the history of Indian involvement in the American Revolution. During the eighteenth century the Iroquois had forcefully established their dominance over neighboring tribes. But the basis of their power had started to disintegrate with the British victory over France in 1763, and their subsequent friendship with Sir William Johnson could not prevent the erosion of their position during the years before 1775. Tribes long resentful of Iroquois power (and of the similar status of the Cherokee in the South) saw little reason to ally themselves with those from whose dominance they had just escaped, even to achieve the goal of preventing white encroachment on their lands. Consequently, during the Revolution most tribes pursued a course that aligned them with neither side, but which (as the American leaders wanted) for the most part kept them out of active involvement in the war.

Thus, although the patriots could never completely ignore the threats posed by loyalists, blacks, neutrals, and Indians, only rarely did fear of these groups seriously hamper the revolutionary movement. Occasionally frontier militia refused to turn out for duty on the seaboard because they feared Indians would attack in their absence. Sometimes southern troops refused to serve in the North because they (and their political leaders) were unwilling to leave the South unprotected against a slave insurrection. But the practical impossibility of a large-scale slave revolt, coupled with tribal feuds and the patriots' successful campaign to disarm and neutralize loyalists, ensured that the revolutionaries would remain firmly in control as they fought for independence.

WAR BEGINS

On January 27, 1775, the secretary of state for America, Lord Dartmouth, addressed a fateful letter to General Thomas Gage in Boston. Expressing his belief that American resistance was nothing more than the response of a "rude rabble without plan," Dartmouth ordered Gage to arrest "the principal actors and abettors in the provincial congress." If such a step were taken swiftly and silently, Dartmouth observed, no bloodshed need occur. Opposition could not be "very formidable," Dartmouth wrote, and even if it were, "it will surely be better that the Conflict should be brought on, upon such ground, than in a riper state of Rebellion."

Because of poor sailing weather, Dartmouth's letter did not reach Gage until April 14. The major patriot leaders had by then already left Boston, and in any event Gage did not believe that arresting them would serve a useful purpose. The order nevertheless spurred him to action: he decided to send an expedition to confiscate provincial military supplies stockpiled at Concord. Bostonians dispatched two messengers, William Dawes and Paul Revere (later joined by a third, Dr. Samuel Prescott), to rouse the countryside. Thus when the

Battles of Lexington and Concord

British vanguard of several hundred men approached Lexington at dawn on April 19, they found a straggling group of seventy militiamen—approximately half the adult male population of the town—drawn up before them on the town common. The Americans' commander, Captain John Parker, ordered his men to withdraw, realizing that they were too few to halt the redcoat advance. But as they began to disperse, a shot rang out; the British soldiers then fired several volleys. When they stopped, eight Americans lay dead and another ten had been wounded. The British moved on to Concord, five miles away (see map).

There the contingents of militia were larger; the men of Concord had been joined by groups from Lincoln, Acton, and other nearby towns. The Americans allowed the British to enter Concord unopposed, but later in the morning they attacked the British infantry companies guarding the North Bridge. The brief exchange of gunfire there spilled the first British blood of the Revolution: three men were killed and nine (including four officers) wounded. On their retreat to Boston, the British were attacked by thousands of militiamen, firing from behind trees, bushes, and houses along the road. By the end of the day, the redcoats had suffered 272 casualties, 70 of whom were dead. Only the arrival of reinforcements from the city and the militia's lack of coordination prevented much heavier British losses. The patriots suffered just 93 casualties.

By the evening of April 20, perhaps as many as twenty thousand American militiamen had gathered around Boston, summoned by local committees that spread the alarm across the New England countryside. Many did not stay long, since they were needed at home for spring planting, but those who remained dug in along siege lines encircling the city. For nearly a year the two armies sat and stared at each other across those lines. During that period the redcoats attacked their besiegers only once, on June 17, when they drove the Americans from trenches atop Breed's Hill in Charlestown. In that misnamed Battle of Bunker Hill, the British incurred their greatest losses of the entire war: over 800 wounded and 228 killed. The Americans, though forced to abandon their position, lost fewer than half that number. During the same eleven-month period, the patriots captured Fort Ticonderoga, a British post on Lake Champlain, acquiring much-needed cannon. In the hope of bringing

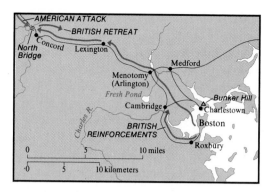

Lexington and Concord, April 19, 1775

Canada into the war on the American side, they also mounted an uncoordinated northern campaign that ended in disaster at Quebec in early 1776. But the chief significance of the first year of the war lay in the long lull in fighting between the main armies at Boston. The delay gave both sides a chance to regroup, organize, and plan their strategies.

Lord North and his new American secretary, Lord George Germain, made three major assumptions about the war they faced. First, they concluded that patriot forces could not withstand the assaults of trained British regulars. They and their generals were convinced that the campaign of 1776 would be the first and last of the war. Accordingly, they dispatched to America the largest single force Great Britain had ever assembled anywhere: 370 transport ships carrying 32,000 troops and tons of supplies, accompanied by 73 naval vessels and 13,000 sailors. Such an extraordinary effort would, they thought, ensure a quick victory. (Among the troops were thousands of mercenaries from the German state of Hesse; eighteenth-century armies were largely composed of such professional soldiers who hired out to the highest bidder.)

Second, British officials and army officers persisted in comparing this war to wars they had fought successfully in Europe. Thus they adopted a conventional strategy of capturing major American cities and defeating the rebel army decisively without suffering serious casualties themselves. Third, they assumed that a clear-cut military victory would automatically bring about their goal of retaining the colonies' allegiance.

British Strategy

All these assumptions proved false. North and Germain, like Lord Dartmouth before them, vastly underestimated the Americans' commitment to armed resistance. Defeats on the battlefield did not lead the patriots to abandon their political aims and sue for peace. The ministers also failed to recognize the significance of the American population's dispersal over an area 1,500 miles long and more than 100 miles wide. Although at one time or another during the war the British would control each of the most important American ports, less than 5 percent of the population lived in those cities. And the coast offered so many excellent harbors that essential commerce was easily rerouted. In other words, the loss of the cities did little to damage the American cause, while the desire for such ports repeatedly led redcoat generals astray.

Most of all, the British did not at first understand that a military victory would not necessarily bring about a political victory. Securing the colonies permanently would require hundreds of thousands of Americans to return to their original allegiance. The conquest of America was thus a far more complicated task than the defeat of France twelve years earlier. The British needed not only to overpower the patriots, but also to convert them. After 1778, they adopted a strategy designed to achieve that goal through the expanded use of loyalist forces and the restoration of civilian authority in occupied areas. But the new policy came too late. The British never fully realized that they were not fighting a conventional European war at all, but rather an entirely new kind of conflict: the first modern war of national liberation.

The British at least had a bureaucracy ready to supervise the war effort. The Americans had only the Second Continental Congress, originally intended merely as a brief gathering of colonial representatives to consider the British response to the Continental Association. Instead, the delegates who convened in Philadelphia on May 10, 1775, found that they had to assume the mantle of intercolonial government. "Such a vast Multitude of objects, civil, political, commercial and military, press and crowd upon us so fast, that we know not what to do first," John Adams wrote a close friend early in the session. Yet as the summer passed, the congress slowly organized the colonies for war. It

Second Continental Congress

authorized the printing of money with which to purchase necessary goods, established a committee to supervise relations with foreign countries, and took steps to strengthen the militia. Most important of all, it created the Continental Army and appointed its generals.

Until the congress met, the Massachusetts provincial congress had taken responsibility for organizing the massive army of militia encamped at Boston. But that army, composed of men from all the New England states, was a heavy drain on limited local resources. Consequently, on May 16 Massachusetts asked the Continental Congress to assume the task of directing the army. First, congress had to choose a commander-in-chief. Since the war had thus far been a wholly northern affair, many delegates recognized the importance of naming a non–New Englander to command the army. There seemed only one obvious candidate: they unanimously selected their fellow delegate, the Virginian George Washington.

Washington was no fiery radical, nor was he a reflective political thinker. He had not played a prominent role in the prerevolutionary agitation, but his devotion to the American cause was unquestioned. He was dignified, conservative, respectable, and a man of unimpeachable integrity. The younger son of a Virginia planter, Washington had not expected to inherit substantial property and had planned to make his living as a surveyor. But the early death of an older brother and his marriage to the wealthy widow Martha Custis had made him a rich man. Though unmistakably an aristocrat, Washington was unswervingly committed to representative government. And he had other desirable traits as well. His stamina was remarkable: in more than eight years of war Washington never had a serious illness and took only one brief leave of absence. Moreover, he both looked and acted like a leader. Six feet tall in an era when most men were five inches shorter, his presence was stately and commanding. Other patriots praised his judgment, steadiness, and discretion, and even a loyalist admitted that Washington could "atone for many demerits by the extraordinary coolness and caution which distinguish his character."

Washington needed all the coolness and caution he could muster when he took command of the army

George Washington: A Portrait of Leadership

outside Boston in July 1775. It took him months to impose hierarchy and discipline on the unruly troops and to bring order to the supply system. But by March 1776, when the arrival of cannon from Ticonderoga enabled him at last to put direct pressure on the redcoats in the city, the army was prepared to act. As it happened, an assault on Boston proved unnecessary. Sir William Howe, who had replaced Gage, had been considering an evacuation for some time; he wanted to transfer his troops to New York City. The patriots' bombardment of Boston early in the month decided the matter. On March 17, the British and more than a thousand of their loyalist allies abandoned Boston forever.

That spring of 1776, as the British fleet left Boston for the temporary haven of Halifax, Nova Scotia, the colonies were moving inexorably toward the act the Massachusetts loyalists on board the ships feared most: a declaration of independence. Even months after fighting had begun, American leaders still denied they sought a break with the empire. Then in January 1776 there appeared a pamphlet by a man who not only thought the unthinkable but advocated it.

Thomas Paine's *Common Sense* exploded on the American scene like a bombshell. Within three months of publication, it sold 120,000 copies. The author, a radical English printer who had lived in America only since 1774, called stridently and stirringly for independence. More than that: Paine challenged many common American assumptions about government and the colonies' relationship to England. Rejecting the notion that a balance of monarchy, aristocracy, and democracy was necessary to preserve freedom, he advocated the establishment of a republic. Instead of acknowledging the benefits of a connection with the mother country, Paine insisted that Britain had exploited the colonies unmercifully. In place of the frequent assertion that an independent America would be weak and divided, he substituted an unlimited confidence in America's strength when freed from European control. These striking statements were clothed in equally striking prose. Scorning the polite, rational style of his classically educated predecessors, Paine adopted a furious, raging tone. Although a printed work, the pamphlet reflected the oral culture of ordinary folk. It was couched in everyday language

Thomas Paine's *Common Sense*

George Washington (1732–1799), painted in his uniform. His stalwart bearing, so vividly conveyed in this portrait, was one of his prime assets as a leader. Washington-Custis-Lee Collection, Washington and Lee University, Virginia.

and relied heavily on the Bible—the only book familiar to most Americans—as a primary source of authority. No wonder the pamphlet had a wider distribution than any other political publication of its day.

There is no way of knowing how many people were converted to the cause of independence by reading *Common Sense*. But by late spring 1776 independence had clearly become inevitable. On May 10, the Second Continental Congress formally recommended that individual colonies "adopt such governments as shall, in the opinion of the representatives of the people, best conduce to the happiness and safety of their constituents in particular, and America in general." From that source grew the first state constitutions. Perceiving the trend of events, the few loyalists still connected with the congress severed their ties to that body.

Then on June 7 came the confirmation of the movement toward independence. Richard Henry Lee

After listening to the first formal reading of the Declaration of Independence in New York City on July 9, 1776, a crowd of soldiers and civilians spontaneously pulled down a statue of George III that stood on the Bowling Green in the heart of the city. Most of the statue was later melted down and made into bullets, but some pieces of it were found a few years ago in Connecticut. Library of Congress.

of Virginia, seconded by John Adams of Massachusetts, introduced the crucial resolution: "that these United Colonies are, and of right ought to be, free and independent States, that they are absolved of all allegiance to the British Crown, and that all political connection between them and the State of Great Britain is, and ought to be, totally dissolved." The congress debated but did not immediately adopt Lee's resolution. Instead, it postponed a vote until early July, to allow time for consultation and public reaction. In the meantime, a committee composed of Thomas Jefferson, John Adams, Benjamin Franklin, Robert R. Livingston of New York, and Roger Sherman of Connecticut was directed to draft a declaration of independence.

Declaration of Independence

The committee in turn assigned primary responsibility for writing the declaration to Jefferson, who was well known for his apt and eloquent style. Years later John Adams recalled that Jefferson had modestly protested his selection, suggesting that Adams prepare the initial draft. The Massachusetts revolutionary recorded his frank response: "You can write ten times better than I can."

Thomas Jefferson was at the time thirty-four years old, a Virginia lawyer educated at the College of William and Mary and in the law offices of the prominent attorney George Wythe. He had read widely in history and political theory and had been a member of the House of Burgesses. His broad knowledge was evident not only in the declaration but also in his draft of the Virginia state constitution, completed just a few days before his appointment to the committee. Jefferson, an intensely private man, loved his home and family deeply. This early stage of his political career was marked by his beloved wife Martha's repeated difficulties in childbearing. While he wrote and debated in Philadelphia during the summer of 1776, she suffered a miscarriage at their home, Monticello. Not until after her death in 1782, from complications following the birth of their sixth (but only third surviving) child in ten years of marriage, did Jefferson fully commit himself to public service.

The draft of the declaration was laid before congress on June 28. The delegates officially voted for independence four days later, then debated the wording of the declaration for two more days, adopting it with some changes on July 4. Since Americans had long since ceased to see themselves as legitimate subjects of Parliament, the Declaration of Independence concentrated on George III (see Appendix). That focus also provided a single identifiable villain on whom to center the charges of misconduct. The document accused the king of attempting to destroy representative government in the colonies and of oppressing Americans through the unjustified use of excessive force. But the declaration's chief long-term importance did not lie in its lengthy catalogue of grievances against George III (including, in a section omitted by congress, Jefferson's charge that the British monarchy had introduced slavery into America). It lay instead in the ringing statements of principle that have served ever since as the ideal to which Americans aspire. "We hold these truths to be self-evident: That all men are created equal; that they are endowed by their Creator with certain unalienable rights; that among these are life, liberty and the pursuit of happiness; that, to secure these rights, governments are instituted among men, deriving their just powers from the consent of the governed; that whenever any form of government becomes destructive of these ends, it is the right of the people to alter or to abolish it, and to institute new government." These phrases have echoed down through American history like no others.

The delegates in Philadelphia who voted to accept the Declaration of Independence did not have the advantage of our two hundred years of hindsight. When they adopted the declaration, they risked their necks: they were committing treason. Thus when they concluded the declaration with the assertion that they "mutually pledge[d] to each other our lives, our fortunes, and our sacred honor," they spoke no less than the truth. The real struggle still lay before them, and few of them had Thomas Paine's boundless confidence in success.

THE LONG STRUGGLE IN THE NORTH

In late June 1776, the first of the ships carrying Sir William Howe's troops from Halifax appeared off the coast of New York. On July 2, the day the congress voted for independence, the redcoats landed on Staten Island. But Howe waited until mid-August, after the arrival of troop transports from England, to begin his attack on the city. The delay gave Washington sufficient time to march his army south to meet the threat. To defend New York, Washington had approximately seventeen thousand soldiers: ten thousand Continentals who had promised to serve until the end of the year, and seven thousand militiamen who had enlisted for shorter terms. Neither he nor most of his men had ever fought a major battle against the British, and their lack of experience led to disastrous mistakes. The difficulty of defending New York City only compounded the errors.

Battle for New York City

Washington's problem was as simple as the geography of the region was complex (see map, page 142). To protect the city adequately, he would have to divide his forces among Long Island, Manhattan Island, and the mainland. But the British fleet under Admiral Lord Richard Howe, Sir William's brother, controlled the harbors and rivers that separated the American forces. The patriots thus constantly courted catastrophe, for swift action by the British navy could cut off the possibility of retreat and perhaps even communication. But despite these dangers, Washington could not afford to surrender New York to the Howes without a fight. Not only did the city occupy a strategic location, but the region that surrounded it was known to contain many loyalist sympathizers. A show of force was essential if the revolutionaries were to retain any hope of persuading waverers to join them.

On August 27, Sir William Howe's forces attacked the American positions on Brooklyn Heights, pushing the untried rebel troops back into their defensive entrenchments. But he failed to press his advantage, even neglecting to send his brother's ships into the

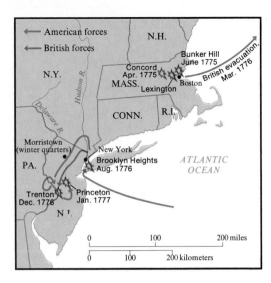

The War in the North, 1775–1777

East River to cut off a retreat. Consequently, the Americans were able to escape; a troop of Marblehead fishermen ferried nine thousand men to the southern tip of Manhattan Island in less than twelve hours on the night of August 29. Washington then moved north along the island, retreating onto the mainland but leaving behind nearly three thousand men in the supposedly impregnable Fort Washington on the west shore of Manhattan. Howe slowly followed him into Westchester County, then turned back to focus his attention on the fort. Its defenses collapsed, and the large garrison surrendered in early November. Only when Charleston fell to the British in May 1780 did the Americans lose more men on a single occasion.

George Washington had defended New York, but he had done a bad job of it. He had repeatedly broken a basic rule of military strategy: never divide your force in the face of a superior enemy. In the end, though, the Howe brothers' failure to move quickly prevented a decisive defeat of the Americans. Although Washington's army had been seriously reduced by battlefield casualties, the surrender of Fort Washington, and the loss of most of the militiamen (who had returned home for the harvest), its core remained. Through November and December, Washington led his men in a retreat across New Jersey. Howe followed at a leisurely pace, setting up a string of outposts manned mostly by Hessian mercenaries. After Washington crossed the Delaware River into Pennsylvania,

the British commander turned back and settled into comfortable winter quarters in New York City.

The British now controlled most of New Jersey. Hundreds of Americans accepted the pardons offered by the Howes. Among them were Joseph Galloway, a delegate to the First Continental Congress, and Richard Stockton, a signer of the Declaration of Independence. Occupying troops met little opposition, and the Revolutionary cause appeared to be in disarray. "These are the times that try men's souls," wrote Thomas Paine in his pamphlet *The Crisis*. "The summer soldier and the sunshine patriot will, in this crisis, shrink from the service of his country; . . . yet we have this consolation with us, that the harder the conflict, the more glorious the triumph."

In the aftermath of battle, as at its height, the British generals let their advantage slip away. The redcoats stationed in New Jersey went on a rampage of rape and plunder. Because loyalists and patriots were indistinguishable to the British and Hessian troops, families on both sides suffered nearly equally. Livestock, crops, and firewood were seized for use by the army. Houses were looted and burned, churches and public buildings desecrated. But nothing was better calculated to rally doubtful Americans to the cause of independence than the wanton murder of innocent civilians and rape of women.

The soldiers' marauding alienated potentially loyal New Jerseyites and Pennsylvanians whose allegiance the British could ill afford to lose. It also spurred Washington's determination to strike back. The enlistments of most of the Continental troops were to expire on December 31, and Washington also wanted to take advantage of short-term Pennsylvania militia who had recently joined him. He moved quickly and attacked the Hessian encampment at Trenton early in the morning of December 26, while the redcoats were still reeling from their Christmas celebration. The patriots captured more than nine hundred Hessians and killed another thirty; only three Americans were wounded. A few days later, after persuading many of his men to stay on beyond the term of their enlistments, Washington attacked again at Princeton. Having gained command of the field and buoyed American spirits with the two swift victories, Washington set up winter quarters at Morristown, New Jersey.

Battle of Trenton

Chapter 5: A Revolution, Indeed, 1775–1783

Jean Baptiste Antoine de Verger, a sublieutenant in the French army in America, painted this watercolor of revolutionary soldiers in his journal. They are, left to right, a black light infantryman, a musketman, a rifleman, and an artilleryman. Brown University Library.

The campaign of 1776 established patterns that were to persist throughout much of the war, despite changes in British leadership and strategy. British forces were usually more numerous and often better led than the Americans. But their ponderous style of maneuvering, lack of familiarity with the terrain, and inability to live off the land without antagonizing the populace helped to offset those advantages. Furthermore, although Washington always seemed to lack regular troops—the Continental Army never numbered more than 18,500 men—he could usually count on the militia to join him at crucial times. American militiamen did not like to sign up for long terms of service or to fight far from home, but when their homes were threatened they would rally to the cause. Washington and his officers frequently complained about the militia's habit of disappearing during planting or harvesting. But time and again their presence, however brief, enabled the Americans to launch an attack or counter an important British thrust.

As the war dragged on, the Continental Army and the militia took on decidedly different characters. State governments, responsible for filling military quotas, discovered that most men willing to enlist for long periods in the regular army were young, single, and footloose. Farmers with families tended to prefer short-term militia duty. As the supply of whites willing to sign up for the Continentals diminished, recruiters in the northern states turned increasingly to blacks, both slave and free. (White southerners continued to resist this approach.) Perhaps as many as five thousand blacks eventually served in the Revolutionary army, and most of them won their freedom as a result. They commonly served in racially integrated units, often being assigned tasks that whites wanted to avoid (such as cooking, foraging for food, or driving wagons).

Also attached to the American forces were a number of women, mostly wives and widows of poor soldiers. Such camp followers worked as cooks, nurses, and launderers, performing vital services for the army in return for rations and low wages. The presence of the women, as well as the militiamen who floated in and out of the American camp at irregular intervals, made for an unwieldy army that its officers found difficult to manage. Yet the army's shapelessness also reflected its greatest strength: an almost unlimited reservoir of man and woman power.

Deborah Sampson (1760–1827), who disguised herself as a man and enlisted in the Continental Army as Robert Shurtleff. She served from May 1782 to October 1783, when her sex was discovered and she was discharged. In later years she gave public lectures describing her wartime experiences. After her death her husband became the only man to receive a pension as the "widow" of a revolutionary soldier. Courtesy of the Rhode Island Historical Society.

In 1777, the chief British effort was planned by the flashy "Gentleman Johnny" Burgoyne, a playboy general as much at home at the gaming tables of London as on the battlefield. Burgoyne, a subordinate of Howe, had spent the winter of 1776 to 1777 in London, where he gained the ear of Lord George Germain. Burgoyne convinced Germain that he could lead an invading force of redcoats and Indians down the Hudson River from Canada, cutting off New England from the rest of the states. He proposed to rendezvous near Albany with a similar force that would move east from Niagara along the Mohawk River valley. The combined force would then pre-

sumably link up with that of Sir William Howe in New York City.

That Burgoyne's scheme would give "Gentleman Johnny" all the glory and relegate Howe to a supporting role did not escape the latter's notice. While Burgoyne was plotting in London, Howe was laying his own plans in New York City. Joseph Galloway and other Pennsylvania loyalists persuaded Howe that Philadelphia could be taken easily and that his troops would be welcomed by many residents of the region. Just as Burgoyne left Howe out of his plans, Howe left Burgoyne out of his. Thus the two major British armies in America would operate independently in 1777, and the result would be a disaster (see map).

Howe accomplished his objective: he captured Philadelphia. But he did so in an inexplicable fashion, delaying for months before beginning the campaign,

Howe Takes Philadelphia

then taking six weeks to transport his troops by sea to the head of Chesapeake Bay instead of marching them overland. That maneuver cost him at least a month, debilitated his men, and depleted his supplies. Incredibly, he was only forty miles closer to Philadelphia at the end of the lengthy voyage than when he started. Two years later, when Parliament formally inquired into the conduct of the war, Howe's critics charged that his errors were so extraordinary he must have deliberately committed treason. Even today, historians have not been able to explain his motives adequately. In any event, by the time Howe was ready to move on Philadelphia, Washington had had time to prepare its defenses. Twice, at Brandywine Creek and again at Germantown, the two armies clashed near the rebel capital. Though the British won both engagements, the Americans handled themselves well. The redcoats took Philadelphia in late September, but to little effect. The campaign season was nearly over; the Revolutionary army had gained confidence in itself and its leaders; few welcoming loyalists had materialized; and, far to the north, Burgoyne was going down to defeat.

Burgoyne and his men had set out from Montreal in mid-June, floating down Lake Champlain into New York in canoes and flat-bottomed boats. In early June they had easily taken Fort Ticonderoga from its outnumbered and outgunned defenders. But trouble

Burgoyne's Campaign in New York

began as Burgoyne started his overland march. His clumsy artillery carriages and baggage wagons foundered in the heavy forests and ravines. Patriot militia felled giant trees across the army's path. As a result, Burgoyne's troops took twenty-four days to travel the twenty-three miles to Fort Edward, on the Hudson River. Short of supplies, the general dispatched eight hundred German mercenaries to forage the countryside. On August 16, American militia companies nearly wiped out the Germans near Bennington. Yet Burgoyne failed to recognize the seriousness of his predicament and continued to dawdle, giving the Americans more than enough time to prepare for his coming. By the time he finally crossed the Hudson in mid-September, bound for Albany, Burgoyne's fate was sealed. After several bloody clashes with the American force commanded by Horatio Gates, Burgoyne was surrounded near Saratoga, New York. On October 17, 1777, he surrendered his entire force of more than six thousand men.

Long before, the 1,400 redcoats and Indians marching along the Mohawk River toward Albany had also been turned back. Under the command of Colonel Barry St. Leger, they had advanced easily until they reached the isolated American outpost at Fort Stanwix in early August. After they had laid siege to the well-fortified structure, they learned that a patriot relief column was en route to the fort. Leaving only a small detachment at Fort Stanwix, the British ambushed the Americans at Oriskany on August 6. The British claimed victory in the ensuing battle, one of the bloodiest of the war, but they and their Indian allies lost their taste for further fighting. The Americans tricked them into believing that another large patriot force was on the way, and in late August the British abandoned the siege and returned to Niagara.

The battle of Oriskany marked a split of the Iroquois Confederacy. In 1776 the Six Nations had formally pledged to remain neutral in the Anglo-American struggle. But two influential Mohawk leaders, Joseph and Mary Brant, worked tirelessly to persuade their fellow Iroquois to join the British. Mary Brant, a powerful tribal matron, was also the widow of the respected Indian

Split of the Iroquois Confederacy

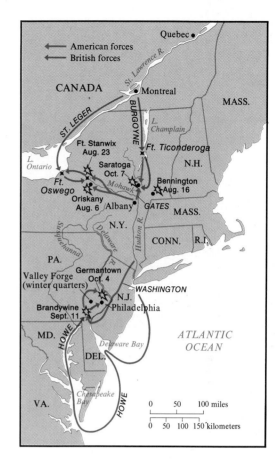

Campaign of 1777

superintendent Sir William Johnson. Her younger brother Joseph, a renowned warrior, was convinced that the Six Nations should ally themselves with the British in order to prevent American encroachment on their lands. As an observer said of Mary, "one word from her goes farther with them [the Iroquois] than a thousand from any white man without exception." The Brants won over to the British the Seneca, Cayuga, and Mohawk, all of whom contributed warriors to St. Leger's expedition. But the Oneida preferred the American side, bringing the Tuscarora with them. (The remaining Iroquois tribe, the Onondaga, split into three factions, one on each side and one supporting neutrality.) At Oriskany, some Oneidas and Tuscaroras joined the patriot militia to fight their Iroquois brethren; thus a league of friendship that had survived over three hundred years was torn apart by the whites' family quarrel.

The Mohawk chief Joseph Brant (1742–1807), painted in London in 1786 by Gilbert Stuart. New York State Historical Association, Cooperstown.

The collapse of Iroquois unity and the confederacy's abandonment of neutrality had important consequences for both whites and Indians in subsequent years. In 1778, Iroquois warriors allied with the British raided the New York frontier villages of Wyoming and Cherry Valley; to retaliate, in the late summer of 1779 the whites dispatched an expedition under General John Sullivan to burn Iroquois crops, orchards, and settlements. The destruction was so thorough that many bands had to leave their ancestral homeland to seek food and shelter with the British north of the Great Lakes during the winter of 1779 to 1780. A large number of Iroquois people never returned to New York, but settled permanently in British Canada.

For the Indians, Oriskany was the most significant battle of the northern campaign; for the whites, it was Saratoga. The news of Burgoyne's surrender brought joy to patriots, discouragement to loyalists and Britons. In exile in London, Thomas Hutchinson wrote of the "universal dejection" among loyalists there. "Everybody in a gloom," he commented; "most of us expect to lay our bones here." The disaster prompted Lord North to authorize a peace commission to offer the Americans everything they had requested in 1774—in effect, a return to the imperial system of 1763. It was, of course, far too late for that: the patriots rejected the overture and the peace commission sailed back to England empty-handed in mid-1778.

Most important of all, the American victory at Saratoga drew France formally into the conflict. Ever since 1763, the French had sought to avenge their defeat in the French and Indian War, and the American Revolution provided them with that opportunity. Even before Benjamin Franklin arrived in Paris in late 1776, France was covertly supplying the revolutionaries with military necessities. Indeed, 90 percent of the gunpowder the Americans used in the first two years of the war came from France.

The Franco-American Alliance of 1778

Franklin worked tirelessly to strengthen the ties between the two nations. Although he was not a Quaker, he deliberately affected a plain style of dress that made him stand out amid the luxury of the court of King Louis XVI. He cleverly presented himself as a representative of American simplicity, playing on the French image of Americans as virtuous yeomen. Franklin's efforts culminated in February 1778 when the countries signed two treaties. In the first, France recognized American independence; the second provided for a formal alliance between the two nations until the war was won. The most visible symbol of Franco-American cooperation in the years that followed was the Marquis de Lafayette, a young nobleman whose father had been killed by the British in King George's War. He volunteered for service with George Washington in 1777 and fought with the American forces until the conflict ended.

The French alliance had two major benefits for the patriot cause. First, France began to aid the Americans openly, sending troops and naval vessels in addition to supplies of arms, ammunition, clothing, and blankets. Second, the British could no longer focus their attention on the American mainland alone, for they had to fight the French in the West Indies and elsewhere. Spain's entry into the war in 1779 as an ally of France (but not the United States) further magnified Britain's problems. Throughout the war, French assistance was important to the Americans, but in the last years of the conflict that aid was especially vital.

Chapter 5: A Revolution, Indeed, 1775–1783

THE LONG STRUGGLE
IN THE SOUTH

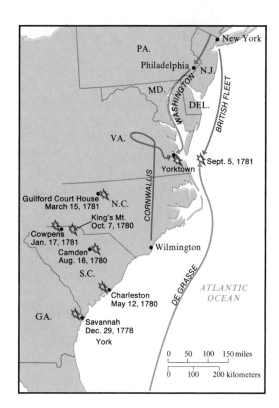

The War in the South

In the aftermath of the Saratoga disaster, Lord George Germain and the military officials in London reassessed their strategy. Maneuvering in the North had done them little good; perhaps shifting the field of battle southward would bring success. The many loyalist exiles in England encouraged this line of thinking. They argued that loyal southerners would welcome the redcoat army as liberators, and that once the region had been pacified and returned to civilian control it could serve as a base for attacking the North.

In early 1778 Sir William Howe was replaced by Sir Henry Clinton. As commander-in-chief, Clinton was also afflicted with sluggishness and lack of resolution. Still, he oversaw the regrouping of British forces in America, ordering the evacuation of Philadelphia in June 1778 and dispatching a small expedition to Georgia at the end of the year. When Savannah and then Augusta fell easily into British hands, Clinton became convinced that a southern strategy would work. In late 1779 he sailed down the coast with 8,500 troops to attack Charleston, the most important American city in the South (see map).

Although the Americans worked hard to bolster Charleston's defenses, the city fell to the British on May 12, 1780. General Benjamin Lincoln surrendered the entire southern army—5,500 **Fall of** men—to the invaders. In the weeks **Charleston** that followed, the redcoats spread through South Carolina, establishing garrisons at key points in the interior. As in New Jersey in 1776, hundreds of South Carolinians renounced allegiance to the United States and proclaimed their loyalty to the crown. Clinton organized loyalist regiments and the process of pacification began.

Yet the British triumph was less complete and secure than it appeared. The success of the southern campaign depended on British control of the seas, for only by sea could the widely dispersed British armies remain in communication with one another.

For the moment the Royal Navy safely dominated the American coastline, but French naval power posed a threat to the entire southern enterprise. Moreover, the redcoats never managed to establish full control of the areas they seized. As a result, patriot bands operated freely throughout the state, and loyalists could not be guaranteed protection against their enemies. Last but not least, the fall of Charleston did not dishearten the patriots; instead, it spurred them to greater exertions. As one Marylander declared confidently, "The Fate of America is not to be decided by the Loss of a Town or Two." Patriot women in four states formed the Ladies Association, which collected money to purchase shirts for needy soldiers. Recruiting efforts were stepped up.

Throughout most of 1780, though, the war in South Carolina went badly for the patriots. In August, a reorganized southern army under the command of Horatio Gates was crushingly defeated at Camden by the forces of Lord Cornwallis, who had been placed in charge of the southern campaign. The British army was joined wherever it went by hundreds, even thousands, of blacks seeking freedom on the basis of

Lord Dunmore's proclamation. Slaves ran away from their patriot masters individually and as families, in such numbers that they seriously disrupted planting and harvesting in 1780 and 1781. More than fifty-five thousand blacks were lost to their owners as a result of the war. Not all of them joined the British or won their freedom if they did, but their flight had just the effect Dunmore wanted. Many served the British well as scouts, guides, and laborers.

After the defeat at Camden, Washington (who had to remain in the North to oppose the British army occupying New York) gave command of the southern campaign to General Na-

Greene Rallies South Carolina thanael Greene of Rhode Island. Greene was appalled by what he found in South Carolina. As he wrote to a friend, "the word difficulty when applied to the state of things here . . . is almost without meaning, it falls so far short" of reality. His troops needed clothing, blankets, and food, but "a great part of this country is already laid waste and in the utmost danger of becoming a desert." The constant guerrilla warfare had, he commented, "so corrupted the principles of the people that they think of nothing but plundering one another." Under such circumstances, Greene had to move cautiously. He adopted a conciliatory policy toward loyalists and neutrals, persuading the governor of South Carolina to offer complete pardons to those who had fought for the British if they would join the patriot militia. He also ordered his troops not to loot loyalist property and to treat captives fairly. Greene recognized that the patriots could win only by convincing the people that they could bring stability to the region. He thus helped the shattered provincial congresses of Georgia and South Carolina to begin re-establishing civilian authority in the interior—a goal the British were never able to accomplish, even along the coast.

Greene also took a conciliatory approach to the southern Indians. With his desperate need for soldiers, he could not afford to have frontier militia companies occupied in defending their homes against Indian attacks. Since he had so few regulars (only 1,600 when he took command), Greene had to rely on western volunteers. Therefore, he negotiated with the Indians.

His policy eventually met with success, although at first royal officials cooperating with the British invasion forces won allies among a number of southern tribes, especially Dragging Canoe's Cherokee band. But the southern Indians, recalling the disastrous defeat the Cherokee had suffered in 1776, never committed themselves wholeheartedly to the British. In 1781 the Cherokee began negotiations with the patriots, and the next year the other tribes too sued for peace. By the end of the war only the Creek remained allied to the redcoats. A group of Chickasaw chiefs explained their reasoning to American agents in July 1782, after Greene's battlefield successes had forced the British to withdraw into Savannah and Charleston: "The English put the Bloody Tomahawk into our hands, telling us that we should have no Goods if we did not Exert ourselves to the greatest point of Resentment against you, but now we find our mistake and Distresses. The English have done their utmost and left us in our adversity. We find them full of Deceit and Dissimulation."

Even before Greene took command of the southern army in December 1780, the tide had begun to turn. At King's Mountain in October, a force of "over-mountain men" from the settlements west of the Appalachians had defeated a large party of redcoats and loyalists. Then in January 1781 Greene's trusted aide, Brigadier General Daniel Morgan, brilliantly defeated the crack British regiment Tarleton's Legion at Cowpens, near the border between North and South Carolina. Greene himself confronted the main body of British troops under Lord Cornwallis at Guilford Court House, North Carolina, in March. Cornwallis controlled the field at the end of the day, but his army had been largely destroyed. He had to retreat to Wilmington, on the coast, to receive supplies and fresh troops from New York by sea. In the meantime Greene returned to South Carolina, where, in a series of swift strikes, he forced the redcoats to abandon their posts in the interior and quickly retire to Charleston.

Cornwallis had already ignored explicit orders not to leave South Carolina unless the state was safely in British hands. Evidently bent on his own destruc-

Surrender at Yorktown tion, he now headed north into Virginia, where he joined forces with a detachment of redcoats commanded by the American traitor Benedict Arnold. (Arnold had fought heroically with the patriots early in the war, but defected to the

In 1781 Charles Willson Peale traveled to Yorktown to commemorate the great victory by the combined American and French forces. That he was present in the immediate aftermath of the battle is indicated by his portrayal of sunken ships in the river and dead horses on the beach. On the right stands Washington with (from left to right) the Marquis de Lafayette, Count Rochambeau, and Tench Tilghman, one of Washington's aides. Maryland Historical Society.

British in 1780 in the belief that the Americans did not fully appreciate him.) Instead of acting decisively with his new army of 7,200 men, Cornwallis withdrew to the tip of the peninsula between the York and James rivers, where he fortified Yorktown and in effect waited for the end. Seizing the opportunity, Washington quickly moved over seven thousand troops south from New York City. When a French fleet under the Comte de Grasse arrived from the West Indies in time to defeat the Royal Navy vessels sent to rescue Cornwallis, the British general was trapped (see map, page 147). On October 19, 1781, four years and two days after Burgoyne's defeat at Saratoga, Cornwallis surrendered to the combined American and French forces while his military band played "The World Turned Upside Down."

When news of the surrender reached England,

Lord North's ministry fell. Parliament voted to cease offensive operations in America and authorized peace negotiations. But guerrilla warfare between patriots and loyalists continued to ravage the Carolinas and Georgia for more than a year, and in the North vicious retaliatory raids by Indians and whites kept the frontier aflame. Indeed, the single most brutal massacre of the war occurred in March 1782, at Gnadenhuetten in the Ohio country. A group of white militiamen, seeking the Indians who had killed a frontier family, encountered a peaceful band of Delawares. The Indians, who had been converted to both Christianity and pacifism by Moravian missionaries, were slaughtered unmercifully. Ninety-six men, women, and children died that day, some burned at the stake, others tomahawked. Two months later, hostile members of the Delaware tribe captured three

1774	First Continental Congress
1775	Battles of Lexington and Concord
	Lord Dunmore's Proclamation
	Second Continental Congress
1776	Thomas Paine, *Common Sense*
	British evacuate Boston
	Declaration of Independence
	New York campaign
1777	British take Philadelphia
	Burgoyne surrenders at Saratoga
1778	French alliance
	British evacuate Philadelphia
1779	Sullivan expedition against Iroquois
	villages
1780	British take Charleston
1781	Cornwallis surrenders at Yorktown
1782	Peace negotiations begin
1783	Treaty of Paris

white militiamen and subjected them to gruesome tortures in reprisal. The persistence of conflict between whites and Indians after Yorktown, all too often overlooked in accounts of the Revolution, serves to underline the degree to which the Indians were the real losers in the war initiated by whites.

The fighting finally ended when Americans and Britons learned of the signing of a preliminary peace treaty at Paris in November 1782. The American negotiators—Benjamin Franklin, **Treaty of Paris** John Jay, and John Adams—ignored their instructions to be guided by France and instead struck a separate agreement with Great Britain. Their instincts were sound: the French government was more an enemy to Britain than a friend to the United States. In fact, French ministers worked secretly behind the scenes to try to prevent the establishment of a strong, unified, independent

government in America. The new British ministry, headed by Lord Shelburne (formerly a persistent critic of Lord North's harsh American policies), was weary of war and made numerous concessions—so many, in fact, that Parliament ousted the ministry shortly after the peace terms were approved.

Under the treaty, signed formally on September 3, 1783, the Americans were granted unconditional independence and unlimited fishing rights off Newfoundland. The boundaries of the new nation were generous: to the north, approximately the current boundary with Canada; to the south, the thirty-first parallel; to the west, the Mississippi River. Florida, which the British had acquired in 1763, was returned to Spain. In ceding so much land unconditionally to the Americans, the British entirely ignored the territorial rights of their Indian allies. Once again, the tribes' interests were sacrificed to the demands of European power politics. Loyalists and British merchants were also poorly served by the British negotiators. The treaty's ambiguously worded clauses pertaining to the payment of prewar debts and the postwar treatment of loyalists caused trouble for years to come and proved impossible to enforce.

The long war finally over, the victorious Americans could look back on their achievement with satisfaction and awe. In 1775, with an inexperienced ragtag army, they had taken on the greatest military power in the world—and eight years later they had won. They had accomplished their goal more through persistence and commitment than through brilliance on the battlefield. Actual victories had been few, but their army had always survived defeat and stand-offs to fight again. Ultimately, the Americans had simply worn their enemy down.

SUGGESTIONS FOR FURTHER READING

General

Edward Countryman, *The American Revolution* (1985); Larry Gerlach, ed., *Legacies of the American Revolution* (1978); *Journal of Interdisciplinary History,* 6, No. 4 (spring 1976),

Interdisciplinary Studies of the American Revolution; Stephen G. Kurtz and James H. Hutson, eds., *Essays on the American Revolution* (1973); Library of Congress, *Symposia on the American Revolution*, 5 vols. (1972–1976); Edmund S. Morgan, *The Challenge of the American Revolution* (1976); *William and Mary Quarterly*, 3rd ser., 33, No. 3 (July 1976), *The American Revolution;* Alfred Young, ed., *The American Revolution: Explorations in the History of American Radicalism* (1976).

Military

John Richard Alden, *The American Revolution 1775–1783* (1964); John C. Dann, ed., *The Revolution Remembered: Eyewitness Accounts of the War for Independence* (1980); Ira Gruber, *The Howe Brothers and the American Revolution* (1972); Richard J. Hargrove, *General John Burgoyne* (1983); Don Higginbotham, *The War of American Independence: Military Attitudes, Policies, and Practice, 1763–1789* (1971); Ronald Hoffman and Peter Albert, eds., *Arms and Independence: The Military Character of the American Revolution* (1984); Piers Mackesy, *The War for America, 1775–1783* (1964); James K. Martin and Mark Lender, *A Respectable Army: The Military Origins of the Republic 1763–1789* (1982); Charles Royster, *A Revolutionary People at War: The Continental Army and American Character, 1775–1783* (1980); John Shy, *A People Numerous & Armed: Reflections on the Military Struggle for American Independence* (1976); William Willcox, *Portrait of a General: Sir Henry Clinton in the War of Independence* (1964).

Local and Regional

Richard V. W. Buel, *Dear Liberty: Connecticut's Mobilization for the Revolutionary War* (1980); Edward Countryman, *A People in Revolution: The American Revolution and Political Society in New York, 1760–1790* (1981); Jeffrey Crow and Larry Tise, eds., *The Southern Experience in the American Revolution* (1978); Robert A. Gross, *The Minutemen and Their World* (1976); Ronald Hoffman, *A Spirit of Dissension: Economics, Politics, and the Revolution in Maryland* (1973); Ronald Hoffman, Thad W. Tate, and Peter Albert, eds., *An Uncivil War: The Southern Backcountry During the American Revolution* (1985); Robert J. Taylor, *Western Massachusetts in the Revolution* (1954).

Indians and Blacks

Barbara Graymont, *The Iroquois in the American Revolution* (1972); Isabel T. Kelsey, *Joseph Brant, 1743–1807: Man of Two Worlds* (1984); Duncan J. MacLeod, *Slavery, Race, and the American Revolution* (1974); James H. O'Donnell, III, *Southern Indians in the American Revolution* (1973); Benjamin Quarles, *The Negro in the American Revolution* (1961); Anthony F. C. Wallace, *The Death and Rebirth of the Seneca* (1969).

Loyalists

Bernard Bailyn, *The Ordeal of Thomas Hutchinson* (1974); Robert McCluer Calhoon, *The Loyalists in Revolutionary America 1760–1781* (1973); William H. Nelson, *The American Tory* (1961); Mary Beth Norton, *The British-Americans: The Loyalist Exiles in England, 1774–1789* (1972); Paul H. Smith, *Loyalists and Redcoats: A Study in British Revolutionary Policy* (1964); James W. St. G. Walker, *The Black Loyalists: The Search for a Promised Land in Nova Scotia and Sierra Leone 1783–1870* (1976).

Women

Linda Grant DePauw and Conover Hunt, *"Remember the Ladies": Women in America 1750–1815* (1976); Linda K. Kerber, *Women of the Republic: Intellect & Ideology in Revolutionary America* (1980); Mary Beth Norton, "Eighteenth-Century American Women in Peace and War: The Case of the Loyalists," *William and Mary Quarterly*, 3rd ser., 33 (1976), 386–409; Mary Beth Norton, *Liberty's Daughters: The Revolutionary Experience of American Women, 1750–1800* (1980).

Foreign Policy

Samuel F. Bemis, *The Diplomacy of the American Revolution* (1935); Felix Gilbert, *To the Farewell Address* (1961); Ronald Hoffman and Peter Albert, eds., *Diplomacy and Revolution: The Franco-American Alliance of 1778* (1981); James H. Hutson, *John Adams and the Diplomacy of the American Revolution* (1980); Lawrence Kaplan, ed., *The American Revolution and a "Candid World"* (1977); Richard B. Morris, *The Peacemakers: The Great Powers and American Independence* (1965); Richard W. Van Alstyne, *Empire and Independence: The International History of the American Revolution* (1965).

Patriot Leaders

Fawn M. Brodie, *Thomas Jefferson: An Intimate History* (1974); Verner W. Crane, *Benjamin Franklin and a Rising People* (1954); Marcus Cunliffe, *George Washington: Man and Monument* (1958); James T. Flexner, *George Washington*, 4 vols. (1965–1972); Eric Foner, *Tom Paine and Revolutionary America* (1976); Claude A. Lopez and Eugenia Herbert, *The Private Franklin: The Man and His Family* (1975); Dumas Malone, *Jefferson and His Time*, 6 vols. (1948–1981); Peter Shaw, *The Character of John Adams* (1976); Garry Wills, *Inventing America: Jefferson's Declaration of Independence* (1977).

Forging a National Republic

1776–1789

Chapter 6

"*In the new* Code of Laws which I suppose it will be necessary for you to make I desire you would Remember the Ladies," Abigail Adams wrote her congressman husband John on March 31, 1776. "Remember all Men would be tyrants if they could," she continued. "If perticuliar care and attention is not paid to the Laidies we are determined to foment a Rebelion, and will not hold ourselves bound by any Laws in which we have no voice, or Representation."

With these words, Abigail Adams took a step that was soon to be duplicated by other disfranchised Americans. She deliberately employed the ideology that had been developed to combat Great Britain's claims to political supremacy, but applied it to purposes white male leaders had never intended. Since men were "Naturally Tyrannical," she argued, America's new legal code should "put it out of the power of the vicious and the Lawless to use us with cruelty and indignity." Thus she called for reformation of the American law of marriage, which made wives wholly subordinate to their husbands.

John Adams failed to take his wife's suggestion seriously. Two weeks later he replied, "As to your extraordinary Code of Laws, I cannot but Laugh. We have been told that our Struggle has loosened the bands of Government every where"—that children, apprentices, slaves, Indians, and college students had all become "disobedient" and "insolent." Her letter was the first sign that "another Tribe more numerous and powerfull than all the rest were grown discontented." But women, he insisted, had little reason for complaint. "In Practice you know We are subjects. We have only the Name of Masters, and rather than give up this, which would compleatly subject Us to the Despotism of the Peticoat, I hope General Washington and all our brave Heroes would fight."

Abigail Adams's famous words have often been cited as the first stirrings of feminism in America. Whether or not such an interpretation is accurate, her comments were, as John Adams recognized, a sign of the impact the Revolution and its ideology had had on American society. Few aspects of American life remained untouched by the Revolution: during and after the war Americans reshaped their political structures, their intellectual world, and their social interactions.

At the core of the changes lay their new commitment to republicanism: the notion that the government should be based wholly on the consent of the people. When they left the British Empire, Americans abandoned the idea that the best system of government balanced monarchy, aristocracy, and democracy. Instead they substituted a belief in the superiority of republicanism, in which the people, not Parliament, were sovereign. Americans disagreed, however, on such critical issues as how to define "the people" and how fully and frequently to obtain their consent. Although almost all white men agreed that women and blacks should be excluded from formal participation in politics, they found it difficult to reach a consensus on how many of their own number should be included. And when should consent be sought: semiannually? annually? at intervals of two or more years? Further, how should governments be structured so as to reflect the people's consent most accurately? Americans replied to these questions in different ways.

Republican political ideas carried with them a host of implications for other areas of American life. Because it was widely believed that the citizens of a republic had to be especially virtuous or the republic would not survive, America's political and intellectual leaders worked hard to inculcate virtue in their fellow countrymen and women. After 1776 American literature, theater, art, and architecture all had moral goals. Each in its own way was intended to inspire its audience to behave virtuously. Women too played a particularly important role in the preservation of virtue. As the mothers of the republic's children, they were primarily responsible for ensuring their nation's future. For the first time America's leaders became concerned about the nature and content of women's education. If the United States was to endure, they concluded, the mothers of the rising generation had to be properly educated.

Other elements of republicanism had more troublesome connotations. Should a republic conduct its dealings with Indian tribes, or with foreign countries,

In the mid-1780s Abigail Adams (1744–1818) and her husband John (1735–1826) sat for these portraits in London. John Adams was then American ambassador to Great Britain. Left, Boston Athenaeum; right: New York State Historical Association, Cooperstown.

any differently from other types of governments? Did republics, in other words, have an obligation to negotiate fairly and honestly at all times? Even more bothersome were Thomas Jefferson's words in the Declaration of Independence: "all men are created equal." Given that bold statement of principle, how could white republicans justify holding Afro-Americans in perpetual bondage? Some answered that question by freeing their slaves or by voting for state laws that abolished slavery. Others responded by denying that blacks were "men" in the same sense as whites.

The most important task facing Americans in these years was the construction of a national government. Before 1765, the English mainland colonies had rarely cooperated on common endeavors. Many things separated them: their diverse economies, varying religious traditions and ethnic compositions, competing land claims (especially in the west), and the differences in their political systems (see Chapters 2 and 3). But fighting the Revolutionary war brought them together and created a new nationalistic spirit, especially in

the ranks of those men who served in the Continental Army or the diplomatic corps. Wartime experiences broke down at least some of the boundaries that had previously divided Americans, replacing loyalties to state and region with loyalties to the nation.

Still, forging a *national* republic (as opposed to a set of loosely connected state republics) was neither easy nor simple. America's first such government, the Articles of Confederation, proved to be inadequate. But the nation's political leaders learned from their experiences and tried another approach when they drafted the Constitution in 1787. Some historians have argued that the Articles of Confederation and the Constitution reflected opposing political philosophies, the Constitution representing an "aristocratic" counterrevolution against the "democratic" Articles. The two documents are more accurately viewed as separate and successive attempts to solve the same problems. Both in part applied theories of republicanism to practical problems of governance; neither was entirely successful in resolving those difficulties.

Creating a Virtuous Republic

Many years after the Revolution, John Dickinson recalled that in 1776, when the colonies declared their independence from Great Britain, "there was no question concerning forms of Government, no enquiry whether a Republic or a limited Monarchy was best. . . . We knew that the people of this country must unite themselves under some form of Government and that this could be no other than the Republican form." But what, precisely, was a republic? And what role would be played in it by previously disfranchised white men? by the white women who displayed a new political consciousness and activism during the 1760s and 1770s? by blacks? During and after the war Americans offered varying answers to these and other related questions.

Three different definitions of republicanism emerged in the new United States. The first, held chiefly by members of the educated elite (for example, the

Varieties of Republicanism

Adamses of Massachusetts), was based directly on ancient history and political theory. It insisted that republics were especially fragile forms of government that risked chronic instability. The histories of popular governments in such places as Greece and Rome seemed to prove that republics could succeed only if they were small in size and homogeneous in population. Furthermore, unless the citizens of a republic were especially virtuous, willing to sacrifice their own private interests for the good of the whole, the government would inevitably collapse. In return for sacrifices, though, a republic offered its citizens equality of opportunity. Under such a government, rank would be based on merit rather than inherited wealth and status. Society would be ruled by members of a "natural aristocracy," men of talent who had risen from what might have been humble beginnings to positions of power and privilege. Rank would not be abolished but instead would be placed on a different footing.

A second definition of republicanism, also advanced by members of the elite but in addition by some skilled craftsmen, drew more on economic than political thought. Instead of perceiving the nation as an organic whole, composed of people sacrificing to the common good, this version of republicanism emphasized individuals' pursuit of rational self-interest. The nation could only benefit from aggressive economic expansion, such men as Alexander Hamilton (see page 186) argued. When republican men sought to improve their own economic and social circumstances, the entire nation would benefit. Republican virtue would be achieved through the advancement of private interests, rather than through their subordination to some communal ideal.

The third notion of republicanism was less influential, because it was popular primarily with people who were illiterate or barely literate, and who thus wrote little to promote their beliefs. But it certainly involved a more egalitarian approach to governance than did either of the other two, both of which contained considerable potential for inequality. In other words, some late-eighteenth-century Americans (like Thomas Paine) can be termed democrats in more or less the modern sense. They emphasized the importance of widespread participation in political activities, wanted government to be responsive to their needs, and openly questioned the gentry's ability to speak for them.

Despite the differences, it is important to recognize that the three strands of republicanism were part of a unified whole, and that they shared many of the same assumptions. For example, all three contrasted a virtuous, industrious America to the corrupt luxury of England and Europe. In the first version, that virtue manifested itself in frugality and self-sacrifice; in the second, it would prevent self-interest from becoming vice; in the third, it was the justification for including even propertyless white men in the ranks of voters. "Virtue, Virtue alone . . . is the basis of a republic," asserted Dr. Benjamin Rush of Philadelphia, an ardent patriot, in 1778. His fellow Americans fully concurred, even if they defined virtue in divergent ways.

As the citizens of the United States set out to construct their republic, then, they believed they were embarking on an unprecedented enterprise. With great pride in their new nation, they wanted to exchange the vices of monarchical Europe for the virtues of republican America. They wanted to embody republican principles not only in their governments (see page 161) but also in their society and their culture. They looked to painting, literature, drama, and architecture to convey messages of nationalism and virtue to the public.

But Americans faced a crucial contradiction at the very outset of their efforts. To some republicans, the fine arts were themselves manifestations of vice. Their

Virtue and the Arts

appearance in a virtuous society, many contended, signaled the arrival of luxury and corruption. What need did a frugal yeoman have for a painting—or, worse yet, a novel? Why should anyone spend hard-earned wages to see a play in a lavishly decorated theater? The first American artists, playwrights, and authors were thus trapped in a dilemma from which escape was nearly impossible. They wanted to produce works embodying virtue, but those very works, regardless of their content, were viewed by many as corrupting.

Still, they tried. William Hill Brown's *The Power of Sympathy* (1789), the first novel written in the United States, was a lurid tale of seduction intended as a warning to young women, who made up a large proportion of America's fiction readers. In Royall Tyler's *The Contrast* (1787), the first successful American play, the virtuous conduct of Colonel Manly was contrasted (hence the title) with the reprehensible behavior of the fop Billy Dimple. The most popular book of the era, Mason Locke Weems's *Life of Washington*, published in 1800 shortly after its subject's death, was, the author declared, designed to "hold up his great Virtues . . . to the imitation of Our Youth." Weems could hardly have been accused of being subtle. The famous tale he invented—six-year-old George bravely admitting cutting down his father's favorite cherry tree—ended with George's father exclaiming, "Run to my arms, you dearest boy. . . . Such an act of heroism in my son, is worth more than a thousand trees, though blossomed with silver, and their fruits of purest gold."

Painting, too, was expected to embody high moral standards. The major artists of the republican period—Gilbert Stuart and John Trumbull—studied in London under Benjamin West and John Singleton Copley, the first great American-born painters, both of whom had emigrated to England before the Revolution. Stuart and Charles Willson Peale (an American-

In the 1780s, this fabric was manufactured in England specifically for the American market. At top left, two cherubs hold a map of America; at top right, Benjamin Franklin and Liberty display a scroll proclaiming, "Where Liberty Dwells There is My Country." Below them George Washington drives a chariot in which an allegorical figure of America carries a sign noting "American Independance 1776," and an Indian carries a banner with Franklin's segmented snake "Unite or Die" motto. Douglas Political Americana Collection, Cornell University.

trained artist) painted innumerable portraits of upstanding republican citizens—the political, economic, and social leaders of the day. Trumbull's vast canvases depicted such milestones of American history as the Battle of Bunker Hill, Burgoyne's surrender at Saratoga, and Cornwallis's capitulation at Yorktown. Both portraits and historical scenes were intended to arouse patriotic virtues in their viewers.

Architects likewise hoped to convey in their buildings a sense of the young republic's ideals, and most of them consciously rejected British models. When the Virginia government asked Thomas Jefferson, then ambassador to France, for advice on the design of a state capitol in Richmond, Jefferson unhesitatingly recommended copying a Roman building, the Maison Carrée at Nîmes. "It is very simple," he explained, "but it is noble beyond expression." Jefferson set forth ideals that would guide American architecture for a generation to come: simplicity of line, harmonious proportions, a feeling of grandeur. Nowhere were these rational goals of republican art manifested more clearly than in Benjamin H. Latrobe's plans for the majestic domed United States Capitol in Washington, built shortly after the turn of the century.

Despite the artists' efforts, or perhaps, some would have said, because of them, some Americans were beginning to detect signs of luxury and corruption by the mid-1780s. The end of the war and resumption of European trade brought a return to fashionable clothing styles for both men and women and abandonment of the simpler homespun garments patriots had once worn with such pride. Balls and concerts resumed in the cities and were attended by well-dressed elite families. Parties no longer seemed complete without gambling and card-playing. Social clubs for young people multiplied; Samuel Adams worried in print about the possibilities for corruption lurking behind innocent plans for tea drinking and genteel conversation among Boston youths. Especially alarming to fervent republicans was the establishment in 1783 of the Society of the Cincinnati, a hereditary organization of Revolutionary War officers and their descendants. Many feared that the group would become the nucleus of a native-born aristocracy. All these developments directly challenged the United States's image as a virtuous republic.

Their deep-seated concern for the future of the infant republic focused Americans' attention on their children, the "rising generation." Education acquired new significance in the context of

Educational Reform

the republic. Since the early days of the colonies, education had been seen chiefly as a private means to personal advancement, and thus of concern only to individual families. Now, though, it would serve a public purpose. If young people were to resist the temptation of vice, they would have to learn the lessons of virtue at home and at school. In fact, the very survival of the nation depended on it. The early republican period was thus a time of major educational reform.

The 1780s and 1790s brought two significant changes in American educational practice. First, some states began to be willing to use tax money to support public elementary schools. Nearly all education in the colonies, at whatever level, had been privately financed. In the republic, though, schools could lay claim to tax dollars. In 1789 Massachusetts became one of the first states to require towns to supply their citizens with free public elementary education.

Second, schooling for girls was improved. Americans' recognition of the importance of the rising generation led to the realization that mothers would have to be properly educated if they were to be able to instruct their children adequately. Therefore Massachusetts insisted in its 1789 law that town elementary schools be open to girls as well as boys. Throughout the United States, private academies were founded to give teenage girls from well-to-do families an opportunity for advanced schooling. No one yet proposed opening colleges to women, but a few fortunate girls could now study history, geography, rhetoric, and mathematics. The academies also trained female students in fancy needlework—the only artistic endeavor open to women.

The chief theorist of women's education in the early republic was Judith Sargent Murray, of Gloucester, Massachusetts. In a series of essays published in

Judith Sargent Murray on Education

the 1780s and 1790s, Murray argued that women and men had equal intellectual capacities, though women's inadequate education might make them seem to be less intelligent. "We can only reason from what we know," she declared, "and if an opportunity of acquiring knowledge hath been denied us, the inferiority of our sex cannot fairly be deduced from thence." Therefore, concluded Murray, boys and girls should be offered equivalent scholastic training. She further contended that girls should be taught to support themselves by their own efforts: "Independence should be placed within their grasp." Because she rejected the prevailing notion that a young woman's chief goal in life should be finding a husband, Judith Sargent Murray deserves the title of the first American feminist. (That distinction is usually accorded to better-known nineteenth-century women like Margaret Fuller or Sarah Grimké.)

Judith Sargent (1751–1820), later Mrs. John Murray, painted by John Singleton Copley when she was in her late teens. Although her steady gaze suggests clear-headed intelligence, there is little in the stylized portrait—typical of Copley's work at the time—to suggest her later emergence as the first notable American feminist theorist. Frick Art Reference Library.

Murray's direct challenge to the traditional colonial belief that (as one man put it) girls "knew quite enough if they could make a shirt and a pudding" was part of a general rethinking of women's position that occurred as a result of the Revolution. Male patriots who enlisted in the army or served in Congress were away from home for long periods of time. In their absence their wives, who had previously handled only the "indoor affairs" of the household, had to shoulder the responsibility for "outdoor affairs" as well. As the wife of a Connecticut militiaman later recalled, her husband "was out more or less during the remainder of the war [after 1777], so much so as to be unable to do anything on our farm. What was done, was done by myself."

In many households, the necessary shift of re-sponsibilities during the war taught men and women that their notions of proper sex roles had to be rethought. Both John and Abigail

Women's Role in the Republic

Adams took great pride in Abigail's developing skills as a "farmeress," and John praised her courage repeatedly. "You are really brave, my dear, you are an Heroine," he told her in 1775. Abigail Adams, like her female contemporaries, stopped calling the farm "yours" in letters to her husband, and began referring to it as "ours"—a revealing change of pronoun. Both men and women realized that female patriots had made a vital contribution to winning the war through their work at home. Thus, in the years after the Revolution, Americans began to develop new ideas about the role women should play in a republican society.

Only a very few thought that role should include the right to vote. Abigail Adams did not press for female suffrage, believing that women's influence was best exerted in the privacy of their homes, through their impact on their husbands and children, especially their sons. But some women thought differently, as events in New Jersey proved. The men who drafted the state constitution in 1776 defined voters loosely as "all free inhabitants" who met certain property qualifications. They thereby unintentionally gave the vote to property-holding white spinsters and widows, as well as to free blacks. In the 1780s and 1790s women successfully claimed the right to vote in New Jersey's local and congressional elections. They continued to exercise that right until 1807, when women and blacks were disfranchised by the state legislature on the grounds that their votes could be easily manipulated. Yet the fact that they had voted at all was evidence of their altered perception of their place in political life.

Such dramatic episodes were unusual. On the whole the re-evaluation of women's position had its greatest impact on private life. The traditional colonial view of marriage had stressed the sub-

Marriage and Motherhood

ordination of wife to husband. But in 1790 a female "Matrimonial Republican" asserted that "marriage ought never to be considered as a contract between a superior and an inferior, but a reciprocal union of interest. . . . The obedience between man and wife is, or ought to be mutual." This new understanding of the marital relationship seems to have contributed to a rising divorce rate after the war. Dissatisfied wives proved less willing to remain in unhappy marriages than they had been previously. At the same time, state judges became more sympathetic to women's desires to be freed from abusive or unfaithful husbands. Even so, divorces were still rare; most marriages were for life. And married women continued to suffer serious legal disabilities. Like John Adams, most political leaders failed to heed calls for reform. It was not until the 1830s that legislators began to change the statutes governing the legal status of married women.

The republican decades witnessed an ever-increasing emphasis on the importance of mothers. In 1790 one woman even argued publicly for female superiority, resting her claim on woman's maternal role. Men, she said, had assumed primacy in the past "on the vain presumption of their being assigned the most important duties of life." But God had clearly intended otherwise, since to women He had "assigned the care of making the first impressions on the infant minds of the whole human race, a trust of more importance than the government of provinces, and the marshalling of armies."

Other Americans did not go that far. To be sure, they were more willing than before to expand the meaning of the phrase "all men are created equal" to apply to women, but they still viewed woman's role in traditional terms. Most eighteenth-century white Americans assumed that women's place was in the home and that their primary function was to be good wives and mothers. They accepted the notion of equality, but within the context of men's and women's separate spheres. Whereas their forebears had seen women as inferior and subordinate to men, members of the revolutionary generation regarded the sexes and their roles as more nearly equal in importance. However, equality did not mean sameness.

Indeed, the differences they perceived between the male and female characters eventually enabled Americans to resolve the conflict between the two most influential strands of republican thought. Because married women could not own property or participate directly in economic life, women in general came to be seen as the embodiment of self-sacrificing, disinterested republicanism. Through female-run char-

itable and other social welfare groups, they assumed responsibility for the welfare of the community as a whole. Yet because they worked chiefly with women and children in familial settings, women continued to be seen primarily as private beings. Thus men were freed from any naggings of conscience as they pursued their economic self-interest (that other republican virtue), secure in the knowledge that their wives and daughters were fulfilling the family's obligation to the common good. The ideal republican man, therefore, was an individualist, seeking advancement for himself and his family; the ideal republican woman, by contrast, always put the well-being of others ahead of her own.

Together white men and women established the context for the creation of a virtuous republic. But nearly 20 percent of the American population was black. How did approximately 700,000 Afro-Americans fit into the developing national plan?

EMANCIPATION AND THE GROWTH OF RACISM

Revolutionary ideology exposed one of the primary contradictions in American society. Just as Abigail Adams pointed out to her husband his failure to apply revolutionary doctrines to the status of women, so too both blacks and whites recognized the irony of slaveholding Americans claiming that one of their aims in taking up arms was to prevent Britain from "enslaving" them.

As early as 1764, James Otis, Jr., had identified the basic problem in his pamphlet *The Rights of the British Colonies Asserted and Proved* (see page 110). If according to natural law all people were born free and equal, that meant *all* humankind, black and white. "Does it follow that 'tis right to enslave a man because he is black?" Otis asked. "Can any logical inference in favor of slavery be drawn from a flat nose, a long or short face?" The same theme was later voiced by other revolutionary leaders. In 1773 the Philadelphia doctor Benjamin Rush called slavery "a vice which degrades human nature," warning ominously that "the plant of liberty is of so tender a nature that it cannot thrive long in the neighborhood of slavery." Common folk too saw the contradiction. When Josiah Atkins, a Connecticut soldier marching south, saw George Washington's plantation, he observed in his journal: "Alas! That persons who pretend to stand for the *rights of mankind* for the *liberties of society*, can delight in oppression, & that even of the worst kind!"

Afro-Americans themselves were quick to recognize the implications of revolutionary ideology. In 1779 a group of slaves from Portsmouth, New Hampshire, asked the state legislature "from what authority [our masters] assume to dispose of our lives, freedom and property," and pleaded "that the name of slave may not more be heard in a land gloriously contending for the sweets of freedom." That same year several black residents of Fairfield, Connecticut, petitioned the legislature for their freedom, characterizing slavery as a "dreadful Evil" and "flagrant Injustice." Surely, they declared pointedly, "your Honours who are nobly contending in the Cause of Liberty, whose Conduct excited the Admiration, and Reverence, of all the great Empires of the World; will not resent, our thus freely animadverting, on this detestable Practice."

Both legislatures responded negatively. But the postwar years did witness the gradual abolition of slavery in the North. Vermont abolished slavery in its 1777 constitution. Massachusetts

Gradual Emancipation courts decided in the 1780s that the clause in the state constitution declaring that "all men are born free and equal, and have certain natural, essential, and unalienable rights" prohibited slavery in the state. Pennsylvania passed an abolition law in 1780; four years later Rhode Island and Connecticut provided for gradual emancipation, followed by New York (1799) and New Jersey (1804). Although New Hampshire did not formally abolish slavery, only eight slaves were reported on the 1800 census and none remained a decade later.

No southern state adopted similar general emancipation laws, but the legislatures of Virginia (1782), Delaware (1787), and Maryland (1790 and 1796) did decide to change laws that had restricted masters' ability to free their slaves. South Carolina and Georgia never considered adopting such acts, though, and North Carolina insisted that all manumissions

(emancipations of individual slaves) be approved by county courts.

Thus revolutionary ideology had limited impact on the well-entrenched economic interests of large slaveholders. Only in the North, where there were few slaves and where little money was invested in human capital, could state legislatures vote to abolish slavery with relative ease. Even there, legislators' concern for property rights—the Revolution was, after all, fought for property as well as life and liberty—led them to favor gradual emancipation over immediate abolition. Most states provided only for the freeing of children born after passage of the law, not for the emancipation of adults. And even those children were to remain slaves until ages ranging from eighteen to twenty-eight. As a result, some northern states still had a few legally held slaves at the time of the Civil War.

Despite the slow progress of abolition, the free black population of the United States grew dramatically in the first years after the Revolution. Before the

Growth of the Free Black Population war there had been few free blacks in America. (According to a 1755 Maryland census, for example, only 4 percent of the Afro-Americans in the colony were free.) Most prewar free blacks were mulattoes, born of unions between white masters and enslaved black women. But wartime disruptions radically changed the size and composition of the free black population. Slaves who had escaped from plantations during the war, others who had served in the American army, and still others who had been emancipated by their owners or by state laws were now free. Because most of them were not mulattoes, dark skin was no longer an automatic sign of slave status. By 1790 there were nearly 60,000 free people of color in the United States; ten years later they numbered more than 108,000 and represented nearly 11 percent of the total black population. The effects of postwar manumissions were felt most sharply in the Chesapeake, where they were fostered by such economic changes as declining soil fertility and the shift from tobacco to grain production. (Since grain cultivation was less labor-intensive than tobacco growing, planters began to complain about "excess" slaves. They often solved that problem by freeing the most favored or least productive of their bondspeople.) The free Negro population of Virginia more

The Reverend Lemuel Haynes was one of the best-known black clergymen of the late eighteenth and early nineteenth centuries. He attacked the institution of slavery both in print and from the pulpit. Here he is shown preaching to an attentive congregation. Rhode Island School of Design.

than doubled between 1790 and 1810, and by the latter year nearly a quarter of Maryland's black population was no longer in legal bondage.

In the 1780s and thereafter, freed people often made their way, as had landless colonists decades before them, to the port cities of the North. They moved to Boston and Philadelphia in particular, where slavery was abolished sooner than it was in New York City. Women outnumbered men among the migrants by a margin of three to two. Like female whites, black women found more opportunities for employment, particularly as domestic servants, in the cities than in the countryside. Some black men also worked in domestic service, but larger numbers were employed as unskilled laborers or seamen. A few of the women and a sizable proportion of men (nearly a third of those in Philadelphia in 1795) were skilled workers or retailers. These freed people chose new names for themselves, exchanging the surnames of their former masters for names like Newman or Brown, and as soon as possible they established independent two-parent nuclear families instead of continuing to live in white households. They also began to cluster their residences in certain neighborhoods, probably as a result of both discrimination by whites and a desire for black solidarity.

Emancipation did not bring equality, though. Even whites who recognized Afro-Americans' right to freedom were unwilling to accept them as equals. Laws discriminated against emancipated blacks as they had against slaves—South Carolina, for example, did not permit free blacks to testify against whites in court. Public schools often refused to educate the children of free black parents. Freedmen found it difficult to purchase property and find good jobs. And though in many areas Afro-Americans were accepted as members—even ministers—of evangelical churches, whites rarely allowed them an equal voice in church affairs.

Gradually free blacks developed their own separate institutions, often based in the neighborhoods in which they lived. In Charleston, mulattoes formed the Brown Fellowship Society, which provided insurance coverage for its members, financed a school for free children, and helped to support black orphans. In 1787 blacks in Philadelphia and Baltimore founded churches that eventually became the African Methodist Episcopal (AME) denomination. AME churches later sponsored schools in a number of cities and, along with African Baptist and African Presbyterian churches, became cultural centers of the free black community. Freed people quickly learned that if they were to survive and prosper they would have to rely on their own collective efforts rather than on the benevolence or goodwill of their white compatriots.

Development of Black Institutions

Their endeavors were all the more important because the postrevolutionary years ironically witnessed the development of a coherent racist theory in the United States. Whites had long regarded blacks as inferior, but the most influential writers on race had attributed that inferiority to environmental, rather than hereditary, factors. That is, they argued that blacks' seemingly debased character derived from their enslavement, instead of enslavement being the consequence of genetic inferiority. In the aftermath of the Revolution, white southerners needed to defend their holding other human beings in bondage against the notion that "*all* men are created equal." Consequently, they began to argue that blacks were less than fully human, that the principles of republican equality applied only to whites. To avoid having to confront the contradiction between their practice and the egalitarian implications of revolutionary theory, in short, they redefined the theory, making it inapplicable to blacks.

Development of Racist Theory

Their racism had several intertwined elements. First was the insistence that, as Thomas Jefferson suggested in 1781, blacks were "inferior to the whites in the endowments both of body and mind." Second came the belief that blacks were congenitally lazy, dishonest, and uncivilized (or uncivilizable). Third,

A woodcut portrait of Benjamin Banneker adorned the cover of his almanac for 1795. *Maryland Historical Society.*

and of crucial importance, was the notion that all blacks were sexually promiscuous and that black men lusted after white women. The specter of interracial sexual intercourse involving black men and white women haunted early American racist thought. The reverse situation, which occurred with far greater frequency (as white masters sexually exploited their female slaves), aroused little comment.

Afro-Americans did not allow these developing racist notions to pass unnoticed. Benjamin Banneker, a free black surveyor, astronomer, and mathematical genius, directly challenged Thomas Jefferson's belief in blacks' intellectual inferiority. In 1791 Banneker sent Jefferson a copy of his latest almanac (which included his astronomical calculations), as an example of blacks' mental powers. Jefferson's response admitted Banneker's capabilities but implied that he regarded Banneker as an exception. The future president insisted that he needed more evidence before he would abandon his previous position.

At its birth, then, the republic was defined as an exclusively white enterprise. Indeed, some historians have argued that the subjection of blacks was a necessary precondition for equality among whites. They have pointed out that identifying a common racial antagonist helped to create white solidarity and to lessen the threat to gentry power posed by the enfranchisement of poorer whites. It was less dangerous to allow whites with little property to participate formally in politics than to open the possibility that they might combine with freed blacks to question the rule of the "better sort." That was one reason why, in the postrevolutionary years, the division of American society between slave and free was transformed into a division between black —some of whom were free—and white. The white male wielders of power ensured their continued dominance in part by making certain that race replaced enslavement as the primary determinant of Afro-Americans' status.

A Republic for Whites Only

DESIGNING REPUBLICAN GOVERNMENTS

On May 10, 1776, even before passage of the Declaration of Independence, the Continental Congress directed the states to devise new republican governments to replace the provincial congresses and committees that had met since 1774. Thus Americans initially concentrated on drafting state constitutions and devoted little attention to their national government— an oversight they were later forced to remedy. At the state level, they immediately faced the problem

Drafting of State Constitutions

of defining just what a constitution was. The British constitution could not serve as a model because it was an unwritten mixture of law and custom; Americans wanted tangible documents specifying the fundamental structures of government. Several years passed before the states agreed that their constitutions could not be drafted by regular legislative bodies, like ordinary laws. Following the lead established by Massachusetts in 1780, they began to call conventions for the sole purpose of drafting constitutions. Thus the states sought direct authorization from the people— the theoretical sovereigns in a republic—before establishing new governments. After the new constitutions had been drawn up, delegates submitted them to the people for ratification.

Those who wrote the state constitutions concerned themselves primarily with outlining the distribution of and limitations on governmental power. Both questions were crucial to the survival of republics. If authority was improperly distributed among the branches of government or not confined within reasonable limits, the states might become tyrannical, as Britain had. Indeed, Americans' experience with British rule affected every provision of their new constitutions.

Under their colonial charters, Americans had learned to fear the power of the governor—in most cases the appointed agent of the king or the proprietor—and to see the legislature as their defender. Accordingly, the first state constitutions typically provided for the governor to be elected annually (usually by the legislature), limited the number of terms any one governor could serve, and gave him little independent authority. At the same time the constitutions expanded the powers of the legislature. They redrew the lines of electoral districts to reflect population patterns more accurately and increased the number of members in both the upper and lower houses. Finally, most states lowered property qualifications for voting. As a result the legislatures came to include some men who before the war would not even have been eligible to vote. Thus the revolutionary era witnessed the first deliberate attempt to broaden the base of American government, a process that has continued into our own day.

But the authors of the state constitutions knew that governments designed to be responsive to the people would not necessarily provide sufficient protection should tyrants be elected to office. Consequently, they included limitations on governmental authority in the documents they composed. Seven of the constitutions contained formal bills of rights, and the others had similar clauses. Most of them guaranteed citizens freedom of the press and of religion, the right to a fair trial, the right of consent to taxation, and protection against general search warrants. An independent judiciary was charged with upholding such rights.

In sum, the constitution-makers put far greater emphasis on preventing state governments from becoming tyrannical than on making them effective wielders of political authority. Their approach to the process of shaping governments was understandable, given the American experience with Great Britain. But establishing such weak political units, especially in wartime, practically ensured that the constitutions would soon need revision. As early as the 1780s some states began to rewrite the constitutions they had drafted in 1776 and 1777. Invariably, the revised versions increased the powers of the governor and reduced the scope of the legislature's authority. Only then, a decade after the Declaration, did Americans start to develop a formal theory of checks and balances as the primary means of controlling governmental power. Once they realized that legislative supremacy did not in itself guarantee good government, Americans attempted to achieve their goal by balancing the powers of the legislative, executive, and judicial branches against one another. The national constitution they drafted in 1787 would embody that principle.

The most heated constitutional debate took place in Pennsylvania. There the adherents of the third— or democratic—philosophy of republicanism early gained the upper hand. They dominated the Pennsylvania Assembly that in spring 1776 drafted the state's first constitution. It abolished the office of governor (replacing the single executive with an executive council) and established a one-house (unicameral) legislature. The constitution extended the right of suffrage to a much larger proportion of the male population than did any other state at the time. It defined voters as men

Pennsylvania's Constitutional Debate

who met minimum age, residency, and tax-paying (but not property-holding) requirements. Believing that the people should have a real and continuing impact on government policies, the constitution-drafters also limited the number of terms officials could serve and ordered that all meetings of the assembly be open to the public. Even more important, they provided that, in order to allow time for public comment, any bill would have to be passed by two separate legislative sessions before it became law.

The Pennsylvania Constitution of 1776 represented such a break with the previous form of government that it immediately aroused intense opposition, chiefly among the educated elite. The critics, who included adherents of both the other two definitions of republicanism, primarily focused on the lack of an upper house and an effective governor. As the debate progressed, both sides appealed to the people, each claiming to be more republican than the other. Each argued that its brand of republicanism would better preserve the people's rights by more effectively limiting the reach of government. The Constitutionalists praised the provisions for frequent rotation of offices and weakening the executive; the Republicans (as the elite critics termed themselves) called for the establishment of another house to represent the people's wishes and stressed the need for a balance of powers among governmental branches. In 1790, when Pennsylvania revised its constitution, the Republicans won the prolonged struggle. Pennsylvania's experiment in direct democracy had proved to be out of step with developing American notions of proper political structure.

The constitutional theories that Americans applied at the state level did not at first influence their conception of the nature of a national government. The powers and structure of the Continental Congress evolved by default early in the war, since Americans had little time to devote to legitimizing their de facto government while organizing the military struggle against Britain. Not until late 1777, after Burgoyne's defeat at Saratoga, did Congress send the Articles of Confederation to the states for ratification.

The articles by and large wrote into law the arrangements that had developed, unplanned and largely unheeded, in the Continental Congress. The chief organ of national government was a unicameral leg-

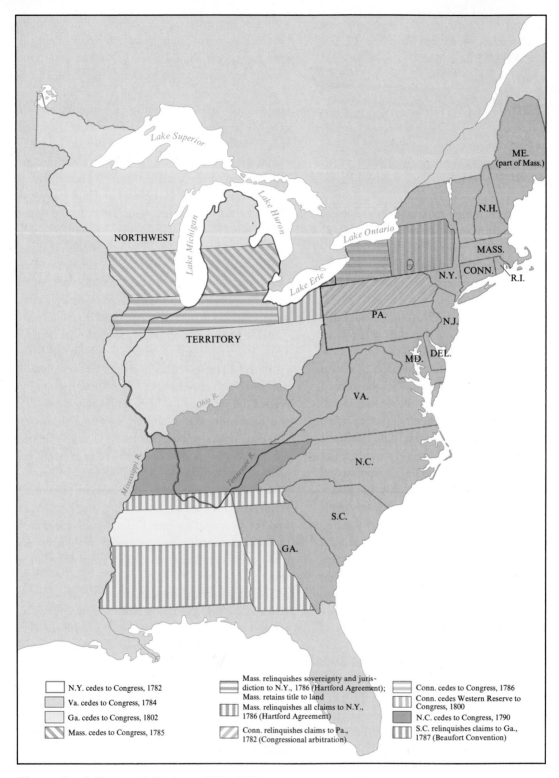

Western Land Claims and Cessions, 1782–1802

Legend:

- N.Y. cedes to Congress, 1782
- Va. cedes to Congress, 1784
- Ga. cedes to Congress, 1802
- Mass. cedes to Congress, 1785
- Mass. relinquishes sovereignty and jurisdiction to N.Y., 1786 (Hartford Agreement); Mass. retains title to land
- Mass. relinquishes all claims to N.Y., 1786 (Hartford Agreement)
- Conn. relinquishes claims to Pa., 1782 (Congressional arbitration)
- Conn. cedes to Congress, 1786
- Conn. cedes Western Reserve to Congress, 1800
- N.C. cedes to Congress, 1790
- S.C. relinquishes claims to Ga., 1787 (Beaufort Convention)

Articles of Confederation islature in which each state had one vote. Its powers included the conduct of foreign relations, the settlement of disputes between states, control over maritime affairs, the regulation of Indian trade, and the valuation of state and national money. The articles did not give the national government the ability to tax effectively or to enforce a uniform commercial policy. The United States of America was described as "a firm league of friendship" in which each state "retains its sovereignty, freedom and independence, and every Power, Jurisdiction and right, which is not by this confederation expressly delegated to the United States, in Congress assembled."

The articles required the unanimous consent of the state legislatures for ratification or amendment, and a clause concerning western lands turned out to be troublesome. The draft accepted by Congress allowed the states to retain all land claims derived from their original colonial charters. But states with definite western boundaries in their charters (like Maryland, Delaware, and New Jersey) wanted the other states to cede the lands west of the Appalachian Mountains to the national government. Otherwise, they feared, states with large claims could expand and overpower their smaller neighbors. Maryland absolutely refused to accept the articles until 1781, when Virginia finally promised to surrender its western holdings to national jurisdiction (see map).

The fact that a single state could delay ratification for three years was a portent of the fate of American government under the Articles of Confederation. The unicameral legislature, whether it was called the Second Continental Congress (until 1781) or the Confederation Congress (thereafter), was too inefficient and unwieldy to govern effectively. The authors of the articles had not given adequate thought to the distribution of power within the national government or to the relationship between the Confederation and the states. The congress they created was simultaneously a legislative body and a collective executive, but it had no independent income and no authority to compel the states to accept its rulings. What is surprising, in other words, is not how poorly the Confederation functioned in the following years, but rather how much the government was able to accomplish.

TRIALS OF THE CONFEDERATION

During and after the war the most persistent problem faced by the American governments, state and national, was finance. Because legislators at all levels were understandably reluctant to levy taxes on their fellow countrymen, both Congress and the states tried to finance the war by simply printing currency. Even though the money was backed by nothing but good faith, it circulated freely and without excessive depreciation during 1775 and most of 1776. Demand for military supplies and civilian goods was high, stimulating trade (especially with France) and local production. Indeed, the amount of money issued in those years was probably no more than what a healthy economy required as a medium of exchange.

But in late 1776, as the American army suffered major battlefield reverses in New York and New Jersey, prices began to rise and inflation set in. The value of the currency rested on Americans' **Monetary Problems** faith in their government, a faith that was sorely tested in the years that followed, especially during the dark days of the early British triumphs in the South (1779 and 1780). Some state governments fought inflation by controlling wages and prices, requiring acceptance of paper currency on an equal footing with hard money, borrowing, and even levying taxes. Their efforts were futile. So too was Congress's attempt to stop printing currency altogether and to rely solely on state contributions. By early 1780 it took forty paper dollars to purchase one in silver. A year later Continental currency was worthless.

The severe wartime inflation seriously affected people on fixed incomes—including many soldiers and civilian leaders of the Revolution. Common laborers, small farmers, clergymen, and poor folk in general could do nothing to stop the declining value of their incomes. Yet there were people who benefited from such economic conditions. Military contractors could make sizable profits. Large-scale farmers who produced surpluses of meat, milk, and grains could sell their goods at high prices to the army or to civilian merchants. People with money could invest in lucrative trading voyages. More risky, but potentially even more profitable, was privateering against enemy shipping—an enterprise that attracted venturesome sailors and wealthy merchants alike.

Such accumulations of private wealth did nothing to help Congress with its financial problems. In 1781, faced with the total collapse of the monetary system, the delegates undertook major reforms. After establishing a department of finance under the wealthy Philadelphia merchant Robert Morris, they asked the states to amend the Articles of Confederation to allow Congress to levy a duty on imported goods. Morris put national finances on a solid footing, but the customs duty was never adopted. First Rhode Island, then New York refused to agree to the tax. The states' resistance reflected genuine fear of a too-powerful central government. As one worried citizen wrote in 1783, "If permanent Funds are given to Congress, the aristocratical Influence, which predominates in more than a major part of the United States, will fully establish an arbitrary Government."

Congress also faced major diplomatic problems at the close of the war. Chief among them were issues involving the peace treaty itself. Article 4, which promised the repayment of prewar debts (most of them owed by Americans to British merchants), and Article 5, which recommended that states allow loyalists to recover their confiscated property, aroused considerable opposition. States passed laws denying British subjects the right to sue for recovery of debts or property in American courts, and town meetings decried the loyalists' return. As residents of Norwalk, Connecticut, put it, few Americans wanted to permit the "Tory Villains" to return "while filial Tears are fresh upon our Cheeks and our Murdered Brethren scarcely cold in their Graves." The state governments also had reason to oppose enforcement of the treaty. Sales of loyalists' land, houses, and other possessions had helped to finance the later stages of the war; since most of the purchasers were prominent patriots, the states had no desire to raise questions about the legitimacy of their property titles.

Failure to Enforce the Treaty of Paris

The failure of state and local governments to comply with Articles 4 and 5 gave Britain an excuse to maintain posts on the Great Lakes long after its troops were supposed to be withdrawn. Furthermore, Congress's inability to convince the states to implement the treaty pointed up its lack of power, even in an area—foreign affairs—in which it had been granted specific authority by the Articles of Confederation. Concerned nationalists argued publicly that enforcement of the treaty, however unpopular, was a crucial test for the republic. "Will foreign nations be willing to undertake anything with us or for us," asked Alexander Hamilton, "when they find that the nature of our governments will allow no dependence to be placed on our engagements?"

Congress's weakness was especially evident in the realm of trade, because the Articles of Confederation specifically denied it the power to establish a national commercial policy. Immediately following the war, Britain, France, and Spain restricted American trade with their colonies. Americans, who had hoped independence would bring about free trade with all nations, were outraged but could do little to change matters. Members of Congress watched helplessly as British manufactured goods flooded the United States while American produce could no longer be sold in the British West Indies, once its prime market. The South Carolina indigo industry, deprived of the British bounty that had supported it, suffered a setback. Though Americans began trading with northern European countries like the Netherlands and opened a profitable trade with China in 1784, neither substituted for access to closer and larger markets.

Congress also had difficulty dealing with the threat posed by Spain's presence on the southern and western borders of the United States. Determined to prevent the new nation's expansion, Spain in 1784 closed the Mississippi River to American navigation. It thus deprived the growing settlements west of the Appalachians of their major access route to the rest of the nation and the world. If Spain's policy were not reversed, westerners might have to accept Spanish sovereignty as the necessary price for survival. Congress opened negotiations with Spain in 1785, but even John Jay, one of the nation's most experienced diplomats, could not win the necessary concessions on navigation. The talks collapsed the following year after Congress divided sharply on the question of whether agreement should be sought on other issues. Southerners, voting as a bloc, insisted on navigation rights on the Mississippi, while northerners were willing to abandon that claim in order to win commercial concessions. The impasse raised doubts about the possibility of a national consensus on foreign affairs.

Diplomatic problems of another sort confronted congressmen when they considered the status of the land on the United States's western borders. Although

Encroachment on Indian Lands

tribal claims were not discussed by British and American diplomats at the end of the war, the United States assumed that the Treaty of Paris (1783) cleared its title to all land east of the Mississippi except the areas still held by Spain. But recognizing that some sort of land cession should be obtained from the major tribes, Congress initiated negotiations with both northern and southern Indians. At Fort Stanwix, New York, in 1784, and at Hopewell, South Carolina, in late 1785 and early 1786, American representatives signed treaties of questionable legality with the Iroquois and with Choctaw, Chickasaw, and Cherokee chiefs respectively (see map). The United States took the treaties as final confirmation of its sovereignty over the Indian territories, and authorized white settlers to move onto the land. Whites soon poured over the southern Appalachians, provoking the Creek tribe—which had not agreed to the Hopewell treaties—to defend its territory by declaring war. Only in 1790, when the Creek chief Alexander McGillivray traveled to New York to negotiate a treaty, did the tribe finally come to terms with the United States.

In the North, meanwhile, the Iroquois Confederacy was in disarray. The members of the Six Nations who had not fled to Canada in 1779 soon found that they had little bargaining power left. In 1786 they formally repudiated the Fort Stanwix treaty and threatened new attacks on frontier settlements, but both whites and Indians knew the threat was an empty one. The flawed treaty was permitted to stand by default. At intervals during the remainder of the decade the state of New York purchased large amounts of land from individual Iroquois tribes. By 1790 the once-proud Iroquois Confederacy was confined to a few scattered reservations.

Western tribes like the Shawnee, Chippewa, Ottawa, and Potawatomi had once allowed the Iroquois to speak for them. After the collapse of Iroquois power, they formed their own confederacy and de-

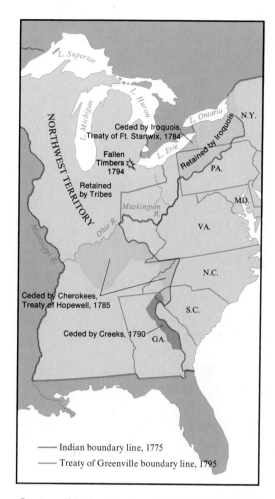

Cession of Indian Lands to U.S., 1775–1790 *Source: Reprinted by permission of Princeton University Press.*

manded direct negotiations with the United States. Their aim was to present a united front, so as to avoid the piecemeal surrender of land by individual tribes.

At first the national government ignored the western Indian confederacy. Shortly after the state land cessions were completed, Congress began to organize the

Northwest Ordinances

Northwest Territory, bounded by the Mississippi River, the Great Lakes, and the Ohio River. Ordinances passed in 1784, 1785, and 1787 outlined the process through which the land could be sold to settlers and formal governments organized. To ensure orderly development, Congress directed that the land be surveyed into townships six miles square, each divided into thirty-six sections of 640

General Anthony Wayne accepting the surrender of the Indian leader Little Turtle after the United States Army's victory in the Battle of Fallen Timbers, August 1794. Chicago Historical Society.

acres (one square mile). Revenue from the sale of the sixteenth section of each township was to be reserved for the support of public schools—the first instance of federal aid to education in American history. The minimum price per acre was set at one dollar, and the minimum sale was to be 640 acres. Congress was not especially concerned about helping the small farmer: the minimum outlay of $640 was beyond the reach of most Americans (except, of course, veterans who had received part of their army pay in land warrants). The proceeds from the land sales were the first independent revenues available to the national government.

The most important ordinance was the third, passed in 1787. The Northwest Ordinance contained a bill of rights guaranteeing settlers in the territory freedom of religion and the right to a jury trial, prohibiting cruel and unusual punishments, and abolishing slavery. It also specified the process by which residents of the territory could eventually organize state governments and seek admission to the union "on an equal footing with the original States." Early in the nation's history, therefore, Congress laid down a policy of admitting new states on the same basis as the old and assuring residents of the territories the same rights as citizens of the original states. Having suffered under the rule of a colonial power, congressmen understood the importance of preparing the United States's first "colony" for eventual self-government. Nineteenth- and twentieth-century Americans were to be less generous in their attitudes toward residents of later territories, many of whom were nonwhite or non-Protestant.

But the nation never fully lost sight of the egalitarian principles of the Northwest Ordinance.

In a sense, though, the ordinance was purely theoretical at the time it was passed. The Miami, Shawnee, and Delaware refused to acknowledge American sovereignty and insisted on their right to the land. They opposed white settlement violently, attacking unwary pioneers who ventured too far north of the Ohio River. In 1788 the Ohio Company, to which Congress had sold a large tract of land at reduced rates, established the town of Marietta at the juncture of the Ohio and Muskingum rivers. But the Indians prevented the company from extending settlement very far into the interior. After General Arthur St. Clair, the first governor of the Northwest Territory, failed to negotiate a meaningful treaty with the tribes in early 1789, it was apparent that the United States could not avoid a clash with a western confederacy, composed of eight tribes and led by the Miami.

War in the Northwest Little Turtle, the able war chief of the Miami confederacy, defeated first General Josiah Harmar (1790) and then St. Clair himself (1791) in major battles near the present border between Indiana and Ohio. More than six hundred of St. Clair's men were killed and scores more wounded; it was the whites' worst defeat in the entire history of the American frontier. In 1793 the Miami confederacy declared that peace could be achieved only if the United States recognized the Ohio River as the boundary between white and Indian lands. But the national government refused to relinquish its claim to the Northwest Territory. A new army under the command of General Anthony Wayne, a Revolutionary War hero, attacked and defeated the tribesmen in August 1794, at the Battle of Fallen Timbers (near Toledo, Ohio). This victory made it possible for serious negotiations to begin.

By the summer of 1795, Wayne had reached agreement with delegates from the Miami confederacy. The Treaty of Greenville gave each side a portion of what it wanted. The United States gained the right to settle much of what was to become the state of Ohio, the tribes retaining only the northwest corner of the region. The Indians received the acknowledgment they had long sought: American recognition of their rights to the soil. At Greenville, the United States formally accepted the principle of Indian sovereignty, by virtue of residence, over all lands the tribes had not yet ceded. Never again would the United States government claim that it had acquired Indian territory solely through negotiation with a European or American country.

The problems the United States encountered in ensuring safe settlement of the Northwest Territory pointed up, once again, the basic weakness of the Confederation government. Not until after the Articles of Confederation were replaced with a new constitution could the United States muster sufficient force to implement all the provisions of the Northwest Ordinance. Thus, although the ordinance is often viewed as one of the few major accomplishments of the Confederation Congress, it must be seen within a context of political impotence.

FROM CRISIS TO A CONSTITUTION

The Americans most deeply concerned about the inadequacies of the Articles of Confederation were those involved in overseas trade and foreign affairs. It was in those areas that the articles were most obviously deficient: Congress could not impose its will on the states to establish a uniform commercial policy or to ensure the enforcement of treaties. The problems involving trade were particularly serious. Less than a year after the end of the war, the American economy slid into a depression; both exporters of staple crops (especially tobacco and rice) and importers of manufactured goods were adversely affected by the postwar restrictions on American commerce imposed by European powers. Although recovery had begun by 1786, the war's effects proved impossible to erase entirely, particularly in the Lower South.

The war, indeed, had wrought permanent change in the American economy. The near-total cessation of commerce in nonmilitary items during the war years proved a great stimulus to domestic manufacturing. Consequently, despite the influx of European goods after 1783, the postwar period witnessed the

A woodcut of Daniel Shays and one of his chief officers, Job Shattuck, in 1787. *National Portrait Gallery, Smithsonian Institution, Washington, D.C.*

stirrings of American industrial development—for example, the first American textile mill began production in Pawtucket, Rhode Island, in 1793. Because of continuing population growth, the domestic market assumed greater relative importance in the overall economy. Moreover, foreign trade patterns shifted from Europe and toward the West Indies, continuing a trend that had begun before the war. Foodstuffs shipped to the French and Dutch Caribbean islands became America's largest single export, replacing tobacco (thus accelerating the Chesapeake's conversion from tobacco to grain production; see page 78).

Recognizing the Confederation Congress's inability to deal with commercial matters, Virginia invited the other states to a conference at Annapolis, Maryland, to discuss trade policy. Although eight states named representatives to the meeting in September 1786, only five delegations attended. Those present realized that they were too few in number to have any real impact on the political system. They issued a call for another convention, to be held in Philadelphia in nine months, "to devise such further provisions as shall . . . appear necessary to render the constitution of the federal government adequate to the exigencies of the Union."

That fall an incident in western Massachusetts helped to convince other Americans that broad changes were necessary in their national government.

Shays' Rebellion

Crowds of farmers angered by high taxes and the low supply of money halted court proceedings in which the state was trying to seize property for nonpayment of taxes. The insurgents were led by Daniel Shays, a farmer who had risen to the rank of captain in the Revolutionary army; many of them were respected war veterans, described as "gentlemen" in contemporary accounts of the riots. Clearly the episode could not be dismissed as the work of an unruly rabble. What did the uprising mean for the future of the republic? Was it a sign of impending anarchy? Those were the questions that worried the nation's political leaders.

The protesters explained their position in an address to the governor and council of Massachusetts. They proclaimed their loyalty to the nation but objected to the state's fiscal policies, which, they said, prevented them from providing adequately for their families. Referring to their experience as revolutionary soldiers, they asserted that they "esteem[ed] one moment of Liberty to be worth an eternity of Bondage."

To residents of eastern Massachusetts and other citizens of the United States, the most frightening aspect of the uprising was the rebels' attempt to forge direct links with the earlier struggle for independence. The state legislature issued an address to the people, asserting that "in a republican government the majority must govern. If the minor part governs it becomes aristocracy; if every one opposed at his pleasure, it is no government, it is anarchy and confusion." Thus Massachusetts officials insisted that the crowd actions that had once been a justifiable response to British tyranny were no longer legitimate. In a republic, reform had to come about through the ballot box rather than by force. If the nation's citizens refused to submit to legitimate authority, the result would be chaos and collapse of the government.

Consequently, Shays' Rebellion symbolically seemed to challenge the existence of the entire United States, though it never seriously threatened even the state of Massachusetts. (The rebels were easily dispersed by militia early in 1787.) Of the major American political thinkers, only Thomas Jefferson could view the Massachusetts incidents without alarm. "What country can preserve its liberties, if its rulers are not warned from time to time that their people preserve the spirit of resistance?" Jefferson wrote from Paris, where he was serving as American ambassador. "What signify a few lives lost in a century or two? The tree of liberty must be refreshed from time to time, with the blood of patriots and tyrants. It is its natural manure."

But Jefferson was clearly exceptional. Shays' Rebellion unquestionably hastened the movement toward comprehensive revision of the Articles of Confederation. In February 1787, after most

Calling of the Constitutional Convention

of the states had already appointed delegates, the Confederation Congress belatedly endorsed the convention. In mid-May, fifty-five men, representing all the states but Rhode Island, assembled in Philadelphia to begin their deliberations.

The vast majority of the delegates were men of property and substance, and they all favored reform; otherwise they would not have come to Philadelphia. Most wanted to invigorate the national government, to give it new authority to solve the problems besetting the United States. Among their number were merchants, planters, physicians, generals, governors, and especially lawyers—twenty-three had studied the law. Most had been born in America, and many came from families that had arrived in the seventeenth century. In an era when only a tiny proportion of the population had any advanced education, more than half had attended college. A few had been educated in Britain, but most were graduates of American institutions: Princeton (ten), William and Mary (four), Yale (three), Harvard and Columbia (two each). The youngest delegate was twenty-six, the oldest—Benjamin Franklin—eighty-one. Like George Washington, whom they elected chairman, most were in their vigorous middle years. A dozen men did the bulk of the convention's work: Oliver Ellsworth and Roger Sherman of Connecticut; Elbridge Gerry and Rufus King of Massachusetts; William Paterson of New Jersey; Gouverneur Morris of New York; James Wilson of Pennsylvania; John Rutledge and Charles Pinckney of South Carolina; and Edmund Randolph, George Mason, and James Madison of Virginia. Of those leaders, Madison was by far the most important; he truly deserves the title Father of the Constitution.

The frail, shy, slightly built James Madison was thirty-six years old in 1787. Raised in the Piedmont country of Virginia, he had attended Princeton, served on the local committee of safety,

James Madison: His Early Life

and been elected successively to the Virginia provincial convention, the state's lower and upper houses, and finally the Continental Congress (1780–1783). Although Madison returned to Virginia to serve in the state legislature in 1784, he remained in touch with national politics, partly through his continuing correspondence with his close friend Thomas Jefferson. A promoter of the Annapolis convention, he strongly supported its call for further reform.

Madison was unique among the delegates in his systematic preparation for the Philadelphia meeting. Through Jefferson in Paris he bought more than two hundred books on history and government, and carefully analyzed their accounts of past confederacies and republics. In April 1787, a month before the convention began, he summed up the results of his research in a lengthy paper entitled "Vices of the Political System of the United States." After listing the eleven major flaws he perceived in the current structure of the government (among them "en-

James Madison (1751–1836), the youthful scholar and skilled politician who earned the title Father of the Constitution.   Collection of Albert E. Leeds.

croachments by the states on the federal authority" and "want of concert in matters where common interest requires it"), Madison revealed the conclusion that would guide his actions over the next few months. What the government most needed, he declared, was "such a modification of the sovereignty as will render it sufficiently neutral between the different interests and factions, to controul one part of the society from invading the rights of another, and at the same time sufficiently controuled itself, from setting up an interest adverse to that of the whole Society."

Thus Madison set forth the principle of checks and balances. The government, he believed, had to be constructed in such a way that it could not become tyrannical or fall wholly under the influence of a particular interest group. He regarded the large size of a potential national republic as an advantage in that respect. Rejecting the common assertion that republics had to be small to survive, Madison argued that a large, diverse republic was in fact to be preferred.

Because the nation would include many different interest groups, no one of them would be able to control the government. Political stability would result from compromises among the contending parties.

Madison's conception of national government was embodied in the so-called Virginia plan, introduced on May 29 by his colleague Edmund Randolph. The

Virginia and New Jersey Plans

plan provided for a two-house legislature with proportional representation in both houses, an executive elected by Congress, a national judiciary, and congressional veto over state laws. It gave Congress the broad power to legislate "in all cases to which the separate states are incompetent." Had the Virginia plan been adopted intact, it would have created a government in which national authority reigned unchallenged and state power was greatly diminished.

But the convention included many delegates who, while recognizing the need for change, believed that the Virginians had gone too far in the direction of national consolidation. After Randolph's proposal had been debated for several weeks, the disaffected delegates united under the leadership of William Paterson. On June 15 Paterson presented an alternative scheme, the New Jersey plan, calling for modifications in the Articles of Confederation rather than a complete overhaul of the government. Even before introducing his proposals, Paterson had made his position clear in debate. On June 9 he asserted that the articles were "the proper basis of all the proceedings of the convention," and warned that if the delegates did not confine themselves to amending the articles they would be charged with "usurpation" by their constituents. All that was needed, Paterson contended, was "to mark the orbits of the states with due precision and provide for the use of coercion" by the national government. Although the delegates rejected Paterson's narrow interpretation of their task, he and his allies won a number of major victories in the months that followed.

The delegates began their work by discussing the structure and functions of Congress. They readily concurred that the new national government, like the states, should have a two-house (bicameral) legislature. But then they discovered that they differed widely in their answers to three key questions: Should there be representation proportional to population in both houses of Congress? How was that representation in either or both houses to be apportioned among the states? And, finally, how were the members of the two houses to be elected?

The last issue was the easiest to resolve. In the words of John Dickinson, the delegates thought it "essential" that members of one branch of Congress be elected directly by the people and "expedient" that members of the other be chosen by the state legislatures. Since the legislatures had selected delegates to the Confederation Congress, they would expect a similar privilege in the new government. Had the convention not agreed to allow state legislatures to elect senators, the Constitution would have aroused significant opposition among political leaders at the state level.

Considerably more difficult was the matter of proportional representation in the Senate. The delegates accepted without much debate the principle of proportional representation in the lower house. But the smaller states, through their spokesman Luther Martin of Maryland, argued for equal representation in the Senate, while large states like Pennsylvania supported a proportional plan for the upper house. Martin argued that "an equal vote in each state was essential to the federal idea," but James Wilson responded with the query, are we forming a government "for *men,* or for the imaginary beings called *states?*" For weeks the convention was deadlocked on the issue, neither side being able to obtain a majority. A committee appointed to work out a compromise recommended equal representation in the Senate, coupled with a proviso that all appropriation bills had to originate in the lower house. But not until the convention accepted Roger Sherman's suggestion that a state's two senators vote as individuals rather than as a unit was a breakdown averted.

Another critical question remained, one that divided the nation along sectional rather than population lines: How was representation in the lower house to be apportioned among the states? Delegates from states with large numbers of slaves wanted all people, black and white, to be counted equally; delegates from states with few slaves wanted only free people to be counted. The issue was resolved by using a formula developed by the Confederation Congress in 1783 to allocate taxation among the states: three-fifths of the slaves would be included in the population

totals. (The formula reflected the delegates' judgment that slaves were less efficient producers of wealth than free people, not that they were 60 percent human and 40 percent property.) After the three-fifths compromise was linked to a clause allowing Congress to stop the slave trade after twenty years (thereby preventing the indefinite increase of the slave population), it was unanimously accepted. Only two delegates, Gouverneur Morris and George Mason, spoke out against the institution of slavery itself.

Once agreement was reached on the knotty problem of representation, the delegates had little difficulty achieving consensus on the other major issues confronting them. Instead of giving Congress the nearly unlimited scope proposed in the Virginia plan, the delegates enumerated congressional powers and then provided for flexibility by granting all authority "necessary and proper" to carry out those powers. Discarding the legislative veto contained in the Virginia plan, the convention implied a judicial veto instead. The Constitution plus national laws and treaties would constitute "the supreme law of the land; and the judges in every state shall be bound thereby." The convention placed primary responsibility for the conduct of foreign affairs in the hands of the president, who was also designated commander-in-chief of the armed forces. The delegates established an elaborate mechanism, the electoral college, to select the president, in order to ensure that the executive would be independent of the national legislature. They also agreed that the chief executive should serve a four-year term but be eligible for re-election.

The final document still showed signs of its origins in the Virginia plan, but compromises had created a system of government less powerful at the national level than Madison and Randolph had envisioned. The key to the Constitution was the distribution of political authority—separation of powers among the executive, legislative, and judicial branches of the national government, and division of powers between states and nation. The branches were balanced against one another, their powers deliberately entwined to prevent them from acting independently. The president was given a veto over congressional legislation, but his treaties and major appointments required the consent of the Senate. Congress could impeach the president and the federal

Separation of Powers

judges, but the courts appeared to have the final say on interpretation of the Constitution. As Madison had intended, the system of checks and balances would make it difficult for the government to become tyrannical. At the same time, though, the elaborate system would sometimes prevent the government from acting quickly and decisively. Furthermore, the line between state and national powers was so ambiguously and vaguely drawn that the United States had to fight a civil war in the next century before the issue was fully resolved. (See Appendix for the full text of the Constitution.)

The convention held its last session on September 17, 1787. Of the forty-two delegates present, only three refused to sign the Constitution. (Two of the three, George Mason and Elbridge Gerry, declined, in part, because of the lack of a bill of rights.) Benjamin Franklin had written a speech calling for unity; because his voice was too weak to be heard, James Wilson read it for him. "I confess that there are several parts of this constitution which I do not at present approve," Franklin admitted. Yet he urged its acceptance "because I expect no better, and because I am not sure, that it is not the best." Only then was the Constitution made public. The convention's proceedings had been entirely secret—and remained so until the delegates' private notes were published in the nineteenth century.

OPPOSITION AND RATIFICATION

Later that same month the Confederation Congress submitted the Constitution to the states but did not formally recommend approval. The ratification clause of the Constitution provided for the new system to take effect once it was approved by special conventions in at least nine states. The delegates to each state convention were to be elected by the people. Thus the national constitution, unlike the Articles of Confederation, would rest directly on popular authority (and the presumably hostile state legislatures would be circumvented).

As the states began to elect delegates to the special conventions, debate over the proposed government grew more heated. Newspapers were filled with essays questioning various clauses of the Constitution, and pamphlets attacked or defended the convention's decisions. It quickly became apparent that the disputes within the Constitutional Convention had been minor compared with the divisions of opinion within the country as a whole. After all, the delegates at Philadelphia had agreed on the need for basic reforms in the American political system. Many citizens, though, not only rejected that conclusion but believed that the proposed government, despite its built-in safeguards, held the potential for tyranny.

Critics of the Constitution, who became known as Antifederalists, fell into two main groups: those who emphasized the threat to the states embodied in the new national government,
Antifederalists and those who stressed the dangers to individuals posed by the lack of a bill of rights. Ultimately, though, the two positions were one. The Antifederalists saw the states as the chief protectors of individual rights, and their weakening as the onset of arbitrary power.

Fundamentally the Antifederalists were traditionalists, fearful of a too-powerful government. Their arguments against the Constitution often consisted largely of lists of potential abuses of the national government's authority. They were the heirs of the Real Whig ideology of the late 1760s and early 1770s, which stressed the need for the people's constant vigilance to avert oppression (see page 109). Indeed, in some instances the Antifederalists were the very men who had originally promulgated those ideas; for example, Samuel Adams and Richard Henry Lee were both leaders of the opposition to the Constitution. Antifederalist ranks were heavily peopled not only by such older Americans (whose political opinions had been shaped prior to the more centralizing, nationalistic Revolution) but also by small farmers, who jealously guarded their property against excessive taxation by either state or nation.

As the months passed and public debate continued, the Antifederalists focused more sharply on the Constitution's lack of a bill of rights. Even if the states were weakened by the new system, they believed, the people could still be protected from tyranny if their rights were specifically guaranteed. The Constitution did contain some prohibitions on congres-

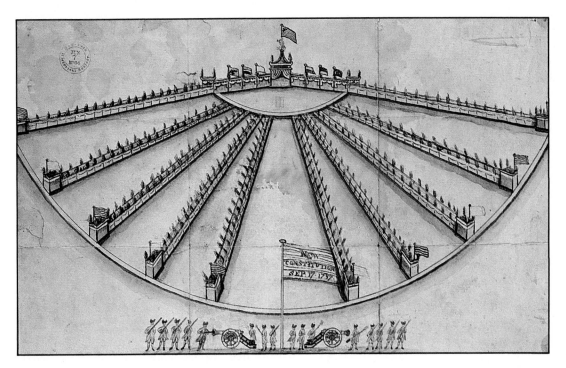

In July 1788, New York City's leaders celebrated their state's ratification of the Constitution at an elaborate banquet served in a pavilion erected for the occasion. Their hopes for an orderly government were symbolized by the orderly arrangement of the tables, separate but linked into a semicircle by the central structure displaying flags and banners. *The New-York Historical Society.*

sional power—for example, the writ of habeas corpus, which prevented arbitrary imprisonment, could not be suspended except in dire emergencies—but the Antifederalists found these provisions inadequate. Nor were they reassured by the Federalists' assertion that, since the new government was one of limited powers, it had no authority to violate the people's rights. *Letters of a Federal Farmer*, perhaps the most widely read Antifederalist pamphlet, listed the rights that should be protected: freedom of the press and of religion, the right to trial by jury, and guarantees against unreasonable search warrants.

From Paris, Thomas Jefferson added his voice to the chorus. Replying to Madison's letter conveying a copy of the Constitution, Jefferson wrote: "I like much the general idea of framing a government which should go on of itself peaceably, without needing continual recurrence to the state legislatures." He also approved of the separation of powers among the

three branches of government and declared himself "captivated" by the compromise between the large and small states. Nevertheless, he added, he did not like "the omission of a bill of rights. . . . A bill of rights is what the people are entitled to against every government on earth, general or particular, and what no just government should refuse, or rest on inference."

As the state conventions met to consider ratification, the lack of a bill of rights loomed larger and larger as a flaw in the new form of government. Four of the first five states to ratify did so unanimously, but

Ratification of the Constitution

serious disagreements then began to surface. Massachusetts ratified by a majority of only 19 votes out of 355 cast; in New Hampshire the Federalists won by a majority of 57 to 47. When New Hampshire ratified, in June 1788, the requirement of nine states had been satisfied. But New York and Virginia had not yet voted, and everyone realized the new constitution could not succeed unless those key states accepted it. In Virginia, despite a valiant effort by the Antifederalist Patrick Henry, the pro-Constitution forces won 89 to 79. In New York James Madison, John Jay, and Alexander Hamilton campaigned for ratification by publishing *The Federalist*, a political tract that explained the theory behind the Constitution and masterfully answered its critics. Their reasoned arguments, coupled with the promise that a bill of rights would be added to the Constitution, helped win the battle. On July 26, 1788, New York ratified the Constitution by the slim margin of 3 votes. The new government was a reality, even though the last state (Rhode Island, which had not participated in the convention) did not formally join the union until 1790.

The experience of fighting a war and of struggling for survival as an independent nation in the 1780s had altered the political context of American life. Whereas at the outset of the war most politically aware Americans believed that "that government which governs best governs least," by the late 1780s many had changed their minds. These were the drafters and supporters of the Constitution, who had concluded from the republic's vicissitudes under the Articles of Confederation that the United States needed a more powerful central government. They won their point when the Constitution was adopted, however narrowly. They contended during the ratification debates that their proposed solution to the nation's problems was just as "republican" in conception (if not more so) as the articles. While disagreeing about details, both sides concurred in their general adherence to republican principles.

White males wholly dominated the new United States. The era that saw the formation of the union also witnessed the systematic formulation of American racist thought, and the two processes were intimately linked. One way to preserve the freedom of all whites was to ensure the continued subjection of all blacks, slave or free. Likewise, one way to preserve the unchallenged economic independence of white men was to ensure the economic and political dependence of white women on their husbands, fathers, and brothers. Even if the leaders of the United States were not consciously aware of adopting such strategies, their decisions had similar effects. Independence had been fought for and won by many Americans—white, black, and red, male and female—but in the new republic only white males would hold political power.

SUGGESTIONS FOR FURTHER READING

General

Joyce Appleby, "The Social Origins of American Revolutionary Ideology," *Journal of American History*, 64 (1978), 935–958; Staughton Lynd, *Class Conflict, Slavery, & the United States Constitution: Ten Essays* (1967); Forrest McDonald, *E Pluribus Unum: The Formation of the American Republic 1776–1790* (1965); Jackson Turner Main, *The Social Structure of Revolutionary America* (1965); Curtis P. Nettels, *The Emergence of a National Economy, 1775–1815* (1962); Robert R. Palmer, *The Age of the Democratic Rev-*

olution: *A Political History of Europe and America 1760–1800*, 2 vols. (1959, 1964); Gordon S. Wood, *The Creation of the American Republic, 1776–1787* (1969).

Continental Congress and Articles of Confederation

E. James Ferguson, *The Power of the Purse: A History of American Public Finance, 1776–1790* (1961); H. James Henderson, *Party Politics in the Continental Congress* (1974); Merrill Jensen, *The Articles of Confederation: An Interpretation of the Social-Constitutional History of the American Revolution, 1774–1781*, 2nd ed. (1959); Merrill Jensen, *The New Nation: A History of the United States During the Confederation, 1781–1789* (1950); Jack N. Rakove, *The Beginnings of National Politics: An Interpretive History of the Continental Congress* (1979).

State Politics

Willi Paul Adams, *The First American Constitutions: Republican Ideology and the Making of the State Constitutions in the Revolutionary Era* (1980); Edward Countryman, *A People in Revolution: The American Revolution and Political Society in New York, 1760–1790* (1981); Ronald Hoffman and Peter Albert, eds., *Sovereign States in an Age of Uncertainty* (1981); Donald Lutz, *Popular Consent and Popular Control: Whig Political Theory in the Early State Constitutions* (1980); Jackson Turner Main, *Political Parties Before the Constitution* (1973); Jackson Turner Main, *The Sovereign States, 1775–1783* (1973); Jackson Turner Main, *The Upper House in Revolutionary America, 1763–1788* (1967); Stephen E. Patterson, *Political Parties in Revolutionary Massachusetts* (1973); J. R. Pole, *Political Representation in England and the Origins of the American Republic* (1966); Marion L. Starkey, *A Little Rebellion* (1955); David P. Szatmary, *Shays' Rebellion: The Making of an Agrarian Insurrection* (1980).

The Constitution

Douglass Adair, *Fame and the Founding Fathers* (1974); Charles A. Beard, *An Economic Interpretation of the Constitution of the United States* (1913); Irving Brant, *James Madison*, 6 vols. (1941–1961); Forrest McDonald, *We the People: The Economic Origins of the Constitution* (1958); Jackson Turner Main, *The Anti-Federalists: Critics of the Constitution, 1781–1788* (1961); Frederick W. Marks, III, *Independence on Trial: Foreign Affairs and the Making of the Constitution* (1973); Clinton Rossiter, *1787: The Grand Convention* (1973); Robert A. Rutland, *The Ordeal of the Constitution: The Antifederalists and the Ratification Struggle of 1787–88* (1966); Abraham Sofaer, *War, Foreign Affairs, and Constitutional Power*, vol. 1: *The Origins* (1976); Carl

Van Doren, *The Great Rehearsal: The Story of the Making and Ratifying of the Constitution of the United States* (1948); Garry Wills, *Explaining America: The Federalist* (1981).

Education and Culture

Lawrence A. Cremin, *American Education: The National Experience, 1783–1876* (1981); Joseph J. Ellis, *After the Revolution: Profiles of Early American Culture* (1979); Carl F. Kaestle, *Pillars of the Republic: Common Schools and American Society, 1780–1860* (1983); Russel B. Nye, *The Cultural Life of the New Nation: 1776–1803* (1960); Kenneth Silverman, *A Cultural History of the American Revolution* (1976).

Women

Charles Akers, *Abigail Adams: An American Woman* (1980); Ruth Bloch, "American Feminine Ideals in Transition: The Rise of the Moral Mother, 1785–1815," *Feminist Studies*, 4, No. 2 (June 1978), 100–126; Nancy F. Cott, "Divorce and the Changing Status of Women in Massachusetts," *William and Mary Quarterly*, 3rd ser., 33 (1976), 586–614; Linda K. Kerber, *Women of the Republic: Intellect & Ideology in Revolutionary America* (1980); Mary Beth Norton, *Liberty's Daughters: The Revolutionary Experience of American Women, 1750–1800* (1980); Lynn Withey, *Dearest Friend: A Life of Abigail Adams* (1980).

Blacks and Slavery

Ira Berlin, *Slaves Without Masters: The Free Negro in the Antebellum South* (1974); Ira Berlin and Ronald Hoffman, eds., *Slavery and Freedom in the Age of the American Revolution* (1983); David Brion Davis, *The Problem of Slavery in the Age of Revolution, 1770–1823* (1975); Carol V. R. George, *Segregated Sabbaths: Richard Allen and the Emergence of Independent Black Churches 1760–1840* (1973); Winthrop Jordan, *White over Black: American Attitudes Toward the Negro, 1550–1812* (1968); Duncan J. Macleod, *Slavery, Race, and the American Revolution* (1974); Donald L. Robinson, *Slavery in the Structure of American Politics 1765–1820* (1971); Arthur Zilversmit, *The First Emancipation: The Abolition of Slavery in the North* (1967).

Indians

Dorothy Jones, *License for Empire: Colonialism by Treaty in Early America* (1982); Francis Paul Prucha, *American Indian Policy in the Formative Years: The Indian Trade and Intercourse Acts 1790–1834* (1962); Bernard Sheehan, *Seeds of Extinction: Jeffersonian Philanthropy and the American Indian* (1973); Anthony F. C. Wallace, *The Death and Rebirth of the Seneca* (1969).

Politics and Society in the Early Republic

1790–1800

Chapter 7

Charles Thomson, secretary to Congress, arrived at Mount Vernon, Virginia, around noon on April 14, 1789. He brought momentous news: the first electoral college convened under the new Constitution had unanimously elected George Washington president of the United States, and Congress had confirmed the choice.

Washington had been expecting the summons to New York City, the nation's capital. Two days later he and Thomson began the journey north. The new president, who disliked pomp, hoped in vain for an uneventful trip. After being honored at formal dinners in Alexandria, Baltimore, and Wilmington, he arrived on April 20 at a bridge across the Schuylkill River. Charles Willson Peale, the painter and naturalist, had turned the crude bridge into a triumphal avenue, beginning and ending with laurel-bedecked arches twenty feet high and flanked on both sides by flags. As Washington rode a white horse beneath the first arch, Peale's daughter Angelica operated a machine that placed a laurel wreath on his head. In Philadelphia, on the other side of the river, more than twenty thousand people lined the streets for a glimpse of the first president of the new republic.

Entering Trenton the next day, Washington rode under another triumphal arch, this one emblazoned with the words, "The Defender of the Mothers will be the Protector of the Daughters." The women of New Jersey had not forgotten that Washington's victories at Princeton and Trenton had put an end to the epidemic of rape they endured when the British occupied the state. A group of girls dressed in white threw flowers in his path while singing an ode composed for the occasion.

Each New Jersey town Washington passed through greeted him with speeches, music, pealing bells, and military salutes. Finally, at Elizabeth on April 23, he was met by a congressional committee sent to escort him to Manhattan. The official party traveled up the Hudson on a specially constructed fifty-foot barge draped in red. When the barge arrived at the foot of Wall Street, church bells rang and thirteen guns fired a salute. On the night of Washington's inauguration one week later, New York City was illuminated by lanterns and the festivities ended with a spectacular two-hour fireworks display.

The United States formally honored its first president with an outpouring of affection and respect that has rarely been equaled since. Washington's inauguration allowed the people to express their pride in the Revolution, the new Constitution, and most of all in the nation itself. The struggle against Britain had nurtured in Americans an intense nationalism. They believed their republican experiment placed them in the vanguard of political reform, and they optimistically expected a future of prosperity, expansion, national unity, and independence from Europe.

Yet Americans were unsuccessful in their quest for unity and unqualified independence during the 1790s. Nowhere was their failure more evident than in the realm of national politics. The fierce battle over the Constitution foreshadowed an even wider division over the major political issues the republic had to confront. To make matters worse, Americans' belief in the efficacy of republicanism prevented them from fully anticipating the political disagreements that characterized the 1790s. They believed that the Constitution would resolve the problems that had arisen during the Confederation period, and they expected the new government to rule largely by consensus. Accordingly, they found it difficult to understand and deal with partisan tensions that developed out of disputes over such fundamental questions as the extent to which authority, especially fiscal authority, should be centralized in the national government; the formulation of foreign policy in an era of continual warfare in Europe; and the limits of dissent within the republic. As the decade closed they still had not come to terms with the implications of partisan politics.

Prosperity and expansion too were not easily attained. The United States economy still depended on the export trade, as it had throughout the colonial era. When warfare between England and France resumed in 1793, Americans found their commerce disrupted once again, with consequent fluctuations in their income and profits. Moreover, the strength of the Miami confederacy blocked the westward expansion of white settlement north of the Ohio River

This flag of the New York Society of Pewterers was carried in the New York City Constitution ratification parade in July 1788. The New-York Historical Society.

until after the Treaty of Greenville in 1795 (see page 171). South of the Ohio, settlements were established west of the mountains as early as the 1770s, but the geographical barrier of the Appalachians tended to isolate them from the eastern seaboard. Not until the last years of the century did the frontier settlements become more fully integrated into American life through the vehicle of the Second Great Awakening, a religious revival that swept both east and west.

BUILDING A WORKABLE GOVERNMENT

In 1788 Americans celebrated the ratification of the Constitution with a series of parades, held in many cities on the Fourth of July. The processions were carefully planned to symbolize the unity of the new nation and to recall its history to the minds of the watching throngs. The parades, like prerevolutionary protest meetings, served as political educators for literate and illiterate Americans alike. Men and women who could not read were thereby informed of the significance of the new Constitution in the life of the nation. They were also instructed about political leaders' hopes for industry and frugality on the part of a virtuous American public.

The Philadelphia parade, planned largely by Charles Willson Peale, was filled with symbols related to those goals. About five thousand people participated in the procession, which stretched for a mile and a half and lasted three hours. Twelve costumed "axemen" representing the first pioneers were followed by a mounted military troop and a group of men with flags symbolizing independence, the peace treaty, the French alliance, and other revolutionary events. A band played a "Federal March" composed for the occasion. There followed a Constitution float, displaying a large framed copy of the Constitution and a thirteen-foot-high eagle. A number of local dignitaries marched in front of the next float, "The Grand Federal Edifice," a domed structure supported by thirteen columns (three of which were left unfinished to signify the states that had not yet ratified).

The remainder of the parade consisted of groups of artisans and professionals marching together and dramatizing their work. One of the farmers scattered seed in the streets; on the manufacturers' float, cloth was being made; the printers operated a press, distributing copies of a poem written to honor the Constitution. More than forty other groups of tradesmen, such as barbers, hatters, and clockmakers, sponsored similar floats. The artisans were followed by lawyers, doctors, clergymen of all denominations, and congressmen. Bringing up the rear was a symbol of the nation's future, a contingent of students from the University of Pennsylvania and other city schools. Marching with their teachers, they carried a flag labeled "The Rising Generation."

The nationalistic spirit expressed in the ratification processions carried over into the first session of Congress. In the congressional elections, held late in 1788, only a few Antifederalists had

First Congress run or been elected to office. Thus the First Congress was composed chiefly of men who were considerably more inclined toward a strong national government than had been the delegates to the Constitutional Convention. Since the Constitution had deliberately left many key issues undecided, the nationalists' domination of Congress meant that their views on those points quickly prevailed.

Congress faced four immediate problems when it convened in April 1789: raising revenue to support the new government, responding to the state ratification conventions' calls for the addition of a bill of rights to the Constitution, setting up executive departments, and organizing the federal judiciary. The latter task was especially important. The Constitution established a Supreme Court but left it to Congress to decide whether to have other federal courts as well.

The Virginian James Madison, who had been elected to the House of Representatives, soon became as influential in Congress as he had been at the Phil-

adelphia convention. Only a few months into the session, he persuaded Congress to impose a tariff on certain imported goods. Consequently, the First Congress quickly achieved what the Confederation Congress never had: an effective national tax law. The new government would have problems, but lack of revenue in its first years was not one of them.

Madison also took the lead on the issue of constitutional amendments. At the convention and thereafter, he had consistently opposed additional limitations on the national govern-

Bill of Rights ment on the grounds that it was unnecessary to guarantee the people's rights when the government was one of limited, delegated powers. But Madison recognized that public opinion, as expressed by the state ratifying conventions, was against him, and accordingly placed nineteen proposed amendments before the House. Congress eventually sent twelve amendments to the states for ratification. Two, having to do with the number of congressmen and their salaries, were not accepted by a sufficient number of states. The other ten amendments officially became part of the Constitution on December 15, 1791. Not for many years, though, did they become known collectively as the Bill of Rights (see Appendix).

The first amendment specifically prohibited Congress from passing any law restricting the people's right to freedom of religion, speech, press, peaceable assembly, or petition. The next two arose directly from the former colonists' fear of standing armies as a threat to freedom. The second amendment guaranteed the people's right "to keep and bear arms" because of the need for a "well-regulated Militia." Thus the constitutional right to bear arms was based on the expectation that most able-bodied men would serve the nation as citizen soldiers, and there would be no need for a standing army. The third amendment defined the circumstances in which troops could be quartered in private homes. The next five pertained to judicial procedures. The fourth amendment prohibited "unreasonable searches and seizures"; the fifth and sixth established the rights of accused persons; the seventh specified the conditions for jury trials in civil, as opposed to criminal, cases; and the eighth forbade "cruel and unusual punishments." Finally, the ninth and tenth amendments reserved to the people and the states other unspecified rights and powers. In short, the authors of the amendments made clear that in listing some rights explicitly they did not mean to preclude the exercise of others.

While debating the proposed amendments, Congress also concerned itself with the organization of the executive branch. It was readily agreed to continue the three administrative departments established under the Articles of Confederation: War, Foreign Affairs (renamed State), and Treasury. Congress also instituted two lesser posts: the attorney general—the nation's official lawyer—and the postmaster general, who would oversee the Post Office. The only serious controversy was whether the president alone could dismiss officials whom he had originally appointed with the consent of the Senate. After some debate, the House and Senate agreed that he had such authority. Thus was established the important principle that the heads of the executive departments are responsible solely to the president. Though it could not have been foreseen at the time, this precedent paved the way for the development of the president's cabinet.

Aside from the constitutional amendments, the most far-reaching piece of legislation enacted by the First Congress was the Judiciary Act of 1789. That

Judiciary Act of 1789

act was largely the work of Senator Oliver Ellsworth of Connecticut, a veteran of the Constitutional Convention who in 1796 would become the third chief justice of the United States. The Judiciary Act provided for the Supreme Court to have six members: a chief justice and five associate justices. It also defined the jurisdiction of the federal judiciary and established thirteen district courts and three circuit courts of appeal.

The act's most important provision may have been Section 25, which allowed appeals from state courts to the federal court system when certain types of constitutional issues were raised. This section was intended to implement Article VI of the Constitution, which stated that federal laws and treaties were to be considered "the supreme Law of the Land." If Article VI was to be enforced uniformly, the national judiciary clearly had to be able to overturn state court decisions in cases involving the Constitution, federal laws, or treaties. Yet nowhere did the Constitution explicitly permit such action by federal courts. The nationalistic First Congress accepted Ellsworth's argument that the right of appeal from state to federal

courts was implied in the wording of Article VI. Eventually, however, judges and legislators committed to the ideal of states' rights were to challenge that interpretation.

During the first decade of its existence, the Supreme Court handled few cases of any importance. Indeed, for its first three years it heard no cases at all. John Jay, the first chief justice, served only until 1795, and only one of the first five associate justices remained on the bench in 1799. But in a significant 1796 decision, *Ware* v. *Hylton*, the Court—acting on the basis of section 25 of the Judiciary Act of 1789— for the first time declared a state law unconstitutional. That same year it also reviewed the constitutionality of an act of Congress, upholding its validity in the case of *Hylton* v. *US*. The most important case of the decade, *Chisholm* v. *Georgia* (1793), established that states could be freely sued in federal courts by citizens of other states; this decision, unpopular with the states, was overruled five years later by the Eleventh Amendment to the Constitution (See Appendix for the text of the Constitution and all amendments.)

DOMESTIC POLICY UNDER WASHINGTON AND HAMILTON

George Washington did not seek the presidency. When he returned to Mount Vernon in 1783, he was eager for the peaceful life of a Virginia planter.

Election of the First President

He rebuilt his house, redesigned his gardens, experimented with new agricultural techniques, improved the breeding of his livestock, and speculated in western lands. Yet his fellow countrymen never regarded Washington as just another private citizen. Although he took little part in the political maneuverings that preceded the Constitutional Convention, he was unanimously elected its presiding officer. As a result, he did not participate in debates, but he consistently voted for a strong national government. Once the proposed structure of the government was presented to the public, Americans concurred that only George Washington had sufficient

The inauguration of George Washington as first president of the United States occurred on the balcony of Federal Hall in New York City. This engraving of the event was printed the following year; it was purchased by many patriotic Americans who wanted personal reminders of the momentous occasion.   Library of Congress.

by which he should be addressed aroused a good deal of controversy (Vice President John Adams favored "His Highness, the President of the United States of America, and Protector of their Liberties"), Washington said nothing; the accepted title soon became a plain "Mr. President." He used the heads of the executive departments collectively as his chief advisors and thus created the cabinet. As the Constitution required, he sent Congress an annual "State of the Union" message (though he did not deliver it in person, as presidents do today). Washington also concluded that he should exercise his veto power over congressional legislation very sparingly—only, indeed, if he was convinced a bill was unconstitutional.

Washington's first major task as president was to choose the men who would head the executive departments. For the War Department he selected an old comrade-in-arms, Henry Knox, who had been his reliable general of artillery during much of the Revolution. His choice for the State Department was his fellow Virginian Thomas Jefferson, who had just returned to the United States from his post as ambassador to France. Finally, for the crucial position of secretary of the treasury, the president chose the brilliant, intensely ambitious Alexander Hamilton.

Alexander Hamilton: His Early Life

The illegitimate son of a Scottish aristocrat and a woman divorced by her husband for adultery and desertion, Hamilton was born in the British West Indies in 1757. His early years were spent in poverty; after his mother's death when he was eleven, he worked as a clerk for a mercantile firm. In 1773 Hamilton enrolled in King's College (later Columbia University) in New York City; only eighteen months later the precocious seventeen-year-old contributed a major pamphlet to the prerevolutionary publication wars of late 1774. Devoted to the patriot cause, Hamilton volunteered for service in the American army, where he came to the attention of George Washington. In 1777 Washington appointed the young man as one of his aides-de-camp, and the two developed great affection for one another. Indeed, in some respects Hamilton became the son Washington never had.

The general's patronage enabled the poor youth of dubious background to marry well. At twenty-three he took as his wife Elizabeth Schuyler, the daughter of a wealthy New York family. After the

prestige to serve as the republic's first president. The vote of the electoral college was just a formality.

Washington was reluctant to return to public life, but knew he could not resist his country's call. Awaiting the summons to New York, he wrote to an old friend, "My movements to the chair of Government will be accompanied by feelings not unlike those of a culprit who is going to the place of his execution. . . . I am sensible, that I am embarking the voice of my Countrymen and a good name of my own, on this voyage, but what returns will be made for them, Heaven alone can foretell."

During his first months in office Washington acted cautiously, knowing that whatever he did would set precedents for the future. He held weekly receptions at which callers could pay their respects and toured different areas of the country in turn. When the title

war, Hamilton practiced law in New York City and served as a delegate first to the Annapolis Convention in 1786 and the following year to the Constitutional Convention. Though he exerted little influence at either convention, his contributions to *The Federalist* in 1788 revealed him to be one of the chief political thinkers in the republic.

In his dual role as secretary of the treasury and one of Washington's major advisors, two traits distinguished Hamilton from most of his contemporaries. First, he displayed an undivided, unquestioning loyalty to the nation as a whole. As a West Indian who had lived on the mainland only briefly before the war, Hamilton had no ties to an individual state. He showed little sympathy for, or understanding of, demands for local autonomy. Thus his fiscal policies aimed always at consolidation of power at the national level. Furthermore, he never feared the exercise of centralized executive authority, as did his older counterparts who had clashed repeatedly with colonial governors.

Second, he regarded his fellow human beings with unvarnished cynicism. Perhaps because of his difficult early life and his own overriding ambition, Hamilton believed people to be motivated primarily, if not entirely, by self-interest—particularly economic self-interest. He placed absolutely no reliance on people's capacity for virtuous and self-sacrificing behavior. That outlook set him apart from those republicans who foresaw a rosy future in which public-spirited citizens would pursue the common good rather than their own private advantage. Although other Americans (like Madison) also stressed the role of private interests in a republic, Hamilton went beyond them in his nearly exclusive emphasis on self-interest as the major motivator of human behavior. And those beliefs significantly influenced the way in which he tackled the monumental task before him: straightening out the new nation's tangled finances.

In 1789 Congress ordered the new secretary of the treasury to study the state of the public debt and to submit recommendations for supporting the government's credit. Hamilton discovered that the country's remaining war debts fell into three categories: those owed by the United States to foreign governments and investors, mostly to France (about $11 million); those owed by the national government to merchants,

National Debt

Alexander Hamilton (1737–1804), painted by John Trumbull in 1792. Hamilton was then at the height of his influence as secretary of the treasury, and his haughty, serene expression reveals his supreme self-confidence. Trumbull, an American student of the English artist Benjamin West, painted the portrait at the request of John Jay. National Gallery of Art, Gift of the Avalon Foundation.

former soldiers, holders of revolutionary bonds, and the like (about $27 million); and, finally, similar debts owed by state governments (roughly estimated at $25 million). With respect to the national debt, there was little disagreement: politically aware Americans recognized that if their new government was to succeed it would have to pay the obligations the nation had incurred while winning independence.

The state debts were quite another matter. Some states—notably Virginia, Maryland, North Carolina, and Georgia—had already paid off most of their war debts. They would oppose the national government's assumption of responsibility for other states' debts, since their citizens would be taxed to pay such obligations in addition to their own. Massachusetts, Connecticut, and South Carolina, on the other hand, still had sizable unpaid debts and would welcome a system of national assumption. The possible assumption of state debts also had political implications. Consolidation of the debt in the hands of the national government would unquestionably help to concentrate both economic and political power at the national level. A contrary policy would reserve greater independence of action for the states.

Hamilton's "Report on Public Credit," sent to Congress in January 1790, reflected both his national loyalty and his cynicism. It proposed that Congress **Hamilton's "Report on Public Credit"** assume outstanding state debts, combine them with national obligations, and issue new securities covering both principal and accumulated unpaid interest. Current holders of state or national debt certificates would have the option of taking a portion of their payment in western lands. Hamilton's aims were clear: he wanted to expand the financial reach of the United States government and reduce the economic power of the states. He also wanted to ensure that the holders of public securities—many of them wealthy merchants and speculators—would have a significant financial stake in the survival of the national government.

Hamilton's plan stimulated lively debate in Congress. The opposition coalesced around his former ally James Madison. Madison opposed the assumption of state debts, since his own state of Virginia had already paid off most of its obligations. As a congressman tied to agrarian rather than moneyed interests, he opposed the notion that only current holders of public securities should receive payments. Believing with some reason that speculators had purchased large quantities of debt certificates at a small fraction of their face value, Madison proposed that the original holders of the debt also be compensated by the government. But Madison's plan, though probably more fair than Hamilton's—in that it would have directly rewarded those people who had actually supplied the revolutionary governments with goods or services— was exceedingly complex and perhaps impossible to administer. The House of Representatives rejected it.

At first, however, the House also rejected the assumption of state debts. Since the Senate, by contrast, adopted Hamilton's plan largely intact, a series of compromises followed. Hamilton agreed to changes in the assumption plan that would benefit Virginia in particular. The assumption bill also became linked in a complex way to the other major controversial issue of that congressional session: the location of the permanent national capital. Northerners and southerners both wanted the capital in their region. The traditional story that Hamilton and Madison agreed over Jefferson's dinner table to exchange assumption of state debts for a southern site is not supported by the surviving evidence, but a political deal was undoubtedly struck. The Potomac River was designated as the site for the capital. Simultaneously, the four congressmen from Maryland and Virginia whose districts contained the most likely locations for the new city switched from opposition to support for assumption. As a result, the first part of Hamilton's financial program became law in August 1790.

Four months later Hamilton submitted to Congress a second report on public credit, recommending the chartering of a national bank. Like his proposal for assumption of the debt, this recommendation too aroused considerable opposition. Unlike the earlier debate, which involved matters of policy, this one focused on constitutional issues. It also arose primarily after Congress had already adopted the bank proposal.

Hamilton modeled his bank on the Bank of England. The Bank of the United States was to be capitalized at $10 million, with only $2 million coming from **First Bank of the United States** public funds. The rest would be supplied by private investors. Its charter was to run for twenty years, and one-fifth of its directors were to be named by the government. Its bank notes would circulate as the nation's currency; it would also act as the collecting and disbursing agent for the treasury, and lend money to the government. Most people recognized that such an institution would benefit the country, especially because it would solve the problem of America's perpetual shortage of an acceptable medium of exchange. But there was another issue: did the Constitution give Congress the power to establish such a bank?

James Madison, for one, answered that question with a resounding no. He pointed out that the delegates at the Philadelphia convention had specifically rejected a clause authorizing Congress to issue corporate charters. Consequently, he argued, that power could not be inferred from other parts of the Constitution.

Washington was sufficiently disturbed by Madison's contention that he decided to request other opinions

Chapter 7: POLITICS AND SOCIETY IN THE EARLY REPUBLIC, 1790–1800

before signing the bill. Edmund Randolph, the attorney general, and Thomas Jefferson, the secretary of state, agreed with Madison that the bank was unconstitutional. Jefferson referred to Article I, Section 8, of the Constitution, which gave Congress the power "to make all Laws which shall be necessary and proper for carrying into Execution the foregoing Powers." *Necessary* was the key word, Jefferson argued: Congress could do what was needed but it could not do what was merely desirable without specific constitutional authorization. Thus Jefferson formulated the strict-constructionist interpretation of the Constitution.

Washington asked Hamilton to reply to these negative assessments of his proposal. Hamilton's "Defense of the Constitutionality of the Bank," presented to Washington in February 1791, was a brilliant exposition of what has become known as the broad-constructionist view of the Constitution. Hamilton argued forcefully that Congress could choose any means not specifically prohibited by the Constitution to achieve a constitutional end. In short, if the end was constitutional and the means was not *unconsti-tutional*, then the means was also constitutional.

Washington was convinced. The bill became law; the bank proved successful. So did the scheme for funding and assumption: the new nation's securities became desirable investments for its own citizens and for wealthy foreigners. But two other aspects of Alexander Hamilton's wide-ranging financial scheme did not fare so well.

In December 1791, Hamilton presented to Congress his "Report on Manufactures," the third and last of his prescriptions for the American economy. In it he outlined an ambitious plan for encouraging and protecting the United States's infant industries, like shoemaking and textile manufacturing. Hamilton argued that the nation could never be truly independent as long as it had to rely heavily on Europe for its manufactured goods. He thus urged Congress to promote the immigration of technicians and laborers, enact protective tariffs, and support industrial development. Although many of Hamilton's ideas were implemented in later decades, few congressmen in 1791 could see much merit in his proposals. They firmly believed that America's future was agrarian. The mainstay of the republic was the virtuous yeoman farmer. Therefore, Congress rejected the report.

That same year Congress did accept the other part of Hamilton's financial program, an excise tax on whiskey, because of the need for additional government revenues and because of the congressmen's desire to reduce the nation's consumption of distilled spirits. (Eighteenth-century Americans were notorious for their heavy drinking habits; annual per capita consumption of alcohol then was about double today's rate.) The import duties adopted in 1789 had raised the price of rum (which was made from imported molasses); the excise tax increased the price of domestically produced whiskey. The new tax most directly affected western farmers, who sold their grain crops in the form of distilled spirits as a means of avoiding the high costs of transporting wagonloads of bulky corn over the mountains.

News of the excise law set off immediate protests in frontier areas of Pennsylvania and the Carolinas. But matters did not come to a head until the summer of 1794, when western Pennsylvania farmers tried to stop a federal marshal from arresting some men charged with violating the law. The only person killed in the disturbances was a leader of the rioters, but President Washington was determined to prevent a recurrence of Shays' Rebellion. On August 7, he issued a proclamation calling on the insurgents to disperse by September 1, and he summoned more than twelve thousand militia from Pennsylvania and neighboring states. By the time the federal forces marched westward in October and November (headed some of the time by Washington himself), the riots had long since ended. The troops, who met no resistance, arrested a number of suspects. Only two were ever convicted of treason, and Washington pardoned both. The rebellion, such as it was, ended almost without bloodshed.

Whiskey Rebellion

The chief importance of the Whiskey Rebellion was not military victory over the rebels—for there was none—but rather the message it forcefully conveyed to the American public. The national government, Washington had demonstrated, would not allow violent organized resistance to its laws. In the new republic, change would be effected peacefully, by legal means. Those who were dissatisfied with the law should try to amend or repeal it, not take extralegal action.

An American artist painted this view of President Washington, in army uniform once again, as he (on October 18, 1794) reviewed the troops that had been summoned to suppress the Whiskey Rebellion. *Metropolitan Museum of Art, Gift of Edgar William and Bernice Chrysler Garbisch, 1963.*

By 1794, a group of Americans had already begun to seek change systematically within the confines of electoral politics, even though traditional political theory regarded organized opposition—especially in a republic—as illegitimate. The leaders of the opposition were Thomas Jefferson and James Madison, who became convinced as early as 1792 that Hamilton and his supporters intended to impose a corrupt, aristocratic government on the United States. Jefferson and Madison justified their opposition to Hamilton and his policies by contending that they were the true heirs of the Revolution, whereas Hamilton was actually plotting to subvert republican principles. To emphasize their point, they and their followers in Congress began calling themselves *Republicans.* Hamilton in turn accused Jefferson and Madison of the same crime: attempting to destroy the republic. To legitimize their claim to being the rightful interpreters of the Constitution, Hamilton and his supporters called themselves *Federalists.* In short, each group accused the other of being an illicit faction that was working to destroy the republican principles of the Revolution. (A faction was, in the traditional sense of the term, by definition opposed to the public good.)

At first, President Washington tried to remain aloof from the political dispute that divided his chief advisors, Hamilton and Jefferson. Even so, the controversy helped to persuade him to seek a second term of office in 1792 in hopes of promoting political unity. But in 1793 and thereafter, a series of developments in foreign affairs magnified the disagreements.

PARTISAN POLITICS AND FOREIGN POLICY

The first years under the Constitution were blessed by international peace. Eventually, however, the French Revolution, which began in 1789, brought about the resumption of hostilities between France, America's wartime ally, and Great Britain, America's most important trading partner.

At first, Americans welcomed the news that France was turning toward republicanism. The French people's success in limiting, then overthrowing, the monarchy seemed to vindicate the United States's own revolution. Now more than ever, Americans could see themselves as being in the vanguard of an inevitable historical trend that would reshape the world for the better. But by the early 1790s the reports from France were disquieting. Outbreaks of violence continued, ministries succeeded each other with bewildering rapidity, and executions were commonplace. The king himself was beheaded in early 1793. Although many Americans, including Jefferson and Madison, retained their sympathy for the French revolutionaries, others began to view France as a prime example of the perversion of republicanism. As might be expected, Alexander Hamilton fell into the latter group.

At that juncture, France declared war on Britain, Spain, and Holland. The Americans thus faced a dilemma. The 1778 treaty with France bound them to that nation "forever," and a mutual commitment to republicanism created ideological bonds. Yet the United States was connected to Great Britain as well. Aside from sharing a common history and language, America and England were economic partners. Americans still purchased most of their manufactured goods from Great Britain and sold their own produce chiefly in British and British colonial markets. Indeed, since the Hamiltonian financial system depended heavily on import tariffs as a source of revenue, and America's imports came primarily from Britain, the nation's economic health in effect required uninterrupted trade with the former mother country.

The political and diplomatic climate was further complicated in April 1793, when Citizen Edmond Genet, a representative of the French government, landed in Charleston. As Genet made his leisurely way northward to New York City, he was wildly cheered and lavishly entertained at every stop. En route, he recruited Americans for expeditions against British and Spanish possessions in the Western Hemisphere and distributed privateering commissions with a generous hand. Genet's arrival raised a series of key questions for President Washington. Should he receive Genet, thus officially recognizing the French revolutionary government? Should he acknowledge an obligation to aid France under the terms of the 1778 treaty? Or should he proclaim American neutrality in the conflict?

Citizen Genet

For once, Hamilton and Jefferson saw eye to eye. Both told Washington that the United States could not afford to ally itself firmly with either side. Washington agreed; thus he received Genet officially, but also issued a proclamation informing the world that the United States would adopt "a conduct friendly and impartial toward the belligerent powers." In deference to Jefferson's continued support for France, the word *neutrality* did not appear in the declaration— but its meaning was nevertheless clear.

Genet himself was removed as a factor in Franco-American relations at the end of the summer. His faction fell from power in Paris, and instead of returning home to face almost-certain execution he sought political asylum in the United States. But his disappearance from the diplomatic scene did not lessen the continuing impact of the French Revolution in America. The domestic divisions Genet helped to widen were perpetuated by clubs called Democratic-Republican societies, formed by Americans sympathetic to the French Revolution and worried about trends in the Washington administration. The societies thus expressed grassroots concern about the same developments that troubled Jefferson and Madison.

Democratic-Republican Societies

More than forty Democratic-Republican societies were organized between 1793 and 1800, in both rural and urban areas. Their members saw themselves as heirs of the Sons of Liberty, seeking the same goal as their predecessors: protection of the people's liberties against encroachments by corrupt and evil rulers. To that end, they publicly protested government policies and published "addresses to the people" warning of impending tyranny. The societies repeatedly proclaimed their belief in "the equal rights of man," stressing in particular the rights to free speech, free press, and assembly. Like the Sons of Liberty, the Democratic-Republican societies were composed chiefly of artisans and craftsmen of various kinds, although professionals, farmers, and merchants also joined.

The rapid growth of such groups, outspoken in their criticism of the Washington administration for its failure to come to the aid of France and for its domestic economic policies, deeply disturbed Hamilton and eventually Washington himself. Newspapers sympathetic to the Federalists charged that the societies were subversive agents of a foreign power. Their "real design," one asserted, was "to involve the country in war, to assume the reins of government and tyrannize over the people." The climax of the attack came in the fall of 1794, when Washington accused the societies of having fomented the Whiskey Rebellion.

In retrospect, Washington's and Hamilton's reaction to the Democratic-Republican societies seems hysterical, overwrought, and entirely out of proportion to whatever challenge they may have posed to the administration. But it must be kept in mind that "faction" was believed to be dangerous to the survival of a republic. In a monarchy, opposition groups were to be expected, even encouraged. In a government of the people, though, serious and sustained disagreement was taken as a sign of corruption and subversion. The Democratic-Republican societies were the first formally organized political dissenters in the United States. As such, they aroused the fear and suspicion of elected officials who had not yet accepted the idea that one component of a free government was an organized loyal opposition.

That same year George Washington decided to send Chief Justice John Jay to England to try to reach agreement on four major unresolved questions affecting Anglo-American affairs. Jay's diplomatic mission had important domestic consequences. The first point at issue was recent British seizures of American merchant ships trading in the French West Indies. The United States wanted to establish the principle of freedom of the seas and to assert its right, as a neutral nation, to trade freely with both sides. Second, Great Britain had not yet carried out its promise in the Treaty of Paris (1783) to evacuate its posts in the American

Northwest. Western settlers believed that the British were responsible for the renewed Indian warfare in the region (see pages 169–171), and they wanted that threat removed. Third and fourth, the Americans hoped for a commercial treaty and sought compensation for the slaves who had left with the British army at the end of the war.

The negotiations in London proved difficult, since Jay had little to offer Britain in exchange for the concessions he wanted. In the end, Britain did agree to evacuate the western forts and ease the restrictions on American trade to England and the West Indies. (Some limitations were retained, however, violating the Americans' stated commitment to open commerce.) No compensation for lost slaves was agreed to, but Jay accepted a provision establishing an arbitration commission to deal with the matter of prewar debts owed to British creditors. A similar commission was to handle the question of compensation for the seizures of American merchant ships. Under the circumstances, Jay had done remarkably well: the treaty averted war with England at a time when the United States, which lacked an effective navy, could not have hoped to win a conflict with its former mother country. Nevertheless, most Americans, including the president, were dissatisfied with at least some parts of the treaty.

Jay Treaty

At first, however, potential opposition was blunted, because the Senate debated and ratified the treaty in secret. Not until after it was formally approved by a vote of 20 to 10 on June 24, 1795, was the public informed of its provisions. The Democratic-Republican societies led protests against the treaty, which were especially intense in the South. Planters criticized Jay's failure to obtain compensation for runaway slaves as well as the commitment to repay prewar debts. Once President Washington had reluctantly signed the treaty, though, there seemed to be little the Republicans could do to prevent it from taking effect. Just one opportunity remained: Congress had to appropriate funds to carry out the treaty provisions, and according to the Constitution money bills had to originate in the House of Representatives.

When the House took up the issue in March 1796, opponents of the treaty tried to prevent approval of the appropriations. To that end, they called on Washington to submit to the House all documents pertinent to the negotiations. In successfully resisting the House's request, Washington established the doctrine of executive privilege—that is, the power of the president to withhold information from Congress if he believes circumstances warrant doing so. Although the treaty's opponents initially appeared to be in the majority, pressure for approval built as time passed. Frontier residents were eager for evacuation of the British posts, fearing a new outbreak of Indian war despite the signing of the Treaty of Greenville the previous year (see page 171). Merchants wanted to reap the benefits of widened trade with the British Empire. Furthermore, Thomas Pinckney of South Carolina had negotiated a treaty with Spain giving the United States navigation privileges on the Mississippi, which would be an economic boost to the West and South. Its popularity (the Senate ratified Pinckney's Treaty unanimously) helped to overcome opposition to the Jay Treaty. For all these reasons the House on April 30, 1796, voted the necessary funds by the narrow margin of 51 to 48.

Analysis of the vote reveals both the regional nature of the division and the growing cohesion of the Republican and Federalist factions in Congress. Voting **Republicans and Federalists** in favor of the appropriations were 44 Federalists and 7 Republicans; voting against were 45 Republicans and 3 Federalists. The final tally was also split by region. The vast majority of votes against the bill were cast by southerners (including the three Federalists, who were Virginians). The bill's supporters were largely from New England and the middle states, with the exception of two South Carolina Federalists. The seven Republicans who voted for the appropriations were from commercial areas in New York, Pennsylvania, and Maryland.

The small number of defectors revealed a new force at work in American politics: partisanship. Voting statistics from the first four congresses show the ever-increasing tendency of members of the House of Representatives to vote as coherent groups, rather than as individuals. If factional loyalty is defined as voting together at least two-thirds of the time on national issues, the percentage of nonaligned congressmen dropped from 42 percent in 1790 to just 7 percent in 1796. Also, the majority slowly shifted from Federalist to Republican. Federalists controlled the first three congresses, through spring 1795; Republicans

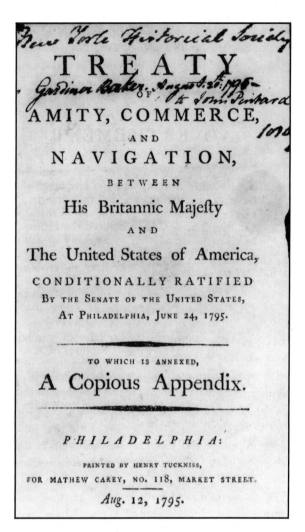

TREATY OF AMITY, COMMERCE, AND NAVIGATION, BETWEEN His Britannic Majesty AND The United States of America, CONDITIONALLY RATIFIED By the Senate of the United States, At Philadelphia, June 24, 1795.

TO WHICH IS ANNEXED, A Copious Appendix.

PHILADELPHIA:

PRINTED BY HENRY TUCKNISS, FOR MATHEW CAREY, NO. 118, MARKET STREET.

Aug. 12, 1795.

Title page of the Jay Treaty. Publication of the document after its secret ratification by the Senate aroused widespread protest against its terms. The House of Representatives tried but failed to halt its implementation.   The New-York Historical Society.

gained the ascendancy in the Fourth Congress; Federalists returned to power with slight majorities in the Fifth and Sixth Congresses; and the Republicans took over in the Seventh Congress in 1801.

To describe these shifts is easier than to explain them. The growing division cannot be accurately explained in the terms used by Jefferson and Madison (aristocrats versus the people) or by Hamilton and Washington (true patriots versus subversive rabble). Simple economic differences between agrarian and commercial interests do not provide the answer either, since more than 90 percent of Americans in the

1790s lived in rural areas. Moreover, Jefferson's vision of a prosperous agrarian America was based on commercial, not self-sufficient, farming. Yet certain distinctions can be made. Republicans tended to be self-assured, confident, and optimistic about both politics and the economy. They did not fear instability, at least among the white population, and they sought to widen the people's participation in government. They foresaw a prosperous future, and looked first to the United States's own resources, second to its position in the world. Republicans also remained sympathetic to France in international affairs.

Federalists, on the other hand, were insecure, uncertain of the future. They stressed the need for order, authority, and regularity in the political world. Unlike Republicans, they had no grassroots political organization and put little emphasis on involving ordinary people in government. The nation was, in their eyes, perpetually threatened by potential enemies, both internal and external, and best protected by a continuing alliance with Great Britain. Their vision of international affairs may have been more accurate, given the warfare in Europe, but it was also narrow and unattractive. Since it held out little hope of a better future to the voters of any region, it is not surprising that the Republicans eventually became dominant.

If the factions' respective attitudes are translated into economic and regional affiliations, the pattern is clear. Northern merchants and commercially oriented farmers, well aware of the uncertainties of international trade, tended to be Federalists. Since New England's soil was poor and agricultural production could not be expanded, northern subsistence farmers also gravitated toward the more conservative party, which wanted to preserve the present (and past) rather than look to the future.

Republican southern planters, on the other hand, firmly in control of their region and of a class of enslaved laborers, could anticipate unlimited westward expansion. Many planters had successfully shifted from the cultivation of soil-draining tobacco to grains and other foodstuffs. The invention of the cotton gin in 1793 allowed southerners to plant many more acres of cotton (see Chapter 11). For their part, small farmers in the South found the Republicans' democratic rhetoric (despite aristocratic leadership) more congenial than the Federalist viewpoint. So too urban artisans,

who stressed their role as independent producers of necessary goods, supported the Republican position.

Finally, the two sides drew supporters from different ethnic groups. Americans of English stock tended to be Federalists, while those of Irish or Scots origin were more likely to be Republicans. Another large group, the Germans, was split fairly evenly at first but eventually moved into the Republican camp. To what degree ethnic antagonisms contributed to the growing political split is impossible to say. But since patterns of migration to and within America (see pages 73–75) rendered regional and ethnic lines largely parallel, it is conceivable that ethnicity was as important as other factors in determining political alignments.

The presence of the two organized groups, not yet parties in the modern sense but nonetheless active contenders for office, made the presidential election of 1796 the first that was seriously contested. George Washington, tired of the criticism to which he had been subjected, decided to retire from office. (Presidents had not yet been limited to two terms by constitutional amendment.) In September Washington published his famous "Farewell Address," most of which was written by Hamilton. Washington outlined two principles that guided American foreign policy at least until the late 1940s: maintain commercial but not political ties to other nations and enter no permanent alliances. He also drew a sharp distinction between the United States and Europe, stressing America's uniqueness and the need for unilateralism (independent action in foreign affairs).

Domestically, Washington lamented the existence of factional divisions among his fellow countrymen. His call for an end to partisan strife has often been interpreted by historians as the statement of a man who could see beyond political affiliations to the good of the whole. But it is more accurately read in the context of its day as an attack on the legitimacy of the Republican opposition. What Washington wanted was unity behind the Federalist banner, which he saw as the only proper political stance. The Federalists (like the Republicans) continued to see themselves as the sole guardians of the truth, the only true heirs of the Revolution, and they perceived their opponents as misguided, unpatriotic troublemakers.

To succeed Washington, the Federalists in Congress put forward the candidacy of Vice President John

Election of 1796 Adams, with the diplomat Thomas Pinckney of South Carolina as his vice-presidential running mate. Congressional Republicans caucused and chose Thomas Jefferson as their candidate; the lawyer, revolutionary war veteran, and active Republican politician Aaron Burr of New York agreed to run for vice president.

That the election was contested did not mean that its outcome was decided by the people. Voters could cast their ballots only for electors, not for the candidates themselves. Many voters did not even have that opportunity, since more than 40 percent of the members of the electoral college that year were chosen by state legislatures, some even before the presidential candidates had been selected. Furthermore, the method of voting prescribed for the electoral college by the Constitution tended to work against the new factions, which was not surprising, since the authors of the Constitution had not foreseen the development of opposing national political organizations. Members of the electoral college were required to vote for two persons, without specifying the office. The man with the highest total became president; the second highest became vice president. In other words, there was no way an elector could explicitly support one person for president and another for vice president.

This procedure proved to be the Federalists' undoing. Adams won the presidency with 71 votes, but a number of Federalist electors (especially those from New England) failed to cast ballots for Pinckney. Thomas Jefferson won 68 votes, 9 more than Pinckney, and became vice president. The incoming administration was thus politically divided. The next four years were to see the new president and vice president, once allies and close friends, become bitter enemies.

JOHN ADAMS AND POLITICAL DISSENT

John Adams took over the presidency peculiarly blind to the partisan developments of the previous four years. As president he never abandoned the outdated notion George Washington had discarded as early as 1794: that the president should be above politics, an independent and dignified figure who did not seek petty factional advantage. Thus Adams kept Washington's cabinet intact, despite its key members' allegiance to his chief rival, Alexander Hamilton. He often adopted a passive posture, letting others (usually Hamilton) take the lead, when he should have acted decisively. As a result his administration gained a reputation for inconsistency. When Adams's term ended, the Federalists were severely divided and the Republicans had won the presidency. But at the same time Adams's detachment from Hamilton's maneuverings enabled him to weather the greatest international crisis the republic had yet faced: the so-called Quasi-War with France.

The Jay Treaty improved America's relationship with England, but it provoked retaliation from France. Angry that the United States had, in effect, abandoned the 1778 French-American treaty, the Directory (the coalition then in power in Paris) ordered French vessels to seize American ships carrying British goods. In response, Adams appointed three special commissioners to try to reach a settlement with France: Elbridge Gerry, an old friend from Massachusetts; John Marshall, a Virginia Federalist; and Charles Cotesworth Pinckney of South Carolina, Thomas's older brother. At the same time Congress increased military spending, authorizing the building of ships and the stockpiling of weapons and ammunition.

For months, the American commissioners futilely sought to open negotiations with Talleyrand, the French foreign minister. But Talleyrand's agents demanded a bribe of $250,000 before **XYZ Affair** talks could begin. The Americans retorted, "No, no; not a sixpence," and reported the incident in dispatches that President Adams received in early March 1798. Adams informed Congress of the impasse and recommended increased appropriations for defense.

Convinced that Adams had deliberately sabotaged the negotiations, congressional Republicans insisted that the dispatches be turned over to Congress. Aware that releasing the reports would work to his advantage, Adams complied. He withheld only the names of the French agents, referring to them as X, Y, and Z. The revelation that the Americans had been treated with utter contempt by the Directory stimulated a wave of anti-French sentiment in the United States. A journalist's version of the commissioners' reply, "Millions for defense, but not a cent for tribute," became the national slogan. Cries for war filled the air. Congress formally abrogated the 1778 treaty and authorized American ships to seize French vessels.

Thus began the United States's first undeclared war. The Quasi-War with France was fought in the West Indies, between French privateers seeking to capture American merchant vessels and warships of the United States Navy. Although initial American losses of merchant shipping were heavy, by early 1799 the navy had established its superiority in Caribbean waters. Its ships captured a total of eight French privateers and naval vessels, easing the threat to America's vital West Indian trade.

The Republicans, who opposed war and continued to sympathize with France, could do little to stem the tide of anti-French feelings. Since Agent Y had boasted of the existence of a "French party in America," Federalists flatly accused the Republicans of traitorous designs. A New York newspaper declared that anyone who remained "lukewarm" after reading the XYZ dispatches was a "criminal—and the man who does not warmly reprobate the conduct of the French must have a soul black enough to be *fit* for *treason Strategems* and *spoils*." John Adams wavered between calling the Republicans traitors and acknowledging their right to oppose administration measures. His wife was less tolerant: "Those whom the French boast of as their Partizans," Abigail Adams told her older sister, deserved to be "adjudged traitors to their country." If Jefferson had been president, "we should all have been sold to the French."

The Federalists saw this climate of opinion as an opportunity to deal a death blow to their Republican opponents. Now that the country seemed to see the truth of what they had been saying ever since the Whiskey Rebellion in 1794—that the Republicans were subversive foreign agents—the Federalists sought to codify that belief into law. In the spring and summer of 1798, the Federalist-controlled Congress adopted a set of four laws known as the Alien and Sedition Acts, intended to suppress dissent and prevent further growth of the Republican party.

Three of the acts were aimed at immigrants, whom the Federalists quite correctly suspected of being Republican in their sympathies. The Naturalization Act

Alien and Sedition Acts lengthened the residency period required for citizenship from five to fourteen years and ordered all resident aliens to register with the federal government. The Alien Enemies Act provided for the detention of enemy aliens in time of war. The Alien Friends Act, which was to be in effect for only two years, gave the president almost unlimited authority to deport any alien he deemed dangerous to the nation's security. (Adams never used that authority. The Alien Enemies Act was not implemented either, since war was never formally declared.)

The fourth law, the Sedition Act, sought to control both citizens and aliens. It outlawed conspiracies to prevent the enforcement of federal laws and set the maximum punishment for such offenses at five years in prison and a $5,000 fine. The act also tried to control speech. Writing, printing, or uttering "false, scandalous and malicious" statements "against the government of the United States, or the President of the United States, with intent to defame . . . or to bring them or either of them, into contempt or disrepute" became a crime punishable by as much as two years imprisonment and a fine of $2,000. Today the Supreme Court would declare unconstitutional any such law punishing speech alone. But in the eighteenth century, when organized political opposition was regarded with suspicion, the Sedition Act was legally acceptable.

In all, there were fifteen indictments and ten convictions under the Sedition Act. Most of the accused were outspoken Republican newspaper editors who failed to mute their criticism of the administration in response to the law. But the first victim—whose story may serve as an example of the rest—was a Republican congressman from Vermont, Matthew Lyon. The Irish-born Lyon, a former indentured servant who had purchased his freedom and fought in the Revolution, was indicted for declaring in print that John Adams had displayed "a continual grasp for power" and "an unbounded thirst for ridiculous pomp, foolish adulation, and selfish avarice." Though convicted, fined $1,000, and sent to prison for four months, Lyon was not silenced. He conducted his re-election campaign from jail, winning an overwhelming majority. The fine, which he could not afford, was ceremoniously paid by contributions from leading Republicans around the country.

Matthew Lyon, the congressman convicted of violating the Sedition Act, had a fiery temper. In January 1798, before his arrest and trial, he engaged in this brawl with a congressman from Connecticut in the chamber of the House of Representatives. *Library of Congress.*

Faced with the prosecutions of their major supporters, Jefferson and Madison sought an effective means of combating the Alien and Sedition Acts.

Virginia and Kentucky Resolutions

Petitioning the Federalist-controlled Congress to repeal the laws would clearly do no good. Furthermore, Federalist judges refused to allow accused persons to question the Sedition Act's constitutionality. Accordingly, the Republican leaders turned to the only other possible mechanism for protest: the state legislatures. Carefully concealing their own role (it would hardly have been desirable for the vice president to be indicted for sedition), Jefferson and Madison each drafted a set of resolutions. Introduced into the Kentucky and Virginia legislatures respectively in the fall of 1798, the resolutions differed somewhat but their import was the same. Since the Constitution was created by a compact among the states, they contended, the people speaking through their states had a legitimate right to judge the constitutionality of actions by the federal government. Both sets of resolutions pronounced the Alien and Sedition Acts null and void and asked other states to join in the protest.

Although no other state replied positively to the Virginia and Kentucky resolutions, they nevertheless had major significance. In the first place, they were superb political propaganda, rallying Republican opinion throughout the country. They placed the opposition party squarely in the revolutionary tradition

This handpainted banner, ca. 1800, celebrating Thomas Jefferson's victory over John Adams, was found in the early 1960s in Massachusetts. The eagle carries a streamer that reads, "T. Jefferson/President of the United States of America/John Adams no more."   Ralph E. Becker Collection, Smithsonian Institution.

of resistance to tyrannical authority. Second, the theory of union they proposed was expanded on by southern states'-rights advocates in the 1830s and thereafter. Jefferson and Madison had identified a key constitutional issue: how far could the states go in opposing the national government? How could a conflict between the two be resolved? These questions were not to be definitively answered until the Civil War.

Ironically, just as the Sedition Act was being implemented and northern state legislatures were rejecting the Virginia and Kentucky resolutions, Federalists split badly over the course of action the United States should take toward France. Hamilton and his supporters still called for a declaration legitimizing the undeclared naval war the two nations had been waging for months. But Adams had received a number of private signals that the Directory now regretted its

treatment of the three American commissioners. Acting on these assurances, he dispatched the envoy William Vans Murray to Paris. The United States asked two things of France: nearly $20 million in compensation for ships the French had seized since 1793, and abrogation of the Treaty of 1778. The Convention of 1800, which ended the Quasi-War, included the latter but not the former. Still, it freed the United States from its only permanent alliance, thus allowing it to follow the independent diplomatic course George Washington had outlined in his Farewell Address (see page 194).

The results of the negotiations were not known in the United States until after the presidential election of 1800. Even so, Adams's decision to seek a peaceful settlement probably cost him re-election because of the divisions it caused in Federalist ranks.

In sharp contrast, the Republicans entered the

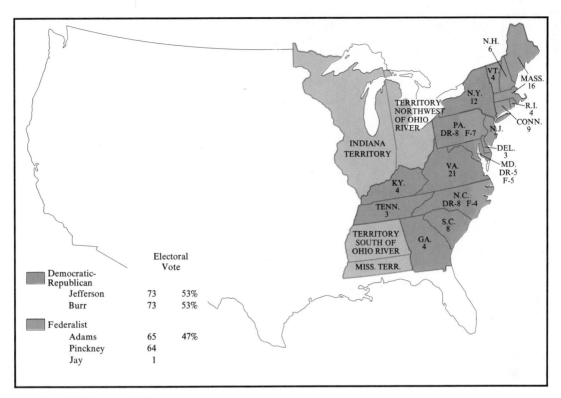

Presidential Election, 1800

Electoral Vote

Democratic-Republican
Jefferson	73	53%
Burr	73	53%

Federalist
Adams	65	47%
Pinckney	64	
Jay	1	

1800 presidential race firmly united behind the Jefferson-Burr ticket. Though they won the election, their lack of foresight almost cost

Election of 1800

them dearly. The problem was caused by the system of voting in the electoral college, which the Federalists understood more clearly than the Republicans. The Federalists arranged in advance for one of their electors to fail to vote for Charles Cotesworth Pinckney, their vice-presidential candidate. John Adams thus received the higher number of Federalist votes (65 to Pinckney's 64). The Republicans failed to make the same distinction between their candidates, and all 73 cast ballots for both Jefferson and Burr (see map). Because neither Republican had a plurality, the Constitution required that the contest be decided in the House of Representatives, with each state's congressmen voting as a unit. Since the new House, dominated by Republicans, would not take office for some months, Federalist congressmen decided the election. It took them thirty-five ballots to decide that Jefferson would be a lesser evil than Burr. As a result of the tangle, the twelfth amendment to the Constitution (1804) changed the method of voting in the electoral college to allow for a party ticket.

WESTWARD EXPANSION, SOCIAL CHANGE, AND RELIGIOUS FERMENT

In the postrevolutionary years, the United States experienced a dramatic increase in internal migration. As much as 5 to 10 percent of the population moved each year, half of them relocating in another state. Young white men were the most mobile segment of the populace, but all groups moved with approximately equal frequency. The major population shifts were from east to west (see map, page 200): from New England to upstate New York, from New Jersey to western Pennsylvania, from the Chesapeake to

Western Expansion, 1785–1805

Chapter 7: POLITICS AND SOCIETY IN THE EARLY REPUBLIC, 1790–1800

the new states of Kentucky and Tennessee, which entered the union in 1792 and 1796, respectively. Very few people moved north or south, the largest proportion being southerners (perhaps yeomen farmers escaping the expansion of slavery) seeking new homes farther north.

Some of these migrants moved west of the Appalachian Mountains. The first permanent white settlements beyond the mountains were established in

White Settlement in the West

western North Carolina in 1771, along the Holston and Wautauga rivers. But not until after the defeat of the Shawnee in 1774 and the Cherokee in 1776 (see pages 135–136) was the way cleared for a more general migration. Small groups of families filtered through the Cumberland Gap into Kentucky, following the Wilderness Road carved out by Daniel Boone in 1775. Once the war had ended, Americans streamed over the mountains in considerably larger numbers. In 1783, only about twelve thousand people lived west of the mountains and south of the Ohio River; less than a decade later, the 1790 census counted more than 100,000 residents of the future states of Kentucky and Tennessee.

North of the Ohio River, white settlements grew more slowly because of the strength of the Miami confederacy. But once the Treaty of Greenville was signed in 1795, Ohio too grew rapidly. Whites migrating to Ohio traveled by land to Pittsburgh, then floated down the river on flatboats and rafts to Marietta or another Ohio River town, where they either stayed or moved farther inland onto farms surveyed under the terms of the land ordinance of 1785 (see pages 169–170).

The westward migration of slaveholding whites, first to Kentucky and Tennessee and then later into the rich lands of western Georgia and eventually the

Blacks in the West

Gulf Coast, had a major adverse impact on Afro-Americans. The web of family connections built up over several generations of residence in the Chesapeake was torn apart by the population movement. Even those few large planters who moved their entire slave force west could not have owned all the members of every family on their plantations. Far more commonly the white migrants were younger sons of eastern slaveholders, whose inheritance included only a portion of the family's slaves, or small farmers who owned just one or two blacks. In the early years of American settlement in the West, the population was widely dispersed; accordingly, Chesapeake blacks who had been raised in the midst of large numbers of kin had to adapt to lonely lives on isolated farms, far from their parents, siblings, or even spouses and children. The approximately 100,000 Afro-Americans forcibly moved west by 1810 had to begin to build new families there to replace those unwillingly left behind in the East. They succeeded well, as will be seen in Chapter 11.

The mobility of both blacks and whites created a volatile population mix in frontier areas. Everyone was new to the region and few had relatives nearby. Since most of the migrants were young single men just starting to lead independent lives, western society was at first unstable. Like the seventeenth-century Chesapeake (see page 27), the late-eighteenth-century American West was a society in which single women married quickly. One genteel Connecticut girl, reluctantly moving to Ohio with relatives in 1810 after the death of her parents, was dismayed to find that other travelers assumed she was going west to find a husband after failing to wed in the East. (She did marry within a year.) The other side of the same coin was that the few women among the migrants lamented their lack of congenial female friends. Isolated, far from familiar surroundings, women and men both strove to create new communities to replace those they had left behind.

Perhaps the most meaningful of the new communities was that supplied by evangelical religion. Among the migrants to Kentucky and Tennessee

Second Great Awakening

were clergymen and committed lay members of the evangelical sects that arose in America after the First Great Awakening: Baptists, Presbyterians, and Methodists. The Awakening had flourished in the southern backcountry much later than it had in New England (see pages 94–96), and therefore the Second Great Awakening, which began around 1800 in the West, can in one sense be seen as simply an extension of the first colonial revival to that region. Laymen and clerics alike spread the doctrine of evangelical Christianity through the countryside, carrying the message of salvation to the rootless and largely uneducated frontier folk.

In the early nineteenth century, a French artist traveling in America drew this picture of Methodists en route to a camp meeting. They carry bundles of food and clothing with them. Note the large proportion of women in the crowd. Library of Congress.

At camp meetings, sometimes attended by thousands of people and usually lasting from three days to a week, clergymen exhorted their audiences to repent their sins and become genuine Christians. They stressed that salvation was open to all, downplaying the doctrine of predestination that had characterized orthodox colonial Protestantism. The emotional nature of the conversion experience was emphasized far more than the need for careful study and preparation. Such preachers thus brought the message of religion to the people in more ways than one. They were in effect "democratizing" American religion, making it available to all rather than to a preselected and educated elite.

The most famous camp meeting took place at Cane Ridge, Kentucky, in 1801. At a time when the largest settlement in the state had no more than two thousand inhabitants, attendance at Cane Ridge was estimated at between ten and twenty-five thousand. One witness, a Presbyterian cleric, marveled that "no sex nor color, class nor description, were exempted from the pervading influence of the spirit; even from the age of eight months to sixty years, there were evident subjects of this marvellous operation." He went on to recount how people responded to the preaching with "loud ejaculations of prayer, . . . some struck with terror, . . . others, trembling, weeping and crying out . . . fainting and swooning away, . . . others surrounding them with melodious songs, or fervent prayers for their happy resurrection, in the love of Christ." Such scenes were to be repeated many times in the decades that followed. Revivals swept across different regions of the country until nearly the middle of the century, leaving an indelible legacy of evangelism to American Protestant churches.

The sources of the Second Great Awakening, which revitalized Protestant Christianity in the United States during the nineteenth century, were embedded in late-eighteenth-century American society in the East as well as the West. From the 1760s through the 1780s, religious concerns had been subordinated to secular affairs, as clergymen and lay people of all denominations had concentrated their energies on war and politics. Indeed, clerics had created a kind of "civil religion" for the nation, in which the fervor of the veneration for the republic sometimes surpassed the fervor of religious worship. Moreover, the orthodox churches, showing the influence of Enlightenment thought, had for decades stressed reason more than revelation. Circumstances were thus ripe for a movement of spiritual renewal that would appeal to the emotional side of people's natures.

In addition, America's largest Protestant denominations had to find new sources of financial and membership support after the Revolution. In the

Disestablishment of Religion

colonial period, most of the provinces had had established, or state-supported, churches. In Massachusetts, for example, the Congregational church had been financed by taxes levied on all residents of the state, not just the members of that church. The same was true of the Church of England in such southern colonies as Virginia and South Carolina. Before the war, the protests of religious dissenters, like Baptists, had fallen on deaf ears. Yet they too—like other disadvantaged groups in American society—learned to use revolutionary ideology for their own purposes. Isaac Backus, a New England Baptist, pointed out forcefully that "many, who are filling the nation with the cry of LIBERTY and against *oppressors* are at the same time themselves violating that dearest of all rights, LIBERTY OF CONSCIENCE." Legislators could not resist the logic of such arguments. Many states dissolved their ties to churches during or immediately after the war, and others vastly reduced state support for established denominations.

These changes meant that congregations could no longer rely on tax revenues and that all churches were placed on the same footing with respect to the government. Church membership was now entirely

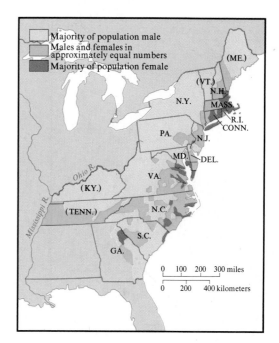

Sex Ratio of White Population, 1790

voluntary, as were monetary contributions from members. If congregations were to survive, they had to generate new sources of support, by increasing their number of enthusiastic members; revivals proved a convenient means of doing so. The revivals represented genuine outpourings of religious sentiment, but their more mundane function must not be overlooked.

An analysis of secular society can help to explain the conversion patterns of the Second Awakening. Unlike the First Great Awakening, when converts

Women and the Second Awakening

were evenly divided by sex, more women than men—particularly young women—answered the call of Christianity during the Second Awakening. The increase in female converts seems to have been directly related to major changes in women's circumstances at the end of the eighteenth century. In some areas of the country, especially New England (where the revival movement flourished), women outnumbered men after 1790, since many young men had migrated westward (see map). Thus eastern girls could no longer count on finding marital partners. The uncertainty of their social and familial position seems to have led them to seek spiritual certainty in the church.

Young women's domestic roles changed dramatically

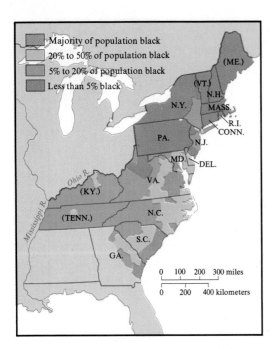

Black Population, 1790: Proportion of Total Population   Source: *Reprinted by permission of Princeton University Press.*

at the same time, as cloth production began to move from the household to the factory (see page 254). Deprived of their chief household role as spinners and weavers, New England daughters found in the church a realm where they could continue to make useful contributions to society. Church missionary societies and charitable associations provided an acceptable outlet for their talents. One of the most striking developments of the early nineteenth century was the creation of hundreds of female associations to aid widows and orphans, collect money for foreign missions, or improve the quality of maternal care. Thus American women collectively assumed the role of keepers of the nation's conscience, taking the lead—via their churches—in charitable enterprise, and freeing their husbands from concern for such moral issues.

The religious ferment among both blacks and whites in frontier regions of the Upper South contributed to racial ferment as well. People of both races attended the camp meetings, and sometimes black preachers exhorted whites in addition to members of their own race. When revivals spread eastward

Blacks and the Second Awakening

into more heavily slaveholding areas, white planters became fearful of the egalitarianism implied in the evangelical message of universal salvation and harmony. At the same time, revivals created a group of respected black leaders—preachers—and provided them with a ready audience for a potentially revolutionary doctrine.

Recent events in the West Indies gave whites ample reason for apprehension. In the 1790s, over the course of several years, mulattoes and blacks in the French colony of Saint Domingue (Haiti) overthrew European rule under the leadership of a mulatto, Toussaint L'Ouverture. The revolt was bloody, vicious, prolonged, and characterized by numerous atrocities committed by both sides. In an attempt to prevent the spread of such unrest to their own slaves, southern state legislators passed laws forbidding white Haitian refugees from bringing their slaves with them. But North American blacks learned about the revolt anyway. Furthermore, the preconditions for racial upheaval did not have to be imported into the South from the West Indies: they already existed on the spot.

The Revolution had caused immense destruction in the South, especially in the states south of Virginia. The heavy losses of slaves and constant guerrilla warfare, not to mention the changes in American trading patterns brought about by withdrawal from the British Empire, wreaked havoc on the southern economy. After the war Lower South planters rushed to replace their lost work force; the postwar decades therefore witnessed the single most massive influx of Africans into North America since the beginnings of the slave trade. Before the legal trade was halted in 1808, more than ninety thousand new Africans had been imported into the United States.

The vast postwar increase in the number of free blacks severely strained the system of race relations that had evolved during the eighteenth century. Color, caste, and slave status no longer coincided, as they had when the few free blacks were all mulattoes (see map). Furthermore, like their white compatriots, blacks (both slave and free) had become familiar with notions of·liberty and equality. They had also witnessed the benefits of fighting collectively for freedom, rather than resisting individually or running away. The circumstances were ripe for an explosion, and the Second Awakening was the match that lit the fuse in both Virginia and North Carolina.

The Virginia revolt was planned by Gabriel Prosser, a blacksmith who argued that blacks should fight to obtain the same rights as whites, and who explicitly placed himself in the tradition of the French and Haitian revolutions. At revival meetings led by his brother Martin, a preacher, Gabriel recruited other blacks like himself—artisans who moved easily in both black and white circles and who lived in semifreedom under minimal white supervision. The artisan leaders then enlisted rural blacks in the cause. The conspirators planned to attack Richmond on the night of August 30, 1800, setting fire to the city, seizing the state capitol, and capturing the governor. Their plan showed considerable political sophistication, but heavy rain made it impossible to execute the plot as scheduled. Several whites then learned of the plan from their slaves and spread the alarm. Gabriel avoided capture for some weeks, but most of the other leaders of the rebellion were quickly arrested and interrogated. The major conspirators, including Prosser himself, were hanged, but in the months that followed other insurrectionary scares continued to frighten Virginia slaveowners.

Gabriel's Rebellion

Two years later a similar wave of fear swept North Carolina and the bordering counties of Virginia. A slave conspiracy to attack planters' homes, kill all whites except small children, and seize the land was uncovered in Bertie County. Similar plots were rumored elsewhere. Again, slave artisans and preachers played prominent roles in the planned uprisings. Nearly fifty blacks were executed as a result of the whites' investigations of the rumors. Some were certainly innocent victims of the planters' hysteria, but there can be no doubt about the existence of most of the plots.

Significantly, the Iroquois were affected by a religious revival at the same time as American whites and blacks were experiencing the Second Great Awakening. Led by their prophet, Handsome Lake, the remaining American Iroquois, who were scattered on small reservations, embraced the traditional values of their culture and renounced such destructive white customs as drinking alcohol and playing cards. At the same time, though, they began abandoning their ancient way of life. With Handsome Lake's approval, Quaker missionaries taught the Iroquois Anglo-American styles of agricultural subsistence; men were

IMPORTANT EVENTS	
1789	George Washington inaugurated
	Judiciary Act of 1789
	French Revolution begins
1790	Alexander Hamilton's first "Report on Public Credit"
1791	First ten amendments (Bill of Rights) ratified
1793	France declares war on Britain, Spain, and Holland
	Neutrality Proclamation
	Democratic-Republican societies founded
1794	Whiskey Rebellion
1795	Jay Treaty
1796	First contested presidential election: John Adams elected president, Thomas Jefferson vice president
1798	XYZ affair
	Alien and Sedition Acts
	Virginia and Kentucky resolutions
1798–99	Quasi-War with France
1800	Franco-American Convention
	Jefferson elected president, Aaron Burr vice president
	Second Great Awakening begins
	Gabriel's Rebellion

now to be cultivators rather than hunters and women housekeepers rather than cultivators. Since the tribes had lost their hunting territories to white farmers, Iroquois men accepted the changes readily. But many women—especially the powerful tribal matrons—resisted the shift in the gender division of labor. They realized that when they surrendered control over food production they would jeopardize their status in the tribe. But Handsome Lake branded as "witches" any women who opposed the changes too vigorously, and eventually he triumphed. A division of work by sex continued to characterize Iroquois economic organization, but the specific tasks assigned to men and women changed completely. In order to maintain some cultural autonomy, the Iroquois had to adopt an economic system resembling that of the dominant whites.

Their plight may be taken as symbolic of that of tribes located west of the Appalachians, for they too would have to find ways of accommodating themselves to the dominant Anglo-American culture. Although most had yet to feel the full force of the whites' westward thrust, the weapon that had served the Iroquois and other interior tribes so well—the countervailing presence of England, France, and Spain—was not available to them. Now that the United States had established its independence, western tribes had no alternative but to confront directly the problems posed by land-hungry whites. They would delay but not halt the expansion of the United States.

As the new century began, then, white, red, and black inhabitants of the United States were moving toward an accommodation to their new circumstances. The United States was starting to take shape as a free nation no longer dependent on England. In domestic politics, the Jeffersonian interpretation of republicanism had prevailed over the Hamiltonian approach. As a result, the country would be characterized by a decentralized economy, minimal government (especially at the national level), and maximum freedom of action and mobility for individual white males.

But that freedom would be purchased at the expense of white females and black men, women, and children. In the decades to come, both groups would be subject to further control. To prevent a recurrence of outbreaks of violence like those of 1800 through 1802, slaveholders increased the severity of the slave codes, further restricting their human property. Before long, all talk of emancipation (gradual or otherwise) ceased, and slavery became even more firmly entrenched as an economic institution and way of life. Likewise, the Revolution's implicit promise for women was never fully realized. Woman's place was still in the home; in the first half of the nineteenth century an unprecedented outpouring of books and magazine articles asserted that conclusion with ever greater force

and fervor. Jeffersonian Republicans, like almost all Americans before them, failed to extend to women the freedom and individuality they recognized as essential for men.

SUGGESTIONS FOR FURTHER READING

National Government and Administration

Ralph Adams Brown, *The Presidency of John Adams* (1975); John R. Howe, *The Changing Political Thought of John Adams* (1966); Richard H. Kohn, *Eagle and Sword: The Federalists and the Creation of the Military Establishment in America, 1783–1802* (1975); Stephen G. Kurtz, *The Presidency of John Adams: The Collapse of Federalism, 1795–1800* (1957); Forrest McDonald, *Alexander Hamilton: A Biography* (1979); Forrest McDonald, *The Presidency of George Washington* (1974); John C. Miller, *The Federalist Era, 1789–1801* (1960); Merrill D. Peterson, *Thomas Jefferson & The New Nation: A Biography* (1970); Carl E. Prince, *The Federalists and the Origins of the U.S. Civil Service* (1978); Leonard D. White, *The Federalists: A Study in Administrative History* (1948); Garry Wills, *Cincinnatus: George Washington and the Enlightenment* (1984).

Partisan Politics

Leland D. Baldwin, *The Whiskey Rebels* (1939); Lance Banning, *The Jeffersonian Persuasion: Evolution of a Party Ideology* (1978); Richard Beeman, *The Old Dominion and the New Nation, 1788–1801* (1972); Richard W. Buel, Jr., *Securing the Revolution: Ideology in American Politics, 1789–1815* (1972); William Nisbet Chambers, *Political Parties in a New Nation: The American Experience, 1776–1809* (1963); Joseph Charles, *The Origins of the American Party System* (1956); Noble E. Cunningham, *The Jeffersonian Republicans: The Formation of Party Organization, 1789–1801* (1957); Manning J. Dauer, *The Adams Federalists* (1953); Paul Goodman, *The Democratic Republicans of Massachusetts* (1964); Richard Hofstadter, *The Idea of a Party System: The Rise of Legitimate Opposition in the United States, 1780–1840* (1970); Adrienne Koch, *Jefferson and Madison: The Great Collaboration* (1950); Eugene P. Link, *Democratic-*

Republican Societies, 1790–1800 (1942); Norman K. Risjord, Chesapeake Politics, 1781–1800 (1978); Patricia Watlington, The Partisan Spirit: Kentucky Politics, 1779–1792 (1972); Alfred F. Young, The Democratic-Republicans of New York: The Origins, 1763–1797 (1967); John Zvesper, Political Philosophy and Rhetoric: A Study of the Origins of American Party Politics (1977).

Foreign Policy

Harry Ammon, The Genet Mission (1973); Samuel F. Bemis, Jay's Treaty, 2nd ed. (1962); Samuel F. Bemis, Pinckney's Treaty, 2nd ed. (1960); Jerald A. Combs, The Jay Treaty (1970); Alexander DeConde, Entangling Alliance: Politics and Diplomacy under George Washington (1958); Alexander DeConde, The Quasi-War: Politics and Diplomacy of the Undeclared War with France, 1797–1801 (1966); Felix Gilbert, To the Farewell Address: Ideas of Early American Foreign Policy (1961); Reginald Horsman, The Diplomacy of the New Republic, 1776–1815 (1985); Bradford Perkins, The First Rapprochement: England and the United States, 1795–1805 (1967); Charles Ritcheson, Aftermath of Revolution: British Policy Toward the United States, 1783–1795 (1969); William Stinchcombe, The XYZ Affair (1981); Paul A. Varg, Foreign Policies of the Founding Fathers (1963).

Civil Liberties

Leonard W. Levy, Origins of the Fifth Amendment (1968); Leonard W. Levy, Legacy of Suppression: Freedom of Speech and Press in Early American History (1960); Robert A. Rutland, The Birth of the Bill of Rights, 1776–1791 (1955); James Morton Smith, Freedom's Fetters: The Alien and Sedition Laws and American Civil Liberties (1956).

Women and Blacks

Ira Berlin and Ronald Hoffman, eds., Slavery and Freedom in the Age of the American Revolution (1983); Nancy F. Cott, The Bonds of Womanhood: "Woman's Sphere" in New England, 1780–1835 (1977); Nancy F. Cott, "Young Women in the Second Great Awakening in New England," Feminist Studies, 3, No. 1/2 (1975), 15–29; Jeffrey J. Crow, "Slave Rebelliousness and Social Conflict in North Carolina, 1775 to 1802," William and Mary Quarterly, 3rd ser., 37 (1980), 79–102; Gerald W. Mullin, Flight and Rebellion: Slave Resistance in Eighteenth-Century Virginia (1972).

Social Change and Westward Expansion

Mary H. Blewett, "Work, Gender, and the Artisan Tradition in New England Shoemaking, 1780–1860," Journal of Social History, 17 (1983), 221–248; Reginald Horsman, The Frontier in the Formative Years 1783–1815 (1970); Howard Rock, Artisans of the New Republic: The Tradesmen of New York City in the Age of Thomas Jefferson (1979); Malcolm Rohrbough, The Trans-Appalachian Frontier: Peoples, Societies, and Institutions, 1775–1850 (1979); W. J. Rorabaugh, The Alcoholic Republic: An American Tradition (1979); Charles G. Steffen, The Mechanics of Baltimore: Workers and Politics in the Age of Revolution, 1763–1812 (1984); Sean Wilentz, Chants Democratic: New York City and the Rise of the American Working Class, 1788–1850 (1984).

Religion

Sydney Ahlstrom, A Religious History of the American People (1972); Catharine Albanese, Sons of the Fathers: The Civil Religion of the American Revolution (1976); Fred J. Hood, Reformed America 1783–1837 (1980); William McLoughlin, Revivals, Awakenings, and Reform (1978).

THE EMPIRE OF LIBERTY
1801–1824

CHAPTER 8

"*I have this* morning witnessed one of the most interesting scenes a free people can ever witness," Margaret B. Smith, a Philadelphian, wrote on March 4, 1801, to her sister-in-law. "The changes of administration, which in every government and in every age have most generally been epochs of confusion, villainy and bloodshed, in this our happy country take place without any species of distraction, or disorder." On that day, Thomas Jefferson strolled from his New Jersey Avenue boardinghouse in the new federal capital of Washington, D.C., to be sworn in as president at the Capitol building. The precedent of an orderly and peaceful change of government had been established.

Jefferson's inauguration marked a change of style in government, at the beginning of a period when Americans were struggling to assert and define their nationalism amid challenges, both foreign and domestic. Almost overnight the formality of the Federalist presidencies of Washington and Adams was significantly altered as Jefferson set the tone for the Republican government. Gone were the aristocratic wigs and breeches (knee-length trousers) the first two presidents had favored; Jefferson wore plainer garb. Though personally richer and with more luxurious tastes than Adams, Jefferson rejected the aristocratic and wealthy pretensions he associated with the Federalists. Republican virtue would be restored.

Ordinary folk who had come to celebrate Jefferson's inaugural overran Washington, causing Federalists to cluck their tongues at the seeming collapse of authority and order. For two weeks following the inauguration, Jefferson still lived and worked at his modest lodgings a few blocks from the Capitol. He ran the presidency from the parlor next to his bedroom and continued to eat at the communal dining table. Not until March 19 did he move to the president's mansion.

The government had moved to Washington from New York in November 1800, and its unfinished federal buildings seemed to symbolize the unfinished nation. Augustus John Foster, a British diplomat, lamented the move. The diplomatic corps, he reported, found it "difficult to digest" moving from "agreeable," urban New York "to what was then scarce any better than a mere swamp." Abigail Adams found it "the very dirtyest Hole," its streets "a quagmire after every rain." On the other hand, Washington offered amusements unlike any other Atlantic capital. "Excellent snipe shooting and even partridge shooting was to be had on each side of the main [Pennsylvania] avenue and even close under the wall of the Capitol," Foster recalled. But the simpler lifestyle seemed to suit the change from the formality of the Federalist government to the less pretentious Republican administration.

The new district, carved out of Maryland and Virginia, had been chosen because of its central location. Washington was thus beholden to neither the colonial past nor any single state. Few buildings were needed to house the government, which essentially collected tariffs, delivered mail, and defended the nation's borders. But a small government suited the republic. Even for the Federalists, the adoption of the Constitution and their holding power in the 1790s had been more a result of dissatisfaction with the Articles of Confederation than a sign of their confidence in central government. The election of the Republican Thomas Jefferson in 1800 began the Virginia dynasty and a swing back to state authority that lasted until 1825. In an age when it took some congressmen more than a week to reach the capital, most Americans favored government closer to home.

The transfer of power to the Republicans from the Federalists intensified political conflict and voter interest. Republican presidents sought, in the Revolutionary War tradition, to limit government and decentralize authority. Federalists prized a stronger national government with more order and authority in a centralized system. With both parties competing for adherents and popular support, the basis was laid for the evolution of democratic party politics. But factionalism and the partisanship of personal disputes within each party prevented the development of true political parties, and the Federalists, unable to build a popular base, slowly disappeared as an organized opposition party.

Events abroad both encouraged and threatened the expansionism of the young nation. Seizing one opportunity, the United States purchased the Louisiana Territory, pushing the frontier further west. But then from the high seas came war. Caught between the British and the French, the United States found itself a victim of European conflict with its shipping rights as a neutral, independent nation ignored and violated. When the humiliation became too great, Americans took up arms in the War of 1812 both to defend their rights as a nation and to expand farther to the west and north. Although unprepared for combat, the United States fought Great Britain to a standstill. The peace treaty merely restored the prewar status quo, but the war and the treaty nevertheless reaffirmed American independence and determination to steer clear of European conflicts, and led to growing accommodation with Great Britain.

The War of 1812 unleashed a wave of nationalism and self-confidence. The disruption of trade with Europe during the war promoted the development of manufacturing in the United States. The war also pointed up the need for better transportation within the country. Following the war, the government became the champion of business and promoted the building of roads and canals. The new spirit encouraged economic growth and western expansion at home and assertiveness throughout the hemisphere, as was evident in the Monroe Doctrine. By the 1820s the United States was no longer an experiment; a new nation had emerged. Free of its colonial past, the country began energetically shaping its own identity.

Growth and expansion did generate new problems, however. A financial panic brought hardship and conflict in 1819, which sowed the seeds for the Jacksonian movement in the 1830s. More ominously, sectional differences and the presence of slavery created divisions that would widen in the wake of further westward expansion during the 1840s and 1850s.

JEFFERSON IN POWER

Jefferson delivered his inaugural address in the Senate chamber, the only part of the Capitol that had been completed. Nearly a thousand people strained to hear his barely audible voice. "We are

Jefferson's Inaugural Address

all Republicans, we are all Federalists," he told the assembly in an appeal for unity. Confidently addressing those with little faith in the people's ability to govern themselves, he called America's republican government "the world's best hope." If "man cannot be trusted with the government of himself," Jefferson argued, "can he, then, be trusted with the government of others? Or have we found angels in the forms of kings to govern him? Let history answer this question."

The new president went on to outline his own and his party's republican goals:

A wise and frugal government, which shall restrain men from injuring one another, which shall leave them otherwise free to regulate their own pursuits. . . .
Equal and exact justice to all men, of whatever state or persuasion, religious or political. . . .
The support of the state governments in all their rights, as the most competent administrators for our domestic concerns and the surest bulwarks against antirepublican tendencies.

At the same time, he assured Federalists that he shared some of their concerns as well:

The preservation of the general government in its whole constitutional vigor. . . .
The honest payment of our debts and sacred preservation of the public faith. . . .
Encouragement of agriculture and of commerce as its handmaid.

Yet Jefferson and his fellow Republicans distrusted the Federalists. They considered them to be antidemocratic and antirepublican at heart and accused them of imitating the court society of England. One of Jefferson's first acts was to extend the grasp of Republicanism over the federal government. Virtually all appointed officials were loyal Federalists: of the six hundred or so appointed under Washington and Adams, only six were known Republicans. To counteract Federalist power and restore government to those who shared his vision of an agrarian republic, Jefferson refused to recognize Adams's last-minute "midnight appointments" to local offices in the District of Columbia. Next he dismissed Federalist customs collectors from New England ports. Vacant treasury and judicial offices were awarded to Republicans,

Trumbull's formal portrait of Thomas Jefferson. Increasingly Jefferson came to disdain wearing a wig and preferred plainer garb. At his inaugural he was simply dressed as he spoke to his fellow citizens of republican virtue and reconciliation. The Metropolitan Museum of Art.

until by July 1803 only 130 of 316 presidentially controlled offices were held by Federalists. Jefferson, in restoring political balance in government, used patronage to reward his friends, to build a party organization, and to compete with the Federalists.

The Republican Congress similarly proceeded to affirm its republicanism. Guided by Secretary of the Treasury Albert Gallatin and John Randolph of Virginia, Jefferson's ally in the House, the federal government went on a diet. Congress repealed all internal taxes, even the whiskey tax. Gallatin cut the army budget in half, to just under $2 million, and reduced the navy budget from $3.5 to $1 million in 1802. Moreover, Gallatin laid plans to reduce the national debt—Alexander Hamilton's engine of economic growth—from $83 to $57 million, as part of a plan

to retire it altogether by 1817. Jefferson even closed two of the nation's five diplomatic missions abroad— the Hague and Berlin—to save money.

More than frugality, however, separated Republicans from Federalists. Opposition to the Alien and Sedition laws of 1798 had helped unite Republicans before Jefferson's election (see pages 196–199). Now as president, Jefferson forswore using the acts against his opponents, as President Adams had, and Congress let them expire in 1801 and 1802. Congress also repealed the Naturalization Act of 1798, which had required fourteen years of residency for citizenship. The 1802 act that replaced it required only five years of residency, acceptance of the Constitution, and the forsaking of foreign allegiance and titles. The new act would remain the basis of naturalized American citizenship into the twentieth century.

The Republicans turned next to the judiciary, the last stronghold of unchecked Federalist power. During the 1790s not a single Republican had been appointed to the federal bench. Moreover, the

Attacks on the Judiciary Judiciary Act of 1801, passed in the last days of the Adams administration, had created fifteen new judgeships (which Adams filled in his midnight appointments, signing appointments until his term was just hours away from expiring) and would reduce by attrition the number of justices on the Supreme Court from six to five. Since that reduction would have denied Jefferson any Supreme Court appointments until two vacancies had occurred, the new Republican-dominated Congress repealed the 1801 act as one of its first moves.

Republicans also targeted opposition judges for removal. Federalist judges had refused to review the Sedition Act, and Federalists had prosecuted critics of the administration under the act. At Jefferson's suggestion, the House impeached (indicted) Federal District Judge John Pickering of New Hampshire; in 1804 the Senate removed him from office. Although he was an alcoholic and emotionally disturbed, Pickering had not committed any crime.

The same day Pickering was convicted, the House impeached Supreme Court Justice Samuel Chase for judicial misconduct. Chase, an arch-Federalist and leader in pressing convictions under the Sedition Act, had repeatedly denounced Jefferson's administration from the bench. The Republicans, however, failed to muster the two-thirds majority necessary to convict him; they had gone too far. Their failure to remove Chase preserved the Court's independence and established a precedent for narrow interpretation of the grounds for impeachment (criminal rather than political). Time soon cured Republican grievances; by the year Jefferson left office, he had appointed three new Supreme Court justices. Nonetheless, under Chief Justice John Marshall, the Court remained a Federalist stronghold.

Marshall was an astute lawyer with keen political sense. A Virginia Federalist who had served under George Washington in the Revolutionary War, he had been minister to France and **John Marshall** then secretary of state under President Adams before being named chief justice. Jefferson considered Marshall a midnight appointment, believing that any appointment after Adams learned of his defeat in the electoral college on December 12, 1800, was wrong and immoral, if not illegal. But Congress approved the appointment in January 1801 before Jefferson was sworn in as president.

Although he was an autocrat by nature, Marshall possessed a grace and openness of manner well suited to the new Republican political style. Under Marshall's domination, the Supreme Court retained a Federalist viewpoint even after Republican justices achieved a majority in 1811. Throughout his tenure (from 1801 until 1835), the Court upheld federal supremacy over the states and protected the interests of commerce and capital.

More important, Marshall made the Court an equal branch of government in practice as well as theory. First, he made a place on the Court a coveted honor. Prior to Marshall it had been difficult to keep the Court filled. Fifteen justices had served on the six-member Court during its first twelve years; after Marshall's appointment it took forty years for fifteen new members to be appointed. Marshall's presence had made the Court worthy of ambitious and talented men. Second, he unifed the Court, influencing the justices to issue single majority opinions rather than individual concurring judgments. Marshall himself became the voice of the majority. From 1801 through 1805 he wrote 24 of the Court's 26 decisions; through 1810 he wrote 85 percent of the 171 opinions, including every important decision.

John Marshall (1755–1835), chief justice of the Supreme Court from 1801 to 1835. This portrait shows the strength of personality that enabled Marshall to make the Court into a Federalist stronghold. Supreme Court of the United States.

Finally, Marshall increased the Court's power. *Marbury v. Madison* (1803) was the landmark case that enabled Marshall to strengthen the Court. William Marbury had been designated **Marbury v.** a justice of the peace in the District **Madison** of Columbia as part of Adams's midnight appointments of March 2, 1801. He now sued the new secretary of state, James Madison, for failing to certify his appointment so that Jefferson could appoint a Republican. In his suit Marbury requested a writ of mandamus (a court order compelling Madison to appoint him).

At first glance, the case presented a political dilemma. Even if the Supreme Court ruled in favor of Marbury and issued a writ of mandamus, the president might not comply. After all, why should the president, sworn to uphold the Constitution, allow the Court to decide for him what was constitutional? On the other hand, if the Court refused to issue the writ, it would be handing the Republicans a victory. Marshall avoided both alternatives. Speaking for the Court, he ruled that Marbury had a right to his commission but that the Court could not compel Madison to honor it, because the Constitution did not grant the Court power to issue a writ of mandamus. Thus Marshall declared unconstitutional Section 13 of the Judiciary Act of 1789, which authorized the Court to issue such writs. Marbury lost his job and the justices denied themselves the power to issue writs of mandamus, but the Supreme Court claimed its power to judge the constitutionality of laws passed by Congress.

In succeeding years Marshall fashioned the theory of judicial review. Since the Constitution was the supreme law, he reasoned, any act of Congress contrary to the Constitution must be null and void. And since the Supreme Court was responsible for upholding the law, it had a duty to decide whether or not a conflict existed between a legislative act and the Constitution. If such a conflict did indeed exist, the Court would declare the congressional act unconstitutional.

Marshall's decision rebuffed Republican criticism of the Court as a partisan instrument. He avoided a confrontation with the Republican-dominated Congress by not ruling on its repeal of the 1801 Judiciary Act. And he enhanced the Court's independence by claiming the power of judicial review.

While President Jefferson fought with the Federalist judiciary and struggled to reduce federal spending, he kept a wary eye on the Louisiana Territory. Lou-

Louisiana Purchase

isiana, France's largest colony in the New World, defined the western United States border along the Mississippi from the Gulf of Mexico to present-day Minnesota. It had been ceded to Spain in 1762 at the end of the French and Indian War (see page 105). Jefferson shared with other Americans the belief that the United States was destined to expand its "empire of liberty." Since the first days of American independence, Louisiana had held a special place in the young nation's expansionist dreams. By 1800, hundreds of thousands of Americans in search of land had trekked into the rich Mississippi and Ohio valleys to settle, often intruding on Indian lands. Down the Mississippi and Ohio rivers to New Orleans they floated their farm goods for export.

Thus, whoever controlled the port of New Orleans had a hand on the throat of the American economy. As long as Spain owned Louisiana, Americans did not fear. But in 1802 Napoleonic France acquired the vast territory in an ambitious bid to rebuild its empire in the New World. The transfer, moaned Jefferson, "works most sorely" on the United States. Fears intensified even more in October 1802, when Spanish officials, on the eve of ceding control to the French, violated Pinckney's Treaty (see page 193), by denying Americans the privilege of storing their products at New Orleans prior to transshipment to foreign markets. Western farmers and eastern merchants thought a devious Napoleon had closed the port; they grumbled and talked war.

To relieve the pressure for war and to prevent westerners from joining Federalists in opposition to his administration, Jefferson simultaneously prepared for war and accelerated talks with the French. In January 1803 he sent James Monroe to France to help the American minister Robert Livingston in negotiating to buy New Orleans. Meanwhile, Congress authorized a call-up of eighty thousand militia if it proved necessary. Arriving in Paris in April, Monroe was astonished to learn that France had already offered to sell all 827,000 square miles of Louisiana to the United States for $15 million. On April 30 Monroe and Livingston signed a treaty to purchase the vast territory, whose borders were left undefined at that time (see map).

The Louisiana Purchase doubled the size of the nation and opened the way for westward expansion across the continent. The acquisition was the single most popular achievement of Jefferson's presidency. Yet for Jefferson, the purchase presented a dilemma. It promised fulfillment of the dream of a continental nation reaching to the Pacific Coast, "with room enough for our descendants to the hundredth and thousandth generation," as he put it. And it offered a solution to Indian-settler conflict in the frontier by providing land to which eastern tribes, North and South, could be removed. But its legality was questionable. The Constitution gave him no clear authority to acquire new territory and incorporate it into the nation. Jefferson considered requesting a constitutional amendment to allow the purchase, but in the end he justified it on the grounds that it was part of the

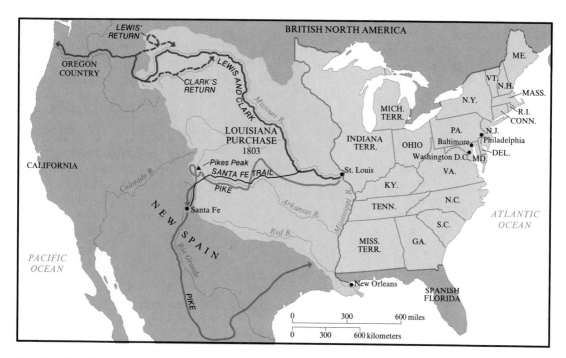

Louisiana Purchase

president's implied powers to protect the nation. The people, he knew, would accept or reject the purchase on election day in 1804.

The president had had a long-standing interest in Louisiana and the West. As early as 1782, as an American envoy in France, Jefferson had suggested sending an exploratory mission across the continent to California. As secretary of state ten years later he commissioned a French emigré, André Michaux, to explore the Missouri River. Allegations of Michaux's complicity in the Genet Affair (see page 191) aborted this mission. In 1803 Jefferson renewed Michaux's instructions when he sent Meri-

Lewis and Clark

wether Lewis and William Clark to the Pacific Ocean via the Missouri and Columbia rivers. Lewis and Clark, from 1804 to 1806, headed the nearly fifty-strong "Corps of Discovery," which was aided by trappers and American Indians along the way. A French-Canadian trader and his young Shoshone wife, Toussaint Charbonneau and Sacajawea, joined the expedition. Sacajawea interpreted both the terrain and the languages of the West to the wanderers in a strange land.

The Lewis and Clark expedition, planned in secrecy before the Louisiana Purchase, reflected both Jefferson's scientific curiosity and his interest in western commercial development, especially the prospects of the fur and China trades. Other explorers soon followed them, led in 1805 and 1806 by Lieutenant Zebulon Pike in search of the source of the Mississippi. A year later Pike attempted to find a navigable path to the Far West and sought the headwaters of the Arkansas River. He reached the Rocky Mountains in present-day Colorado, though he never made it to the top of the peak that bears his name. Pike and his men wandered into Spanish territory to the south, where the Spanish arrested them and held them captive for several months in Santa Fe. After his release, Pike wrote an account of his experiences that set commercial minds spinning. He described a potential commercial market in southwestern Spanish cities as well as the bounty of furs and precious minerals to be had. The vision of the road to the Southwest became a reality with the opening of the Santa Fe Trail in the 1820s. Over the next few decades Americans avidly read published accounts of western exploration. Expansion and the West had caught their imagination, and Jefferson considered the acquisition of Louisiana and the opening of the West among his greatest presidential accomplishments.

REPUBLICANS VERSUS FEDERALISTS

Campaigning for re-election in 1804, Jefferson claimed credit for western expansion and the restoration of republican values. He removed the

1804 Election

Federalist threat to liberty by allowing the Alien and Sedition and Judiciary Acts to expire. At the same time he reduced the size and cost of government by cutting spending. And despite his opponents' charges, he proved that Republicans supported commerce. He removed major obstacles to American commercial growth by purchasing the Louisiana Territory, including New Orleans, and by having Congress repeal the Federalist excise and property taxes. And further American trade with Europe flourished. Unwisely, Federalists who had earlier criticized Jefferson for not seizing Louisiana now attacked the president for paying too much for the territory or for exceeding his powers. Charles Cotesworth Pinckney, a wealthy South Carolina lawyer and former Revolutionary War aide to General George Washington, carried the opposition standard against Jefferson. Pinckney had been Adams's vice-presidential candidate in 1800 and inherited the Federalist party leadership. Jefferson and his running mate, George Clinton of New York, swamped Pinckney and Rufus King in the electoral college by 162 votes to 14, carrying fifteen of the seventeen states.

Jefferson's re-election was both a personal and a party triumph. The political dissenters of the 1790s had turned their Democratic-Republican societies into a political party—an organization for the purpose of winning elections. More than anything else, opposition to the Federalists had molded and unified them. Indeed, it was where the Federalists were strongest— in commercial New York and Pennsylvania in the 1790s and in New England in the 1800s—that the Republicans had organized most effectively.

Until the Republican successes in 1800 and 1804, Federalists had disdained popular campaigning. They believed in government by the "best" people—those whose education, wealth, and experience marked them as leaders. For candidates to debate their qualifications before their inferiors—the voters—was unnecessary and undignified. The direct appeals of the Republicans therefore struck them as a subversion of the natural political order.

But after their resounding defeat in 1800, a younger generation of Federalists began to imitate the Republicans. They organized statewide and, led by men

Younger Federalists

like Josiah Quincy, a young congressman from Massachusetts, they began to campaign for popular support. Quincy cleverly identified the Federalists as the people's party, attacking Republicans as autocratic planters. "Jeffersonian Democracy," Quincy satirized in 1804, was "an indian word, signifying '*a great tobacco planter who had herds of black slaves.*'" In attacking frugal government, the self-styled Younger Federalists played on fears of a weakened army and navy. Merchants depended on a strong navy to protect ocean trade while westerners, encroaching on Indian tribes, looked for federal support.

In the states where both parties organized and ran candidates, participation in elections increased markedly. In some states more than 90 percent of the eligible voters—nearly all of whom were white males— cast ballots between 1804 and 1816. People became more interested in politics generally, especially at the local level; and as participation in elections increased, the states expanded suffrage. Nevertheless, the popular base of the parties was still restricted. Property qualifications for voting and holding office remained common and in six states the legislatures still selected presidential electors in 1804. Even Republicans were restrained in committing themselves to party organization. Most leaders, fearing the divisiveness of partisanship, were suspicious of cohesive political movements.

Yet party competition, spurred on by a vigorous press which saw its primary role as political advocacy, led to grassroots campaigning. The political barbecue symbolized the new style as the parties responded to

Citizens gather at the State House in Philadelphia to whip up support for their candidates and parties. This picture, drawn on Election Day in 1816, suggests the overwhelmingly white, exclusively male composition of the electorate. Library of Congress.

increasing voter involvement in politics. In New York they roasted oxen; on the New England coast they baked clams; in Maryland they served oysters. The guests washed down their meals with beer and punch and sometimes competed in corn shuckings or horse pulls. During the barbecue, candidates and party leaders spoke from the stump. Oratory was a popular form of entertainment, and the speakers delivered lengthy and uninhibited speeches. They often made wild accusations, which—given the slow speed of communications—might not be answered until after the election. In 1808, for example, a New England Republican accused the Federalists of causing the Boston Massacre.

Soon both parties were using barbecues to appeal directly to voters. But although the Younger Federalists adopted the political barbecue, the Federalist party never fully mastered the art of wooing voters. Older Federalists still opposed such blatant campaigns. And though they were strong in a few states like Connecticut and Delaware, the Federalists never offered the Republicans sustained competition. Divisions between Older and Younger Federalists often hindered them, and the extremism of some Older Federalists tended to discredit the party. A case in point was Timothy Pickering, a Massachusetts congressman and former secretary of state who opposed the Louisiana Purchase, feared Jefferson's re-election, and urged the secession of New England in 1803 and 1804. Pickering won some support among the few Federalists in Congress, but others opposed his plan for a northern confederacy. When Vice President Aaron Burr lost his bid to become governor of New York in 1804, the plan collapsed. Burr, more an opportunist than a loyal Republican, was to have led New York into secession, with the other states to follow.

Both political parties suffered from factionalism and individuals' personal ambitions, which undermined party loyalty and cohesiveness. For a long time, for instance, Aaron Burr and Alexander Hamilton had crossed swords in political conflict. Burr had an affinity for conspiracies and it seemed to him that Hamilton always blocked his path. Hamilton had thwarted Burr's attempt to steal the 1800 election from Jefferson (see page 199) and in the 1804 New York gubernatorial race the Federalist Hamilton backed a rival Republican faction against Burr. Burr, his political career in ruins, turned his resentment on Hamilton and challenged him to a duel. The specific insult was Hamilton's description of Burr as dangerous and unfit to hold office. With his honor at stake, Hamilton accepted Burr's challenge, although he found dueling repugnant. They withdrew to New Jersey since New York had outlawed dueling. On July 11, 1804, at Weehawken, New Jersey, Hamilton deliberately fired astray. He paid for that decision with his life. Burr was indicted for murder in New York and New Jersey and faced immediate arrest if he returned to either state.

Hamilton-Burr Duel

With his political career over in the United States, Burr plotted to build an empire in the Southwest, using Louisiana as a base from which to launch an attack against Spanish lands. He planned to raise a private army, but the United States commander in the Mississippi Valley, General James Wilkinson, informed President Jefferson of Burr's plans. In 1807 Burr was tried and acquitted of treason but fled to Europe to avoid further prosecution.

The Burr-Hamilton conflict highlights some of the limitations of the early party system. Personal animosities often prompted the crossing of party lines and the appearance of new, temporary factions. Moreover, although politicians appealed for voter support and participation in politics broadened, the electoral base remained narrow. As the election of 1804 revealed, the Federalists could offer only weak competition at the national level. And where Federalists were too weak to be a threat, Republicans succumbed to the temptation to fight among themselves.

Thus, although this period is commonly called the era of the first party system, parties as such never fully developed. Competition encouraged party organization, but personal ambition, personality clashes, and local, state, and regional loyalties worked against it. Increasingly, external events intruded, and these would occupy most of Jefferson's time in his second administration.

PRESERVING AMERICAN NEUTRALITY IN A WORLD AT WAR

"Peace, commerce, and honest friendship with all nations, entangling alliance with none," President Jefferson had sensibly proclaimed in his first inaugural address. And Jefferson's efforts to stand clear of European conflict worked until 1805. Thereafter he found peace and undisturbed commerce an elusive goal, though pursuit of it occupied nearly his entire second administration.

After the Senate ratified the Jay Treaty in 1795 (see pages 192–193), the United States and Great Britain had appeared to reconcile their differences. Britain withdrew from its western forts and interfered less in American trade with France. More importantly, trade between the United States and Britain increased: the republic became Britain's best customer, and the British Empire in turn bought the bulk of American exports.

But renewal of the Napoleonic wars in May 1803—two weeks after Napoleon sold Louisiana to the United States—again trapped the nation between the two unfriendly superpowers. For two years American commerce actually benefited from the conflict. As the world's largest neutral carrier, the United States became the chief supplier of food to Europe. American merchants also gained control of most of the West Indian trade, which was often transshipped through American ports to Europe.

Meanwhile, the United States victory over Tripolitan pirates on the north coast of Africa (the Barbary states) provided Jefferson with his one clear success in protecting American trading rights. In 1801 Jefferson had refused the demands of the Sultan of Tripoli for payment of tribute to exempt American ships from seizure by Barbary Coast pirates. Instead he sent a naval squadron to the Mediterranean to protect American merchant ships. In 1803 and 1804, under Lieutenant Stephen Decatur, the navy blockaded Tripoli harbor while marines marched overland from Egypt to seize the port of Derna. The United States signed a peace treaty with Tripoli in 1805, but continued to pay tribute to other Barbary states.

That same year American merchants became victims of Anglo-French enmity. First Britain tightened its control over the high seas with its victory over the French and Spanish fleets at the Battle of Trafalgar in October 1805. Two months later Napoleon defeated the Russian and Austrian armies at Austerlitz. Stalemated, the two powers waged commercial war, blockading and counterblockading each other's trade. As a trading partner of both countries, the United States paid a high price.

The British navy at the same time stepped up impressments of American sailors. Britain, whose navy was the world's largest, was suffering a severe shortage of sailors. Few enlisted, and those already in service frequently deserted, discouraged by poor food and living conditions and brutal discipline. The Royal Navy resorted to stopping American ships and forcibly removing British deserters, British-born naturalized American seamen, and other unlucky sailors mistakenly suspected of being British. It is estimated that six to eight thousand Americans were drafted in this manner between 1803 and 1812.

Impressment of American Sailors

Americans saw impressment as a direct assault on their new republic. It violated America's rights as a neutral nation, and the British principle of "once a British subject, always a British subject" ignored American citizenship and sovereignty. Moreover, the practice exposed the weakness of the new nation;

the United States was in effect unable to protect its citizens from impressment.

In February 1806 the Senate denounced British impressment as aggression and a violation of neutral rights. To protest the insult Congress passed the Non-Importation Act, prohibiting importation from Great Britain of a long list of cloth and metal articles. In November Jefferson suspended the act temporarily while William Pinckney, a leading Baltimore lawyer, joined James Monroe in London in an attempt to negotiate a settlement. But the treaty Monroe and Pinckney carried home violated their instructions— it did not mention impressment—and Jefferson never submitted it to the Senate for ratification.

Less than a year later the *Chesapeake* Affair exposed American military weakness and revealed the emotional impact of impressment on the public. In June 1807 the forty-gun frigate U.S.S. *Chesapeake* left Norfolk, Virginia, on a mission to protect American ships trading in the Mediterranean. About ten miles out, still inside American territorial waters, it met the fifty-gun British frigate *Leopard*. When the *Chesapeake* refused to be searched for deserters, the *Leopard* repeatedly emptied its guns broadside into the American ship. Three Americans were killed and eighteen wounded, including the ship's captain, Commodore James Barron. Four sailors were impressed—three of them American citizens, all of them deserters from the Royal Navy. Wounded and humiliated, the *Chesapeake* crept back into port.

Chesapeake Affair

Had the United States been better prepared militarily, the howl of public indignation that resulted might have brought about a declaration of war. But the United States was ill equipped to defend its neutral rights with force; it was no match for the British navy. Fortunately, Congress was not in session at the time of the *Chesapeake* Affair, and Jefferson was able to avoid hostilities. The president responded instead by strengthening the military and putting economic pressure on Great Britain: in July Jefferson closed American waters to British warships to prevent similar incidents and soon thereafter he increased military and naval expenditures. On December 14, 1807, Jefferson again invoked the Non-Importation Act, followed eight days later by a new measure, the Embargo Act.

THE IMPRESSMENT OF AN

American Sailor Boy,

SUNG ON BOARD THE BRITISH PRISON SHIP CROWN PRINCE, THE FOURTH OF JULY, 1814
BY A NUMBER OF THE AMERICAN PRISONERS.

THE youthful sailor mounts the bark,
    And bids each weeping friend adieu :
Fair blows the gale, the canvass swells :
    Slow sinks the uplands from his view.

Three mornings, from his ocean bed,
    Resplendent beams the God of day :
The fourth. high looming in the mist,
    A war-ship's floating banners play.

Her yawl is launch'd ; light o'er the deep,
    Too kind, she wafts a ruffian band :
Her blue track lengthens to the bark,
    And soon on deck the miscreants stand.

Around they throw the baleful glance :
    Suspense holds mute the anxious crew—
Who is their prey ? poor sailor boy !
    The baleful glance is fix'd on you.

Nay. why that useless scrip unfold ?
    They damn'd the " lying yankee scrawl,"
Torn from thine hand, it strews the wave—
    They force thee trembling to the yawl.

Sick was thine heart as from the deck,
    The hand of friendship wav'd farewell ;
Mad was thy brain, as far behind,
    In the grey mist thy vessel fell.

One hope, yet, to thy bosom clung,
    The captain mercy might impart ;

Vain was that hope, which bade thee look,
    For mercy in a Pirate's heart.

What woes can man on man inflict,
    When malice joins with uncheck'd power ;
Such woes, unpitied and unknown,
    For many a month the sailor bore !

Oft gem'd his eye the bursting tear,
    As mem'ry linger'd on past joy ;
As oft they flung the cruel jeer,
    And damn'd the " chicken liver'd boy."

When sick at heart, with " hope defer'd."
    Kind sleep his wasting form embrac'd,
Some ready minion ply'd the lash,
    And the lov'd dream of freedom chas'd.

Fast to an end his miseries drew :
    The deadly hectic flush'd his cheek :
On his pale brow the cold dew hung,
    He sigh'd, and sunk upon the deck !

The sailor's woes drew forth no sigh ;
No hand would close the sailor's eye :
Remorseless, his pale corse they gave,
Unshrouded to the friendly wave.

And as he sunk beneath the tide,
    A hellish shout arose ;
Exultingly the demons cried,
    " So fare all Albion's Rebel Foes ! "

Ballad of an American Sailor impressed by the British during the War of 1812. References to the British captain as a "Pirate" and the British crew as "demons" reveal the intense indignation felt by the American public.   The New-York Historical Society.

Intended as a short-term measure, the Embargo Act forbade virtually all exports from the United States to any country. Imports came

Embargo Act   to a halt as well, since foreign ships delivering goods would have to leave American ports with empty holds. Smuggling blossomed overnight.

Few American policies were as well intentioned but as unpopular and unsuccessful as Jefferson's embargo. Although the notion of "peaceable coercion" was an enlightened concept in international affairs, some Republicans felt uneasy about using coercive federal power. Federalists felt no unease; commercially minded and generally pro-British, they opposed the embargo vociferously. Some feared its impact internationally; "If England sink," Rufus King said in 1808, "her fall will prove the grave of our liberties." For mercantile New Englanders, it dug another grave. Their region, the heart of Federalist opposition to the Virginian presidents, felt the brunt of the resulting depression. Shipping collapsed as exports fell by 80 percent from 1807 to 1808. In the winter of 1808 to 1809, talk of secession spread through New England port cities. Although unemployment soared, some benefited. Merchants with ships abroad at the time of the embargo or those willing to trade illegally and risk the weak and lax enforcement could garner enormous profits. Similarly, United States manufacturers received a boost, since the domestic market was theirs exclusively.

Great Britain, in contrast, was only mildly affected by the embargo. Those British citizens hurt most—West Indians and English factory workers—had no voice in policy. English merchants actually gained, since they took over the Atlantic carrying trade from the stalled American merchant marine. Moreover, because the British blockade of Europe had already ended most trade with France, the embargo had little practical effect on the French. Indeed, it gave France an excuse to privateer against American ships that had managed to escape the embargo by avoiding American ports. The French argued that such ships must be British ships in disguise, since the embargo barred American ships from the seas.

In the election of 1808, the Republicans faced the Federalists, the embargo, and factional dissent in their own party. Jefferson followed Washington's example, renouncing a third term and supporting James Madison, his secretary of state, as the Republican standard-bearer. Madison won the endorsement of the congressional caucus, but Virginia Republicans put forth James Monroe (who later withdrew), and some eastern Republicans supported Vice President George Clinton. This was the first time the Republican nomination had been contested.

Charles Cotesworth Pinckney and Rufus King again headed the Federalist ticket, but with new vigor. The Younger Federalists, led by Harrison Gray Otis and other Bostonians, pounded away at the widespread disaffection with Republican policy, especially the embargo. Although Pinckney received only 47 electoral votes to Madison's 122, the Federalists did manage to make the election a race. Pinckney carried all of New England except Vermont, and won Delaware and some electoral votes in two other states as well. Federalists also gained seats in Congress and captured the New York state legislature. For the Younger Federalists, the future looked promising.

As for the embargo, it eventually collapsed under the pressure of domestic opposition. Jefferson felt the weight of his failure; "never did a prisoner, released

Non-Intercourse Act   from his chains," Jefferson wrote on leaving office, "feel such relief as I in shaking off the shackles of power." In his last days in office he had tried to lighten the burden by working

to replace the embargo with the Non-Intercourse Act of 1809. The act reopened trade with all nations except Britain and France and authorized the president to resume trade with either country if it ceased to violate neutral rights. But the new act solved only the problems that had been created by the embargo; it did not convince Britain and France to change their policies. For one brief moment it appeared to work: President Madison reopened trade with England in June 1809 after the British minister to the United States assured him that Britain would offer the concessions he sought. His Majesty's government in London, however, repudiated the minister's assurances, and Madison renewed nonintercourse.

When the Non-Intercourse Act expired in spring 1810, Congress created a variant, relabeled Macon's Bill Number 2. The bill reopened trade with both Great Britain and France, but provided that if either nation ceased to violate American rights, the president could shut down American commerce with the other. Madison, eager to use the bill rather than go to war, was tricked at his own game. When Napoleon declared that French edicts against United States shipping would be lifted, Madison declared nonintercourse against Great Britain in March 1811. But Napoleon did not keep his word. The French continued to seize American ships, and nonintercourse failed a second time.

Britain, not France, was the main target of American hostility, since the Royal Navy controlled the Atlantic. New York harbor was virtually blockaded by the British, so reopening trade with any nation had little practical effect. Angry American leaders tended to blame even Indian resistance in the West on British agitation, ignoring the Indians' legitimate protests against white encroachment and treaty violations. Frustrated and having exhausted all efforts to alter British policy, the United States in 1811 and 1812 drifted into war with Great Britain.

Meanwhile, unknown to the president and Congress, Great Britain was changing its policy. The Anglo-French conflict had ended much of British commerce with the European continent, and exports to the United States had fallen 80 percent. Depression had hit the British Isles. On June 16, 1812, Britain opened the seas to American shipping. But two days later, before word had crossed the Atlantic, Congress declared war.

The War of 1812 was the logical outcome of United States policy after the renewal of war in Europe in 1803. The grievances enumerated in President Madison's message to Congress on June 1, 1812, were old ones: impressment, interference with neutral commerce, and the British alliances with western Indians. Unmentioned was the resolve to defend American independence and honor—and the thirst of expansionists for British Canada. Yet Congress and the country were divided. Much of the sentiment for war came from the War Hawks, land-hungry southerners and westerners led by Henry Clay of Kentucky and John C. Calhoun of South Carolina. They were concerned equally with national honor and expansion. Most representatives from the coastal states opposed war, since armed conflict with the great naval power threatened to close down all Amer-

ican shipping. The vote for war—79 to 49 in the House, 19 to 13 in the Senate—reflected these sharp regional differences. The split would also be reflected in the way Americans fought the war.

THE WAR OF 1812

War was a foolish adventure for the United States in 1812; despite six months of preparation, American forces remained ill equipped. Because the army had neither an able staff nor an adequate force of enlisted men, the burden of fighting fell on the state militias—and not all the states cooperated. The navy did have a corps of well-trained, experienced officers who had proven their mettle in protecting American merchantmen from Mediterranean pirates. But next to the Royal Navy, the ruler of the seas, the U.S. Navy was minuscule. Jefferson's warning that "our constitution is a peace establishment—it is not calculated for war" proved a wise one. Fortunately for the United States, the war consisted mostly of scuffles and skirmishes; full-scale battles were rare.

For the United States, the only readily available battlefront on which to confront Great Britain was Canada. The mighty Royal Navy was useless on the

Invasion of Canada

waters separating the United States and Canada, since no river afforded it access from the sea. Invasion of Canada, thousands of miles from British supply sources, therefore might give the United States an edge. And England, preoccupied with fighting Napoleon on the European continent, was unlikely to reduce its continental forces to defend Canada.

Begun with high hopes, the invasion of Canada ended as a disaster. The American strategy was to concentrate on the West, splitting Canadian forces and isolating the Shawnee, Potawatomi, and other tribes who supported the British. General William Hull, governor of Michigan Territory, marched his troops into Lower Canada, near Detroit. More experienced as a politician than a soldier, Hull surrounded himself with newly minted colonels equally politically

Major Campaigns of the War of 1812

astute and militarily ignorant. The British anticipated the invasion, mobilized their Indian allies, moved troops into the area, and demanded Hull's surrender. When a pro-British, mostly Potawatomi, contingent captured Fort Dearborn, near Detroit, Hull capitulated (see map). Farther to the west, other American forts surrendered. By the winter of 1812 and 1813, the British controlled about half the Old Northwest (Ohio, Indiana, Illinois, Michigan, and Wisconsin).

The United States had no greater success on the Niagara front, where New York borders Canada. At the Battle of Queenstown, north of Niagara, the United States regular army met defeat because the New York state militia refused to leave the state. This scene was repeated near Lake Champlain, where American plans to attack Montreal were foiled when the militia declined to cross the border.

The navy provided the only bright note in the

first year of the war: the U.S.S. *Constitution*, the U.S.S. *Wasp*, and the U.S.S. *United States* all bested British warships on the Atlantic. But their victories gave the United States only a brief advantage. In defeat the British lost just 1 percent of their strength; in victory the Americans lost 20 percent. The British admiralty simply shifted its fleet away from the American ships, and by 1813 the Royal Navy again commanded the seas.

In 1813 the two sides also vied for control of the Great Lakes, the key to the war in the Northwest.

Great Lakes Campaign
The contest was largely a shipbuilding race. Under Master Commandant Oliver Hazard Perry and shipbuilder Noah Brown, the United States outbuilt the British on Lake Erie and defeated them at the bloody Battle of Put-in-Bay on September 10. The ships fought fiercely and at close range; of 103 men on duty on the U.S.S. *Lawrence*, 21 were killed and 63 wounded. With this costly victory, the Americans gained control of Lake Erie.

General William Henry Harrison then began the march that proved to be the United States's most successful moment in the war. Harrison's 4,500-man force, mostly Kentucky volunteers, crossed Lake Erie and pursued the British, Shawnee, and Chippewa forces into Canada, defeating them at the Battle of the Thames on October 5. The Shawnee and Chippewa warriors continued to fight after the British had surrendered in the battle; defeat came when the great Shawnee chief Tecumseh died, ending the Indian confederacy he had formed to resist American expansion (see pages 285–286). Harrison's campaign gave the United States virtual control of the Old Northwest.

The American success on Lake Erie could not be repeated on Lake Ontario. After the Battle of the Thames, both sides seemed to favor petty victories over strategic goals in the Northwest. The Americans raided York (now Toronto), the Canadian capital, and looted and burned the Parliament before withdrawing, too few in number to hold the city.

Outside the Old Northwest the British set Americans back. In December 1812 the Royal Navy blockaded the Chesapeake and Delaware bays. By May 1813 the blockade had closed nearly

British Naval Blockade
all southern and Gulf of Mexico ports, and by November it had reached north to Long Island Sound. By 1814 all New England ports were closed. American trade had declined nearly 90 percent since 1811, and the decline in revenues from customs duties threatened to bankrupt the federal government.

Following their defeat of Napoleon in April 1814, the British stepped up the land campaign against the United States, concentrating their efforts in the Chesapeake. In retaliation for the burning of York—and to divert American troops from Lake Champlain, where the British planned a new offensive—royal troops occupied Washington and set it to the torch, leaving the Executive Mansion scarred by fire. The attack on the capital was, however, only a raid. The major battle occurred at Baltimore, where the Americans held firm. Although the British inflicted heavy damages both materially and psychologically, they achieved no more than a stalemate. The British offensive at Lake Champlain proved equally unsuccessful. An American fleet forced a British flotilla to turn back at Plattsburgh on Lake Champlain, and the offensive was discontinued.

The last campaign of the war was waged in the South, along the Gulf of Mexico. It began when Tennessee militia general Andrew Jackson defeated the Creek Indians at the Battle of Horseshoe Bend in March 1814. The battle ended the year-long Creek War, which had begun after a series of skirmishes between Indians and settlers. As a result, the Creek nation ceded two-thirds of its land and withdrew to southern and western Alabama. Jackson became a major general in the regular army and continued south toward the Gulf. To forestall a British invasion at Pensacola Bay, which provided an overland route to New Orleans, Jackson seized Pensacola—in Spanish Florida—on November 7, 1814. After securing Mobile, he marched on to New Orleans and prepared for a British attempt to capture the city.

The Battle of New Orleans was the final military engagement. Early in December the British fleet landed 1,500 men east of New Orleans, hoping to gain control of the Mississippi River.

Battle of New Orleans
They faced an American force of regular army troops, plus a larger contingent of Tennessee and Kentucky frontiersmen and two companies of free black volunteers from New Orleans. For three weeks the

Oliver Hazard Perry's victory at Put-in-Bay (1813), in which the United States gained control of Lake Erie. New York State Historical Association, Cooperstown.

British under Sir Edward Pakenham and the Americans under Jackson played cat-and-mouse, each trying to gain a major strategic position. Finally, on January 8, 1815, the two forces met head on. Jackson and his mostly untrained army held their ground against two frontal assaults and a reinforced British contingent of 6,000. It was a massacre. More than 2,000 British soldiers lay dead or wounded at the day's end; the Americans suffered only 21 casualties. Andrew Jackson emerged a national hero. Ironically, the Battle of

New Orleans was fought two weeks after the end of the war; unknown to Jackson, a treaty had been signed in Ghent, Belgium, on December 24, 1814.

The United States government had gone to war only reluctantly and during the conflict had continued to probe for a diplomatic end to hostilities. In 1813, for instance, President Madison had eagerly accepted a Russian offer to mediate, but Great Britain had refused it. Three months later, British Foreign Minister Lord Castlereagh suggested opening peace talks. It took over ten months to arrange meetings, but in August 1814 a team of American negotiators, including John Quincy Adams and Henry Clay, began talks with the British in Ghent.

The Ghent treaty made no mention of the issues that had led to war. The United States received no satisfaction on impressment, blockades, or other maritime rights for neutrals. Likewise, British demands for an Indian buffer state in the Northwest and territorial cessions from Maine to Minnesota went unmet. Essentially, the Treaty of Ghent restored the prewar status quo. It provided for an end to hostilities, release of prisoners, restoration of conquered territory, and arbitration of boundary disputes. Other questions—notably compensation for losses and fishing rights—would be negotiated by joint commissions.

Treaty of Ghent

Why did the negotiators settle for so little? Events in Europe had made peace and the status quo acceptable at the end of 1814, as they had not been in 1812. Napoleon's fall from power allowed the United States to abandon its demands, since peace in Europe made impressment and interference with American commerce moot questions. Similarly, war-weary Britain, its treasury nearly depleted, gave up pressing for a military victory.

The War of 1812 reaffirmed the independence of the young American republic. Although conflict with Great Britain continued, it never again led to war. The experience strengthened America's resolve to steer clear of European politics, for it had been the British-French conflict that had drawn the United States into war. For the rest of the century the nation would shun involvement in European political issues and wars.

Effects of War of 1812

The war had disastrous results for most Indian tribes. With the death of Tecumseh, they lost their most powerful political and military leader; with the withdrawal of the British, they lost their strongest ally. Although in the peace treaty the United States agreed to return Indian lands seized after 1811, the collapse of Indian leadership and British withdrawal made this provision moot. The Shawnee, Potawatomi, Chippewa, and other midwestern tribes had lost most of the resources with which they could have resisted American expansion (see pages 284–290).

Domestically, the war exposed weaknesses in defense and transportation, which were vital for westward expansion. American generals had found American roads inadequate to move an army and its supplies among widely scattered fronts. In the Northwest, General Harrison's troops had depended on homemade cartridges and gifts of clothing from Ohio residents, and in Maine troops had melted down spoons to make bullets. Clearly, improved transportation and a well-equipped army were major priorities. In 1815 President Madison responded by centralizing control of the military, and Congress voted a standing army of 10,000 men, one-third of the army's wartime strength but three times the size it was during Jefferson's administration.

Possibly most important of all, the war stimulated economic change. The embargo, the Non-Importation and Non-Intercourse Acts, and the war itself had spurred the production of manufactured goods—cloth and metal—to replace banned imports. And in the absence of commercial opportunities abroad, New England capitalists had begun to invest in manufactures. The effects of these changes were to be far-reaching (see Chapter 9).

And, finally, the war sealed the fate of the Federalist party. Realizing that their chances of winning a presidential election in wartime were slight, the Federalists had joined dissatisfied Republicans in supporting De Witt Clinton of New York in 1812. This was the high point of Federalist organization at the state level, and the Younger Federalists campaigned hard. Clinton nevertheless lost to President Madison by 128 to 89 electoral votes; areas that favored the war (the South and West) voted solidly Republican. The Federalists did, however, gain some congressional seats, and they carried many local elections.

But once again extremism undermined the Federalists. During the war Older Federalists had revived talk of secession, and from December 15, 1814, to January 5, 1815, Federalist delegates from New England met in Hartford, Connecticut. With the war in a stalemate and trade in ruins, they plotted to revise the national compact or pull out of the republic. Moderates prevented a resolution of secession, but convention members condemned the war and the embargo, and endorsed radical changes

Hartford Convention

in the Constitution. In particular, they wanted constitutional amendments restricting the presidency to one term and requiring a two-thirds congressional vote to admit new states. They also hoped to abolish the three-fifths compromise, whereby slaves were counted in the apportionment of congressional representatives, and to forbid naturalized citizens from holding office. These proposals were aimed at the growing West and South—the heart of Republican electoral strength—and at Irish immigrants.

If nothing else, the timing of the Hartford Convention proved fatal. The victory at New Orleans and news of the peace treaty made the Hartford Convention, with its talk of secession and proposed constitutional amendments, look ridiculous, if not treasonous. Rather than harassing a beleaguered wartime administration, the Federalists now retreated before a rising tide of nationalism. Though it remained strong in a handful of states until the 1820s, the Federalist party began to dissolve. The war, at first a source of revival as opponents of war flocked to the Federalist banner, helped kill the party.

POSTWAR NATIONALISM AND DIPLOMACY

With peace came a new sense of American nationalism. Self-confidently, the nation asserted itself at home and abroad as Republicans aped Federalists in encouraging economic development and commerce. In his last message to Congress in December 1815, President Madison embraced Federalist doctrine by recommending military expansion and a program to stimulate economic growth. Wartime experiences had, he said, demonstrated the need for a national bank (the first bank had expired) and for better transportation. To raise government revenues and perpetuate the wartime growth in manufacturing, Madison called for a protective tariff—a tax on imported goods. Yet in straying from Jeffersonian Republicanism, Madison did so within limits. Only a constitutional amendment, he argued, could give the federal government authority to build roads and canals that were less than national in scope.

The congressional leadership pushed Madison's nationalist program energetically. Congressman John C. Calhoun and Speaker of the House Henry Clay,

American System

who named the program the American System, believed it would unify the country. They looked to the tariff on imported goods to stimulate industry. New mills would purchase raw materials; new millworkers would buy food from the agricultural South and West. New roads would make possible the flow of produce and goods, and tariff revenues would provide the money to build them. Finally, a national bank would facilitate all these transactions.

Indeed, Hamilton's original plan for a Bank of the United States became fundamental to the new Republican policy. Fearing the concentration of economic power in a central bank, the Republicans had allowed the charter of the first Bank of the United States to expire in 1811. State banks, however, proved inadequate to the nation's needs. Their resources had been insufficient to assist the government in financing the War of 1812. Moreover, people distrusted currency issued by banks in distant localities. Because many banks issued notes without gold to back them up, and counterfeit notes were common, merchants hesitated to accept strange currency. Republicans therefore came to favor a national bank. In 1816 Congress chartered the Second Bank of the United States for twenty years, with its headquarters, like those of the first Bank of the United States, in Philadelphia. The government provided $7 million of the $35 million capital and appointed one-fifth of the directors, and the bank opened its doors on January 1, 1817.

Congress did not share Madison's reservations about the constitutionality of using federal funds to build local roads. "Let us, then, bind the republic together," Calhoun declared, "with a perfect system of roads and canals." But Madison vetoed Calhoun's internal improvements bill, which provided for the construction of roads of mostly local benefit, adamantly insisting that it was unconstitutional. Internal improvements were the province of the states and of private enterprise. (Madison did, however, approve funds for the continuation of the National Road to Ohio, on the grounds that it was a military necessity.)

This watercolor by George Tattersall shows the primitive state of American roads in the early nineteenth century. Museum of Fine Arts, Boston, M. and M. Karolik Collection.

Protective tariffs completed Madison's nationalist program. Though the embargo and the war had stimulated domestic industry, especially cloth and iron manufacturing, resumption of trade after the war brought competition from abroad. Americans charged that British firms were dumping their goods on the American market at below cost to stifle American manufacturing. To aid the new industries, Madison recommended and Congress passed the Tariff of 1816, the first protective tariff in American history. The act levied taxes on imported woolens and cottons, especially inexpensive ones, and on iron, leather, hats, paper, and sugar. In effect it raised the cost of these imported goods. Some New England representatives viewed the tariff as interference in free trade, and southern representatives (except Calhoun and a few others) opposed it because it raised the cost of imported goods to southern farmers. But the western and Middle Atlantic states backed it, and the tariff passed.

James Monroe, Madison's successor as president, retained Madison's domestic program, supporting the bank and tariffs and vetoing internal improvements on constitutional grounds. Monroe was the third member of the Virginia dynasty that held the presidency from 1801 through 1825. A former United States senator, twice governor of Virginia and an experienced diplomat, he served under Madison as secretary of state and of war. As secretary of state he received the nomination of the Republican congressional caucus in 1816. Later that year he easily defeated Rufus King, the last Federalist nominee, sweeping all the states except the Federalist strongholds of Massachusetts, Connecticut, and Delaware. Monroe optimistically declared that "discord does not belong to our system." The American people were, he said, "one great family with a common interest." A Boston newspaper dubbed the one-party period the "Era of Good Feelings." And for Monroe's first term that seemed true.

Under Chief Justice John Marshall, the Supreme Court during this period also became the bulwark of a nationalist point of view. In *McCulloch v. Maryland* (1819), the Court struck down a

McCulloch v. Maryland

Maryland law taxing the federally chartered Second Bank of the United States. Maryland had adopted the tax in an effort to destroy the bank's Baltimore branch. The issue was thus one of state versus federal power. Speaking for a unanimous Court, Marshall asserted the supremacy of the federal government over the states. "The Constitution and the laws thereof are supreme," he declared; "they control the constitution and laws of the respective states and cannot be controlled by them."

Having established federal supremacy, the Court in *McCulloch v. Maryland* went on to consider whether Congress could issue a bank charter. No such power was specified in the Constitution. But Marshall noted that Congress had the authority to pass "all laws which shall be necessary and proper for carrying into execution" the enumerated powers of the government (Article I, Section 8). Therefore Congress could legally exercise "those great powers on which the welfare of the nation essentially depends." If the ends were legitimate and the means were not prohibited, Marshall ruled, a law was constitutional. The Constitution was, in Marshall's words, "intended to endure for ages to come, and consequently, to be adapted to the various causes of human affairs." The bank charter was declared legal.

In *McCulloch v. Maryland* Marshall combined Federalist nationalism with Federalist economic views. By asserting federal supremacy he was protecting the commercial and industrial interests that favored a national bank. This was Federalism in the tradition of Alexander Hamilton. The decision was only one in a series. In *Fletcher v. Peck* (1810) the Court voided a Georgia law that violated individuals' right of contract. Similarly, in the famous *Dartmouth College v. Woodward* (1819), the Court nullified a New Hampshire act altering the charter of Dartmouth College, which Marshall ruled constituted a contract. In protecting such contracts, Marshall thwarted state interference in commerce and business.

John Quincy Adams, Monroe's secretary of state, matched the self-confident Marshall Court in nationalism and assertiveness. From 1817 to 1825 he

John Quincy Adams as Secretary of State

managed the nation's foreign policy brilliantly. He was the son of John and Abigail Adams, an experienced diplomat who had served abroad and negotiated the Treaty of Ghent. Adams stubbornly pushed for expansion, fishing rights for Americans in Atlantic waters, political distance from the Old World, and peace. An ardent expansionist, he nonetheless placed limits on expansion: it must come through negotiations, not war, and newly acquired territories must not permit slavery. In appearance a small, austere man, once described by a British official as a "bulldog among spaniels," Adams was a superb diplomat who knew six languages.

Despite being an Anglophobe, Adams worked to strengthen the peace with Great Britain. In April 1817 the two nations agreed in the Rush-Bagot Treaty to limit their Great Lakes naval forces to one ship each on Lakes Ontario and Champlain and two vessels each on the other lakes. This first disarmament treaty of modern times led to the demilitarization of the United States–Canadian border.

Adams then pushed for the Convention of 1818 which fixed the United States–Canadian border from the Lake of the Woods in Minnesota west to the Rockies along the 49th parallel. When agreement could not be reached on the territory west of the mountains, Britain and the United States settled on joint occupation of Oregon for ten years, which was renewed for another ten years in 1827. Adams wanted to fix the border along the 49th parallel right through to the Pacific Ocean, which would gain the important inland waterways of Juan de Fuca Strait and Puget Sound for the United States. He hoped for a better negotiating position when the treaty lapsed.

Adams's next move was to settle long-term disputes with Spain. Although the 1803 Louisiana Treaty had omitted reference to Spanish-ruled West Florida, the United States claimed the territory as far as the Perdido River (the present-day Florida-Alabama border), but only occupied a small finger of that area. During the

War of 1812 the United States seized Mobile and the remainder of West Florida. Afterward it took advantage of Spain's preoccupation with domestic and colonial troubles to negotiate for the purchase of East Florida. Talks took place in 1818, while General Andrew Jackson's troops occupied much of Florida on the pretext of suppressing Seminole raids against American settlements across the border. Adams was furious with Jackson, but defended his brazen act. The following year, on behalf of Spain, Don Luís de Onís, Spanish minister to the United States, agreed to cede Florida to the United States without payment. In this Transcontinental, or Adams-Onís Treaty, the United States also defined the southern boundary of the Louisiana Purchase. The border zigzagged across the West from Texas to the Pacific Ocean (see map, page 232). In return, the United States government assumed $5 million worth of claims by American citizens against Spain and gave up its dubious claim to Texas. Expansion had thus been achieved at little cost and without war, and American territorial claims now stretched from the Atlantic to the Pacific.

Adams-Onís Treaty

While the Rush-Bagot Treaty, the Convention of 1818, and the Adams-Onís Treaty temporarily resolved conflict between the United States and European nations, events to the south still threatened United States interests. John Quincy Adams's desire to insulate the United States and the Western Hemisphere from European conflict led to his greatest achievement: the Monroe Doctrine.

Specifically, the thorny issue of the recognition of new governments in Latin America had to be confronted. The United Provinces of the Río de la Plata (present-day northern Argentina, Paraguay, and Uruguay), Chile, Peru, Columbia, and Mexico had all broken free from Spain between 1808 and 1822. Many Americans wanted to recognize the independence of these former colonies because they seemed to be following the United States's revolutionary tradition. But Monroe and Adams moved cautiously. They sought to avoid conflict with Spain and its allies and to assure themselves of the stability of the revolutionary regimes. But in 1822, shortly after the Adams-Onís Treaty with Spain was safely signed and ratified, the United States became the first nation outside Latin America to recognize the new states.

Soon events in Europe again threatened the stability of the New World. Spain suffered a domestic revolt, and France occupied Spain in an attempt to bolster the weak monarchy against the rebels. The United States feared that France would seek to restore the new Latin American states to Spanish rule. Similarly distrustful of France, Great Britain proposed a joint United States–British declaration against European intervention in the hemisphere and a joint disavowal of British and American territorial ambitions in the region. But Adams rejected the British overture; he insisted that the United States act independently in accordance with the principle of avoiding foreign entanglements.

Determined to thwart joint action with Great Britain, the unbending Adams tenaciously outargued other cabinet members. Those who favored joint action believed that the United States needed British naval power to prevent French or Russian intervention. They were supported by former president Jefferson, then in retirement at Monticello. Adams, however, won. "It would be more candid, as well as more dignified," he argued, "to avow our principles explicitly to Russia and France, than to come in as a cockboat in the wake of the British man-of-war." Moreover, he rejected the British proposal to abdicate territorial ambitions as a deliberate attempt at preventing further American expansion.

President Monroe presented the American position—the Monroe Doctrine—in his last message to Congress on December 2, 1823. He called for, first, *noncolonization* of the Western Hemisphere by European nations, a principle that expressed American anxiety not only about Latin America but also about Russian expansion on the West Coast. Second, he demanded *nonintervention* by Europe in the affairs of independent New World nations. Finally, Monroe pledged *noninterference* by the United States in European affairs, including those of Europe's existing New World colonies.

Monroe Doctrine

The Monroe Doctrine proved popular at home as an anti-British, anti-European assertion of American nationalism, and it eventually became the foundation of American policy in the Western Hemisphere. Monroe's words, however, carried no force. Indeed, the policy could not have succeeded without the support of the British, who were already committed

John Quincy Adams (1767–1848), secretary of state from 1817 to 1825 and architect of the Monroe Doctrine, in an early daguerreotype taken by Southworth and Hawes shortly before his death. This famous photograph suggests Adams's bulldog tenacity. The Metropolitan Museum of Art, Gift of I. N. Phelps Stokes, Edward S. Hawes, Alice Mary Hawes, Marion Augusta Hawes, 1937.

to keeping other European nations out of the New World. Europeans ignored the doctrine; it was the Royal Navy they respected, not American policy.

THE PANIC OF 1819 AND RENEWED SECTIONALISM

Monroe's domestic achievements could not match the diplomatic successes that John Quincy Adams brought to his administration. By 1819 postwar nationalism and confidence had eroded,

and financial panic darkened the land. (Neither panic nor the resurgence of sectionalism hurt Monroe politically; without a rival political party to rally opposition, he won a second term in 1820 unopposed.)

But hard times spread. The postwar expansion had been built on loose money and widespread speculation. State banks extended credit and printed notes too freely, fueling a speculative western land boom. When it slowed, the manufacturing depression that had begun in 1818 deepened, and prices spiraled downward. The Second Bank of the United States, in order to protect its assets, reduced loans, thus accelerating the contraction in the economy. Distressed urban workers lobbied for relief and began to take a more active role in politics. Farmers clamored for lower tariffs. Hurt by a sharp decline in the price of cotton, southern planters railed at the protective Tariff of 1816, which had raised prices at the same time their incomes were falling sharply. The Virginia Agricultural Society of Fredericksburg, for example, argued that the tariff violated the very principles on which the nation had been founded. In a protest to Congress in January 1820, the society called the tariff an unequal tax that awarded exclusive privileges to "oppressive monopolies, which are ultimately to grind both us and our children after us 'into dust and ashes.' " Manufacturers, on the other hand, demanded greater tariff protection—and eventually got it in the Tariff of 1824.

Economic Depression

Western farmers suffered too. Those who had purchased public land on credit could not repay their loans. To avoid mass bankruptcy, Congress delayed payment of the money, and western state legislatures passed "stay laws" restricting mortgage foreclosures. Many westerners blamed the panic on the Second Bank of the United States for tightening the money supply. Many state banks, in debt to the national bank, folded, and westerners bitterly accused the bank of saving itself while the nation went to ruin. Although the economy recovered in the mid-1820s, the seeds of the Jacksonian movement (see pages 335–339) had been sown.

Even more divisive was the question of slavery. Ever since the drafting of the Constitution, political leaders had largely avoided the issue. The one exception was the 1807 act closing the slave trade after January 1, 1808, which passed without much op-

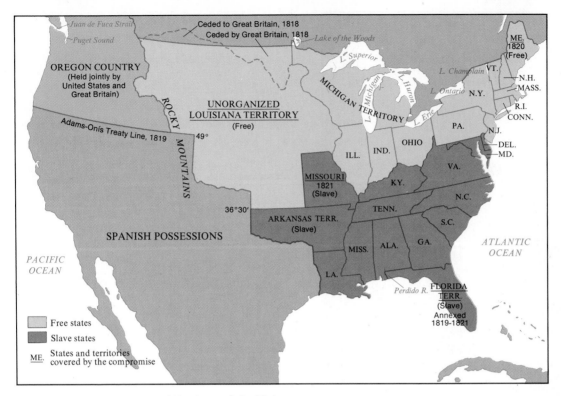

The Missouri Compromise and the State of the Union, 1820

position. It had been taken for granted that once the Constitutional ban (Article I, Section 9) on

Slavery Question

closing the slave trade expired in 1808, Congress would act. In February 1819, however, slavery finally crept onto the political agenda when Missouri residents petitioned Congress for admission to the Union as a slave state. For the next two-and-one-half years the issue dominated all congressional action. "This momentous question," Thomas Jefferson wrote, fearful for the life of the Union, "like a fire bell in the night, awakened and filled me with terror."

The debate transcended slavery in Missouri. At stake was the undoing of the compromises that had kept the issue quarantined since the Constitutional Convention. Five new states had joined the Union since 1812—Louisiana (1812), Indiana (1816), Mississippi (1817), Illinois (1818), and Alabama (1819)— and of these, Louisiana, Mississippi, and Alabama were slave states. Missouri was on the same latitude as free Illinois, Indiana, and Ohio (a state since

1803), and its admission as a slave state would thus thrust slavery further northward. It would also tilt the political balance toward the states committed to slavery. In 1819 the Union consisted of an uneasy balance of eleven slave and eleven free states. If Missouri entered as a slave state, the slave states would have a two-vote edge in the Senate.

But what made the issue so divisive was not the politics of admission to statehood, but white people's emotional attitudes toward slavery. The settlers of Missouri were mostly Kentuckians and Tennesseeans who had grown up with slavery. But in the North, slavery was slowly dying out, and many northerners had come to the conclusion that it was evil. During the Second Great Awakening, there arose a groundswell for reform, including abolition, especially among women (see Chapter 12). Thus when Representative James Tallmadge, Jr., of New York introduced an amendment providing for gradual emancipation in Missouri, it led to passionate and sometimes violent debate on moral grounds. The House, which had a northern majority, passed the Tallmadge amendment, but the Senate rejected it. The two sides were deadlocked.

A compromise emerged in 1820 under pressure from House Speaker Henry Clay: the admission of free Maine, carved out of Massachusetts, was linked with that of slave Missouri. In the **Missouri Compromise** rest of the Louisiana Territory north of 36°30′ (Missouri's southern boundary), slavery was prohibited forever (see map). The compromise carried, but the agreement almost came apart in November when Missouri submitted a constitution that barred free blacks from settling in the state. Opponents contended that the proposed state constitution violated the federal Constitution's provision that "the citizens of each State shall be entitled to all privileges and immunities of citizens in the several States." Advocates argued that restrictions on free blacks were common in state law both North and South. In 1821 Clay produced a second compromise: Missouri guaranteed that none of its laws would discriminate against citizens of other states. (Once admitted to the Union, however, Missouri twice adopted laws banning free blacks.)

Although political leaders had successfully removed slavery from the congressional agenda, sectional issues undermined Republican unity and ended the reign of the Virginia dynasty. The Republican party would come apart in 1824 as presidential candidates from different sections of the country scrambled for caucus support (see pages 336–337).

Sectionalism and the question of slavery would ultimately threaten the Union itself. Still, the first decades of the nineteenth century were a time of nationalism and growth for the young republic. Political parties channeled and limited partisan divisions, and a tradition of peaceful transition of power through presidential elections was established. A second war with Britain—the War of 1812—had to be fought to reaffirm American independence; thereafter the nation was able to settle many disputes at the bargaining table. The foreign policy problems confronting the infant republic from the turn of the century through the mid-1820s strikingly resemble those faced today by the newly established nations of the Third World. The mother country often treated its former colony as if it had not won its independence. And

COUNTIES	Free white males	Free white females	Free persons of color	Slaves	Persons bound to service for a term of years	Total	Representatives
Boone,	1679	1466	1	576		3392	3
Cooper,	1612	1419	12	440		3483	3
Callaway	712	642		443		1797	1
Cole	582	444		52		1028	1
Chariton,	583	541	7	290	5	1416	1
Cape Girardeau	3526	3200	44	1082		7852	6
Franklin	880	853	9	186		1928	2
Gasconade	650	463	1	60		1174	1
Howard	3219	2690	2	1400	3	7321	5
Jefferson	875	749	4	200	1	1834	2
Lincoln	823	636	2	911	2	1674	1
Lillard	695	515		130		1340	1
Montgomery	923	802		308		2032	2
Madison	858	715	5	344	3	1907	1
New madrid	1155	972	7	310		2444	2
Pike	1286	1014	2	495		2677	2
Perry	740	623	1	929	6	1592	1
Ralls	742	581	1	358	2	1684	1
Ray	912	732	2	141	2	1732	2*
St. Louis	3564	2858	141	1608	24	8190	5
St. Charles	1856	1453	11	733	5	4055	3
St. Genevieve	1317	1081	62	717	4	3181	2
Saline	519	476	2	178	1	1176	1
Washington	1816	1302	2	550		4772	3
Wayne	720	645	1	946	2	1614	1
	32120	26903	321	11254	60	70647	54

*County divided. County of St. Francois 1
55

With the Missouri Compromise of 1820, Missouri and Maine joined the Union as slave and free states respectively. The first census of the new state (1821) enumerated the large slave population and the small number of free blacks whom many Missourians wished to bar from settlement. Library of Congress.

like Third World nations today, the young United States steered clear of alliances with superpowers, preferring neutrality and unilateralism. The War of 1812 and diplomatic assertiveness brought a sense of national security and confidence.

After the war, all branches of the government, responding to the popular mood, pursued a more vigorous national policy. The Supreme Court further advanced national unity by extending federal power over the states and encouraging commerce and economic growth. In spite of Jefferson's vision of an agrarian society of independent farmers and artisans, the country was gradually changing to a market economy in which people produced goods not just for their own use but to sell to others (see Chapter 9).

IMPORTANT EVENTS

1801	John Marshall becomes Chief Justice
	Jefferson inaugurated
1801–05	Tripoli War
1803	*Marbury v. Madison*
	Louisiana Purchase
1804	Jefferson re-elected
1804–06	Lewis and Clark expedition
1807	*Chesapeake* Affair
	Embargo Act
1808	Madison elected president
1812–15	War of 1812
1814	Treaty of Ghent
1814–15	Hartford Convention
1815	Battle of New Orleans
1816	Monroe elected president
	Second Bank of the United States chartered
1817	Rush-Bagot Treaty
1819	*McCulloch v. Maryland*
	Adams-Onís Treaty
1819–23	Financial panic; depression
1820	Missouri Compromise
	Monroe re-elected
1823	Monroe Doctrine

Disruption of trade during the war had promoted the manufacturing of goods in the United States, instead of dependence on imports from Europe. The development of faster transportation further promoted the economy, and old cities expanded in the market-oriented North as new ones sprouted up in the West on trade and transportation routes (see Chapter 10).

But along with the nationalism and growth of the country came the problem of sectionalism. While the manufacturers and commercial interests in the North were becoming increasingly connected with the agricultural producers in the West through transportation and trade, the South was developing its own economy and culture based on cotton crops, export markets, a plantation system, and slavery (see Chapter 11). Politicians kept the question of slavery off the national agenda as long as possible and worked out the Missouri Compromise as a stopgap measure. But new land acquisitions and further westward expansion in the 1840s and 1850s, combined with a rising tide of reform impulse, eventually made the question of slavery unavoidable (see Chapters 12 and 13). Americans would finally settle the issue in the Civil War.

SUGGESTIONS FOR FURTHER READING

General

Henry Adams, *History of the United States of America During the Administration of Thomas Jefferson and of James Madison*, 9 vols. (1889–1891); George Dangerfield, *The Awakening of American Nationalism, 1815–1828* (1965); George Dangerfield, *The Era of Good Feelings* (1952); John Mayfield, *The New Nation, 1800–1845* (1981); Glover Moore, *The Missouri Compromise, 1819–1821* (1953); Murray N. Rothbard, *The Panic of 1819* (1962); Marshall Smelser, *The Democratic Republic, 1801–1815* (1968).

Party Politics

James M. Banner, *To the Hartford Convention: The Federalists and the Origins of Party Politics in the Early Republic, 1789–1815* (1967); James Broussard, *The Southern Federalists 1800–1816* (1978); Noble E. Cunningham, Jr., *The Jeffersonian Republicans in Power: Party Operations, 1801–1809* (1963); David Hackett Fischer, *The Revolution of American Conservatism: The Federalist Party in the Era of Jeffersonian Democracy* (1965); Linda K. Kerber, *Federalists in Dissent* (1970);

Shaw Livermore, *Twilight of Federalism: The Disintegration of the Federalist Party, 1815–1830* (1962); Milton Lomask, *Aaron Burr*, 2 vols. (1979, 1983); Richard P. McCormick, *The Presidential Game. The Origins of American Presidential Politics* (1982); James Sterling Young, *The Washington Community, 1800–1828* (1966).

The Virginia Presidents

Harry Ammon, *James Monroe: The Quest for National Identity* (1971); Irving Brant, *James Madison*, 6 vols. (1941–1961); Irving Brant, *The Fourth President: A Life of James Madison* (1970); Noble E. Cunningham, Jr., *The Process of Government Under Jefferson* (1978); James Ketcham, *James Madison* (1970); Forrest McDonald, *The Presidency of Thomas Jefferson* (1976); Dumas Malone, *Jefferson and His Time*, 6 vols. (1948–1981); Merrill D. Peterson, *The Jefferson Image in the American Mind* (1960); Merrill D. Peterson, *Thomas Jefferson and the New Nation* (1970).

The Supreme Court and the Law

Leonard Baker, *John Marshall: A Life in Law* (1974); Albert Beveridge, *The Life of John Marshall*, 4 vols. (1916–1919); Richard E. Ellis, *The Jeffersonian Crisis: Courts and Politics in the Young Republic* (1971); Charles G. Haines, *The Role of the Supreme Court in American Government and Politics, 1789–1835* (1944); Morton J. Horowitz, *The Transformation of American Law, 1780–1860* (1977); R. Kent Newmyer,

The Supreme Court Under Marshall and Taney (1968); Francis N. Stites, *John Marshall: Defender of the Constitution* (1981).

Expansion and the War of 1812

Roger H. Brown, *The Republic in Peril: 1812* (1964); A. L. Burt, *The United States, Great Britain, and British North America* (1940); Harry L. Coles, *The War of 1812* (1965); Alexander De Conde, *This Affair of Louisiana* (1976); Clifford L. Egan, *Neither Peace nor War: Franco-American Relations, 1803–1812* (1983); Reginald Horsman, *The War of 1812* (1969); Donald Jackson, ed., *Letters of the Lewis and Clark Expedition with Related Documents, 1783–1854* (1962); Bradford Perkins, *Prologue to War: England and the United States, 1805–1812* (1961); Julius W. Pratt, *Expansionists of 1812* (1925); Burton Spivak, *Jefferson's English Crisis: Commerce, Embargo, and the Republican Revolution* (1974); J. C. A. Stagg, *Mr. Madison's War. Politics, Diplomacy, and Warfare in the Early Republic, 1783–1830* (1983).

The Monroe Doctrine

Samuel F. Bemis, *John Quincy Adams and the Foundations of American Foreign Policy* (1949); Walter LaFeber, ed., *John Quincy Adams and American Continental Empire* (1965): Ernest R. May, *The Making of the Monroe Doctrine* (1976); Dexter Perkins, *The Monroe Doctrine 1823–1826* (1927); Dexter Perkins, *Hands Off: A History of the Monroe Doctrine* (1941).

A MARKET AND
INDUSTRIAL ECONOMY
1800–1860

CHAPTER 9

John Jervis suffered from canal fever and railroad fever nearly all his life. He first contracted the obsession in 1817, when at age twenty-two he left his father's upstate New York farm to clear a cedar swamp for the Erie Canal. Like the other laborers, as well as the men directing the project, Jervis had no experience in canal construction. Indeed, he had never built anything according to a plan or diagram.

Together the directors and workers learned enough on the job to construct 363 well-engineered miles of canal. Jervis's education began his first day. Though he was an expert axeman, he had never downed a line of trees along an exact path. With ingenuity, he learned to hew with precision. Jervis learned new skills each year, advancing from axeman to surveyor to engineer to superintendent of a division. He was the most famous engineer to have received his training from the Erie Canal "School of Engineering."

When the Erie Canal was completed in 1825, Jervis signed on as second-in-command of the Delaware and Hudson Canal project. To reduce costs, he substituted a railroad line for the last seventeen miles of the canal. Since there was not a single locomotive in the United States in 1828, Jervis had one sent from England. The engine that was delivered, however, was heavier than the one he had ordered, and on both tests it crushed the hemlock rails.

Undaunted, the self-trained engineer left the Delaware canal company to supervise construction of another early rail experiment, the Mohawk and Hudson Railroad from Albany to Schenectady. In building the railroad Jervis redesigned the locomotive's wheel assembly, and his design became standard throughout America.

Jervis spent the next two decades building the 98-mile Chenango Canal and the fresh-water supply for New York City—consisting of the Croton Reservoir, a 33-mile aqueduct, and pumping system. Later he built other railroads, including the Michigan Southern, the Rock Island, and the Nickel Plate. In 1864, at age sixty-nine, Jervis returned home to Rome, New York, and organized an iron mill. He had spent his life constructing the mechanisms—canals and railroads—that would change America.

John Jervis's life bridged the old and the new. His roots lay in the rural farm country that was typical of the United States at the beginning of the nineteenth century. Born at Huntington, Long Island, in 1795, he was taken to western New York in 1798 by his carpenter father, who moved to the frontier to farm. He learned to read and write during occasional attendance at common school, and to farm and handle an axe from his father. But in 1817 he left behind much of that tradition and became involved in undertakings that would lead to a new, far different nation. He had to acquire skills not used on the farm: the ability to follow and create construction plans, to calculate weight stresses, and to work precisely in tandem with others. A religious man, he extolled the pioneer virtues of hard work and independence, and he prided himself on his rise from farm boy to world-class engineer. Yet, by the time of his death in 1885 engineering leadership had passed to the university-trained.

The canals and railroads that John Jervis and others built were the most visible signs of economic development and the best-known links in the growing national economy from 1800 through 1860. The canal boat, the steamboat, the locomotive, and the telegraph all helped to open up the frontier and to encourage greater farm production for markets at home and abroad. They made it possible for New England mill girls to turn slave-produced southern cotton into factory-made cloth that was purchased by women in New York, Cincinnati, San Francisco, and thousands of smaller towns across America. Increasingly, farmers grew more for market while urban producers worked for wages. Thus, if transportation was the most visible change, less tangible but equally significant was the increased specialization in agriculture, manufacturing, and finance that eventually brought about a national, capitalist market economy.

The dramatic transformation of the United States between 1800 and 1860 was manifest nearly everywhere. In 1800 most of the 5.3 million Americans earned a living working the land and serving those who did. Except in Kentucky and Tennessee, settlement had not stretched far to the west. By 1860,

Chapter 9: A Market and Industrial Economy, 1800–1860

31.4 million Americans had spread across the continent; in the Midwest some farms were 1500 miles from the Atlantic; and on the Pacific Slope, settlement boomed. A continental nation had been forged. Though still primarily agricultural, the economy was being transformed by an enormous commercial and industrial expansion.

Promotion of economic growth became the hallmark of government, especially in the nationalist mood after the War of 1812. Government sought to encourage individual freedom and choice by furthering an environment in which farming and industry could flourish. New financial institutions amassed the capital for large-scale enterprises like factories and railroads. Mechanization took root; factories and precision-made machinery began to replace home workshops and handmade goods, while reapers and sowers revolutionized farming.

New problems and tensions accompanied the rewards of economic expansion. Not everyone profited, as John Jervis did, in wealth and opportunity. The journeyman tailor who was replaced by new retailers and cheaper labor had a far different experience from the new merchant princes. New England farm daughters found their world changing no less radically. Moreover the cycles of boom and bust became part of the fabric of ordinary life. Whatever the benefits and drawbacks, however, economic development and change were irreversible.

THE MARKET ECONOMY

Most farmers in the early nineteenth century geared production to family needs. They lived in interdependent communities and kept detailed account books of labor and goods exchanged with neighbors. Farm families tended to produce much of what they needed—foodstuffs, clothing, candles, soap, and the like—but traded agricultural surpluses for or purchased items they could not produce, such as cooking pots, shoes for animals, coffee, tea, and white sugar. On most such farms, men selling cordwood and women selling eggs, butter, cheese, and poultry produced the family's only cash. By the Civil War,

however, the United States had an industrializing economy in which an increasing number of men and women worked in factories or offices for a wage, and in which most citizens—farmers and workers alike—had become dependent on store-bought necessities.

In the market economy crops were grown and goods were produced for sale in the marketplace, at home or abroad. The money received in market transactions, whether from the sale of goods or of a person's labor, purchased items produced by other people—such as the candles and soap no longer made at home. Such a system encouraged specialization. Formerly self-sufficient farmers, for example, began to grow just one or two crops, or to concentrate on raising only cows, pigs, or sheep for market. Farm women gave up spinning and weaving at home and purchased fabric produced by wage-earning farm girls in Massachusetts textile mills.

Definition of a Market Economy

Sustained growth was the result of this economic evolution. Improvements in transportation and technology, the division of labor, and new methods of financing all fueled expansion of the economy—that is, the multiplication of goods and services. In turn, this growth prompted new improvements. The effect was cumulative; by the 1840s the economy was growing more rapidly than in the previous four decades. Per capita income doubled between 1800 and 1860.

The Ohio dairy industry illustrates this process. In the first decades of the century, Ohio farm women made whatever cheese they needed for their own tables. Some made cheese to sell elsewhere, but only because they had a surplus of milk. However, the development of canals and railroads in the 1830s and 1840s changed Ohio farming. Farmers began to specialize, finding it more profitable to invest in better tools and spend all their time on one product. Some chose to grow wheat or tobacco for market, and to purchase whatever dairy products they needed. Others, especially in northeastern Ohio, decided to devote themselves full time to dairy farming. Beginning in 1847, entrepreneurs built cheese factories in rural towns and contracted to buy curd from these local dairy farmers. In 1851 one such factory in Gustavus, Ohio, produced a daily average of 5,000 pounds of cheese from the milk of 2,500 cows. The cheese was shipped by canal and railroad to cities and eastern

Traditionally cheese making was a woman's chore. The work was physically arduous and continuous, requiring daily attention to the curds. Evan Jones, The World of Cheese, *Knopf, 1976.*

ports. In Boston and New York, some merchants turned to handling cheese and other dairy products exclusively, selling to consumers as far away as California, England, and China. By 1860 Ohio dairymen were producing 21.6 million pounds of cheese a year for market—a huge leap in production over the early 1800s.

The changes in Ohio dairy husbandry altered farm life. Traditionally the making of cheese was a family industry in which men fed and tended the cows, men or women milked them, and women made the cheese. As cheese production increased, women's work on family-run dairy farms intensified as they added cheesemaking to their regular tasks. The work was physically arduous and continuous, requiring daily attention both to the new day's curds and to the previous days' cheese, which needed to be pressed and turned. The *Ohio Cultivator* in 1848 noted that "the condition of women in dairies is frequently little better than servitude." In large, commercial dairies, however, where making cheese was a male task, gender roles had shifted under the pressure of market demands.

Though economic change and growth were sustained, their pace was uneven. Prosperity reigned during two long periods, from 1823 to 1835 and from 1843 to 1857. But there were long stretches of economic contraction as well. During the time from

Boom-and-Bust Cycles Jefferson's 1807 embargo through the War of 1812, the interruption in trade contributed to a negative growth rate—that is, fewer goods and services were produced. Contraction and deflation occurred again during the depressions of 1819 through 1823, 1839 through 1843, and 1857. These periods were characterized by the collapse of banks, business bankruptcies, and a decline in wages and prices. Workers faced increasing insecurity as a result of these cycles; on the down side, they suffered not only lower incomes but also unemployment.

Working people, a Baltimore physician noted during the depression of 1819, felt hard times "a thousand fold more than the merchants." Yet even during good times wage earners could not build up sufficient financial reserves to get them through the next depression; often they could not make it through the winter without drawing on charity for food, clothing, and firewood. In the 1820s and 1830s, free laborers in Baltimore found steady work from March through October and unemployment and hunger from November through February.

If good times were hard on workers and their families, depressions devastated them. In 1839 in Baltimore, small manufacturers for the local market closed their doors; tailors, shoemakers, milliners, and shipyard and construction workers lost their jobs. Ninety miles to the north, Philadelphia took on an eerie aura. "The streets seemed deserted," Sidney George Fisher observed in 1842; "the largest [merchant] houses are shut up and to rent, there is no business . . . no money, no confidence." Only auctions boomed, as the sheriff sold off seized property at a quarter of predepression prices. Elsewhere in the city, soup societies fed the hungry. In New York, breadlines and beggars crowded the sidewalks. In smaller cities like Lynn, Massachusetts, the poor who did not leave became scavengers, digging for clams and harvesting dandelions.

In 1857 hard times struck again. The Mercantile Agency recorded 5,123 bankruptcies in 1857—nearly double the number in the previous year. The bankrupt firms had a total debt of $300 million, only half of which would be paid off. Contemporary reports estimated 20,000 to 30,000 unemployed in Philadelphia, and 30,000 to 40,000 in New York City. Female benevolent societies expanded their soup kitchens

Chapter 9: A MARKET AND INDUSTRIAL ECONOMY, 1800–1860

and distributed free firewood to the needy. In Chicago, charities reorganized to meet the needs of the poor; in New York, the city hired the unemployed to fix streets and develop Central Park. And in Fall River, Massachusetts, a citizens' committee disbursed public funds on a weekly basis to nine hundred families. The soup kitchen, the breadline, and public aid had become fixtures in urban America.

What caused the cycles of boom and bust that brought about such suffering? In general, they were a direct result of the new market economy. Prosperity inevitably stimulated greater demand for staples and finished goods. In-

Cause of Boom-and-Bust Cycles

creased demand led in turn to higher prices and still higher production, to speculation in land, and to the flow of foreign currency into the country. Eventually production surpassed demand, leading to lower prices and wages; and speculation outstripped the true value of land and stocks. The inflow of foreign money led first to easy credit and then to collapse when unhappy investors withdrew their funds.

Some economists considered this process beneficial—a self-adjusting cycle in which unprofitable economic ventures were eliminated. In theory, people concentrated on the activities they did best, and the economy as a whole became more efficient. Advocates of the system argued also that it furthered individual freedom, since ideally each seller, whether of goods or labor, was free to determine the conditions of the sale. But in fact the system put workers on a perpetual rollercoaster; they had become dependent on wages—and the availability of jobs—for their very existence.

Many also felt a distinct loss of status. For Joseph T. Buckingham, foreman of the Boston printing shop of West & Richardson, wage labor represented failure. Buckingham had been a master printer, running the shop of Thomas & Andrews on commission and doing some publishing of his own. In 1814 he purchased the shop, but did not get enough work to pay his debts. Without the capital to sustain his losses or to compete with larger shops, Buckingham had to sell his presses at auction. He became a wage earner, albeit a foreman. Though his wages were about the equal of an ordinary printer's income, Buckingham was unhappy. In his own words, he was "nothing more than a journeyman, except in responsibility."

GOVERNMENT PROMOTES ECONOMIC GROWTH

The eighteenth-century political ideas which had captured the imagination of the Revolutionary War generation and found expression in the ideal of republican virtue were paralleled in economic thought by the writings of Adam Smith, a Scottish political economist. Smith's *The Wealth of Nations* first appeared in 1776, the year of the Declaration of Independence; both works emphasized individual liberty, one economic, the other political. Both were reactions against forceful government: Jefferson attacked monarchy and distant government while Smith attacked mercantilism, government regulation of the economy to benefit the state (see page 61). They believed that virtue was lodged in individual freedom and that the entire community would benefit most from individuals pursuing their own self-interest. As president, Jefferson put these political and economic beliefs into action by reducing the role of government.

Jefferson, influenced by the economic and egalitarian ideas of republicanism (see pages 156–157), recognized that government was nonetheless a necessary instrument in promoting individual freedom. Freedom, he believed, thrived where individuals had room for independence, creativity, and choices; individuals fettered by government, monopoly, or economic dependence could not be free. Committed to the idea that a republican democracy would flourish best in a nation of independent farmers and artisans and an atmosphere of widespread political participation, Jefferson worked to realize those ideals. Beginning with the purchase of Louisiana in 1803, Republican party policy, no less than that of the Federalists, turned to using government as an active promoter of the economy. Belief in a limited government was not an end in itself, but only a means to greater individual freedom.

Once Louisiana had been acquired, the federal government played an active role in promoting economic growth and in fulfilling the spirit of manifest destiny by encouraging westward expansion and settlement and by promoting agriculture. The Lewis and

Clark expedition from 1804 to 1806 (see page 215) was the beginning of a continuing federal interest in geographic and geologic surveying and the first step in the opening of western lands to exploitation and settlement.

New steps followed quickly. In 1817 and 1818 Henry Rowe Schoolcraft explored the Missouri and Arkansas region, reporting on its geologic features and mineral resources. In 1819 and 1820 Major Stephen Long explored the Great Plains, mapping the area between the Platte and Canadian rivers. Between 1827 and 1840 the government surveyed about fifty railroad routes. The final door to western settlement was opened in 1843 and 1844 by John C. Frémont's expedition, which followed the Oregon Trail to the Pacific, then traveled south to California and returned east by way of the Great Salt Lake. Frémont, later a California senator and 1856 Republican presidential candidate, gained fame as a soldier-surveyor of the West. His report of his journey dispelled a long-standing myth that the center of the continent was a desert.

To encourage western agriculture, the federal government offered public lands for sale at reasonable prices (see page 263) and evicted Indian tribes from their traditional lands. And because transportation was crucial to development of the frontier, the government financed roads and subsidized railroad construction through land grants. Even the State Department aided agriculture: its consular offices overseas collected horticultural information, seeds, and cuttings and published technical reports in an effort to improve American farming.

The federal government played a key role in technological and industrial growth. Federal arsenals pioneered new manufacturing techniques and helped to develop the machine-tool industry. The United States Military Academy at West Point, founded in 1802, emphasized technical and scientific subjects in its curriculum. And the U.S. Post Office stimulated interregional trade and played a brief but crucial role in the development of the telegraph: the first telegraph line, from Washington to Baltimore, was constructed under a government grant, and during 1845 the Post Office ran it, employing inventor Samuel F. B. Morse as superintendent. Finally, to create an atmosphere conducive to economic growth and individual creativity, the government protected inventions and do-

mestic industries. Patent laws gave inventors a seventeen-year monopoly on their inventions, and tariffs protected American industry from foreign competition.

The federal judiciary validated government promotion of the economy and encouraged business enterprise. In *Gibbons* v. *Ogden* (1824), the Supreme

Legal Foundations of Commerce

Court overturned a New York state law that had given Robert Fulton and Robert Livingston a monopoly on the New York–New Jersey steamboat trade. Ogden, their successor, lost his monopoly when Chief Justice John Marshall ruled that the trade fell under the sway of the commerce clause of the Constitution. Thus Congress, not New York, had the controlling power. Since the federal government issued such licenses on a nonexclusive basis, the decision ended monopolies on waterways throughout the nation. Within a year, forty-three steamboats were plying Ogden's route.

In defining interstate commerce broadly, the Marshall Court expanded federal powers over the economy while limiting the ability of states to control economic activity within their borders. Its action was consistent with its earlier decision in *Dartmouth College* v. *Woodward* (1819), which protected the sanctity of contracts against interference by the states (see page 229). "If business is to prosper," Marshall wrote, "men must have assurance that contracts will be enforced."

Federal and state courts, in conjunction with state legislatures, also encouraged the proliferation of corporations—groups of investors that could hold property and transact business as one person. In 1800 the United States had about 300 incorporated firms; in 1817 about 2,000. By 1830 the New England states alone had issued 1,900 charters, one-third to manufacturing and mining firms. At first each firm needed a special legislative act to incorporate, but after the 1830s applications became so numerous that incorporation was authorized by general state laws. Though legislative action created corporations, the courts played a crucial role in defining their status, extending their powers, and protecting them.

A further encouragement to economic development, corporate development, and free enterprise was the Supreme Court's ruling in *Charles River Bridge* v. *Warren Bridge* (1837) that new enterprises could not be restrained by implied privileges under old charters.

Chapter 9: A MARKET AND INDUSTRIAL ECONOMY, 1800–1860

*The Marshall Court encouraged business competition by
ending the state-licensed monopolies on inland waterways.
Gibbons v. Ogden (1824) opened up the New York–New
Jersey trade to new lines, and within a short time dozens of
steamboats ferried passengers and freight across the Hudson
River.   The New-York Historical Society.*

The case involved issues of great importance: should a new interest be able to compete against existing, older privileges, and should the state protect existing privilege or encourage innovation to benefit all? In 1785 the Massachusetts legislature chartered the Charles River Bridge Company, and in 1791 extended its charter to a seventy-year term. In return for the risk of building the bridge between Charlestown and Boston, the owners received the privilege of collecting tolls. In 1828 the legislature chartered another company to build the Warren Bridge across the Charles, with the right to collect tolls for six years, after which the bridge would be turned over to the state and be toll-free. With the terminus of the new bridge only ninety yards away from its own, the Charles River Bridge Company sued in 1829, claiming that the new bridge breached the earlier charter and contradicted the principles in *Dartmouth College* v. *Woodward*. Justice Roger Taney, speaking for the Court majority, noted that the original charter did not confer the privilege of monopoly and therefore exclusivity could not be implied. Focusing on the question of corporate privilege rather than the right of contracts, Taney ruled that charter grants should be interpreted narrowly and that ambiguities would be decided in favor of the public interest. New enterprises should not be restricted under old charters, and economic growth would best be served by narrowing the application of the *Dartmouth College* decision. Thus, the judiciary supported economic expansion and individual economic opportunity.

State governments far surpassed the federal government in promoting the economy. From 1815 through 1860, for example, 73 percent of the $135 million invested in canals was government money, mostly from the states. In the 1830s the states shifted their investments to rail construction. Even though the federal government played a larger role in building railroads than canals, state and local governments provided more than half of southern rail capital. In the nineteenth century, railroads received 131 million acres in land subsidies, 48 million of which was provided by the states. State governments also invested in corporation and bank stocks, providing those institutions with much-needed capital. Pennsylvania, probably the most active of the states in promoting its economy, invested a total of $100 million in canals, railroads, banks, and manufacturing firms; its appointees sat on more than 150 corporate boards of directors.

State Promotion of the Economy

States actually equaled or surpassed private enterprise in their investments. But they did more than invest in industry. By establishing bounties for agricultural prizes, they stimulated commercial agriculture, especially sheep raising and wool manufacture (see page 258). Through special acts and general incorporation laws, states regulated the nature and activities of both corporations and banks. They also used their licensing capacity to regulate industry; in Georgia, for example, grading and marketing of tobacco was regulated by the state.

From the end of the War of 1812 until 1860 the United States experienced uneven but sustained economic growth largely as a result of these government efforts. Though political controversy raged over questions of state versus federal activity—especially with regard to internal improvements and banking—all parties agreed on the general goal of economic expansion (see Chapters 8 and 12). Indeed, the major restraint on government action during these years was not philosophical but financial: both the government and the public purse were small. As the private sector grew stronger, entrepreneurs looked less to government for financial support and states played less of an investment role. In either case, government provided an atmosphere conducive to business and economic growth.

TRANSPORTATION AND REGIONALIZATION

From 1800 through 1860 the North, South, and West followed distinctly different paths economically. Everywhere agriculture remained the foundation of the American economy. Nevertheless, industry, commerce, and finance came to characterize the North, plantations and subsistence farms the South, and commercialized family farms, agricultural processing, and implement manufacturing the West. Paradoxically, this tendency toward regional specialization made the sections at once more different and more dependent on each other.

The revolution in transportation and communications was probably the single most important cause of these changes. It was the North's heavy investment in canals and railroads that made it the center of American commerce; its growing seaboard cities distributed western produce and New England textiles. New York financial and commercial houses linked the southern cotton-exporting economy to the North and Europe. The South, with most of its capital invested in slave labor, built fewer canals, railroads, and factories and remained largely rural and undeveloped (see Chapter 11).

Before the canal fever of the 1820s and 1830s and the railroad fever of the 1830s and after became epidemic, it was by no means self-evident that New England and the Middle Atlantic states would dominate American economic life. In fact, the natural orientation of the 1800 frontier—Tennessee, Kentucky, and Ohio—was to the South. The southward-flowing Ohio and Mississippi rivers were the lifelines of early western settlement. Flatboats transported western grain and hogs southward for consumption or transfer to oceangoing vessels at New Orleans. Southern products—first tobacco, then lumber and cotton—flowed directly to Europe. Settlement of southern Illinois and Indiana and the appearance of steamboats on western rivers only intensified this pattern.

Change in Trade Routes

But the pattern changed in the 1820s and 1830s. New roads and turnpikes opened up east-west travel. The National Road, a stone-based, gravel-topped highway beginning in Cumberland, Maryland, reached Wheeling (then in Virginia) in 1818 and Columbus, Ohio, in 1833. More important, the Erie Canal, completed in 1825, forged an east-west axis from the Hudson River to Lake Erie, linking the Greak Lakes with New York City and the Atlantic Ocean. The canal carried easterners and then immigrants to settle the Old Northwest and the frontier beyond; in the opposite direction, it bore western grain to the large and growing eastern markets. Railroads and later the telegraph would solidify these east-west links. By contrast, only at one place—Bowling Green, Kentucky—did a northern railroad actually connect with a southern one. Although trade still continued southward along the Ohio and Mississippi rivers, the bulk of western trade flowed eastward by 1850. Thus, by the eve of the Civil War, the northern and Middle Atlantic states were closely tied to the former frontier of the Old Northwest.

Construction of the 363-mile-long Erie Canal was a visionary enterprise. When the state of New York authorized it in 1817, the longest existing American canal was only 28 miles long. Vig-

Canals

orously promoted by Governor De Witt Clinton, the Erie cost $7 million, much of it raised by loans from British investors. The canal shortened the journey between Buffalo and New York City from twenty to six days and reduced freight charges from $100 to $5 a ton. By 1835 traffic was so heavy that the Erie had to be widened from forty to seventy feet and deepened from four to seven feet. The skeptics who had called the canal "Clinton's big ditch" had long since been silenced by the success of the enterprise.

The Erie triggered an explosion of canal building. Other states and cities, sensing the advantage New York had gained, rushed to follow suit. By 1840 canals crisscrossed the Northeast and Midwest, and canal mileage in the United States had reached 3,300—an increase of more than 2,000 miles in a single decade. Unfortunately for investors, none of these canals enjoyed the financial success achieved by the Erie. The high cost of construction and economic contraction after 1837 lowered profitability.

A mid-nineteenth-century poster boasts of the superior services of the New York Central Railroad. American Antiquarian Society.

As a result, investment in canals began to slump in the 1830s. By 1850 more miles were being abandoned than built, and the canal era had ended.

Meanwhile, railroad construction was on the upswing, and visionaries like John Jervis left canals for railroads. The railroad era began in 1830 when Peter Cooper's locomotive *Tom Thumb*

Railroads

first steamed along 13 miles of track constructed by the Baltimore and Ohio Railroad. In 1833 a second railroad ran 136 miles from Charleston to Hamburg, South Carolina. By 1850 the United States had nearly 9,000 miles of railroad; by 1860, roughly 31,000 (see map, page 246). Canal fever stimulated this early railroad construction. Promoters of the Baltimore and Ohio had turned to the railroad in an effort to compete with the canal. Similarly, the line between Boston and Worcester, Massachusetts, was intended as the first link in a line to Albany, at the eastern end of the Erie Canal.

The earliest railroads connected two cities or one city and its surrounding area. Not until the 1850s would railroads offer long-distance service at reasonable rates. And the early lines also had technical problems

Major Railroads, Canals, and Roads in 1860

to contend with. As John Jervis had discovered, locomotives heavy enough to climb steep grades and pull long trains required strong rails and resilient roadbeds. Engineers met those needs by replacing wooden track with iron rails and by supporting the rails with ties embedded in gravel. John Jervis's wheel alignment—called the swivel truck—removed another major obstacle by enabling engines to hold the track on sharp curves. Other problems persisted, though: notably the continued use of hand brakes, which severely restricted speed, and the lack of a standard gauge for track. The Pennsylvania and Ohio railroads, for instance, had no fewer than seven different track widths. Thus a journey from Philadelphia to Charleston, South Carolina, involved eight changes in gauge.

In the 1850s technological improvements, competition, and economic recovery prompted the de-

velopment of regional and later national rail networks. The West too experienced a railroad boom. By 1853 rail lines linked New York to Chicago, and a year later track had reached the Mississippi River. By 1860 rails stretched as far west as St. Joseph, Missouri—the edge of the frontier. In that year the railroad network east of the Mississippi approximated its physical pattern for the next century, but the process of corporate integration had only begun. In 1853 seven short lines combined to form the New York Central system, and the Pennsylvania Railroad was unified from Philadelphia to Pittsburgh. Most lines, however, were still independently run, separated by gauge, scheduling, differences in car design, and a commitment to serve their home towns first and foremost.

Railroads did not completely replace water transportation. Steamboats, introduced in 1807 when

Chapter 9: A MARKET AND INDUSTRIAL ECONOMY, 1800–1860

Steamboats Robert Fulton's *Clermont* paddled up the Hudson from New York City, still plied the rivers. They had proven their value on western rivers in 1815 when the *Enterprise* first carried cargo upstream on the Mississippi and Ohio rivers. Until the 1850s, when western rail development blossomed, steamboats outdid railroads in carrying freight. Great Lakes steamers managed to hold their own even into the 1850s, for the sealike lakes permitted the construction of giant ships and the widespread adoption of propellers in place of paddle wheels. These leviathans were especially well suited to carrying heavy bulk cargoes like lumber, grain, and ore.

Gradually steamboats replaced sailing vessels on the high seas. In days gone by, sailing ships—whalers, sleek clippers, and square-rigged packets—had been the pride of American commerce. But sailing ships were dependent on prevailing winds and weather, and thus could not schedule regular crossings. In 1818 steam-powered packets made four round trips a year between New York and Liverpool, sailing on schedule rather than waiting for a full cargo as had ships before then. The breakthrough came in 1848, though, when Samuel Cunard introduced regularly scheduled steamships to the Atlantic run between Liverpool and New York, reducing travel time from twenty-five days eastbound and forty-nine days westbound to ten to fourteen days each way. Sailing ships quickly lost first-class passengers and light cargo to these swift steamships. For the next decade they continued to carry immigrants and bulk cargo, but by 1860 only the freight trade remained to them.

By far the fastest spreading technological advance of the era was the magnetic telegraph. Samuel F. B. Morse's invention freed messages from the restraint of traveling no faster than the mes-

Telegraph senger; instantaneous communication became possible even over long distances. By 1853, only nine years after construction of the first experimental line, 23,000 miles of telegraph wire spread across the United States; by 1860, 50,000. In 1861 the telegraph bridged the continent, connecting the east and west coasts. The new invention revolutionized news-gathering, provided advance information for railroads and steamships, and altered patterns of business and finance. Rarely has innovation had so great an impact so quickly.

The changes in transportation and communications from 1800 to 1860 were revolutionary. Railroads reduced the number of loadings and unloadings, were cheap to build over difficult terrain, and remained in use all year, unlike water transport which was frozen out in winter. But time was the key. In 1800 it took four days to travel from New York City to Baltimore, and nearly four weeks to reach Detroit. By 1830 Baltimore was only a day-and-a-half away and Detroit only a two-week journey. By 1857 Detroit was but an overnight trip; in a week one could reach Texas, Kansas, or Nebraska. This reduced travel time saved money and facilitated commerce. During the first two decades of the century, wagon transportation cost 30 to 70 cents per ton per mile. By 1860, railroads in New York State carried freight at an average charge of 2.2 cents per ton per mile; wheat moved from Chicago to New York for 1.2 cents a ton-mile. In sum, the transportation revolution had transformed the economy—and with it the relationships of the North, West, and South.

THE RISE OF MANUFACTURING AND COMMERCE

The McCormick reaper, ridiculed the London *Times*, looked like "a cross between a flying-machine, a wheelbarrow, and an Astley chariot." In one continuous motion, the horse-drawn reaper used a revolving drum to position the stalks before a blade, with the cut grain falling onto a platform. Put to a competitive test through rain-soaked wheat, the Chicago-made reaper alone passed, to the cheers of the skeptical English spectators. The reaper and hundreds of other American products made their international debut at the 1851 London Crystal Palace Exhibition, the first modern world's fair. There the design and quality of American machines and wares—from familiar farm tools to such exotic devices as an ice-cream freezer and the reaper—astonished observers. American manufacturers returned home with dozens of medals, including all three prizes for piano making. Most impressive to the Europeans were three simple machines: Alfred C. Hobb's unpickable padlocks, Samuel Colt's revolvers, and Robbins and Lawrence's six rifles with completely interchangeable parts. All were machine- rather than hand-tooled, products of what the British called the American system of manufacturing.

So impressed were the British—the leading industrial nation of the time—that in 1853 they sent a parliamentary commission to study the American system. A year later a second committee returned to examine the firearms industry in detail. In their report, the committee described an astonishing experiment performed at the federal armory in Springfield, Massachusetts. To test the interchangeability of machine-made muskets, they selected rifles made in each of the previous ten years. While the committee watched, the guns were dismantled "and the parts placed in a row of boxes, mixed up together." The Englishmen "then requested the workman, whose duty it is to 'assemble' the arms, to put them together, which he did—the Committee handing him the parts, taken at hazard—with the use of a turnscrew only, and as quickly as though they had been English muskets, whose parts had carefully been kept separate." Britain's Enfield arsenal subsequently converted to American equipment. Within the next few years other nations followed Great Britain's lead, sending delegations across the Atlantic to bring back American machines.

The American system of manufacturing used precision machinery to produce interchangeable parts that needed no filing or fitting. In 1798 Eli Whitney had used a primitive system of interchangeable parts when he contracted with the federal government to make ten thousand rifles in twenty-eight months. By the 1820s the Connecticut manufacturer Simeon North, the Springfield, Massachusetts, Arsenal, and the Harpers Ferry, Virginia, Armory were all producing machine-made interchangeable parts for firearms. From the arsenals the American system spread, giving birth to the machine-tool industry—the mass manufacture of specialized machines for other industries. One by-product was an explosion in consumer goods: since the time and skill involved in manufacturing had been greatly reduced, the new system permitted mass production at low cost. Waltham watches, Yale locks,

American System of Manufacturing

and Singer sewing machines became household items, inexpensive yet of uniformly high quality.

Interchangeable parts and the machine-tool industry were uniquely American contributions to the industrial revolution. Both paved the way for America's swift industrialization following the Civil War. The process of industrialization began, however, in a simple and traditional way, not unlike that of other nations. In 1800 manufacturing was relatively unimportant to the American economy. What manufacturing there was took place mostly in small workshops or homes, where journeymen and apprentices worked with and under master craftsmen, or women spun thread and wove cloth alone at home. Tailors, shoemakers, and blacksmiths made articles by hand for a specific customer.

The clothing trades illustrate well the nineteenth-century changes in manufacturing and distribution. In the eighteenth century, most men wore clothes made by their mothers, wives, or daughters, or occasionally bought used clothing. Wealthy men had clothing made by tailors who cut and sewed unique garments to fit them. A tailor was a master craftsman whose journeymen and apprentices worked with him to produce goods made to order. By the 1820s and 1830s, clothiers and clothing manufacturers had replaced most, though not all, of the old craftsmen and journeymen. In the 1820s clothiers appeared with stocks of ready-made clothes. T. S. Whitmarsh of Boston advertised in 1827 that "he keeps constantly for Sale, from 5 to 10,000 Fashionable ready-made Garments." In 1830, J. T. Jacobs of New York boasted that "Gentlemen can rely upon being as well fitted from the shelves as if their measures were taken—their stock being very extensive and their sizes well assorted."

Clothing Trades

The early mass-produced clothes, crude and limited to a variety of loose-fitting sizes, were mainly produced for men. They sold to men who lived in city boarding and rooming houses, away from the female kin who would previously have made their clothes. Most women made their own clothes, since nearly all girls were expected to acquire sewing skills, but those women who could afford it employed seamstresses to make their tailored garments.

Upon entering Whitmarsh's or Jacobs's emporium

L. J. Levy and Company, exclusively a dry goods retail store, sold ready-to-wear clothing and helped make Chestnut Street a fashionable shopping street in Philadelphia. The Free Library of Philadelphia.

a customer found row after row of ready-made goods without a sign of tailors or a workshop. Unlike the eighteenth-century tailor, the nineteenth-century ready-to-wear clothier was exclusively a retailer. The merchant most likely bought the goods wholesale; if he manufactured them himself, it would not be in his retail shop. Nor were the goods made under the master-journeyman-apprentice system. The former master tailor, now often an entrepreneur, might employ a journeyman to cut out fabric panels, but most of the sewing was put out at piece rates to unskilled or semiskilled labor. In 1832 Boston tailors employed 300 journeymen tailors at $2.00 per day and 100 boys and 1,300 women at 50 cents a day. Most of the women worked in their own homes sewing straight seams. Apprentices, if used at all, were no longer learning a trade but were a permanent source of

cheap labor. Sewing skills were learned within a different type of master-apprentice system; they were passed down from mother to daughter.

Essential to this change in the clothing industry was the rise of the cotton textile mill. First in England, then in the United States, mills insatiably processed the increasing supply of cotton grown in the slave South. At the same time, the expanding market economy, fed by the population boom, bought the manufactured cotton goods. The first American textile mill, built in Pawtucket, Rhode Island, in 1790, used water-powered spinning machines constructed from British models by the English immigrant Samuel Slater. Slater employed women and children as cheap labor and sold manufactured thread from Maine to Maryland. Soon other mills sprang up, stimulated by the embargo on British imports from 1807 through 1815. From

1809 through 1813 alone, 151 cotton and woolen companies incorporated.

Early mills also used the putting-out system. Traditionally women had spun their own thread and woven it into cloth for their own families; now many women received thread from the mills and returned finished cloth. The change was subtle but significant: although the work itself was familiar, women now operated their looms for piece-rate wages and produced cloth for the market, not for their own use.

Textile manufacturing was radically transformed in 1813 by the construction of the first American power loom and the chartering of the Boston Manufacturing Company. The corpo-

Waltham (Lowell) System

ration was capitalized at $400,000— ten times the amount behind the Rhode Island mills—by Francis Cabot Lowell and other Boston merchants. Its goal was to eliminate problems of timing, shipping, coordination, and quality control inherent in the putting-out system. The owners erected their factories in Waltham, Massachusetts, combining all the manufacturing processes at a single location. They also employed a resident manager to run the mill, thus separating ownership from management. The company produced cloth suitable for the mass market so inexpensively that most women began to purchase rather than make their own cloth. Nonetheless, spinning and weaving remained women's work in many rural homes. And not until the end of the century would a majority of women purchase ready-made clothing (see page 542).

In the rural setting of Waltham not enough hands could be found to staff the mill, so the managers recruited New England farm daughters, accepting responsibility for their living conditions and their virtue. To persuade young women to come, they offered cash wages, company-run boardinghouses, and such cultural events as evening lectures—none of which were available on the farm. This paternalistic approach, called the Waltham or Lowell system, was adopted in other mills erected alongside New England rivers. The Hamilton Corporation (1825), the Appleton and Lowell corporations (1828), and the Suffolk, Tremont, and Lawrence firms (1831) all followed.

By 1860 a cotton mill resembled a modern factory. A majority of the mill work force by this time were immigrant Irish women, who lived at home; the mills did not provide subsidized housing for them. New England farm girls continued to stay in the remaining boardinghouses, but they had become few in number. Technological improvements in the looms and other machinery made the work tasks less skilled and more alike. The mills could thus pay lower wages, and with increased immigration during the nineteenth century, they always had a reservoir of unskilled labor to draw from. The factory had radically altered work relationships in America.

Textile manufacturing changed New England. Lowell, the famous "city of spindles" that came to symbolize early American industrialization, grew from 2,500 people in 1826 to 33,000 in 1850. The textile industry became the most important in the nation before the Civil War, employing 115,000 workers in 1860, more than half of whom were women and immigrants. The key to its success was that the machines, not the women, spun the thread and wove the cloth. The workers watched the machines and intervened to maintain smooth operation. When a thread broke, for instance, the machine stopped automatically; the worker would find the break, piece the ends together, and restart the machine. The mills used increasingly specialized machines, relying heavily on advances in the machine-tool industry. Here was the American system of manufacturing applied.

Though textile mills were in the vanguard of industrialization, manufacturing grew in many areas. Woolen textiles, farm implements, machine tools, iron, glass, and finished consumer goods all became major industries. "White coal"—water power—was widely used to run the machines. Yet by 1860, the United States was still predominantly an agricultural nation; just over one-half of the work force was engaged in agriculture. Manufacturing accounted for only a third of total production, even though that percentage had doubled in twenty years.

To a great extent, industrialization in this period can be seen as flowing from other changes in American life rather than the agent of change. Ever since Alexander Hamilton's report on manufactures (see page 189), national self-consciousness and pride had emphasized the development of American industry. Contrary to Hamilton's hopes, however, more money flowed into the merchant marine than into industry between 1789 and 1808. In the early republic, greater profits could be made by transporting British products to the United States than by producing the same items at home. But the embargo and the War of 1812 reversed the situation, and merchants began to shift their capital from shipping to manufacturing (see pages 221–226). It was in this new economic environment that the Waltham system took root.

Other factors also helped to stimulate industry. Population growth, especially in urban areas and the Old Northwest, created a large domestic market for finished goods (see maps, page 252). The rise of commercial agriculture brought farmers more fully into the market economy. Specialty merchants and new modes of transportation speeded up the development of these new markets. And the relative scarcity of skilled craftsmen encouraged mechanization—as more workers moved westward than entered the factories, merchants had to find some way to produce more goods with less labor. Finally, beginning with the Tariff of 1816 and culminating in the Tariff of Abominations of 1828, Congress passed tariffs more to protect the market for domestic manufactures than to increase government revenue.

Essential to the rise of manufacturing was the growth of, and specialization in, commerce. Cotton, for instance, had once been traded by plantation agents who handled all the goods produced and bought by the owners, extending credit where needed. As cotton became a great staple export following the invention of the cotton gin in 1793, exports rose from half a

Specialization of Commerce

million pounds in that year to 83 million pounds in 1815. Gradually some agents came to specialize in finance alone: cotton brokers appeared, men who for a commission brought together buyers and sellers. Similarly, wheat and hog brokers sprang up in the West—in Cincinnati, Louisville, and St. Louis. The supply of finished goods also became more specialized. Wholesalers bought large quantities of a particular item from manufacturers, and jobbers broke down the wholesale lots for retail stores and country merchants.

In small towns the general merchant persisted for a longer time. Such merchants continued to sell some goods through exchange with farm women—trading flour or pots and pans for eggs or other local produce. They left the sale of finished goods, such as shoes and clothing, to local craftsmen. In rural areas and on the frontier, peddlers acted as general merchants.

But as transportation improved and towns grew, even small-town merchants began to specialize.

Commercial specialization made some traders in the big cities, especially New York, virtual merchant princes. New York had emerged as the dominant port in the late 1790s, outstripping Philadelphia and Boston. When the Erie Canal opened, the city became a standard stop on every major trade route—from Europe, the ports of the South, and the West. New York traders were the middlemen in southern cotton and western grain trading; in fact, New York was the nation's major cotton-exporting city. Merchants in other cities played a similar role within their own regions.

These newly rich traders invested their profits in processing and then manufacturing, further stimulating the growth of northern cities. Some cities became leaders in specific industries: Rochester became a milling center and Cincinnati—"Porkopolis"—the first meat-packing center.

To support their complex commercial transactions, many merchants required large office staffs. In an age before typewriters and carbon paper, much of

Counting House and Credit Systems

the office staff—all male—worked on high stools laboriously copying business forms and correspondence. The scratch of their pens was the early-nineteenth-century equivalent of the typewriter's clatter. At the bottom of the office hierarchy were messenger boys, often pre-teenagers, who delivered documents. Above them were the ordinary copyists, who hand-copied documents in ink as many times as needed. Clerks handled such assignments as customs-house clearances and duties, shipping papers, and translations. Above them were the bookkeeper and the confidential chief clerk. Those seeking employment in such an office, called a counting house, could take a course from a writing master to acquire a "good hand." All hoped to rise to the status of partner.

Banking and other financial institutions played a significant role in the expansion of commerce and manufacturing and were themselves an important industry. The new financial institutions (banks, insurance companies, and corporations) linked savers—those who put money in the bank—with

Banking and Credit Systems

producers or speculators—those who wished to borrow money for equip-

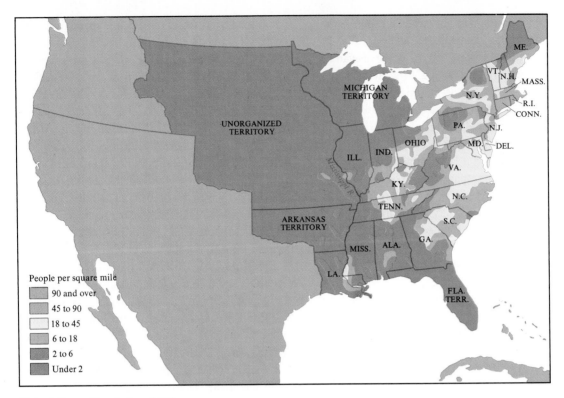

United States Population, 1820

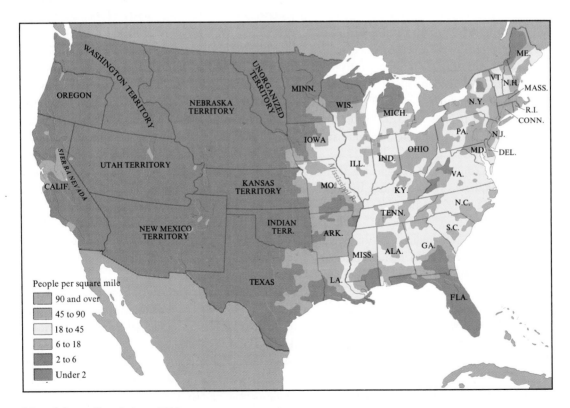

United States Population, 1860

Chapter 9: A Market and Industrial Economy, 1800–1860

ment. The expiration of the first Bank of the United States in 1811 after Congress refused to renew its charter acted as a stimulus to state-chartered banks, and in the next five years the number of banks more than doubled. Nonetheless, state banks proved inadequate to spur national growth, and in 1816 Congress chartered the Second Bank of the United States (see page 227). From then until 1832, however, many farmers, local bankers, and politicians denounced the bank as a monster, and they finally succeeded in killing it (see page 341).

The closing of the Second Bank in 1836 caused a nationwide credit shortage that, along with the Panic of 1837, stimulated major reforms in banking. Michigan and New York introduced charter laws promoting what was called *free banking*. Previously every new bank had required a special legislative charter, which made each bank incorporation a political decision. Under the new laws, any proposed bank that met certain minimum conditions—amount of money, notes issued, and types of loans to be made—would automatically receive a state charter. Although banks were thus freer to incorporate, more restrictions were placed on their practices, slightly reducing the risk of bank failure. Other states soon followed suit.

Free banking proved a significant stimulus to the economy in the late 1840s and 1850s. New banks sprang up everywhere, providing merchants and manufacturers with the credit they needed. The free banking laws also served as a precedent for general incorporation statutes, which allowed manufacturing firms to receive state charters without special acts. Investors in corporations, called shareholders, were granted *limited liability,* or freedom from responsibility for the company's debts. An attractive feature to potential investors, limited liability thus encouraged people to back new business ventures.

Business itself became more sophisticated. Merchants learned to evaluate their customers carefully before shipping them goods on credit. One response to the need to minimize risk was Lewis Tappan's mercantile agency, founded in 1841. The forerunner of Dun and Bradstreet, Tappan furnished his subscribers with confidential credit reports on country merchants. One such report read:

James Samson is a peddler, aged 30; he comes to Albany to buy his goods, and then peddles them out along the canal from Albany to Buffalo. He is worth $2,000; owns a wooden house at Lockport . . . has a wife and three children . . . drinks two glasses cider brandy, plain, morning and evening—never more; drinks water after each; chews fine cut; never smokes; good teeth generally; has lost a large double tooth on lower jaw, back, second from throat on left . . . purchases principally jewelry and fancy articles.

Changes in insurance firms also promoted industrialization. In the course of business, insurance companies accumulated large amounts of money as reserves against future claims. Then as now, their greatest profits came from investing those reserves. Beginning in the 1840s and 1850s, insurance companies lent money for longer periods than banks, and they bought shares in corporations. They were able to do so by persuading customers to buy whole-life policies rather than annual term insurance. They also took advantage of improvements in communications to establish networks of local agencies, thus expanding the number of customers they served.

In the 1850s, with credit and capital both more easily obtainable, the pace of industrialization increased. In the North, industry began to rival agriculture and commerce in dollar volume. Meanwhile commercial farming, financed by the credit boom, integrated the early frontier into the northern economy. By 1860 six northern states—Massachusetts, New York, Pennsylvania, Connecticut, Rhode Island, and Ohio—were highly industrialized. The clothing, textile, and shoe industries employed more than 100,000 workers each, lumber 75,000, iron 65,000, and woolens and leather 50,000. Although agriculture still predominated even in these states, industrial employment would soon surpass it.

MILL GIRLS AND MECHANICS

Oh, sing me the song of the Factory Girl!
So merry and glad and free!
The bloom in her cheeks, of health how it speaks,
Oh! a happy creature is she!
She tends the loom, she watches the spindle,

And cheerfully toileth away,
Amid the din of wheels, how her bright eyes
  kindle,
And her bosom is ever gay.

Oh, sing me the song of the Factory Girl!
Whose fabric doth clothe the world.
From the king and his peers to the jolly tars
With our flag o'er all seas unfurled.
From the California's seas, to the tainted breeze
Which sweeps the smokened rooms,
Where "God save the Queen" to cry are seen
The slaves of the British looms.

This idyllic portrait of factory work was an anachronism when it appeared in the Chicopee, Massachusetts, *Telegraph* in 1850. But it was a fitting song for the teenage, single women who first left the villages and farms of New England to work in the mills. The mill owners, believing that the degradation of English factory workers arose from their living conditions and not from the work itself, designed a model community offering airy courtyards and river views, secure dormitories, prepared meals, and cultural activities. Housekeepers enforced strict curfews, banned alcohol, and reported to the corporations on workers' behavior and church attendance.

Kinship ties, the promise of steady work, and good pay at first lured rural young women into the mills. Many pairs of sisters and cousins worked in the same mill and lived in the same boardinghouse. They helped each other adjust, and letters home brought other kin to the mills. Girls then had few opportunities for work outside their own homes, and at the same time their families had less need for their labor. The commercial production of thread and cloth had reduced a good part of the work done in farm households by New England daughters, whereas sons were still needed to assist their fathers. Moreover, the mills paid better wages than did farm work, domestic service, or sewing. Yet the New England daughters, who averaged sixteen and one-half years of age when they entered the mills, usually stayed there only about five years. Few intended to stay longer. Mill earnings brought a special satisfaction: feelings of independence and of freedom of choice in spending or saving their money. That satisfaction was not sufficient, however, to change their life's ambitions to be wives and mothers, not mill girls. Most left the mills to marry, only to be replaced by other women.

In the 1840s factory girls rebelled against the mill and mill town. They expressed their feelings in many ways, as in the song "The Factory Girl's Come-All-Ye" (about 1850):

No more I'll take my bobbins out,
No more I'll put them in,
No more the overseer will say
"You're weaving your cloth too thin!"

No more will I eat cold pudding,
No more will I eat hard bread,
No more will I eat those half-baked beans,
For I vow! They're killing me dead!

I'm going back to Boston town
And live on Tremont Street;
And I want all you fact'ry girls
To come to my house and eat!

What had happened to dash the hopes of these young women? The corporation's goal of building an industrial empire had taken precedence over its concern for workers' living conditions. In the race for profits, owners had lengthened hours, cut wages, and tightened discipline. Eliza R. Hemingway, a six-year veteran of the Massachusetts mills, told an 1845 state House of Representatives committee that the worker's hours were too long, "her time for meals too limited. In the summer season, the work is commenced at 5 o'clock, A.M., and continued 'til 7 o'clock, P.M., with half an hour for breakfast and three quarters of an hour for dinner." When Hemingway worked evenings—which was compulsory—lamps provided dim light in the room. There was no bloom of health in her cheeks.

New England mill workers responded to their deteriorating working conditions by organizing and striking. In 1834, in reaction to a 25-percent wage cut, they unsuccessfully "turned out" **Mill Girl** (struck) against the Lowell mills. **Protests** Two years later, when boardinghouse rates were raised, they turned out again. Following the period from 1837 to 1842, when most mills ran only part-time because of a decline in demand for cloth, managers applied still greater pressures on workers. The speedup, the stretch-out, and the premium system became common methods of increasing production. The speedup increased the speed of the machines; the stretch-out increased the number of machines each worker had to operate.

Premiums were paid to overseers whose departments produced the most cloth. The result was that in Lowell between 1836 and 1850, the number of spindles and looms increased 150 and 140 percent respectively, while the number of workers increased by only 50 percent. Some mill workers began to think of themselves as slaves.

As conditions worsened, workers changed their methods of resistance. In the 1840s strikes gave way to a concerted effort to shorten the workday. Massachusetts mill women joined forces with other workers to press for legislation mandating a ten-hour day. They aired their complaints in worker-run newspapers—the *Factory Girl* appeared in New Hampshire and the *Wampanoag and Operatives' Journal* in Massachusetts, both in 1842. Two years later the *Factory Girl's Garland* and the *Voice of Industry*, nicknamed "the factory girl's voice," were founded. Even the *Lowell Offering*, the owner-sponsored paper that was the pride of mill workers and managers alike, became embroiled in controversy when some workers charged that articles critical of working conditions had been suppressed.

But not all the militant native-born mill workers stayed on to fight the managers and owners, and gradually fewer New England daughters entered the mills. The immigrant women, mostly Irish, who constituted a majority of mill workers by the end of the 1850s were driven to the mills by the need to support their families. Most could not afford to complain about their working conditions.

What happened in the New England mills occurred in less dramatic fashion throughout the nation. Work tasks and workplaces changed, as did relations between workers and supervisors. In the traditional workshops and households, work relationships were intensely personal. People worked within family settings and shared a sense of unity and purpose; men and women had a feeling of control over the quality, value (wages), and conditions of their labor.

But textile mills, insurance companies, wholesale stores, canals, and railroads were the antithesis of the old workshop and household production tradition. Factories and counting houses lacked the reciprocity that had characterized earlier relationships. Workers lost their sense of autonomy, and impersonal market forces seemed to dominate. Stiff

Changes in the Workplace

This 1853 timetable from the Lowell Mills illustrates the regimentation workers had to submit to in the new environment of the factory. Note that workers frequently began before daylight, finished after sunset, and were given only half an hour for meals. Merrimack Valley Textile Museum.

competition among mills in the growing textile industry of the 1820s and 1830s led to layoffs and replacement of operatives with cheaper, less-skilled workers or children. The formal rules of the factory contrasted sharply with the conditions in workshops or farm households. Supervisors separated the workers from the owners. The division of labor and the use of machines reduced the skills required of workers. And the coming and going of the large work forces was governed by the bell, the steam whistle, or the clock. In 1844 the *Factory Girl's Garland* published a poem describing how the ringing of the factory bell controlled when the workers awoke, ate, began and ended work, and went to sleep. The central problem, of course, was the quickening of the work between the bells. Since owners and managers no longer shared the workers' tasks, it was easier for them to expect faster and faster performance.

Like the mill women, most workers at first welcomed the new manufacturing methods; new jobs and higher wages seemed adequate compensation. But later wage reductions, speedups, and stretch-outs changed their minds. Other adjustments were difficult too. Young women in the mills had to tolerate the roar of the looms, and all workers on power machines risked accidents that could kill or maim. Most demoralizing of all, they had to accept that their future was relatively fixed. Opportunities to become an owner or manager in the new system were virtually nil.

Changes in the workplace transformed workers. Initially, mill girls used kinship, village, and gender ties to build supportive networks in factories. In the 1840s and after, as Irish women came to predominate, more workers were strangers before they entered the mills, so that what they had in common, the bases for friendship and mutual support, were their work and job experiences. Yet as a sense of distance from their employers increased, so did deep-seated differences among workers. Nationality, religion, education, and future prospects separated Irish and Yankee mill workers. For many Irish women, mill work was not a stage in their lives; it would be permanent. Unlike their Yankee sisters, they could not risk striking and loss of their jobs; they and their families were dependent upon their earnings. With legions of unskilled immigrants looking for work, Irish mill girls and women considered themselves fortunate to hold on to their jobs, even though the mills cut wages three times in the 1850s and continued the speedups and stretch-outs. Many of the New England women resented the immigrants who came to the mill villages, and management set one against the other through selective hiring and promotions. Though the Irish workers assisted one another as much as possible, formal action was limited.

Eroded too were the republican virtues that artisans shared with the revolutionary war generation. Thomas Jefferson had hoped to preserve these values with the purchase of the Louisiana Territory, but the market economy, in which artisans and household workers were transformed into wage workers, undermined the Jeffersonian hopes with accumulating force and rapidity. Those who stayed in the master-journeyman-apprentice system or remained on farms after the 1830s saw themselves as distinct from the new wage workers. So too did many Yankee mill workers, for whom factory work remained merely a stage in their lifecycle before marriage.

One response to these changes was the active participation of workers in reform politics. In the 1820s labor parties arose in Pennsylvania, New York, and Massachusetts; they eventually spread to a dozen states. These parties advocated free public education, abolition of imprisonment for debt, revision of the militia system (in which workers bore the greatest burden) and opposition to banks and monopolies. Workers' reform often crossed paths with middle-class benevolent movements, since the two groups shared a concern not only for public education but also for public morals: temperance, observance of the Sabbath, and suppression of vice (see Chapter 12). Ironically, however, reform politics tended to divide workers. Many of the reforms—moral education, temperance, Sabbath closings—served merchants and industrialists seeking a more disciplined work force. Others broadened the divisions between native-born and immigrant workers. Anti-immigrant and anti-Catholic movements spread.

Emergence of a Labor Movement

Because of these divisions and economic upheaval, organized labor was not a strong force during this period. Labor unions tended to be local in nature; the strongest resembled medieval guilds. The first unions arose among urban journeymen in printing, woodworking, shoemaking, and tailoring. These craftsmen sought to protect themselves against the competition of inferior workmen by regulating apprenticeship and establishing minimum wages. In the 1820s and 1830s craft unions—unions organized by occupation—forged larger umbrella organizations in the cities, including the National Trades Union (1834). But in the depression of 1839 through 1843, the movement fell apart amidst wage reductions and unemployment. In the 1850s the deterioration of working conditions strengthened the labor movement again. Workers won a reduction in hours, and the ten-hour day became standard. Though the Panic of 1857 wiped out the umbrella organizations, some of the new national unions for specific trade groups—notably printers, hat finishers, and stonecutters—survived. By 1860 five more national unions had been organized by the painters, cordwainers, cotton spinners, iron molders, and machinists.

Organized labor's greatest achievement during this

Women shoe workers strike for higher wages at Lynn, Massachusetts, in 1860. Library of Congress.

period was in gaining recognition of its right to exist. When journeymen shoemakers organized in the first decade of the century, employers **Right to Strike** turned to the courts, charging criminal conspiracy. The cordwainers' conspiracy cases, which involved six trials from 1806 through 1815, left labor organizations in a tenuous position. Although the journeymen's right to organize was recognized, the courts ruled unlawful any coercive action that harmed other businesses or the public. In effect strikes were illegal. Eventually a Massachusetts case, *Commonwealth* v. *Hunt* (1842), effectively reversed the decision when Chief Justice Lemuel Shaw ruled that Boston journeymen bootmakers could combine and strike "in such manner as best to subserve their own interests."

The impact of economic and technological change, however, fell more heavily on individual workers than on their organizations. As a group, the workers' share of the national wealth declined after the 1830s. Individual producers—craftsmen, factory workers, and farmers—had less economic power than they had had a generation or two before. And workers were increasingly losing control over their own work.

COMMERCIAL FARMING

Beyond the town and city limits, agriculture remained the backbone of the economy. Although urban areas were growing quickly, so too were rural districts, and America was still overwhelmingly rural; even in 1860 rural residents far outnumbered urban dwellers. Indeed, it was rural population growth that transformed so many farm villages into bustling small cities. And it was the ability of farmers to feed the growing town and village populations that made possible the concentration of population and the development of commerce and industry.

New England and Middle Atlantic farmers in 1800 worked as their fathers and mothers had. They tilled relatively small plots of land centered around a household economy in which the needs of the family and the labor it supplied mostly determined what was produced and in what amounts. Most of their implements were homemade—wooden plows, rakes, shovels, and yokes. For iron parts, they turned to the local blacksmith.

But then canals and railroads began transporting grains, especially wheat, eastward from the fertile Old Northwest. And at the same time, northeastern agriculture developed some serious problems. Northeastern farmers had already cultivated all the land they could; expansion was impossible. Moreover, these small New England farms with their uneven terrain did not lend themselves to the new labor-saving farm implements introduced in the 1830s—mechanical sowers, reapers, threshers, and balers. Many northeastern farms also suffered from soil exhaustion: the worn-out land produced lower yields while requiring a greater investment in seed.

Northeastern Agriculture

In response to these problems and to competition from the West, many northern farmers either went west or gave up farming for jobs in the merchant houses and factories. For eastern farm sons and daughters, western New York was the first frontier. After the Erie Canal was completed, these Yankees and Yorkers settled on more fertile, cheaper land in Ohio and Illinois, and then in Michigan, Indiana, and Wisconsin. Farm daughters who did not go west flocked to the early textile mills. Still other New Englanders—urban, better educated, and often experienced in trade—entered the counting houses of New York and other cities.

Neither the counting house nor the factory, however, depleted New England agriculture. The farmers who remained proved as adaptable at farming as their children did at copy desks and water-powered looms. By the 1850s New England and Middle Atlantic farmers were successfully adjusting to competition from western agricultural products. They abandoned commercial production of wheat and corn and stopped tilling poor land. Instead they improved their livestock, especially cattle, and specialized in vegetable and fruit production and dairy farming. They financed these changes through land sales or borrowing. In fact, their greatest profit was made from increasing land values, not from farming itself.

Yet many could not buy farm land. Indeed, the growing division between worker and owner was mirrored in commercial agriculture by the gap between hired hands or tenants and farm owners. Though the United States was still primarily an agricultural nation—and many saw the frontier farm as the antidote to commerce and industrialization—not all farmers were yeomen. Farm laborers, once scarce in the United States, had become commonplace. In the North in 1860 there was one hired hand for every 2.3 farms. Given the high cost of land and of farming by that time, hired hands had little opportunity to acquire farms of their own. By the 1850s it took from ten to twenty years for a rural laborer to save enough money to farm for himself. For the same reason, the number of tenant farmers increased.

Nonetheless, state governments still energetically promoted commercial agriculture in order to spur economic growth and sustain the values of an agrarian-based republic. Massachusetts in 1817 and New York in 1819 subsidized agricultural prizes and county fairs. New York required contestants to submit written descriptions of how they grew their prize crops; the state then published the best essays to encourage the use of new methods and to promote specialization. Farm journals also helped to familiarize farmers with developments in agriculture. By 1860 there were nearly sixty journals with a combined circulation of from 250,000 to 300,000.

Even so, the Old Northwest gradually and inevitably replaced the northeastern states as the center of American family agriculture. Farms in the Old Northwest were much larger than northeastern ones and better suited to the new mechanized farming implements. The farmers of the region bought machines such as the McCormick reaper on credit and paid for them with the profits from their high yields. By 1847 Cyrus McCormick was selling a thousand reapers a year. Using interchangeable

Mechanization of Agriculture

parts, he expanded production to five thousand a year, but still demand outstripped supply. Similarly, John Deere's steel plow, invented in 1837, replaced the inadequate iron plow; steel blades kept the soil from sticking and were tough enough to break the roots of prairie grass. By 1856, Deere's sixty-five employees were making 13,500 plows a year.

These machines eased the problem of scarce farm labor and permitted a 70-percent surge in wheat production in the 1850s alone. By that time the area that had been the western wilderness in 1800 had become one of the world's leading agricultural regions. Midwestern farmers fed an entire nation and a generation of immigrants, and had food to export.

THE WESTERN FRONTIER

B etween 1800 and 1860 the frontier moved westward at an incredible pace. In 1800 the edge of settlement formed an arc from western New York through the new states of Kentucky and Tennessee, south to Georgia. Twenty years later it had shifted to Ohio, Indiana, and Illinois in the North and Louisiana, Alabama, and Mississippi in the South. By 1860 settlement had reached the West Coast; the 1800 frontier was long-settled, and once-unexplored regions were dotted with farms and mines, towns and villages. Unsettled land remained—mostly between the Mississippi River and the Sierra Nevada—but essentially the frontier and its native inhabitants, the Indians, had given way to white settlement (see pages 287–290). All that remained for whites was to people the plains and mountain territories.

Movement of the Frontier

The legal boundaries of the country also changed rapidly during this period. Between 1803 and 1853 the United States pushed its original boundaries to their present continental limits (except for Alaska). The Louisiana Purchase roughly doubled the nation's size, and the acquisition of Florida from Spain in 1819 secured the Southeast. In the 1840s the United States annexed the Republic of Texas, defined its northern border with Canada, and acquired through war California, Nevada, Utah, and most of Arizona from Mexico (see pages 349, 357). In the 1850s the Gadsden Purchase added southern Arizona and New Mexico.

The lore of the vanishing frontier forms part of the mythology of America. It includes fur trappers, explorers, and pioneers braving an unknown environment and hostile Indians; settlers crossing the arid plains and snow-covered Rockies by Conestoga wagon to bring civilization to the wilderness; Mormons finding Zion in the Great American Desert; forty-niners sailing on clipper ships to California in search of gold.

Americans have only recently come to recognize that there are other sides to these familiar stories. Women, Indians, and blacks as well as white men were pioneers. Explorers and pioneers did not discover North America by themselves, nor did the wagon trains fight their way across the plains—Indians guided them along traditional paths and led them to food and water. And rather than civilizing the frontier, settlers at first brought a rather primitive economy and society, which did not compare favorably with the well-ordered Indian civilizations. In the South, frontier settlement carried with it slavery. The Mormons who sought a new Jerusalem by Salt Lake were fleeing the gehenna (hell) imposed on them by intolerant, violent frontier folk farther east (see page 329). And all those who sought furs, gold, and lumber spoiled the natural landscape in the name of progress and development.

This was the ironic contrast between the ideal and the reality of the frontier. If pioneers were attracted by the beauty and bounty of the American wilderness, if they were lured by the opportunity to live a simple, rewarding life close to the soil, they were also destroying the natural landscape in the process. It was almost as if the vast forests, prairies, and lakes were enemies to be conquered and bent to their will. Millions of trees were felled to make way for farms. Michigan lumbermen denuded the land. And farther west, miners in search of gold leveled the hills.

No figure has come to symbolize the frontier more aptly than the footloose, rugged fur trapper, who roamed thousands of unmapped miles in search of pelts. The trapper, with his backpack, rifle, and kegs of whiskey, spearheaded America's manifest destiny (see page 346), extending the United States

Fur Trade

Spring rendezvous at Green River, Wyoming, painted by
W. H. Jackson.   United States Department of the Interior,
National Park Service.

presence to the Pacific Slope. Fur trading, especially for beaver, had been economically important since the early colonial period. Traders were the link in an elaborate network that reached from beyond the settled frontier to sophisticated European shops. But after 1800 American investors organized to compete with foreign trading companies such as Hudson's Bay. The German immigrant John Jacob Astor, for instance, became a millionaire through his American Fur Trading Company. And Americans also changed the method by which furs were acquired. In 1825 the St. Louis merchant William Henry Ashley pioneered the rendezvous system. Instead of buying beaver furs from Indians, Ashley sent out non-Indian trappers to roam the Rockies and farther west; at a meeting on the Green River, in present-day Wyoming, at season's end, the trappers exchanged their pelts for goods Ashley had brought in from St. Louis. This annual spring rendezvous was the hallmark of the American fur-trading system through the late 1830s, when silk hats replaced beaver ones and trapping declined. In many areas the beaver had been virtually trapped out of existence.

Throughout the West trappers sought the cooperation of neighboring tribes in their territory, and nearly 40 percent wed Indian women. Most often the trapper or trader followed the tribe's custom, negotiating with her parents for the match. When a chief's daughter wed a fur merchant, separate cultures convened to celebrate, as when Archibald McDonald of the Hudson's Bay Company and Koale-xoa, daughter of a Chinook chief, were married in traditional ceremonies at the mouth of the Columbia River. Since in Indian and white frontier societies there was little distinction between public and private spheres, an Indian wife played an important "public" role in bridging trapper culture and economy and Indian society. Moreover, Indian women brought special trading privileges as well as family ties and experiences of life on the frontier. Over time, Métis or mixed bloods (Indian-white offspring) and white women replaced Indian women as trappers' wives; not only did this change trapper culture but in itself it was a sign of the decline of the fur trade. It signaled the coming of settled, agrarian society.

The history of trapping was in essence the history

The gold rush brought treasure seekers—men and women, white and black, native and foreign born—to California. Few found their fortune in gold, but most stayed to settle the West Coast. California State Library.

of the frontier. Early fur traders exploited friendly Indian tribes; then pioneers (mountain trappers) monopolized the trade through the systematic organization and financial backing of trading companies. Soon settlements and towns sprang up along the trappers' routes. With the decline in the fur trade, some trappers settled down. In Oregon in 1843 former trappers helped organize the first provisional government and pressured for United States statehood. In the mountain states the mining and cattle frontiers were to continue for another half-century, following the development of the fur-trading frontier.

But not all regions followed this pattern. By contrast, California was settled almost overnight. In January 1848 James Marshall, a carpenter, spotted a few gold-like particles in the millrace at Sutter's Mill (now Coloma, California). Word of the discovery spread, and other Californians rushed to garner instant fortunes. When John C. Frémont reached San Francisco in June 1848, he found that "all, or nearly all, its male inhabitants had gone to the mines." The town, "which a few months before was so busy and thriving, was then almost deserted."

California Gold Rush

By 1849 the news had spread eastward; hundreds of thousands of fortune-seekers flooded in. Most forty-niners never found enough gold to pay their expenses. "The stories you hear frequently in the States," one gold-seeker wrote home, "are the most extravagant lies imaginable—the mines are a humbug. . . . the almost universal feeling is to get home." But many stayed, unable to afford the passage back home, or tempted by the growing labor shortage in California's cities and agricultural districts. San Francisco, the gateway from the coast to the interior, became an instant city, ballooning from 1,000 people in 1848 to 35,000 just two years later.

Although those who came produced almost nothing, they had to be fed. Thus began the great California agricultural boom, centered along the natural waterways in the fertile interior of the state. Wheat was the great staple; it required minimal investment, was easily planted, and offered a quick return at the end of a relatively short growing season. California farmers became eager importers of machinery, since wages were high in the labor-scarce district and the extensive flat, treeless plains were well suited to horse-drawn machines. By the mid-1850s, California was exporting wheat. In its growing cities, merchant princes arose to supply, feed, and clothe the new settlers. One such merchant was Levi Strauss, whose tough mining pants became synonymous with American jeans.

Still food had to be cooked and clothes washed. In the western frontier women were relatively few in number. Unlike the Midwest, where family farms were the basic unit of production

Frontier Women

and life, in California gold and ore mining, grazing, and large-scale wheat farming were overwhelmingly male occupations. The women who comprised about one-seventh of the travelers on the overland trails found that their domestic skills were therefore in great demand. They received high fees for cooking, laundering, and sewing, and inevitably the boardinghouses and hotels were run by women, as men shunned domestic work. Not all women were entrepreneurs. Some found their domestic skills offered free by over-hospitable husbands. Abigail Scott Duniway, a leading western crusader for women's suffrage and a veteran of the Overland Trail to Oregon, wrote of one woman's experience. "It was a hospitable neighborhood composed chiefly of bachelors," she wrote in 1859, "who found comfort in mobilizing at meal time at the homes of the few married men of the township, and seemed especially fond of congregating at the hospitable cabin home of my good husband, who was never quite so much in his glory as when entertaining men at this fireside, while I,

if not washing, scrubbing, churning, or nursing the baby, was preparing their meals in our lean-to kitchen."

Gold altered the pattern of settlement along the entire Pacific Coast. Before 1848 most overland traffic flowed north over the Oregon Trail; fewer pioneers turned south to California or used the Santa Fe Trail. But by 1849 a pioneer observed that the Oregon Trail "bore no evidence of having been much traveled this year." Traffic was instead flowing south, and California was becoming the new population center of the Pacific Slope. One measure of the shift was the overland mail routes. In the 1840s the Oregon Trail had been the major communications link between the Pacific and the Midwest. But the Post Office officials who organized mail routes in the 1850s terminated them in California; there was no route farther north than Sacramento.

By 1860 California, like the Great Plains and prairies farther east, had become a farmers' and merchants' frontier. Though the story of these settlers is less

Farming Frontier

dramatic than that of the trappers and forty-niners, it is nevertheless the story of the overwhelming majority of westerners before 1860. The farming frontier started first on the western fringes of the eastern seaboard states and in the Old Northwest, then moved to the edge of the Great Plains and California. Pioneer families cleared the land of trees or prairie grass, hoed in corn and wheat, fenced in animals, and constructed cabins of logs or sod. If they were successful—and many were not—they slowly cleared more land. As settled areas expanded, farmers built roads to carry their stock and produce to market and bring back supplies they could not produce themselves. Growth brought specialization; as western farmers shifted from self-sufficiency to commercial farming, they too tended to concentrate on one crop. By this time the area was no longer a frontier, and families seeking new land had to go farther west. In John Jervis's time a farmer from Rome, New York, might have gone to Michigan via the Erie Canal and Lake Erie. A later generation would go farther west to Iowa, Nebraska, or even California.

What made farm settlement possible was the availability of land and credit. Some public lands were granted as a reward for military ser-

Land Grants and Sales

vice: veterans of the War of 1812 received 160 acres; veterans of the

The greatest wealth was to be found in supplying, feeding, and clothing the gold seekers. Men and women opened stores for and provided services to the miners; overnight towns like Marysville, California, sprang up in the gold district. Library of Congress.

Mexican War (see Chapter 13) could purchase land at reduced prices. And until 1820, civilians could buy government land at $2 an acre (a relatively high price) on a liberal four-year payment plan. More important, from 1800 to 1817 the government successively reduced the minimum purchase from 640 to 80 acres. However, when the availability of land prompted a flurry of land speculation that ended in the Panic of 1819, the government discontinued credit sales. Instead it reduced the price further, to $1.25 an acre.

Some eager pioneers settled land before it had been surveyed and put up for sale. Such illegal settlers, or squatters, then had to buy the land they lived on at auction, and faced the risk of being unable to purchase it. In 1841, to facilitate settlement, simplify

land sales, and end property disputes, Congress passed the Pre-emption Act, which legalized settlement prior to surveying.

Since most settlers, squatters or not, needed to borrow money, private credit systems arose. Banks, private investors, country storekeepers, and speculators all extended credit to farmers. Railroads also sold land on credit—land they had received from the government as construction subsidies. (The Illinois Central, for example, received 2.6 million acres in 1850.) Indeed, nearly all economic activity in the West involved credit, from land sales to the shipping of produce to railroad construction. And again in 1836, 1855, and 1856 easy credit helped to boost land prices. When the speculative bubbles burst, much land fell into the hands of speculators, and as a

IMPORTANT EVENTS

1807	Fulton's steamboat, *Clermont*
1812–15	War of 1812
1813	Boston Manufacturing Company founded
1818	National Road reaches Wheeling, Virginia
1819	*Dartmouth College v. Woodward*
1819–23	Depression
1820s	New England textile mills expand
1824	*Gibbons v. Ogden*
1825	Erie Canal completed
1830	Baltimore and Ohio Railroad begins operation
1831	McCormick invents the reaper
1834	Mill women strike at Lowell
1837	*Charles River Bridge v. Warren Bridge*
1839–43	Depression
1844	Baltimore-Washington telegraph line
1849	California gold rush
1853	British study of American system of manufacturing
1854	Railroad reaches the Mississippi
1857	Depression

spearheaded settlement farther west. Steamboats connected eastern markets and ports with these river and lake cities, carrying grain east and returning with finished goods. As in the Northeast, these western cities eventually developed into manufacturing centers when merchants shifted their investments from commerce to industry. Chicago became a center for the manufacture of farm implements, Louisville of textiles, and Cleveland of iron. Smaller cities specialized in flour mills, and all produced consumer goods for the hinterlands.

Urban growth in the West was so spectacular that by 1860 Cincinnati, St. Louis, and Chicago had populations exceeding 100,000, and Buffalo, Louisville, San Francisco, Pittsburgh, Detroit, Milwaukee, and Cleveland had surpassed 40,000. Thus commerce, urbanization, and industrialization overtook the farmers' frontier, wedding the Old Northwest and areas beyond to the Northeast.

For the nation as a whole, the period from 1800 through 1860 was one of sustained growth. Population increased sixfold. Settlement, once restricted to the Atlantic seaboard and the eastern rivers, extended more than a thousand miles inland by 1860 and was spreading east from the Pacific Ocean as well. Whereas agriculture had completely dominated the nation at the turn of the century, by midcentury farming was being challenged by a booming manufacturing sector. And agriculture itself was becoming mechanized.

Economic development changed the American landscape and the way people lived. Canals, railroads, steamboats, and telegraph lines linked together economic activities hundreds and thousands of miles apart. The market economy brought both sustained growth and cycles of boom and bust. Hard times and unemployment became frequent occurrences.

At the same time, commercial and industrial growth altered production and consumption. Manufactured goods changed farm work as farmers began to purchase goods produced formerly by wives and daughters. Many New England farm daughters left the farms to become the first factory workers in the new textile industry. As factories grew larger and as factory production replaced the master-journeyman-apprentice system, workplace relations became more impersonal and conditions harsher. Immigrants began to form a new industrial group, and some workers organized labor unions.

consequence tenancy became more common in the West than it had been in New England.

Towns and cities were the lifelines of the agricultural West. Cities along the Ohio and Mississippi rivers— Pittsburgh, Louisville, Cincinnati, and St. Louis— preceded most of the settlement of the early frontier.

Frontier Cities A generation later the lake cities of Cleveland, Detroit, and Chicago

Chapter 9: A MARKET AND INDUSTRIAL ECONOMY, 1800–1860

The American people too were changing. Immigration and western expansion made the people and society more diverse. Urbanization, commerce, and industry produced significant divisions among Americans. And their reach extended deeply into the home as well as the workshop.

SUGGESTIONS FOR FURTHER READING

General

Stuart Bruchey, *The Roots of American Economic Growth, 1607–1861: An Essay in Social Causation* (1965); David Klingaman and Richard Vedder, eds., *Essays in 19th Century History* (1975); Susan Previant Lee and Peter Passell, *A New Economic View of American History* (1979); Otto Mayr and Robert C. Post, eds., *Yankee Enterprise. The Rise of the American System of Manufactures* (1981); Douglass C. North, *Economic Growth of the United States, 1790–1860* (1966); Nathan Rosenberg, *Technology and American Economic Growth* (1972).

Transportation

Robert G. Albion, *The Rise of New York Port, 1815–1860* (1939); Albert Fishlow, *American Railroads and the Transformation of the Ante-Bellum Economy* (1965); Carter Goodrich, *Government Promotion of American Canals and Railroads, 1800–1890* (1960); Louis C. Hunter, *Steamboats on the Western Rivers* (1949); Harry N. Scheiber, *Ohio Canal Era: A Case Study of Government and the Economy, 1820–1861* (1969); Ronald E. Shaw, *Erie Water West: Erie Canal, 1797–1854* (1966); George R. Taylor, *The Transportation Revolution, 1815–1860* (1951).

Commerce and Manufacturing

Alfred D. Chandler, Jr., *The Visible Hand: Managerial Revolution in American Business* (1977); Thomas C. Cochran, *Frontiers of Change: Early Industrialization in America* (1981); H. J. Habakkuk, *American and British Technology in the Nineteenth Century* (1962); Louis Hartz, *Economic Policy and Democratic Thought: Pennsylvania, 1776–1860* (1954); David J. Jeremy, *Transatlantic Industrial Revolution: The Diffusion of Textile Technologies Between Britain and America, 1790s–1830s* (1981); Stanley I. Kutler, *Privilege and Creative*

Destruction. The Charles River Bridge Case (1971); James D. Norris, *R. G. Dun & Co. 1841–1900* (1978); Merritt Roe Smith, *Harpers Ferry Armory and the New Technology* (1977); Caroline F. Ware, *Early New England Cotton Manufacturing* (1931).

Agriculture

Percy Bidwell and John Falconer, *History of Agriculture in the Northern United States 1620–1860* (1925); Allan G. Bogue, *From Prairie to Corn Belt: Farming on the Illinois and Iowa Prairies in the Nineteenth Century* (1963); Clarence Danhof, *Change in Agriculture: The Northern United States, 1820–1870* (1969); Paul W. Gates, *The Farmer's Age: Agriculture, 1815–1860* (1962); Benjamin H. Hibbard, *A History of Public Land Policies* (1939); Robert Leslie Jones, *History of Agriculture in Ohio to 1880* (1983); Edward C. Kendall, *John Deere's Steel Plow* (1959).

The Western Frontier

Ray A. Billington, *The Far Western Frontier, 1830–1860* (1956); Ray A. Billington and Martin Ridge, *Westward Expansion*, 5th ed., (1982); John Mack Faragher, *Women and Men on the Overland Trail* (1979); William H. Goetzmann, *Exploration and Empire: The Explorer and the Scientist in the Winning of the American West* (1966); Leroy R. Hafen, ed., *The Mountain Men and the Fur Trade of the Far West*, 10 vols. (1965–1972); John A. Hawgood, *America's Western Frontier: The Exploration and Settlement of the Trans-Mississippi West* (1967); Julie Roy Jeffrey, *Frontier Women. The Trans-Mississippi West 1840–1880* (1979); Theodore J. Karamanski, *Fur Trade and Exploration. Opening the Far Northwest 1821–1852* (1983); John D. Unruh, Jr., *The Overland Emigrants and the Trans-Mississippi West, 1840–1860* (1979); David J. Wishart, *The Fur Trade of the American West, 1807–1840* (1979).

Workers

Alan Dawley, *Class and Community: The Industrial Revolution in Lynn* (1977); Thomas Dublin, *Women at Work: The Transformation of Work and Community in Lowell, Massachusetts, 1826–1860* (1979); Thomas Dublin, ed., *Farm to Factory. Women's Letters, 1830–1860* (1981); Susan E. Hirsch, *Roots of the American Working Class: The Industrialization of Crafts in Newark, 1800–1860* (1978); Alice Kessler-Harris, *Out to Work. A History of Wage-Earning Women in the United States* (1982); Bruce Laurie, *Working People of Philadelphia, 1800–1850* (1980); Norman Ware, *The Industrial Worker, 1840–1860* (1924); Sean Willentz, *Chants Democratic: New York City and the Rise of the American Working Class, 1788–1850* (1984).

Toward Greater Diversity:
The American People
1800–1860

Chapter 10

For twenty years actors Edwin Forrest and his English rival William Charles Macready had vied for the favor of American audiences. Literary and intellectual circles lionized Macready; artisans and mechanics preferred Forrest, an American who stressed his love of flag, country, and democracy. When the two actors appeared simultaneously in New York City in May 1849, posters went up challenging Macready.

WORKING MEN,
shall
AMERICANS OR ENGLISH RULE
in this city?

Macready's opening night was ruined by noise and a barrage of objects, including four chairs, thrown from the gallery. Later in his run a crowd gathered outside the theater, protesting Macready's appearance as a symbol of "English *ARISTOCRATS!!* and Foreign Rule!" Adding to the fray were Anglophobic Irish immigrants, recently escaped from famine and English rule. As Macready left the theater under police protection, the mob surged. The militia, on guard to maintain order, fired in the air, missing the rioters but felling dozens of bystanders. Twenty-two people were killed, thirty-six injured.

This incident was an extreme version of the chaos typical of theaters. The Englishwoman Frances Trollope, in her *Domestic Manners of the Americans* (1832), described the audience at a Cincinnati theater: "The spitting was incessant," accompanied by "the mixed smell of onions and whiskey. . . . The noises, too, were perpetual, and of the most unpleasant kind." An 1830 theater poster forbade "personal altercations in any part of the house," "the uncourteous habit of throwing nut shells, apples, etc., into the Pit," and "clambering over the balustrade into the Boxes, either during or at the end of the Performance." Indeed, theater regularly evoked the strongest of passions among Americans. "When a patriotic fit seized them, and 'Yankee Doodle' was called for," Trollope observed, "every man seemed to think his reputation as a citizen depended on the noise he made."

The theater, a pre-eminent institution in American life, reflected the class, race, ethnic, gender, and patriotic divisions and conflicts of the times. On the floor of the theater were the benches of the pit, where the mass of mechanics and artisans sat. In the tiers of boxes beyond the pit were the most expensive seats, where merchants, professionals, and ladies gathered. The third tier of boxes was generally reserved for less respectable women—boardinghouse keepers and other gainfully employed women. Above these boxes, farthest from the stage, was the gallery (balcony). If the theater permitted blacks, they sat in the gallery, along with prostitutes and those of the working class unable to afford a seat in the pit.

As the American scene changed, so did the theater. As cities and towns grew larger, they boasted more than one or two theaters, and different houses began to cater to different classes. In New York, the Park Theater enjoyed the patronage of the carriage trade, the Bowery drew the middle class, and the Chatham attracted workers. The opera house generally became the upper-class playhouse. Again, the theater mirrored society, for with the increasing pace of urbanization and industrialization, the gap between the sexes and classes yawned wider. It was economic hardship as much as patriotism that sent Edwin Forrest's admirers into the streets of New York in 1849. The theater was the stage for their much larger drama.

Indeed, as the United States grew, its society became at once more diverse and more turbulent. Communities changed as they grew larger everywhere, and, with increased mobility, one year's frontier became the next year's settled town. More and more people lived in cities, where poverty, overcrowding, and crime set them against each other. Opulent mansions existed within sight of notorious slums, and both wealth and poverty reached extremes unknown in traditional agrarian America.

Private space—the family—underwent changes too. With increasing industrialization, the home began to lose its function as a workplace. Especially among the middle and upper classes, it became woman's domain, a refuge from man's world. At the same time, birth control was more widely practiced and families were smaller.

Immigration further increased social diversity.

Chapter 10: TOWARD GREATER DIVERSITY: THE AMERICAN PEOPLE, 1800–1860

Within large cities and in the countryside, whole districts became European enclaves. In hiring themselves out to build transportation and industry, immigrants reshaped American culture in the process.

The position of free blacks and Indians within this society was uncertain. Their very presence disturbed many Americans. Free people of color were second-class citizens at best, struggling to better their lot against overwhelming legal and racial barriers. Eastern Indians, forced to abandon their lands for resettlement beyond the Mississippi River, fared no better.

To a great degree, many Americans were uncomfortable with the new direction of American life. Antipathy toward immigrants was common among native-born Americans, who feared competition for jobs. Blacks fought unceasingly for equality, and Indians tried unsuccessfully to resist forced removal. And some women began to raise their voices against the restrictions they faced. In a society growing ever more diverse and complex, conflict became common.

COUNTRY LIFE, CITY LIFE

Communities, and life within them, changed significantly in the first half of the nineteenth century. Within a generation many frontier settlements became sources rather than recipients of migration. Villages in western New York State lured the sons and daughters of New England in the first two decades of the century. Yet in the 1820s and 1830s, after the best land was settled and tilled and the Erie Canal opened (1825), young people moved from New York villages to the new frontier in the Old Northwest. Later, Ohio and Michigan towns and farms would send their young people further west. Similarly, migrants from the Upper South went to Illinois and Ohio as people on the move further south settled the Gulf states.

Widespread settlement and the development of towns rapidly overtook the frontier so that the isolated pioneers of the 1840s and 1850s—the hunter, the trapper, the homesteader—were more than one thousand miles from where their counterparts had been in the 1800s and 1810s. For all the romance of pioneering, many longed for a sense of community. In the late 1820s Mrs. Trollope visited a farm family living near Cincinnati. The family grew or produced all their necessities except for coffee, tea, and whiskey, which they got by sending butter or chickens to market. But until other settlers came to live near them, they lacked the human contact that a community offered. For their inexpensive land and self-sufficiency they paid the price of isolation and loneliness. " 'Tis strange to us to see company," lamented the mother. "I expect the sun may rise and set a hundred times before I shall see another *human* that does not belong to the family."

Throughout the United States, however, the farm community rather than the isolated family dominated rural America. The farm village was the center of rural life—the farmers' link with religion, politics, and the outside world. But rural social life was not limited to trips to the village; families gathered on each other's farms to do as a community what they could not do individually. Barn-raising was among the activities that regularly brought people together. In preparation for the event, the farmer and an itinerant carpenter built a platform and cut beams, posts, and joists. When the neighbors arrived by buggy and wagon, they put together the sides and raised them into position. After the roof was up, everyone celebrated with a communal meal, and perhaps with singing and dancing. Similar gatherings took place at harvest time and on special occasions.

Farm Communities

Rural women met more formally than did men. Farm men had frequent opportunities to mix at general stores, markets, and taverns. Women had to prearrange their regular work and social gatherings: after-church dinners; sewing, quilting, and corn-husking bees; and preparations for marriages and baptisms. These were times to exchange experiences and thoughts, offer each other support, and swap letters, books, and news.

Irene Hardy, who spent her childhood in rural southwestern Ohio in the 1840s, left a record of the gatherings she attended as a girl. Most vivid in her memory fifty years later were the apple bees, when neighbors gathered to make apple butter or preserves. "Usually invitations were sent about by word of mouth," she recalled. " 'Married folks' came and

Country people looked forward to combining work and play in communal bees. At the annual fall apple bee, depicted above, young and old gathered to socialize, gossip, play, eat, court, and make apple preserves. Library of Congress.

worked all day or afternoon." A dinner feast followed, for which the visiting women made biscuits, vegetables, and coffee. After cleaning up, "the old folks went home to send their young ones for their share of work and fun." The elders gossiped to pass the time; the youngsters joked and teased each other in a comic-serious precourting ritual. "Then came supper, apple and pumpkin pies, cider, doughnuts, cakes, cold chicken and turkey," Hardy wrote, "after which games, 'Forfeits,' 'Building a Bridge,' 'Snatchability,' even 'Blind Man's Buff' and 'Pussy Wants a Corner.' "

Traditional country bees had their town counterparts. Fredrika Bremer, a Swedish visitor to the United States, described a sewing bee in 1849 in Cambridge, Massachusetts, at which neighborhood women made clothes for "a family who had lost all their clothing by fire." Yet these town bees were not the all-day family affairs typical of the countryside, and when the Hardy family moved to the town of Eaton in 1851, young Irene missed the country gatherings. The families of Eaton seldom held bees; they purchased their goods at the store.

Everywhere cities were growing, especially in the North. The transportation revolution and the ex-

pansion of commerce and manufacturing, fed by immigration and internal migration, caused cities to burst their colonial boundaries. Between 1800 and 1860, the number of Americans increased sixfold to 31.4 million. As the population grew, the frontier receded, and rural settlements became towns. In 1800 the nation had only 33 towns with 2,500 or more people and only 3 with more than 25,000. By 1860, 392 towns exceeded 2,500 in population and 35 had more than 25,000.

In the Northeast, the percentage of people living in urban areas grew from 9 to 35 percent from 1800 to 1860. Significantly, most of this growth occurred in northern and western commu-

Growth of Cities

nities located along the new transportation routes, where increased commerce created new jobs and opportunities. Kingston, New York, ninety miles north of New York City on the Hudson River, was one example. The Delaware and Hudson Canal, which extended from the Hudson Valley to the coalfields of Pennsylvania, rapidly transformed Kingston from a sleepy farm village of 1,000 in the 1820s to an urban community of more than 10,000 in 1850.

The hundreds of small new cities like Kingston were surpassed by stars of even greater magnitude: the great metropolitan cities. In 1860 twenty-one cities exceeded 40,000 in population and nine exceeded 100,000 (see maps, page 272). By 1810 New York City had overtaken Philadelphia as the nation's most populous city, and major port and commercial center; its population soared thereafter, reaching 1,174,779 in 1860. Baltimore and New Orleans dominated the South, and San Francisco became the leading West Coast city. In the Midwest the new lake cities (Chicago, Detroit, and Cleveland) began to overtake the frontier river cities (Cincinnati, Louisville, and Pittsburgh) founded a generation earlier. These cities formed a nationwide urban network, linked by canals, roads, and railroads, connecting the great metropolises of the North (see Chapter 9).

Rapid urban growth in turn brought about a radical change in American commerce and trade. In 1800 most merchants performed the functions of retailer, wholesaler, importer and exporter, and banker. But in New York and Philadelphia in the 1790s, and increasingly in all large cities after the War of 1812, the general merchant gave way to the specialist. As a result, the distribution of goods became more systematic. By the 1830s and 1840s, urban centers had been transformed into a pattern we would recognize today: retail shops featured such specialized lines as shoes, wines and spirits, dry goods, and hardware. Within the downtown area importers and exporters, wholesalers, bankers, and insurance brokers clustered on particular streets, near transportation and the merchant exchanges that catered to specialized trades.

Thus Kingston in the 1850s differed from Kingston in the 1820s not just in size and population density but also in the complexity of its institutions. In the small rural village of the 1820s, homes and workplaces were often combined; thirty years later Kingston had separate commercial and residential districts. By 1858 Kingston's downtown boasted china shops, clothing stores, fancy-goods outlets, and dry-goods stores, as well as other retail shops, doctors' and lawyers' offices, and financial firms. Beyond the commercial center, two small industrial zones housed nearly all of the city's manufacturing.

Other city institutions became more complex as well. As the workplace and home grew apart, there were fewer opportunities to turn work into festivals

City Life or family gatherings as rural folk did in barn-raisings and sewing bees. In cities, amusements were more organized than in the country. Entertainment became part of specialized commerce; one purchased a ticket—to the theater, the circus, or P. T. Barnum's American Museum; or in the 1840s, to the racetrack; or a decade later, to the baseball park. The concentration of population in cities supported this diversity of activities.

Though population density and cultural diversity animated city life, they also became problems in themselves. Sporting events became so crowded that one New Yorker doubted whether it was worth battling the mobs of people to attend the racetrack. The "crowd and the dust and the danger and the difficulty of getting on and off the course with a carriage," Philip Hone wrote in 1842, "are scarcely compensated by any pleasure to be derived from the amusement." Everywhere there seemed to be mobs of people. When P. T. Barnum brought Jenny Lind, the famous Swedish soprano, to New York in September 1850, twenty thousand people mobbed the hotel entrance for a glimpse of her.

As cities grew in size, public transportation made it easier to get around. Horse-drawn buses appeared in New York in 1827, and the Harlem Railroad, completed in 1832, ran the length of Manhattan. By the 1850s all big cities had streetcars. And they needed them. Cities grew so fast, they seemed to leap overnight into the countryside. George Templeton Strong, a New York lawyer and devoted diarist, recorded in 1856 that he had attended a party at a Judge Hoffman's "in thirty-seventh!!!—it seems but the other day that thirty-seventh Street was an imaginary line running through a rural district and grazed over by cows."

Strong and other upper-class New Yorkers found the density and diversity of the city repugnant. He especially disliked mixing with the masses on the city railroad. One day in 1852, suffering from a "splitting headache," Strong expressed his disgust at the immigrant population that crowded the city's public transportation. In "the choky, hot railroad car," he gagged on the "stale, sickly odors from sweaty Irishmen in their shirt sleeves." The other people repelled him as well: "German Jew shop-boys in white coats, pink faces, and waistcoats that looked like virulent prickly heat; fat old women, with dirty-nosed babies; one

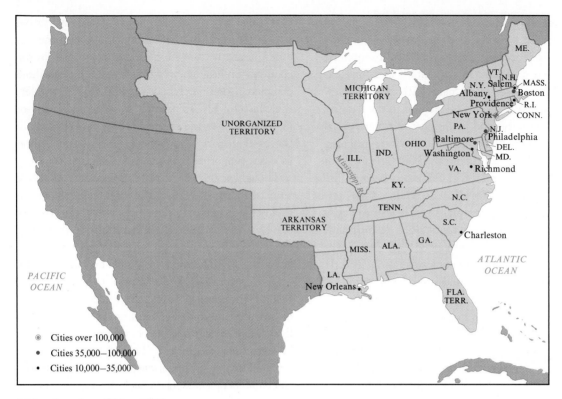

Major American Cities, 1820

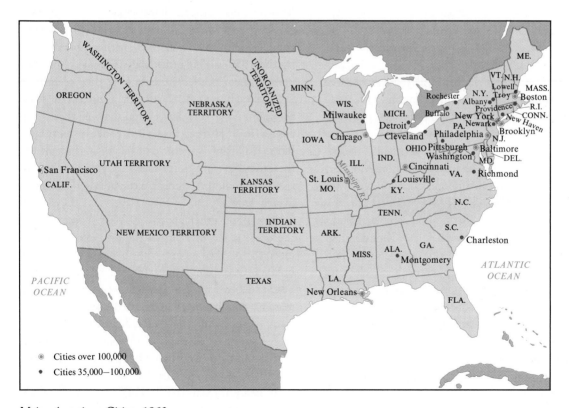

Major American Cities, 1860

Chapter 10: TOWARD GREATER DIVERSITY: THE AMERICAN PEOPLE, 1800–1860

sporting man with black whiskers, miraculously crisp and curly, and a shirt collar insulting stiff, who contributed a reminiscence of tobacco smoke—the spiritual body of ten thousand bad cigars."

Strong's prejudices reflect one man's responses to immigration and city life in the period. Yet, by twentieth-century standards, early-nineteenth-century cities were certainly disorderly, unsafe, and unhealthy. Expansion occurred so suddenly that few cities could handle the problems it brought. For example, migrants from rural areas were used to relieving themselves and throwing refuse in any vacant area. But in the city waste spread disease, created water pollution, and gave off obnoxious odors. New York City solved part of the problem in the 1840s by abandoning wells in favor of reservoir water piped into buildings and outdoor fountains. In some districts scavengers and refuse collectors carted away garbage and human waste, but in much of the city it just lay on the ground until it rotted.

Crime was another problem. To keep order and provide for public safety, Boston supplemented (1837) and New York replaced (1845) their colonial watchmen and constables with paid policemen. Nonetheless, middle-class men and women did not venture out alone at night, and during the day they stayed clear of many city districts. And the influx of immigrants to the cities compounded social tensions by pitting people of different backgrounds against each other in the contest for jobs and housing. Ironically, in the midst of the dirt, the noise, the crime, and the conflict, as if to tempt those who struggled to survive, rose the opulent residences of the very rich.

EXTREMES OF WEALTH

Some observers, notably the young French visitor Alexis de Tocqueville, saw the United States before the Civil War as a place of equality and opportunity. Over a nine-month period in 1831 and 1832, Tocqueville and his companion Gustave de Beaumont traveled four thousand miles and visited all twenty-four states. He later introduced *Democracy in America,* his classic analysis of the American people and nation, with the statement: "No novelty in the United States struck me more vividly during my stay there than the equality of conditions."

Tocqueville believed American equality—the relative fluidity of the social order in the United States—derived from its citizens' geographic mobility. Migration offered people opportunities to start anew regardless of where they came from or who they were. Prior wealth or family mattered little; a person could be known by deeds alone. And indeed, ambition for security and success drove Americans on; sometimes they seemed unable to stop. "An American will build a house in which to pass his old age," Tocqueville wrote, "and sell it before the roof is on; he will plant a garden and rent it just as the trees are coming into bearing; he will clear a field and leave others to reap the harvest; he will take up a profession and leave it, settle in one place and soon go off elsewhere with his changing desires."

Talent and hard work, many Americans believed, found their just reward in such an atmosphere. It was common advice that anyone could advance by working hard and saving money. A local legend from Newburyport, Massachusetts, sounded this popular theme. Tristram Dalton, a Federalist lawyer, wanted his carriage repaired. Moses Brown, an energetic mechanic, refused to wait for Dalton's servants to tow the carriage to his shop; he sought out the vehicle and fixed it on the spot. After Dalton's death his heirs squandered the family fortune, but Brown's industriousness paid off. Through hard work the humble carriage craftsman became one of Massachusetts' richest men. Eventually he bought the Dalton homestead and lived out his life there. The message was clear: "Men succeed or fail . . . not from accident or external surroundings," as the *Newburyport Herald* put it in 1856, but from "possessing or wanting the elements of success in themselves."

But other observers recorded the rise of a new aristocracy based on wealth and power, and growing class and ethnic divisions. Among those who disagreed with the egalitarian view of American life was *New York Sun* publisher Moses Yale Beach, author of twelve editions of *Wealth and Biography of the Wealthy Citizens of New York City.* In 1845 Beach listed a thousand New Yorkers with assets of $100,000

Differences in Wealth

or more. (John Jacob Astor led with a $25-million fortune.) Combining gossip-column tidbits with often erroneous guesses at people's wealth, Beach's book nevertheless suggests the enormous wealth of New York's upper class. Tocqueville himself, ever sensitive to the conflicting trends in American life, had described the growth of an American aristocracy based on industrial wealth. The rich and well educated "come forward to exploit industries," Tocqueville wrote, and become "more and more like the administrators of a huge empire. . . . What is this if not an aristocracy?"

Wealth throughout the United States was becoming concentrated in the hands of a relatively small number of people. In Brooklyn in 1810 two-thirds of the families owned only 10 percent of the wealth; by 1841 their share had decreased to almost nothing. In New York City between 1828 and 1845, the wealthiest 4 percent of the city's population increased their holdings from an estimated 63 percent to 80 percent of all individual wealth. By 1860 the top 5 percent of American families owned more than half the nation's wealth; the top tenth owned over 70 percent.

Inequality, urbanization, and immigration contributed to the renewal of urban conflict as rioting and sporadic incidents of violence became frequent.

Urban Riots The colonial tradition of crowd action, in which disfranchised people took to the streets (see Chapter 4), had diminished in the first three decades of the nineteenth century. In the 1830s riots again became commonplace as professionals and merchants, skilled craftsmen, and ordinary laborers vented their rage against their opponents. "Gentlemen of property and standing," unnerved by the abolitionist attack on American society and traditional leadership, sacked abolitionist newspapers and offices and attacked antislavery advocates throughout the nation. In the 1840s "respectable" citizens waged war against the Mormons, driving them from Illinois and Missouri. Skilled workers raged against new migrants to the cities and other symbols of the new industrial order. In Philadelphia, for instance, native-born workers fought Irish weavers in 1828; whites and blacks rioted on the docks in 1834 and 1835. And in North Philadelphia from 1840 to 1842, residents took to the streets continuously until the construction of a railroad

through their neighborhood was abandoned. These disturbances climaxed in the great riots of 1844, in which mostly Protestant skilled workers fought Irish Catholics. In the 1850s nativist riots peaked. By 1840 more than 125 people had died in urban riots, and by 1860 more than 1,000.

A cloud of uncertainty hung over working men and women. Many were afraid that in periods of economic depression they would become part of the urban flotsam and jetsam of able-bodied men and women, white and black, who could not find steady work. They feared the competition of immigrant and slave labor. They feared the insecurities and indignities of poverty, chronic illness, disability, old age, widowhood, and desertion. And they had good reason.

Indeed, poverty and squalor stalked the urban working class as cities grew. Cities were notorious for the dilapidated districts where newly arrived immigrants, indigent blacks, working **Urban Slums** poor and thieves, beggars, and prostitutes lived. Five Points in New York City's Sixth Ward became the worst slum in pre–Civil War America. Dominated by the Old Brewery, which in 1837 had been converted to housing for hundreds of adults and children, the neighborhood was equally divided between Irish and blacks. Ill-suited to human habitation and lacking such amenities as running water and sewers, it exemplified the worst of urban life.

In New York and other large cities lived "street rats," children and young men who earned their living off the streets by bootblacking or petty thievery. They slept on boats, in haylofts, or in warehouses. Charles Loring Brace, a founder of the Children's Aid Society (1853), described the street rats in his *Dangerous Classes of New York* (1872): "Like the rats, they were too quick and cunning to be often caught in their petty plunderings, so they gnawed away at the foundations of society undisturbed." To Brace and others, such rootless persons threatened American society. They represented a threat far different from Shay's Rebellion, Burr's conspiracies, or the Hartford Convention. "They will vote—they will have the same rights as we ourselves," warned the first report of the Children's Aid Society in 1854, "though they have grown up ignorant of moral principle, as any savage or Indian." Moreover, "they will perhaps be embittered at the wealth and luxuries they never

The infamous Five Points section of New York City's Sixth Ward, probably the worst slum in pre-Civil War America. Immodestly dressed prostitutes cruise the streets or gaze from windows, while a pig roots for garbage in their midst. Courtesy of the New-York Historical Society.

share. Then let society beware, when the vicious, reckless multitude of New York boys, swarming now in every foul alley and low street, come to know their power and *use it!*"

A world apart from Five Points and the people of the streets was the upper-class elite society of Philip Hone, one-time mayor of New York. Hone's diary, meticulously kept from 1826 until his death in 1851, records the activities of an American aristocrat.

Urban Elite

On February 28, 1840, for instance, Hone attended a masked ball at the Fifth Avenue mansion of Henry Breevoort, Jr., and Laura Carson Breevoort. The ball began at the fashionable hour of 10 P.M., and the five hundred ladies and gentlemen who filled the mansion wore costumes adorned with ermine and gold. For more than a week, Hone believed, the affair "occupied the minds of the people of all stations, ranks, and employments." Few balls attained such grandeur, but at one time or another similar parties were held in Boston, Philadelphia, Baltimore, and Charleston.

At a less rarefied level, Hone's social calendar was filled with elegant dinner parties featuring fine cuisine and imported wines. The New York elite who filled the pages of Hone's diary—the 1 percent of the population who owned 50 percent of the city's wealth—lived in large townhouses and mansions, attended by a corps of servants. They comprised the "carriage trade" for whom Broadway merchants filled their shop windows with luxuries from around the world. In the summer, country estates, ocean resorts, mineral spas, and grand tours of Europe offered them relief from the winter and spring social seasons.

A world apart from the slums was the upper-class society. This lithograph depicts Boston's elite dancing the quadrille at a fashionable Tremont House ball around 1840. The American Antiquarian Society.

The basis of this new wealth tended to be inherited. For every John Jacob Astor who made his millions in the western fur trade, or George Law who left a farm to become a millionaire contractor and investor in railroads and banks, there were ten who built additional wealth on money they inherited or married. Andrew H. Mickle, a poor Irish immigrant, became a millionaire and mayor of New York City, but his fortune came from marrying the daughter of his employer. Many of the wealthiest bore the names of the colonial commercial elite—Beekman, Breevoort, Roosevelt, Van Rensselaer, and Whitney. Yet these men were not an idle class; they devoted energy to increasing their fortunes and power. Urban capitalists like Philip Hone profited enormously from the transportation, commercial, and manufacturing revolutions; hardly a major canal, railroad, bank, or mill venture lacked the names and investments of the fashionable elite. Wealth begat wealth, and family ties through inheritance and marriage were essential in that world.

More modest in wealth though hard working were those in the expanding middle class. The growth and specialization of trade had rapidly increased their numbers, and they were a distinct part of the urban scene. The men were businessmen or professionals, the women homemakers. They were the backbone of the rich associational life that Tocqueville had discovered in America. They filled the family pews in church on Sundays; their children pursued whatever educational opportunities were available. Often they dreamed of Philip Hone's world while mindful that the gulf between them and manual workers was narrow.

WOMEN AND THE FAMILY

E conomic change transformed women and families too, and made them more diverse. What had been fairly similar backgrounds of native-born white women began to splinter and to show differences by class, life cycle, and place of residence. Families too varied greatly, and change affected them at different rates and in varying ways.

Increasingly, women's and men's work grew apart, as men left their homes to "go to work." On farms, there was still an overlap, but in the new shops, offices, and factories, tasks diverged. Specialization in business and production accompanied specialization in work tasks; men acquired new, narrower skills which were applied in set ways with purposefully designed tools and systems. Authority within the work environment, removed from the household, became more formal and impersonal.

Some women shared these experiences for brief periods in their lives. New England farm daughters who were the first textile-mill workers left home to perform new, specialized work tasks. In the 1840s the new urban department stores hired young women as clerks and cash runners. Others worked in the expanding needle trades. Paid employment represented merely a stage in their life cycle, a brief period between their parental and marital households.

Working Women

Working-class women—the poor, widows, free blacks—worked for wages most of their lives. Leaving their parental homes as early as twelve or thirteen, they earned wages most of their lives, with only short respites for bearing children and rearing infants. Unlike men, however, most of these women did not work in the new shops and factories. Instead they sold their domestic skills for wages outside of their own households. Unmarried girls and women worked as domestic servants in other women's homes; married and widowed women worked as laundresses, seamstresses, cooks, and boardinghouse keepers.

Increasingly work took on greater gender meaning and segregation. Most women's work centered, as it always had, on the home. As the family lost its importance in the production of goods, household upkeep and childrearing continued to magnify in importance, requiring women's full-time attention. Education, religion, morality, domestic arts, and culture began to overshadow the productive functions of the family. These roles became associated for many with ideal female characteristics, what has come to be called woman's sphere or the cult of domesticity of the nineteenth century.

Many American women and men placed great im-

A watercolor-and-ink portrait of a scrubwoman, made in 1807. Domestic work was still the most common job held by women working outside the home in the early nineteenth century.   The New-York Historical Society.

portance on the family. The role of the mother in the early republic was to ensure the nation's future by rearing her children and providing her husband with a spiritual and virtuous environment. The family was to be a moral institution where selflessness and cooperation ruled. Thus women were idealized as the embodiment of self-sacrificing republicanism. This contrasted with the world outside the home, one increasingly identified with men. The world of work— the market economy—was seen as one of conflict, dominated by base self-interest. Amidst a rapidly changing world in which single men and women left their parental homes and villages, in which factories and stores replaced traditional production and distribution, the family was supposed to be a rock of stability and traditional values.

The domestic ideal limited the paying jobs middle-class women could hold outside of the home. Most paid work was viewed with disapproval since it conflicted with the ideal of domesticity. One occupation did come to be recognized as consistent with the genteel female nature: teaching. In 1823 Catharine

While sensitive to the changing life cycles of women, the above lithograph emphasizes the domestic ideal to which most women aspired. But in depicting the roles of daughter, wife, and mother, it neglects woman's paid employment. Library of Congress.

Beecher established a female academy with her sister Mary. Their Hartford Female Seminary added philosophy, history, and science to the traditional women's curriculum of domestic arts and religious education. In the 1830s Catharine Beecher campaigned to establish schools for girls and training seminaries for female teachers. Viewing formal education as an extension of women's nurturing role, Beecher had great success in spreading her message. By the 1850s schoolteaching became a major woman's vocation, with women teachers in the majority in most large cities. The employment of female teachers served to enlarge the work opportunities open to educated women. Not only did many consider education an appropriate nurturing role for women, but men shunned it because of the low pay. Even then, women were often hired at half the wages paid to male teachers. For society, it was a bargain that worked as long as talented, educated women had relatively limited opportunities to use their education in other occupations.

While woman's work outside the home remained limited, family size was shrinking. In 1800 an American woman bore, on the average, six children; in 1860 she would bear five, and by 1900 four. This decline occurred even **Decline in the** while many immigrants with large-**Birth Rate** family traditions were settling in the United States; thus the birth rate for native-born women declined even more sharply. Although rural families were larger than urban ones, birth rates in both areas declined to the same degree.

A number of factors reduced family size. Increasingly, small families were viewed as desirable. Children would have greater opportunities in smaller families; parents could pay more attention to them and would be better able to educate them and help them financially. Also, contemporary marriage manuals stressed the harmful effects of too many births on a woman's health; too many children weakened women physically and overworked them as mothers.

All this evidence suggests that wives and husbands made deliberate decisions to limit the size of families. In those areas where farm land was relatively expensive, families were smaller than in other agricultural districts. It appears that parents who foresaw difficulty setting up their children as independent farmers chose to have fewer children. Similarly, in urban areas children were more an economic burden than an asset. As the family lost its role as a producer of goods, the length of time during which children were only consumers grew, as did the economic costs to parents.

How did men and women limit their families in the early nineteenth century? Many married later, thus shortening the period of childbearing. And women had their last child at a younger

Birth Control age, dropping from around forty in the mid-eighteenth century to around thirty-five in the mid-nineteenth century. More important, however, was the widespread use of birth control. The popular marriage guide by the physician Charles Knowlton, *Fruits of Philosophy; or, the Private Companion of Young Married People* (1832), provides us with a glimpse of contemporary birth control methods. Probably the most widespread practice was *coitus interruptus,* or withdrawal of the male before completion of the sexual act. But medical devices were beginning to compete with this ancient folk practice. Although animal-skin condoms imported from France were too expensive for popular use, cheap rubber condoms were widely adopted when they became available in the 1850s. Some couples used the rhythm method—attempting to confine intercourse to a woman's infertile periods. Knowledge of the "safe period," however, was uncertain even among physicians. Another method was abstinence, or less frequent sexual intercourse.

If all else failed, abortion was widely available, especially after 1830. Ineffective folk remedies for self-induced abortion had been around for centuries, but in the 1830s surgical abortions became common. Abortionists advertised their services in large cities, and middle-class and elite women asked their doctors to perform abortions. One sign of the upswing in abortions was the increase in legislation against it. Between 1821 and 1841, ten states and one territory prohibited abortions; by 1860, twenty states had outlawed it. Only three of those twenty punished the mother, however, and the laws were rarely enforced.

Significantly, the birth-control methods women themselves controlled—douching, the rhythm method, abstinence, and abortion—were the ones that were increasing in popularity. For the new emphasis on women's domesticity encouraged women's autonomy in the home and gave them greater control over their own bodies. According to the cult of domesticity, the refinement and purity of women ruled the household, including the bedroom; as one woman put it, "woman's duty was to subdue male passions, not to kindle them."

In turn, smaller families and fewer births changed the position and living conditions of women. At one time birth and infant care had occupied the entire span of women's adult lives, and few mothers had lived to see their youngest child reach maturity. But after the 1830s many women had time for other activities. Smaller families also allowed women to devote more time to their older children, and slowly childhood came to be perceived as a distinct part of the life span. The beginnings of public education in the 1830s (see page 331) and the policy of grouping school children by age tended to reinforce this trend.

Sarah Ripley of Massachusetts, an eighteenth-century young girl and a nineteenth-century adult, revealed in her diaries the changes American society

Sarah Ripley Stearns was experiencing. Daughter of a Greenfield shopkeeper, her childhood was a privileged one both at home and boarding school. After completing school she returned home to work as a shop assistant in her father's store. In 1812, after a five-year courtship, she married Charles Stearns of Shelburn. "I have now acquitted the abode of my youth, left the protection of my parents and given up the name I have always borne," she recorded in her diary. "May the grace of God enable me to fulfill with prudence and piety the great and important duties which now evolve on me." Yet she missed the bustle of the shop, as she confessed in her diary.

Sarah Ripley Stearns's life was not a settled one; change was everywhere. Motherhood occupied her, as she bore three children within four years. Her brother moved west; after marriage she left her parents' home and village; she moved with her family three times during her marriage; and in 1818 she became a widow. Amidst all, Sarah Ripley Stearns found religion an anchor. When a revival visited her village in the 1810s, Stearns declared her faith. Rather than leading to introspection, religion promoted social interaction. With her neighbors she formed a "little band of associated females" and sponsored a school society and juvenile home.

Revival and reform had come early to Sarah Ripley Stearns in northwestern Massachusetts, but it was an experience many other women shared during this period. The ideal of domesticity, however, did not confine these middle-class women to their homes. Visits and meetings in parlors and churches led women into a public sphere that was an extension of their domestic concerns. Stearns's benevolent society work not only aided poor children but also provided its female participants with experience and opportunities in organizing, chairing meetings, raising funds, and cultivating an extended network of other women. Thus religion and charity stimulated new directions for women's roles (see pages 325–327).

At the same time, working women were pioneering new roles for women beyond the home. Many found teaching a rewarding profession and preferred it to marriage and domesticity. Mill girls forged new roles for women, as did the women who assembled at Seneca Falls, New York, in 1848. Modeling their protest on the Declaration of Independence, they called for political, social, and economic equality for women (see page 332). Free black women, however, had little choice between paid employment and maintaining households and rearing children. Their different tasks had to be accomplished simultaneously. Immigrant women, too, often had to combine many roles at the same time and, like black women, they found that gender and class were but part of the burdens they carried; ethnic and religious differences created a separate set of problems.

IMMIGRANT LIVES IN AMERICA

No less than gender, ethnic and religious differences divided Americans. In numbers alone immigrants drastically altered the United States. The 5 million immigrants who settled in the states between 1820 and 1860 outnumbered the entire population of the country at the first census in 1790. They came from all continents, though Europeans made up the vast majority. The peak period of pre–Civil War immigration was from 1847 through 1857; in that eleven-year period, 3.3 million immigrants entered the United States, 1.3 million from Ireland and 1.1 million from the German states. By 1860, 15 percent of the white population was foreign-born.

This massive migration had been set in motion decades earlier. In Europe around the turn of the nineteenth century, the Napoleonic wars had begun one of the greatest population shifts in history, which was to last more than a century. One part of the movement, increasingly significant as time went on, was emigration of Europeans to the United States. War, revolution, famine, industrialization, and religious persecution oppressed weary Europeans. Meanwhile, the United States beckoned. Millions of unplowed acres there awaited Europeans, offering them economic opportunity and religious freedom.

European Immigration

Large construction projects and mines needed strong young laborers. Textile mills and city homes recruited young women workers. Europeans' awareness of the United States heightened as employers, states, and shipping companies advertised the opportunities to be found across the Atlantic. Often the message was stark: work and prosper in America or starve in Europe. With regularly scheduled sailing ships commuting across the ocean, the cost of transatlantic travel was within easy reach of millions of Europeans.

So they came, enduring the hardships of travel and of settling in a strange land. The journey was difficult. The average crossing took six weeks; in bad weather it could take three months. Disease spread unchecked among people huddled together like cattle

In 1855, New York State established Castle Garden, in the background above, as an immigrant center. There at the tip of Manhattan Island, many immigrants first touched American soil. The painting depicts immigrants ending their long sea voyage from Ireland. Museum of the City of New York.

in steerage. More than 17,000 immigrants, mostly Irish, died from "ship fever" in 1847. On disembarking, immigrants became fair game for the con artists and swindlers who worked the docks. Agents greeted them and tried to lure them from their chosen destinations. In 1855, in response to the immigrants' plight, New York State's commissioners of emigration established Castle Garden as an immigrant center. There, at the tip of Manhattan Island, the major port of entry, immigrants were somewhat sheltered from fraud. Authorized transportation companies maintained offices in the large rotunda and assisted immigrants with their travel plans.

Most immigrants gravitated toward the cities, since only a minority had farming experience or the means to purchase land and equipment. Many stayed in New York itself. By 1845, 35 percent of the city's 371,000 people were of foreign birth. Ten years later 52 percent of its 623,000 inhabitants were immigrants, 28 percent from Ireland and 16 percent from Germany. In the Sixth Ward, home of Five Points, no fewer than 70 percent of the residents were immigrants. Boston, an important entry point for the Irish, took on a European tone. Throughout the 1850s the city was about 35 percent foreign-born, of whom more than two-thirds were Irish. In the South, too, major cities had large immigrant populations. In 1860 New Orleans was 44 percent foreign-born, Savannah 33 percent, and the border city of St. Louis, 61 percent. On the West Coast, San Francisco had a foreign-born majority.

Some immigrants, however, did settle in rural areas. In particular, German, Dutch, and Scandinavian farmers gravitated toward the Midwest. Greater percentages of Scandinavians and Netherlanders took up farming than other nationalities; both groups came mostly as religious dissenters and migrated in family units. The Dutch who founded the American Holland in Michigan and Wisconsin, for instance, had seceded from the official Reformed Church of the Netherlands. Under such leaders as Albertus C. Van Raalte, they fled persecution in their native land to establish new and more pious communities—Holland and Zeeland, Michigan, among them.

Success in America bred further emigration. "I wish, and do often say that we wish you were all in this happy land," wrote shoemaker John West of Germantown, Pennsylvania, to his **Promotion of** kin in Corsley, England, in 1831. **Immigration** "A man nor woman need not stay out of employment one hour here," he advised. John Down, a weaver from Frome, England, settled in New York City without his family. Writing to his wife in August 1830, he described the bountiful meal he had shared with a farmer's family: "They had on the table puddings, pyes, and fruit of all kind that was in season, and preserves, pickles, vegetables, meats, and everything that a person would wish, and the servants [farm hands] set down at the same table with their masters." Though Down missed his family dearly, he wrote, "I do not repent of coming, for you know that there was nothing but poverty before me, and to see you and the dear children want was what I could not bear. *I would rather cross the Atlantic ten times than hear my children cry for victuals once.*" To those skeptics who claimed the United States was filling up, he advised, "There is plenty of room yet, and will be for a thousand years to come." These letters and others were widely circulated in Europe to advertise the success of pauper immigrants in America.

American institutions, both public and private, actively recruited European emigrants. Western states lured potential settlers in the interest of promoting their economies. In the 1850s, for instance, Wisconsin appointed a commissioner of emigration, who ad-

vertised the state's advantages in American and European newspapers. Wisconsin also opened a New York office and hired European agents to compete with other states and with firms like the Illinois Central Railroad for immigrants' attention.

Before the potato blight hit Ireland, tens of thousands of Irish were lured to America by recruiters. They came to swing picks and shovels on American canals and railroads, to dig the foundations of mills and factories. The popular folksong "Working on the Railroad" records their story:

Oh in eighteen hundred and forty-three
I sailed away across the sea,
I sailed away across the sea,
To work upon the railway, the railway.
I'm weary of the railway;
Oh poor Paddy works on the railway!

. . .

Oh in eighteen hundred and forty-six
I changed my trade to carrying bricks,
I changed my trade to carrying bricks,
From working on the railway, the railway . . .

Oh in eighteen hundred and forty-seven
Poor Paddy was thinking of going to Heaven,
Poor Paddy was thinking of going to Heaven,
After working on the railway, the railway,
He was weary of the railway;
Oh poor Paddy worked on the railway!

But as other verses reveal, not all the Irish immigrants were successful; tens of thousands of them returned to their homeland. Among them was Michael Gaugin, who had the misfortune to **Immigrant** arrive in New York City during the **Disenchant-** financial panic of 1837. Gaugin, for **ment** thirteen years an assistant engineer in the construction of a Dublin canal, had been attracted to the United States by the promise that "he should soon become a wealthy man." The Dublin agent for a New York firm convinced Gaugin to quit his job, which included a house and an acre of ground, in order to emigrate to the United States. Within two months of arriving in the United States, Gaugin had become a pauper. In August 1837 he declared he was "now without means for the support of himself and his family, and has no employment, and has already suffered great deprivation since he arrived in this country; and is now soliciting means to enable him to return with his family home to Ireland." Many of those who had come with the Gaugins had already returned home.

Such experiences did not deter Irish men and women from coming to the United States. Ireland was the most densely populated European country, and among the most impoverished. From 1815 on, small harvests prompted a steady stream of Irish to emigrate to America. Then in 1845 and 1846 potatoes—the basic Irish food—rotted in the fields. From 1845 to 1849, death in the form of starvation, malnutrition, and typhus spread. In all, 1 million died and about 1.5 million fled, two-thirds of them to the United States. People became Ireland's major export.

Irish Immigrants

In the 1840s and 1850s a total of 1.7 million Irish men and women entered the United States. At the peak of Irish immigration, from 1847 to 1854, 1.2 million came. By the end of the century there would be more Irish in the United States than in Ireland.

The new Irish immigrants differed greatly from those who had left Ireland to settle in the American colonies. In the eighteenth century, the Scotch-Irish predominated (see pages 74–75), and their journey had involved moving from one part of the British Empire to another. The nineteenth-century Roman Catholic Irish travelers to America, however, moved from still-colonial Ireland to an independent republic, and the political and religious differences made their cultural adaptation that much more difficult. In comparison with the Scotch-Irish, the newer immigrants from Ireland tended to be younger, increasingly female, and mostly from the rural provinces. With eldest sons heirs to the family farms and with eldest daughters staying home to care for parents, the younger children who came alone to the United States were expendable in Ireland's declining economy. Farmers' daughters could find work only as domestic servants, and poverty-stricken Ireland could not absorb all of them. In American cities they found work in factories and households. If they married, they would marry late, as did their sisters in Ireland. They helped support their families still at home and built Catholic churches and organizations in United States cities.

In the urban areas where they clustered in poverty, most Irish immigrants met growing anti-immigrant,

Anti-Catholicism

anti-Catholic sentiment. Everywhere "No Irish Need Apply" signs appeared. During the colonial period, white Protestant settlers had feared "popery" as a system of tyranny and had discriminated against the few Catholics in America. Following the Revolution, anti-Catholicism receded. But in the 1830s the trend reversed, and anti-Catholicism appeared wherever the Irish did. Attacks on the papacy and the church circulated widely in the form of libelous texts like *The Awful Disclosures of Maria Monk* (1836), which alleged sexual orgies among priests and nuns. Nowhere was anti-Catholicism more open and nasty than in Boston, though such sentiments were widespread. Anti-Catholic riots were almost commonplace. In Charlestown, Massachusetts, a mob burned a convent (1834); a Philadelphia crowd attacked priests and nuns and vandalized churches (1844); and in Lawrence, Massachusetts, a mob leveled the Irish neighborhood (1854).

The native-born who embraced anti-Catholicism were motivated largely by anxiety. They feared that a militant Roman church would subvert American society, that unskilled Irish workers would displace American craftsmen, and that the slums inhabited in part by the Irish were undermining the nation's values. Every American problem from immorality and the evils of alcohol to poverty and economic upheaval was blamed on immigrant Irish Catholics. Impoverished workers complained to the Massachusetts legislature that the Irish displaced "the honest and respectable laborers of the State . . . and from their manner of living . . . work for much less per day . . . being satisfied with food to support the animal existence alone." American workers, on the other hand, "not only labor for the body but for the mind, the soul, and the State." Friction increased as Irish-American men fought back against anti-Irish and anti-Catholic prejudice; in the 1850s they began to vote and to become active in politics.

Though potato blight also sent many Germans to the United States in the 1840s, other hardships contributed to the steady stream of German immigrants.

German Immigrants

Many came from areas where small landholdings made it hard to eke out a living and to pass on land to their sons. Others were craftsmen displaced by the industrial revolution. These refugees were joined by middle-class Germans who had sought to unify the three dozen or so German states in a liberal republic. Frustration with abortive revolutions like one that occurred in 1848 led them to emigrate to the United States. For some, the only other choice was jail.

Unlike the Irish, who tended to congregate in towns and cities, Germans settled everywhere. Many came on German cotton boats, disembarked at New Orleans, and traveled up the Mississippi. In the South they became peddlers and merchants; in the North and West they worked as farmers, urban laborers, and businessmen. Also unlike the Irish, they tended to migrate in families. A strong desire to maintain the German language and culture prompted them to colonize areas as a group.

German immigrants transplanted their Old World institutions in the New World, creating New Germanies in rural areas and transforming the tone and culture of established cities like Cincinnati and Milwaukee. *Turnvereine*—German physical-culture clubs—sprouted in villages and cities; by 1853 sixty such societies were hosting exercise groups and German-language lectures.

In adhering to German traditions, German-Americans too met with antiforeign attitudes. More than half the German immigrants were Catholic, and their Sabbath practices were different from the Protestants'. On Sundays German families typically gathered at beer gardens to eat and drink beer, to dance, sing, and listen to band music, and sometimes to play cards. Protestants were outraged by such violations of the Lord's day. In Chicago riots broke out when Protestants enforced the Sunday prohibition laws.

Their persistence in using the German language and their different religious beliefs set them apart. Besides the Catholic majority, a significant number of German immigrants were Jewish. And even the Protestants—mostly Lutherans—founded their own churches and often educated their children in German-language schools. Not all Germans, however, were religious. The failure of the revolution of 1848 had sent to the United States a whole generation of liberals and freethinkers, some of whom were socialists, communists, and anarchists. The freethinkers entered politics with a loud voice, embracing abolitionism and the Republican party.

The conflict between the immigrants and the society they joined paralleled the inner tensions most immigrants experienced. On the one hand they felt impelled to commit themselves wholeheartedly to their new country, to learn the language and adapt themselves to American ways. On the other hand they were rooted in their own cultural traditions—the comfortable, tested customs of the country of their birth, the familiar ways and words that came intuitively and required no education.

For immigrants, conflict centered around their desire to be part of American society, albeit for some on their own terms. Once here, they claimed their right to a fair economic and political share. Indians, on the other hand, had to defend what they conceived of as prior rights. Their land, their religion, their way of life came under constant attack as they were most often viewed as an obstacle to expansion and economic growth.

INDIAN RESISTANCE AND REMOVAL

The clash between Indians and the larger society had been inherited from the colonial past. Population growth, westward expansion, the transportation revolution, and invigorated capitalism underlay the designs and demands on Indian land. At best Indians could hope for mutual understanding, but when that rare event occurred, it was only on a personal level. Whatever good intentions motivated the leaders of the republic, they were subordinated to the desire for Indian land. Indian resistance proved incapable of protecting either their land or their traditional culture, and the great Indian nations were removed to lands west of the Mississippi.

As the colonial powers in North America had done, the United States treated Indian tribes as sovereign nations until Congress ended the practice in 1871. In its relations with tribal leaders, the government followed the ritual of international protocol. Indian chiefs and delegations who visited Washington were received with the appropriate pomp and ceremony. Leaders exchanged presents as tokens of

The Shawnee Chiefs Prophet (left) and Tecumseh (right). The two brothers led a revival of traditional Shawnee culture and preached Indian federation against white encroachment. In the War of 1812, they allied themselves with the British, but Tecumseh's death at the Battle of Thames (1813) and British indifference thereafter caused Indian resistance and unity to collapse. Prophet: National Museum of American Art; Tecumseh: Field Museum of Natural History, Chicago.

friendship, and commemorative flags and silver medals with presidents' likenesses became prized possessions among Indian chiefs. Agreements between a tribe and the United States were signed, sealed, and ratified as was any international pact.

In practice, however, Indian sovereignty was a fiction. Though protocol seemed to acknowledge independence and mutual respect, treaty negotiations exposed the fiction. Essentially, treaty-making was a process used to acquire Indian land. Differences in power made it less than the bargaining of two equal nations. Treaties were often made between victors and vanquished. In a context of coercion, old treaties often gave way to new ones in which the Indians ceded their traditional holdings in return for different lands in the West. Beginning with President Jefferson,

the government withheld payments due to tribes for previous land cessions to pressure them to sign new treaties.

The War of 1812 snuffed out whatever realistic hopes Indian leaders might have had of resisting American expansion by warfare. Armed resistance persisted, and it was bloody on both sides, as in the Seminole Wars, but only the revived idea of pan-Indian federation offered any hope to counter the military might of the United States. The Shawnee chiefs Prophet and Tecumseh attempted to build such a movement, taking advantage of Anglo-American friction in the decade before the War of 1812, but in the end it failed. And with it died the most significant resistance to the federal government's treaty-making tactics.

Prophet's early experiences mirror the fate that befell many frontier tribes. Born in 1775, a few months after his father had died in battle, Prophet was afterward abandoned by his mother, who rejoined her native tribe further west. He was raised by his sister and called Lalawethika (noisemaker) as a young man. He was among the defeated Shawnee at the Battle of Fallen Timbers and among the Indians expelled under the 1795 Treaty of Greenville (see page 171). He joined a small band of his tribe in Ohio, then moved with them to Indiana. Within the shrunken territory granted to them under the treaty, game became scarce and Lalawethika found it difficult to feed his family. Encroachment by whites and the periodic ravages of disease brought further misery to Indian villages and tribes; economic and social instability went hand in hand. Like other Indians, Lalawethika turned to whiskey. He was befriended by a local shaman, who shared his traditional folk knowledge of medicine and Indian lore. When the medicine man died in 1804, he was succeeded by his young disciple. But Lalawethika was a failure; his medicine could not stop the white man's viral illnesses from ravaging his village.

Prophet

Lalawethika emerged from his own battle with illness in 1805 as a new man, called Prophet. Claiming to have died and been resurrected, he told a visionary tale of this experience and warned of damnation for those who drank whiskey. In the following years, Prophet traveled widely in the Northwest as a holy man, attacking the decline of moral values among Indians, condemning intertribal battles, and stressing harmony and respect for elders. In essence he preached the revitalization of traditional Shawnee culture. Return to the old ways, he told the Indians of the Old Northwest, abandon white customs. Hunt with bows and arrows, he said, not guns; release domestic animals and discard the wearing of hats; refrain from eating bread and cultivate corn and beans.

Prophet's message was a reassuring one to the Shawnee, Potawatomi, and other Indians of the Old Northwest who felt unsettled and threatened by whites. Prophet won converts by performing miracles—he darkened the sun by coinciding this act with an eclipse—and used opposition to federal Indian policy to draw others into his camp.

The government and white settlers were alarmed by the religious revival led by Prophet. With his brother, Tecumseh, who was seven years older, he refused to leave lands claimed by the government. In 1808 Prophet and his brother began to turn from a message of spiritual renewal to one of resistance to white aggression. In repudiating land sales to the government under the Treaty of Fort Wayne (1809), Tecumseh told Indiana's Governor William Henry Harrison at Vincennes in 1810 that "the only way to check and stop this evil is, for all the red men to unite in claiming a common and equal right in the land, as it was at first, and should be yet; for it never was divided, but belongs to all, for the use of each. . . . No part has a right to sell, even to each other, much less to strangers."

Tecumseh

At that point Tecumseh, the towering six-foot warrior and magnetic orator, replaced Prophet as Shawnee leader. Prophet's medicine could not stop white encroachment, so the young warriors looked to Tecumseh for political leadership. Convinced that only a federation of tribes could stop the advance of white settlement, Tecumseh sought to unify northern and southern Indians. He warned Harrison that the Indians would resist white occupation of the 2.5 million acres on the Wabash that they had ceded in the Treaty of Fort Wayne.

A year later, using a Potawatomi raid on an Illinois settlement as an excuse, Harrison attacked and demolished Prophet's Town, Tecumseh's headquarters on Tippecanoe Creek in Indiana Territory. Losses on both sides were heavy. Indian warriors throughout the Midwest came to Tecumseh's side; Harrison appealed for help to President Madison. When the War of 1812 started, Tecumseh joined the British in return for a promise of an Indian country in the Great Lakes region. But he was killed in the Battle of the Thames in October 1813, and with his death Indian unity collapsed (see pages 224 and 226).

After Tecumseh's death, Prophet attempted to rally the remnants of the movement, but he lacked the political and military skills of his brother. Prophet remained under British protection in Canada after the War of 1812 even though most of his followers returned to the United States. Finally he came back to the United States in 1825 and worked for the emigration of the remaining Shawnee to Indian territory in Kansas. He made the trip west, but it was a bitter and miserable one since the promised government assistance never came. Prophet died in Kansas in 1836, all but forgotten.

By 1820 Indians in Ohio, southern Indiana and Illinois, southwestern Michigan, most of Missouri, central Alabama, and southern Mississippi had been

Indian Policy forced to cede their lands. They had given up nearly 200 million acres for pennies an acre. But white settlers' appetites were insatiable; the expansion of commercial farming in the Midwest and of cotton plantations in the South increased demands for Indian land and for Indians to assimilate. One instrument that served both purposes was the Indian agency system, which monopolized trade with Indians in a designated locality and paid out the rations, supplies, and annuities that Indians received in exchange for abandoning their land. The tribes became dependent on these government payments—a dependency intended to make them more docile in treaty negotiations.

At the same time, reformers sought to assimilate Indians into American society by educating and Christianizing them. Motivated by a sincere concern for Indians and influenced by the Second Great Awakening, female missionary and benevolent societies assisted in founding four Christian schools for Indians by 1819. In that year, under missionary lobbying, Congress appropriated $10,000 annually for the "civilization of the tribes adjoining the frontier settlements." This "civilization act" was a means to teach Indians to live like white settlers. Within five years thirty-two schools appeared, scattered throughout the country, and government financial support rose. The new boarding schools, unlike the earlier ones, substituted English for native Indian languages and taught agricultural techniques in addition to the Gospel.

To settlers eyeing Indian land, assimilation through education was too slow a process, and Indians themselves questioned the instruction. There were never more than one thousand students at any one time in all the schools; at that rate it would take centuries to assimilate all Indians. And after 1826, when Congress reduced its annual appropriations to $10,000, missionary societies failed to make up the deficit. Some Indian tribes found the missionary message repugnant. The Creek nation permitted the schools

only after being assured that there would be no preaching. Zealous missionaries violated the agreement, preaching to the Creek and their black slaves. With no other recourse available, a band of Creek sacked the school. Similarly, the Passamaquoddy tribe of New England, many of whom were Catholics, opposed teachers' efforts to make them Episcopalians. Even the vocational aspects seemed unpromising; graduates who returned to their tribal villages had no way of applying the commercial agricultural skills acquired in the schools.

It became apparent in the 1820s that neither economic dependency nor education could force Indians voluntarily to cede much more land to meet the demands of expansionists. Attention focused on the Cherokee, Creek, Choctaw, Chickasaw, and Seminole tribes in the South because much of their land remained intact after the War of 1812 and because they aggressively resisted white encroachment. They had more formal political institutions than the northern Indians and thus were better organized to resist.

In his last annual message in December 1824, President James Monroe suggested to Congress that all Indians settle beyond the Mississippi River. Secretary of War John C. Calhoun

Indian Removal agreed, and three days later the president sent a special message to Congress advocating removal. Stressing the positive aspects, Monroe believed his proposal an "honorable" one that would protect Indians from invasion, and provide them with independence for "improvement and civilization." Monroe felt that force would be unnecessary; the promise of a home free from white encroachment would be sufficient to win Indian acceptance.

The southern tribes unanimously rejected Monroe's offer. The Cherokee, Creek, Choctaw, and Chickasaw tribes to whom the program was directed wanted to be left alone. Between 1789 and 1825 they had negotiated a total of thirty individual treaties with the United States; they had reached their limits. They wished to remain on what was left of their ancestral land.

Pressure from Georgia had prompted Monroe's policy. Most Cherokee and some Creek lived in northwestern Georgia, and in the 1820s the state accused the federal government of not fulfilling its 1802 promise to remove the Indians in return for the state's re-

The French genre painter Alfred Boisseau recorded the passage of the Choctaw through Louisiana from Mississippi to Indian Territory. With dignity they made the forced march. Isaac Delgado Museum of Art, New Orleans.

nunciation of its claim to western lands. Georgia sought complete removal and was not satisfied by Monroe's removal messages nor by further Creek cessions. Although in 1826 the Creek nation, under federal pressure, ceded all but a small strip of its Georgia lands, Governor George M. Troup wanted all their land. Troup sent surveyors to the one remaining strip; President John Quincy Adams then threatened to send the army to protect the Indians' claims, and Troup countered with his own threats. Only the eventual removal of the Georgia Creek to the west in 1826 prevented a clash between the state and the federal government. For the Creek the outcome was a devastating defeat. In attempting to hold fast to the remainder of their traditional lands, they had significantly altered their political structure. In 1829 they centralized tribal authority, strengthening their national council at the expense of traditional village autonomy, and had forbidden any chief from negotiating land cessions. In 1827 the Cherokee tried

to resist forced removal by adopting a written constitution modeled after the United States system and by organizing themselves officially as an independent nation. But in 1828 the Georgia legislature annulled the constitution, extended state sovereignty over the Cherokee, and ordered the seizure of tribal lands.

In 1829 the Cherokee, with the support of sympathetic whites but without the support of the new president, Andrew Jackson, turned to the federal courts to defend their treaty with **Cherokee** the United States and prevent **Nation v.** Georgia's seizure of their land. In **Georgia** *Cherokee Nation* v. *Georgia* (1831), Chief Justice John Marshall ruled that under the federal Constitution an Indian tribe was neither a foreign nation nor a state, and therefore had no standing in federal courts. Nonetheless, said Marshall, the Indians had an unquestioned right to their lands; they could lose title only by voluntarily giving it up. A year later, in *Worcester* v. *Georgia*,

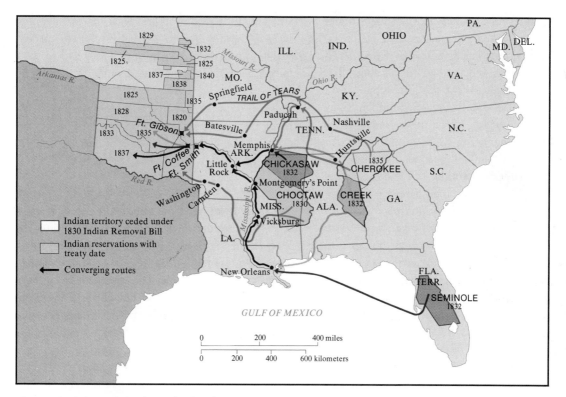

Removal of the Indians from the South, 1820–1840
Source: Redrawn by permission of Macmillan Publishing
Company, Inc. From American History Atlas by Martin
Gilbert, cartography by Peter Kingsland. Copyright © 1968
by Martin Gilbert.

Marshall defined the Cherokee position more clearly. The Indian nation was, he declared, a distinct political community in which "the laws of Georgia can have no force" and into which Georgians could not enter without permission or treaty privilege.

President Andrew Jackson, who as a general had led the expedition against the Seminole in Spanish Florida in 1818, had little sympathy for the Indians and ignored the Supreme Court's ruling. Keen to open up new lands for settlement, he was determined to remove the Cherokee at all costs. In the Removal Act of 1830 Congress provided Jackson the funds he needed to negotiate new treaties and resettle the resistant tribes west of the Missis-

Trail of Tears sippi. The Choctaw were the first to go; in the winter of 1831 and 1832, they made the forced journey from Mississippi and Alabama to the West (see map). Alexis de Tocqueville was visiting Memphis when they arrived there, "the wounded, the sick, newborn babies, and

the old men on the point of death. . . . I saw them embark to cross the great river," he wrote, "and the sight will never fade from my memory. Neither sob nor complaint rose from that silent assembly. Their afflictions were of long standing, and they felt them to be irremediable."

Soon other tribes were forced west. The Creek in Alabama delayed removal until 1836, when the army pushed them westward. A year later the Chickasaw followed. The Cherokee, having fought through the courts to stay, found themselves divided. Some recognized the hopelessness of further resistance and accepted removal as the only chance to preserve their civilization. The leaders of this minority signed a treaty in 1835 in which they agreed to exchange their southern home for western land. But when the time for evacuation came in 1838, most Cherokee refused to move. President Martin Van Buren then sent federal troops to round up the Indians. About twenty thousand Cherokee were evicted, held in detention camps, and marched to Oklahoma under military escort. Nearly one-quarter died of disease and exhaustion on the infamous Trail of Tears. When it was all over, the Indians had traded about 100 million acres of land east of the Mississippi for 32 million acres west of the river plus $68 million. Only a few scattered remnants of the tribes, among them the Seminole, remained in the East and South.

A small band of Seminole successfully resisted removal and remained in Florida. In the 1832 Treaty of Payne's Landing, tribal chiefs agreed to relocate to the West within three years. Under **Seminole War** der Osceola, however, a minority refused to vacate their homes, and from 1835 on they waged a fierce guerrilla war against the United States. The army in turn attempted, ruthlessly but unsuccessfully, to exterminate the Seminole. In 1842 the United States finally abandoned the Seminole War; it had cost 1,500 soldiers' lives and $20 million. Osceola's followers remained in Florida.

To open up the West to white settlement, Commissioner of Indian Affairs William Medill in 1848 proposed gathering the western Indians into two great reservations, one northern and one southern. The Kansas and Platte valleys separated the two areas, creating a wide corridor for white settlers to use on their way westward. In 1853, however, the government took back most of the northern lands in a new round of treaties, and Kansas and Nebraska were opened to white settlement.

A complex set of attitudes drove whites to force Indian removal. Most merely wanted Indian lands; they had little or no respect for the rights or culture of the Indians. Manifest destiny and westward migration justified bulldozing Indians aside. Others were aware of the injustice, but believed the Indians must inevitably give way to white settlement. Some, like John Quincy Adams, believed the only way to preserve Indian civilization was to remove the tribes and establish a buffer zone between Indians and whites. Others, including Thomas Jefferson, doubted that white civilization and Indian "savagery" could coexist. Supported by missionaries and educators, they hoped to "civilize" the Indians and assimilate them slowly into American culture. Whatever the source of white behavior, the outcome was the same: the devastation of Native American people and their culture.

Another minority experienced insecurity and struggled for recognition and legal rights. Like most Indians, they too were involuntarily a part of American society. Unlike Indians, however, they wished to be fully a part of the American people.

FREE PEOPLE OF COLOR

No black person was safe, wrote the abolitionist and former slave Frederick Douglass after the Philadelphia riot of 1849. "His life—his property—and all that he holds dear are in the hands of a mob, which may come upon him at any moment—at midnight or mid-day, and deprive him of his all." Between 1832 and 1849 five major antiblack riots occurred in Philadelphia. Mobs stormed black dwellings and churches, set them to the torch, and killed the people inside. For free people of color, mobs could take many forms. They could come in the shape of slave hunters, seeking fugitive slaves but as likely to kidnap a free black as a slave. Or they could take the form of civil authority, as in Cincinnati in 1829, when city officials, frightened by the growing black population, drove one to two thousand blacks from the city by enforcing a law requiring cash bonds for good behavior. In whatever form, free blacks faced insecurity daily.

Under federal law, blacks held an uncertain position. The Bill of Rights seemed to apply to free blacks; the Fifth Amendment specified that "no person shall . . . be deprived of life, liberty, or property, without due process of law." Yet the racist theory of the eighteenth century that defined a republic as being only for whites seemed to exclude blacks (see pages 163–164). This exclusion was reflected in early federal legislation. In 1790 naturalization was limited to white aliens, and in 1792 the militia was limited to white male citizens. Moreover, Congress approved the admission to the Union of states whose constitutions restricted the rights of blacks. Following the admission of Missouri in 1821, every new state admitted until the Civil War banned blacks from voting. And when the Oregon and New Mexico territories were organized, public land grants were limited to whites.

In the North blacks faced legal restrictions nearly

everywhere; Massachusetts was the major exception. Many states barred entry to free blacks or required bonds of $500 to $1,000 to guarantee their good behavior, as in Ohio (1804), Illinois (1819), Michigan (1827), and Oregon (1857). Although seldom enforced, these laws clearly indicated the less-than-free status of blacks. Only in Massachusetts, New Hampshire, Vermont, and Maine could blacks vote on an equal basis with whites throughout the pre–Civil War period. Blacks gained the right to vote in Rhode Island in 1842, but they had lost it earlier in Pennsylvania and Connecticut. No state but Massachusetts permitted blacks to serve on juries; four midwestern states and California did not allow blacks to testify against whites. In Oregon blacks could not own real estate, make contracts, or sue in court.

Legal status was important, but practice and custom were crucial. Although Ohio repealed its law barring black testimony against whites in 1849, the exclusion persisted as custom in southern Ohio counties. Throughout the North free people of color were either excluded from or segregated in public places. Abolitionist Frederick Douglass was repeatedly turned away from public facilities during a speaking tour of the North in 1844. A doorkeeper refused him admission to a circus in Boston, saying "We don't allow niggers in here." He met the same reply when he tried to attend a revival meeting in New Bedford. At a restaurant in Boston and on an omnibus in Weymouth, Massachusetts, he heard the familiar words. Hotels and restaurants were closed to blacks, as were most theaters and churches.

Exclusion and Segregation of Blacks

Probably no practice inflicted greater injury than the general discrimination in hiring. The counting houses, retail stores, and factories that characterized the expanding economy refused to hire black men other than as janitors and general handymen. New England mills hired only white women. Other than a small professional and commercial and skilled elite, northern free black men found steady work difficult to obtain; most toiled as unskilled daily laborers. Black women more easily found jobs as their domestic skills were in great demand in the burgeoning urban society, and they worked as domestic servants, cooks, laundresses, and seamstresses. Unlike their white counterparts, however, these women did not view paid employment as a distinct period in their life

A free black man being expelled from a whites-only railway car in Philadelphia. Prior to the Civil War, blacks were commonly segregated or excluded from public places in the North. Library of Congress.

cycle; around 40 percent of black women worked for wages during marriage and the childrearing years. Given the lower wages black workers received, not many black families could survive on one income.

Free people of color faced more severe legal and social barriers in the southern slave states, where their presence was often viewed as an incentive to insurrection. Indeed, southern states responded to fear of mass rebellion by tightening the restrictions on free blacks and forcing them to leave small towns and interior counties. After a successful slave rebellion in Haiti in the 1790s and Gabriel Prosser's Virginia slave revolt in 1800 (see page 205), southern states barred the entry of free blacks for two decades. And in 1806 Virginia required newly freed blacks to leave the state. Following Nat Turner's slave uprising in Southampton County in 1831, the position of free blacks weakened further. Within five years nearly all the southern states prohibited the freeing of any slaves without legislative or court approval, and by the 1850s Texas, Mississippi, and Georgia had banned manumission altogether.

BLACK POPULATION OF THE UNITED STATES, 1800–1860

Year	Total Black Population	Percentage of Total U.S. Population	Free People of Color	Free Blacks as a Percentage of Black Population
1800	1,002,000	18.9	108,000	10.8
1810	1,378,000	19.0	186,000	13.5
1820	1,772,000	18.4	234,000	13.2
1830	2,329,000	18.1	320,000	13.7
1840	2,874,000	16.8	386,000	13.4
1850	3,639,000	15.7	435,000	11.9
1860	4,442,000	14.1	488,000	11.0

To restrict free blacks and encourage them to migrate north, southern states adopted elaborate "black codes." Blacks were required to have licenses for certain occupations and were barred from others (for example, Virginia and Georgia banned black river captains and pilots). Some states forbade blacks to assemble without a license; some prohibited blacks from being taught to read and write. In the late 1830s, when these black codes were enforced with vigor for the first time, free blacks increasingly moved northward, even though northern states discouraged the migration.

Black Codes

In spite of these obstacles, the free black population rose dramatically in the first part of the nineteenth century, from 108,000 in 1800 to almost 500,000 in 1860 (see table). Nearly half lived in the North, occasionally in rural settlements like Hammond County, Indiana, but more often in cities like Philadelphia, New York, or Cincinnati. Baltimore had the largest free black community; sizable free black populations also existed in New Orleans, Charleston, and Mobile (see pages 305–306).

The ranks of free blacks were constantly increased by ex-slaves. Some, like Frederick Douglass and Harriet Tubman, were fugitives. Douglass had hired himself out as a ship caulker in Baltimore, paying $3 monthly to his owner.

Fugitive Slaves

Living among free workers made him yearn to escape slavery. By masquerading as a free black with the help of borrowed seaman's papers, he bluffed his way to Philadelphia and freedom. Tubman, a slave on the eastern shore of Maryland, escaped to Philadelphia in 1849 when her master's death led to rumors that she would be sold out of the state. Within the next two years she returned twice to free her two children, her sister, her mother, and her brother and his family. Other slaves were voluntarily freed by their owners. Some, like a Virginia planter named Sanders who settled his slaves as freedmen in Michigan, sought to cleanse their souls by freeing their slaves in their wills. Some freed elderly slaves after a lifetime of service rather than support them in old age. The parents of the slave Isabella (Sojourner Truth) were freed when whites who inherited the family would not support the father, who was too old to work.

Sojourner Truth's experience in New York reveals that the gradual emancipation laws of northern states had little effect as long as slavery existed elsewhere. In 1817 New York State adopted an emancipation plan whereby all slaves over forty years old were freed, and young slaves would serve ten more years. But owners tried to thwart the law by selling their slaves into other states. In 1826, fearing sale to the South, Sojourner Truth found refuge with a nearby

Sojourner Truth (about 1797–1883), the spellbinding preacher, abolitionist, and crusader for women's rights.   Sophia Smith Collection, Smith College.

industry, and morality, thus equipping their members to improve their lot. But no amount of effort could counteract white prejudice. Blacks remained second-class in status.

The network of societies among urban free black men and women provided a base for black protest. From 1830 to 1835, and thereafter irregularly, free blacks held national conventions with delegates drawn from ad hoc city and state organizations. Under the leadership of the small black middle class, which included the Philadelphia sail manufacturer James Forten and the orator Reverend Henry Highland Garnet, the convention movement served as a forum to attack slavery and agitate for equal rights. The militant new black newspapers joined the struggle. *Freedom's Journal,* the first black weekly, appeared in March 1827; in 1837 the *Weekly Advocate* began publication in New York City. Both papers circulated throughout the North, spreading black thought and activism.

Although abolitionism and civil rights remained at the top of the blacks' agenda, the mood of free blacks began to shift in the late 1840s and 1850s.

Black Nationalism
Many were frustrated by the failure of the abolitionist movement and by the passage of the Fugitive Slave Law of 1850 (see page 361). Some black leaders became more militant, and a few joined John Brown in his plans for rebellion. But many more were swept up in the tide of black nationalism, which stressed racial solidarity and unity, self-help, and a growing interest in Africa. Before this time, efforts to send Afro-Americans "back to Africa" had originated with whites seeking to solve racial problems by ridding the United States of blacks. But in the 1850s blacks held emigrationist conventions of their own under the leadership of Henry Bibb and Martin Delany. In 1859 Delany led a Niger Valley exploration party as the emissary of a black convention. He signed a treaty with Yoruba rulers allowing him to settle American blacks in that African kingdom (the plan was never carried out). Nothing better illustrates the ironic position of free blacks in the United States than the flight of blacks to Canada and Africa, in search of freedom, while millions of European migrants were coming to the United States for liberty and opportunity. With the coming of the Civil War and emancipation, however, the status of blacks, free and

abolitionist couple. With their help she sued successfully for the freedom of her son Peter, who had been sold unlawfully to an Alabaman. One can only guess how many blacks did not receive such help and were permanently deprived of their freedom.

In response to their oppression, free blacks founded strong, independent self-help societies to meet their unique needs and fight their less-than-equal status.

Founding of Black Institutions
Revival and reform influenced blacks as well. In every black community there appeared black churches, fraternal and benevolent associations, literary societies, and schools. In Philadelphia in the 1840s, more than half the black population belonged to mutual beneficiary societies, and female benevolent societies and schools flourished. The black Masons grew to more than fifty lodges in seventeen states by 1860. Many black leaders believed that these mutual aid societies would encourage thrift,

IMPORTANT EVENTS

1805	Prophet emerges as Shawnee leader
1810	New York surpasses Philadelphia in population
1813	Death of Tecumseh
1819	Indian "Civilization Act"
1823	Beechers' Hartford Female Seminary established
1824	Monroe proposes Indian removal
1827	*Freedom's Journal* first published
1830s–1850s	Urban riots
1831	*Cherokee Nation* v. *Georgia*
1831–38	Trail of Tears
1835–42	Seminole War
1837	Boston employs paid policemen
1845	Start of Irish potato famine
1848	Abortive German revolution
1849	New York theater riot

to insulate their homes from the competition of the market economy. Many women found fulfillment in the domestic ideal, although others found it confining. More and more, urban women became associated with nurturing roles, first in homes and schools, then in churches and reform societies.

In Europe, famine and religious and political oppression sent millions of people across the Atlantic. They were drawn to the United States by the promise of jobs and of political and religious toleration. Yet most found the going rough even though conditions were often better than in their native lands. In the process they changed the profile of the American people; Americans differed from each other more and more and shared common traditions and experiences less and less. Competition and diversity bred intolerance and prejudice. None were to feel that more painfully than Indians and free blacks, who were most often made to feel as aliens in their own land. Indians were expelled from their traditional lands while free people of color were second-class citizens.

But change was not limited to the North and West. The agrarian, slave South too was undergoing a transformation.

SUGGESTIONS FOR FURTHER READING

slave, would move back onto the national political agenda, and Afro-Americans would focus with renewed intensity on their position at home.

The United States in 1860 was a far more diverse and complex society than it had been in 1800. Industrialization, specialization, urbanization, and immigration had altered the ways people lived and worked. Economic growth not only created new jobs in towns and cities but also caused clearer distinctions in wealth and status. Inequality increased everywhere, and competition and insecurity produced resentments and conflict. Increasingly, cities housed ostentatious wealth and abject poverty, and violence and disorder became commonplace.

Amidst these changes, middle-class families sought

Communities and Inequality

Stuart M. Blumin, *The Urban Threshold: Growth and Change in a Nineteenth-Century American Community* (1976); Don H. Doyle, *The Social Order of a Frontier Community: Jacksonville, Illinois, 1825–1870* (1978); Roger W. Lotchin, *San Francisco, 1846–1856: From Hamlet to City* (1974); Raymond A. Mohl, *Poverty in New York, 1783–1825* (1971); Edward Pessen, *Riches, Class and Power Before the Civil War* (1973); Jonathan Prude, *The Coming of Industrial Order. Town and Factory Life in Rural Massachusetts, 1810–1860* (1983); Edward K. Spann, *The New Metropolis. New York City, 1840–1857* (1981); Stephan Thernstrom, *Poverty and Progress: Social Mobility in a Nineteenth Century City* (1964); Alexis de Tocqueville, *Democracy in America*, 2 vols. (1835–1840); Richard C. Wade, *The Urban Frontier: 1790–1830*

(1957); Anthony F. C. Wallace, *Rockdale: The Growth of an American Village in the Early Industrial Revolution* (1978).

Women and the Family

Nancy F. Cott, *The Bonds of Womanhood: "Woman's Sphere" in New England, 1780–1835* (1977); Carl N. Degler, *At Odds: Women and the Family in America from the Revolution to the Present* (1980); Hasia R. Diner, *Erin's Daughters in America. Irish Immigrant Women in the Nineteenth Century* (1983); Linda Gordon, *Woman's Body, Woman's Rights: A Social History of Birth Control in America* (1976); James C. Mohr, *Abortion in America: The Origins and Evolution of National Policy, 1800–1900* (1978); James Reed, *From Private Vice to Public Virtue: The Birth Control Movement and American Society Since 1830* (1978); Mary P. Ryan, *Cradle of the Middle Class. The Family in Oneida County, New York, 1790–1865* (1981); Kathryn Kish Sklar, *Catharine Beecher: A Study in American Domesticity* (1973); Maris A. Vinovskis, *Fertility in Massachusetts from the Revolution to the Civil War* (1981); Robert V. Wells, *Revolutions in Americans' Lives* (1982); Barbara Welter, "The Cult of True Womanhood, 1820–1860," *American Quarterly*, 18 (Summer 1966), 151–174.

Immigrants

Rowland Berthoff, *British Immigrants in Industrial America* (1953); Theodore C. Blegen, *Norwegian Migration to America, 1825–1860* (1931); Kathleen Neils Conzen, *Immigrant Milwaukee: 1836–1860* (1976); Jay P. Dolan, *The Immigrant Church: New York's Irish and German Catholics, 1815–1865* (1975); Charlotte Erickson, *Invisible Immigrants* (1972); Robert Ernst, *Immigrant Life in New York City, 1825–1863* (1949); Oscar Handlin, *Boston's Immigrants: A Study in Acculturation*, rev. ed. (1959); Harold Runblom and Hans Norman, *From Sweden to America* (1976); Philip Taylor, *The Distant Magnet: European Emigration to the United States of America* (1971); Mark Wyman, *Immigrants in the Valley.*

Irish, Germans and Americans in the Upper Mississippi, 1830–1860 (1984).

Native Americans

Robert F. Berkhofer, Jr., *The White Man's Indian* (1978); Arthur De Rosier, *Removal of the Choctaw Indians* (1970); R. David Edmunds, *The Shawnee Prophet* (1983); Grant Foreman, *Indian Removal: The Emigration of the Five Civilized Tribes of Indians*, rev. ed. (1953); Michael D. Green, *The Politics of Indian Removal. Creek Government and Society in Crisis* (1982); Charles Hudson, *The Southeastern Indians* (1976); John K. Mahon, *History of the Second Seminole War, 1835–1842* (1967); Francis P. Prucha, *American Indian Policy in the Formative Years* (1962); Ronald N. Satz, *American Indian Policy in the Jacksonian Era* (1975); Herman J. Viola, *Thomas L. McKenney. Architect of America's Early Indian Policy: 1816–1830* (1974); Wilcomb E. Washburn, *The Indian in America* (1975); Thurman Wilkin, *Cherokee Tragedy* (1970).

Free People of Color

Ira Berlin, *Slaves Without Masters: The Free Negro in the Antebellum South* (1974); Leonard P. Curry, *The Free Black in Urban America 1800–1850* (1981); James Horton and Lois Horton, *Black Bostonians: Family Life and Community Struggle in the Antebellum North* (1979); Luther Porter Jackson, *Free Negro Labor and Property Holding in Virginia, 1830–1860* (1942); David M. Katzman, *Before the Ghetto: Black Detroit in the Nineteenth Century* (1973); Rudolph M. Lapp, *Blacks in Gold Rush California* (1977); Leon Litwack, *North of Slavery: The Negro in the Free States, 1790–1860* (1961); Floyd J. Miller, *The Search for a Black Nationality: Black Colonization and Emigration 1787–1863* (1975); Emma Lou Thornbrough, *The Negro in Indiana* (1957); Juliet E. K. Walker, *Free Frank. A Black Pioneer on the Antebellum Frontier* (1983); Arthur Zilversmit, *The First Emancipation: The Abolition of Slavery in the North* (1967).

SLAVERY AND THE GROWTH OF THE SOUTH

1800–1860

CHAPTER 11

He was weeping, sobbing. In a humble voice he had begged his master not to give him to Mr. King, who was going away to Alabama, but it had done no good. Now his voice rose and he uttered "an absolute cry of despair." Raving and "almost in a state of frenzy," he declared that he would never leave the Georgia plantation that was home to his father, mother, wife, and children. He twisted his hat between clenched fists and flung it to the ground; he would kill himself, he said, before he lost his family and all that made life worth living.

To Fanny Kemble, watching from the doorway, it was a horrifying and disorienting scene. One of the most famous British actresses ever to tour America, Fanny had grown up breathing England's antislavery tradition as naturally as the air. In New England she had become friends with such enlightened antislavery thinkers as William Ellery Channing, the liberal Boston minister who founded Unitarianism; Catharine Maria Sedgwick, America's foremost woman novelist; and Elizabeth Dwight Sedgwick, an educator and Catharine's sister-in-law. Amid such company, Fanny understandably assumed that attitudes in America were advanced and civilized. Then the man she married took her away from New England to a Georgia rice plantation, where hundreds of dark-skinned slaves produced the white grain that was his source of wealth.

Pierce Butler, Fanny's husband, was all that a cultured Philadelphia gentleman should be. He had lived all his life in the North, though part of his family's fortune had always sprung from southern slavery. When Fanny chose him from dozens of suitors, he had seemed an attractive exemplar of American culture. Yet now he shattered his slave's hopes without hesitation. Quietly "leaning against a table with his arms folded," Butler advised the distraught black man not to "make a fuss about what there was no help for."

Fanny wondered what America was really like. In the South, the northerner she thought she knew seemed a different man. Only with tears and vehement pleas was she able to convince Butler to keep the slave family together. He finally agreed as a favor to her, not on principle or because she had a right to be consulted.

This incident, which occurred in 1839, illustrates both the similarities between South and North and the differences that were beginning to emerge. Though racism existed in the North, its influence was far more visible on southern society. And though some northerners, like Pierce Butler, were undisturbed by the idea of human bondage, a growing number considered it shocking and backward. In the years after the Revolution, these northerners, possessing few slaves and influenced by the revolutionary ideal of natural rights, had adopted gradual emancipation laws (see page 161). At the same time they had developed a widening market economy and embarked on an industrial revolution. These changes increased production, spurred mechanization, and rendered forced labor obsolete.

In the South too, the years from 1800 to 1860 were a time of growth and prosperity; new lands were settled and new states peopled. But as the North grew and changed, economically the South merely grew; change there only reinforced existing economic patterns. Steadily the South emerged as the world's most extensive and vigorous slave economy. Its people were slaves, slaveholders, and nonslaveholders rather than farmers, merchants, mechanics, and manufacturers. Its well-being depended on agriculture alone, rather than agriculture plus commerce and manufacturing. Its population was almost wholly rural rather than rural and urban.

These facts meant that the social lives of southerners were unavoidably distinct from those of northerners. Nonslaveholders operated their family farms in a society dominated by slaveholding planters. A handful of planters developed an aristocratic lifestyle, while slaves—one-third of the South's people—lived without freedom, struggling to develop a culture that sustained hope. The influence of slavery spread throughout the social system, affecting not just southern economics but southern values, customs, and laws. It created a society that was noticeably different from the society of the north.

THE SOUTH REMAINS RURAL

The South in the early 1800s was the product of precisely the kind of resource-exploiting commercial agriculture that most of the early colonies had aspired to develop. Only there, nonmechanized agriculture remained highly profitable, as it did not in the Northeast. Southern planters were not sentimentalists who held onto their slaves for noneconomic reasons even in the face of the industrial revolution. Like other Americans, they were profit-oriented. But circumstances allowed them to continue to profit from a plantation economy.

At the time of the Revolution, slave-based agriculture was not exceedingly lucrative. Debt hung heavily over most of Virginia's extravagant and aristocratic tobacco growers, prodding them to consider the disadvantages of slavery. Cotton was a lucrative export crop only for sea-island planters, who grew the luxurious long-staple variety. The short-staple cotton that grew readily in the interior was unmarketable because its sticky seeds lay tangled in the fibers. But in spite of the limited usefulness of slavery, much wealth was tied up in it. Social inertia and fear of slave revolts prevented its abolition.

Then England's burgeoning textile industry changed the southern economy. English mills needed more and more cotton. Sea-island cotton was so profitable between 1785 and 1795 that thousands of farmers in the interior experimented with the short-staple variety; by the early 1790s southern farmers were growing 2 to 3 million pounds of it each year. Some of this cotton was meant for domestic use, but most was grown in the hope that some innovation would make the crop salable to the English. In such circumstances the invention of a cotton gin was almost inevitable, and Eli Whitney responded in 1793 with a simple machine that removed the seeds from the fibers. By 1800 cotton was spreading rapidly westward from the seaboard states.

So the antebellum South, or Old South, became primarily a cotton South. Tobacco continued to be grown in Virginia and North Carolina, and rice and sugar were still very important in certain coastal areas,

Rise of the Cotton South especially in South Carolina, Georgia, and Louisiana. But cotton was the largest crop, the most widespread, and the force behind the South's hunger for new territory. Ambitious cotton growers poured across the Appalachians into the West, pushing the Indians off their fabulously fertile Gulf lands (see pages 287–290). The boom in the cotton economy came in the 1830s in Alabama and Mississippi. But not until the 1850s did the wave of cotton expansion cross Louisiana and pour into Texas (see maps, page 300).

Thus the Old South was not old at all; in 1860 it was young and still growing. For although prices plunged sharply at least once a decade after 1820, overall demand for cotton soared. Since English mills would buy virtually all the cotton a planter could grow, eager southerners bought more slaves and more land. Soon they were exporting more than three-quarters of their crop and supplying almost the same proportion of England's purchases. In just a few decades some of these planters amassed great personal fortunes and rose to an aristocratic position in society. Though some old Virginia and South Carolina families were represented among the proud new "cotton snobs," most of the wealthy were newly rich.

To the hard-working and lucky, riches came quickly. A good example is the family of Jefferson Davis. Like Abraham Lincoln, Davis was born in humble circumstances. His father was one of

Jefferson Davis: His Early Life the thousands of American farmers on the frontier who moved frequently, unwisely buying land when prices were high and selling when they were low, never making his fortune. Luckily for Davis, his older brother migrated to Mississippi and became successful. Settling on rich bottomlands next to the Mississippi River, Joseph Davis made profits, expanded his holdings of land and slaves, and made more profits. Soon he was an established figure in society, and he used his position to arrange an education at West Point for his younger brother. A large plantation awaited Jefferson's resignation from the army. Thus the Davis family became aristocrats in one generation.

A less-fortunate consequence of the cotton boom was the relative indifference of farmers to the long-term fertility of the soil. In an expanding economy,

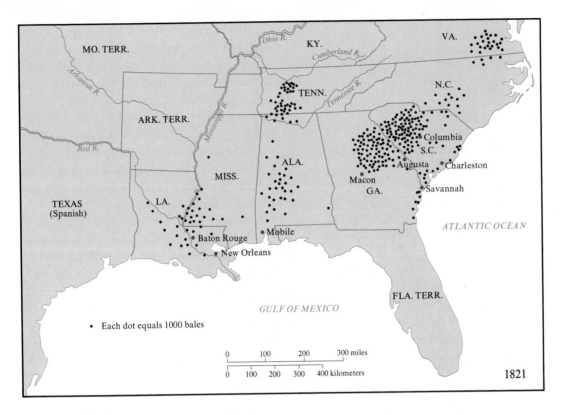

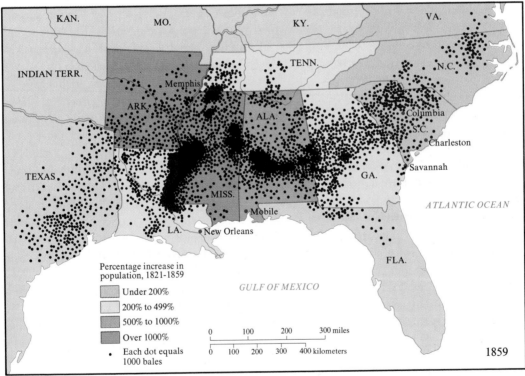

Cotton Production in the South

Jefferson Davis became a stiff and formal aristocrat. Varina Howell Davis, despite her glum expression here, was lively and clever, a social asset to her husband. Library of Congress.

with cheap and superior land available farther west, most people preferred to exhaust the land and move on rather than invest heavily in preserving it. Only in the older states of the Upper South, where the major landholders stayed behind, and where the cotton boom had less impact, did serious interest in diversified farming develop.

An even more important consequence of the boom was thin population distribution. Producers spread out over as large an area as possible in order to maximize production and income. Because farms were far apart, southern society remained predominantly rural. Population density, low even in the older plantation states, was especially so in the frontier areas being brought under cultivation. In 1860 there were only 2.3 people per square mile in Texas, 15.6 in Louisiana, and 18.0 in Georgia. By contrast, population density in the nonslaveholding states east of the Mississippi River was almost three

Population Distribution

times higher. The Northeast had an average of 65.4 persons per square mile, and in some places the density was much higher. Massachusetts had 153.1 people per square mile, and New York City, where overcrowding reached epic proportions, compressed 86,400 people into each square mile.

Even in the 1850s, much of the South seemed almost uninhabited, a virtual wilderness. Frederick Law Olmsted, a northerner who later became famous as a landscape architect, made several trips through the South in the 1850s as a reporter. He found that the few trains and stagecoaches available to travelers offered only rough accommodations and kept their schedules poorly. Indeed, he had to do most of his traveling on horseback along primitive trails. Passing from Columbus, Georgia, to Montgomery, Alabama, Olmsted observed "a hilly wilderness, with a few dreary villages, and many isolated cotton farms." Alabama, of course, had been frontier as recently as 1800, but Olmsted encountered the same conditions

John Blake White's painting, Perspective of Broad Street *(1836), which depicts the arrival of the mail, suggests the excitement of an urban world in Charleston, one of the South's few cities. The City of Charleston, South Carolina, City Hall Collection.*

in parts of eastern Virginia: "For hours and hours one has to ride through the unlimited, continual, all-shadowing, all-embracing forest, following roads in the making of which no more labor has been given than was necessary to remove the timber which would obstruct the passage of wagons; and even for days and days he may sometimes travel and see never two dwellings of mankind within sight of each other."

Society in such rural areas was characterized by relatively weak institutions, for it takes people to create and support organized activity. Where the concentration of people was low, it was difficult to finance and operate schools, churches, libraries, or even hotels, restaurants, and other urban amenities. Southerners were strongly committed to their churches, and some believed in the importance of universities, but all such institutions were far less developed than those in the North.

The few southern cities were likewise smaller and less developed than those in the North. As exporters, southerners did not need large cities; a small group of merchants working in connection with northern brokers sufficed to ship their cotton overseas and to import necessary supplies and luxuries. As planters, southerners invested most of their capital in slaves; they had little money left to build factories—another source of urban growth. A few southerners did invest in iron or textiles on a small scale. But the largest southern "industry" was lumbering and the largest factories were cigar factories, where slaves finished tobacco products. As a result, in 1860 only 49,000 out of 704,000 South Carolinians lived in towns with 2,500 or more residents. Less than 3 percent of Mississippi's population lived in places of comparable size. In 1860 the population of Charleston was only 41,000, Richmond 38,000, and Mobile 29,000. New Orleans, by far the largest southern city, had only 169,000 residents, and it was being left behind because it was not part of the national railroad network.

Weak Urban Sector

Thus, although it was economically attuned to an international market, the South was only semideveloped in comparison with other sections of the country. Its people prospered, but neither as rapidly nor as independently as residents of the North. There commerce and industry brought unprecedented advances in productivity, widening the range of affordable goods and services and raising the average person's standard of living. In the South, change was quantitative rather than qualitative; farming techniques remained essentially the same. To prosper, southern planters increased their acreage and hoped for continued high demand from foreign customers—decisions that worked to the ultimate disadvantage of the region. Subsistence farmers merely worked harder and hoped to grow a bit more.

The society that developed in this largely agrarian economy was a society of extremes. The social distance between a wealthy planter and a small slaveholder was as great as the distance between a slaveholder and a nonslaveholder, to say nothing of the distance between whites and slaves. And, contrary to popular belief, planters were neither the most numerous nor the most typical group. The typical white southerner was a yeoman farmer.

YEOMAN FARMERS

More than two-thirds of white southern families owned no slaves. Some of them lived in towns and ran stores or businesses, but most were farmers who owned their own land and grew their own food. Independent and motivated by a hearty share of frontier individualism, these people lived a self-sufficient farming life. They had little connection with the market or its type of progress. Families might raise a small surplus to trade for needed items or spending cash, but they were far from major market networks and therefore not particularly concerned about a larger cash income. They valued instead their self-reliance and freedom from others' control. Absorbed in their isolated but demanding rural life, they formed an important, though sometimes silent, part of southern society. If their rights were threatened, however, they could react strongly.

Yeomen pioneered the southern wilderness as herders of livestock and then as farmers. In successive waves they moved down the southern Appalachians into new Gulf lands following the War of 1812. The herdsmen grazed their cattle and pigs on the abundant natural vegetation in the woods. Before long, however, the next wave of settlers arrived and broke ground for crops. These yeoman farmers forced many herdsmen farther west, and eventually across the Mississippi.

Migration became almost a way of life for some yeoman families. Lured by stories of the good land over the horizon, men often uprooted their families repeatedly. They worked hard in each new place to clear fields and establish a farm, while their wives performed their tasks in the household economy and patiently recreated a few social ties—to relatives, neighbors, church members—that enriched experience. "We have been [moving] all our lives," recalled one woman. "As soon as ever we git comfortably settled, it is time to be off to something new." Maria Lides's father took the family from South Carolina to Alabama, but "his having such a good crop" there, lamented Maria, "seems to make him more anxious to move." She almost wished he would decide on California, because "he would be obliged to stop then for he could go no farther."

Some yeomen acquired large tracts of level land and became wealthy planters. Others clung to the beautiful mountainous areas they loved, or pressed farther into the wilds because they "couldn't stand the sound of another man's axe." As they moved, they tended to stick to the climate and soils they knew best. Yeomen could not afford the richest bottomlands, which were swampy and required expensive draining, but they owned land almost everywhere else.

Observers sometimes concluded that these people were poor and idle, especially the herdsmen who sat on their cabin porches while their stock foraged in the woods. It is more accurate to say that they were frontiersmen and farmers who did not manage to become rich. They worked hard, as farmers do everywhere, and enjoyed a folk culture based on family, church, and community. They spoke with a drawl and their inflections were reminiscent of their Scottish and Irish backgrounds. Once a year they flocked to religious revivals called protracted meetings or camp meetings, and in between they enjoyed events such as house-raisings, logrollings, quilting bees, and corn-shuckings. These combined work with fun and provided a fellowship that was especially welcome to isolated rural dwellers. There was food in abundance and often some liquor. The men did most of the farming; though the women occasionally helped in the fields, they commonly spent their time preserving and preparing food, making clothes, blankets, and candles, and tending to household matters. Both sexes worked hard for the family economy, continuing the colonial tradition of outdoor work for men and indoor work for women.

Beyond these basic facts, historians know little about the yeomen. Because their means were modest, they did not generate the voluminous legal papers, such as contracts, wills, and inventories of estates, that document the activities of the rich. Only a few letters have found their way into libraries and archives. It is reasonable to suppose, though, that yeomen held a variety of opinions and pursued individual goals. Some envied the planters and strove to be rich; others were content with their independence, recreation, family life, and religion.

At the first extreme was a North Carolinian named John F. Flintoff, whose rare diary records the ambitions

Folk Culture of the Yeoman

Like the figures in George Caleb Bingham's painting, The Squatters *(1850), southern yeomen were tough, independent people who tamed the frontier.   Museum of Fine Arts, Boston.*

of a nonslaveholder who hungered to be rich. Flintoff was born in 1823 and at age eighteen went to Mississippi to seek his fortune. Like other aspiring yeomen, he worked as an overseer, but often found it impossible to please his employers. At one time he gave up and returned to North Carolina, where he married and lived in his parents' house. But Flintoff was "impatient to get along in the world," so he tried Louisiana next and then Mississippi again.

For Flintoff, the fertile Gulf region had its disadvantages. "My health has been very bad here," he noted; "chills and fever occasionally has hold of me." "First rate employment" alternated with "very low wages." Moreover, as a young man working on isolated plantations, Flintoff often felt "all alone." Even a revival meeting in 1844 proved "an extremely cold time" with "little warm feeling." His uncle and other employers found fault with his work, and in 1846 Flintoff concluded in despair that "managing negroes and large farms is soul destroying."

Still, a desire to succeed kept him going. At twenty-six, before he owned a foot of land, Flintoff bought his first slave, "a negro boy 7 years old." Soon he had purchased two more children, the cheapest slaves available. Conscious of his status as a slaveowner, Flintoff resented the low wages he was paid and complained that his uncle offered him *"hand pay,"* the wages of a day laborer rather than a slaveowner and manager. In 1853, with nine young slaves and a growing family, Flintoff faced "the most unhappy time of my life." He was fired by his uncle, "treated shamefully." Finally he said, "I will have to sell some of my negroes to buy land. This I must have. I want *a home."*

Returning to North Carolina, Flintoff purchased 124 acres with help from his in-laws. He grew corn, wheat, and tobacco and earned extra cash hauling wood in his wagon. By 1860 he owned 3 horses, 26 hogs, 10 cattle, and several slaves, and was paying off his debts. Eventually Flintoff owned 217 acres and became a fairly prosperous tobacco and grain farmer. He was able to send his sons to college, and prided himself that he had freed his wife from much of the labor of yeoman women, so that she "lived a *Lady*." But the struggle upward had not been easy, and Flintoff never became the cotton planter he had aspired to be.

Probably more typical of the southern yeoman was Ferdinand L. Steel. As a young man Steel moved from North Carolina to Tennessee to work as a hatter and river boatman, but he eventually settled down to farming in Mississippi. He rose every day at five and worked until sundown. With the help of his family he raised corn, wheat, pork, and vegetables for the family table. Cotton was his cash crop: like other yeomen he sold five or six bales a year to obtain money for sugar, coffee, salt, calico, gunpowder, and a few other store-bought goods.

Steel picked his cotton himself (never exceeding 120 pounds per day—less than many slaves averaged) and regretted that cotton cultivation was so arduous and time-consuming. He was not tempted to grow more of it. The market fluctuated, and if cotton prices fell, a small grower like himself could be driven into debt and lose his farm. Steel, in fact, wanted to grow less cotton. "We are too weak handed" to manage it, he noted in his diary. "We had better raise small grain and corn and let cotton alone, raise corn and keep out of debt and we will have no necessity of raising cotton."

Steel's life in Mississippi in the 1840s retained much of the flavor of the frontier. He made all the family's shoes; his wife and sister sewed dresses, shirts, and "pantiloons." The Steel women also rendered their own soap, and spun and wove cotton into cloth; the men hunted for game. House-raisings and corn-shuckings provided entertainment, and Steel doctored his illnesses with boneset tea and other herbs.

The focus of Steel's life was his family and his religion. The family prayed together every morning and night, and he prayed and studied Scripture for an hour after lunch. Steel joined a temperance society and looked forward to church and camp meetings. "My Faith increases, & I enjoy much of that peace which the world cannot give," he wrote in 1841. Seeking to improve himself and be "ready" for judgment, Steel borrowed histories, Latin and Greek grammars, and religious books from his church. Eventually he became a traveling Methodist minister. "My life is one of toil," he reflected, "but blessed be God that it is as well with me as it is."

Toil, with even less security, was the lot of two other groups of free southerners: landless whites and free blacks. From 25 to 40 percent of the white workers in the South were laborers who owned no land. Their property consisted of a few household items and some animals—usually pigs—that could feed themselves on the open range. These animals were a major economic asset, for good, steady employment was uncertain in a region whose large producers relied on slave labor. In addition to unskilled laborers in the countryside and towns, the landless included some immigrants, especially Irish, who did heavy and dangerous work such as building railroads and digging ditches.

The white farm laborers were people struggling to become yeomen. They faced low wages or, if they rented, they were dependent on the unpredictable market price for their crops. Some fell into debt and were frequently sued; others, by scrimping and saving and finding odd jobs, managed to climb into the ranks of yeomen. When James and Nancy Bennitt of North Carolina succeeded in their ten-year struggle to buy land, they decided to avoid the unstable market as much as possible; thereafter they raised extra corn and wheat as sources of cash.

There were nearly a quarter of a million free blacks in the South in 1860, people whose conditions were worse than the yeoman's and often little better than the slave's. The free blacks of the

Free Blacks Upper South were usually decendants of men and women emancipated by their owners in the 1780s and 1790s, a period of postrevolutionary idealism that coincided with a decline in tobacco prices. They had few material advantages; most did not own land and had to labor in someone else's field, frequently beside slaves. By law they could not own a gun or liquor, violate curfew, assemble except in church, testify in court, or (everywhere after 1835) vote. Despite these obstacles, a minority bought land, and others found jobs as artisans, draymen, boatmen, and fishermen. A few owned slaves, who were almost always their wives and children, purchased from bondage.

Farther south, in the cotton and Gulf regions, a large proportion of free blacks were mulattoes, the privileged offspring of wealthy planters. Some received good educations and financial backing from their fathers, who recognized a moral obligation to them. In a few cities such as New Orleans and Mobile, extensive interracial sex had produced a mulatto population that was recognized as a distinct class. These mulattoes formed a society of their own and sought a status above slaves and other freedmen, if not equal to planters. But outside New Orleans, Mobile, and Charleston such groups were rare, and most mulattoes encountered disadvantages more frequently than they enjoyed benefits from their light skin tone. (For a more detailed discussion of free blacks during this period, see Chapter 10).

SLAVEHOLDING PLANTERS

At the opposite end of the spectrum from free blacks were the slaveholders. As a group slaveowners lived well, on incomes that enabled them to enjoy superior housing, food, clothing, and luxuries. But most did not live on the opulent scale that legend suggests. A few statistics tell the story: 88 percent of southern slaveholders had fewer than twenty slaves; 72 percent had fewer than ten; 50 percent had fewer than five. Thus the average slaveholder was not a man of great wealth but an aspring farmer. Nor was he a polished aristocrat, but more usually a person of humble origins, with little formal education and many rough edges to his manner. In fact, he probably had little beyond a degree of wealth and a growing ambition to distinguish him from a nonslaveholder.

Even wealthy slaveowners often lacked the refined manner of aristocrats. Many in the Gulf states were new to wealth, and their desire to plant more cotton and buy more slaves often caused them to postpone the enjoyment of luxuries. First-generation planters often lived for decades in their original log cabin,

improved only by clapboards or a frame addition. A Mississippi gentleman admitted, "If you wish to see people worth millions living as they were not worth hundreds, come down here." Yet the planters' wealth put ease and refinement within their grasp.

A Louisiana planter named Bennet Barrow, to take an example, was neither especially polished nor unusually coarse. Barrow's plantation lay in a wealthy parish in Louisiana, but his wealth was new and Barrow was preoccupied with moneymaking. He worried constantly over his cotton crop, filling his diary with tedious weather reports and gloomy predictions of his yields. Yet Barrow also strove to appear above such worries, and in boom times he grandly endorsed notes for men who left him saddled with debt.

Barrow hunted frequently, and he had a passion for racing horses and raising hounds. Each year he set aside several weeks to attend the races in New Orleans, where he entered stallions brought from as far away as Tennessee. Barrow could report the loss of a slave without feeling, but emotion shattered his laconic manner when misfortune struck his sporting animals. "Never was a person more unlucky than I am," he complained; "My favorite pup never lives." His strongest feelings surfaced when his horse Jos Bell—equal to "the best Horse in the South"—"broke down in running a mile . . . ruined for Ever." That same day the distraught Barrow gave his field hands a "general Whipping." Barrow was rich, but his wealth had not softened his rough, direct style of life.

The wealth of the greatest planters gave ambitious men like Barrow something to aspire to. If most planters lived in spacious, comfortable farmhouses, some did live in mansions. If most slaveowners sat down at mealtimes to an abundance of tempting country foods—pork and ham, beef and game, fresh vegetables and fruits, tasty breads and biscuits, cakes and jams—the sophisticated elite consumed such delights as "gumbo, ducks and olives, *supreme de volaille*, chickens in jelly, oysters, lettuce salad, chocolate cream, jelly cake, claret cup, etc." On formal and business occasions such as county court days, a traveler in Mississippi would see gentlemen decked out in "black cloth coats, black cravats and satin or embroidered silk waistcoats; all, too, sleek as if just from a barber's hands, and redolent of perfumes."

The ladies wore the latest fashions to parties and balls and made many other occasions sources of mer-

The North Carolina planter Duncan Cameron (1776–1853) built this spacious and comfortable farmhouse for his bride, Rebecca Bennehan, in 1804. The house, called Fairntosh, is more typical of the average planter's home than the elaborate Greek-revival-style mansions of popular legend. Library of Congress.

riment. Relations and friends often visited each other for several days or weeks at a time, enjoying good food and good company. Courtship was a major attraction at the larger parties or dances. Between social occasions women and many men kept up their close friendships through constant letter-writing.

Among the wealthiest and oldest families, slaveholding men dominated through a paternalistic ideology. Instead of stressing the acquisitive aspects of commercial agriculture, they focused on *noblesse oblige*. They saw themselves as custodians of the welfare of society as a whole and of the black families who depended on them. The paternalistic planter saw himself not as an oppressor but as the benevolent guardian of an inferior race. He developed affectionate feelings toward his slaves (as long as they kept in their place) and was genuinely shocked at outside criticism of his behavior.

Southern Paternalism

The letters of Paul Carrington Cameron, North Carolina's largest slaveholder, illustrate this mentality. After a period of sickness among his one thousand North Carolina slaves (he had hundreds more in Alabama and Mississippi), Cameron wrote, "I fear the Negroes have suffered much from the want of proper attention and kindness under this late distemper . . . no love of lucre shall ever induce me to be cruel, or even to make or permit to be made any great exposure of their persons at inclement seasons." On another occasion he described to his sister the sense of responsibility he felt: "I cannot better follow the example of our venerated Mother than in doing my duty to her faithful old slaves and their descendants. Do you remember a cold & frosty morning, during her illness, when she said to me 'Paul my son the people ought to be shod' this is ever in my ears, whenever I see any ones shoes in bad order; and in my ears it will be, so long as I am master."

There is no doubt that the richest southern planters saw themselves in this way. It was comforting to do so, and slaves, accommodating themselves to the realities of power, encouraged their masters to think their benevolence was appreciated. Paternalism also provided a welcome defense against abolitionist criticism. Still, for most planters, paternalism affected the manner and not the substance of their behavior. It was a matter of style. Its softness and warmth covered harsher assumptions: blacks were inferior; planters should make money. As discussion of owners' duties increased, theories about the complete and permanent inferiority of blacks also multiplied.

Even Paul Cameron's concern vanished with changed circumstances. Following the Civil War he bristled at their efforts to be free and made sweeping economic decisions without regard to their welfare. Writing on Christmas Day, 1865, Cameron showed little Christian charity (but a healthy profit motive) when he expressed his desire to get "free . . . of the negro. I am convinced that the people who gets rid of the free negro first will be the first to advance in improved agriculture. Have made no effort to retain any of mine [and] will not attempt a crop beyond the capacity of 30 hands." With that he turned out nearly a thousand black agriculturalists, rented his lands to several white farmers, and invested in industry.

Relations between men and women in the planter class were similarly paternalistic. An upper-class southern woman typically was raised and educated to be the subordinate companion **Woman's Role** of men. Her proper responsibility was home management. She was not to venture into politics and other worldly affairs. In a social system based on the coercion of an entire race, no woman could be allowed to challenge society's rules. If she defied or questioned the status quo, she risked universal condemnation.

Within the domestic circle the husband reigned supreme. For the fortunate woman, like North Carolina diarist Catherine Devereux Edmondston, whose marriage joined two people of shared tastes and habits, the husband's authority weighed lightly or not at all. But other women, even some who considered themselves happily married, were acutely conscious of that authority. "He is master of the house," wrote South Carolina's Mary Boykin Chesnut. "To hear is to obey

. . . all the comfort of my life depends upon his being in a good humor." In a darker mood Chesnut once observed that "there is no slave . . . like a wife." Unquestionably there were some, possibly many, close and satisfying relationships between men and women in the planter class, but many women were dissatisfied.

The upper-class southern woman had to clear several barriers in the way of happiness. Making the right choice of a husband was especially important. With this decision a young woman moved from the rather narrow experience that society had permitted her into a restricted lifetime role. After spending her early years within the family circle, a planter's daughter usually attended one of the South's rapidly multiplying academies or boarding schools. There she formed friendships with other girls and received an education that emphasized grammar, composition, penmanship, geography, literature, and languages, but much less of science and mathematics. As she developed some sense of herself, the young woman typically maintained dutiful and affectionate ties with her parents. But very soon she had to commit herself for life to a man whom she generally had known for only a brief time.

Once married, she lost most of her legal rights to her husband, became part of his family, and was expected to get along with numerous in-laws during extended visits. Most of the year, she was isolated on a large plantation, where she had to learn a host of new duties. Although free from much of the labor of yeoman women, the plantation mistress was not free from care. She had to supervise many tasks: overseeing the cooking and preserving of food, managing the house, caring for the children, and attending sick slaves. As a woman she was forbidden to travel and visit unless accompanied by men. All the circumstances of her future life depended on the man she chose.

It is not surprising that the intelligent and perceptive young woman sometimes approached marriage with a feeling akin to dread. Lucy Breckinridge, a wealthy Virginia girl, sensed how much autonomy she would have to surrender on her wedding day. She realized that thereafter her life would depend on men, who though chivalrous in manner, expected to be the center of attention. In her diary she recorded this unvarnished observation on marriage: "If [husbands] care for their wives at all it is only as a sort of servant, a being made to attend to their comforts and to keep the children out of the way. . . . A woman's life after she is married, unless there is an immense amount of love, is nothing but suffering and hard work."

Lucy loved young children but knew that childbearing often involved grief and sorrow. On learning of a relative's death, Lucy said, "It is a happy release for her, for her married life has been a long term of suffering. She has been married about seven years and had five children." This case was not too unusual, for in 1840 the birthrate for southern women in their fertile years was almost 20 percent higher than the national average. At the beginning of the nineteenth century, the average southern woman could expect to bear eight children; by 1860 the figure had decreased only to six, and one or more miscarriages were likely among so many pregnancies. The high birthrate took a toll on women's health, for complications of childbirth were a major cause of death.

Moreover, a mother had to endure the loss of many of the infants she bore. Infant mortality in the first year of life exceeded 10 percent and remained high during the next few years. In the South in 1860 almost five out of ten children died before age five, and among South Carolinians younger than twenty, fewer than four in ten survived to reach the twenty- to sixty-year-old category. For those women who wanted to plan their families, methods of contraception were not always reliable. And doctors had few remedies for infection or irritation of the reproductive tract.

Slavery was another source of trouble, a nasty sore that women sometimes had to bandage but were not supposed to notice. "Violations of the moral law . . . made mulattoes as common as blackberries," protested a woman in Georgia, but wives had to play "the ostrich game." "A magnate who runs a hideous black harem," wrote Mrs. Chesnut, "under the same roof with his lovely white wife, and his beautiful accomplished daughters . . . poses as the model of all human virtues to these poor women whom God and the laws have given him. From the height of his awful majesty, he scolds and thunders at them, as if he never did wrong in his life."

In the early 1800s, some southern women, especially Quakers, had spoken out against slavery. Even when they did not criticize the "peculiar institution," white women approached it differently than men, seeing it less as a system and more as a series of relationships with individuals. Perhaps southern men sensed this, for they wanted no discussion by women of the slavery issue. In the 1840s and 1850s, as national and international criticism of slavery increased, southern men published a barrage of articles stressing that women should restrict their concerns to the home. A writer in the *Southern Literary Messenger* bemoaned "these days of Women's Rights." Disapproving of women with political opinions, the *Southern Quarterly Review* declared, "The proper place for a woman is at home. One of her highest privileges, to be politically merged in the existence of her husband." Thomas Dew, one of the nineteenth century's first proslavery theorists, advised that "women are precisely what the men make them," and another writer promoted "affection, reverence, and duty" as a woman's proper attitudes.

But southern women were beginning to chafe at their customary exclusion from financial matters. A study of women in Petersburg, Virginia, has revealed behavior that amounted to an implicit criticism of the institution of marriage and the loss of autonomy it entailed. During several decades before 1860 the proportion of women who had not married, or not remarried after the death of a spouse, grew to exceed 33 percent. Likewise the number of women who worked for wages, controlled their own property, or even ran businesses increased. In managing property these women benefited from legal reforms, beginning with Mississippi's Married Women's Property Act of 1839, that were not designed to increase female independence. Rather, to offset business panics and recessions, the law gave women some property rights in order to protect families from ruin caused by the husband's indebtedness. But some women saw the resulting opportunity and took it. In the countryside southern women had fewer options, but Petersburg's women were seeking to use the talents they had and the education they had gained.

Restrictions on freedom and the use of education were not limited to upper-class women. For a large category of southern men and women, freedom was wholly denied and education in any form was not allowed. Male or female, slaves were expected to accept bondage and ignorance as their condition.

SLAVES AND THE CONDITIONS OF THEIR SERVITUDE

For Afro-Americans, slavery was a curse that brought no blessings other than the strengths they developed to survive it. Slaves knew a life of poverty, coercion, toil, heartbreak, and resentment. They had few hopes that were not denied; often they had to bear separation from their loved ones; and they were despised as an inferior race. That they endured and found loyalty and strength among themselves is a tribute to their courage, but it could not make up for a life without freedom or opportunity.

Southern slaves enjoyed few material comforts beyond the bare necessities. Their diet was plain and limited, though generally they had enough to eat.

Slave Diet, Clothing, and Housing
The basic ration was cornmeal, fat pork, molasses, and occasionally coffee. Many masters allowed slaves to tend gardens, which provided the variety and extra nutrition of greens and sweet potatoes. Fishing and hunting benefited some slaves. "It was nothin' fine," recalled one woman, "but it was good plain eatin' what filled you up."[1] Most slaveowners were innocent of the charge that they starved their slaves, but there is considerable evidence that slaves often suffered the effects of beriberi, pellegra, and other dietary-deficiency diseases.

Clothing too was plain, coarse, and inexpensive. Children of both sexes ran naked in hot weather and wore long cotton shirts in cool. When they were big enough to go to the fields, the boys received a work shirt and a pair of breeches and the girls a simple dress. On many plantations slave women made their own clothing of osnaburg, a coarse cotton fabric known as "nigger cloth." Probably few received more

than one or two changes of clothing for hot and cold seasons and one blanket each winter. Those who could earn a little money by doing extra work often bought additional clothing. Many slaves had to go without shoes until December, even as far north as Virginia. The shoes they received were frequent objects of complaint—uncomfortable brass-toed brogans or stiff wraparounds made from leather tanned on the plantation.

Summer and winter, slaves lived in small one-room cabins with a door and possibly a window opening, but no glass. Logs chinked with mud formed the walls, dirt was the only floor, and a wattle-and-daub or stone chimney vented the fireplace that provided heat and light. Bedding consisted of heaps of straw, straw mattresses, or wooden bedframes lashed to the walls with rope. A few crude pieces of furniture and cooking utensils completed the furnishings of most cabins. More substantial houses survive today from some of the richer plantations, but the average slave lived in crude accommodations. The gravest drawback of slave cabins was not their appearance and lack of comfort but their unhealthfulness. In each small cabin lived one or two whole families. Crowding and lack of sanitation fostered the spread of infection and contagious diseases. Many slaves (and whites) carried worms and intestinal parasites picked up from fecal matter or the soil. Lice were widespread among both races, and flies and other insects spread such virulent diseases as typhoid fever, malaria, and dysentery.

Hard work was the central fact of the slaves' existence. In Gulf-coast cotton districts long hours and large work gangs suggested factories in the field rather than the small-scale, isolated work patterns of slaves in the eighteenth-century Chesapeake. Overseers rang the morning bell before dawn, so early that some slaves remembered being in the fields "before it was light enough to see clearly . . . holding their hoes and other implements—afraid to start work for fear that they would cover the cotton plants with dirt because they couldn't see clearly." And, as one woman testified, when interviewed by workers in the Federal Writers' Project of the 1930s, "it was way after sundown 'fore they could stop that field work. Then they had to hustle to finish their night work in time for supper, or go to bed without it." Except in urban settings and on some rice plantations, where

Slave Work Routines

---

[1] Accounts by ex-slaves are quoted from *The American Slave: A Composite Autobiography*, edited by George P. Rawick (Westport, Conn.: Greenwood Press, First Reprint Edition 1972, Second Reprint Edition 1974), from materials gathered by the Federal Writers' Project and originally published in 1941. The spelling in these accounts has been standardized.

slaves were assigned daily tasks to complete at their own pace, working from "sun to sun" became universal in the South. These long hours and hard work were at the heart of the advantage of slave labor. As one planter put it, slaves were the best labor because "you could command them and *make* them do what was right." White workers, by contrast, were few and couldn't be *driven*; "they wouldn't stand it."

Planters aimed to keep all their laborers busy all the time. Profit took precedence over paternalism's "protection" of women: slave women did heavy field work, often as much as the men and even during pregnancy. Old people—of whom there were few— were kept busy caring for young children, doing light chores, or carding, ginning, or spinning cotton. Children had to gather kindling for the fire, carry water to the fields, or sweep the yard. But slaves had a variety of ways to keep from being worked to death. It was impossible for the master to supervise every slave every minute, and slaves slacked off when they were not being watched. Thus travelers frequently described lackadaisical slaves who seemed "to go through the motions of labor without putting strength into them," and owners complained that slaves "never would lay out their strength freely . . . it was impossible to make them do it." Stubborn misunderstanding and literal-mindedness was another defense. One exasperated Virginia planter exclaimed, "You can make a nigger work, *but you cannot make him think.*"

Of course the slave could not slow his labor too much, because the owner enjoyed a monopoly on force and violence. Whites throughout the South believed that Negroes "can't be governed except with the whip." One South Carolinian frankly explained to a northern journalist that he had whipped his slaves occasionally, "say once a fortnight; . . . the Negroes knew they would be whipped if they didn't behave themselves, and the fear of the lash kept them in good order." Evidence suggests that whippings were less frequent on small farms than on large plantations, but the reports of former slaves show that a large majority even of small farmers plied the lash. These beatings symbolized authority to the master and tyranny to the slaves, who made them a benchmark for evaluating a master. In the words of former slaves, a good owner was one who did not "whip too much,"

Physical and Mental Abuse of Slaves

To maximize the return on their investment, slaveowners put young and old to work, especially at harvest. This family of slaves was picking cotton outside Savannah in 1855. *The New-York Historical Society.*

whereas a bad owner "whipped till he'd bloodied you and blistered you."

As this testimony suggests, terrible abuses could and did occur. The master wielded virtually absolute authority on his plantation, and courts did not recognize the word of a chattel. Pregnant women were whipped, and there were burnings, mutilations, tortures, and murders. Yet the physical cruelty of slavery may have been less in the United States than elsewhere in the New World. In sugar-growing or mining regions of the Western Hemisphere in the 1800s, slaves were regarded as an expendable resource to be replaced after seven years. Treatment was so poor and families so uncommon that death rates were high and the heavily male slave population did not replace itself, and rapidly shrank in size. In the United States, by contrast, the slave population showed a steady natural increase, as births exceeded deaths, and each generation grew larger.

The worst evil of American slavery was not its physical cruelty but the fact of slavery itself: coercion, loss of freedom, belonging to another person. Recalling their days in bondage, some former slaves emphasized the physical abuse—those were "bullwhip days" to one woman; another said, "What I think 'bout slavery? Huh—nigger get back cut in slavery time, didn't he?" But their comments focused on the tyranny of whipping as much as the pain. A woman named Delia Garlic cut to the core when she said, "It's bad to belong to folks that own you soul an' body. I could tell you 'bout it all day, but even then you couldn't guess the awfulness of it." And a man named Thomas Lewis put it this way: "There was no such thing as being good to slaves. Many people were better than others, but a slave belonged to his master and there was no way to get out of it."

As these comments show, American slaves retained their mental independence and self-respect despite their bondage. They hated their oppression, and contrary to some whites' perceptions, they were not grateful to their oppressors. Although they had to be subservient and speak honeyed words in the presence of their masters, they talked quite differently later on among themselves. The evidence of their resistant attitudes comes from their actions and from their own life stories.

Former slaves reported some kind feelings between masters and slaves, but the overwhelming picture was one of antagonism and resistance. Slaves mistrusted kindness from whites and suspected self-interest in their owners. A woman whose mistress "was good to us Niggers" said her owner was kind " 'cause she was raisin' us to work for her." A man recalled that his owners "always thought lots of their niggers and Grandma Maria say, 'Why shouldn't they—it was their money.' " Christmas presents of clothing from the master did not mean anything, observed another, " 'cause he was going to [buy] that anyhow."

Slaves' Attitudes Toward Whites

Slaves also saw their owners as people who used human beings as beasts of burden. "Master was pretty good," said one man. "He treated us just about like you would a good mule." Another said that his master "fed us reg'lar on good, 'stantial food, just like you'd tend to your horse, if you had a real good one." A third recalled his master saying, " 'A well-fed, healthy nigger, next to a mule, is the best propersition a man can invest his money in.' "

Slaves were sensitive to the thousand daily signs of their degraded status. One man recalled the general rule that slaves ate cornbread and owners ate biscuits. If blacks did get biscuits, "the flour that we made the biscuits out of was the third-grade shorts." A woman reported that on her plantation "Old Master hunted a heap, but us never did get none of what he brought in." "Us catch lots of 'possums, but mighty few of 'em us Niggers ever got a chance to eat or rabbits neither," said another. "They made Niggers go out and hunt 'em and the white folks ate 'em." If the owner took slaves' garden produce to town and sold it for them, the slaves suspected him of pocketing part of the profits.

Suspicion and resentment often grew into hatred. According to a former slave from Virginia, "the white folks treated the nigger so mean that all the slaves prayed God to punish their cruel masters." When a yellow fever epidemic struck in 1852, many slaves saw it as God's retribution. As late as the 1930s an elderly woman named Minnie Fulkes cherished the conviction that God was going to punish white people for their cruelty to blacks. She described the whippings that her mother had had to endure and then exclaimed, "Lord, Lord, I hate white people and the flood waters goin' to drown some more." A young slave girl who had suffered abuse as a house servant admitted that she took cruel advantage of her mistress when the woman had a stroke. Instead of fanning the mistress to keep flies away, the young slave struck her in the face with the fan whenever they were alone. "I done that woman bad," the slave confessed, but "she was so mean to me."

The bitterness between blacks and whites was vividly expressed by a former slave named Savilla Burrell, who visited her former master on his deathbed long after the Civil War. Sitting beside him, she reflected on the lines that "sorrow had plowed on that old face and I remembered he'd been a captain on horseback in the war. It come into my remembrance the song of Moses: 'the Lord had triumphed glorily and the horse and his rider have been throwed into the sea.' " She felt sympathy for a dying man, but she also felt satisfaction at God's revenge.

On the plantation, of course, slaves had to keep such thoughts to themselves. Often they expressed one feeling to whites, another within their own race and culture.

The Old Plantation. *Slaves do the Juba, a dance of Yo-ruba origin, to the music of a stringed* molo *and a gudu-gudu (drum). The women's colorful headscarves recall Afri-can styles and customs, as does the man's use of a cane in his dance. Drawn in the late eighteenth century on a planta-tion between Charleston and Orangeburg. The Abby Ald-ridge Rockefeller Folk Art Center, Williamsburg, Virginia.*

SLAVE CULTURE AND
EVERYDAY LIFE

The force that helped slaves to maintain such defiance was their culture. They had their own view of the world, a body of beliefs and values born of both their past and their present, as well as the fellowship and support of their own community. With power overwhelmingly in the hands of whites, it was not possible for slaves to change their world. But drawing strength from their culture, they could resist their condition and struggle on against it.

Slave culture changed significantly after the turn of the century. Between 1790 and 1808, when Congress banned further importation of slaves, there was a rush to import Africans. After that the proportion of native-born blacks rose steadily, reaching 96 percent in 1840 and almost 100 percent in 1860. (For this reason blacks can trace their American ancestry back further than many white Americans.) Meanwhile, more and more slaves adopted Christianity. With time the old African culture faded further into memory as an Afro-American culture matured.

In one sense African influences remained primary. For African practices and beliefs reminded the slaves that they were and ought to be different from their oppressors, and thus encouraged them to resist. The most visible aspects of African culture were the slaves'

Remnants of African Culture

dress and recreation. Some slave men plaited their hair into rows and fancy designs; slave women often wore their hair "in string"—tied in small bunches with a string or piece of cloth. A few men and many women wrapped their heads in kerchiefs following the styles and colors of West Africa.

For entertainment slaves made musical instruments with carved motifs that resembled some African stringed instruments. Their drumming and dancing clearly followed African patterns; whites marveled at them. One visitor to Georgia in the 1860s described a ritual dance of African origin: "A ring of singers is formed. . . . They then utter a kind of melodious chant, which gradually increases in strength, and in noise, until it fairly shakes the house, and it can be heard for a long distance." This observer also noted the agility of the dancers and the call-and-response pattern in their chanting.

Many slaves continued to see and believe in spirits. Whites also believed in ghosts, but the belief was more widespread among slaves. It closely resembled the African concept of the living dead—the idea that deceased relatives visited the earth for many years until the process of dying was complete. Slaves also practiced conjuration, voodoo, and quasi-magical root medicine. By 1860 the most notable conjurers and root doctors were reputed to live in South Carolina, Georgia, Louisiana, and other isolated coastal areas of heavy slave importation.

These cultural survivals provided slaves with a sense of their separate past. Black achievement in music and dance was so exceptional that whites felt entirely cut off from it; in this one area some whites became aware that they did not "know" their slaves and that the slave community was a different world. Conjuration and folklore also directly fed resistance; slaves could cast a spell or direct the power of a hand (a bag of articles belonging to the person to be conjured) against the master. Not all masters felt confident enough to dismiss such a threat.

In adopting Christianity, slaves fashioned it too into an instrument of support and resistance. Theirs was a religion of justice quite unlike that of the propaganda their masters pushed at them. Former slaves scorned the preaching arranged by their masters. "You

Slave Religion

ought to have heard that preachin'," said one man. " 'Obey your master and mistress, don't steal chickens and eggs and meat,' but nary a word about havin' a soul to save." To the slaves, Jesus cared about their souls and their present plight. They rejected the idea that in heaven whites would have "the colored folks . . . there to wait on em." Instead, when God's justice came, the slaveholders would be "broilin' in hell for their sin." "God is punishin' some of them ol' suckers and their children right now for the way they used to treat us poor colored folks," said one woman.

For slaves Christianity was a religion of personal and group salvation. Devout men and women worshipped and prayed every day, "in the field or by the side of the road," or in special "prayer grounds" such as a "twisted thick-rooted muscadine bush" that afforded privacy. Beyond seeking personal guidance, these worshippers prayed "for deliverance of the slaves." Some waited "until the overseer got behind a hill" and then laid down their hoes and called on God to free them. Others held fervent secret prayer meetings that lasted far into the night. From such activities many slaves gained the unshakable belief that God would end their bondage. As one man asserted, "it was the plans of God to free us niggers." This faith and the joy and emotional release that accompanied their worship sustained blacks.

Slaves also developed a sense of racial identity. The whole experience of southern blacks taught them that whites despised their race. White people, as one ex-slave put it, "have been and are now and always will be against the Negro." Even "the best white woman that ever broke bread wasn't much," said another, " 'cause they all hated the poor nigger." Blacks naturally drew together, helping each other in danger, need, and resistance. "We never told on each other," one woman declared. Former slaves were virtually unanimous in denouncing those who betrayed the group or sought personal advantage through allegiance to whites.

Of course, different jobs and circumstances created natural variations in attitude among slaves. But for most slaves, there was no overriding class system within the black community. Only one-quarter of all slaves lived on plantations of fifty blacks or more, so few knew a wide chasm between exalted house servants and lowly field hands. In fact, many slaves did both housework and field work, depending on their age and the season. Their primary loyalty was to each other.

The main source of support was the family. Slave families faced severe dangers. At any moment the master could sell a husband or wife, give a slave child away as a wedding present, or die in debt, forcing a division of his property. Many families were broken in such ways. Others were uprooted in the trans-Appalachian expansion of the South, which caused a large interregional movement of the black population. Between 1810 and 1820 alone, 137,000 slaves were forced to move from North Carolina and the Chesapeake states to Alabama, Mississippi, and other western regions. An estimated 2 million persons were sold between 1820 and 1860. When the Union Army registered thousands of black marriages in Mississippi and Louisiana in 1864 and 1865, 25 percent of the men over forty reported that they had been forcibly separated from a previous wife. A similar proportion of former slaves later recalled that slavery had destroyed one of their marriages. Probably a substantial minority of slave families suffered disruption of one kind or another.

Slave Family Life

But this did not mean that slave families could not exist. American slaves clung tenaciously to the personal relationships that gave meaning to life. For although American law did not protect slave families, masters permitted them. In fact, slaveowners expected slaves to form families and have children. As a result, even along the rapidly expanding edge of the cotton kingdom, where the effects of the slave trade would have been most visible, there remained a normal ratio of men to women, young to old.

Following African kinship taboos, Afro-Americans avoided marriage between cousins (a frequent occurrence among aristocratic slaveowners). Adapting to the circumstances of their captivity, they did not condemn unwed mothers, although they did expect a young girl to form a stable marriage after one pregnancy, if not before. By naming their children after relatives of past generations, Afro-Americans emphasized their family histories. If they chose to bear the surname of a white slaveowner, it was often not their current master's but that of the owner under whom their family had begun.

Slaves abhorred interference in their family lives. Some of their strongest protests sought to prevent the breakup of a family. Indeed, some individuals refused to accept such separations and struggled for years to maintain or re-establish contact. Rape was a horror for both men and women. Some husbands faced death rather than permit their wives to be sexually abused, and women sometimes fought back. In other cases slaves seethed with anger at the injustice but could do nothing except soothe each other with human sympathy and understanding. Significantly, blacks condemned the guilty party, not the victim.

Slave men did not dominate their wives in a manner similar to white husbands, but it is misleading to say that slave women enjoyed equality of power in sex roles and family life. The larger truth is that all black people, men *and* women, were denied the opportunity to provide for or protect their families. Slavery's cruelties put black men and women in the same dilemma. Under the pressures of bondage they had to share the responsibilities of parenthood. Each might have to stand in for the other and assume extra duties. Similarly, uncles, aunts, and grandparents sometimes raised the children of those who had been sold away.

In two other respects, however, distinct gender roles remained very important in slave families and experience. First, after work in the fields was done, men's activities focused on traditional "outdoor" tasks while women did "indoor" work. Slave men hunted and fished for the family stewpot, fashioned a rough piece of furniture, or repaired implements; women cooked the food, mended garments, and cleaned house. It is clear, too, that slave families resembled white families in the fact that black men held a respected place in their homes.

Sex Roles

Second, the life cycle and pattern of work routines frequently placed slave women in close associations with each other that heightened their sense of sisterhood. On plantations young girls worked together as house servants, nursing mothers shared opportunities to feed and care for their children, adults worked together in many common tasks from soapmaking to quilting, and old women were assigned to spin thread or supervise a nursery. Female slaves thus lived significant portions of their lives as part of a group of women, a fact that emphasized the gender-based element of their experience.

Although slave marriage ceremonies were often brief, usually involving jumping over a broomstick in the master's presence, partners "stuck lots closer then," in one woman's words. "[When] they marries they stayed married," said another. When husbands and wives lived on neighboring plantations, visits on Wednesday and Saturday nights included big dinners of welcome and celebration. Christmas was a similarly joyous time " 'cause husbands is coming home and families is getting united again."

Slaves brought to their efforts at resistance the same common sense, determination, and practicality that characterized their family lives. American slavery produced some fearless and implacable revolutionaries. Gabriel's conspiracy apparently was known to more than a thousand slaves when it was discovered in 1800, just before it was put into motion (see page 205). A similar conspiracy in Charleston in 1822, headed by a free black named Denmark Vesey, involved many of the most trusted slaves of leading families. But the most famous rebel of all, Nat Turner, rose in violence in Southampton County, Virginia, in 1831.

Resistance to Slavery

The son of an African woman who passionately hated her enslavement, Nat was a precocious child who learned to read very young. Encouraged by his first owner to study the Bible, he enjoyed some special privileges but also knew changes of masters and hard work. His father, who successfully ran away to freedom, stood always before him as an example of defiance. In time young Nat became a preacher, an impressive orator with a reputation among whites as well as blacks. He also developed a tendency toward mysticism, and he became increasingly withdrawn. After nurturing his plan for several years, Turner led a band of rebels from house to house in the predawn darkness of August 22, 1831. The group severed limbs and crushed skulls with axes or killed their victims with guns. Before they were stopped, Nat Turner and his followers had slaughtered sixty whites of both sexes and all ages. Nat and perhaps two hundred blacks, including many innocent victims of marauding whites, lost their lives as a result of the rebellion.

But most slave resistance was not violent, for the odds against revolution were especially poor in North America. The South had the highest ratio of whites to blacks in the hemisphere; at the same time plantations were relatively small, which meant that whites had ample opportunity to supervise the slaves' activities. There was thus literal truth to one slave's remark that "the white man was the slave's jail." Moreover, the South lacked vital geographic and demographic features that had aided revolution elsewhere. The land offered relatively few jungles and mountain fastnesses to which rebels could flee. And compared with South America, southern slave importations were neither large nor prolonged. The South therefore lacked a preponderance of young male slaves. Nor were its military forces weak and overtaxed, like those of many Latin American nations and colonies.

Thus the scales weighed heavily against revolution, and the slaves knew it. Consequently they directed their energies toward creating means of survival and resistance within slavery. A desperate slave could run away for good, but as often or probably more often slaves simply ran off temporarily to hide in the woods. There they were close to friends and allies who could help them escape capture in an area they knew well. Every day that a slave "lay out" in this way the master lost a day's labor. Most owners chose not to mount an exhaustive search and sent word instead that the slave's grievances would be redressed. The runaway would then return to bargain with the master. Most owners would let the matter pass, for, like the owner of a valuable cook, they were "glad to get her back."

Other modes of resistance had the same object: to resist but survive under bondage. Appropriating food (stealing, in the master's eyes) was so common that even whites sang humorous songs about it. Blacks were also alert to the attitudes of individual whites, and learned to ingratiate themselves or play off one white person against another. Field hands frequently tested a new overseer to intimidate him or win more favorable working conditions. Other blacks fought with patrollers. Some slaves engaged in verbal arguments and even physical violence to deter or resist beatings. The harshest masters were the most strongly resisted. "Good masters had good slaves 'cause they treated 'em good," but "where the old master was mean an' ornery," his slaves were ornery too.

HARMONY AND TENSION IN A SLAVE SOCIETY

Not only for blacks but for whites too, slave labor stood at the heart of the South's social system. A host of consequences flowed from its existence, from the organization of society to an individual's personal values.

For blacks, the nineteenth century brought a strengthening and expansion of the legal restrictions of slavery. In all things, from their workaday movements to Sunday worship, slaves fell under the supervision of whites. Courts held that a slave "has no civil right" and could not even hold property "except at the will and pleasure of his master." When slaves revolted, legislators tightened the legal straitjacket: after the Nat Turner insurrection in 1832, for example, they prohibited owners from teaching their slaves to read.

The weight of this legal and social framework fell on nonblacks as well. All white male citizens bore an obligation to ride in patrols to discourage slave movements at night. Whites in strategic positions, such as ship captains and harbor masters, were required to scrutinize the papers of blacks who might be attempting to escape bondage. White southerners who criticized the slave system out of moral conviction or class resentment were intimidated, attacked, or legally prosecuted. (Some, like James Birney, went north to join the antislavery movement, and two sisters from Charleston, Angelina and Sarah Grimké, became leading advocates of both abolition and women's rights—see pages 331–332.) Urban residents who did not supervise their domestic slaves as closely as planters found themselves subject to criticism. And the South's few manufacturers felt pressure to use slave rather than free labor.

Slavery had a deep effect on southern values because it was the main determinant of wealth in the South. Ownership of slaves guaranteed the labor to produce cotton and other crops on a large scale—labor otherwise unavailable in a rural society. Slaves were therefore vital to the acquisition of a fortune. Beyond

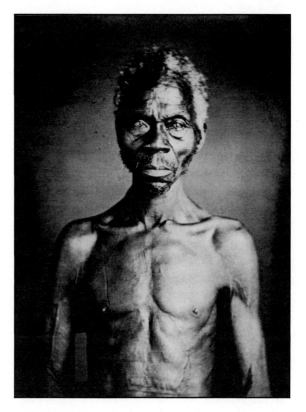

Slave property was tangible wealth—an investment—to whites. Increasingly they tried to deny that slaves were people who suffered, as this rare photograph of Renty, an elderly "Congo" field hand, reminds us.   Harvard University.

Slavery as the Basis of Wealth and Social Standing that, slaves were a commodity and an investment, much like gold; people bought them on speculation, hoping for a steady rise in their value. In fact, for southern society as a whole, slaveholding indicated wealth in general with remarkable precision. Important economic enterprises not based on slavery were so rare that the correspondence between geographic variations in wealth and variations in slaveholding was nearly one-to-one.

It was therefore natural that slaveholding should be the main determinant of a man's social position, with women deriving high status from their husband's or father's ownership of slaves. Wealth in slaves was also the foundation on which the ambitious built their reputations. Ownership of slaves brought political power: a solid majority of political officeholders were slaveholders, and the most powerful of them were generally large slaveholders. Though lawyers and newspaper editors were sometimes influential, they did not hold independent positions in the economy or society. Dependent on the planters for business and support, they served planters' interests and reflected their outlook.

As slavery became entrenched, its influence spread throughout the social system until even the values and mores of nonslaveholders bore its imprint. For one thing, the availability of slave labor tended to devalue free labor. Where strenuous work under another was reserved for an enslaved race, few free people relished working "like a nigger." Nonslaveholders therefore preferred to work for themselves rather than to hire out. Whites who had to sell their labor tended to resent or reject tasks that seemed degrading. This kind of thinking engendered an aristocratic value system ill-suited to a newly established democracy.

In modified form the attitudes characteristic of the planter elite gained a considerable foothold among the masses. The ideal of the aristocrat emphasized lineage, privilege, power, pride, and refinement of person and manner. Some of those qualities were in short supply in the recently settled, expanding cotton kingdom, however; they mingled with and were modified by the tradition of the frontier. In particular, independence, and defense of one's honor were highly valued by planter and frontier farmer alike.

Aristocratic Values and Frontier Individualism

Fights and even duels over personal slights were not uncommon in southern communities. This custom sprang from both frontier lawlessness and aristocratic tradition. Throughout the sparsely settled regions of America in the early nineteenth century, pugnacious people took the law into their own hands. Thus it was not unusual for a southern slaveowner who had warned patrollers to stay off his property to shoot at the next group of trespassers. But instead of gradually disappearing, as it did in the North, the code duello, which required men to defend their honor through the rituals of a duel, hung on in the South and gained an acceptance that spread throughout the society.

An incident that occurred in North Carolina in 1851 will illustrate. A wealthy planter named Samuel Fleming responded to a series of disputes with the rising lawyer William Waightstill Avery by whipping or "cowhiding" him on a public street. According to the code, Avery had two choices: to redeem his honor through violence or to brand himself a coward through inaction. Three weeks later Avery shot Fleming dead at pointblank range during a session of Burke County Superior Court, with Judge William Battle and numerous spectators looking on. A jury took just ten minutes to find Avery not guilty, and the spectators gave him a standing ovation. Some people, including Judge Battle, were troubled by the victory of the unwritten code over the law, but most white males seemed satisfied.

Other aristocratic values that marked the planters as a class were less acceptable to the average citizen. Simply put, planters believed they were better than other people. In their pride, they expected not only to wield power but to receive special treatment. By the 1850s, some planters openly rejected the democratic creed, vilifying Jefferson for his statement that all men were equal.

These ideas shaped the outlook of the southern elite for generations, but they were never acceptable to the individualistic members of the yeoman class. Independent and proud of their position, yeomen resisted any infringement of their rights. They believed that they were as good as anyone, and many belonged to evangelical faiths that exalted values far removed from the planters' love of wealth. They were conscious, too, that they lived in a nation in which democratic ideals were gaining strength. Thus there were occasional conflicts between aristocratic pretensions and democratic zeal. As Mary Boykin Chesnut pointed out, a wealthy planter who sought public office could not announce his status too haughtily. She described the plight of Colonel John S. Preston, a South Carolinian with great ambitions. Preston, a perfect aristocrat, carried his high-flown manners too far; he refused to make the necessary gestures of respect toward the average voter—mingling with the crowd, exchanging jokes and compliments. Thus his highest aspiration, political leadership, could never be fulfilled. The voters would not accept him.

Such tensions found significant expression in the western parts of the seaboard states during the 1820s and 1830s. There yeoman farmers and citizens resented their underrepresentation in state legislatures, corruption in government, and undemocratic control

Democratic Reform Movements

over local government. After vigorous debate, the reformers won most of their battles. Five states—Alabama, Mississippi, Tennessee, Arkansas, and Texas—adopted what was for that time a thoroughly democratic system: popular election of governors; white manhood suffrage; legislative apportionment based on the white population; and locally chosen county government. Kentucky was democratically governed except in its counties. Georgia, Florida, and Louisiana were not far behind, and reformers won significant concessions in Maryland and some adjustments in North Carolina. Only South Carolina and Virginia effectively defended property qualifications for office, legislative malapportionment, appointment of county officials, and selection of the governor by the lawmakers. Democracy had expanded with the cotton kingdom.

Even in Virginia, nonslaveholding westerners raised a basic challenge to the slave system. Following the Nat Turner rebellion, advocates of gradual abolition forced a two-week legislative debate on slavery, arguing that it was injurious to the state and inherently dangerous. When the House of Delegates finally voted, the motion favoring abolition lost by just 73 to 58. This was the last major debate on slavery in the antebellum South.

With such tension in evidence, it was perhaps remarkable that slaveholders and nonslaveholders did not experience frequent and serious conflict. Why were class confrontations among whites so infrequent? Historians who have considered this question have given many answers. In a rural society, family bonds and kinship ties are valued, and some of the poor nonslaveholding whites were related to the rich new planters. The experience of frontier living must also have created a relatively informal, egalitarian atmosphere. And there is no doubt that the South's racial ideology, which stressed whites' superiority to blacks and race, not class, as the social dividing line, tended to reduce conflict among whites.

Also, it is important to remember that the South was a new and mobile society. Many people had risen in status, and far more were moving away geographically. Yeomen often moved several times during a lifetime of farming, and many slaveowners did too. Even in cotton-rich Alabama in the 1850s, fewer than half the richest families in a county belonged

to its elite category ten years later. Most had not died or lost their wealth; they had merely moved on to some new state. This constant mobility meant that southern society had not settled into a rigid, unchanging pattern.

But two other factors, social and economic, were probably more important. First, the South was rural and uncrowded. Travel was difficult, and people stayed much to themselves. Consequently slaveowners and nonslaveowners rarely collided or confronted each other as groups. Classes, as collective, competing objects, were rarely visible. Second, the two groups functioned quite independently of each other. The yeomen farmed for themselves; planters farmed for themselves and for the market. The complementary growing patterns of corn and cotton allowed planters to raise food for their animals and laborers without lowering cotton production: from spring through December, cotton and corn needed attention alternately, but never at the same time. Thus the planter did not need to depend on the nonslaveholder, and yeomen needed nothing from the planters. In politics, too, national issues that affected planters economically often had less meaning to yeomen who stayed largely outside the market economy.

There were signs, however, that the relative lack of conflict between slaveholders and nonslaveholders was coming to an end. As the region grew older,

Hardening of Class Lines

nonslaveholders saw their opportunities beginning to narrow; meanwhile wealthy planters enjoyed an expanding horizon. The risks of cotton production were becoming too great and the cost of slaves too high for many yeomen to rise in society. Thus from 1830 to 1860 the percentage of white southern families holding slaves declined steadily from 36 to 25 percent. At the same time, the monetary gap between the classes was widening. Although nonslaveholders were becoming more prosperous, slaveowners' wealth was increasing much faster. And though slaveowners made up a smaller portion of the population in 1860, their share of the South's agricultural wealth remained at between 90 and 95 percent. In fact, the average slaveholder was almost fourteen times as rich as the average nonslaveholder.

Urban artisans and mechanics felt the pinch acutely. Their numbers were few, their place in society was hardly recognized, and in bad times they were often the first to lose work. Moreover, they faced stiff competition from urban slaves, whose masters wanted them to hire their time and bring in money by practicing a trade. White workers in Charleston, Wilmington, and elsewhere staged protests and demanded that economic competition from slaves be forbidden. This demand was always ignored—the powerful slaveowners would not tolerate interference with their property or the income they derived from it. But the angry protests of white workers resulted in harsh restrictions on *free* black workers and craftsmen, who lacked any powerful allies to stand behind them. In Charleston on the eve of the Civil War, many successful free blacks actually felt compelled to leave the city.

Pre–Civil War politics reflected these tensions. Facing the prospect of a war to defend slavery, slaveowners expressed growing fear about the loyalty of nonslaveholders and discussed schemes to widen slave ownership, including reopening of the African slave trade. In North Carolina, a prolonged and increasingly bitter controversy over the combination of high taxes on land and low taxes on slaves erupted, and a class-conscious nonslaveholder named Hinton R. Helper denounced the slave system. Convinced that slavery had impoverished many whites and retarded the whole region, Helper attacked the institution in his book *The Impending Crisis,* published in New York in 1857. Discerning planters knew that such fiery controversies lay close at hand in every southern state.

But for the moment slaveowners stood secure. They held from 50 to 85 percent of the seats in state legislatures and a similarly high percentage of the South's congressional seats. In addition to their near-monopoly on political office, they had established their point of view in all the other major social institutions. Professors who criticized slavery had been dismissed from colleges and universities; schoolbooks that contained "unsound" ideas had been replaced. And almost all the Methodist and Baptist clergy, some of whom had criticized slavery in the 1790s, had given up preaching against the institution. In fact, except for a few obscure persons of conscience, southern clergy had become its most vocal defenders. Society as southerners knew it seemed stable, if not unthreatened.

Elsewhere in the nation, however, society was anything but stable. Change had become one of the major characteristics of the northern economy and society, and social conflict was an increasingly common phenomenon. Throughout the North, in a variety of ways, people were trying to cope with change.

SUGGESTIONS FOR FURTHER READING

Southern Society

Edward L. Ayers, *Vengeance and Justice* (1984); W. J. Cash, *The Mind of the South* (1941); Avery O. Craven, *The Growth of Southern Nationalism, 1848–1861* (1953); Clement Eaton, *The Growth of Southern Civilization, 1790–1860* (1961); Clement Eaton, *Freedom of Thought in the Old South* (1940); Alison Goodyear Freehling, *Drift Toward Dissolution* (1982); William W. Freehling, *Prelude to Civil War* (1965); Eugene D. Genovese, "Yeoman Farmers in a Slaveholders' Democracy," *Agricultural History,* 49 (April 1975), 331–342; Eugene D. Genovese, *The World the Slaveholders Made* (1964); William Sumner Jenkins, *Pro-Slavery Thought in the Old South* (1935); Donald G. Mathews, *Religion in the Old South* (1977); Robert McColley, *Slavery and Jeffersonian Virginia* (1964); Frederick Law Olmsted, *The Slave States,* ed. Harvey Wish (1959); Edward Phifer, "Slavery in Microcosm: Burke County, North Carolina," *Journal of Southern History,* XXVIII (May 1962), 137–165; Charles S. Sydnor, *The Development of Southern Sectionalism, 1819–1848* (1948); Ralph A. Wooster, *Politicians, Planters, and Plain Folk* (1975); Ralph A. Wooster, *The People in Power* (1969); Gavin Wright, *The Political Economy of the Cotton South* (1978); Bertram Wyatt-Brown, *Southern Honor* (1982).

Slaveholders and Nonslaveholders

Bennet H. Barrow, *Plantation Life in the Florida Parishes of Louisiana, as Reflected in the Diary of Bennet H. Barrow,* ed. Edwin Adams Davis (1943); Ira Berlin, *Slaves Without Masters* (1974); William J. Cooper, *The South and the Politics of Slavery, 1828–1856* (1978); Everett Dick, *The Dixie Frontier* (1948); Clement Eaton, *The Mind of the Old South* (1967); Drew Faust, *James Henry Hammond and the Old South* (1982); Drew Faust, *A Sacred Circle: The Dilemma of the Intellectual in the Old South* (1977); John Hope Franklin, *The Militant South, 1800–1861* (1956); John Hope Franklin, *The Free Negro in North Carolina, 1790–1860* (1943); Luther P. Jackson, *Free Negro Labor and Property Holding in Virginia,*

1830–1860 (1942); Michael P. Johnson and James L. Roark, *Black Masters* (1984); Frances Anne Kemble, *Journal of a Residence on a Georgian Plantation in 1838–1839* (1863); Robert Manson Myers, ed., *The Children of Pride* (1972); James Oakes, *The Ruling Race* (1982); Frank L. Owsley, *Plain Folk of the Old South* (1949); J. Mills Thornton, III, *Politics and Power in a Slave Society* (1978); C. Vann Woodward, ed., *Mary Chesnut's Civil War*, (1981).

Southern Women

Carol Bleser, *The Hammonds of Redcliffe* (1981); Jane Turner Censer, *North Carolina Planters and Their Children, 1800–1860* (1984); Catherine Clinton, *The Plantation Mistress* (1982); Jacqueline Jones, *Labor of Love, Labor of Sorrow* (1985); Suzanne Lebsock, *Free Women of Petersburg* (1983); Elisabeth Muhlenfeld, *Mary Boykin Chesnut* (1981); Mary D. Robertson, ed., *Lucy Breckinridge of Grove Hill* (1979); Ann Firor Scott, *The Southern Lady* (1970); Deborah G. White, *Arn't I a Woman?* (1985); C. Vann Woodward and Elisabeth Muhlenfeld, eds., *The Private Mary Chesnut* (1985).

Conditions of Slavery

Kenneth F. Kiple and Virginia H. Kiple, "Black Tongue and Black Men," *Journal of Southern History*, XLIII (August 1977), 411–428; Ronald L. Lewis, *Coal, Iron, and Slaves* (1979); Richard G. Lowe and Randolph B. Campbell, "The Slave Breeding Hypothesis," *Journal of Southern History*, XLII (August 1976), 400–412; Leslie Howard Owens, *This Species of Property* (1976); Willie Lee Rose, ed., *A Documentary History of Slavery in North America* (1976); Todd L. Savitt, *Medicine and Slavery* (1978); Kenneth M. Stampp, *The Peculiar Institution* (1956); Robert S. Starobin, *Industrial Slavery in the Old South* (1970).

Slave Culture and Resistance

Herbert Aptheker, *American Negro Slave Revolts* (1943); John W. Blassingame, *The Slave Community* (1972); Judith Wragg Chase, *Afro-American Art and Craft* (1971); Jeffrey J. Crow, *The Black Experience in Revolutionary North Carolina* (1977); Dena J. Epstein, *Sinful Tunes and Spirituals* (1977); Paul D. Escott, *Slavery Remembered* (1979); Eric Foner, ed., *Nat Turner* (1971); Eugene D. Genovese, *From Rebellion to Revolution* (1979); Eugene D. Genovese, *Roll, Jordan, Roll* (1974); Herbert G. Gutman, *The Black Family in Slavery and Freedom, 1750–1925* (1976); Vincent Harding, *There Is a River* (1981); Charles Joyner, *Down by the Riverside* (1984); Lawrence W. Levine, *Black Culture and Black Consciousness* (1977); Gerald W. Mullin, *Flight and Rebellion* (1972); Stephen B. Oates, *The Fires of Jubilee* (1975); Albert J. Raboteau, *Slave Religion* (1978); Robert S. Starobin, *Denmark Vesey* (1970); Peter H. Wood, *Black Majority* (1974).

Reform, Politics, and Expansion

1824–1844

Chapter 12

The gaunt, bearded New Englander Henry David Thoreau was skeptical of the value of the artifacts of a changing economy and society: railroads, steamboats, the telegraph, factories, and cities. "There is an illusion about" such improvements, he wrote in *Walden, or Life in the Woods* (1854). "There is not always a positive advance. . . . Men think that it is essential that the *Nation* have commerce, and export ice, and talk through a telegraph, and ride thirty miles an hour . . . but whether we should live like baboons or like men, is a little uncertain."

Thoreau was seeking to escape the marketplace, to forgo the world of cities and factories, to live simply in the landscape that existed before the plow and the engine, when he retreated to the wilderness shores of Walden Pond in Concord, Massachusetts. Yet for all his idealization of the simple life, Thoreau did not withdraw from the world, much less from Concord. While at Walden he dined with townsfolk, joined the men congregating around the grocery-store stove, and hosted picnics. In reality his everyday life was infused with all those modern improvements he seemed to spurn. Thoreau even raised a cash crop—beans—and sold it to support himself at Walden. As he said in his own journal, he loved "society as much as most." But he was caught up in a basic ambivalence toward industrialization and urbanization that he shared with millions of other Americans. They were lured on the one hand by the simplicity and beauty of pastoral days gone by, pulled on the other by their belief in progress and the promise of machine-generated prosperity and happiness.

In the early nineteenth century, reformers of all kinds sought to find or impose harmony on a society in which economic change and discord had reached a crescendo. Prompted by the evangelical ardor of the Second Great Awakening and convinced of the perfectibility of the human race, they crusaded for individual improvement. Some withdrew from the everyday competitive world to seek perfection in utopian communities. Others sought to improve themselves by renouncing alcohol. Inevitably the personal impulse to reform oneself led to the creation and reshaping of institutions. Schools, penitentiaries, and other institutions all underwent scrutiny and reform. Women were prominent in the reform movement, and the role of women in public life became an issue in itself.

Eventually one concern overrode all others: antislavery. No single issue evoked the depth of passion that slavery did. On a personal level it pitted neighbor against neighbor, settler against settler, section against section. Territorial expansion in the 1840s and 1850s would make it politically explosive as well.

Once reformers of various causes became a cohesive group, they naturally turned to the state as an effective instrument of social and economic change. The line between social reform and politics was not always distinguishable. Their opponents were no less concerned with social problems. What set them apart from reformers was their skepticism about human perfectibility and their distrust of institutions and power, both public and private. To them, coercion was the greater evil. They sought to reverse, not shape, change.

In the late 1820s the opponents of reform found a champion in Andrew Jackson and a home in the Democratic party. Jackson reversed the emphasis of previous presidents on an activist national government, believing that a strong federal government restricted individual freedom by favoring one group over another. In response, reformers rallied around the new Whig party, which became the vehicle for humanitarian reform. The two parties competed energetically in the second party system, a system marked by strong organizations, intensely loyal followings, and religious and ethnic differences.

During the economically prosperous 1840s, both Democrats and Whigs eagerly promoted westward expansion to further their goals. Democrats saw the agrarian West as an antidote to urbanization and industrialization; Whigs focused on new commercial opportunities. The idea of expansion from coast to coast seemed to Americans to be the inevitable manifest destiny of the United States. The politics of territorial expansion would collide with the antislavery movement with explosive results in the 1850s and 1860s.

The Lackawanna Valley (1855) by George Inness. Hired by the Lackawanna Railroad to paint a railroad scene, Inness blended landscape and machine into an organic whole. American industrialism, Inness seemed to say, belonged to the landscape; it would neither overpower nor obliterate the land. National Gallery of Art, Washington, Gift of Mrs. Huttleston Rogers.

REFORM AND RELIGIOUS REVIVAL

While the South was becoming more entrenched in a plantation system and slave society, the vast changes taking place in the rest of the country were having an unsettling effect. Population growth, immigration, internal migration, loosening family and community ties, the advancing frontier, and territorial expansion all contributed to the remaking of the United States. But the undisputed symbol of change was the machine—that fine-tooled, power-driven substitute for men's and women's own hands, stamping out interchangeable parts for other machines. Some feared it would turn America into a giant factory, in which everything would be viewed as a commodity to be sold at the marketplace.

Many people felt they were no longer masters of their own fate. Change was occurring so rapidly that people had difficulty keeping up with it. An apprentice tailor could find his trade obsolete by the time he became a journeyman; a student could find himself lacking sufficient arithmetic to enter a counting house when he graduated; a young rural woman could find her tasks unneeded on her family's farm. Americans had fought the Revolution to make themselves independent; poverty and obsolescent trades and education made them dependent. Other aspects of change were simply unpleasant or culturally alien. Respectable citizens found their safety threatened by urban mobs and paupers, and the Protestant majority feared the growing Catholic minority, with their distinctive customs and beliefs. Protestants had waged war to preserve the rights they claimed as Englishmen, not to protect alien cultures and religions. To many, all these changes seemed to undermine republican virtues.

Disturbed by change, yet convinced that the world could be improved, and confident that they could do something about it, various reformers and reform movements began to emerge and coalesce during the 1820s. Basically, reformers sought to restore order to a society made disorderly by economic, social, and cultural change. They were so active from 1820 through the 1850s that the period became known as an age of reform.

Reform was at its core an attempt to impose more direction on society. The movement encompassed both individual improvement (religion, temperance, health) and institutional reform (antislavery, women's rights, and education). Some reformers were motivated more by fear than by hope—Antimasonic, nativist, and anti-Catholic. Not all the problems that reformers addressed were new to the nineteenth century; some were generations old. Slavery had existed in the United States for two centuries, and alcohol had been a colonial problem; yet neither became a national issue until the 1820s and after, when the reformist ferment prompted action.

Though reform movements played an important role in all sections of the country, most were northern. In the South, slavery and the complex issues surrounding that institution tended to suppress the reform impulse. Fear of educating blacks, for instance, led even antislavery southerners to ignore the movement for educational reform.

The prime motivating force behind organized reform was probably religion. Starting in the late 1790s, a tremendous religious revival, the Second Great Awakening, galvanized Protestants, especially women (see pages 201–204). The Awakening began in small villages in the East, intensified in the 1820s in western New York, and continued

Second Great Awakening

through the late 1840s. Under its influence, Christians in all parts of the country tried to right the wrongs of the world.

Evangelical Christianity was a religion of the heart, not the head. In 1821 Charles G. Finney, "the father of modern revivalism," experienced a soul-shaking conversion, which, he said, brought him "a retainer from the Lord Jesus Christ to plead his cause." Finney, a former teacher and lawyer, immediately began his career as a converter of souls, preaching that salvation could be achieved through spontaneous conversion or spiritual rebirth like his own. In everyday language, he told his audiences that "God has made man a moral free agent." In other words, evil was avoidable; Christians were not doomed by original sin. Hence anyone could achieve salvation. Finney's brand of revivalism transcended sects, wealth, and race. Presbyterians, Baptists, and Congregationalists became evangelists, as did some Methodists.

The Second Great Awakening also raised people's hopes for the Second Coming of the Christian messiah and the establishment of the Kingdom of God on earth. Revivalists set out to speed the Second Coming by creating a heaven on earth. They joined the forces of good and light—reform—to combat those of evil and darkness. Some revivalists even believed that the United States had a special mission in God's design, and therefore a special role in eliminating evil.

Regardless of theology, all shared a belief in individual perfection as a moving force. In this way the Second Great Awakening bred reform, and evangelical Protestants became missionaries for both religious and secular salvation. Wherever they preached, voluntary societies arose. Evangelists organized an association for each issue—temperance, education, Sabbath observance, antidueling, and later antislavery; collectively these groups formed a national web of benevolent and moral reform societies.

As social change accelerated in the 1830s and 1840s, so did reform. In western New York and Ohio, Charles G. Finney's preaching was a catalyst to reform. Western New York experienced such continuous and heated waves of revivalism that it became known as the "burned-over" district. The opening of the Erie Canal and the migration of New Englanders carried the reform ferment farther westward. There, revivalist institutions—Ohio's Lane Seminary and Oberlin

College were the most famous—sent committed graduates out into the world to spread the gospel of reform. Evangelists also organized grassroots political movements. In the late 1830s and 1840s they rallied around the Whig party in an attempt to use government as an instrument of reform. Their efforts stirred nonevangelical Protestants, Catholics, and Jews as well as evangelical Christians.

Women were the earliest converts, and they tended to sustain the Second Great Awakening. When Finney led daytime prayer meetings in Rochester, New York, for instance, pious middle-class women visited families while the men were away at work. Slowly they brought their families and husbands into the churches and under the influence of reform. Women more than men tended to feel personally responsible for the increasingly secular orientation of the expanding market economy. Many women felt guilty for neglecting their religious duties, and the emotionally charged conversion experience set them on the right path again.

At first, revival seemed to reinforce the cult of domesticity since piety and religious values were associated with the domestic sphere (see Chapter 10). In the conversion experience, women declared their submissiveness to the will of Providence, vowing to purge themselves and the world of wickedness. Yet the commitment to spread the word, to become evangelicals, led to new, public roles for women. The organized prayer groups and female missionary societies that preceded and accompanied the Second Great Awakening were soon surpassed by greater organized reform and religious activity. Thus revival prompted and legitimized woman's public role, providing a path of certainty and stability amidst a rapidly changing economy and society.

From Revival to Reform

The establishment and work of female reform societies were not merely responses to inner voices; they were reactions to the poverty and wretched urban conditions found in the growing cities. At the turn of the nineteenth century, most of the expanding cities had women's societies to help needy women and orphans, as did Salem, Massachusetts, with its Female Charitable Society. The spread of poverty and vice that accompanied urbanization increasingly affected women, especially those caught up in the fervor of revival.

An 1830 exposé of prostitution in New York City revealed the diverging concerns and responses of men and women and demonstrated the convergence of urban problems, revival, and reform. John R. McDowall, a divinity student, detailed how prostitution had taken hold on New York City. Philip Hone, one of the city's leaders (see page 275), called McDowall's *Magdalen Report* "a disgraceful document," and he and other New York men united to defend the city's good name against "those base slanders." Their condemnation led the male-run New York Magdalen Society to cease its work. Women, on the other hand, moved by the plight of "fallen women," responded by forming two new societies concerned with prostitutes and prostitution. In revival and reform, women acted in the face of men's opposition and indifference.

The Female Moral Reform Society, in particular, led the crusade against prostitution. Over the next decade, the New York–based association expanded its activities and geographical scope as the American Female Moral Reform Society. By 1840, it had 555 affiliated female societies among the converted across the nation. These women not only fought the evils of prostitution but also assisted poor women and orphans and entered the political sphere. In New York State in the 1840s the movement fostered public morality by successfully crusading for criminal sanctions against seducers and prostitutes.

Another response to change was the interest in utopian communities. Such settlements offered an antidote to the market economy and to the untamed growth of large urban communities, and an opportunity to restore tradition and social cohesion. Whatever their particular philosophy, utopians sought order and regularity in their daily lives and a cooperative rather than competitive environment. Some experimented with communal living and nontraditional work, family, and gender roles.

America's earliest utopian experiments were organized by the Shakers, who derived their name from the way they danced and swayed at worship services.

Shakers

An offshoot of the Quakers, their sect was established in America in 1774 by the English Shaker Ann Lee. Shakers believed that the end of the world was near, and that sin entered the world through sexual intercourse. They regarded existing churches as too

Etching of a Shaker dance during worship.   *Library of Congress.*

worldly and considered the Shaker family the in-strument of salvation.

After the death of Mother Ann Lee in 1784, the Shakers turned to communal living to fulfill their mission. In 1787 they "gathered in" at New Lebanon, New York, to live, worship, and work communally. Other colonies soon followed. At its peak, between 1820 and 1860, the sect had about six thousand members in twenty settlements in eight states. Shaker communities emphasized agriculture and crafts; most managed to become self-sufficient, profitable enter-prises. In particular, Shaker furniture became famous for its excellent construction, utility, and beauty of design.

Though economically conservative, the Shakers were social radicals. They abolished individual families, practiced celibacy, and treated men and women equally in their communities. Each colony was one large family. The Shaker ministry was headed by a woman, Lucy Wright, during its period of greatest growth. Celibacy, however, led to the withering away of the communities. Unable to reproduce naturally, the col-onies succumbed to death by attrition in the twentieth century.

Not all utopian communities were founded by re-ligious groups. Robert Owen's New Harmony was a short-lived attempt to found a socialist utopia in Indiana. A wealthy Scottish industrialist, Owen es-tablished the cooperative community in 1825. Ac-cording to his plan, its nine hundred members were to exchange their labor for goods at a communal store. Handicrafts (hat- and boot-making) flourished at New Harmony. But the economic base of the community, its textile mill, failed after Owen gave it to the community to run. Turnover in membership was too great for the community to develop any cohesion, and by 1827 the experiment had ended.

More successful were the New Englanders who lived and worked at the Brook Farm cooperative in West Roxbury, Massachusetts. Inspired by the tran-scendental philosophy that the **Brook Farm** spiritual rises above the worldly, its members rejected materialism and sought satisfaction in a communal life combining spirituality, work, and play. Founded in 1841 by the Unitarian minister George Ripley, Brook Farm at-tracted not only farmers and skilled craftsmen but teachers and writers, among them Nathaniel Haw-thorne. Indeed, the fame of Brook Farm rested on the intellectual achievements of its members. Its school drew students from outside the community, and its residents contributed regularly to the *Dial*, the leading transcendentalist journal. In 1845 Brook Farm's hundred members organized themselves into model phalanxes (work-living units) in keeping with the philosophy of the French utopian Charles Fourier. Rigid regimentation replaced individualism, and membership dropped. Following a disastrous fire in 1846, the experiment collapsed.

Though short-lived, Brook Farm played a significant part in the Romantic movement. During these years Hawthorne, Emerson, and the *Dial*'s editor Margaret Fuller joined Thoreau, James Fenimore Cooper, Herman Melville, and others in creating what is known today as the American Renaissance—the flowering of a national literature. In poetry and prose these Romanticists praised individualism and intuition, rejecting or modifying the ordered world of the Enlightenment in favor of the mysteries of nature. Rebelling against convention, both social and literary, they probed and celebrated the American character and the American experience. Cooper, for instance, wrote of the frontier in the Leatherstocking Tales, and Melville wrote of great spiritual quests in the guise of seafaring adventures. Their themes were universal, their settings and people, American.

Ralph Waldo Emerson was the "high priest" of the American Renaissance and the center of the transcendental movement. He had followed his father and grandfather into the ministry, but quit his Boston Unitarian pulpit in 1831. He returned from a two-year pilgrimage in Europe to lecture and write, preaching individualism and self-reliance. His message stressed that each person could experience God directly and intuitively through the "Oversoul." What gave Emerson's writings such force was his simple, direct prose. Others admired him, and he influenced Thoreau, Margaret Fuller, Nathaniel Hawthorne, and the members of Brook Farm. They followed his advice in *Nature* (1836) and "The American Scholar" (1837), turning to American themes and reform.

Far and away the most successful communitarians were the Mormons, who originated in the burned-over district of western New York. Organized by Joseph Smith in 1830 as the Church of Jesus Christ of Latter-day Saints, the church established communities dedicated to Christian cooperation.

Mormon Community of Saints

Fleeing persecution in Ohio, Illinois, and Missouri because of their claims of divine sanction and their newly adopted practice of polygamy (having more than one wife at the same time), the Mormons trekked across the continent in 1846 and 1847 to found a New Zion in the Great Salt Lake Valley. There, under Brigham Young, head of the Twelve Apostles (their governing body), they established a cohesive community of Saints—a heaven on earth. The Mormons created agricultural settlements and distributed land according to family size. An extensive irrigation system, constructed by men who contributed their labor according to the quantity of land they received and the amount of water they expected to use, transformed the arid valley into a rich oasis. As the colony developed, its cooperative principles gradually gave way to benevolent corporate authority, and the church elders came to control water, trade, industry, and even the territorial government of Utah. As the Mormon experience demonstrates, revival and reform could pursue and combine many diverse directions.

TEMPERANCE, PUBLIC EDUCATION, AND FEMINISM

One of the most successful reform efforts was the campaign against the consumption of alcohol, which was more widespread in the early nineteenth century than it is today. As a group, American men liked to drink alcoholic spirits—whiskey, rum, and hard cider. They gathered in public houses, saloons, and rural inns to gossip, discuss politics, play cards, escape work and home pressures, and drink. Men drank on all occasions: contracts were sealed with a drink; celebrations were toasted with spirits; barn-raisings and harvests ended with liquor. And though respectable women did not drink in public, many regularly tippled alcohol-based patent medicines promoted as cure-alls. Moreover, immigration brought more people for whom drinking was part of everyday life.

Why then did temperance become such a vital issue? And why were women specially active in the movement? As with all reform, temperance had a strong religious base. "The Holy Spirit," a temperance pamphlet proclaimed, "will not visit, much less dwell with him who is under the polluting, debasing effects of intoxicating drink." To evangelicals, the selling of whiskey was a chronic symbol of Sabbath violation, for workers commonly labored six days a week, then spent Sunday at the public house drinking and socializing. Alcohol was seen as a destroyer of families as well, since men who drank heavily either neglected their families or could not adequately support them. Temperance literature was laced with domestic images—abandoned wives, prodigal sons, drunken fathers. Outside the home, the habit of drinking could not be tolerated in the new world of the factory. Employers complained that drinkers took "St. Monday" as a holiday to recover from Sunday. Whatever they felt about other reforms, industrialists supported temperance as part of the new work habits needed for factory work. Timothy Shay Arthur dramatized all these evils in *Ten Nights in a Barroom* (1853), a classic American melodrama.

Demon rum thus became a major target of reformers. As the movement gained momentum, they shifted their emphasis from temperate use of spirits to voluntary abstinence and finally to a crusade to prohibit the manufacture and sale of spirits. The American Society for the Promotion of Temperance, organized in 1826 to urge drinkers to sign a pledge of abstinence, shortly thereafter became a pressure group for state prohibition legislation. By the mid-1830s there were some five thousand state and local temperance societies, and more than a million people had taken the pledge. By the 1840s the movement's success was reflected in a sharp decline in alcohol consumption in the United States. Between 1800 and 1830, annual per capita consumption of alcohol had risen from three to more than five gallons; by the mid-1840s, however, it had dropped below two gallons. Success bred more victories. In 1851 Maine prohibited the manufacture and sale of alcohol except for medicinal purposes, and by 1855 similar laws had been enacted throughout New England, the Old Northwest, and in New York and Pennsylvania.

Temperance Societies

Even though consumption of alcohol was declining, opposition to it did not weaken. Many reformers believed that alcohol was an evil introduced and perpetuated by Catholic immigrants. From the 1820s

This certificate of membership in a temperance society, for display, announced the virtues of the household to all visitors. In the illustration, the man signs with the support of wife and child; demon rum and its accompanying evils were banished from this home. Library of Congress.

on, antiliquor reformers based much of their argument on this false prejudice. The Irish and Germans, the *American Protestant Magazine* complained in 1849, "bring the grog shops like the frogs of Egypt upon us." Rum and immigrants defiled the Sabbath; rum and immigrants brought poverty; rum and immigrants supported the feared papacy. Some Catholics did join with nonevangelical Protestant sects like the Lutherans to oppose temperance legislation. But other Catholics took the pledge of abstinence and formed their own temperance organizations, such as the St. Mary's Mutual Benevolent Total Abstinence Society in Boston. Even nondrinking Catholics tended to oppose state regulation of drinking, however; temperance seemed to them a question of individual choice, not state coercion. They favored self, not societal, control.

Another important part of the reform impulse was the development of new institutions to meet the social needs of citizens. The list of organizations founded during this era is a long one—Protestant denominations, Catholic orders, reform Judaism; schools and colleges, hospitals, asylums, orphanages, and penitentiaries; new political parties; and myriad reform societies. Many of these institutions experimented with new techniques for handling old problems. New York State's penitentiary at Auburn, for example, placed prisoners in rehabilitative cooperative labor programs during the day, confining them only at night. Other states soon followed New York's lead.

Public education was one of the more lasting results of the age of institution building. In 1800 there were no public schools outside New England; by 1860 every state had some public education. Massachusetts took the lead, especially under Horace Mann, secretary of the state board of education from 1837 to 1848. Under Mann, Massachusetts established a minimum school year of six months, increased the number of high schools, formalized the training of teachers, and emphasized secular subjects and applied skills rather than religious training. In the process, teaching became a woman's profession.

Horace Mann on Education

Horace Mann was an evangelist of public education and school reform; his preaching on behalf of free state education changed schooling throughout the nation. "If we do not prepare children to become good citizens," Mann prophesied, "if we do not develop their capacities, . . . imbue their hearts with the love of truth and duty, and a reverence for all things sacred and holy, then our republic must go down to destruction." The abolition of ignorance, Mann claimed, would end misery, crime, and suffering. "The only sphere . . . left open for our patriotism," he wrote, "is the improvement of our children,—not the few, but the many; not a part of them but all."

In laying the basis of free public schools, Mann also broadened the scope of education. Previously, education had focused exclusively on literacy, religious training, and discipline. Thus most parents were indifferent to whether or not their children continued their schooling. Under Mann's leadership, the school curriculum became more secular and appropriate for future clerks, farmers, and workers. Students now studied geography, American history, arithmetic, and science. Moral education was retained, but direct religious indoctrination was dropped.

Many traditionalists, including New England Congregationalists, fought to maintain the old ties between education and religion. Some feared secular public education was a sign of the decline of American morality and virtue. But others, including many deeply religious people reborn in the Second Great Awakening, believed that public education would strengthen religious and family values. Mann's ideals and motives—the general betterment of society—were similar to theirs, and they saw merit in a democratic school system available to all, rich and poor. They noted, furthermore, that the Bible remained the centerpiece of elementary school education. And free public education would enable Sunday schools to devote full time to their students' religious needs without having to teach reading and writing as well. Thus Sunday-school teachers became Mann's allies.

A more controversial reform movement was the rise of American feminism in the 1840s. Ironically, it was women's traditional image as pious and spiritual that brought them into the public sphere. Revivalism, with its emphasis on conversion through the heart, served to elevate women; they were thought to be more emotional than men, and emotion was the most important element in being reborn. Organized into groups like the American Female Moral Reform Society, women slowly entered the public arena.

Reaction to the growing involvement of women in reform movements led many women to re-examine their position in society. In 1837 two antislavery lecturers, Angelina and Sarah Grimké, became particular objects of controversy. Natives of Charleston, South Carolina, they moved north in the 1820s to speak and write more openly and forcefully against slavery. They received a hostile reception for speaking before mixed groups of men and women. Some New England Congregationalists and even abolitionists joined in the criticism; as one pastoral letter put it, women should obey, not lecture, men. This reaction turned the Grimkés' attention from slavery to women's condition. The two attacked the concept of "subordination to man," insisting that both men and women had the "same rights and same duties." Sarah Grimké's *Letters on the Condition of Women and the Equality of the Sexes* (1838) and her sister's *Letters to Catharine E. Beecher*, published the same year, were the opening volleys in the war against the legal and social inequality of women.

Angelina and Sarah Grimké

In arguing against slavery, some women noticed the similarities between their own position and that of slaves. They saw parallels in their legal disabilities—

inability to vote or control their own property, except in widowhood—and their social restrictions—exclusion from advanced schooling and from most occupations. "The investigation of the rights of the slave," Angelina Grimké confessed, "has led me to a better understanding of my own." Some of the women who worked in the Lowell mills came to the same conclusion in the 1840s.

Unlike other reform movements, which succeeded in building a broad base of individual and organizational support, the movement for women's rights was limited. Some men joined the ranks, notably abolitionist William Lloyd Garrison and ex-slave Frederick Douglass, but most were actively opposed. In the 1840s the question of women's rights split the antislavery movement, the majority declaring themselves opposed. At a Woman's Rights Convention at Seneca Falls, New York, in 1848, led by Elizabeth Cady Stanton and Lucretia Mott, a much-published indictment of the injustices suffered by women was issued. If women had the vote, these reformers argued, they would be able both to protect themselves and to realize their potential as moral and spiritual leaders. Their argument won few over to their cause. By the 1850s feminists were focusing more and more on the single issue of suffrage. But another cause would eclipse their movement, at least for a time.

THE ANTISLAVERY MOVEMENT

Antislavery began as one among many reform movements. But, sparked by territorial expansion, the issue of slavery eventually became so overpowering that it consumed all other reforms. Passions would become so heated that they would threaten the nation itself. Above all else, those opposed to slavery saw it as a moral issue, evidence of the sinfulness of the American nation. When territorial questions in the 1850s forced the issue of slavery to center stage, the antislavery forces were well prepared (see Chapter 13).

Prior to the 1820s antislavery had played on the conscience of the individual slaveholder. Quakers had led the first antislavery movement in the eighteenth century, freeing their slaves and preaching that bondage was a Christian sin. But in the North, where most states had abolished slavery by 1800, whites took little interest in an issue that did not concern them directly. It was in the Upper South that antislavery sentiment was strongest, at least until the 1820s. But the movement there seemed to be as much concerned with preparing society for the natural death of slavery as with the plight of the slaves themselves.

Through the 1820s only free people of color demanded an immediate end to slavery. By 1830 there were at least fifty black antislavery societies in major

Black Antislavery Movement

black communities. These associations assisted fugitive slaves, attacked slavery at every turn, and reminded the nation that its mission as defined in the Declaration of Independence remained unfulfilled. A free black press helped to spread their word. Black abolitionists Frederick Douglass, Sojourner Truth, and Harriet Tubman then joined forces with white reformers in the American Anti-Slavery Society. These crusaders also stirred European support for their militant and unrelenting campaign. "Brethren, arise, arise, arise!" Henry Highland Garnet commanded the 1843 National Colored Convention. "Strike for your lives and liberties. Now is the day and hour. Let every slave in the land do this and the days of slavery are numbered. Rather die freemen than live to be slaves."

In the 1830s a small minority of white reformers made antislavery their primary commitment and made abolitionism a crusade. The most prominent and uncompromising abolitionist, though

William Lloyd Garrison

clearly not the most representative, was William Lloyd Garrison, who demanded "immediate and complete emancipation." Garrison had begun his career in the late 1820s editing the *National Philanthropist*, a weekly paper devoted to general reform, but especially to prohibition. It was in 1828, when Benjamin Lundy recruited him to another journal, *The Genius of Universal Emancipation*, that Garrison entered the ranks of the abolitionists. But Lundy favored colonization and sought to end slavery through persuasion, a position Garrison came to reject. In January 1831 Garrison broke with gradualists like Lundy and published the first issue of the *Liberator*, which was to be his

Chapter 12: REFORM, POLITICS, AND EXPANSION, 1824–1844

major weapon against slavery for thirty-five years. "I am in earnest—I will not equivocate—I will not excuse—I will not retreat a single inch—and *I will be heard*," he wrote in the first issue.

Garrison's refusal to work with anyone who even indirectly delayed emancipation left him isolated. He even forswore political action, on the grounds that it was governments that permitted slavery. (On July 4, 1854, Garrison burned a copy of the Constitution, proclaiming, "So perish all compromises with tyranny.") Through sheer force of rhetoric, Garrison helped to make antislavery the prevailing issue. His "immediatism" is probably best defined as tolerating no delay in ending slavery; he had no specific plan for abolishing it. In essence, Garrison called for an antislavery revival—all those who held slaves or cooperated with institutions supporting slavery should cast off their sins, repent, and do battle against evil.

Garrison alone could not have made antislavery a central issue. By the 1830s many northern reformers were recognizing the evils of slavery and preparing to act. Moral and religious ferment in the burned-over district and the Old Northwest had primed evangelists to enter the fray. And the reform activities of the 1820s, including antislavery, had built a network of interrelated organizations. In Michigan, for example, reformers convened one day as a temperance group and reconvened the next day as an antislavery society.

Ironically, it was in defense of the constitutional rights of abolitionists, not slaves, that many whites entered the struggle. Wherever they went, abolitionists found their civil rights in danger, especially their right of free speech. Unruly audiences found their rhetoric dangerous and a threat to the preservation of the Union. Using the new steam press, the American Anti-Slavery Society had increased its distribution of antislavery propaganda tenfold between 1834 and 1835, sending out 1.1 million pieces in 1835. But southern mobs seized and destroyed much of the mail, and South Carolina intercepted and burned abolitionist literature that entered the state (with the approval of the postmaster general). President Andrew Jackson even proposed a law prohibiting the mailing of antislavery tracts.

Another civil rights confrontation developed in Congress. Exercising their constitutional right to petition Congress, abolitionists mounted a campaign to abolish slavery and the slave trade in the District

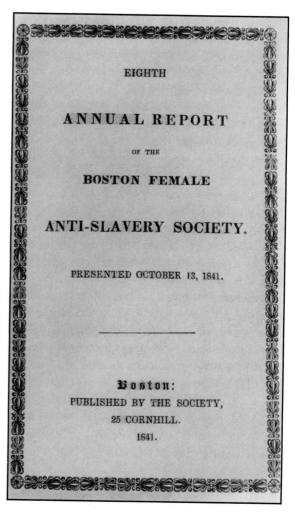

Women organized in Boston in 1833 to fight the evils of slavery. This annual report of their society was published in 1841. *Sophia Smith Collection, Smith College.*

of Columbia. (Since the district was under federal rule, states'-rights arguments against interfering with slavery did not apply there.) But Congress responded in 1836 by adopting the so-called gag rule, which automatically tabled abolitionist petitions, effectively preventing debate on them. In a dramatic defense of the right of petition, ex-president John Quincy Adams, then a Massachusetts representative, took to the floor repeatedly to defy the gag rule and eventually succeeded in getting it repealed (1844).

Gag Rule

Antislavery speakers often faced hostile crowds, and their presses were under constant threat of attack. The martyrdom of Elijah P. Lovejoy at the hands of a mob in Alton, Illinois, in 1837, drew attention to proslavery violence. Lovejoy, who had been driven out of slaveholding Missouri, had re-established his printing plant just across the river in Illinois. A mob sacked his office, with the cooperation of local authorities, and killed the abolitionist editor. Public outrage at Lovejoy's murder, as with the gag rule and censorship of the mails, only served to broaden the base of antislavery support in the North.

Frustration with the federal government also fed northern support for antislavery. By and large, politicians and government officials sought to avoid the question of slavery. The Missouri Compromise of 1820 had been an effort to quarantine the issue by adopting a simple formula—banning slavery north of 36°30′, Missouri's southern boundary—that would make debate on the slave or free status of new states unnecessary. Censorship of the mails and the gag rule were similar attempts to keep the issue out of the political arena. Yet the more national leaders, especially Democrats, sought to avoid the matter, the more they hardened the resolve of the antislavery forces.

The effect of the unlawful, violent, and obstructionist tactics used by proslavery advocates cannot be overestimated. Antislavery was not at the outset a unified movement. It was splintered and factionalized, and its adherents fought each other as often as they fought the defenders of slavery. They were divided over Garrison's emphasis on "moral suasion" versus the more practical political approach of James G. Birney, the Liberty party's candidate for president in 1844 (see page 349). They were split over support of other reforms, especially the rights of women. And they disagreed over the place of free black people in American society. Even so, abolitionists eventually managed to unify and make antislavery a major issue in the politics of the 1850s.

ANTIMASONRY

Antimasonry did not have the lasting appeal that antislavery had, but for a brief time it matched the intensity of abolitionism. The Antimasonry movement appeared like a comet in the burned-over district of western New York in 1826, and it stirred political activity before disappearing in the 1840s. As in antislavery, the line between reform and politics faded. The political arena quickly absorbed Antimasonry, but its short life illustrates the close tie between politics and reform from the 1820s through the 1840s.

Antimasonry was a reaction to Freemasonry, which had come to the United States from England in the eighteenth century. Freemasonry was a secret middle- and upper-class fraternity that attracted the sons of the Enlightenment, such as Benjamin Franklin and George Washington, with its emphasis on the Deity as opposed to organized religion and on brotherhood as opposed to one church. In the early nineteenth century it spread in the growing towns, attracting many commercial and political leaders. For ambitious young men, the Masons offered access to and fellowship with community leaders.

The Morgan affair was the catalyst for Antimasonry as an organized movement. In 1826, William Morgan, a disillusioned Mason, wrote an exposé of Masonry, *The Illustration of Masonry, By One*

Morgan Affair *of the Fraternity Who Has Devoted Thirty Years to the Subject,* to which his printer David Miller had added a scathing attack on the order. On September 12, 1826, prior to the book's appearance, a group of Masons abducted Morgan outside the Canandaigua, New York, jail. It was widely believed that the Masons had murdered Morgan, whose body was never found.

What energized the Antimasonry crusade was that its worst fears and charges seemed to be confirmed. Many of the officeholders in western New York, especially prosecutors, were Masons and they appeared to obstruct the investigation of Morgan's abduction. Public outcry and opposing political factions pressed for justice, and a series of notorious trials from 1827 through 1831 led many to suspect a conspiracy at work. The cover-up became as much the issue as Masonry itself, and the movement spilled over from the burned-over district to other states. In the Morgan affair, Antimason claims of a secret conspiracy seemed to be justified. Opponents of Masonry charged that the order's secrecy was antidemocratic and antirepublican, as was its elite membership and its use of regalia and such terms as knights and priests. As

In this contemporary Antimason cut, Freemasonry is represented as a Hydra-headed monster, with its tail strangling the Tree of Liberty. William Morgan, at the far right with an open book, is unmasking the monster, assisted by Antimasons. The winged figures are the Angels of Light and Truth with a holy mandate to finish off the monster. Library of Congress.

church leaders took up the moral crusade against Masonry, evangelicals labeled the order satanic.

As a moral crusade, however, Antimasonry crossed over into politics almost immediately. The issue itself was a political one since obstruction of justice was a signal element. Antimasonry attracted the lower and middle classes, pitting them against higher-status Masons and exploiting the general public's distrust and envy of local political leaders. And always there were factional leaders like Governor DeWitt Clinton of New York, willing to join the public outrage and pit his faction against others.

Unwittingly the Masons stoked the fires of Antimasonry. The silence of the order seemed to condone the murder of Morgan, and the construction of monumental lodges, like the one in Boston, advertised their determination to remain a public force. When editors who were Masons ignored the crusade against Masonry, the Antimasons started their own newspapers. The struggle, carried out within and without political parties, aroused public interest in politics.

Antimasonry spread as a popular movement and introduced the convention system for choosing political candidates. In defense of public morality and the republic, the Antimasons held conventions in 1827

Convention System to oppose Masons running for public office. In 1828 the conventions supported the National Republican candidate, John Quincy Adams, and opposed Andrew Jackson because he was a Mason. In 1831 the Antimasons held the first national political convention in Baltimore, and a year later nominated in convention William Wirt as their presidential candidate. Thus the Antimasons became one rallying point for those opposed to President Andrew Jackson.

By the mid-1830s Antimasonry had lost force as a moral and political movement. Most Antimasons found a comfortable anti-Jackson vehicle in the Whig party. Yet the movement left an indelible mark on the politics of the era. As a moral crusade concerned about public officeholders, it inspired and welcomed wider participation in the political process. In the burned-over district, wherever religious fervor appeared, and wherever families entered the market economy, Antimasonry arose. The revivalist and reform impulses in movements like Antimasonry further stimulated and awakened disagreements over values and ideology that were reinforced by conflicts over wealth, religion, and status. These differences helped polarize politics and shape parties as organizations to express those differences. The Antimasons contributed specifically to party development by pioneering the convention system and by stimulating greater grassroots involvement.

JACKSONIANISM AND THE BEGINNINGS OF MODERN PARTY POLITICS

The distinction between reform and politics eroded in the 1820s and after as reform inched its way into politics. The Antimasons, and then the abolitionists, appealed directly to voters. Although their means often differed, party leaders too sought to deal with the problems created by an expanding, urbanizing, market-oriented nation. President John

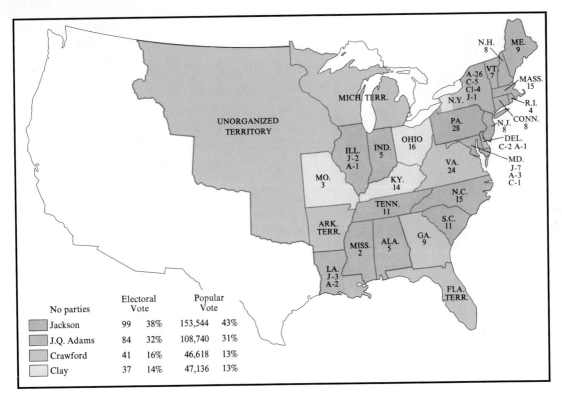

No parties	Electoral Vote		Popular Vote	
Jackson	99	38%	153,544	43%
J.Q. Adams	84	32%	108,740	31%
Crawford	41	16%	46,618	13%
Clay	37	14%	47,136	13%

Presidential Election, 1824

Quincy Adams advocated a nationalist program and an activist federal government; Andrew Jackson and his followers adhered to the Jeffersonian ideal of a more limited federal government.

The election of 1824, in which Adams and Jackson faced each other for the first time, signaled the beginning of a new, more open political system. The

End of the Caucus System

Federalist party had died out after the election of 1816, and Monroe had run unopposed in 1820 as the Republican candidate. In 1824, however, the Republicans were unable to agree on a candidate. From 1800 through 1820 a caucus in the House of Representatives had chosen the Republican presidential nominees: Jefferson, Madison, and Monroe. Jefferson and Madison had both indicated to the caucus that their secretaries of state should succeed them, and the system had worked efficiently. Of course, such a system restricted voter involvement—but this was not a real drawback at first, since in 1800 only five of sixteen states selected presidential electors by popular vote. (In most, legislators designated the electors.) In 1816, however, ten out of

nineteen states chose electors by popular vote, and in 1824, eighteen out of twenty-four did so.

Moreover, President Monroe never designated an heir apparent. Without direction from the president, therefore, the caucus in 1824 chose William H. Crawford, secretary of the treasury. But other Republicans, encouraged by the opportunity to appeal directly to the voters in most states, challenged Crawford. Secretary of State John Quincy Adams drew support from New England, and westerners backed Speaker of the House Henry Clay of Kentucky. Secretary of War John C. Calhoun looked to the South for support, and hoped to win Pennsylvania as well. Andrew Jackson, a popular military hero whose political views were unknown, was nominated by resolution of the Tennessee legislature and won support everywhere. But Crawford, who had declined to oppose Monroe in 1816 and 1820, had the most widespread support in Washington. Since his choice by the caucus was a foregone conclusion, the other four candidates joined in attacking the caucus system as undemocratic. When their supporters boycotted the deliberations, Crawford's victory became hollow,

Chapter 12: REFORM, POLITICS, AND EXPANSION, 1824–1844

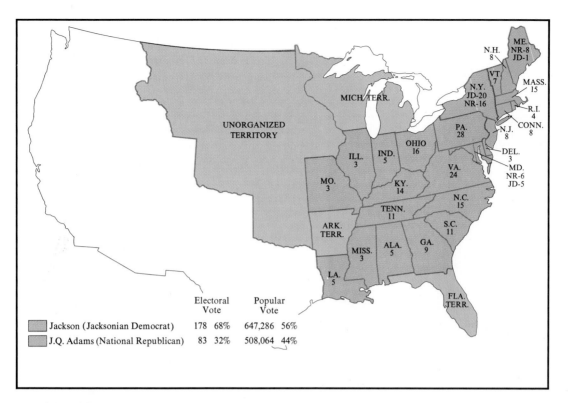

Presidential Election, 1828

Electoral Vote / Popular Vote legend:

	Electoral Vote	Popular Vote
Jackson (Jacksonian Democrat)	178 68%	647,286 56%
J.Q. Adams (National Republican)	83 32%	508,064 44%

Map labels: ME. NR-8 JD-1; N.H. 8; VT. 7; MASS. 15; N.Y. JD-20 NR-16; R.I. 4; CONN. 8; N.J. 8; PA. 28; DEL. 3; MD. NR-6 JD-5; MICH. TERR.; OHIO 16; IND. 5; ILL. 3; VA. 24; KY. 14; MO. 3; N.C. 15; TENN. 11; S.C. 11; ARK. TERR.; MISS. 3; ALA. 5; GA. 9; LA. 5; FLA. TERR.; UNORGANIZED TERRITORY

based on a minority vote. The role of the congressional caucus in nominating presidents ended.

Though Andrew Jackson led in both popular and electoral votes in the four-way presidential election of 1824, no one received a majority (see map). Adams finished second, and Clay and Crawford trailed far behind. (Calhoun dropped out of the race before the election.) Under the Constitution, the selection of a president in such circumstances fell to the House of Representatives, which would vote by state delegation, one vote to a state. Crawford, a stroke victim, never received serious consideration; Clay, who had received the fewest votes, was dropped. But Clay, as Speaker of the House and leader of the Ohio Valley states, backed Adams, who received the votes of thirteen out of twenty-four state delegations. Clay was rewarded with the position of secretary of state in the Adams administration—the traditional stepping-stone to the presidency. Angry Jacksonians denounced the arrangement as a "corrupt bargain" that had stolen the office from the clear frontrunner.

As president, John Quincy Adams took a strong nationalist position emphasizing Henry Clay's Amer-

ican System of protective tariffs, a national bank, and internal improvements (see page 227). Adams believed the federal government should take an activist role not only in the economy but in education, science, and the arts; accordingly, he proposed a national university in Washington, D.C.

Brilliant as a diplomat and secretary of state, Adams was sadly inept as president. He underestimated the lingering effects of the Panic of 1819 and the ensuing bitter opposition to a national bank and protective tariffs. Meanwhile, supporters of Andrew Jackson sabotaged Adams's administration at every opportunity.

The 1828 campaign between Adams and Jackson was an intensely personal conflict. Whatever principles the two men stood for were obscured by the mud-slinging both sides indulged in. Jackson's supporters claimed that the presidency had been stolen from the general in 1824. Adams, son of John Adams and a former Federalist, distrusted party organization, and as president he did not use his patronage power to aid his policies or his re-election. Though Adams won the same states as in 1824, the opposition was unified, and Jackson swamped him (see map).

Andrew Jackson in 1832, at the peak of his success and power. Library of Congress.

Jackson polled 56 percent of the popular vote and won in the electoral college, 178 to 83. For him and his supporters, the election of 1828 was the culmination of a long-fought, well-organized campaign based on party organization. Through a lavishly financed coalition of state parties, political leaders, and newspaper editors, a popular movement had elected a president. An era had ended, and the Democratic party became the first truly modern political party in the United States. The future belonged to well-organized political parties and leaders who engaged in party politics.

Andrew Jackson was nicknamed "Old Hickory," after the toughest American hardwood. A rough-and-tumble, ambitious man, he rose from humble

Andrew Jackson

birth to become a wealthy planter and slaveholder. Jackson was the first American president not born into comfortable circumstances, a self-made man at ease among both frontiersmen and southern planters.

Few Americans have been celebrated in myth and legend as has Andrew Jackson. As a general in the Tennessee militia, Jackson had led the battle to remove the Creek from the Alabama and Georgia frontier. He burst onto the national scene as the great hero of the War of 1812, and in 1818 enhanced his glory in an expedition against the Seminole in Spanish Florida. Jackson also served as a congressional representative and senator from Tennessee, as a judge in his home state, and as the first territorial governor of Florida (1821) before running for president in 1824. He was an active presidential aspirant until he won the office in 1828.

Jackson and his supporters offered a distinct alternative to the strong national government Adams had advocated. They and their party, the Democratic-Republicans (shortened to Democrats),

Democrats

represented a wide range of beliefs but shared some common ideals. Fundamentally, they sought to foster the Jeffersonian concept of an agrarian society, harkening back to the belief that a strong central government was the enemy of individual liberty, a tyranny to be feared. Thus, like Jefferson, they favored limited government and emphasized state sovereignty.

Jacksonians were as fearful of the concentration of economic power as they were of political power. They saw government intervention in the economy as benefiting special-interest groups and creating corporate monopolies, and thus rejected an activist economic program as favoring the rich. Jacksonians sought to restore the independence of the individual—the artisan and the yeoman farmer—by ending federal support of banks and corporations and restricting the use of paper currency. Their concept of the proper role of government tended to be negative, and Jackson's political power was largely expressed in negative acts; he used the veto more than all previous presidents combined.

Finally, Jackson and his supporters were hostile to reform as a movement and an ideology. Reformers were increasingly calling for an activist and interventionist government as they organized to turn their programs into legislation. But Democrats tended to oppose programs like educational reform and the establishment of public education. They believed, for instance, that public schools restricted individual liberty by interfering with parental responsibility, and undermined freedom of religion by replacing church schools. Nor did Jackson share reformers' humanitarian concerns. He showed little sympathy for the Indians, ordering their removal from the Southeast to make way for white agricultural settlement (see page 289).

Yet Jackson and the Jacksonians considered themselves reformers in a different way. In following Jefferson's notion of restraint in government and in emphasizing individualism, Jackson and his followers sought to restore old republican virtues. Individual traits such as industriousness, prudence, sobriety, and economy were highly prized. No less than reformers he favored human goodness. He believed that his party, headed by a politically sensitive and astute leader, was the best instrument to restore those traditional values.

Like Jefferson, Jackson strengthened the executive branch of government at the same time as he tended to weaken the federal role. Given his popularity and the strength of his personality, this concentration of power in the presidency was perhaps inevitable; but his deliberate policy of combining the roles of party leader and chief of state centralized even greater power in the White House. Enamored of power, Jackson never hesitated to confront his opponents with all the weapons at his command. Among his followers he commanded enormous loyalty, and he rewarded them handsomely. Invoking the principle that rotating officeholders would make government more responsive to the public will, Jackson used the spoils system to reward loyal Democrats with appointments to office. Though he removed fewer than one-quarter of federal officeholders in his two terms, his use of patronage nevertheless strengthened party organization and loyalty.

Among Jackson's opponents animosity grew year by year. "When he comes," Daniel Webster wrote in 1829 of the soon-to-be-inaugurated Jackson, "he will bring a breeze with him. Which way it will blow I cannot tell . . . , but my *fear* is greater than my hope." Once in office, Jackson was mocked as King Andrew I for his quick and firm actions. Critics attempted to undermine his claim of restoring republican virtue and of inheriting the mantle of Jefferson. They charged him with recklessly and impulsively destroying the economy.

Jackson invigorated the philosophy of limited government. In 1830 he vetoed the Maysville Road bill, which would have provided a federal subsidy to construct a sixty-mile turnpike from Maysville to Lexington, Kentucky. Jackson insisted that an internal improvement confined to one state was unconstitutional, and that such projects were properly a state responsibility. The veto undermined Henry Clay's American System and personally embarrassed Clay, since the project was in his home district.

THE NULLIFICATION AND BANK CONTROVERSIES

Jackson had to face more directly the question of the proper division of sovereignty between state and central government. The growing reform crusades, especially antislavery, had made the southern states fearful of federal power—and none more so than South Carolina, where the planter class was strongest and slavery most concentrated. Having watched the growth of abolitionist sentiment in Great Britain, which resulted in 1833 in emancipation in the West Indies, South Carolinians feared the same thing would happen at home. Hard hit by the Panic of 1819, from which they never fully recovered, they also resented the high prices of imported goods created by protectionist tariffs.

To protect their interests, South Carolinian political leaders developed the doctrine of *nullification,* according to which a state had the right to overrule, or nullify, federal legislation that conflicted with its own. The act that directly inspired this doctrine was the passage in 1828 of the Tariff of Abominations. In his unsigned *Exposition and Protest,* John C. Calhoun argued that in any disagreement between the federal government and a state, a special state convention—like those called to ratify the Constitution—would decide the conflict by either nullifying or accepting the federal law. Only the power of nullification could protect the minority against the tyranny of the majority, Calhoun asserted.

In public, John C. Calhoun let others take the lead in advancing nullification. As Jackson's running mate in 1828, he avoided publicly identifying with nullification and thus embarrassing the ticket. And as vice president, he hoped to win Jackson's support as Democratic presidential nominee over Martin Van Buren. Thus a silent Calhoun presided over the Senate and its packed galleries when Senators Daniel Webster (New Hampshire) and Robert Y. Hayne (South Carolina) debated nullification in January 1830. The debate explored North-South grievances and the question of the nature of the Union. With Calhoun nodding agreement in the chair, Hayne charged that the Hartford Convention at the end of the War of 1812 had been an act of disunity (see page 226). Over two days Webster defended the New England states and his beloved republic in eloquent rhetoric. Though debating Hayne, he aimed his remarks at Calhoun as he depicted the nation as a compact of people, not merely states. In the climax of his career as a debator, he invoked two images. One, which he hoped he would not see, was the outcome of nullification: "states dissevered, discordant, belligerent; on a land rent with civil feuds, or drenched . . . in fraternal blood!" The other was a patriotic vision of a great nation flourishing under the motto "Liberty *and* Union, now and forever, one and inseparable."

Webster-Hayne Debate

Though sympathetic to states' rights, Jackson shared Webster's dread and distrust of nullification. Soon after the Webster-Hayne debate, the president made his position clear at a Jefferson Day dinner, with the toast: "Our Federal Union, it *must* and *shall be* preserved." Calhoun, when it came to his turn, offered: "The Federal Union—next to our liberty the most dear." Calhoun, torn between devotion to the Union and loyalty to his state, had revealed his preference for states' rights. Politically and personally Calhoun and Jackson grew apart, and it soon became apparent that Jackson favored Secretary of State Martin Van Buren, not Calhoun, as his successor.

South Carolina first invoked its theory of nullification against the tariff of 1832. Though this tariff had the effect of reducing some duties, it retained high taxes on imported iron, cottons, and woolens. A majority of southern representatives supported the new tariff, but South Carolinians refused to go along. In their view, their constitutional right to control their own destiny had been sacrificed to the demands of northern industrialists. They feared

Nullification Crisis

the consequences of accepting such an act; it could set a precedent for congressional legislation on slavery. In November 1832 a South Carolina state convention nullified the tariff, making it unlawful for officials to collect duties in the state after February 1, 1833. Immediately recruiters began to organize a volunteer army to ensure nonenforcement of the tariff.

"Old Hickory" responded with toughness. Privately, he threatened to invade South Carolina and hang Calhoun, his vice president; publicly, he sought to avoid the use of force. On December 10, 1832, Jackson issued his own proclamation nullifying nullification. He moved troops to federal forts in South Carolina and prepared United States marshals to collect the required duties. At Jackson's request, Congress passed the Force Act, which supposedly renewed Jackson's authority to call up troops; it was actually a scheme to avoid the use of force by collecting duties before ships reached South Carolina. At the same time, Jackson extended the olive branch by recommending tariff reductions. Calhoun, disturbed by South Carolina's drift toward separatism, resigned as vice president and became a South Carolina senator. In the Senate he worked with Henry Clay to draw up the compromise tariff of 1833. Quickly passed by Congress and signed by the president, the revision lengthened the list of duty-free items and reduced duties over the next nine years. Satisfied, South Carolina's convention repealed its nullification law, and in a final salvo nullified Jackson's Force Act. Jackson ignored the gesture.

Although fought over the practical issue of tariffs (and the unspoken issue of slavery), the nullification controversy did represent a genuine debate on the true nature and principles of the republic. Each side believed it was upholding the Constitution. Both felt they were fighting special privilege and subversion of republican values. South Carolina was fighting the tyranny of the federal government and the manufacturers who sought tariff protection; Jackson was fighting the tyranny of South Carolina, whose refusal to bow to federal authority threatened to split the republic. Neither side won a clear victory, though both claimed to have done so. Another issue, that of a central bank, would define the powers of the federal government more clearly.

At stake was the rechartering of the Second Bank of the United States, whose twenty-year charter expired in 1836. Like its predecessor, the bank served

Second Bank of the United States

as a depository for federal funds, on which it paid no interest; and it served the republic in many other ways. Its bank notes circulated as currency throughout the country; they could be readily exchanged for gold, and the federal government accepted them as payment in all transactions. Through its twenty-five branch offices, the bank acted as a clearing-house for state banks, keeping them honest by refusing to accept their notes if they had insufficient gold in reserve.

But the bank had enemies. Most state banks resented the central bank's police role; by presenting state bank notes for redemption all at once, the Second Bank could easily ruin a state bank. Moreover, state banks, with less money in reserve, found themselves unable to compete on an equal footing with the Second Bank. Many state governments regarded the national bank, with its headquarters in Philadelphia, as unresponsive to local needs. Westerners and urban workers remembered with bitterness the bank's conservative credit policies during the Panic of 1819—and there was some truth to their complaints. Though the Second Bank served some of the functions of a central bank, it was still a private profit-making institution, and its policies reflected the self-interest of its owners. Its president, Nicholas Biddle, controlled the bank completely. Conservative and anti-Jacksonian, Biddle symbolized all that westerners found wrong with the bank. Moreover, the bank had great political influence. Many members of Congress and business leaders were beholden to it, and the only check on that power was at rechartering time.

Although the bank's charter would not expire until 1836, Biddle, aware of Jackson's hostility and encouraged by the National Republican presidential candidate, Henry Clay, sought to make it an issue in the campaign of 1832. His strategy backfired. Biddle's success with Congress did not deter Jackson; in July 1832 Jackson vetoed the rechartering bill, and the Senate failed to override the veto. Jackson's veto message was an emotional attack on the undemocratic nature of the bank. "It is to be regretted," he said, "that the rich and powerful too often bend the acts of government to their selfish purposes." Rechartering would grant "exclusive privileges, to make the rich richer and the potent more powerful."

The bank became the major symbol and issue in the presidential campaign of 1832. Jackson ignored its constitutionality and its functions; instead he denounced special privilege and economic power. The Jacksonians had organized a highly effective party, and they used it in the election. Operating in a system in which all the states but South Carolina now chose electors by popular vote, the Jacksonians mobilized voters by advertising the presidential election as the focal point of the political system. The Antimasons adopted a party platform, the first in the nation's history. The Democrats and the major opposition party, the National Republicans, quickly followed suit. Jackson and Martin Van Buren were nominated at the Democratic convention, Clay and John Sergeant at the National Republican. John Floyd ran as South Carolina's candidate. Jackson was re-elected easily in a Democratic party triumph.

After his victory and second inauguration in 1833, Jackson moved not only to dismantle the Second Bank of the United States but to ensure that it would not be resurrected. He deposited federal funds in favored state-chartered ("pet") banks; without federal money, the bank shriveled. When its federal charter expired in 1836, it became just another Pennsylvania-chartered private bank. In 1841 it closed its doors.

As part of the coup de grâce delivered to the Bank of the United States, Congress, with Jackson's support, passed the Deposit Act of 1836. Under this act, the secretary of the treasury designated one bank in each state and territory to provide the services formerly performed by the Bank of the United States. The act provided that the federal surplus in excess of $5 million be distributed to the states as interest-free loans beginning in 1837, and these loans were never recalled—a fitting Jacksonian hold on the federal purse.

Jackson was worried about more than just restraining the government. The surplus had derived from wholesale speculation in public lands. Purchasers bought public land on credit, borrowed from banks against the land to purchase additional acreage, and repeated the cycle. Between 1834 and 1836 federal receipts from land sales rose from $5 to $25 million. Banks issued bank notes in providing loans, and Jackson, an opponent of paper money, feared that the speculative craze threatened the state banks while closing the door to settlers, who could not compete with speculators in bidding for the best land.

When New York state banks stopped redeeming bank notes for gold or silver during the Panic of 1837, Whigs blamed the crisis on Jackson's opposition to the Second Bank of the United States. This satirical six-cent note drawn on the Humbug Glory Bank ridicules Jackson and Van Buren. Notice the Democratic donkey and the hickory leaf on the face of the paper. *The New-York Historical Society.*

Following his hard-money instinct and his opposition to paper currency, President Jackson ordered Treasury Secretary Levi Woodbury to issue the Specie Circular.

Specie Circular

It provided that after August 15, 1836, only specie—gold or silver—or Virginia land scrip would be accepted as payment for federal lands. The circular stated that it sought to end "the monopoly of the public lands in the hands of speculators and capitalists" and the "ruinous extension" of bank notes and credit. By ending credit sales, the circular reduced significantly public land purchases and forced a halt to the distribution of the surplus to the states; the final payments were never made since the surplus evaporated.

The policy was a disaster on many fronts. Although federal land sales were sharply reduced, speculation still continued as available land for sale became a scarce commodity. The ensuing increased demand for specie squeezed banks, and many suspended specie payment (the redemption of bank notes for specie). This led to further credit contraction, as banks issued fewer notes and gave less credit. Equally damaging was the way Jackson attacked the problem. He pursued a tight money policy instinctively, and was indifferent to the impact of his policies. More important, the Specie Circular, issued in July 1836, was similar to a bill defeated in the Senate nearly three months earlier. His opponents saw King Andrew at work. Congress voted to repeal the circular in the waning days of Jackson's administration, but the president pocket-vetoed the bill. Finally in May 1838, a joint resolution of Congress overturned the circular.

Jackson used the veto power more often than did all his predecessors combined. From Washington to John Quincy Adams, presidents had vetoed nine bills; Jackson vetoed twelve. And he was the first to use the pocket veto—refusing to sign or veto a bill at the end of a congressional session, thus killing it. Previous presidents believed that vetoes were justified only on constitutional grounds, but Jackson, as in the veto of the Second Bank of the United States, negated bills merely because he disagreed with them. He made the veto an important weapon in controlling Congress, since representatives and senators had to consider the possibility of a presidential veto on any bill. In effect, he made the executive power equal to that of two-thirds of both houses of Congress.

The Whig Challenge and the Second Party System

Once historians described the 1830s and 1840s as the Age of Jackson, and the personalities of the leading political figures dominated history books. Increasingly, however, historians have viewed these years as an age of popularly based political parties and reformers. For it was only when the passionate concerns of evangelicals and reformers spilled into politics that party differences became important again and party loyalties solidified. For the first time grassroots political groups, organized from the bottom up, set the tone of political life.

In the 1830s the Democrats' opponents, including remnants of the now-disorganized National Republican party, found shelter under a common umbrella, the Whig party. Resentful of Jackson's domination of Congress, the Whigs borrowed their name from the British party that had opposed the tyranny of Hanoverian monarchs in the eighteenth century. From the congressional elections of 1834 through the 1840s, they and the Democrats competed nearly equally; only a few percentage points separated the two parties in national elections. They fought at every level—city, county, and state—and achieved a stability previously unknown in American politics. Both parties built strong organizations, commanded the loyalty of legislators, and attracted mass popular followings.

The two parties emphasized responsiveness to their supporters, a priority that reflected significant changes in the electoral process. At the local level, direct voting had replaced nomination and election by legislators and electors. And though many states still permitted only taxpayers to vote in local elections, by the 1830s only a handful significantly restricted adult white male suffrage in nonlocal elections. Some even allowed immigrants who had taken out their first citizenship papers to vote. The effect of these changes was a sharp increase in the number of votes cast in presidential elections. Between 1824 and 1828 the number of votes cast for president increased threefold, from 360,000 to over 1.1 million. In 1840, 2.4 million men cast votes. The proportion of eligible voters who cast ballots also increased. In 1824 an estimated 27 percent of those eligible voted; from 1828 through 1836, about 55 percent, in 1840, more than 80 percent.

On the political agenda during these years were numerous fundamental issues. At the national level, officials struggled with the question of the proper constitutional roles of the federal and state governments, national expansion, and Indian policy. Also during this period, many state conventions were drafting new constitutions and deliberating over such basic issues as the rights of individuals and corporations; the rights of labor and capital; government aid to business; currency and sources of revenue; and public education, temperance, and antislavery.

Increasingly the two parties differed in their approaches to these issues. Though both favored economic expansion, the Whigs sought it through an activist government, the Democrats through limited central government.

Whigs

Thus the Whigs supported corporate charters, a national bank, and paper currency; the Democrats were opposed. The Whigs also favored more humanitarian reforms than did the Democrats—public schools, abolition of capital punishment, temperance, and prison and asylum reform.

In general, Whigs were simply more optimistic than Democrats, and more enterprising. They did not hesitate to help one group if doing so would promote the general welfare. The chartering of corporations, they argued, expanded economic opportunity for everyone, providing work for laborers and increasing demand for food from farmers. Meanwhile the Democrats, distrustful of the concentration of economic power and of moral and economic coercion, held fast to their Jeffersonian principle of limited government.

For all the rank economic inequality that characterized the era, it was not the major issue that divided the parties. Nor were the conflicts over the bank and government or the issuing of corporate charters battles between the haves and have-nots. Although the Whigs attracted more of the upper and middle class, both sides drew support from manufacturers, merchants, laborers, and farmers. Instead, it was religion and ethnicity that determined party membership. In the North, the Whigs' concern for energetic government and humanitarian and moral reform won the favor of native-born and British-American evangelical Protestants, especially those involved in religious revival. These Presbyterians, Baptists, and Congregationalists were overwhelmingly Whigs, as were the relatively small number of free black voters. Democrats, on the other hand, tended to be foreign-born Catholics and nonevangelical Protestants, both groups that preferred to keep religious and secular affairs separate.

The Whig party thus became the vehicle of evangelical Christianity. In many locales, the membership of reform societies overlapped that of the party. Indeed,

Whigs and Reformers

Whigs practiced a kind of political revivalism. Their rallies resembled camp meetings; their speeches echoed evangelical rhetoric; their programs embodied the perfectionist beliefs of reformers. This potent blend of religion and politics—which, as Tocqueville noted, were "intimately united" in America—greatly intensified political loyalties.

In unifying evangelicals, the Whigs alienated members of other faiths. The evangelicals' ideal Christian state had no room for Catholics, Mormons, Unitarians, Universalists, or religious freethinkers. Sabbath laws, temperance legislation, and Protestant-inspired public education threatened the religious freedom and individual liberty of these groups, which generally opposed state interference in moral and religious questions. As a result, more than 95 percent of Irish Catholics, 90 percent of Reformed Dutch, and 80 percent of German Catholics voted Democratic.

Vice President Martin Van Buren headed the Democratic ticket in the presidential election of 1836. Hand-picked by Jackson, Van Buren was a shrewd politician who had built the Democratic party in New York. The Whigs, who had not yet coalesced into a national party, entered three sectional candidates: Daniel Webster of New England, Hugh White of the South, and William Henry Harrison of the West. By splintering the vote, they hoped to throw the election into the House, but Van Buren squeaked through with a 25,000-vote edge out of a total of 1.5 million. No vice-presidential candidate received a majority of electoral votes, though, and for the only time in American history the Senate chose a vice president: the Democratic candidate, Richard M. Johnson.

Van Buren took office just weeks before the American credit system collapsed. The economic boom of the 1830s was over. In May 1837 New York banks

Martin Van Buren and Hard Times

stopped redeeming paper currency in gold, and soon all banks suspended payments in hard coin. As confidence faded, banks curtailed loans. The credit contraction only made things worse; after a brief recovery, full-scale depression set in, and persisted from 1839 to 1843.

Not surprisingly, economic issues were paramount during these years. Unfortunately, Van Buren followed Jackson's hard-money policies. He curtailed federal spending, thus accelerating deflation, and opposed the Whigs' advocacy of a national bank, which would have expanded credit. Even worse, Van Buren proposed a new treasury system under which the government would keep its funds in regional treasury offices rather than banks. The treasury branches would accept and pay out only gold and silver coin; they would not accept paper currency or checks drawn on state banks. Van Buren's independent treasury bill was passed in 1840. By creating a constant demand for hard coin, it deprived banks of gold and added to the general deflation.

Undaunted, the Whigs fought the Democrats at the state level over these issues, since great economic advantages were at stake. The Whigs favored new banks, more paper currency, and more corporations. As the party of hard money, the Democrats favored eliminating paper currency altogether and using only gold or silver coin. Increasingly the Democrats became distrustful even of state banks, and by the mid-1840s a majority favored eliminating all bank corporations. The Whigs, riding the wave of economic distress into office, made banking and corporate charters more readily available.

With the nation in a depression, the Whigs confidently prepared for the election of 1840. Their strategy was simple: keep their loyal supporters and win over independents distressed by hard

Election of 1840

times. The Democrats renominated President Van Buren in a somber convention. The Whigs rallied behind the military hero General William Henry Harrison, conqueror of Prophet Town or Tippecanoe Creek in 1811. Harrison and his running mate, John Tyler of Virginia, ran a "log cabin and hard cider" campaign—a people's crusade against the artistocratic president in the Palace, as the Whigs called the White House. Using many of the techniques of twentieth-century politics—huge rallies, parades, songs, posters, and campaign hats—the Whigs wooed supporters and independents alike. Harrison stayed carefully above the issues, earning the nickname General Mum, but party hacks bluntly blamed the depression on the Democrats. In a huge turnout in which 80 percent of eligible voters cast ballots, Harrison won the popular vote by a narrow margin but swept the electoral college 234 to 60.

Immediately after taking office in 1841, President Harrison called a special session of Congress to enact the Whig economic program: repeal of the independent treasury system; a new national bank; and a higher protective tariff. Unfortunately for the Whigs, Harrison died within a month of his inauguration. His successor, John Tyler, a former Democrat who had left the party in opposition to Jackson's nullification proclamation, turned out to be more of a Democrat than a Whig. Tyler consistently opposed the Whig congressional program. He repeatedly vetoed Henry Clay's protective tariffs, bills promoting internal improvements, and bills aimed at reviving the Bank of the United States. The only important measures that became law under his administration were the repeal of the independent treasury and a higher tariff. Two days after Tyler's second veto of a bank bill, the entire cabinet except Secretary of State Daniel Webster resigned. Webster, involved in negotiating a new treaty with Great Britain, left shortly thereafter. Tyler became a president without a party, and the Whigs lost the presidency without an election.

Virtually expelled from the Whig party and at war with them over domestic policy, Tyler tended to territorial questions. During the late 1830s, Anglo-American relations, friendly since the War of 1812, again became tense. Southern alarm over West Indian emancipation; northern comercial rivalry with Britain; the default of state governments and corporations on British-held debts during the Panic of 1837; rebellion in Canada; boundary disputes; and American expansionism—all fueled Anglo-American tensions.

Anglo-American Tensions

One of the most troublesome of these disputes arose from the *Caroline* affair, in which a United States citizen, Amos Durfee, had been killed when

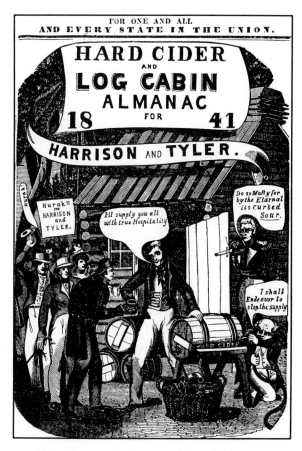

Using many of the techniques of twentieth-century politics, General William Henry Harrison ran a "log cabin and hard cider" campaign—a popular crusade—against Jackson heir, President Martin Van Buren. The almanac cover shows a victorious Harrison receiving the people's acclaim while Jackson's cider—popularity—has turned sour and Van Buren is unable to stem the Whig's appeal.   Library of Congress.

Canadian militia set the privately owned steamer *Caroline* afire in the Niagara River. (The *Caroline* had supported an unsuccessful uprising against Great Britain in Upper Canada in 1837.) Britain refused to apologize for its revenge, and patriotic Americans seethed with rage. Fearing that popular support for the Canadian rebels would ignite war, President Van Buren posted troops at the border to discourage border raids. Tensions subsided in November 1840 when Alexander McLeod, a Canadian deputy sheriff, was arrested in New York for the murder of Durfee. McLeod was eventually acquitted; had he been found guilty and executed, Lord Palmerston, the British foreign minister, might have sought war.

At about the same time another quarrel threatened Anglo-American relations. The Treaty of Ghent that ended the War of 1812 had not solved the boundary dispute between Maine and New Brunswick. Moreover, although Great Britain had accepted an 1831 arbitration decision fixing a new boundary, the United States Senate had rejected it in 1832. Thus when Canadians began to log the disputed region in the winter of 1838 and 1839, the citizens of Maine attempted to expel them. Soon the lumbermen had captured the Maine land agent and posse; both sides had mobilized their militia; and Congress had authorized a call-up of fifty thousand men. No blood was spilled, though. General Winfield Scott, who had patrolled the border during the *Caroline* affair, was dispatched to Aroostook, Maine. Scott arranged a truce between the warring state and province, and the two sides compromised on their conflicting claims in the Webster-Ashburton Treaty (1842).

These border disputes with Great Britain prefigured an issue that became prominent in national politics in the mid- to late 1840s: the westward expansion of the United States. Tyler's succession to power in 1841 and a Democratic victory in the presidential election of 1844 ended activist, energetic government on the federal level for the rest of the decade. Meanwhile economic issues were eclipsed by debate over the nation's destiny to stretch from coast to coast. Reform, however, was not dead. Its passions would resurface in the 1850s in the debate over slavery in the territories.

MANIFEST DESTINY

The belief that American expansion westward and southward was inevitable, divinely ordained, and just was first called *manifest destiny* by a Democrat, the newspaperman John L. O'Sullivan. The annexation of Texas, O'Sullivan wrote in 1845, was "the fulfillment of our manifest destiny to overspread the continent allotted by Providence for the free development of our yearly multiplying millions." Americans had thought similarly for decades, but during the 1840s they used such rhetoric to hurry the inexorable process along and to justify war and threats of war in the quest for more territory.

Americans had been hungry for new lands ever since the colonists first turned their eyes westward. There lay fertile soil, valuable minerals, and the chance for a better life or a new beginning. Acquisition of the Louisiana Territory and the Floridas had set the process in motion (see map). Agrarian Democrats saw the West as an antidote to urbanization and industrialization. Enterprising Whigs looked to the new commercial opportunities the West offered. No wonder that between 1833 and 1860 the proportion of Americans living west of the Appalachians grew from one-quarter to one-half.

A fierce national pride also spurred the quest for western land. Dampened during times of depression, it reasserted itself during recoveries and booms, as in the 1840s. North or South, Whig or Democrat, Americans were convinced that theirs was the greatest country on earth, with a special role to play in the world. What better evidence of such a role could there be than expansion from coast to coast?

Americans also idealistically believed that westward expansion would extend American freedom and democracy. The acquisition of new territory would, they reasoned, bring the benefits of America's republican system of government to less fortunate people. Of course such idealism was self-serving, and it contained an undercurrent of racism as well. Indians were perceived as savages best removed from their homes east of the Mississippi and confined to small areas in the West. Mexicans and Central and South Americans were also seen as inferior peoples, fit to be controlled or conquered. Thus the same racism that justified slavery in the South and discrimination in the North supported expansion in the West.

Finally, the expansionist fever of the 1840s was fed by the desire to secure the nation from perceived external enemies. The internal enemies of the 1830s—a monster bank, corporations, paper currency, alcohol, Sabbath violation—seemed to pale before the threats Americans found on their borders in the 1840s. Expansion, some believed, was necessary to preserve American independence.

Among the long-standing objectives of expansionists was the Republic of Texas, which included parts of present-day Oklahoma, Kansas, Colorado, Wyoming, and New Mexico as well as all of Texas. This territory

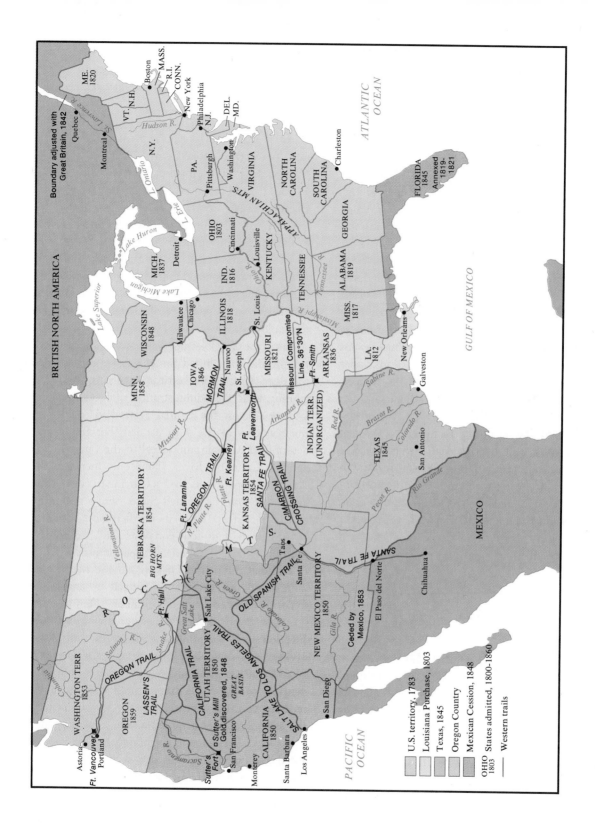

Westward Expansion, 1800–1860

Legend:
- U.S. territory, 1783
- Louisiana Purchase, 1803
- Texas, 1845
- Oregon Country
- Mexican Cession, 1848
- OHIO 1803 — States admitted, 1800–1860
- — Western trails

Map labels:

BRITISH NORTH AMERICA

ME. 1820
Boston
MASS.
R.I.
CONN.
New York
N.Y.
VT. N.H.
Boundary adjusted with Great Britain, 1842
Quebec
St. Lawrence R.
Montreal
Hudson R.
PA.
Pittsburgh
DEL.
N.J.
Philadelphia
Washington
MD.
VIRGINIA
NORTH CAROLINA
SOUTH CAROLINA
Charleston
ATLANTIC OCEAN
APPALACHIAN MTS.
FLORIDA 1845
Annexed 1819–1821
GEORGIA
ALABAMA 1819
TENNESSEE
KENTUCKY
Louisville
Cincinnati
OHIO 1803
Detroit
MICH. 1837
Lake Huron
Lake Michigan
Lake Superior
L. Ontario
L. Erie
Ohio R.
Tennessee R.
MISS. 1817
LA. 1812
New Orleans
Galveston
GULF OF MEXICO
Mississippi R.
Sabine R.
ARKANSAS 1836
Ft. Smith
Missouri Compromise Line, 36°30'N
MISSOURI 1821
St. Louis
ILLINOIS 1818
IND. 1816
Chicago
Milwaukee
WISCONSIN 1848
MINN. 1858
IOWA 1846
Nauvoo
St. Joseph
MORMON TRAIL
Ft. Leavenworth
Ft. Kearney
OREGON TRAIL
SANTA FE TRAIL
KANSAS TERRITORY 1854
INDIAN TERR. (UNORGANIZED)
Arkansas R.
Red River
Brazos R.
Colorado R.
TEXAS 1845
San Antonio
Rio Grande
MEXICO
Pecos R.
Chihuahua
El Paso del Norte
SANTA FE TRAIL
CIMARRON CROSSING TRAIL
Santa Fe
Taos
NEW MEXICO TERRITORY 1850
Ceded by Mexico, 1853
Gila R.
San Diego
OLD SPANISH TRAIL
SALT LAKE TO LOS ANGELES TRAIL
Los Angeles
Santa Barbara
Monterey
San Francisco
Sutter's Fort
Sutter's Mill Gold discovered, 1848
Sacramento R.
CALIFORNIA 1850
GREAT BASIN
Salt Lake City
Great Salt Lake
UTAH TERRITORY 1850
CALIFORNIA TRAIL
Green R.
Colorado R.
NEBRASKA TERRITORY 1854
BIG HORN MTS.
Ft. Laramie
N. Platte R.
Platte R.
Missouri R.
Yellowstone R.
ROCKY MTS.
Ft. Hall
Snake R.
Salmon R.
Columbia R.
OREGON 1859
WASHINGTON TERR. 1853
Astoria
Ft. Vancouver
Portland
LASSEN'S TRAIL
OREGON TRAIL
PACIFIC OCEAN

347

Republic of Texas was originally a part of Mexico. After winning its independence from Spain in 1821, the government of Mexico encouraged the development of these rich but remote northern provinces, offering large tracts of land to certain settlers called *empresarios* who agreed to bring two hundred or more families into the area. Americans like Moses and Stephen Austin, who had helped to formulate the policy, responded eagerly, for Mexico was offering land virtually free in return for settlers' promises to become Mexican citizens and adopt the Catholic religion.

By 1835, 35,000 Americans, including many slaveholders, lived in Texas. These new settlers ignored local laws and oppressed native Mexicans, and when the Mexican government attempted to tighten its control over the region, a rebellion erupted. At the Alamo in San Antonio in 1836, fewer than 200 Texans made a heroic stand against 3,000 Mexicans under General Santa Anna. All the defenders of the fort, including Davy Crockett and Colonel James Bowie, died in the battle, and "Remember the Alamo" became the Texans' rallying cry. By the end of the year the Texans had won independence, delighting most Americans, some of whom saw the victory as a triumph of white Protestantism over Catholic Mexico.

Although they established an independent republic, Texans soon sought annexation to the United States. To many white Texans, an independent republic was but a means to joining the Union. President Sam Houston opened negotiations with Washington, but the issue became politically explosive. Southerners favored annexing the proslavery territory; antislavery forces, many northerners, and most Whigs opposed it. In view of the political dangers, President Jackson delayed recognition of Texas until after the election of 1836, and President Van Buren ignored annexation.

Rebuffed by the United States, Texans talked about developing close ties with the British and extending their republic all the way to the Pacific Coast. Faced with the specter of a rival republic to the south, and with British colonies already entrenched to the north, some Americans feared encirclement. If Texas reached the ocean and became an English ally, would not American independence be threatened?

Now President Tyler—committed to expansion, fearful of the Texans' talk of ties with the British, and eager to build political support in the South—pushed for annexation. But in April 1844 the Senate rejected a treaty of annexation. A letter from Secretary of State Calhoun to the British minister justifying annexation as a step in protecting slavery so outraged senators that the treaty was defeated 16 to 35.

Just as southerners sought expansion to the Southwest, northerners looked to the Northwest. In 1841 "Oregon fever" struck thousands. Lured by the glowing reports of missionaries, who seemed **Oregon Fever** to show as much interest in the Northwest's richness and beauty as in the conversion of the Indians, migrants organized hundreds of wagon trains and embarked on the Oregon Trail. The two-thousand-mile journey took six months or more, but within a few years five thousand settlers had arrived in the fertile Willamette Valley south of the Columbia River.

Since the Anglo-American convention of 1818, Britain and the United States had jointly occupied the disputed Oregon Territory (see page 229). Beginning with the administration of President John Quincy Adams, the United States had tried to fix the boundary at the 49th parallel, but Britain was determined to maintain access to the Puget Sound and the Columbia River. Time only increased the American appetite. In 1843 a Cincinnati convention demanded that the United States obtain the entire Oregon Territory, up to its northernmost border of 54°40′. Soon "Fifty-four Forty or Fight" had become the rallying cry of American expansionists.

The expansion into Oregon and the rejection of annexation of Texas, both favored by antislavery forces, heightened southern pessimism. Thus southern leaders became anxious about their **Election of** diminishing ability to control the **1844** debate over slavery. Calhoun persuaded the 1844 Democratic convention to adopt a rule that the presidential nominee receive two-thirds of the convention votes. In effect, the southern states acquired a veto, and they used it to block Van Buren as the nominee. Calhoun had hated Van Buren since their days as rivals for Jackson's favor, and most southerners objected to his antislavery stance and opposition to Texas annexation. Instead, the party chose House Speaker James K. Polk, a hardmoney Jacksonian and avid expansionist from Tennessee. The Whig leader Henry Clay, who opposed annexation, won his party's unanimous designation.

"Oregon Fever" lured thousands of men, women, and children to make the six-month, two-thousand-mile journey across the plains and mountains. They both succumbed to and fueled the spirit of Manifest Destiny. National Park Service.

The main plank of the Democratic platform called for occupation of the entire Oregon Territory and annexation of Texas. The Whigs, though they favored expansion, argued that the Democrats' belligerent nationalism would lead the nation to war with Great Britain or Mexico or both. Clay favored expansion through negotiation, not force.

But few militant expansionists supported Clay, and Polk and the Democrats captured the White House by 170 electoral votes to 105 (they won the popular vote by just 38,000 out of 2.7 million). Polk carried New York's 36 electoral votes by just 6,000 votes; abolitionist James G. Birney, the Liberty party candidate, drew almost 16,000 votes away from Clay, handing the state and the election to Polk. Thus abolitionist forces had influenced the choice of a president.

Interpreting Polk's victory as a mandate for annexation, President Tyler proposed in his last days in office that Texas be admitted by joint resolution of Congress. (The usual method of annexation, by treaty negotiation, required a two-thirds vote in the Senate—which expansionists clearly did not have. Joint resolution required only a simple majority in both houses.) Proslavery and antislavery congressmen debated the extension of slavery into the territory, and the resolution passed the House 120 to 98 and the Senate 27 to 25. Three days before leaving office, Tyler signed the measure. Mexico immediately broke relations with the United States; war loomed.

Politics, the reform spirit, and expansionism commingled in the 1830s and 1840s. Reform imbued with revivalism sought to bring order in a rapidly changing society. But reformers had no monopoly on claims of republican virtue; their opponents too claimed descent from the revolutionary values that held dear individual liberty. Once reform entered politics, it sparked a broader-based interest. Political organization and conflict stimulated even greater interest in campaigns and political issues. Eventually, however, one issue absorbed nearly all attention and created a crisis in the Union: slavery.

IMPORTANT EVENTS

1790s–1840s	Second Great Awakening
1825	House of Representatives elects John Quincy Adams president
1826	American Society for the Promotion of Temperance founded Morgan affair
1828	Tariff of Abominations Jackson elected president
1830	Webster–Hayne debate
1830s–1840s	Second party system
1831	*Liberator* begins publication First national Antimason Convention
1832	Veto of Second Bank of the United States recharter Jackson re-elected
1832–33	Nullification crisis
1836	Republic of Texas established Specie Circular Van Buren elected president
1837	Financial panic
1837–39	U.S.–Canada border tensions
1837–48	Horace Mann heads Massachusetts Board of Education
1839–43	Depression
1840	Whigs under Harrison win presidency
1841–47	Brook Farm
1841	Tyler assumes the presidency Oregon fever
1844	Polk elected president
1845	Texas admitted to the Union
1846–47	Mormon trek to the Great Salt Lake
1848	Woman's Rights Convention, Seneca Falls, New York

SUGGESTIONS FOR FURTHER READING

Religion and Revivalism

Leonard J. Arrington and Davis Bitton, *The Mormon Experience. A History of the Latter-day Saints* (1979); Whitney R. Cross, *The Burned-Over District* (1950); Leon A. Jick, *The Americanization of the Synagogue, 1820–1870* (1976); Charles A. Johnson, *The Frontier Camp Meeting* (1955); Paul E. Johnson, *A Shopkeeper's Millennium: Society and Revivals in Rochester, New York, 1815–1837* (1978); William G. McLoughlin, *Revivals, Awakenings, and Reform: An Essay on Religion and Social Change in America, 1607–1977* (1978); Perry Miller, *The Life of the Mind in America: From the Revolution to the Civil War* (1966); Timothy L. Smith, *Revivalism and Social Reform in Mid-Nineteenth Century America* (1957); William W. Sweet, *Revivalism in America* (1949).

Reform

Ray Allen Billington, *The Protestant Crusade, 1800–1860: A Study of the Origins of American Nativism* (1938); Henri Desroche, *The American Shakers from Neo-Christianity to Pre-Socialism* (1971); Lawrence Foster, *Religion and Sexuality: Three American Communal Experiments of the Nineteenth Century* (1981); Clifford S. Griffin, *The Ferment of Reform, 1830–1860* (1967); Clifford S. Griffin, *Their Brother's Keepers: Moral Stewardship in the United States, 1800–1865* (1960); Raymond Muncy, *Sex and Marriage in Utopian Communities:*

19th Century America (1973); Russel B. Nye, Society and Culture in America, 1830–1860 (1974); David J. Rothman, The Discovery of the Asylum: Social Order and Disorder in the New Republic (1971); Mary P. Ryan, Cradle of the Middle Class. The Family in Oneida County, New York, 1790–1865 (1981); Wallace Stegner, The Gathering of Zion: The Story of the Mormon Trail (1964); Alice Felt Tyler, Freedom's Ferment (1944); Ronald G. Walter, American Reformers, 1815–1860 (1978).

Temperance, Education, and Feminism

Barbara J. Berg, The Remembered Gate: Origins of American Feminism. The Woman and the City, 1800–1860 (1977); Lawrence A. Cremin, American Education: The National Experience, 1783–1876 (1980); Ellen C. Du Bois, Feminism and Suffrage: The Emergence of an Independent Woman's Movement in America 1848–1869 (1978); Barbara Leslie Epstein, The Politics of Domesticity. Women, Evangelism, and Temperance in Nineteenth-Century America (1981); Carl Kaestle, Pillars of the Republic: Common Schools and American Society, 1780–1860 (1982); Michael Katz, The Irony of Early School Reform (1968); Jonathan Messerli, Horace Mann (1972); W. J. Rorabaugh, The Alcoholic Republic: An American Tradition (1979); Ian R. Tyrrell, Sobering Up: From Temperance to Prohibition in Antebellum America, 1800–1860 (1979).

Antislavery and Abolitionism

Frederick Douglass, Life and Times of Frederick Douglass (1881); Martin Duberman, ed., The Anti-Slavery Vanguard (1965); Aileen S. Kraditor, Means and Ends in American Abolitionism: Garrison and His Critics on Strategy and Tactics (1967); Gerda Lerner, The Grimké Sisters of South Carolina (1967); William H. Pease and Jane H. Pease, They Would Be Free: Blacks' Search for Freedom, 1830–1861 (1974); Lewis Perry and Michael Fellman, eds., Antislavery Reconsidered (1979); Benjamin Quarles, Black Abolitionists (1969); Leonard L. Richards, "Gentlemen of Property and Standing": Anti-Abolition Mobs in Jacksonian America (1970); John L. Thomas, The Liberator: William Lloyd Garrison (1963); Ronald G. Walters, The Antislavery Appeal: American Abolitionism After 1830 (1976); Bertram Wyatt-Brown, Lewis Tappan and the Evangelical War Against Slavery (1969).

Andrew Jackson and the Jacksonians

Lee Benson, The Concept of Jacksonian Democracy: New York as a Test Case (1964); Richard B. Latner, The Presidency of Andrew Jackson (1979); Marvin Meyers, The Jacksonian Persuasion (1960); John Niven, Martin Van Buren (1983); Edward Pessen, Jacksonian America: Society, Personality, and Politics, rev. ed. (1979); Robert V. Remini, Andrew Jackson and the Course of American Democracy (1984); Robert V. Remini, Andrew Jackson and the Course of American Freedom, 1822–1832 (1981); Robert V. Remini, Andrew Jackson and the Bank War (1967); Arthur M. Schlesinger, Jr., The Age of Jackson (1945); John William Ward, Andrew Jackson: Symbol for an Age (1955); Harry L. Watson, Jacksonian Politics and Community Conflict. The Emergence of the Second American Party System in Cumberland County, North Carolina (1981); Major L. Wilson, The Presidency of Martin Van Buren (1984).

Democrats and Whigs

Ronald P. Formisano, The Transformation of Political Culture. Massachusetts Parties, 1790s–1840s (1983); Ronald P. Formisano, The Birth of Mass Political Parties: Michigan, 1827–1861 (1971); William W. Freehling, Prelude to Civil War: The Nullification Controversy in South Carolina (1966); Daniel Walker Howe, The Political Culture of the American Whigs (1979); Kathleen Smith Kutolowski, "Antimasonry Reexamined: Social Bases of the Grass-Roots Party," Journal of American History, 71 (September 1984), 269–293; Richard P. McCormick, The Second American Party System: Party Formation in the Jacksonian Era (1966); James Roger Sharp, The Jacksonians Versus the Banks. Politics in the States After the Panic of 1837 (1970); William Preston Vaughn, The Antimasonic Party in the United States 1826–1843 (1983).

Manifest Destiny and Foreign Policy

Norman B. Graebner, ed., Manifest Destiny (1968); Reginald Horsman, Race and Manifest Destiny (1981); Frederick Merk, Manifest Destiny and Mission in American History (1963); David M. Pletcher, The Diplomacy of Annexation: Texas, Oregon, and the Mexican War (1973); Charles G. Sellers, Jr., James K. Polk: Continentalist, 1843–1846 (1966); Paul A. Varg, United States Foreign Relations, 1820–1860 (1979); Albert K. Weinberg, Manifest Destiny (1935).

Territorial Expansion and Slavery: The Road to War

1845–1861

Chapter 13

"*Our people have* filled the eastern valley of the Mississippi, adventurously ascended the Missouri to its headsprings, and are already engaged in establishing the blessings of self-government in valleys of which the rivers flow to the Pacific. Our title to the country of Oregon," continued James K. Polk, "is 'clear and unquestionable.'" With these words, spoken in 1845, a new president made territorial expansion the centerpiece of his administration's agenda and pledged his support for Americans' expansionist energies. Many shared President Polk's enthusiasm and rejoiced when the nation obtained a vast western domain through war with Mexico. But expansion stirred conflict along with celebration, as Polk had reason to know. One year before, as a dark-horse candidate for the presidential nomination, Polk had little chance until that issue divided the Democratic party's convention. From the deadlocked convention he eventually emerged, victorious.

Fifteen years later the nation's territories figured prominently in another political gathering. In 1860 tense and angry Democrats gathered at Charleston for another nominating convention. Again the convention deadlocked, but this time there was no successful resolution. Charging that southern rights in the territories were being denied, delegates from six deep-South states walked out of the meeting amid cheers and applause from the Charleston gallery. That walkout destroyed the last remaining national party and began the destruction of the Union. Americans' fascination with new land had brought Texas, the West Coast, and the Southwest into the nation and launched the settling of the Great Plains, but ultimately it disrupted the Union.

Some experienced politicians had foreseen just such a result, because slavery lay at the root of territorial controversies. Each time the nation expanded it confronted a thorny issue—whether new territories and states should be slave or free. Over this question there were disagreements too violent to compromise. Sensing that fact, John C. Calhoun called Mexico "the forbidden fruit; the penalty of eating it would be to subject our institutions to political death." A host of political leaders, including Henry Clay, Lewis Cass, Stephen A. Douglas, and Presidents Jackson and Van Buren, labored from the 1830s through the 1850s to postpone or compromise disagreements about slavery in the territories. But repeatedly these disputes injected the bitterness surrounding slavery into national politics. If slavery was the sore spot in the body politic, territorial disputes were like salt rubbed into the sore.

Moreover, as Americans fought over slavery in the territories, the conflict broadened to encompass many other issues. The United States had always been a heterogeneous, diverse society, not a cohesive unit, but now various concerns became linked to one divisive issue instead of balancing each other off. Northerners came to believe that their liberties, political rights, and economic interests were under attack by an aggressive South. Southerners began to fear that their safety, rights, and prosperity were in peril from a hostile North. Citizens in both sections, North and South, worried that opportunity, a precious social commodity for themselves and their children, was at stake.

Battles over slavery in the territories broke the second party system apart and then shaped a realigned system that emphasized sectional enmity. Sectional parties replaced nationwide organizations. No matter how diverse the following of these sectional parties was, their rise was alarming; it seemed to confirm the trend toward disunion. In addition, it removed intraparty pressures for compromise and strengthened the hand of intransigent elements.

As parties clamored for support, and as citizens reflected on events, the feeling grew that North and South were too different to thrive within the same country. A northern ideology advanced by the new Republican party suggested that progress depended on the free labor, civil liberties, and economic change that the South opposed. A southern ideology depicted northern society as unstable, lacking in respect for the Constitution, and prone to interfere with slavery, which southerners claimed was the foundation of white equality and republicanism. Some concluded that the two sections had to separate.

Not all Americans were obsessed with these conflicts. In fact, the results of the 1860 presidential election strongly suggested that most voters wanted neither disunion nor civil war. Yet within six months they had both. By 1860 the cloud over the territories had grown into a storm. Both sections felt threatened and anxious, and an area of disagreement that once had been limited to a small minority of extremists now engaged two powerful groups: the victorious Republican party and defensive southern slaveholders. These groups were on a collision course, and they chose not to accept any of the desperate, last-minute compromises offered to resolve their differences. Because neither side gave in, conflict was inevitable. Because thousands who disagreed with the antagonists shared many of their fears, a vast Civil War began.

James K. Polk was an effective president who achieved his goals. But territorial expansion led to sectional conflict. Painting by George Peter Alexander Healy in the Collection of the Corcoran Gallery of Art.

CONFLICT BEGINS: THE MEXICAN WAR

The Mexican War evoked enthusiasm and conflict, national pride and sectional suspicions. Americans learned of bold advances in the military theater and key victories by their soldiers. In the political theater Americans found themselves embroiled in serious and long-lasting divisions. The war introduced other, broader issues and entangled politicians in a growing number of problems related to slavery.

James K. Polk's territorial ambitions pushed events in the direction of war. Despite his claim, the United States's title to Oregon was not "clear and unquestionable." Since 1818 America and Britain had jointly occupied the disputed territory, and for over twenty years the British had refused to accept a boundary dividing the two nations' jurisdictions at the 49th parallel. But when he entered office, Polk found that Texas was the more pressing crisis. Congress's annexation of Texas had outraged Mexican leaders. They had severed relations with the United States, yet American ambitions in that region remained undiminished. Observers knew that war could break out at any time (see page 349).

Faced with imminent war in the Southwest, President Polk decided to use diplomacy to avoid a second conflict with Great Britain in the Northwest. Dropping the demand for a boundary at 54°40′, he kept up pressure on the British to accept the 49th parallel. Eventually, in 1846 Great Britain agreed. In the Oregon Treaty, the United States gained all of present-day Oregon, Washington, and Idaho and parts of Wyoming and Montana (see map, page 356).

Determined to acquire California and New Mexico in addition to all the land claimed by Texas, Polk charted a firm course in regard to Mexico. He ordered American troops to defend the border claimed by Texas but disputed by Mexico, and he attempted to buy a huge tract of land in the Southwest from the resentful Mexicans. After purchase failed Polk resolved to ask Congress for a declaration of war and set to work compiling a list of grievances. This task became unnecessary when word arrived that Mexican forces had engaged a body of American troops in disputed territory. American blood had been shed. Eagerly Polk declared that "war exists by the act of Mexico itself" and summoned the nation to arms.

Congress voted to recognize a state of war between

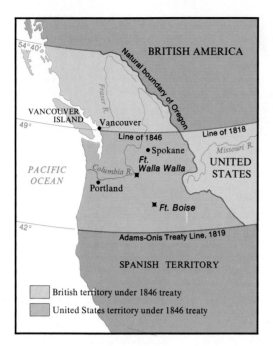

American Expansion in Oregon

1836, when Congress passed the gag rule (see page 333). Many white northerners, even those who saw nothing wrong with slavery, had viewed John Quincy Adams's stand against the rule as a defense of free speech and the right to petition. The fight over the gag rule increased the influence of the largely unpopular abolitionists. Anxieties about free speech and civil liberties first made the idea of a Slave Power credible.

Now the Mexican War increased fears of this sinister power. Sectional acrimony took a marked turn for the worse as Congress debated the conduct of the war. A Democratic representative from Pennsylvania, David Wilmot, rose to offer an amendment to an appropriations bill in support of the war. Wilmot's Proviso added a simple but fateful condition: "neither slavery nor involuntary servitude shall ever exist" in any territory gained from Mexico. The proviso did not pass, and some observers did not immediately sense its significance. But within a few years the Wilmot Proviso became a rallying cry for abolitionists and Free-Soilers, and eventually fourteen northern legislatures endorsed it.

Wilmot Proviso

David Wilmot, significantly, was neither an abolitionist nor a Free-Soiler. He denied having any "squeamish sensitiveness upon the subject of slavery" or "morbid sympathy for the slave" and explained that his goal was to defend "the rights of white freemen." Wilmot wanted California "for free white labor"; he was fighting for opportunity for "the sons of toil, of my own race and own color." His involvement in antislavery controversy showed the alarming ability of the slavery issue to broaden through territorial questions.

Like Wilmot, most northerners were racists, not abolitionists. But fear of the Slave Power was transforming the abolitionist impulse into a broader and more potent antislavery movement, which terrified southern spokesmen. Northern voters, even antiblack voters, were becoming opponents of slavery. Their concern was to protect themselves, not southern blacks, from the Slave Power. As the issues of the day broadened, they excited larger numbers of people: more northerners cared about the Slave Power than about the extension of slavery, and more cared about slavery extension than about abolition. In the form of territorial controversies, issues that had at first alarmed only a few claimed the attention of many.

Mexico and the United States in May 1846, but controversy rapidly grew. Public opinion about the war was sharply divided, with southwesterners enthusiastic and New Englanders strenuously opposed. In Congress Whigs charged that Polk had "literally provoked" an unnecessary war and "usurped the power of Congress by making war upon Mexico." The aged John Quincy Adams passionately opposed the war, dying after delivery of a powerful speech against it, and a tall young Whig from Illinois named Abraham Lincoln questioned its justification. Moreover, a small minority of antislavery Whigs agreed with abolitionists—the war was no less than a plot to extend slavery. Joshua Giddings of Ohio charged on the floor of the House that Polk's purpose was "to render slavery secure in Texas" and to extend the slave domain to vast expanses of new territory.

These charges fed fear of the Slave Power. Abolitionists long had warned that there was a Slave Power—a slaveholding oligarchy in control of the South and intent on controlling the nation. In the South these dangerous aristocrats had gained power by persecuting critics of slavery and suppressing their ideas. The Slave Power's assault on northern liberties, abolitionists argued, had begun in

Idea of a Slave Power

Despite this dissension at home, events on the battlefield went well for American troops, who as in previous wars were mainly volunteers furnished by the states. General Zachary Taylor's forces attacked and occupied Monterrey, securing northeastern Mexico (see map, page 359.) Polk then ordered Colonel Stephen Kearny and a small detachment to invade the remote and relatively unpopulated provinces of New Mexico and California. Taking Santa Fe without opposition, Kearney pushed into California, where he joined forces with rebellious American settlers, led by Captain John C. Frémont, and a couple of United States naval units. A quick victory was followed by reverses, but American soldiers soon re-established their dominance in distant and thinly populated California.

Meanwhile, General Winfield Scott led fourteen thousand men from Veracruz, on the Gulf of Mexico, toward Mexico City. This daring invasion was the

Treaty of Guadalupe Hidalgo

decisive campaign of the war. After a series of hard-fought battles, Scott's men captured the Mexican capital and brought the war to an end. On February 2, 1848, representatives of both countries signed the Treaty of Guadalupe Hidalgo. The United States gained California and New Mexico (including present-day Nevada, Utah, and Arizona) and recognition of the Rio Grande as the southern boundary of Texas. In return, the American government agreed to settle the claims of its citizens against Mexico and to pay Mexico a mere $15 million.

The cost of the war included thirteen thousand Americans and fifty thousand Mexicans dead, plus Mexican-American enmity lasting into the twentieth century. But the domestic cost may have been even higher. The acquisition of new territory only fed sectional distrust and acrimony. Northerners and southerners disagreed with each other more frequently, and under the pressure of sectional issues, party unity for both Democrats and Whigs began to loosen.

Hoping to stem growing factionalism among Democrats, Polk had renounced a second term early in his administration. He also offered regular Democrats nearly all they could ask for in the way of traditional Jacksonian economic policy. He persuaded Congress to reinstitute the independent treasury system and to remove protectionist features from the tariff, and he vetoed internal improvements. But slavery in the

As this broadside shows, suspicion that the Slave Power sought additional territory and influence preceded the Mexican War and was deeply rooted. Library of Congress.

territories was one issue beyond solution by him or anyone else. When Polk recommended that Oregon be a free territory, southerners felt anew the old fear that congressional power would be used against slavery. Some northern expansionists, on the other hand, thought that Texas had received priority over Oregon due to a Slave Power plot.

In the presidential election of 1848 slavery in the territories was the one overriding issue. Both parties tried to push this question into the background, but

Election of 1848 and Popular Sovereignty

it dominated the conventions, the campaign, and the election. The Democrats tried to avoid sectional conflict by nominating General Lewis Cass of Michigan for president and General William Butler of Kentucky for vice president. Cass devised the idea of "popular sovereignty" for the territories—letting residents in the territories decide the question of slavery for themselves. His party's platform declared that Congress did not have the power to interfere with slavery and criticized those who pressed the question. The Whigs nominated General Zachary Taylor, who was a southern slaveholder as well as a military hero, along with Millard Fillmore for vice president. Their convention similarly refused to assert

There was more to the Mexican War than romance and glory. Several fierce battles took place along the route of General Scott's invasion. West Point Museum.

that Congress had power over slavery in the territories. But the issue would not stay in the background.

Antislavery Whigs in the North were not satisfied with their party's stand, and many southern Democrats apparently voted for Taylor because he was a slaveholder. Some northern Democrats broke with their party and nominated former president Van Buren, who received support from the Liberty party and abolitionist Whigs and became the Free-Soil candidate. This new party, whose slogan was "Free soil, free speech, free labor, and free men," drew many northern votes away from Cass. In New York support for Free-Soil pulled enough votes away from the Democrat, Cass, to put Zachary Taylor in the White House. Sectional concerns were fragmenting the parties, and antislavery forces again had influenced the outcome of the election.

The election of 1848 and the conflict over slavery in the territories shaped politics in the 1850s. At the national level, all issues would be seen through the prism of sectional conflict over slavery in the territories. The nation's uncertain attempts to deal with economic and social change would give way to more pressing questions about the nature of the Union itself. And the second party system would itself succumb to crisis.

TERRITORIAL PROBLEMS ARE COMPROMISED BUT RE-EMERGE

The first sectional battle of the decade involved the territory of California. More than eighty thousand Americans flooded into California in 1849. President Taylor, seeing a simple solution to the challenge of governing lands acquired from Mexico, urged the settlers to apply for admission to the Union. They promptly did so, submitting a proposed state

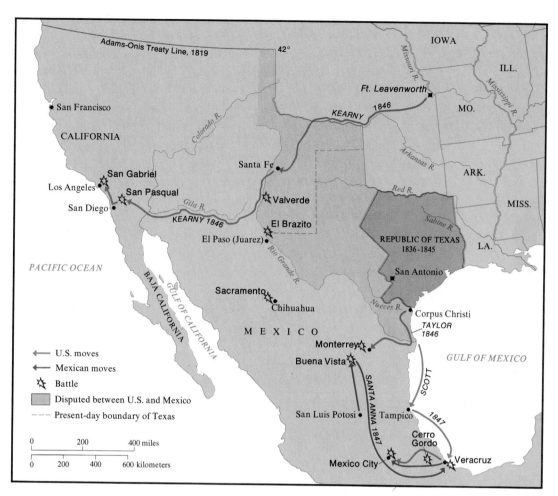

The Mexican War

constitution that did not allow for slavery. But southern politicians wanted to make California slave territory, or at least to extend the Missouri Compromise line west through California. Representatives from nine southern states met in an unofficial convention in Nashville to assert the South's right to part of the territory.

Sensing that the Union was in peril, the venerable Whig leader Henry Clay marshalled his energies once more. Twice before, in 1820 and 1833, the "Great Pacificator" had taken the lead in shaping sectional compromise; now he labored one last time to preserve the nation. To hushed Senate galleries Clay presented a series of compromise measures. Over the weeks that followed, Clay and Senator Stephen A. Douglas of Illinois steered their omnibus bill, or package of compromises, through debate and amendment.

The problems to be solved were thorny indeed. Would California or a part of it become a free state? How should the land acquired from Mexico be organized? Texas, which allowed slavery, claimed large portions of the new land as far west as Santa Fe, so that claim too had to be settled. And in addition to southern complaints that fugitive slaves were not being returned, as the Constitution required, and northern objections to the sale of human beings in the nation's capital, the lawmakers had to deal with competing theories of settlers' rights in the territories. It was these theories that proved most troublesome in the continuing debate over the territories.

Clay and Douglas hoped to avoid a specific formula and preserve the ambiguity that existed about settlers' rights in the territories. Lewis Cass's idea of popular sovereignty, for example, had both an attractive ring

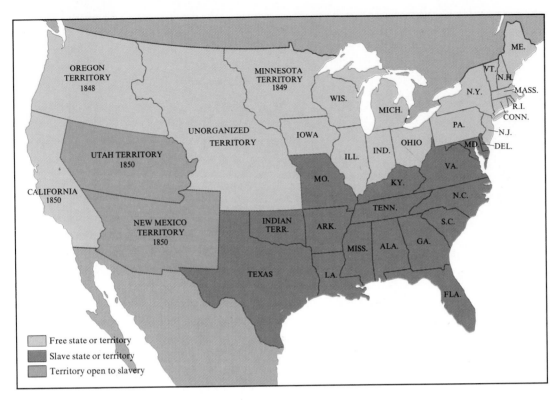

The Compromise of 1850

to it and a useful vagueness. Cass had observed that Congress could stay out of the territorial wrangle. Ultimately it would have to approve statehood for a territory, but Congress should "in the meantime," Cass said, allow the people living there "to regulate their own concerns in their own way." These few words, seemingly clear, proved highly ambiguous, disagreement centering on the meaning of "meantime."

When could settlers bar slavery? Southerners claimed that they had equal rights in the territories as well as in the nation. Therefore neither Congress nor a territorial legislature could bar slavery. Only when settlers framed a state constitution could they take that step. Northerners, meanwhile, argued that Americans living in a territory were entitled to local self-government, and thus could outlaw slavery at any time, if they allowed it at all. To avoid dissension within their party, northern and southern Democrats had explained Cass's statement to their constituents in these two incompatible ways. Their conflicting interpretations caused strong disagreement in the debate on Clay's proposals.

After months of labor, Clay and Douglas finally brought their package to a vote, and met defeat. But the determined Douglas had not given up. With Clay sick and absent from Washington, Douglas brought the compromise measures up again, one at a time. Congress lacked a majority to approve the package, but Douglas shrewdly realized that different majorities might be created for each of the measures. The strategy worked, and Douglas's resourcefulness salvaged a positive result from six months of congressional effort. The Compromise of 1850, as it was called, became law.

Under the terms of its various measures, California was admitted as a free state, and the Texan boundary was set at its present limits (see map). The United States paid Texas $10 million in consideration of the boundary agreement. And the territories of New Mexico and Utah were organized with power to legislate on "all rightful subjects . . . consistent with the Constitution." A stronger fugitive slave law and an act to suppress the slave trade in the District of Columbia completed the compromise.

Compromise of 1850

Chapter 13: TERRITORIAL EXPANSION AND SLAVERY, 1845–1861

Jubilation greeted passage of the Compromise of 1850; in Washington, crowds celebrated the happy news. "On one glorious night," records a modern historian, "the word went abroad that it was the duty of every patriot to get drunk. Before the next morning many a citizen had proved his patriotism," and several prominent senators "were reported stricken with a variety of implausible maladies—headaches, heat prostration, or overindulgence in fruit."

In reality, there was less cause for celebration than citizens thought. Fundamentally, the Compromise of 1850 was not a settlement of sectional disputes. It was at best an artful evasion. Douglas had found a way to pass his proposals without getting northerners and southerners to come to agreement on them; neither side had given up anything. Though this compromise bought time for the nation, it did not create guidelines for the settlement of future territorial questions. It merely put them off.

Furthermore, the compromise had two basic flaws. The first pertained to popular sovereignty. What were "rightful subjects of legislation, consistent with the Constitution"? During debate, southerners asserted that this meant there would be no prohibition of slavery during the territorial stage; northerners declared that settlers could bar slavery whenever they wished. After passage of the compromise, legislators from the two sections went home and explained the act in these different ways, as if there were two different compromises. (In fact, the compromise admitted the disagreement by providing for the appeal of a territorial legislature's action to the Supreme Court. But no such case ever arose.) Thus, in the controversy over popular sovereignty, nothing had been settled. In one politician's words, the legislators seemed to have enacted a lawsuit instead of a law.

The second flaw lay in the Fugitive Slave Act, which stirred up controversy instead of laying it to rest. The new law empowered slaveowners to go into

Fugitive Slave Act

court in their own states and present evidence that a slave who owed them service had escaped. The transcript of such a proceeding, including a description of the fugitive, was to be taken as conclusive proof of a person's slave status, even in free states and territories. Legal authorities had to decide only whether the black person brought before them was the person described, not whether

he or she was indeed a slave. Fees and penalties encouraged U.S. marshals to assist in apprehending fugitives and discouraged citizens from harboring them. (Authorities were paid $10 if the alleged fugitive was turned over to the slaveowner, $5 if he was not.)

Abolitionist newspapers quickly attacked the fugitive slave law as a violation of the Bill of Rights. Why were alleged fugitives denied a trial by jury before being sent to bondage in a slave state? Why did suspected fugitives have no right to present evidence or cross-examine witnesses? Did not the law give authorities a financial incentive to turn prisoners over to slaveowners? These arguments convinced some northerners that free blacks could be sent into slavery, mistakenly or otherwise, with no means to defend themselves. Protest meetings were held in Massachusetts, New York, Pennsylvania, northern Ohio, northern Illinois, and elsewhere. In Boston in 1851, a mob grabbed a runaway slave from a U.S. marshal and sent him to safety in Canada.

At this point a relatively unknown writer dramatized the plight of the slave in a way that captured the sympathies of millions of northerners. Harriet Beecher Stowe, daughter of a religious New England family that had produced many prominent ministers, wrote *Uncle Tom's Cabin* out of deep moral conviction. Her book, published in March 1852, showed how slavery brutalized the men and women who suffered under it. Stowe also portrayed slavery's evil effects on slaveholders, indicting the institution itself more harshly than the southerners caught in its web. In nine months the book sold over 300,000 copies; by mid-1853, over a million. Countless people saw *Uncle Tom's Cabin* performed as a stage play or read similar novels inspired by it. Stowe had brought the issue of slavery home to many who had never before given it much thought.

Uncle Tom's Cabin

The popularity of *Uncle Tom's Cabin* alarmed and appalled many southerners, who had long been sensitive about slavery. Southern leaders were intelligent men who were fully aware of the worldwide movement away from slavery and the forces gathering against it within the United States. They were also men who tended to see the world from the perspective of their plantations. Human bondage was so central to their world that life without slavery was almost unimaginable to them. They had built their fortunes

Holy Bible.
Thou shalt not deliver unto the master his servant which has escaped from his master unto thee. He shall dwell with thee. Even among you in that place which he shall choose in one of thy gates where it liketh him best Thou shalt not oppress him
Deut XXIII 16

Effects of the Fugitive-Slave-Law.

Declaration of independence.
We hold that all men are created equal, that they are endowed by their Creator with certain unalienable rights, that among these are life liberty and the pursuit of happiness

Despite their racial prejudice, many northerners disapproved of slavery and viewed summary proceedings that could send a man into slavery as contrary to the Bill of Rights. Library of Congress.

and their society on the institution of slavery, and they wanted to keep the world they knew. Accordingly, they fought every battle in the sectional crisis with a white-hot intensity. In so doing, they developed a variety of proslavery arguments.

Some southerners tried to prove the necessity of expanding slavery into the territories. Expansion was essential to the welfare of the Negro, they declared, for prejudice lessened as the concentration of blacks decreased. It was necessary to the prosperity of the South, they argued, for rich opportunities lay waiting in the territories, while older areas of declining fertility had surplus slave populations. Yet there was a noticeable absence of huge migrations of slaveholders into the territories. A more likely cause of southern concern over the territories was the fear that if nearby areas became free soil, they would be used as bases from which to spread abolitionism into the slave states. Jefferson Davis of Mississippi voiced such a concern when he wrote in 1855 that "abolitionism would gain but little in excluding slavery from the territories, if it were never to disturb that institution in the States."

To counter indictments of slavery as a moral wrong, proslavery theorists elaborated numerous arguments based on partially scientific or pseudoscientific data.

Proslavery Theories

At a moment's notice southern writers or politicians could discuss anthropological evidence for the separate origin of the races; physicians' views on the inferiority of the black body; and sociological arguments for the superiority of the slave-labor system. Writers explained the history of ancient races or the new "science" of phrenology. Its data on the external dimensions of human skulls and the volume of the cranial cavity "proved" that blacks were a separate and inferior race. One southern sociologist, a Virginian named George Fitzhugh, focused on relations between management and labor in both the North and the South. He concluded that wage labor in industry was more inhumane than slavery because employers cared nothing about wage laborers as people and turned them out when they grew old or sick, in contrast to paternalistic slaveowners. From these points Fitzhugh drew an extreme conclusion—slavery ought to be practiced in all societies, whatever their racial composition.

But in private and in their hearts, most of these men fell back on two rationales: a belief that blacks were inferior and biblical accounts of slaveholding. Among friends, Jefferson Davis ignored all the latest racist theories and reverted to the eighteenth-century argument that southerners were doing the best they could with a situation they had inherited. "Is it well to denounce an evil for which there is no cure?" he asked. On another occasion, repeating the widespread belief that living with a sizable free black population was impossible, he protested to a friend that Congress never discussed "any thing but that over which we have no control, slavery of the negro."

To try to control Congress, southern leaders relied on their chief tool in defending slavery: constitutional theory. They developed an interpretation of the Constitution and the principles of American government that linked them to the founding fathers and the original purposes of the nation. Drawing on Thomas Jefferson's concept of strict construction, they emphasized that the nation arose from a compact among sovereign states; that the states were primary and the central government secondary; that the states retained all powers not expressly granted to the central government; and that the states were to be treated equally. Along with these theories went the philosophy that the power of the federal government should be kept to a minimum. By keeping government close to home, southerners hoped to maintain slavery.

Many of them hoped that slavery would be secure and allowed to expand under the administration of a new president. Franklin Pierce, a Democrat from New Hampshire, won a smashing victory in 1852 over the Whig presidential nominee, General Winfield Scott. Pierce's victory derived less from his strengths than from his opponents' weaknesses. The Whigs had been a congressional party that was competitive with the Democrats in the states and strong in the nation's legislature, but lacked commanding presidents in an era of strong leaders like Jackson and Polk. Sectional discord was steadily splitting the party up into southern and northern

Election of 1852

wings that cooperated less and less. The deaths of President Taylor (1850), Daniel Webster (1852), and Henry Clay (1852) deprived the party of the few dominant personalities it had, and no new leaders emerged to solve its problems. The Whig party in 1852 ran on little but its past reputation, and many politicians were predicting its demise.

But southerners were pleased that Pierce made no secret of his belief that the defense of each section's rights was essential to the nation's unity. Americans hoped that Pierce's firm support for the Compromise of 1850 might end sectional divisions. By comparison Scott's views on the compromise were unknown, and the Free-Soil candidate, John P. Hale of New Hampshire, openly repudiated it. Thus Pierce's victory seemed to confirm most Americans' support for the Compromise of 1850.

But Pierce did not seem able to avoid sectional conflict. His proposal for a transcontinental railroad ran into congressional dispute over where it should be built, North or South. His attempts to acquire foreign territory stirred up more trouble. An annexation treaty with Hawaii failed because southern senators would not vote for another free state, and Pierce's efforts to annex Cuba angered antislavery northerners. Pierce tried to purchase Cuba from Spain in 1854. When publication of a government document, the Ostend Manifesto, revealed that three administration officials had rashly talked of "wresting" Cuba from Spain, some northerners concluded that Pierce was determined to acquire more slave territory. The new president's efforts to avoid slavery controversies were heading toward failure when another territorial bill threw Congress, and the nation, into a bitter conflict that had significant results.

TERRITORIAL PROBLEMS SHATTER THE PARTY SYSTEM

The new controversy began in a surprising way. Stephen A. Douglas, one of the architects and manager of the Compromise of 1850, introduced a bill to establish the Kansas and Nebraska territories.

Although Douglas had no reason to attack the compromise, which lent him fame, he did have other concerns and goals. Douglas was from Illinois, a state whose economy benefited from settlement on the Great Plains. A midwestern transcontinental railroad would accelerate this process, but a necessary precondition for such a railroad was the organization of the territory it would cross. Thus it was probably in the interest of building such a railroad that Douglas introduced a bill that inflamed sectional passions, completed the destruction of the Whig party, damaged the northern wing of the Democratic party, gave birth to the Republican party, and injured his own ambitions for national office.

The Kansas-Nebraska bill exposed the first flaw of the Compromise of 1850, and conflict over popular sovereignty erupted once more. Douglas's bill clearly left "all questions pertaining to slavery in the Territories . . . to the people residing therein," but northerners and southerners still disagreed violently over what territorial settlers could constitutionally do. Moreover, the Kansas-Nebraska bill opened a new Pandora's box. The new territories lay within the Louisiana Purchase, and under the Missouri Compromise all that land from 36°30′ north to the Canadian border was off-limits to slavery. Thus, if popular sovereignty were to mean anything in Kansas or Nebraska, it had to mean that the Missouri Compromise no longer was in force. If settlers were to have a choice, they could choose slavery.

Kansas-Nebraska Bill

Southern congressmen, anxious to establish the slaveholders' right to take their slaves into any territory, pressed Douglas to concede this point. He needed southern votes to win passage of his bill, and southerners demanded an explicit repeal of the 36°30′ limitation as the price of their support. During a carriage ride with Senator Archibald Dixon of Kentucky, Douglas debated the point at length. Finally he made an impulsive decision: "By God, Sir, you are right. I will incorporate it in my bill, though I know it will raise a hell of a storm."

Douglas did not regard his bill as a proslavery measure, for he believed that conditions of climate and soil would effectively keep slavery out of Kansas and Nebraska. But the fact remained that his bill threw land open to slavery where it had been prohibited before. This fact immediately generated opposition from free-soil and antislavery forces. The struggle in Congress was titanic and lasted three and one-half months. Douglas obtained the support of President Pierce, and eventually he prevailed: the bill became law in May 1854 (see map). Unfortunately the storm—far more violent than Douglas had imagined—was just beginning. The Kansas-Nebraska Act inflamed fears and angers that had only simmered before. Abolitionists charged that the act was sinister aggression by the Slave Power, its most brazen yet. Concern over the fugitive slave law deepened: between 1855 and 1859 Connecticut, Rhode Island, Massachusetts, Michigan, Maine, Ohio, and Wisconsin passed personal liberty laws designed to interfere with the swift action of the Fugitive Slave Act. These laws, which provided counsel for alleged fugitives and sought to guarantee trial by jury, revealed the strength of northern fear of the Slave Power. To the South, they were outrageous signs of bad faith, a refusal to honor the Compromise of 1850. Even more important, however, was the devastating impact of the Kansas-Nebraska Act on political parties.

The Kansas-Nebraska Act cemented the division of the Whig party into northern and southern wings so irrevocably that it ceased to exist as a national organization and could no longer compete politically. One of the two great parties in the second party system was now gone. The Democrats survived, but their support in the North fell drastically in the 1854 elections. Northern Democrats lost sixty-six of the ninety-one congressional seats they had won in free states in 1852.

Moreover, anger over the territorial issue created a new political party. During debate on the Kansas-Nebraska bill, six congressmen had published an "Appeal of the Independent Democrats," attacking Douglas's legislation as "a gross violation of a sacred pledge" (the Missouri Compromise) and a "criminal betrayal of precious rights" that would make free territory a "dreary region of despotism." This appeal sparked other protests. In the summer and fall of 1854, antislavery Whigs and Democrats, Free-Soilers, and other reformers throughout the Northwest met to form a new Republican party, dedicated to keeping slavery out of the territories. The Republicans' influence rapidly spread to the East, and they won a stunning victory

The New Republican Party

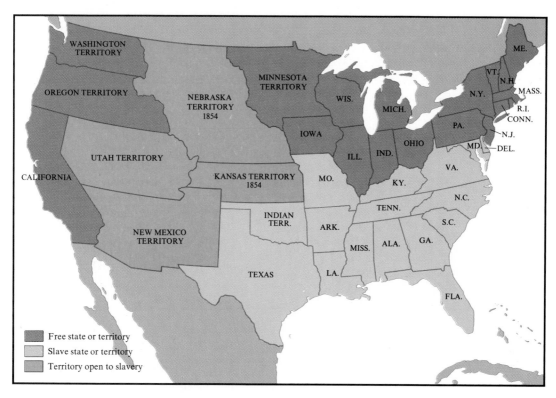

The Kansas-Nebraska Act, 1854

in the 1854 elections. In the party's first appearance on the ballot, Republicans captured a majority of House seats in the North.

For the first time, a sectional party based on a sectional issue had gained significant power in the political system. In the second party system, Whigs and Democrats had been strong in both the North and the South. The national base of support enjoyed by each had moderated sectional conflict, as party leaders compromised to achieve unity. To compete more effectively for national office, the two parties had always papered over their own sectional differences. But now the Whigs were gone, and politics in the 1850s would never be the same. Henceforth, Democrats would struggle to maintain a national following while the new Republican party flourished in a sectional context by exploiting sectional concerns.

Nor were Republicans the only new party. An anti-immigrant organization, the American party, also seemed likely for a few years to replace the Whigs.

Know-Nothings

This party, popularly known as the Know-Nothings (because its members at first kept their purposes secret, answering all queries with the words "I know nothing"), exploited nativist fear of foreigners. Between 1848 and 1860, nearly 3.5 million immigrants came to the United States—proportionally the heaviest influx of foreigners in American history (see pages 280–284). The Democratic party diligently ministered to the needs of these new citizens and relied on their votes in elections. But native-born Americans harbored serious misgivings about them. The temperance movement gained new strength early in these years, promising to stamp out the evils associated with liquor and immigrants. It was in this context that the Know-Nothings became prominent, campaigning to reinforce Protestant morality and restrict voting and office-holding to the native-born.

By the mid-1850s the American party was powerful and growing; in 1854 so many new congressmen won office with anti-immigrant as well as antislavery support that Know-Nothings could claim they outnumbered Republicans. But like the Whigs, the Know-Nothings could not keep their northern and southern wings together, and they melted away after 1856. That left the field to the Republicans, who wooed the nativists

POLITICAL SUCCESSORS TO THE WHIG PARTY

Party	Period of Influence	Area of Influence	Outcome
Free-Soil party	1848–1854	North	Merged with Republican party
Know-Nothings (American party)	1853–1856	Nationwide	Disappeared, freeing some northern voters to join Republican party
Republican party	1854–present	North (later nationwide)	Became rival of Democratic party in third party system

and in several states passed temperance ordinances and laws postponing suffrage for naturalized citizens (see table).

Republicans, Know-Nothings, and Democrats were all scrambling to attract former Whig voters. The death of that party insured a major realignment of the political system. For practical politicians the grand prize was the old Whig following, a magnificent block of voters that once had accounted for approximately half the electorate. To woo these homeless Whigs, the remaining parties stressed a variety of issues chosen to appeal for one reason or another. Immigration, temperance, homestead bills, the tariff, internal improvements—all played an important role in attracting voters during the 1850s. For many Americans it was these issues, not the controversy over slavery, that were the real stuff of politics.

Realignment of Political System

The Republicans appealed strongly to groups interested in the economic development of the West. Commercial agriculture was booming in the Ohio–Mississippi–Great Lakes area, but residents of that region needed more canals, roads, and river and harbor improvements to reap the full benefit of their labors. Because credit was scarce, there was also widespread interest in a federal land-grant program: its proponents argued that western land should be

Republican Appeals

made available free to those who would use it. The Whigs had favored all these things before their party collapsed, but the Democrats resolutely opposed them. Following long-standing party principles, Democratic presidents vetoed internal improvements bills and a homestead bill as late as 1859. Seizing their opportunity, the Republicans added internal improvements and land-grant planks to their platform. They also backed higher tariffs as an enticement to industrialists and businessmen, whose interest in tariffs was quickened by a panic, or recession, in 1857.

Another major feature of the realigned political system was ideology, and ideological appeals had a significant impact on the sectional crisis. In the North, Republicans attracted many voters through effective use of ideology. They spoke to the image that northerners had of themselves, their society, and their future when they preached "Free Soil, Free Labor, Free Men." These phrases resonated with traditional ideals of equality, liberty, and opportunity under self-government—the heritage of republicanism. Use of that heritage also undercut charges that the Republican party was radical and unreliable.

"Free Soil, Free Labor, Free Men" seemed to fit with a northern economy that was energetic, expanding, and prosperous. Untold thousands of farmers had moved west to establish productive farms and growing communities. Midwestern farmers were using machines that multiplied their yields. Railroads were

Republican support for roads, canals, river and harbor improvements, and free homesteads appealed powerfully to those who were settling the thriving states of the upper Middle West. Copyright © 1971, The R. W. Norton Art Gallery, Shreveport, La. Used by permission.

carrying their crops to market. And industry was beginning to perform wonders of production, making available goods that had hitherto been beyond the reach of the average person. As northerners surveyed the general growth and prosperity, they thought they saw a reason for it.

The key to progress seemed, in the eyes of many, to be free labor. People believed in the dignity of labor and the incentive of opportunity. Any hard-working, virtuous person, it was thought, could improve his condition and gain economic independence by applying himself to opportunities that the country had to offer. Republicans pointed out that the South, which relied on slave labor and was not industrializing, appeared backward

Republican Ideology

and retrograde in comparison. Praising both laborers and opportunity, the Republican party projected an ideology that captured much of the spirit of the age in the North.

In the tradition of Republicanism the virtuous citizen, unhindered by aristocrats and strong by virtue of his liberty, character, and aspirations, was the backbone of the country. As a contemporary symbol of the tradition, Republicans held up Abraham Lincoln as an example of a person of humble origins who had improved his lot and became a successful lawyer and political leader. They portrayed their party as the guardian of economic opportunity, working to ensure that individuals could continue to apply their energies to the land's resources and attain success. In the words of an Iowa Republican, the United

The Republicans had to appeal to various reformers and interests in order to build a winning coalition. This Democratic cartoon tries to ridicule the new party as a collection of dangerous and selfish cranks. Library of Congress.

States was thriving because its "door is thrown open to all, and even the poorest and humblest in the land, may, by industry and application, gain a position which will entitle him to the respect and confidence of his fellow-men."

Thus the Republican party picked up support from a variety of sources. Opposition to the extension of slavery had brought the party together, but party members carefully broadened their appeal by adopting the causes of other groups, whether or not those groups were alarmed by slavery. They were wise to do so. As the newspaper editor Horace Greeley wrote in 1856, "It is beaten into my bones that the American people are not yet anti-slavery." Four years later Greeley observed again, "An Anti-Slavery man *per se* cannot be elected." But, he added, "a Tariff, River-and-Harbor, Pacific Railroad, Free Homestead man, *may* succeed *although* he is Anti-Slavery."

Greeley's last remark was insightful. The Republican party was an amalgam of many interests, but functionally it had only one stand in the North-South controversy. Since a high proportion of the original activist Republicans were strongly opposed to slavery, the party's position on slavery and the territories was immune to change. Thus all Republicans, whatever their reasons for joining the coalition, weighed as antislavery voters in the minds of nervous southerners. Republican strength was antislavery strength. The process of party building was linking voters to the sectional conflict, whether the issue of slavery seemed important to them or not.

A similar process was under way in the South. The disintegration of the Whig party had left many southerners at loose ends politically, including a good number of wealthy planters, small-town businessmen,

Southern Democrats

Chapter 13: TERRITORIAL EXPANSION AND SLAVERY, 1845–1861

and slaveholders. Some of these people gravitated to the American party, but not for long. In the increasingly tense atmosphere of sectional crisis, they were highly susceptible to strong states'-rights positions, which provided a handy defense for slavery. Democratic leaders markedly increased their use of such appeals during the 1850s and managed to convert most of the formerly Whig slaveholders. Democrats spoke to the class interests of slaveholders, and the slaveholders responded.

Most Democrats south of the Mason-Dixon line, however, were not slaveholders. Since Andrew Jackson's day, small farmers had been the heart of the Democratic party. Democratic politicians, though often slaveowners themselves, had lauded the common man and argued that their policies advanced his interests. According to the southern version of republicanism, white citizens in a slave society enjoyed liberty and social equality because the black race was enslaved. Slavery supposedly prevented the evil of aristocracy by making all white men equal. As Jefferson Davis put it in 1851, other societies undermined the status of the common white because in them social distinctions were drawn "by property, between the rich and the poor." In the South, however, slavery elevated every white person's status and allowed the non-slaveholder to *"stand upon the broad level of equality with the rich man."* To retain the support of ordinary whites, southern Democrats emphasized this argument and appealed to racism. The issue in the sectional crisis, they warned, was "shall negroes govern white men, or white men govern negroes?"

Southern leaders also portrayed sectional controversies as matters of injustice and insult to all southerners. The rights of all southerners, they argued, were in jeopardy because antislavery and Free-Soil forces were undermining the principle of self-government. They were attacking an institution protected by the Constitution, and thus northern agitators were damaging rights precious to southerners. Although the stable, well-ordered South was the true defender of constitutional principles, runaway change in the North was subverting the government.

These arguments had their effect, and racial fears and traditional political loyalties helped keep the political alliance between yeoman farmers and planters intact through the 1850s. No viable party emerged in the South to replace the Whigs. The result was a one-party system there that emphasized sectional issues. No one raised potential conflicts of interest between slaveholders and nonslaveholders. Instead, in the South as in the North, political realignment obscured support for the Union and made sectional divisions seem even sharper and deeper than they really were.

In both sections political leaders were arguing that opportunity was threatened. The *Montgomery* (Alabama) *Mail* blatantly claimed that the aim of the Republicans was "to free the negroes and force amalgamation between them and the children of the poor men of the South. The rich will be able to keep out of the way of the contamination." Republicans likewise were charging that if slavery entered the territories, the great reservoir of opportunity for decent people without means would be poisoned. The North's free labor system had to be extended to the territories if coming generations were to prosper. These claims and counterclaims aroused anxieties and fears and made the gap between the sections even wider.

Like successive hammer blows, events also continued to drive North and South further apart. Controversy over Kansas did not subside; it grew. For among the settlers in the territory were partisans of both sides, each determined to make Kansas free or slave. Abolitionists and religious groups sent Free-Soil settlers to save the territory from slavery; southerners sent their own reinforcements, fearing that "northern hordes" were about to steal Kansas away. Clashes between the two groups led to violence, and soon the whole nation was talking about "Bleeding Kansas."

Indeed, political processes in the territory resembled war more than democracy. When elections for a territorial legislature were held in 1855, thousands **Bleeding** of proslavery Missourians invaded **Kansas** the polls and ran up a large but unlawful majority for slavery candidates. The legislature that resulted promptly legalized slavery, and in response Free-Soilers called an unauthorized convention and created their own government and constitution. A proslavery posse sent to arrest the Free-Soil leaders sacked the town of Lawrence; in revenge, John Brown, a fanatic who saw himself as God's instrument to destroy slavery, murdered five proslavery settlers. Soon armed bands of guerrillas roamed the state, battling over land claims as well as slavery.

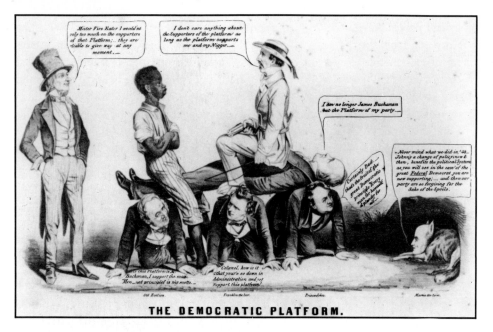

THE DEMOCRATIC PLATFORM.

Growing divisions within the Democratic party provided the opportunity for this Republican cartoon, which suggests that violent slaveholders run a party held together only by Buchanan's unknown views and the lust for spoils. Library of Congress.

The passion generated by this conflict erupted in the chamber of the United States Senate in May 1856, when Charles Sumner of Massachusetts denounced "the Crime against Kansas." Idealistic and radical in his antislavery views, Sumner censored the president, the South, and Senator Andrew P. Butler of South Carolina. Soon thereafter Butler's nephew, Representative Preston Brooks, approached Sumner at his Senate desk and beat him brutally with a cane. Voters in Massachusetts and South Carolina seethed; the country was becoming polarized.

The election of 1856 showed how far the polarization had gone. When Democrats met to select a nominee, they shied away from prominent leaders whose views on the territories were well known. Instead they chose James Buchanan of Pennsylvania, whose chief virtue was that he had been in Britain for four years, serving as ambassador, and thus had not been involved in territorial controversies. This anonymity and superior party organization helped Buchanan win 1.8 million votes and the election, but he owed his victory to southern support. Eleven of sixteen free states voted against him, and Democrats did not regain power in those states for decades. The Republican candidate, John C. Frémont, won those eleven free states and 1.3 million votes; Republicans had become the dominant party in the North. The Know-Nothing candidate, Millard Fillmore, won almost 1 million votes, but this election was his party's last hurrah. The future battle was between a sectional Republican party and an increasingly divided Democratic party.

CONTROVERSY DEEPENS INTO CONFRONTATION

For years the issue of slavery in the territories had convulsed Congress, and for years the members of Congress had tried to settle the issue with vague formulas. In 1857 a different branch of government stepped onto the scene with a different approach. The Supreme Court addressed this emotion-charged subject and attempted to lay controversy to rest with a definitive verdict.

A Missouri slave named Dred Scott had sued his owner for his freedom. Dred Scott based his suit on the fact that his former owner, an army surgeon,

Dred Scott Case had taken him for several years into Illinois, a free state, and into the Wisconsin Territory, from which slavery had been barred by the Missouri Compromise. Scott first won and then lost his case as it moved on appeal through the state courts, into the federal system, and finally after eleven years to the Supreme Court.

Normally this was the type of case that the Supreme Court avoided. Its justices were reluctant, as a rule, to inject themselves into political battles, and it seemed likely that the Court would stay out of this one. An 1851 decision had declared that state courts had the last word in determining the status of Negroes who lived within their jurisdiction. The Supreme Court had only to follow this precedent to avoid ruling on substantive, and very controversial, matters.

The case raised an array of potentially disturbing questions: Was a Negro like Dred Scott a citizen and eligible to sue? Had residence in free territory made him free? And did Congress have the power to prohibit slavery in a territory or to delegate that power to a territorial legislature? Behind that last question lay all the disagreement that Lewis Cass, Henry Clay, Stephen Douglas, and others had tried to paper over.

For a long time it appeared that the Supreme Court would dispose of *Dred Scott* v. *Sanford* by following the 1851 precedent. At its conference the Court had even assigned one justice the task of writing such an opinion. Then the Court suddenly decided to change its plan and to rule on the Missouri Compromise. The change occurred for a number of reasons. Two northerners on the Court indicated that they would dissent from the planned ruling and argue for Scott's freedom and for the constitutionality of the Missouri Compromise. Their action pressured those who disagreed with them to answer their arguments. Southern members of the Court also had some desire to declare the 1820 compromise unconstitutional, and many of the justices felt the Court should try to resolve an issue whose uncertainties had caused so much strife.

Thus, on March 6, 1857, Chief Justice Roger B.

Roger B. Taney, Chief Justice of the Supreme Court from 1836 to 1864, presided over many major cases. But his decision in Dred Scott v. Sanford *fanned the fires of sectional conflict. Supreme Court of the United States.*

Taney delivered the majority opinion of a divided Court. Taney declared that Scott was not a citizen either of the United States or Missouri; that residence in free territory did not make Scott free; and most important, that Congress lacked the power to bar slavery from a territory, as it had done in the Missouri Compromise. Not only did the decision overturn a sectional compromise that had been venerated for years, it also said that the basic ideas of the Wilmot Proviso, and probably popular sovereignty, were not valid. In addition to being controversial in content, the decision had been reached in a manner that aroused sectional suspicions. The majority of the justices were southern; only one northerner had agreed with them. Three northern justices actively dissented or refused to concur in crucial parts of the decision.

A storm of angry reaction broke in the North. The decision alarmed a wide variety of northerners—abolitionists, would-be settlers in the West, and those who hated black people but feared the influence of the South. Every charge against the aggressive Slave Power seemed now to be confirmed. "There is such a thing as THE SLAVE POWER," warned the *Cincinnati Daily Commercial.* "It has marched over and annihilated the boundaries of the states. We are now one great homogenous slaveholding community." And the *Cincinnati Freeman* asked, "What security have the Germans and Irish that their children will not, within a hundred years, be reduced to slavery in this land of their adoption?" Echoed the *Atlantic Monthly,* "Where will it end? Is the success of this conspiracy to be final and eternal?" The poet James Russell Lowell both stimulated and expressed the anxieties of poor northern whites when he had his Yankee narrator, Ezekiel Biglow, say,

Wy, it's jest ez clear ez figgers,
   Clear ez one an' one make two,
Chaps thet make black slaves o' niggers,
   Want to make wite slaves o' you.

Republican politicians capitalized on these fears, building their coalition of abolitionists, who opposed slavery on moral grounds, and racists, who feared that slavery jeopardized their in-

Abraham Lincoln on the Slave Power

terests. Indeed, Abraham Lincoln's greatest achievement in the 1850s, one historian has pointed out, was as a Republican political propagandist against slavery. Lincoln cloaked the crudest charges against the Slave Power in language of biblical majesty, chilling thousands of voters. The South threatened democracy, he argued, and slavery threatened all whites.

At the crux of the matter was the self-interest of whites. Pointing to the southern obsession with the territories, Lincoln had declared as early as 1854 that "the whole nation is interested that the best use shall be made of these Territories. We want them for homes of free white people. This they cannot be, to any considerable extent, if slavery shall be planted within them." The territories must be reserved, he now insisted, "as an outlet for *free white people everywhere*" so that immigrants could come to America and "find new homes and better their condition in life." After the Dred Scott decision, Lincoln charged that the next step in the unfolding Slave Power conspiracy would be a Supreme Court decision "declaring that the Constitution does not permit a State

to exclude slavery from its limits. . . . We shall lie down pleasantly, dreaming that the people of Missouri are on the verge of making their State free; and we shall awake to the reality instead, that the Supreme Court has made Illinois a slave State." The proslavery argument's denigration of freedom and southerners' harping on the inferiority of blacks, Lincoln warned, were signs of a desire "to make *things* out of poor white men."

Lincoln's most eloquent statement against the Slave Power was his famous House Divided speech. In it Lincoln declared: "I do not expect the Union to be dissolved—I do not expect the House to fall—but I do expect it to cease to be divided. It will become all one thing or all the other. Either the opponents of slavery will arrest the further spread of it, and place it where the public mind shall rest in the belief that it is in the course of ultimate extinction; or its advocates will push it forward, till it shall become alike lawful in all the States, old as well as new, North as well as South. Have we no tendency to the latter condition?" The concluding question was the key element of the passage, for it drove home the idea that slaveholders were trying to extend bondage over the entire nation.

The brilliance of Republican tactics offset the difficulties the Dred Scott decision posed for them. By endorsing southern constitutional arguments, the Court had invalidated the central position of the Republican party: no extension of slavery. Republicans could only repudiate the decision, appealing to a "higher law," or hope to change the personnel of the Court. They did both, and by charging that the Supreme Court had become part of the Slave Power they probably gained politically.

For northern Democrats like Stephen Douglas, however, the Court's decision posed an awful dilemma. Northerners were alarmed by the prospect that the territories would be opened up to slavery. To retain support in the North, therefore, Douglas had to find some way to hedge, to reassure voters. Yet he had to do so without alienating southern Democrats. Douglas's task was problematic even at best; given the emotions of the time, it proved impossible.

Douglas chose to stand by his principle of popular sovereignty, which encountered a second test in Kansas in 1857. There, after Free-Soil settlers boycotted an election, proslavery forces met at Lecompton and wrote a constitution that permitted slavery. New elections to the territorial legislature, however, returned an antislavery majority, and the legislature promptly called for a popular vote on the new constitution, which was defeated by more than ten thousand votes. Despite this overwhelming evidence that Kansans did not want slavery, President Buchanan tried to force the Lecompton constitution through Congress. Douglas threw his weight against a document the people had rejected; he gauged their feelings correctly, and in 1858 Kansas voters rejected the constitution a third time. But his action infuriated southern Democrats.

In his well-publicized debates with Abraham Lincoln, his challenger for the Illinois Senate seat in 1858, Douglas further alienated the southern wing of his party. Speaking at Freeport,

Stephen Douglas Proposes the Freeport Doctrine

Illinois, he attempted to revive the notion of popular sovereignty with some tortured extensions of his old arguments. Asserting that the Court had not ruled on the powers of a *territorial* legislature, Douglas claimed that a territorial legislature could bar slavery either by passing a law against it or by doing nothing. Without the patrol laws and police regulations that support slavery, he reasoned, the institution could not exist. This argument, called the Freeport Doctrine, temporarily shored up Douglas's crumbling position in the North. But it gave southern Democrats further evidence that Douglas was unreliable, and some turned viciously against him. A few southerners, like William L. Yancey of Alabama, studied the trend in northern opinion and concluded that southern rights would be safe only in a separate southern nation.

A growing number of slaveholders were similarly deciding that slavery could not be safe within the Union. Such concern was not new. As early as 1838, the Louisiana planter Bennet Barrow had written in his diary, "Northern States medling with slavery . . . openly speaking of the sin of Slavery in the southern states . . . must eventually cause a separation of the Union." And in 1856, a calmer, more polished Georgian named Charles Colcock Jones, Jr., rejoiced at the Democrat James Buchanan's defeat of Republican John C. Frémont for the presidency. The result guaranteed four more years of peace and prosperity, wrote Jones, but "beyond that period . . . we scarce dare

expect a continuance of our present relations." Increasingly slaveowners agreed with Jones and Barrow.

The immediate problem, however, was that the Dred Scott decision had hardened the position of southerners dramatically. Most southerners, probably most slaveowners, were not ready to decide that slavery could be safe only in a southern nation. But after Dred Scott they *were* ready to demand what they saw as their rights. Through years of controversy southern political leaders had fought for the rights flowing from Calhoun's theory of the Constitution and the territories. Now the Supreme Court had affirmed those rights, and southern leaders determined to demand them, both from the nation and from their party.

Thus the territorial issue continued to generate wider and more dangerous conflict, even though it had diminishing practical significance. By 1858 even Jefferson Davis had given up on agricultural development in the Southwest and admitted his uncertainty that slavery could succeed in Kansas. In territories outside Kansas the number of settlers was small, and everywhere the number of blacks was negligible— less than 1 percent of the population in Kansas and New Mexico. Nevertheless, men like Davis and Douglas spent many hours attacking each other's theories on the floor of the Senate. And the general public, both North and South, moved from anxiety to alarm and anger. The situation had become explosive.

THE BREAKUP OF THE UNION

Again, events gave the nation no rest from the growing sectional confrontation. One year before the 1860 presidential election, violence inflamed passions further when John Brown led a small band in an attack on Harpers Ferry, Virginia, hoping to trigger a slave rebellion. Brown failed miserably, and was quickly captured, tried, and executed. It came to light, however, that Brown had had the financial backing of several prominent abolitionists, and northern intellectuals such as Emerson and Thoreau praised him as a hero and a martyr. Since slave rebellion excited the deepest fears in the white South, these disclosures multiplied southerners' fear and anger many times over. The unity of the nation was now in peril.

Many observers feared that the election of 1860 would decide the fate of the Union. An ominous occurrence at the beginning of the campaign did nothing to reassure them. The baneful effects of the Dred Scott decision came to rest on the Democratic party. With southern Democrats intent on their territorial rights and northern Democrats eager to remain competitive in an increasingly free-soil North, the results for the party—and the nation—were bitter.

For several years, the Democratic party had been the only remaining organization that was truly national in scope. Even religious denominations had split into northern and southern wings during the 1840s and 1850s. "One after another," wrote a Mississippi newspaper editor, "the links which have bound the North and the South together, have been severed . . . [but] the Democratic party looms gradually up, its nationality intact, and waves the olive branch over the troubled waters of politics." At its 1860 convention, however, the Democratic party broke in two.

Stephen A. Douglas wanted the party's presidential nomination, but could not afford to alienate northern opinion by accepting a strongly southern position on the territories. Southern Democrats like William L. Yancey, on the other hand, were determined to have their rights recognized, and they moved to block Douglas's nomination. When Douglas nevertheless marshalled a majority for his version of the platform, delegates from the five Gulf states plus South Carolina, Georgia, and Arkansas walked out of the convention hall in Charleston. Efforts at compromise failed, so the Democrats presented two nominees: Douglas for the northern wing, Vice President John C. Breckinridge of Kentucky for the southern. The Republicans nominated Abraham Lincoln; a Constitutional Union party, formed to preserve the nation but strong only in Virginia and the Upper South, nominated John Bell of Tennessee.

Splintering of the Democratic Party

In the ensuing campaign three of the candidates stressed their support for the Union. Bell's only issue was the need to preserve the Union intact. Douglas clearly preferred saving the Union to endangering it, and Breckinridge quickly backed away from any appearance of extremism. His supporters in several states declared that he was not a threat to the Union. Then the *New Orleans Bee* charged that every disunionist in the land was enthusiastic for Breckinridge, and a Texas paper made an earthy reference to his association with radicals: "Mr. Breckinridge claims that he isn't a disunionist. An animal not willing to pass for a pig shouldn't stay in the stye." Frightened by such criticism, Breckinridge went even further to disavow secession. He altered his plan to do no speaking during the campaign and delivered one address in which he flatly denied that his aim was secession. Thereafter his supporters stressed his loyalty and even went so far as to ridicule the possibility of secession in case of a Republican victory.

The results of the balloting were sectional in character, but, if one judges by the candidates' stands, they clearly indicated that most voters were satisfied in the Union. Douglas, Breckinridge, and Bell together received far more votes than Lincoln. Douglas had broad-based support but won few states; Breckinridge carried nine southern states, with his strength concentrated in the Deep South; Bell won pluralities in Virginia, Kentucky, and Tennessee. Lincoln prevailed in the North, but in the states that ultimately remained loyal to the Union he won only a plurality, not a majority (see table). Lincoln's victory was won in the electoral college.

Election of 1860

Given the heterogeneous nature of Republican voters, it is likely that most of even Lincoln's supporters did not view the issue of slavery in the territories as paramount. Thus the majority of voters had not cast ballots for extreme action. In such circumstances, partisan leaders had an opportunity either to work for compromise or to accentuate the conflict.

Determined minorities, however, also had an opportunity to exert pressure and bend the situation toward their goals. They did so, in both North and South. Abolitionists and free-soilers in the North worked through the press and the party to keep the Republicans from compromising on their territorial stand. Proslavery advocates and secessionists whipped up public opinion in the South and shrewdly manipulated state conventions.

Perhaps the most crucial decision was made by

PRESIDENTIAL VOTE IN 1860

	Lincoln	Other Candidates
Entire United States	1,866,452	2,815,617
North plus border and southern states that rejected secession prior to war[1]	1,866,452	2,421,752
North plus border states that fought for union[2]	1,864,523	1,960,842

Note the large vote for other candidates in the righthand column.
[1]Kentucky, Missouri, Maryland, Delaware, Virginia, North Carolina, Tennessee, Arkansas
[2]Kentucky, Missouri, Maryland, Delaware

Source: David Potter, *Lincoln and His Party in the Secession Crisis* (New Haven and London: Yale University Press, 1942, 1967), p. 189.

Lincoln, who decided not to soften his party's position on the territories. In his inaugural address he spoke of the necessity of maintaining the bond of faith between voter and candidate, of declining to set "the minority over the majority." But Lincoln's party was *not* the majority. His refusal to compromise probably had more to do with the unity of the Republican party than with the integrity of the democratic process. For though many conservative Republicans—eastern businessmen and former Whigs who did not feel strongly about slavery—hoped for a compromise, the original and strongest Republicans—antislavery voters and "conscience Whigs"—would not abandon Free Soil. To preserve the unity of his party, then, Lincoln had to take a position that endangered the Union.

Southern leaders in the Senate were willing, conditionally, to accept a compromise formula drawn up by Senator John J. Crittenden of Kentucky. Crittenden, hoping to don the mantle of Henry Clay and avert disaster, had suggested that the two sections divide the territories between them at 36°30′. But the southerners would agree to this *only* if the Republicans did too, for they wanted no less and knew that extremists in the South would demand much more. When Lincoln rejected the possibility that Republicans would make concessions on the territorial issue, Crittenden's peacemaking effort collapsed. Vir-

ginians called for a special convention in Washington, to which several states sent representatives. But this gathering, too, failed to find a magical formula or to reach unanimity on disputed questions.

Political leaders in the North and the South had communicated clearly with each other about the Crittenden proposal, but in a larger sense they tragically misjudged each other. As the historian David Potter has shown, Lincoln and other prominent Republicans believed that southerners were bluffing when they threatened secession; they expected a pro-Union majority in the South to assert itself. Therefore Lincoln determined not to yield to threats, but to call the southerners' bluff. On their side, moderate southern leaders had become convinced, with more accuracy, that northerners were not taking them seriously, and that a posture of strength was necessary to win respect for their position. "To rally the men of the North, who would preserve the government as our fathers found it, we . . . should offer no doubtful or divided front," wrote Jefferson Davis. Thus southern leaders who hoped to avert disaster did not offer compromise, for fear of inviting aggression. Nor did northern leaders who loved the Union, believing compromise would be unnecessary and unwise. With such attitudes controlling leaders' actions, the prospects for a solution were dim.

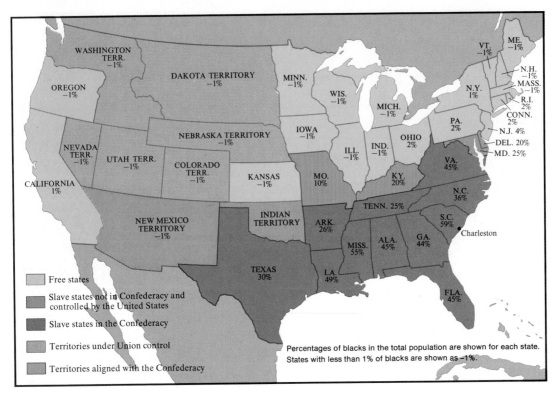

The Divided Nation—Slave and Free Areas, 1861

Map legend:
- Free states
- Slave states not in Confederacy and controlled by the United States
- Slave states in the Confederacy
- Territories under Union control
- Territories aligned with the Confederacy

Percentages of blacks in the total population are shown for each state. States with less than 1% of blacks are shown as −1%.

Meanwhile the Union was being destroyed. On December 20, 1860, South Carolina passed an ordinance of secession amid jubilation and cheering.

Secession of South Carolina This step marked the inauguration of a strategy known as separate-state secession. Foes of the Union, despairing of persuading all the southern states to challenge the federal government simultaneously, had concentrated their hopes on the most extreme proslavery state. With South Carolina out of the Union, they hoped other states would follow suit and momentum would build toward disunion.

The strategy proved effective. By reclaiming its independence, South Carolina had raised the stakes in the sectional confrontation. No longer was secession an unthinkable step; the Union was broken. Now, argued extremists, other states should secede to support South Carolina. Those who wanted to compromise would surely be able to make a better deal outside the Union than in it. Moderates found it difficult to dismiss such arguments, since most of them—even those who felt deep affection for the Union—were committed to defending southern rights and the southern way of life.

In these circumstances, southern extremists soon got their way. Overwhelming their opposition, they quickly called conventions and passed secession ordinances in six other states: Mis-

Confederate States of America sissippi, Florida, Alabama, Georgia, Louisiana, and Texas. By February 1861 these states had joined with South Carolina to form a new government in Montgomery, Alabama: the Confederate States of America. Choosing Jefferson Davis as their president, they began to function independently of the United States.

Yet this apparent unanimity of action was deceiving. Confused and dissatisfied with the alternatives, many voters who had cast a ballot for president stayed home rather than vote for delegates who would consider secession. In some conventions the vote to secede had been close, the balance tipped by the overrepresentation of plantation districts. Furthermore, the conventions were noticeably reluctant to seek ratification of their acts by the people. Four states in the Upper South—Virginia, North Carolina, Tennessee, and Arkansas—flatly rejected secession, and did not join the Confederacy until after the fighting had started. In Kentucky and Missouri popular sentiment was too divided for decisive action; these states remained under Union control, along with Maryland and Delaware (see map).

Misgivings about secession were not surprising, since it posed new and troubling issues for southerners, not the least of them the possibility of war and the question of who would be sacrificed. A careful look at election returns indicates that slaveholders and nonslaveholders were beginning to part company politically. Heavily slaveholding counties drew together in strong support of secession. But nonslaveholding areas that had been willing to support Breckinridge proved far less willing to support secession. Many counties with few slaves took an antisecession position or were staunchly Unionist. Large numbers of yeomen also sat out the election. In other words, nonslaveholders were beginning to consider their class interests, as planters had been doing for some time. With the threat of war on the horizon, nonslaveholders began to ask themselves how far they would go to support slavery and the slaveowners.

Finally, there was still considerable love for the Union in the South. Some opposition to secession was fervently pro-Union, as is apparent in the comment of a northern Alabama delegate after his convention had approved secession: "Here I sit & from my window see the nasty little thing flaunting in the breeze which has taken the place of that glorious banner which has been the pride of millions of Americans and the boast of freemen the wide world over." Such sentiments presented problems for the Confederacy, though they were not sufficiently developed to prevent secession.

The dilemma facing President Lincoln on inauguration day in March 1861 was how to maintain the authority of the federal government without provoking war in the states that had left the Union. He decided to proceed cautiously; by holding onto federal fortifications, he reasoned, he could assert federal sovereignty while waiting for a restoration of relations. But Jefferson Davis, who could not claim to lead a sovereign nation if its ports and military facilities were under foreign control, would not cooperate. A collision was inevitable.

It came in the early morning hours of April 12,

After a fierce bombardment, the Confederate flag replaced the Stars and Stripes over Fort Sumter. The nation's bloodiest war had begun. *National Archives.*

1861, at Fort Sumter in Charleston harbor. A federal garrison there was running low on food. Lincoln had decided to send a supply ship and had notified the South Carolinians of his intention. For the Montgomery government, the only alternative to an attack on the fort was submission to Lincoln's authority. Accordingly, orders were sent to obtain surrender or attack the fort. Under heavy bombardment for two days, the federal garrison finally surrendered. The Confederates permitted the soldiers to sail away on unarmed vessels while the residents of Charleston celebrated. Thus the bloodiest war in the nation's history began in a deceptively gala spirit.

Attack on Fort Sumter

Throughout the 1840s and 1850s many able leaders had worked diligently to avert this outcome. North and South, most had hoped to keep the nation together. As late as 1858 even Jefferson Davis had declared, "This great country will continue united." He had explained sincerely that the United States "is my country and to the innermost fibers of my heart I love it all, and every part." Secession dismayed northern editors and voters, but it also plunged some planters into depression. Paul Cameron, the largest slaveowner in North Carolina, confessed that he was "very unhappy. I love the Union." Why, then, had the war occurred? Why had all the efforts to prevent it failed?

Slavery was an issue that could not be compromised. The conflict over slavery was fundamental and beyond adjustment. Too many powerful emotions were engaged in attacking or defending it. Too many important economic and social interests were involved in maintaining or destroying it. It was entwined with a host of other issues that mattered deeply to people. Ultimately each section regarded slavery as too important to the future to ignore.

Even after extreme views were put aside, the North and the South had different approaches to the institution. The logic of Republican ideology tended in the direction of abolishing slavery, though Republicans denied any such intention. Similarly, the logic of arguments by southern leaders led toward establishing slavery everywhere, though southerners also denied that they sought any such thing. Lincoln put the problem succinctly. Soon after the 1860 election he assured his old friend, Alexander Stephens of Georgia, that the Republican party would not attack slavery in the states where it existed. But Lincoln continued, "You think slavery is *right* and ought to be extended; while we think it is *wrong* and ought to be restricted. That I suppose is the rub."

Fundamental disagreements have not always led to war. It is possible for a nation to encounter unresolvable issues yet manage to get past them. New events can capture people's attention. Time can alter interests and attitudes—if in the intervening years conflict is contained or restricted. That is precisely what America's compromisers sought to achieve. They tried to soothe passions and buy time for the nation, to avoid a conflict that could not be settled and conserve the many areas of consensus among Americans. Their efforts were well intentioned and patriotic, but they were doomed to failure.

The issue of slavery in the territories made conflict impossible to avoid. Territorial expansion generated disputes so frequently that the nation never gained a breathing space. And as the conflict recurred it spread to other questions that were broader and therefore more dangerous. The possibility of sectional

peace receded swiftly as abolitionism broadened into antislavery, as criticism of slaveholding expanded into the idea of the Slave Power, and as alarmed slaveholders became more insistent in their demands.

By 1860 fear added an irrational and complicating element. Its effect was visible in the ironies that prevailed on the eve of war. A vigorous, industrializing, rapidly growing North saw itself as the victim of southern domination. A frightened, defensive, and increasingly isolated South issued belligerent demands and ultimatums. Each section accused the other of violating its rights. Mutual suspicions poisoned trust and carried both sections away from values they held in common. In the end even those who did not want war could find no way to prevent it.

In the profoundest sense, slavery was tied up with the war. Concerns about slavery had driven all the other conflicts, but the fighting began with this, its central issue, shrouded in confusion. How would the Civil War affect slavery, its place in the law, and black people's place in society? The answers to those questions, and the degree to which answers were sought, would be matters of fateful import.

Suggestions for Further Reading

Politics: General

Thomas B. Alexander, *Sectional Stress and Party Strength* (1967); Ray Allen Billington, *The Protestant Crusade, 1800–1860* (1938 and 1964); Stanley W. Campbell, *The Slave Catchers* (1968); Avery O. Craven, *The Coming of the Civil War* (1942); Don E. Fehrenbacher, *The Dred Scott Case* (1978); George M. Fredrickson, *The Black Image in the White Mind* (1971); Holman Hamilton, *Prologue to Conflict* (1964); Michael F. Holt, *The Political Crisis of the 1850s* (1978); Stephen E. Maizlish and John J. Kushma, eds., *Essays on American Antebellum Politics, 1840–1860* (1982); Paul D. Nagle, *One Nation Indivisible* (1964); Roy F. Nichols, *The Disruption of American Democracy* (1948); Russell B. Nye, *Fettered Freedom* (1949); Stephen B. Oates, *To Purge This Land with Blood*, 2nd ed. (1984); David M. Potter, *The Impending Crisis, 1848–1861* (1976); James A. Rawley, *Race and Politics* (1969); Joel H. Silbey, *The Transformation*

IMPORTANT EVENTS

1846	War with Mexico Wilmot Proviso	1856	Preston Brooks attacks Charles Sumner in Senate chamber Bleeding Kansas Buchanan elected president
1847	Lewis Cass proposes idea of popular sovereignty	1857	*Dred Scott v. Sanford* Lecompton Constitution
1848	Taylor elected president		
1849	California applies for admission to Union as free state	1858	Voters reject Lecompton Constitution Lincoln-Douglas debates Freeport Doctrine
1850	Compromise of 1850		
1851	Mob rescues fugitive slave in Boston		
1852	Harriet Beecher Stowe, *Uncle Tom's Cabin* Pierce elected president	1859	John Brown raids Harpers Ferry
1854	Kansas-Nebraska bill "Appeal of the Independent Democrats" Republican party formed Democrats lose ground in congressional elections	1860	Democratic party splits in half Lincoln elected president Crittenden Compromise fails South Carolina secedes from Union
		1861	Six more southern states secede Confederacy established Attack on Fort Sumter

of American Politics, 1840–1860 (1967); Kenneth M. Stampp, *And the War Came* (1950); Gerald W. Wolff, *The Kansas-Nebraska Bill* (1977).

The South and Slavery

William L. Barney, *The Secessionist Impulse* (1974); Drew G. Faust, *The Ideology of Slavery* (1981); Drew G. Faust, *A Sacred Circle: The Dilemma of the Intellectual in the Old South* (1978); Eugene D. Genovese, *The World the Slaveholders Made* (1969); Eugene D. Genovese, *The Political Economy of Slavery* (1967); William Sumner Jenkins, *Pro-Slavery Thought in the Old South* (1935); David M. Potter, *The South and the Sectional Conflict* (1968); William R. Stanton, *The Leopard's Spots* (1960); J. Mills Thornton, III, *Politics and Power in a Slave Society* (1978).

The North and Antislavery

Eugene H. Berwanger, *The Frontier Against Slavery* (1967); Louis Filler, *The Crusade Against Slavery, 1830–1860* (1960);

Eric Foner, *Free Soil, Free Labor, Free Men* (1970); William E. Gienapp, *The Origins of the Republican Party, 1852–1856* (1986); Henry V. Jaffa, *Crisis of the House Divided* (1959); Aileen S. Kraditor, *Means and Ends in American Abolitionism* (1969); Lewis Perry and Michael Fellman, eds., *Antislavery Reconsidered* (1979); Jeffrey Rossbach, *Ambivalent Conspirators* (1982); Alice Felt Tyler, *Freedom's Ferment* (1944); Ronald G. Walters, *American Reformers* (1978).

The Mexican War and Foreign Policy

Reginald Horsman, *Race and Manifest Destiny* (1981); Ernest M. Lander, Jr., *Reluctant Imperialists: Calhoun, the South Carolinians, and the Mexican War* (1980); Robert E. May, *The Southern Dream of a Caribbean Empire, 1854–1861* (1973); Frederick Merk, *The Oregon Question* (1967); David M. Pletcher, *The Diplomacy of Annexation: Texas, Oregon, and the Mexican War* (1973); John H. Schroeder, *Mr. Polk's War* (1973); Otis A. Singletary, *The Mexican War* (1960).

Transforming Fire:
The Civil War
1861–1865

Chapter 14

They came from many different places. They held many different points of view. Perhaps the only thing that united them was the fact that they were caught in a gigantic struggle. Each felt dwarfed by the immense force of the Civil War, a vast and complex event beyond any individual's control.

Moncure Conway, a Virginian who had converted to abolitionism and settled in New England, saw the Civil War as a momentous opportunity to bring justice to human affairs. The progress of reform in the North, Conway wrote in an earnest pamphlet, heralded the dawn of "Humanity's advancing day." Before this dawn, "Slavery, hoary tyrant of the ages," cried out " 'Back! back . . . into the chambers of Night!' " Conway urged northerners to accept slavery's challenge and defeat it, so that "the rays of Freedom and Justice" could shine throughout America. Then the United States would stand as a beacon not only of commercial power but of moral righteousness.

Conway's lofty idealism was far removed from the motives that drove most federal soldiers to march grimly to their death. Though slaves believed they were witnessing God's "Holy War for the liberation of the poor African slave people," Union troops often took a different perspective. When a Yankee soldier ransacked a slave family's cabin and stole their best quilts, the mother exclaimed, "Why you nasty, stinkin' rascal. You say you come down here to fight for the niggers, and now you're stealin' from em." The soldier replied, "You're a G-- D--- liar, I'm fightin' for $14 a month and the Union."

Southerners too acted from limited and pragmatic motives, fighting in self-defense or out of regional loyalty. A Union officer interrogating Confederate prisoners noticed the poverty of one captive. Clearly the man was no slaveholder, so the officer asked him why he was fighting. "Because y'all are down here," replied the Confederate.

The great suffering and frustration of the war were apparent in the bitter words of another southerner, a civilian. Impoverished by the conflict, this farmer had endured inflation, taxes, and shortages to support the Confederacy. Then an impressment agent arrived to take from him still more—grain and meat, horses and mules and wagons. In return the agent offered only a certificate promising repayment sometime in the future. Angry and fed up, the farmer bluntly declared, "the sooner this damned Government falls to pieces, the better it will be for us."

In contrast, many northern businessmen looked to the economic effects of the war with optimism and anticipation. The conflict ensured vast government expenditures, a heavy demand for products, and lucrative government contracts. *Harper's Monthly* reported that an eminent financier expected a long war, the kind of war that would mean huge purchases, paper money, active speculation, and rising prices. "The battle of Bull Run," predicted the financier, "makes the fortune of every man in Wall Street who is not a natural idiot."

For each of these people and millions of others, the Civil War was a life-changing event. It obliterated the normal circumstances of life, sweeping millions of men into training camps and battle units. Armies numbering in the hundreds of thousands marched over the South, devastating once-peaceful countrysides. Families struggled to survive without their men; businesses tried to cope with the loss of workers. Women, North and South, faced added responsibilities in the home and moved into new jobs in the work force. Nothing seemed untouched.

Change was most drastic in the South, where the leaders of the secession movement had launched a revolution for the purpose of keeping things unchanged. Never were men more mistaken: their revolutionary means were fundamentally incompatible with their conservative purpose. Southern whites had feared that a peacetime government of Republicans would interfere with slavery and upset the routine of plantation life. Instead their own actions led to a war that turned southern life upside down and imperiled the very existence of slavery. The Civil War forced changes in every phase of southern society, and the leadership of Jefferson Davis resulted in policies more objectionable to the elite than any proposed by Lincoln. The Confederacy proved to be a shockingly unsouthern experience.

War altered the North as well, but not as deeply.

Since the bulk of the fighting took place on southern soil, most northern farms and factories remained physically unscathed. The drafting of workers and the changing needs for products slowed the pace of industrialization somewhat, but factories and businesses remained busy. Though workers lost ground to inflation, the economy hummed. And a new probusiness atmosphere dominated Congress, where southern representatives no longer filled their seats. To the discomfort of many, the powers of the federal government and the president increased during the war.

The war strained society, both North and South. Disaffection was strongest in the Confederacy, where the sufferings of ordinary citizens were greatest. There poverty and class resentment fed a lower-class antagonism to the war that threatened the Confederacy from within as federal armies assailed it from without. But dissent also flourished in the North, where antiwar sentiment occasionally erupted into violence.

Ultimately, the Civil War forced new social and racial arrangements on the nation. Its greatest effect was to compel leaders and citizens to deal with an issue they had often tried to avoid: slavery. This issue had, in complex and indirect ways, given rise to the war; now the scope and demands of the war forced reluctant Americans to deal with it.

THE SOUTH GOES TO WAR

In the first bright days of the southern nation, few foresaw the changes that were in store. Lincoln's call for troops to put down the Confederate insurrection stimulated an outpouring of regional loyalty that unified the classes. Though four border slave states—Missouri, Kentucky, Maryland, and Delaware—and western Virginia refused to secede, the rest of the Upper South promptly joined the Confederacy. From every quarter southerners flocked to defend their region against Yankee aggression. In the first few months of the war half a million men volunteered to fight; there were so many would-be soldiers that the government could not arm them all.

This ground swell of popular support for the Confederacy generated a mood of optimism and gaiety.

Women sewed dashing, colorful uniforms for men who would before long be lucky to wear drab gray or butternut homespun. Confident recruits boasted of whipping the Yankees and returning home in time

**Battle of
Bull Run**

for dinner. And the first major battle of the war only increased such cockiness. On July 21, 1861, General Irvin McDowell and thirty thousand federal troops attacked General P. G. T. Beauregard's twenty-two thousand southerners at a stream called Bull Run, near Manassas Junction, Virginia. Both armies were ill-trained, and confusion reigned on the battlefield. But nine thousand Confederate reinforcements and a timely stand by General Thomas Jackson (thereafter known as "Stonewall" Jackson) won the day for the South. Union troops fled back to Washington in disarray, and shocked northern picnickers who had expected to witness a victory suddenly feared their capital would be taken.

As 1861 faded into 1862, however, the North undertook a massive buildup of troops in northern Virginia. In the wake of Bull Run, Lincoln had given command of the army to General George B. McClellan, an officer who had always been better at organization and training than at fighting. McClellan devoted the fall and winter to readying a formidable force of a quarter of a million men. "The vast preparation of the enemy," wrote one Confederate soldier, produced a "feeling of despondency" among southerners.

The North also moved to blockade southern ports in order to choke off the Confederacy's avenues of commerce and supply. At first the handful of available steamers proved woefully inadequate to the task of patrolling 3,550 miles of coastline. But the Union Navy gradually increased the blockade's effectiveness, though it never bottled up southern commerce completely.

In the fall of 1861 Union naval power came ashore in the South. Federal squadrons captured Cape Hat-

**Union Naval
Campaign**

teras and Hilton Head, part of the Sea Islands off Port Royal, South Carolina. A few months later, similar operations secured Albemarle and Pamlico sounds, Roanoke Island, and New Bern in North Carolina, as well as Fort Pulaski, which defended Savannah. Then in April 1862 ships commanded by Admiral David Farragut smashed through log booms on the Mississippi River and

After the tension of the secession crisis, both sides welcomed action and military preparations. Thomas Nast captured the festive atmosphere at a parade of New York's Seventh Regiment on April 19, 1861. Seventh Regiment National Guard Armory, New York.

fought their way upstream to capture New Orleans (see map).

The coastal victories off South Carolina foreshadowed another major development in the unraveling of the southern status quo. At the gunboats' approach, frightened planters abandoned their lands and fled. Their slaves, who thus became the first to escape slavery through military action, greeted what they hoped to be freedom with rejoicing and destruction of the cotton gins, symbols of their travail. Their jubilation and the constantly growing stream of runaways who poured into the Union lines removed any doubt about which side the slaves would support, given the opportunity. Ironically the federal government, unwilling at first to wage a war against slavery, did not acknowledge the slaves' freedom—though it

did set to work finding ways to use them in the national cause.

With the approach of spring 1862, the military outlook for the Confederacy darkened again, this time in northern Tennessee. There a hard-drinking, hitherto unsuccessful general named Ulysses S. Grant recognized the strategic importance of Forts Henry and Donelson, the Confederate outposts guarding the Tennessee and Cumberland rivers. Grant saw that if federal troops could capture these forts, two prime routes into the heartland of the Confederacy would lie open. In the space of ten days he seized the forts, using his forces so well that he was able to demand unconditional surrender of Fort Donelson's defenders. A path into

Grant's Campaign in Tennessee

Chapter 14: TRANSFORMING FIRE: THE CIVIL WAR, 1861–1865

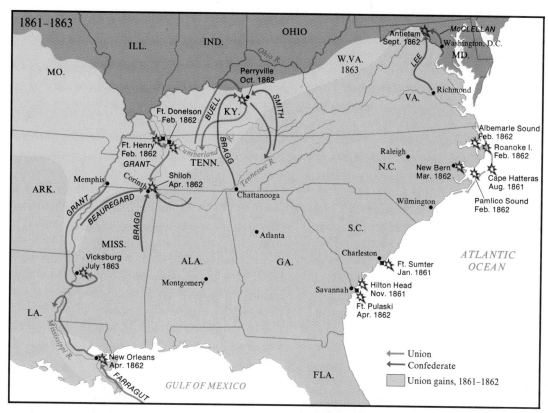

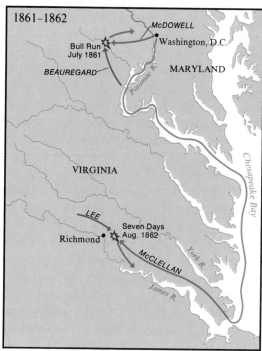

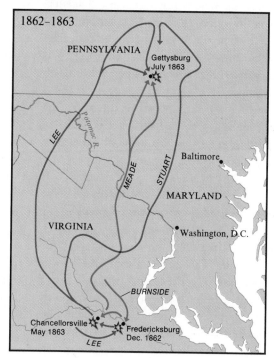

The Civil War, 1861–1863

Tennessee, Alabama, and Mississippi now lay open before the Union army.

On April 6, Confederate General Albert Sidney Johnston caught Grant's army in an undesirable position at Pittsburg Landing in southern Tennessee. The Confederates inflicted heavy damage in fierce fighting. Close to victory, however, General Johnston was struck by a ball that severed an artery in his thigh; within minutes he was dead. Deprived of their leader, southern troops faced a reinforced Union army the next day, and the tide of battle turned. After ten hours of heavy combat, Grant's men forced the Confederates to withdraw to Corinth, Mississippi. Though the Battle of Shiloh was a Union victory, destruction reigned. Northern troops lost 13,000 of 63,000 men; southerners sacrificed 11,000 out of 40,000.

Both soldiers and civilians were beginning to recognize the enormous costs of this war. Never before in Europe or America had such massive forces pummeled each other with weapons of such destructive power. Yet the Civil War's armies seemed virtually indestructible. Even in the bloodiest engagements the losing army was never destroyed—only men died. Many citizens, like soldier (later Supreme Court Justice) Oliver Wendell Holmes, wondered at "the butcher's bill." The improved range of modern rifles multiplied casualties. Since medical knowledge was rudimentary, even minor wounds often led to death through infection.

The slaughter was most vivid, of course, to the soldiers themselves, who saw the blasted bodies of their friends and comrades. "Any one who goes over a battlefield after a battle," wrote one Confederate, "never cares to go over another . . . again. . . . It is a sad sight to see the dead and if possible more sad to see the wounded—shot in every possible way you can imagine."

Troops learned the hard way that soldiering was far from glorious. "The dirt of a camp life knocks all its poetry into a cocked hat," wrote a North Carolina volunteer in 1862. One year later he marveled at his earlier innocence. Fighting had taught him "the realities of a soldier's life. We had no tents after the 6th August, but slept on the ground, in the woods or open fields, without regard to the weather. . . . I learned to eat fat bacon raw, and to like it. . . . Without time to wash our clothes or our persons, and sleeping on the ground all huddled together, the

whole army became lousy more or less with body lice. It was a necessary and unavoidable incident to our arduous campaign."

The scope and duration of the conflict began to have unexpected effects. As the spring of 1862 approached, southern officials worried about the strength of their armies. Tens of thousands of Confederate soldiers had volunteered for just one year's service, planning to return home in the spring to plant their crops. To keep southern armies in the field, the War Department offered bounties and furloughs to all who would reenlist. Officials then called for new volunteers; but, as one admitted, "the spirit of volunteering had died out." Three states threatened or instituted a draft. Finally, still faced with a critical shortage of troops, the Confederate government enacted the first national conscription law in American history. The war had forced an unprecedented change on the states that had seceded for fear of change.

Confederacy Resorts to a Draft

With their ranks reinforced, southern armies moved into heavier fighting. Early in 1862 most of the combat centered on Virginia, where the Confederacy had relocated its capital. General McClellan sailed his troops to the York peninsula and advanced on Richmond from the east. By May and June the sheer size of the federal armies outside the South's capital was highly threatening. But when McClellan sent his legions into combat, Generals Jackson and Lee managed to stave off his attacks. First, Jackson maneuvered into the Shenandoah Valley, behind Union forces, and threatened Washington, drawing some of the federals away from Richmond to protect their own capital. Then, in a series of engagements culminating in the Seven Days' battles, Lee held McClellan off. On August 3 McClellan withdrew to the Potomac, and Richmond was safe for almost two more years.

Buoyed by these results, Jefferson Davis conceived an ambitious plan to turn the tide of the war and compel the United States to recognize the Confederacy. He ordered a general offensive, sending Lee north to Maryland and Generals Kirby Smith and Braxton Bragg to Kentucky. The South would abandon the defensive and take the war north. Davis and his commanders issued a proclamation to the people of Maryland and Kentucky asserting

Davis Orders an Offensive

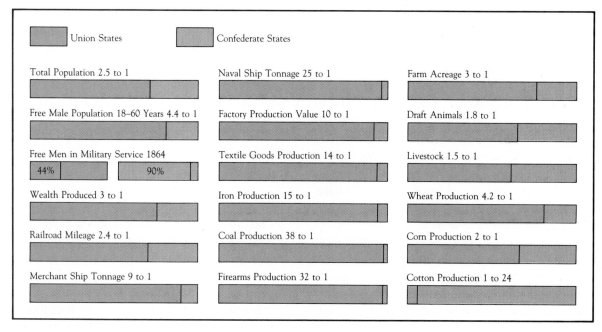

Union States   Confederate States

Total Population 2.5 to 1

Free Male Population 18–60 Years 4.4 to 1

Free Men in Military Service 1864
44%   90%

Wealth Produced 3 to 1

Railroad Mileage 2.4 to 1

Merchant Ship Tonnage 9 to 1

Naval Ship Tonnage 25 to 1

Factory Production Value 10 to 1

Textile Goods Production 14 to 1

Iron Production 15 to 1

Coal Production 38 to 1

Firearms Production 32 to 1

Farm Acreage 3 to 1

Draft Animals 1.8 to 1

Livestock 1.5 to 1

Wheat Production 4.2 to 1

Corn Production 2 to 1

Cotton Production 1 to 24

Comparative Resources, Union and Confederate States, 1861. *Source:* Times Atlas of World History. *Times Books, London, 1978.*

that the Confederates sought only the right of self-government. Lincoln's refusal to grant them independence forced them to attack "those who persist in their refusal to make peace." Davis urged invaded states to make a separate peace with his government and invited the Northwest, whose trade followed the Mississippi to New Orleans, to leave the Union.

The plan was promising, and Davis rejoiced that his outnumbered forces were ready to take the initiative. Every part of the offensive failed, however. In the bloodiest single day of fighting, September 17, 1862, McClellan turned Lee back in the Battle of Antietam near Sharpsburg, Maryland. Smith and Bragg had to withdraw from Kentucky just one day after Bragg had attended the inauguration of a provisional Confederate governor. The entire effort had collapsed.

But southern arms were not exhausted. Jeb Stuart executed a daring cavalry raid into Pennsylvania on October 10 through 12, and Lee decimated General Ambrose Burnside's soldiers as they charged his fortified positions at Fredericksburg, Virginia, on December 13. The Confederate Army of Northern Virginia performed so bravely and controlled the engagement so thoroughly that Lee, a restrained and humane

man, was moved to say, "It is well that war is so terrible. We should grow too fond of it."

Nevertheless, the Confederacy had marshalled all its strength for a breakthrough and failed utterly. Outnumbered and disadvantaged in resources (see figure), the South could not continue its offensive. Meanwhile the North still had reserves of every kind on which to draw. Profoundly disappointed, Davis admitted to a committee of Confederate representatives that southerners had entered "the darkest and most dangerous period we have yet had." Tenacious defense and stoical endurance now seemed the South's only long-range hope. Perceptive southerners shared their president's despair.

WAR TRANSFORMS THE SOUTH

E ven more than the fighting itself, changes in civilian life robbed southerners of their gaiety and nonchalance. The war altered southern society beyond all expectations and with astonishing speed. One of the first traditions to fall was the southern preference for local government.

The South had been an area of little government. States' rights had been its motto, but even the state governments were weak and sketchy affairs by modern standards. To withstand the massive power of the North, however, the South had to centralize; like the colonial revolutionaries, southerners faced a choice of join or die. No one saw the necessity of centralization more clearly than Jefferson Davis. If the states insisted on fighting separately, said Davis, "we had better make terms as soon as we can."

From the outset, Davis pressed to bring all arms, supplies, and troops under his control. He advocated conscription when the states failed to enroll enough new soldiers. And he took a strong

Centralization of Power in the South

leadership role toward the Confederate congress, which raised taxes and later passed a tax-in-kind—a levy not on money but on wheat, corn, oats, rye, cotton, peas, and other farm products. Almost three thousand agents dispersed to collect the tax, assisted by almost fifteen hundred appraisers. Where opposition arose, the government suspended the writ of habeas corpus and imposed martial law. In the face of a political opposition that cherished states' rights, Davis proved unyielding.

To replace the food that soldiers would have grown, Davis exhorted farmers to switch from cash crops to food crops; he encouraged the states to require that they do so. But the army was still short of food and labor. In emergencies the War Department resorted to impressing slaves for labor on fortifications, or took meat and grain in lieu of forced labor. After 1861, the government relied heavily on food impressment to feed the armies. Officers swooped down on farms in the line of march and carted away grain, meat, and other food, plus wagons and draft animals to carry it.

Soon the Richmond administration was taking virtually complete direction of the southern economy. Because it controlled the supply of labor through conscription, the administration could regulate industry, compelling factories to work on government contracts to supply government needs. In addition, the Confederate congress passed laws giving the central government almost full control of the railroads; and

later shipping, too, came under extensive regulation. New statutes even limited corporate profits and dividends. A large bureaucracy sprang up to administer these operations: over seventy thousand civilians were needed to run the Confederate war machine. By the war's end the southern bureaucracy was proportionally larger than its northern counterpart.

The mushrooming bureaucracy expanded the cities. Clerks and subordinate officials, many of them women, crowded the towns and cities where Confederate departments had their offices. These

Effects of War on Southern Cities and Industry

sudden population booms stretched the existing housing supply and stimulated new construction. The pressure was especially great in Richmond, whose population increased two-and-a-half times. Before the war's end Confederate officials were planning the relocation of entire departments to diminish crowding in that city. Mobile's population jumped from 29,000 to 41,000; Atlanta began to grow; and 10,000 people poured into war industries in little Selma, Alabama.

Another prime cause of urban growth was industrialization. Because of the Union blockade, which interrupted imports of manufactured products, the traditionally agricultural South became interested in industry. Davis exulted that southerners were manufacturing their own goods, thus "becoming more and more independent of the rest of the world." Many planters shared his expectations, remembering their battles against tariffs and hoping that their agrarian nation would industrialize enough to win "deliverance, full and unrestricted, from all commercial dependence" on the North. And indeed, though the Confederacy started from scratch, it achieved tremendous feats of industrial development. Chief of Ordnance Josiah Gorgas was able to increase the capacity of the Tredegar Iron Works and other factories to the point that his Ordnance Bureau was supplying all Confederate small arms and ammunition by 1865.

As a result of these changes southerners adopted new values. Women, sheltered in the patriarchal antebellum society, gained substantial new responsibilities. The wives and mothers of soldiers became

Change in the Southern Woman's Role

heads of households and undertook what had previously been considered men's work. To them fell the added tasks of raising crops and tending

Male doctors often resisted women as nurses, yet the women took real risks. This photograph of a nurse and her patients was taken on the front lines right after the battle of Fredericksburg. Armed Forces Institute of Pathology.

animals. Though wives of nonslaveowners had a harder time cultivating their fields than women whose families owned slaves, the latter had to struggle with the management of field hands unused to feminine oversight. Only among the very rich were there enough servants to take up the slack and leave a woman's routine undisturbed. In the cities, white women, who had been virtually excluded from the labor force, found a limited number of new, respectable, paying jobs. Clerks had always been males, but now the war changed that, too. "Government girls" staffed the Confederate bureaucracy, and female schoolteachers became a familiar sight for the first time. Such experiences, though restricted in scope, undermined the image of the omnipotent male and gave thousands of women new confidence in their abilities.

One of those who acquired such confidence as a result of the war was a young North Carolinian named Janie Smith. Raised in a rural area by prosperous parents, she had faced few challenges or grim realities. Then suddenly the war reached her farm, and the troops turned her home into a hospital. "It makes me shudder when I think of the awful sights I witnessed that morning," she wrote to a friend. "Ambulance after ambulance drove up with our wounded. . . . Under every shed and tree, the tables were carried for amputating the limbs. . . . The blood lay in puddles in the grove; the groans of the dying and complaints of those undergoing amputation were hor-

rible." But Janie Smith learned to cope with crisis. She helped to nurse the wounded and ended her account with the proud words "I can dress amputated limbs now and do most anything in the way of nursing wounded soldiers."

The Confederate experience introduced and sustained many other new values. Legislative bodies yielded power to the executive branch of government, which could act more decisively in time of war. The traditional emphasis on aristocratic lineage gave way to respect for achievement and bravery under fire. Thus many men of ordinary background, such as Josiah Gorgas, Stonewall Jackson, and General Nathan Bedford Forrest, gained distinction in industry and on the battlefield that would have been beyond their grasp in time of peace. Finally, sacrifice for the cause discouraged the pursuit of pleasure; hostesses gave "cold water parties" (at which water was the only refreshment) to demonstrate their patriotism.

For the elite such sacrifice was symbolic, but for millions of ordinary southerners it was terrifyingly real. Mass poverty descended on the South, afflicting for the first time a large minority of the white population. The crux of the problem was that many yeoman families had lost their breadwinners to the army. As a South Carolina newspaper put it, "The duties of war have called away from home the sole supports of many, many families. . . . Help must be given, or the poor will suffer." The poor sought such help from relatives, neighbors, friends, anyone. Sometimes they took their cases to the Confederate government, as did an elderly Virginian who pleaded, "If you dount send [my son] home I am bound to louse my crop and cum to suffer. I am eaighty one years of adge." One woman wrote: "I ask in the name of humanity to discharge my husband he is not able to do your government much good and he might do his children some good and thare is no use in keeping a man thare to kill and leave widows and poor little orphen children to suffer . . . my poor children have no home nor no Father."

Human Suffering in the South

Other factors aggravated the effect of the labor shortage. The South was in many places so sparsely populated that the conscription of one skilled craftsman could work a hardship on the people of an entire county. Often they begged in unison for the exemption or discharge of the local miller or the neighborhood

The war separated many young lovers forever. Probably some girl treasured the photo on the left of Private Edwin Francis Jennison of Georgia, killed at Malvern Hill shortly after the picture was taken. The portrait on the right was found beside the body of a Confederate who fell on the battlefield at Chancellorsville. Left: Library of Congress; right: Museum of the Confederacy.

tanner, wheelwright, or potter. Physicians were also in short supply. Most serious, however, was the loss of a blacksmith. As a petition from Alabama explained, "our Section of County [is] left entirely Destitute of any man that is able to keep in order any kind of Farming Tules, Such as the few aged Farmers and families of Those that is gone to defend their rites is Compeled to have to make a Support With."

The blockade created further shortages of common but important items—salt, sugar, coffee, nails—and speculation and hoarding made them worse. Avaricious businessmen moved to corner the supply of some commodities; prosperous citizens tried to stock up on food. The *Richmond Enquirer* criticized one man for hoarding seven hundred barrels of flour; another man, a planter,

Hoarding and Runaway Inflation in the South

purchased so many wagonloads of supplies that his "lawn and paths looked like a wharf covered with a ship's loads." Some people bought up the entire stock of a store and held the goods to sell later at higher prices. "This disposition to speculate upon the yeomanry of the country," lamented the *Richmond Examiner*, "is the most mortifying feature of the war." North Carolina's Governor Zebulon Vance asked where it would all stop: "the cry of distress comes up from the poor wives and children of our soldiers. . . . What will become of them?"

Inflation raged out of control until prices had increased almost 7,000 percent. This fact imperiled urban dwellers and the many who could no longer provide for themselves. As early as 1861 and 1862, newspapers were reporting that "the poor of our . . . country will be unable to live at all" and that "want

Chapter 14: TRANSFORMING FIRE: THE CIVIL WAR, 1861–1865

and starvation are staring thousands in the face." Officials warned of "great suffering next year," predicting that "women and children are bound to come to suffering if not starvation."

Some concerned citizens tried to help. "Free markets," which dispersed goods as charity, sprang up in various cities; some families came to the aid of their neighbors. But there were other citizens who would not cooperate: "It is folly for a poor mother to call on the rich people about here," raged one woman. "Their hearts are of steel they would sooner throw what they have to spare to their dogs than give it to a starving child." The need was so vast that it overwhelmed private charity. A rudimentary relief program organized by the Confederacy offered hope, but was soon curtailed to supply the armies. Southern yeomen sank into poverty and suffering.

As their fortunes declined, these people of once-modest means looked around them and found abundant evidence that all classes were not sacrificing equally.

Inequities of the Confederate Draft
They saw that the wealthy curtailed only their luxuries, while many poor families went without necessities. They saw that the government contributed to these inequities through policies that favored the upper class. Until the last year of the war, for example, prosperous southerners could avoid military service by furnishing a hired substitute. Prices for substitutes skyrocketed, until it was common for a man of means to pay $5,000 or $6,000 to send someone to the front. Well over fifty thousand upper-class southerners purchased such substitutes; Mary Boykin Chesnut knew of one young aristocrat who had "spent a fortune in substitutes. Two have been taken from him [when *they* were conscripted], and two he paid to change with him when he was ordered to the front. He is at the end of his row now, for all able-bodied men are ordered to the front. I hear he is going as some general's courier."

As Chesnut's last remark indicates, the rich also traded on their social connections to avoid danger. "It's a notorious fact," complained an angry Georgian, that "if a man has influential friends—or a little money to spare he will never be enrolled." The Confederate senator from Mississippi, James Phelan, informed Jefferson Davis that apparently "nine tenths of the youngsters of the land whose relatives are conspicuous in society, wealthy, or influential obtain some safe perch where they can doze with their heads under their wings."

Anger at such discrimination exploded when in October 1862 the Confederate congress exempted from military duty anyone who was supervising at least twenty slaves. This "twenty nigger law" became notorious. "Never did a law meet with more universal odium," observed one representative. "Its influence upon the poor is most calamitous." Immediately protests arose from every corner of the Confederacy, and North Carolina's legislators formally condemned the law. Its defenders argued, however, that the exemption preserved order and aided food production, and the statute remained on the books.

Dissension spread as growing numbers of citizens concluded that the struggle was "a rich man's war and a poor man's fight." Alert politicians and newspaper editors warned that class resentment was building to a dangerous level; letters to Confederate officials during this period contained a bitterness that suggested the depth of the people's anger. "If I and my little children suffer [and] die while there Father is in service," threatened one woman, "I invoke God Almighty that our blood rest upon the South." Another woman swore to the secretary of war that

an allwise god . . . will send down his fury and judgment in a very grate manar [on] all those our leading men and those that are in power if thare is no more favors shone to . . . the wives and mothers of those who in poverty has with patrootism stood the fence Battles. . . . I tell you that with out some grate and speadly alterating in the conduckting of afares in this our little nation god will frown on it.

Trouble was brewing in the Confederacy.

THE NORTHERN ECONOMY
COPES WITH WAR

With the onset of war, a tidal wave of change rolled over the North, just as it had over the South. Factories and citizens' associations geared up to support the war, and the federal government and its executive branch gained power they had never had before. Civil liberties were restricted; social values were influenced by both personal sacrifice and wartime riches. Idealism and greed flourished together.

But there was an important difference between North and South: the war did not destroy the North's prosperity. Northern factories ran overtime, and unemployment was low. Furthermore, northern farms and factories came through the war unscathed, whereas most areas of the South suffered extensive destruction. To Union soldiers on the battlefield, sacrifice was a grim reality; but northern civilians experienced only the bustle and energy of wartime production.

Initially, the war was a shock to business. With the sudden closing of the southern market, firms could no longer predict the demand for their goods; many companies had to redirect their activities in order to remain open. And southern debts became uncollectible, jeopardizing not only merchants but many western banks. In farming regions, families struggled with an aggravated shortage of labor. For reasons such as these, the war initially caused an economic slump.

Initial Slump in Northern Business

A few enterprises never pulled out of the tailspin: cotton mills lacked cotton; construction declined; shoe manufacturers sold fewer of the cheap shoes planters had bought for their slaves. Overall the war slowed industrialization in the North. But historians have shown that the war's economic impact was not all negative. Certain entrepreneurs, such as wool producers, benefited from shortages of competing products, and soaring demand for war-related goods swept some businesses to new heights of production. To feed the voracious war machine the federal government pumped unprecedented amounts of money into the economy. The treasury issued $3.2 billion in bonds and paper money called greenbacks, while the War Department spent over $360 million in tax revenues. Government contracts soon totaled more than $1 billion.

Secretary of War Edwin M. Stanton's list of supplies for the Ordnance Department indicates the scope of government demand: "7,892 cannon, 11,787 artillery carriages, 4,022,130 small-arms . . . 1,022,176,474 cartridges for small-arms, 1,220,555,435 percussion caps . . . 14,507,682 cannon primers and fuses, 12,875,294 pounds of artillery projectiles, 26,440,054 pounds of gunpowder, 6,395,152 pounds of niter, and 90,416,295 pounds of lead." Stanton's list covered only weapons; the government also purchased innumerable quantities of uniforms, boots, food, camp equipment, saddles, ships, and other necessaries.

War-related spending revived business in many northern states. In 1863, a merchants' magazine examined the effects of the war in Massachusetts: "Seldom, if ever, has the business of Massachusetts been more active or profitable than during the past year. . . . Labor has been in great demand . . . trade is again in a high state of prosperity. Wealth has flowed into the State in no stinted measure, despite war and heavy taxes. In every department of labor the government has been, directly or indirectly, the chief employer and paymaster." Government contracts had a particularly beneficial impact on the state's wool, metal, and shipbuilding industries, and saved shoe manufacturers there from ruin.

War production also promoted the development of heavy industry in the North. The output of coal rose substantially. Iron makers improved the quality of their product while boosting the production of pig iron from 920,000 tons in 1860 to 1,136,000 tons in 1864. And although new railroad construction slowed, the manufacture of rails increased. Of considerable significance for the future were the railroad industry's adoption of a standard gauge for track and foundries' development of new and less expensive ways to make steel.

Effects of War on Northern Industry and Agriculture

Another strength of the northern economy was the complementary relationship between agriculture and industry. The mechanization of agriculture had begun well before the war. Now, though, wartime recruitment and conscription gave western farmers an added incentive to purchase labor-saving machinery. This shift from human labor to machines had a doubly beneficial effect, creating new markets for industry and expanding the food supply for the urban industrial work force.

The boom in the sale of agricultural tools was tremendous. Cyrus and William McCormick built an industrial empire in Chicago from their sale of reapers. Between 1862 and 1864 the manufacture of mowers and reapers doubled to 70,000 yearly; manufacturers

HARPER'S WEEKLY.

A
JOURNAL OF CIVILIZATION.

Vol. V.—No. 238.] NEW YORK, SATURDAY, JULY 20, 1861. [SINGLE COPIES SIX CENTS.
[$2.50 PER YEAR IN ADVANCE.

Entered according to Act of Congress, in the Year 1861, by Harper & Brothers, in the Clerk's Office of the District Court for the Southern District of New York.

FILLING CARTRIDGES AT THE UNITED STATES ARSENAL AT WATERTOWN, MASSACHUSETTS.—[See next page.]

In both North and South women entered the factories to boost wartime production. This Harper's Weekly *cover shows women filling cartridges in the United States arsenal at Watertown, Massachusetts.   Library of Congress.*

could not supply the demand. By the end of the war, there were 375,000 reapers in use, triple the number in 1861. Large-scale commercial agriculture had become a reality. As a result, farm families whose breadwinners had gone to war did not suffer as they did in the South. "We have seen," one magazine observed, "a stout matron whose sons are in the army, cutting hay with her team . . . and she cut seven acres with ease in a day, riding leisurely upon her cutter."

Northern industrial and urban workers did not fare as well. Though jobs were plentiful following the initial slump, inflation took much of a worker's paycheck. By 1863 nine-cent-a-pound beef was selling for eighteen cents. The price of coffee had tripled; rice and sugar had doubled; and clothing, fuel, and rent had all climbed. Studies of the cost of living indicate that between 1860 and 1864 consumer prices rose at least 76 percent; meanwhile daily wages rose only 42 percent. To make up the difference, workers' families had to do without.

As their real wages shrank, industrial workers also lost job security. To increase production, some employers were replacing workers with labor-saving machines. Other employers urged the government to liberalize immigration procedures so they could import cheap labor. Workers responded by forming unions and sometimes by striking. Skilled craftsmen organized to combat the loss of their jobs and status to machines; women and unskilled workers, excluded by the craftsmen, formed their own unions. And in recognition of the increasingly national scope of business activity, thirteen occupational groups—including tailors, coalminers, and railway engineers—formed national unions during the Civil War. Because of the tight labor market, unions were able to win many of their demands without striking; but still the number of strikes rose steadily.

New Militancy Among Northern Workers

Employers reacted negatively to this new spirit among workers—a spirit that William H. Sylvis, leader of the iron molders, called a "feeling of manly independence." Manufacturers viewed labor activism as a threat to their property rights and freedom of action, and accordingly they too formed statewide or craft-based associations to cooperate and pool information. These employers compiled blacklists of union members and required new workers to sign "yellow dog" contracts, or promises not to join a union. To put down strikes, they hired strikebreakers from the ranks of the poor and desperate—blacks, immigrants, and women—and sometimes received additional help from federal troops.

Troublesome as unions were, they did not prevent many employers from making a profit. The highest profits were made in profiteering on government contracts. Unscrupulous businessmen took advantage of the sudden immense demand for goods for the army by selling clothing and blankets made of "shoddy"—wool fibers reclaimed from rags or worn cloth. The goods often came apart in the rain; most of the shoes purchased in the early months of the war were worthless too. Contractors sold inferior guns for double the usual price and tainted meat for the price of good. Corruption was so widespread that it led to a year-long investigation by the House of Representatives. One group of contractors that had demanded $50 million for their products had to reduce their claims to $17 million as a result of the findings of the investigation.

Wartime Benefits to Northern Business

Legitimate enterprises also turned a neat profit. The output of woolen mills increased so dramatically that dividends in the industry nearly tripled. Some cotton mills, though they reduced their output, made record profits on what they sold. Brokerage houses worked until midnight and earned unheard-of commissions. And railroads carried immense quantities of freight and passengers, increasing their business to the point that railroad stocks doubled or even tripled. Erie Railroad stock skyrocketed from $17 to $126 a share.

In fact, railroads were a leading beneficiary of government largesse. Congress had failed in the 1850s to resolve the question of a northern versus a southern route for the first transcontinental railroad. But with the South out of Congress, the northern route quickly prevailed. In 1862 and 1864 Congress chartered two corporations, the Union Pacific Railroad and the Central Pacific Railroad, and assisted them financially in connecting Omaha, Nebraska, with Sacramento, California. For each mile of track laid, the railroads received a loan of $16,000 to $48,000 plus twenty square miles of land along a free four-hundred-foot-

Like the Union volunteers boarding this large group train, soldiers North and South found that they were entering bureaucratic organizations whose scale, though suggestive of the future, was comparatively unknown in the past. Free Library of Philadelphia.

wide right of way. Overall, the two corporations gained approximately 20 million acres of land and nearly $60 million in loans.

Other businessmen benefited handsomely from the Morrill Land Grant Act (1862). To promote public education in agriculture, engineering, and military science, Congress granted each state 30,000 acres of public land for each of its congressional representatives. The states were free to sell the land as they saw fit, as long as they used the income for the purposes Congress had intended. Though the law eventually fostered sixty-nine colleges and universities, one of its immediate effects was to enrich a few prominent speculators. Hard-pressed to meet wartime expenses, some states sold their land cheaply to wealthy entrepreneurs. Ezra Cornell, for example, purchased 500,000 acres in the Midwest.

Higher tariffs also pleased many businessmen. Northern businesses did not uniformly favor high import duties; some manufacturers desired cheap imported raw materials more than they feared foreign competition. But northeastern congressmen tradi-

tionally supported higher tariffs, and after southern lawmakers left Washington, they had their way: the Tariff Act of 1864 raised tariffs generously. According to one scholar, manufacturers had only to mention the rate they considered necessary and that rate was declared. And, as one would expect, some healthy industries made artificially high profits by raising their prices to a level just below that of the foreign competition. By the end of the war, tariff rates averaged 47 percent, more than double the rates of 1857.

WARTIME SOCIETY IN THE NORTH

The frantic wartime activity, the booming economy, and the Republican alliance with business combined to create a new atmosphere in Washington.

The balance of opinion shifted against consumers and wage earners and toward large corporations; the notion spread that government should aid businessmen but not interfere with them. This was the golden hour of untrammeled capitalism, and railroad builders and industrialists—men such as Leland Stanford, Collis P. Huntington, John D. Rockefeller, John M. Forbes, and Jay Gould—took advantage of it. Their enterprises grew with the aid of government loans, grants, and tariffs.

As long as the war lasted, the powers of the federal government and the president continued to grow. Abraham Lincoln found, as had Jefferson Davis, that

Wartime Powers of the U.S. Executive war required active presidential leadership. At the beginning of the conflict, Lincoln launched a major shipbuilding program without waiting for Congress to assemble. The lawmakers later approved his decision, and Lincoln continued to act in advance of Congress when he deemed it necessary. In one striking exercise of executive power, Lincoln suspended the writ of habeas corpus for all people living between Washington and Philadelphia. The justification for this action was practical rather than legal; Lincoln was ensuring the loyalty of Maryland. Later in the war, with congressional approval, Lincoln repeatedly suspended the writ and invoked martial law. Roughly ten to twenty thousand United States citizens were arrested on suspicion of disloyal acts.

On occasion Lincoln used his wartime authority to bolster his political power. He and his generals proved adept at arranging furloughs for soldiers who could vote in close elections. Needless to say, the citizens in arms whom Lincoln helped to vote usually voted Republican. In another instance, when the Republican governor of Indiana found himself short of funds because of Democratic opposition, Lincoln generously supplied eight times the amount of money the governor needed to get through the emergency situation.

Among the clearest examples of the wartime expansion of federal authority were the National Banking Acts of 1863, 1864, and 1865. Prior to the Civil War the nation did not have a uniform currency. Banks operating under a variety of state charters issued no fewer than seven thousand different kinds of notes, which had to be distinguished from a variety of forgeries. Now, acting on the recommendations of Secretary of the Treasury Salmon Chase, Congress established a national banking system empowered to issue a maximum number of national bank notes. At the close of the war in 1865, Congress laid a prohibitive tax on state bank notes and forced most major institutions to join the system. This process led to a sounder currency and a simpler monetary system, but also to an inflexibility in the money supply and an eastern-oriented financial structure.

Soldiers may have sensed the increasing scale of things better than anyone else. Most federal troops were young; eighteen was the most common age, followed by twenty-one. Many soldiers went straight from small towns and farms into large armies supplied by extensive bureaucracies. By December 1861 there were 640,000 volunteers in arms, a stupendous increase over the regular army of 20,000 men. The increase occurred so rapidly that it is remarkable the troops were supplied and organized as well as they were. But many soldiers' first experiences with large organizations were unfortunate.

Blankets, clothing, and arms were often inferior. Vermin were commonplace. Hospitals were badly managed at first. Rules of hygiene in large camps were badly written or unenforced; latrines were poorly made or carelessly used. One investigation turned up "an area of over three acres, encircling the camp as a broad belt, on which is deposited an almost perfect layer of human excrement." Water supplies were unsafe and typhoid fever epidemics common. About 57,000 army men died from dysentery and diarrhea.

The situation would have been much worse but for the U.S. Sanitary Commission. A voluntary civilian organization, the commission worked to improve conditions in camps and to aid sick and wounded soldiers. Still, 224,000 Union troops died from disease or accidents, far more than the 140,000 who died in battle.

Such conditions would hardly have predisposed the soldier to sympathize with changing social attitudes on the home front. Amid the excitement of money-making, a gaudy culture of vulgar display flourished in the largest cities. A visitor to Chicago commented that "so far as

Self-indulgence Versus Sacrifice in the North

lavish display is concerned, the South Side in some portions has no rival in Chicago, and perhaps not outside New York." Its new residences boasted "marble fronts and expensive ornamentation" that created "a glittering, heartless appearance." As William Cullen Bryant, the distinguished editor of the *New York Evening Post,* observed sadly, "Extravagance, luxury, these are the signs of the times. . . . What business have Americans at any time with such vain show, with such useless magnificence? But especially how can they justify it . . . in this time of war?"

The newly rich did not bother to justify it. *Harper's Monthly* reported that "the suddenly enriched contractors, speculators, and stock-jobbers . . . are spending money with a profusion never before witnessed in our country, at no time remarkable for its frugality. . . . The ordinary sources of expenditure seem to have been exhausted, and these ingenious prodigals have invented new ones. The men button their waistcoats with diamonds . . . and the women powder their hair with gold and silver dust." The *New York Herald* summarized that city's atmosphere:

All our theatres are open . . . and they are all crowded nightly. . . . The most costly accommodations, in both hotels and theatres, are the first and most eagerly taken. . . . The richest silks, laces and jewelry are the soonest sold. . . . Not to keep a carriage, not to wear diamonds, not to be attired in a robe which cost a small fortune, is now equivalent to being a nobody. This war has entirely changed the American character. . . . The individual who makes the most money—no matter how—and spends the most—no matter for what—is considered the greatest man. . . .

The world has seen its iron age, its silver age, its golden age, and its brazen age. This is the age of shoddy.

Yet strong elements of idealism coexisted with ostentation. Abolitionists, after initial uncertainty over whether to fight the South or allow division of the Union to separate the North from slavery, campaigned to turn the war into a war against slavery. Free black communities and churches both black and white responded to the needs of slaves who flocked to the Union lines. They sent clothing, ministers, and teachers in generous measure to aid the runaways in every possible way.

Northern women, like their southern counterparts, took on new roles. Those who stayed home organized over ten thousand soldiers' aid societies, rolled innumerable bandages, and raised $3 million. Thousands served as nurses in front-line hospitals, where they pressed for better care of the wounded. The professionalization of medicine since the Revolution had created a medical system dominated by men; thus dedicated and able female nurses had to fight both military regulations and professional hostility to win the chance to make their contribution. In the hospitals they quickly proved their worth, but only the wounded welcomed them. Even Clara Barton, the most famous female nurse, was ousted from her post during the winter of 1863.

The poet Walt Whitman, who became a daily visitor to wounded soldiers in Washington, D.C., left a record of his experiences as a volunteer nurse.

Walt Whitman As he dressed wounds and tried to comfort suffering and lonely men, Whitman found "the marrow of the tragedy concentrated in those Army Hospitals." But despite "indescribably horrid wounds . . . the groan that could not be repress'd . . . [the] emaciated face and glassy eye," he also found in the hospitals inspiration and a deepening faith in American democracy. Whitman admired the "incredible dauntlessness" and sacrifice of the common soldier who fought for the Union. "The genius of the United States is not best or most in its executives or legislatures," he had written in the Preface to his great work *Leaves of Grass* (1855), "but always most in the common people." Whitman worked this idealization of the common man into his poetry, rejecting the lofty meter and rhyme characteristic of European verse and striving instead for a "genuineness" that would appeal to the masses.

Thus northern society embraced strangely contradictory tendencies. Materialism and greed flourished alongside idealism, religious conviction, and self-sacrifice. While wealthy men purchased 118,000 substitutes and almost 87,000 commutations at $300 each to avoid service in the Union army, other soldiers risked their lives out of a desire to preserve the Union or extend freedom. It was as if there were several different wars under way, each of them serving different motives.

THE STRANGE ADVENT OF EMANCIPATION

At the very highest levels of government there was a similar lack of clarity about the purpose of the war. Through the first several months of the struggle, both Davis and Lincoln studiously avoided references to slavery, the crux of the matter. For his part, Davis was intelligent enough to realize that emphasis on the issue might increase class conflict in the South. Earlier in his career he had struggled on occasion to convince nonslaveholders that defense of the planters' slaves was in their interest. Rather than face that challenge again, Davis articulated a conservative ideology. He told southerners they were fighting for constitutional liberty: northern betrayal of the founding fathers' legacy had necessitated secession. As long as Lincoln also avoided making slavery an issue, Davis's line seemed to work.

Lincoln had his own reasons for refraining from mention of slavery. For some time he clung to the hopeful but mistaken idea that a pro-Union majority would assert itself in the South. Perhaps it would be possible, he thought, to coax the South back into the Union and end the fighting. Raising the slavery issue would effectively end any such possibility of compromise.

Powerful political considerations also dictated that Lincoln remain silent. The Republican party was a young and unwieldy coalition. Some Republicans burned with moral outrage over slavery, while others were frankly racist, dedicated to protecting free whites from the Slave Power and the competition of cheap slave labor. Still others saw the tariff or immigration or some other issue as paramount. A forthright stand by Lincoln on the subject of slavery could split the party, pleasing some groups and alienating others. Until a consensus developed among the party's various wings, or until Lincoln found a way to appeal to all the elements of the party, silence was the best approach.

The president's hesitancy ran counter to some of his personal feelings. Lincoln was a sensitive and compassionate man whose self-awareness, humility, and moral anguish during the war were evident in his speeches and writings. But as a politician, Lincoln kept his moral convictions to himself. He distinguished between the personal and the official; he would not let his feelings determine his political acts. As a result, his political positions were studied and complex, calculated for maximum advantage. Frederick Douglass, the astute and courageous black protest leader, sensed that Lincoln the man was without prejudice toward black people. Yet Douglass judged him "preeminently the white man's president."

Lincoln first broached the subject of slavery in a major way in March 1862, when he proposed that the states consider emancipation on their own. He asked Congress to pass a resolution promising aid to any state that decided to emancipate, and he appealed to border-state representatives to give the idea of emancipation serious consideration. What Lincoln was talking about was gradual emancipation, with compensation for slaveholders and colonization of the freed slaves outside the United States. To a delegation of free blacks he explained that "it is better for us both . . . to be separated." Until well into 1864 Lincoln steadfastly promoted an unpromising and in national terms wholly impractical scheme to colonize blacks in some region like Central America. Despite Secretary of State William H. Seward's care to insert phrases such as "with their consent," the word *deportation* crept into one of Lincoln's speeches in place of *colonization*. Thus his was as conservative a scheme as could be devised. Moreover, since the states would make the decision voluntarily, no responsibility for it would attach to Lincoln.

Lincoln's Plan for Gradual Emancipation

But others wanted to go much further. A group of congressional Republicans known as the Radicals had dedicated themselves to seeing that the war was prosecuted vigorously. They had been instrumental in creating a joint committee on the conduct of the war, which investigated Union reverses, sought to increase the efficiency of the war effort, and prodded the executive to take stronger measures. Early in the war these Radicals, with support from other representatives, turned their attention to slavery.

In August 1861, at the Radicals' instigation, Congress passed its first confiscation act. Designed to punish the Confederate rebels, the law confiscated

Chapter 14: TRANSFORMING FIRE: THE CIVIL WAR, 1861–1865

Confiscation Acts all property used for "insurrectionary purposes." That is, if the South used slaves in a hostile action, those slaves were declared seized and liberated from their owners' possession. A second confiscation act (July 1862) was much more drastic: it confiscated the property of all those who supported the rebellion, even those who merely resided in the South and paid Confederate taxes. Their slaves were "forever free of their servitude, and not again [to be] held as slaves." The logic behind these acts was that the insurrection—as Lincoln always termed it—was a serious revolution requiring strong measures. Let the government use its full powers, free the slaves, and crush the revolution, urged the Radicals.

Lincoln chose not to go that far. He stood by his proposal of voluntary gradual emancipation by the states and made no effort to enforce the second confiscation act. His stance brought a public protest from Horace Greeley, editor of the powerful *New York Tribune*. In an open letter to the president entitled "The Prayer of Twenty Millions," Greeley wrote, "We require of you . . . that you execute the laws. . . . We think you are strangely and disastrously remiss . . . with regard to the emancipating provisions of the new Confiscation Act. . . . We complain that the Union cause has suffered from mistaken deference to Rebel Slavery." Reaching the nub of the issue, the influential editor went on, "On the face of this wide earth, Mr. President, there is not one disinterested, determined, intelligent champion of the Union cause who does not feel that all attempts to put down the Rebellion and at the same time uphold its inciting cause are preposterous and futile."

Lincoln's letter in reply was an explicit statement of his complex and calculated approach to the question. He disagreed, he said, with all those who would make the saving or destroying of slavery the paramount issue of the war. "I would save the Union," announced Lincoln. "If I could save the Union without freeing *any* slave I would do it, and if I could save it by freeing *all* the slaves I would do it; and if I could save it by freeing some and leaving others alone I would also do that. What I do about slavery, and the colored race, I do because I believe it helps to save the Union." Lincoln closed with a personal disclaimer: "I have here stated my purpose according to my view of *official* duty; and I intend no modification of my oft-expressed *personal* wish that all men everywhere could be free."

When he wrote those words, Lincoln had already decided to take a new step: issuance of the Emancipation Proclamation. On the advice of the cabinet, however, he was waiting for a major Union victory before announcing it, so the proclamation would not appear to be an act of desperation. Yet the letter to Greeley was not simply an effort to stall; it was an integral part of Lincoln's approach to the future of slavery, as the text of the Emancipation Proclamation would show.

On September 22, 1862, shortly after the Battle of Antietam, Lincoln issued the first part of his two-part proclamation. Invoking his powers as commander-in-chief of the armed forces, he an-
Emancipation Proclamations nounced that on January 1, 1863, he would emancipate the slaves in states whose people "shall then be in rebellion against the United States." The January proclamation would designate the areas in rebellion based on the presence or absence of bona fide representatives in Congress.

The September proclamation was less a declaration of the right of slaves to be free than it was a threat to southerners to end the war. "Knowing the value that was set on the slaves by the rebels," said Garrison Frazier, a black Georgian, "the President thought that his proclamation would stimulate them to lay down their arms . . . and their not doing so has now made the freedom of the slaves a part of the war." Lincoln may not actually have expected southerners to give up their effort, but he was careful to offer them the option, thus putting the onus of emancipation on them.

Lincoln's designation of the areas in rebellion on January 1 is worth noting. He excepted from his list every Confederate county or city that had fallen under Union control. Those areas, he declared, "are, for the present, left precisely as if this proclamation were not issued." And in a telling omission, Lincoln neglected to liberate slaves in the border slave states that remained in the Union.

"The President has purposely made the proclamation inoperative in all places where . . . the slaves [are] accessible," complained the antiadministration *New York World*. "He has proclaimed emancipation only where he has notoriously no power to execute it."

Black troops soon proved to doubters that they could fight, and 186,000 black men (approximately 150,000 of whom were former slaves) made a vital contribution to the Union armies and navies. Ohio Historical Society.

The exceptions, said the paper, "render the proclamation not merely futile, but ridiculous." Partisanship aside, even Secretary of State Seward, a moderate Republican, said sarcastically that, "we show our sympathy with slavery by emancipating slaves where we cannot reach them and holding them in bondage where we can set them free." A British official, Lord Russell, commented on the "very strange nature" of the document, noting that it did not declare "a principle adverse to slavery."

Furthermore, by making the liberation of the slaves "a fit and necessary war measure," Lincoln raised a variety of legal questions. How long did a war measure have force? Did its power cease with the suppression of a rebellion? The proclamation did little to clarify the status or citizenship of the freed slaves. And a reference to garrison duty in one of the closing par-

agraphs suggested that slaves would have inferior duties and rank in the army. (For many months, in fact, their pay and treatment were inferior.)

Thus the Emancipation Proclamation was a puzzling and ambiguous document that said less than it seemed to say. Physically it freed no bondsmen, and major limitations were embedded in its language. But if as a moral and legal document it was wanting, as a political document it was nearly flawless. Because the proclamation defined the war as a war against slavery, liberals could applaud it. Yet at the same time it protected Lincoln's position with conservatives, leaving him room to retreat if he chose and forcing no immediate changes on the border slave states. The president had not gone as far as Congress had, and he had taken no position he could not change later if necessary.

In June 1864, however, Lincoln gave his support to the constitutional end of slavery. On the eve of the Republican national convention, he called the party's chairman to the White House and instructed him to have the party "put into the platform as the keystone, the amendment of the Constitution abolishing and prohibiting slavery forever." It was done; the party called for a new constitutional amendment, the thirteenth. Although Republican delegates probably would have adopted such a plank without his urging, Lincoln showed his commitment by lobbying Congress for quick approval of the measure. He succeeded, and the proposed amendment went to the states for ratification or rejection. Lincoln's strong support for the Thirteenth Amendment—an unequivocal prohibition of slavery—constitutes his best claim to the title Great Emancipator.

Yet Lincoln soon clouded that clear stand, for in 1865 the newly re-elected president considered allowing the defeated southern states to re-enter the Union and delay or defeat the amendment. In February he and Secretary of State Seward met with three Confederate commissioners at Hampton Roads, Virginia. The end of the war was clearly in sight, and southern representatives angled vainly for an armistice that would allow southern independence. But Lincoln was doing some political maneuvering of his own, apparently contemplating the creation of a new and broader party based on a postwar alliance with southern Whigs

Hampton Roads Conference

and moderates. The cement for the coalition would be concessions to planter interests.

Pointing out that the Emancipation Proclamation was only a war measure, Lincoln predicted that the courts would decide whether it had granted all, some, or none of the slaves their freedom. Seward observed that the Thirteenth Amendment, which would be definitive, was not yet ratified; re-entry into the Union would allow the southern states to vote against it and block it. Lincoln did not contradict him, but spoke in favor of "prospective" ratification—ratification with a five-year delay. He also promised to seek $400 million in compensation for slaveholders and to consider their position on such related questions as confiscation. Such financial aid would provide an economic incentive for planters to rejoin the Union, and capital to ease the transition to freedom for both races.

These were startling propositions from a president who was on the verge of military victory. Most northerners opposed them, and only the opposition of Jefferson Davis, who set himself against anything short of independence, prevented discussion of the proposals in the South. They indicated that even at the end of the war, Lincoln was keeping his options open, maintaining the line he had drawn between "*official* duty" and "*personal* wish." Contrary to legend, then, Lincoln did not attempt to lead public opinion on race, as did advocates of equality in one direction and racist Democrats in the other. Instead he moved cautiously, constructing complex and ambiguous positions. He avoided the great risks inherent in challenging, educating, or inspiring national conscience.

Before the war was over, the Confederacy too addressed the issue of emancipation. Ironically, a strong proposal in favor of liberation came from Jefferson Davis. Though emancipation was far less popular in the South than in the North, Davis did not flinch or conceal his purpose. He was dedicated to independence, and he was willing to sacrifice slavery to achieve that goal. After considering the alternatives for some time, Davis concluded in the fall of 1864 that it was necessary to act.

Davis's Plan for Emancipation

Reasoning that the military situation of the Confederacy was desperate, and that independence with emancipation was preferable to defeat with emancipation, Davis proposed that the central government purchase and train forty thousand male Negro laborers. The men would work for the army under a promise of emancipation and future residence in the South. Later Davis upgraded his proposal, calling for the recruitment and arming of slave soldiers. The wives and children of these soldiers, he made plain, must also receive freedom from the states. Davis and his advisors did not favor full equality—they envisioned "an intermediate stage of serfage or peonage." Thus they shared with Lincoln and their whole generation a racial pessimism and blindness that tried to ignore the massive changes underway.

Still, Davis had proposed a radical change for the conservative, slaveholding South. Bitter debate resounded through the Confederacy, but Davis stood his ground. When the Confederate congress approved enlistments without the promise of freedom, Davis insisted on more. He issued an executive order to guarantee that owners would cooperate with the emancipation of slave soldiers, and his allies in the states started to work for emancipation of the soldiers' families. Some black troops started to drill as the end of the war approached.

Confederate emancipation began too late to revive southern armies or win diplomatic advantages with antislavery Europeans. But Lincoln's Emancipation Proclamation stimulated a vital infusion of forces into the Union armies. Beginning in 1863 slaves shouldered arms for the North. Before the war was over, 150,000 of them had fought for freedom and the Union. Their participation was crucial to northern victory, and it discouraged recognition of the Confederacy by foreign governments. Lincoln's policy, despite its limitations and its lack of clarity, had great practical effect.

THE DISINTEGRATION OF CONFEDERATE UNITY

During the final two years of fighting, both northern and southern governments waged the war in the face of increasing opposition at home. Dissatisfaction that had surfaced earlier grew more intense and sometimes even violent. The unrest was connected to the military stalemate: neither side was close to victory in 1863, though the war had become gigantic in scope and costly in lives. But protest also arose from fundamental stresses in the social structures of the North and the South.

The Confederacy's problems were both more serious and more deeply rooted than the North's. Vastly disadvantaged in terms of industrial capacity, natural resources, and labor, southerners felt the cost of the war more quickly, more directly, and more painfully than northerners. But even more fundamental were the Confederacy's internal problems; crises that were integrally connected with the southern class system threatened the Confederate cause.

One ominous development was the increasing opposition of planters to their own government, whose actions often had a negative effect on them. Not only did the Richmond government impose high taxes and a tax-in-kind, Confederate military authorities also impressed slaves to build fortifications. And when Union forces advanced on plantation areas, Confederate commanders sent detachments through the countryside to burn stores of cotton that lay in the enemy's path. Such interference with plantation routines and financial interests was not what planters had expected of their government, and they resisted. Many taxes went unpaid, and many planters continued to grow and ship cotton, despite the government's desire to withhold it from world markets as a diplomatic weapon.

Nor were the centralizing policies of the Davis administration popular. Many planters agreed with the *Charleston Mercury* that the southern states had seceded because the federal government had grown and "usurped powers not granted—progressively trenched upon State Rights." The increasing size and power of the Richmond administration therefore startled and alarmed them.

The Confederate constitution, drawn up by the leading political thinkers of the South, had in fact granted substantial powers to the central government, especially in time of war. But for many planters, states' rights had become virtually synonymous with complete state sovereignty. R. B. Rhett, editor of the *Charleston Mercury*, wishfully (and inaccurately) described the Confederate constitution: "[It] leaves the States untouched in their Sovereignty, and com-

mits to the Confederate Government only a few simple objects, and a few simple powers to enforce them." Governor Joseph E. Brown of Georgia took a similarly exalted view of the importance of the states. During the brief interval between Georgia's secession from the Union and its admission to the Confederacy, Brown sent an ambassador to Europe to seek recognition for the sovereign republic of Georgia from Queen Victoria, Napoleon III, and the King of Belgium. His mentality harkened back to the 1770s and the Articles of Confederation, not to the Constitution of 1789 or the Confederate constitution.

In effect, years of opposition to the federal government within the Union had frozen southerners in a defensive posture. Now they erected the barrier of states' rights as a defense against change, hiding behind it while their capacity for creative statesmanship atrophied. Planters sought a guarantee that their plantations and their lives would remain untouched; they were deeply committed neither to building a southern nation nor to winning independence. If the Confederacy had been allowed to depart from the Union in peace and continue as a semideveloped cotton-growing region, they would have been content. When secession revolutionized their world, they could not or would not adjust to it.

Confused and embittered, southerners struck out instead at Jefferson Davis. Conscription, thundered Governor Brown, was "subversive of [Georgia's] sovereignty, and at war with all the principles for the support of which Georgia entered into this revolution." Searching for ways to frustrate the law, Brown bickered over draft exemptions and ordered local enrollment officials not to cooperate with the Confederacy. The *Charleston Mercury* told readers that "conscription . . . is . . . the very embodiment of Lincolnism, which our gallant armies are today fighting." And in a gesture of stubborn selfishness, planter Robert Toombs of Georgia, a former U.S. Senator, defied the government, the newspapers, and his neighbors' petitions by continuing to grow large amounts of cotton. His action bespoke the inflexibility and frustration of the southern elite at a crucial point in the Confederacy's struggle to survive.

The southern courts ultimately upheld Davis's power to conscript. He continued to provide strong leadership and drove through the legislature measures that gave

A southern family flees its home as the battle lines draw near. Photographed by Matthew Brady.   National Archives.

the Confederacy a fighting chance. Despite his cold formality and inability to disarm critics, Davis possessed two important virtues: iron determination and total dedication to independence. These qualities kept the Confederacy afloat, for he implemented his measures and enforced them. But his actions earned him the hatred of most influential and elite citizens.

Meanwhile, at the bottom of southern society, there were other difficulties. Food riots occurred in the spring of 1863 in Atlanta, Macon, Columbus, and Augusta, Georgia; and in Salisbury and High Point, North Carolina. On April 2, a crowd assembled in the Confederate capital of Richmond to demand relief from Governor Letcher. A passerby, noticing the excitement, asked a young girl, "Is there some celebration?" "There is," replied the girl. "We celebrate our right to live. We are starving. As soon as enough of us get together we are going to the bakeries and each of us will take a loaf of bread." Soon they did just

Food Riots in Southern Cities

that, sparking a riot that Davis himself had to quell at gunpoint. Later that year, another group of angry rioters ransacked a street in Mobile, Alabama.

Throughout the rural South, ordinary people resisted more quietly—by refusing to cooperate with impressments of food, conscription, or tax collection. "In all the States impressments are evaded by every means which ingenuity can suggest, and in some openly resisted," wrote a high-ranking commissary officer. Farmers who did provide food refused to accept certificates of credit or government bonds in lieu of cash, as required by law. And conscription officers increasingly found no one to draft—men of draft age were hiding out in the forests. "The disposition to avoid military service," observed one of Georgia's senators in 1864, "is general." In some areas tax agents were killed in the line of duty.

Davis was ill-equipped to deal with such discontent. Austere and private by nature, he failed to communicate with the masses. For long stretches of time he buried himself in military affairs or administrative details, until a crisis forced him to rush off on a speaking tour to revive the spirit of resistance. His class perspective also distanced him from the sufferings of the common people. While his social circle in Richmond dined on duck and oysters, ordinary southerners leached salt from the smokehouse floor and went hungry. State governors who saw to the common people's needs won the public's loyalty, but Davis failed to reach out to them and thus lost the support of the plain folk.

Such civil discontent was certain to affect the Confederate armies. "What man is there that would stay in the army and no that his family is sufring at home?" an angry citizen wrote anonymously to the secretary of war. An upcountry South Carolina newspaper agreed, asking, "What would sooner make our soldiers falter than the cry from their families?" Spurred by concern for their loved ones and resentment of the rich man's war, large numbers of men did indeed leave the armies, supported by their friends and neighbors. Mary Boykin Chesnut observed a man being dragged back to the army as his wife looked on. "Desert agin, Jake!" she cried openly. "You desert agin, quick as you kin. Come back to your wife and children."

Desertions from the Confederate Army

Desertion did not become a serious problem for the Confederacy until the summer of 1862, and stiffer policing solved the problem that year. But from 1863 on, the number of men on duty fell rapidly as desertions soared. By the summer of 1863, John A. Campbell, the South's assistant secretary of war, wondered whether "so general a habit" as desertion could be considered a crime. Campbell estimated that 40,000 to 50,000 troops were absent without leave and that 100,000 were evading duty in some way. Liberal furloughs, amnesty proclamations, and appeals to return had little effect; by November 1863, Secretary of War James Seddon admitted that one-third of the army could not be accounted for. And the situation was to worsen.

The gallantry of those who stayed on in Lee's army and the daring of their commander made for a deceptively positive start to the 1863 campaign. On May 2 and 3 at Chancellorsville, Virginia, 130,000 members of the Union Army of the Potomac bore down on fewer than 60,000 Confederates. Acting as

Battle of Chancellorsville

if they enjoyed being outnumbered, Lee and Stonewall Jackson boldly divided their forces, ordering 30,000 men under Jackson on a day-long march westward and to the rear for a flank attack. Jackson arrived at his position late in the afternoon to witness unprepared Union troops "laughing, smoking," playing cards, and waiting for dinner. "Push right ahead," Jackson said, and his weary but excited corps swooped down on the Federals and drove their right wing back in confusion. The Union forces left Chancellorsville the next day defeated. Though Stonewall Jackson had been fatally wounded, it was a remarkable southern victory.

But two critical battles in July 1863 brought crushing defeats to the Confederacy. General Ulysses S. Grant, after months of searching through swamps and bayous, had succeeded in finding an advantageous approach to Vicksburg, and promptly laid siege to that vital western fortification. If Vicksburg fell, U.S. forces would control the Mississippi, cutting the Confederacy in half and gaining an open path into the interior. Meanwhile, with no serious threat to Richmond, General Robert E. Lee proposed a Confederate invasion of the North, to turn the tables on the Union and divert attention from Vicksburg. Both movements drew toward conclusion early in July.

In the North, Lee's troops streamed through western Maryland and into Pennsylvania, threatening both Washington and Baltimore. The possibility of a major victory before the Union capital became more and more likely. But along the Mississippi, Confederate prospects darkened. Davis and Secretary of War Seddon repeatedly wired General Joseph E. Johnston to concentrate his forces and attack Grant's army. "Vicksburg must not be lost, at least without a struggle," they insisted. Johnston, however, either failed in imagination or did not understand the possibilities of his command. "I consider saving Vicksburg hopeless," he telegraphed at one point, and despite prodding he did nothing to relieve the garrison. In the meantime, Grant's men were supplying themselves by drawing on the agricultural riches of the Mississippi River valley. With such provisions, they could continue their siege indefinitely. In fact, their rich meat-and-vegetables diet had become so tiresome to them that one day, as Grant rode by, a private looked up and muttered, "Hardtack" (pilot biscuit). Soon a line

Chapter 14: TRANSFORMING FIRE: THE CIVIL WAR, 1861–1865

These dead Union soldiers helped to repulse Confederate troops who charged valiantly but futilely up Gettysburg's gentle hills. Library of Congress.

of soldiers was shouting "Hardtack! Hardtack!" demanding respite from turkey and sweet potatoes.

In such circumstances the fall of Vicksburg was inevitable, and on July 4, 1863, its commander surrendered. That same day a battle that had been raging since July 1 concluded at Gettysburg, Pennsylvania. On July 1 and 2, the Union and Confederate forces had both made gains in furious fighting. Then on July 3 Lee ordered a direct assault on Union fortifications atop Cemetery Ridge. Full of foreboding, General James Longstreet warned Lee that "no 15,000 men ever arrayed for battle can take that position." But Lee, hoping success might force the Union to accept peace with independence, stuck to his plan. His brave troops rushed the position, and a hundred momentarily breached the enemy's line. But most fell in heavy slaughter. On July 4 Lee had to withdraw, having suffered almost 4,000 killed and approximately 24,000 missing and wounded. The Confederate general reported to Jefferson Davis that "I am alone to blame," and tendered his resignation. Davis replied that to find a more capable commander was "an impossibility."

Battle of Gettysburg

Though southern troops had displayed a courage and dedication that would never be forgotten, the results had been disastrous. Josiah Gorgas, the genius of Confederate ordnance operations, confided to his diary, "Today absolute ruin seems our portion. The Confederacy totters to its destruction." In desperation President Davis and several state governors resorted to threats and racial scare tactics to drive southern whites to further sacrifice. Defeat, Davis warned, would mean "extermination of yourselves, your wives, and children." Governor Charles Clark of Mississippi predicted "elevation of the black race to a position of equality—aye, of superiority, that will make them your masters and rulers." Abroad, British officials held back the delivery of badly needed warships, and diplomats postponed any thought of recognizing the Confederate government.

From this point on, the internal disintegration of the Confederacy quickened. A few newspapers and a few bold politicians began to call openly for peace. "We are for peace," admitted the *Raleigh* (North Carolina) *Daily Progress,* "because there has been enough of blood and carnage, enough of widows and orphans." A neighboring journal, the *North Carolina*

Standard, vowed to "tell the truth," tacitly admitted that defeat was inevitable, and called for negotiations. Similar proposals were made in several state legislatures, though they were presented as plans for independence on honorable terms. But more important, Confederate leaders had begun to realize that they were losing the support of the common people. A prominent Texan noted in his diary that secession had been the work of political leaders operating without the firm support of "the mass of the people without property." Governor Zebulon Vance of North Carolina, who agreed, wrote privately that independence would require more "blood and misery . . . and our people will not pay this price I am satisfied for their independence. . . . The great popular heart is not now & never has been in this war."

In North Carolina a peace movement grew under the leadership of William W. Holden, a popular Democratic politician and editor. In the summer of **Southern Peace Movements** 1863 over one hundred public meetings took place in support of peace negotiations; many established figures believed that Holden had the majority of the people behind him. In Georgia early in 1864, Governor Brown and Alexander H. Stephens, vice president of the Confederacy, led a similar effort. Ultimately, however, these movements came to naught. The lack of a two-party system threw into question the legitimacy of any criticism of the government; even Holden and Brown could not entirely escape the taint of dishonor and disloyalty. That the movement existed despite the risks suggested deep disaffection.

The results of the 1863 congressional elections continued the tendency toward dissent. Everywhere secessionists and supporters of the administration lost seats to men who were not identified with the government. Many of the new representatives, who were often former Whigs, openly opposed the administration or publicly favored peace. In the last years of the war, Davis depended heavily on support from Union-occupied districts to maintain a majority in the congress. Having secured the legislation he needed, he used the bureaucracy and the army to enforce his unpopular policies. Ironically, as the South's situation grew desperate, former critics such as the *Charleston Mercury* became supporters of the administration. They and a solid core of courageous and determined

soldiers kept the Confederacy alive in the face of disintegrating popular support.

By 1864 much of the opposition to the war had moved entirely outside politics. Southerners were simply giving up the struggle, withdrawing their cooperation from the government, and forming a sort of counter-society. Deserters joined with ordinary citizens who were sick of the war to dominate whole towns and counties. Secret societies dedicated to reunion, such as the Heroes of America and the Red Strings, sprang up. Active dissent spread throughout the South but was particularly common in upland and mountain regions. "The condition of things in the mountain districts of North Carolina, South Carolina, Georgia, and Alabama," admitted Assistant Secretary of War John A. Campbell, "menaces the existence of the Confederacy as fatally as either of the armies of the United States." Confederate officials tried using the army to round up deserters and compel obedience, but this approach was only temporarily effective. The government was losing the support of its citizens.

ANTIWAR SENTIMENT IN THE NORTH

In the North opposition to the war was similar in many ways, but not as severe. There was concern over the growing centralization of government, and war-weariness was a frequent complaint. Discrimination and injustice in the draft sparked protest among poor citizens, just as they had in the South. But the Union was so much richer than the South in human resources that none of these problems ever threatened the stability of the government. Fresh recruits were always available, and food and other necessaries were not subject to severe shortages.

What was more, Lincoln possessed a talent that Davis lacked: he knew how to stay in touch with the ordinary citizen. Through letters to newspapers and to soldiers' families, he reached the common people and demonstrated that he had not forgotten them. Their grief was his also, for the war was his personal tragedy. After scrambling to the summit of political ambition, Lincoln had seen the glory of the presidency turn to horror. The daily carnage, the tortuous political problems, and the ceaseless criticism weighed heavily on him. In moving language, this president with the demeanor of a self-educated man of humble origins was able to communicate his suffering. His words helped to contain northern discontent, though they could not remove it.

Much of this wartime protest sprang from politics. The Democratic party, though nudged from its dominant position by the Republican surge of the late

Peace Democrats

1850s, remained strong. Its leaders were determined to regain power, and they found much to criticize in Lincoln's policies: the carnage and length of the war, the expansion of federal powers, inflation and the high tariff, and the improved status of blacks. Accordingly, they attacked the continuation of the war, calling for reunion on the basis of "the Constitution as it is and the Union as it was." The Democrats denounced conscription and martial law, and defended states' rights and the interests of agriculture. They charged repeatedly that Republican policies were designed to flood the North with blacks, depriving white males of their status, jobs, and women. Their stand appealed to southerners who had settled north of the Ohio River, to conservatives, to many poor people, and to some eastern merchants who had lost profitable southern trade. In the 1862 elections, the Democrats made a strong comeback. And during the war, peace Democrats influenced New York State and won majorities in the legislatures of Illinois and Indiana.

Led by outspoken men like Clement L. Vallandigham of Ohio, the peace Democrats were highly visible. Vallandigham criticized Lincoln as a dictator who had suspended the writ of habeas corpus without congressional authority and arrested thousands of innocent citizens. Like other Democrats, he condemned both conscription and emancipation and urged voters to use their power at the polling place to depose "King Abraham." Vallandigham stayed carefully within legal bounds, but his attacks were so damaging to the war effort that military authorities arrested him after Lincoln suspended habeas corpus. Fearing that Vallandigham might gain the stature of a martyr, the president decided against a jail term and exiled

him to the Confederacy. Thus Lincoln rid himself of a troublesome critic, in the process saddling puzzled Confederates with a man who insisted on talking about "our country." Eventually Vallandigham returned to the North through Canada.

Lincoln believed that antiwar Democrats were linked to secret organizations, such as the Knights of the Golden Circle and the Order of American Knights, that harbored traitorous ideas. These societies, he feared, stimulated draft resistance, discouraged enlistment, sabotaged communications, and plotted to aid the Confederacy. Likening such groups to a poisonous snake striking at the government, Republicans sometimes branded them—and by extension the peace Democrats—as Copperheads. Though Democrats were connected with these organizations, most engaged in politics rather than treason. And though some saboteurs and Confederate agents were active in the North, they never effected any major demonstration of support for the Confederacy. Whether Lincoln overreacted in arresting his critics and suppressing opposition is still a matter of debate, but it is certain that he acted with a heavier hand and with less provocation than Jefferson Davis.

More violent opposition to the government came from ordinary citizens facing the draft, especially the urban poor. Conscription was a massive but poorly organized affair. Federal enrolling officers made up the list of eligibles, a procedure open to personal favoritism and ethnic or class prejudice. Lists of those conscripted reveal that poor men were called more often than rich, and that disproportionate numbers of immigrants were called. (Approximately 200,000 men born in Germany and 150,000 born in Ireland served in the Union Army.) And rich men could furnish substitutes or pay a commutation to avoid service.

As a result, there were scores of disturbances and melees. Enrolling officers received rough treatment in many parts of the North, and riots occurred in

New York City Draft Riot

Ohio, Indiana, Pennsylvania, Illinois, and Wisconsin, and in such cities as Troy, Albany, and Newark.

By far the most serious outbreak of violence, however, occurred in New York City in July 1863. The war was unpopular in that Democratic stronghold, and ethnic and class tensions ran high. Shippers had recently broken a longshoremen's strike

These photographers capture the very different personal styles of Grant (left) and Lee (right). Their costly battles stimulated war weariness in 1864 but eventually made the end of the war more clear.   Left: Library of Congress; right: National Archives.

by hiring black strikebreakers who worked under police protection. Working-class New Yorkers feared an influx of such black labor from the South and regarded blacks as the cause of an unpopular war. Irish workers, often recently arrived and poor themselves, resented being forced to serve in the place of others. And indeed, local draft lists certified that the poor foreign-born were going to have to bear the burden of service.

The provost marshal's office came under attack first. Then mobs crying "Down with the rich" looted wealthy homes and stores. But blacks proved to be the rioters' special target. Luckless blacks who happened to be in the rioters' path were beaten; soon the mob rampaged through black neighborhoods, destroying an orphans' asylum. At least seventy-four people died during the violence, which raged out of control for three days. Only the dispatch of army units fresh from Gettysburg ended the episode.

Once inducted, northern soldiers felt many of the same anxieties and grievances as their southern counterparts. Federal troops too had to cope with loneliness and concern for their loved ones, disease, and the tedium of camp life. Thousands of men slipped away from authorities. Given the problems plaguing the draft and the discouragement in the North over lack of progress in the war, it is not surprising that the Union Army struggled with a desertion rate as high as the Confederates'.

Discouragement and war-weariness neared their peak during the summer of 1864. At that point the Democratic party nominated the popular General George B. McClellan for president and put a qualified peace plank into its platform. The plank, written by Vallandigham, condemned "four years of failure to restore the Union by the experiment of war" and called for an armistice. Lincoln concluded that it was "exceedingly probable that this Administration will not be re-elected."

Then, during a publicized interchange with Confederate emissaries in Canada, Lincoln insisted that the terms for peace include reunion and "the abandonment of slavery." A wave of protest rose in the North, for many voters were weary of war and unready to demand terms beyond preservation of the Union. Lincoln quickly backtracked, denying that his offer meant "that nothing *else* or *less* would be considered, if offered." He would insist on freedom only for those slaves (about 150,000) who had joined the Union

army under his promise of emancipation. Thus Lincoln in effect acknowledged the danger that he would not be re-elected. The fortunes of war, however, soon changed the electoral situation.

NORTHERN PRESSURE AND SOUTHERN WILL

The year 1864 brought to fruition the North's long-term diplomatic strategy. From the outset, the North had pursued one paramount diplomatic goal: to prevent recognition of the Confederacy by European nations. Foreign recognition would damage the North's claim that it was fighting an illegal rebellion, not a separate nation. But more important, recognition would open the way to the foreign military and financial aid that could assure Confederate independence. Among the British elite, there was considerable sympathy for southern planters, whose aristocratic values were similar to their own. And in terms of power politics, both England and France stood to benefit from a divided America, which would necessarily be a weaker rival. Thus Lincoln and Secretary of State Seward faced a difficult task. To achieve their goal, they needed to avoid both major military defeats and unnecessary controversies with the European powers.

Northern Diplomatic Strategy

Southerners aided them by an overconfident reliance on "King Cotton" diplomacy. Knowing that the textile industry, directly or indirectly, employed one-fifth of the British population, southern leaders declared that "Cotton is King." They believed that the British government, concerned to obtain cotton for the country's mills, would *have* to recognize the Confederacy. But though cotton was a good card to play, it was not a trump. At the beginning of the war British mills had a 50-percent surplus of cotton on hand. New sources of supply in India, Egypt, and Brazil helped to fill their needs later on, and some southern cotton continued to reach Europe, despite the Confederacy's recommendation that its citizens plant and ship no cotton. The British government, refusing to be stampeded into recognition, kept its eye on the battlefield. France, though sympathetic to the South, was unwilling to act without the British. Confederate agents were able to purchase valuable arms and supplies in Europe and obtained some loans from European financiers, but they never achieved a diplomatic breakthrough.

More than once the Union strategy nearly broke down. A major crisis occurred in 1861 when the overzealous commander of an American frigate stopped the British steamer *Trent* and abducted two Confederate ambassadors. The British reacted strongly, but Lincoln and Seward were able to delay until a less-excited public opinion allowed them to back down and return the ambassadors. In a series of confrontations, the United States protested against the building and sale of warships to the Confederacy. A few ships built in Britain, notably the *Alabama,* reached open water to serve the Confederacy. Over twenty-two months, without entering a southern port, the *Alabama* destroyed or captured more than sixty northern ships. But soon the British government began to bar delivery to the Confederacy of warships such as the Laird rams, formidable vessels whose pointed prows were designed to break the Union blockade.

Back on American battlefields, the northern victory was far from won. Most engagements had demonstrated the advantages enjoyed by the defense and the extreme difficulty of destroying an opposing army. As General William Tecumseh Sherman recognized, the North had to "keep the war South until they are not only ruined, exhausted, but humbled in pride and spirit." Yet the world's recognized military authorities agreed that deep invasion was extremely difficult and risky. The farther an army penetrated enemy territory, the more vulnerable its own communications and support became. Moreover, noted the Prussian expert Karl von Clausewitz, if the invader encountered a "truly national" resistance, his troops would be "everywhere exposed to attacks by an insurgent population." Thus, if southerners were determined enough to mount a "truly national" resistance, their defiance and the vast size of their country would make a northern victory virtually impossible.

General Grant decided to test these obstacles—and southern will—with an innovation of his own: the strategy of raids. Raids were not new, but what

Grant had in mind was on a massive scale. He proposed to use whole armies, not just cavalry, to destroy Confederate railroads, thus denying the enemy rail transportation and damaging the South's economy. Federal armies, abandoning their lines of support, would live off the land while they laid waste all resources useful to the Confederacy. After General George H. Thomas's troops won the Battle of Chattanooga in November 1863 by ignoring orders and charging up Missionary Ridge, the heartland of the South lay open. Moving to the Virginia theater, Grant entrusted General Sherman with 100,000 men for such a raid deep into the South, toward Atlanta.

Jefferson Davis countered by placing the army of General Johnston in Sherman's path. Davis's entire political strategy for 1864 depended on the demonstration of Confederate military strength and a successful defense of Atlanta. With the federal elections of 1864 approaching, Davis hoped that a display of strength and resolution by the South would defeat Lincoln and elect a president who would sue for peace. When Johnston slowly but steadily fell back toward Atlanta, Davis grew anxious and pressed his commander for information and assurances that Atlanta would be held. From a purely military point of view, Johnston was conducting the defense skillfully, but Jefferson Davis could not take a purely military point of view. When Johnston remained uninformative and continued to drop back, Davis replaced him with the one-legged General John Hood, who knew his job was to fight. "Our all depends on that army at Atlanta," wrote Mary Boykin Chesnut. "If that fails us, the game is up."

And for southern morale, the game was up. Hood attacked but was beaten, and Sherman's army occupied Atlanta on September 2, 1864. The victory buoyed northern spirits and assured Lincoln's re-election. Mary Chesnut moaned, "There is no hope," and a government clerk in Richmond wrote, "Our fondly-cherished visions of peace have vanished like a mirage of the desert." Though Davis exhorted southerners to fight on and win new victories before the federal elections, he had to admit that "two-thirds of our men are absent . . . most of them absent without leave." Hood's army marched north to cut Sherman's supply lines and force him to retreat, but Sherman, planning to live off the land, marched the greater

Chapter 14: TRANSFORMING FIRE: THE CIVIL WAR, 1861–1865

Sherman's march demonstrated, as nothing before had, the enormous destructiveness and total, economic character of modern war. The ordnance trains and rolling mill above were blown up at Atlanta. Library of Congress.

part of his army straight to the sea, destroying Confederate resources as he went (see map, page 412.)

As he moved across Georgia Sherman cut a path fifty to sixty miles wide; the totality of the destruction was awesome. A Georgia woman described the "Burnt Country" this way: "The fields were trampled down and the road was lined with carcasses of horses, hogs, and cattle that the invaders, unable either to consume or to carry away with them, had wantonly shot down to starve our people and prevent them from making their crops. The stench in some places was unbearable." Such devastation diminished the South's material resources, but, more importantly, it was bound to impact on the faltering southern will to resist.

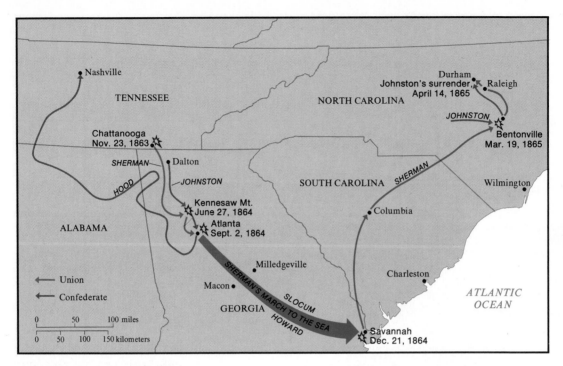

Sherman's March to the Sea

After reaching Savannah in December, Sherman turned north and marched his armies into the Carolinas. Wreaking great destruction as he moved through South Carolina into North Carolina, Sherman encountered little resistance. The opposing army of General Johnston was small, but Sherman's men should have been prime targets for guerrilla raids and harassing attacks by local defense units. The absence of both led South Carolina's James Chesnut, Jr., to write that his state "was shamefully and unnecessarily lost. . . . We had time, opportunity and means to destroy him. But there was wholly wanting the energy and ability required by the occasion." Southerners were reaching the limit of their endurance.

Sherman's march brought additional human resources to the Union cause. In Georgia alone as many as nineteen thousand slaves gladly took the opportunity to escape bondage and join the Union army as it passed through the countryside. Others held back to await the end of the war on the plantations, either from an ingrained wariness of whites or from negative experiences with the federal soldiers. The destruction of food harmed slaves as well as white rebels; many blacks lost blankets, shoes, and other valuables to

their liberators. In fact, the brutality of Sherman's troops shocked these veterans of the whip. "I've seen them cut the hams off of a live pig or ox and go off leavin' the animal groanin'," recalled one man. "The master had 'em kilt then, but it was awful."

It was awful, too, in Virginia, where the preliminaries to victory proved to be protracted and ghastly. Throughout the spring and summer Grant hurled his troops at Lee's army and suffered appalling losses: almost 18,000 casualties in the Battle of the Wilderness, more than 8,000 at Spotsylvania, and 12,000 in the space of a few hours at Cold Harbor (see map). Before the last battle, Union troops pinned scraps of paper bearing their names and addresses to their backs, certain that they would be mowed down as they rushed Lee's trenches. In four weeks in May and June, Grant lost as many men as were enrolled in Lee's entire army. Undaunted, Grant remarked, "I propose to fight it out along this line if it takes all summer." And the heavy fighting did prepare the way for eventual victory: Lee's army shrank to the point that offensive action was no longer possible, while the Union army kept replenishing its forces with new recruits.

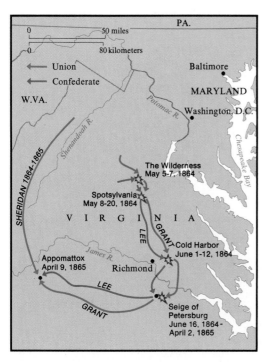

The War in Virginia, 1864–1865

The end finally came in the spring of 1865. Grant kept battering at Lee, who tried but failed to break through the federal line east of Petersburg on March 25. With the numerical superiority of Grant's army now upwards of two-to-one, Confederate defeat was inevitable. On April 2 Lee abandoned Richmond and Petersburg. On April 9, hemmed in by federal troops, short of rations, and with fewer than 30,000 men left, Lee surrendered to Grant. At Appomattox Courthouse the Union general treated his rival with respect and paroled the defeated troops. Within weeks Jefferson Davis was captured, and the remaining Confederate forces laid down their arms and surrendered. The war was over at last.

Heavy Losses Force Lee's Surrender

Lincoln did not live to see the last surrenders. On the evening of Good Friday, April 14, he went to Ford's Theatre in Washington, where an assassin named John Wilkes Booth shot him at pointblank range. Lincoln died the next day. The Union had lost its wartime leader, and to many, relief at the war's end was tempered by uncertainty about the future.

COSTS AND EFFECTS

The costs of the Civil War were enormous. Although precise figures on enlistments are impossible to obtain, it appears that during the course of the conflict the Confederate armies claimed the services of 700,000 to 800,000 men. Far more, possibly 2.3 million, served in the Union armies. Northern reserves were so great that more men were legally subject to the draft at the end of the war than at the beginning.

Statistics on casualties are more precise and more appalling. Approximately 364,222 federal soldiers died, 140,070 of them from wounds suffered in battle.

Casualties

Another 275,175 Union soldiers were wounded but survived. On the Confederate side, an estimated 258,000 lost their lives, and even a conservative estimate of Confederate wounded brings the total number of casualties on both sides to more than 1 million—a frightful toll for a nation of 31 million people. More men died in the Civil War than in all other American wars before Vietnam combined.

Such carnage seems a terrible price to pay over a disagreement in which some possibilities of compromise—such as a national convention—were never tried. But any democratic system requires an underlying degree of consensus in order to function. That consensus had failed in 1860 and 1861. Although most voters in 1860 had not wanted war, and surely not a bloody war like this, the disagreements between North and South had become too deep and too great to manage. Powerful interests had refused to compromise. A fundamental clash of wills, which would continue to trouble Reconstruction, had caused unprecedented loss of life.

Property damage and financial costs were also enormous, though difficult to tally. Federal loans and taxes during the conflict totaled almost $3 billion, and interest on the war debt was $2.8 billion. The Confederacy borrowed over $2 billion but lost far more in the destruction of homes, fences, crops, livestock, and other property. To give just one example of the wreckage that attended four

Financial Cost of the War

Lincoln's face betrays the strain of four years of war. Compare his youthful appearance in Springfield, Illinois, on August 13, 1860, left, with the photograph on the right, taken in Washington, April 10, 1865, four days before his assassination. *Library of Congress.*

years of conflict on southern soil, the number of hogs in South Carolina plummeted from 965,000 in 1860 to approximately 150,000 in 1865. Thoughtful scholars have noted that small farmers lost just as much, proportionally, as planters whose slaves were emancipated.

Estimates of the total cost of the war exceed $20 billion—five times the total expenditure of the federal government from its creation to 1865. The northern government increased its spending by a factor of seven in the first full year of the war; by the last year its spending had soared to twenty times the prewar level. By 1865 the federal government accounted for over 26 percent of the gross national product.

These changes were more or less permanent. In the 1880s, interest on the war debt still accounted for approximately 40 percent of the federal budget, and soldiers' pensions for as much as 20 percent. Thus, although many southerners had hoped to separate government from the economy, the war made such separation an impossibility. And although federal expenditures shrank after the war, they stabilized at twice the prewar level, or 4 percent of the gross national product. Wartime emergency measures had brought the banking and transportation systems under federal control, and the government had put its power behind manufacturing and business interests through tariffs, loans, and subsidies. In political terms too, national power increased. Extreme forms of the states'

IMPORTANT EVENTS

1861	Four more southern states secede from Union
	Battle of Bull Run
	General McClellan organizes Union Army
	Union blockade begins
	First Confiscation Act
1862	Capture of Forts Henry and Donelson
	Capture of New Orleans
	Battle of Shiloh
	Confederacy adopts conscription
	McClellan attacks Virginia
	Second Confiscation Act
	Confederacy mounts offensive
	Battle of Antietam
1863	Emancipation Proclamation
	National Banking Act
	Union adopts conscription
	Black soldiers join Union Army
	Food riots in southern cities
	Battle of Chancellorsville
	Battle of Gettysburg and surrender of Vicksburg
	Draft riots in New York City
1864	Battle of Cold Harbor
	Lincoln requests party plank abolishing slavery
	General Sherman enters Atlanta
	Lincoln re-elected
	Jefferson Davis proposes Confederate emancipation
	Sherman marches through Georgia
1865	Sherman drives through Carolinas
	Congress approves Thirteenth Amendment
	Hampton Roads Conference
	Lee surrenders at Appomattox
	Lincoln assassinated

rights controversy were dead, though Americans continued to favor a state-centered federalism.

Yet despite all these changes, one crucial question remained unanswered: what was the place of black men and women in American life? The Union victory provided a partial answer: slavery as it had existed before the war could not persist. But what would replace it? About 186,000 black soldiers had rallied to the Union cause, infusing it with new strength. Did their sacrifice entitle them to full citizenship? They and other former slaves eagerly awaited an answer, which would have to be found during Reconstruction.

SUGGESTIONS FOR FURTHER READING

The War and the South

Thomas B. Alexander and Richard E. Beringer, *The Anatomy of the Confederate Congress* (1972); Robert F. Durden, *The Gray and the Black* (1972); Clement Eaton, *A History of the Southern Confederacy* (1954); Paul D. Escott, *Many Excellent People* (1985); Paul D. Escott, *After Secession* (1978); Paul D. Escott, " 'The Cry of the Sufferers': The Problem of Poverty in the Confederacy," *Civil War History*, XXIII (September 1977), 228-240; Archer Jones *et al.*, *Why the South Lost the Civil War* (1985); J. B. Jones, *A Rebel War Clerk's Diary*, 2 vols., ed. Howard Swiggett (1935); Stanley Lebergott, "Why the South Lost," *Journal of American History*, 70 (June, 1983), 58–74; Ella Lonn, *Desertion During the Civil War* (1928); Larry E. Nelson, *Bullets, Ballots, and Rhetoric* (1980); Harry P. Owens and James J. Cooke, eds., *The Old South in the Crucible of War* (1983); Frank L. Owsley, *State Rights in the Confederacy* (1925); Charles W. Ramsdell, *Behind the Lines in the Southern Confederacy*, ed. Wendell H. Stephenson (1944); James L. Roark, *Masters Without Slaves* (1977); Georgia Lee Tatum, *Disloyalty in the Confederacy* (1934); Emory M. Thomas, *The Confederate Nation* (1979); Emory M. Thomas, *The Confederacy as a Revolutionary Experience* (1971); Emory M. Thomas, *The Confederate State of Richmond* (1971); Bell Irvin Wiley, *The Life of Johnny Reb* (1943); Bell Irvin Wiley, *The Plain People of the Confederacy* (1943); W. Buck Yearns, ed., *The Confederate Governors* (1985); W. Buck

Yearns and John G. Barrett, *North Carolina Civil War Documentary* (1980).

The War and the North

Ralph Andreano, ed., *The Economic Impact of the American Civil War* (1962); Robert Cruden, *The War That Never Ended* (1973); Wood Gray, *The Hidden Civil War* (1942); Frank L. Klement, *The Copperheads in the Middle West* (1960); Susan Previant Lee and Peter Passell, *A New Economic View of American History* (1979); George Winston Smith and Charles Burnet Judah, *Life in the North During the Civil War* (1966); George Templeton Strong, *Diary*, 4 vols., ed. Allan Nevins and Milton Halsey Thomas (1952); Paul Studenski, *Financial History of the United States* (1952); Bell Irvin Wiley, *The Life of Billy Yank* (1952).

Women

John R. Brumgardt, ed., *Civil War Nurse: The Diary and Letters of Hannah Ropes* (1980); Beth Gilbert Crabtree and James W. Patton, eds., *"Journal of a Secesh Lady": The Diary of Catherine Ann Devereux Edmondston, 1860–1866* (1979); Jacqueline Jones, *Labor of Love, Labor of Sorrow* (1985); Mary D. Robertson, ed., *Lucy Breckinridge of Grove Hill: The Journal of a Virginia Girl, 1862–1864* (1979); C. Vann Woodward and Elisabeth Muhlenfeld, eds., *The Private Mary Chesnut* (1984); C. Vann Woodward, ed., *Mary Chesnut's Civil War* (1981).

Blacks

Ira Berlin, ed., *Freedom: A Documentary History of Emancipation, 1861–1867*, Series II, *The Black Military Experience* (1982); Dudley Cornish, *The Sable Arm* (1956); James M. McPherson, *The Negro's Civil War* (1965); James M. McPherson, *The Struggle for Equality* (1964); Benjamin Quarles, *The Negro in the Civil War* (1953).

Military History

Bern Anderson, *By Sea and by River* (1962); Bruce Catton, *Grant Takes Command* (1969); Bruce Catton, *Grant Moves South* (1960); Thomas L. Connelly and Archer Jones, *The Politics of Command* (1973); Burke Davis, *Sherman's March* (1980); William C. Davis, ed., *The Image of War*, multivolume (1983–1985); Shelby Foote, *The Civil War, a Narrative*, 3 vols. (1958–1974); William A. Frassanito, *Grant and Lee: The Virginia Campaigns, 1864–1865* (1983); Douglas Southall Freeman, *Lee's Lieutenants*, 3 vols. (1942–1944);

Douglas Southall Freeman, *R. E. Lee*, 4 vols. (1934–1935); Herman Hattaway and Archer Jones, *How the North Won* (1983); Archer Jones et al., *Why the South Lost the Civil War* (1986); Archer Jones, *Confederate Strategy from Shiloh to Vicksburg* (1961); Thomas L. Livermore, *Numbers and Losses in the Civil War in America* (1957); James Lee McDonough, *Chattanooga* (1984); James Lee McDonough and Thomas L. Connelly, *Five Tragic Hours* (1984); Grady McWhiney and Perry D. Jamieson, *Attack and Die* (1982); J. B. Mitchell, *Decisive Battles of the Civil War* (1955); Frank E. Vandiver, *Rebel Brass* (1956).

Diplomatic History

Stuart L. Bernath, *Squall Across the Atlantic: American Civil War Prize Cases and Diplomacy* (1970); Kinley J. Brauer, "The Slavery Problem in the Diplomacy of the American Civil War," *Pacific Historical Review*, XLVI, no. 3 (1977), 439–469; David P. Crook, *Diplomacy During the American Civil War* (1975); David P. Crook, *The North, the South, and the Powers, 1861–1865* (1974); Charles P. Cullop, *Confederate Propaganda in Europe* (1969); Norman A. Graebner, "Northern Diplomacy and European Neutrality," in David Donald, ed., *Why the North Won the Civil War* (1960); Frank J. Merli, *Great Britain and the Confederate Navy* (1970); Frank L. Owsley and Harriet Owsley, *King Cotton Diplomacy* (1959); Gordon H. Warren, *Fountain of Discontent: The Trent Affair and Freedom of the Seas* (1981); Gordon H. Warren, "The King Cotton Theory," in Alexander DeConde, ed., *Encyclopedia of American Foreign Policy*, 3 vols. (1978).

Abraham Lincoln and the Union Government

Fawn Brodie, *Thaddeus Stevens* (1959); LaWanda Cox, *Lincoln and Black Freedom* (1981); Richard N. Current, *The Lincoln Nobody Knows* (1958); David Donald, *Charles Sumner and the Rights of Man* (1970); Ludwell H. Johnson, "Lincoln's Solution to the Problem of Peace Terms, 1864–1865," *Journal of Southern History*, XXXIV (November 1968); 441-447; Peyton McCrary, *Abraham Lincoln and Reconstruction* (1978); Stephen B. Oates, *Our Fiery Trial* (1979); Stephen B. Oates, *With Malice Toward None* (1977); James G. Randall, *Mr. Lincoln* (1957); Benjamin F. Thomas, *Abraham Lincoln* (1952); Hans L. Trefousse, *The Radical Republicans* (1969); Glyndon G. Van Deusen, *William Henry Seward* (1967); T. Harry Williams, *Lincoln and His Generals* (1952); T. Harry Williams, *Lincoln and the Radicals* (1941).

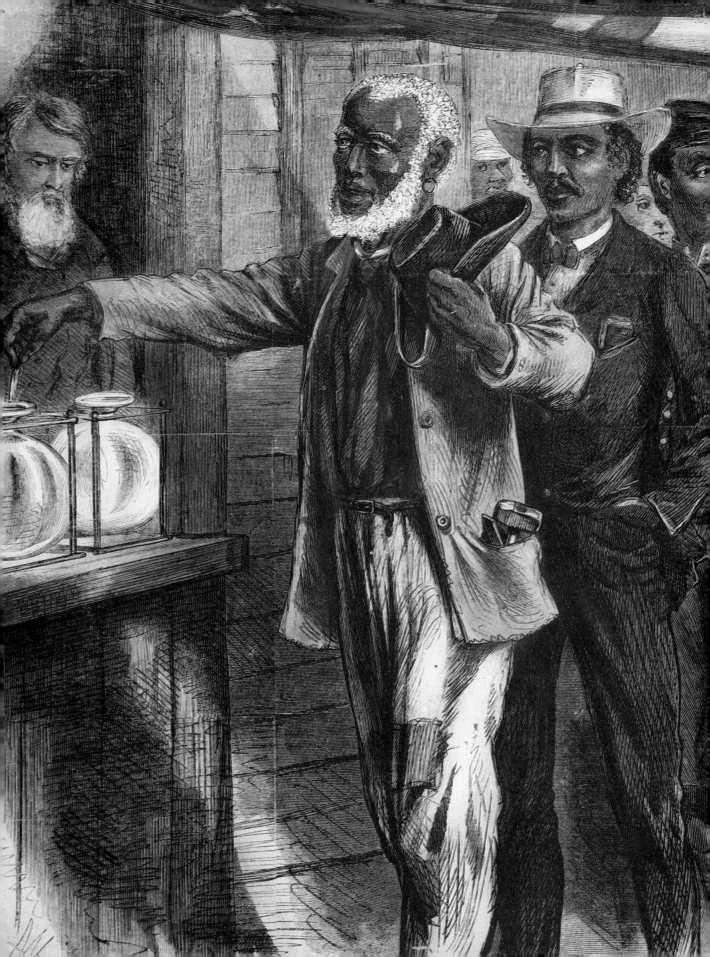

Reconstruction by Trial and Error

1865–1877

Chapter 15

It was a beautiful spring day in 1868. Sunlight and balmy weather bathed the nation's capital on Saturday, May 16, but few people paused to relax or enjoy their surroundings. All of Washington was tense with excitement. Professional gamblers had flooded into the city, outnumbered perhaps only by the reporters who leapt upon every rumor or scrap of information. As the morning passed, a crowd gathered around the Senate chamber. Foreign dignitaries filled the diplomatic box, and spectators packed the Senate galleries. Outside the chamber thousands milled about, choking the hallways and spilling onto the terraces and streets outside.

Precisely at noon the Chief Justice of the United States entered the Senate. Managers and counsel stood ready. Soon two senators who were seriously ill slowly made their way into the chamber, bringing the number of senators present to its full fifty-four. All principals in this solemn drama were present before the High Court of Impeachment except the accused: Andrew Johnson, President of the United States. Johnson, who never appeared to defend himself in person, waited anxiously at the White House as Chief Justice Salmon Chase ordered the calling of the roll. To each senator he put the questions, "How say you? Is the respondent, Andrew Johnson, President of the United States, guilty or not guilty of a high misdemeanor, as charged in this article?" Thirty-five senators answered, "Guilty," nineteen, "Not guilty." The total was one short of a two-thirds majority. The nation had come within one vote of removing its president from office.

How had this extraordinary event come about? What had brought the executive and legislative branches of government into such severe conflict? An unprecedented problem—the reconstruction of the Union—furnished the occasion, and deepening differences over the proper policy to pursue had led to the confrontation. Obviously, by 1868 president and Congress had reached a point of bitter antagonism, with some congressmen charging that the president was siding with traitors.

In 1865, at the end of the war, such a result seemed most unlikely. Although he was a southerner from Tennessee, Johnson had built his career upon criticizing the wealthy planters and championing the South's small farmers. When an assassin's bullet thrust him into the presidency, many former slaveowners shared the worries of a North Carolina lady who wrote, "Think of Andy Johnson [as] the president! What will become of us—'the aristocrats of the South' as we are termed?" Northern Radicals who sounded out the new president on his views also felt confident that he would deal sternly with the South. When one of them suggested the exile or execution of ten or twelve leading rebels to set an example, Johnson had vigorously replied, "How are you going to pick out so small a number? Robbery is a crime; rape is a crime; *treason* is a crime; and *crime* must be punished."

Moreover, fundamental change was already under way in the South. During his army's last campaign, General William T. Sherman had issued Special Field Order No. 15, which set aside for Negro settlement the Sea Islands and all abandoned coastal lands thirty miles to the interior, from Charleston to the Saint John's River in northern Florida. Black refugees quickly poured into these lands; by the middle of 1865, forty thousand freed people were living in their new homes. One former slaveowner who visited his old plantation in Beaufort, South Carolina, received friendly and courteous treatment. But his ex-slaves "firmly and respectfully" informed him that "we own this land now. Put it out of your head that it will ever be yours again."

Before the end of 1865, however, these signs of change were reversed. Although Jefferson Davis was imprisoned for two years, no Confederate leaders were executed, and southern aristocrats soon came to view Andrew Johnson not as their enemy but as their friend and protector. Johnson pardoned rebel leaders liberally, allowed them to take high offices, and ordered government officials to reclaim the freedmen's land and give it back to the original owners. One man in South Carolina expressed blacks' dismay: "Why do you take away our lands? You take them from us who have always been true, always true to the Government! You give them to our all-time enemies! That is not right!"

The unexpected outcome of Johnson's program led Congress to examine his policies and design new plans for Reconstruction. Out of negotiations in Congress and clashes between the president and the legislators, there emerged first one, and then two, new plans for Reconstruction. Before the process was over, the nation had adopted the Fourteenth and Fifteenth Amendments and impeached its president.

Racism did not disappear. During the war the federal government had been reluctant to give even black troops fair treatment, and in Congress northern Democrats continued to oppose equality. Republicans were often divided among themselves, but a mixture of idealism and party purposes drove them forward. Ultimately, fear of losing the peace proved decisive with northern voters. The United States enfranchised the freedmen and gave them a role in reconstructing the South.

Blacks benefited from greater control over their personal lives and took the risks of voting and participating in politics. But they knew that the success of Reconstruction also depended on the determination and support of the North. Southern opposition to Reconstruction grew steadily. By 1869 a secret terrorist organization known as the Ku Klux Klan had added large-scale violence to southern whites' repertoire of resistance. Despite federal efforts to protect them, black people were intimidated at the polls, robbed of their earnings, beaten, or murdered. Prosecution of Klansmen rarely succeeded, and Republicans lost their offices in an increasing number of southern states. By the early 1870s the failure of Reconstruction was apparent. Republican leaders and northern voters had to decide how far they would persist in their efforts to reform the South.

As the 1870s advanced, other issues drew attention away from Reconstruction. Industrial growth accelerated, creating new opportunities and raising new problems. Interest in territorial expansion revived. Political corruption became a nationwide scandal and bribery a way of doing business. North Carolina's Jonathan Worth, an old-line Whig who had opposed secession as strongly as he now fought Reconstruction, deplored the atmosphere of greed. "Money has become the God of this country," he wrote in disgust, "and men, otherwise good men, are almost compelled to worship at her shrine." Eventually these other forces triumphed, politics moved on to new concerns, and

the courts turned their attention away from civil rights. Even northern Republicans gave up on racial reform in 1877.

Thus the nation stumbled, by trial and error, toward a policy that attempted to reconstruct the South. Congress insisted on equality before the law for black people and gave black men the right to vote. It took the unprecedented step of impeaching the president. But more far-reaching measures to advance black freedom never had much support in Congress, and when suffrage alone proved insufficient to remake the South, the nation soon lost interest. Reconstruction proclaimed anew the American principle of human equality but failed to secure it in reality.

EQUALITY:

THE UNRESOLVED ISSUE

For America's former slaves, Reconstruction had one paramount meaning: a chance to explore freedom. A southern white woman admitted in her diary that the black people "showed a natural and exultant joy at being free." Former slaves remembered rejoicing and singing far into the night after federal troops reached their plantations. The slaves on one Texas plantation jumped up and down and clapped their hands as one man shouted, "We is free—no more whippings and beatings."

A few blacks gave in to the natural desire to do what had been impossible before. One grandmother who had long resented her treatment "dropped her hoe" and ran to confront the mistress. "I'm free!" she yelled at her. "Yes, I'm free! Ain't got to work for you no more! You can't put me in your pocket [sell me] now!" Another man recalled that he and others "started on the move" and left the plantation, either to search for family members or just to exercise their new-found freedom of movement. As he traveled, one man sang about being free as a frog, " 'cause a frog had freedom to get on a log and jump off when he pleases."

Most freedmen reacted more cautiously and shrewdly, taking care to test the boundaries of their

In the changed circumstances after emancipation, former slaves and former slaveowners had to work out the terms of a new relationship. Winslow Homer suggested some of the complexity of their encounters in A Visit from the Old Mistress *(1876). National Museum of American Art, Smithsonian Institution, Washington, D.C., Gift of William T. Evans.*

new condition. "After the war was over," explained one man, "we was afraid to move. Just like tarpins or turtles after emancipation. Just stick our heads out to see how the land lay." As slaves they had learned to expect hostility from white people, and they did not presume it would instantly disappear. Life in freedom, they knew, might still be a matter of what was allowed, not what was right. "You got to say master?" asked a freedman in Georgia. "Naw," answered his fellows, but "they said it all the same. They said it for a long time."

One sign of this shrewd caution was the way freedmen evaluated potential employers. "Most all the niggers that had good owners stayed with 'em, but the others left. Some of 'em come back and some

didn't," explained one man. If a white person had been relatively considerate to blacks in bondage, blacks reasoned that he might prove a desirable employer in freedom. Other blacks left their plantation all at once, for, as one put it, "that master am sure mean and if we doesn't have to stay we shouldn't, not with that master."

Even more urgently than a fair employer, the freedmen wanted land of their own. Land represented their chance to farm for themselves, to have an independent life. It represented

Blacks' Desire for Land compensation for their generations of travail in bondage. A northern observer noted that freedmen made "plain, straight-forward" inquiries as they settled the land set aside for them by Sherman. They wanted to be sure the land "would be theirs after they had improved it." Not just in the Sea Island region but everywhere, blacks young and old thirsted for homes of their own. One southerner noted with surprise in her diary that

Uncle Lewis, the pious, the honored, the venerated, gets his poor old head turned with false notions of freedom and independence, runs off to the Yankees with a pack of lies against his mistress, and sets up a claim to part of her land!

Lewis simply wanted a new beginning. Like millions of other freedmen, he hoped to leave slavery behind.

But no one could say how much of a chance the whites, who were in power, would give to blacks. During the war the federal government had refused to arm black volunteers. Many whites agreed with Corporal Felix Brannigan of the Seventy-fourth New York Regiment. "We don't want to fight side and side with the nigger," he said. "We think we are a too superior race for that." In September 1862 Abraham Lincoln said, "If we were to arm [the Negroes], I fear that in a few weeks the arms would be in the hands of the rebels."

Necessity forced a change in policy; because the war was going badly the administration authorized black enlistments. By spring 1863 black troops were proving their value. One general reported that his "colored regiments" possessed "remarkable aptitude for military training," and another observer said, "They fight like fiends." Lincoln came to see "the colored population" as "the great *available* and yet *unavailed of* force for restoring the Union," and recruitment proceeded rapidly.

Black leaders hoped that military service would secure equal rights for their people. Once the black soldier had fought for the Union, wrote Frederick Douglass, "there is no power on earth which can deny that he has earned the right of citizenship in the United States." If black soldiers turned the tide, asked another man, "Would the nation refuse us our rights . . .? Would it refuse us our vote?"

Wartime experience seemed to prove it would. Despite their valor, black soldiers faced persistent discrimination. In Ohio, for example, a mob shouting "Kill the nigger" attacked an off-duty soldier; on

duty, blacks did most of the "fatigue duty," or heavy labor. Moreover, black soldiers were expected to accept inferior pay as they risked their lives. The government paid white privates $13 per month plus a clothing allowance of $3.50. Black troops earned $10 per month less $3 deducted for clothing. Blacks resented this injustice so deeply that in protest two regiments refused to accept any pay, and eventually Congress remedied the discrimination.

Still, this was only a small victory over prejudice; the general attitude of northerners on racial questions was mixed. Abolitionists and many Republicans helped black Americans fight for equal rights, and they won some victories. In 1864 the federal courts accepted black testimony, and New York City desegregated its streetcars. The District of Columbia did the same in 1865, the year the Thirteenth Amendment won ratification. One state, Massachusetts, enacted a comprehensive public accommodations law. On the other hand, there were many more signs of resistance to racial equality. The Democratic party fought against equality, charging that Republicans favored race-mixing and were undermining the status of the white worker. Voters in three states—Connecticut, Minnesota, and Wisconsin—rejected black suffrage in 1865. The racial attitudes of northerners seemed mixed and uncertain.

This was a significant fact, for the history of emancipation in the British Caribbean indicated that, if equality were to be won, the North would have to take a strong and determined stand. In 1833 Great Britain had abolished slavery in its possessions, providing slaveowners with £20 million in compensation plus the benefit of a six-year apprenticeship over all former agricultural slaves. Despite such generosity to the slaveowners, the transition to free labor had not been easy.

Everywhere in the British Caribbean planters fought tenaciously to maintain control over their laborers. Retaining control of local government, the planters fashioned laws, taxes, and administrative decisions with an eye to keeping freedmen on the plantations. With equal determination, the former slaves attempted to move onto small plots of land and raise food crops instead of sugar. They wanted independence and were not interested in raising export crops for the world market. The British, even abolitionists, however,

These schoolteachers were part of Gideon's Band, volunteers sent by northern religious organizations to aid the freed people in Beaufort and Port Royal, South Carolina. Thousands followed their example during Reconstruction. Western Reserve Historical Society, Cleveland, Ohio.

judged the success of emancipation by the volume of production for the market. Their concern for the freedmen soon faded, and before long the authorities assisted planters further by allowing the importation of indentured "coolie" labor from India.

In the United States, some of the same tendencies had appeared on the Sea Islands long before the war ended. The planters had fled and therefore were not present to try to control their former slaves. The freedmen, however, showed a strong desire to leave the plantations and establish small, self-sufficient farms of their own. Northern missionaries, soldiers, and officials brought education and aid to the freedmen but also wanted them to grow cotton. They disapproved of charity and emphasized the values of competitive capitalism. "The danger to the Negro," wrote one worker in the Sea Islands, was "too high wages."

Indeed it would be "most unwise and injurious," declared another worker, to give former slaves free land.

"The Yankees preach nothing but cotton, cotton!" complained one Sea Island black. "We wants land," wrote another, "this very land that is rich with the sweat of we face and the blood of we back." Asking only for a chance to buy land, this man complained that "they make the lots too big, and cut we out." Indeed, the government did sell thousands of acres in the Sea Islands for nonpayment of taxes, but when blacks pooled their earnings to buy almost 2,000 of the 16,749 acres sold in March 1863, 90 percent of the land went to wealthy investors from the North. Thus even among their northern supporters, the former slaves had received only partial support. How much opportunity would freedom bring? That was a major question to be answered during Reconstruction, and the answer depended on the evolution of policy in Washington.

JOHNSON'S RECONSTRUCTION PLAN

Throughout 1865 the formation of Reconstruction policy rested solely with Andrew Johnson, for shortly before he became president Congress recessed and did not reconvene until December. In the nearly eight months that intervened, Johnson devised his own plan and put it into operation. He decided to form new governments in the South by using his power to grant pardons.

Johnson had a few precedents to follow in Lincoln's wartime plans for Reconstruction. In December 1863 Lincoln has proposed a "10-percent" plan for a gov-
Lincoln's Reconstruction Plan ernment being organized in captured portions of Louisiana. According to this plan, a state government could be established as soon as 10 percent of those who had voted in 1860 took an oath of future loyalty. Only high-ranking Confederate officials would be denied a chance to take the oath, and Lincoln urged that at least a few well-qualified blacks be given the ballot. Radicals bristled, however, at such a mild plan, and a majority of Congress (in the Wade-Davis bill, which Lincoln pocket-vetoed) favored stiffer requirements and stronger proof of loyalty.

Later, in 1865, Lincoln suggested but then abandoned more lenient terms. At Hampton Roads, where he raised questions about the extent of emancipation (see page 401), Lincoln discussed compensation and restoration to the Union, with full rights, of the very state governments that had tried to leave it. Then in April he considered allowing the Virginia legislature to convene in order to withdraw its support from the Confederate war effort. Faced with strong opposition in his cabinet, however, Lincoln reversed himself, denying that he had intended to confer legitimacy

Combative and inflexible, President Andrew Johnson contributed greatly to the failure and rejection of his own reconstruction program. Library of Congress.

on a rebel government. At the time of his death, Lincoln had given general approval to a plan drafted by Secretary of War Stanton that would have imposed military authority and provisional governors as steps toward new state governments. Beyond these general outlines, it is impossible to say what Lincoln would have done had he survived.

Johnson began with the plan Stanton had drafted for consideration by the cabinet. At a cabinet meeting on May 9, 1865, Johnson's advisors split evenly on the question of voting rights for freedmen in the South. Johnson said that he favored black suffrage, but only if the southern states adopted it voluntarily. A champion of states' rights, he regarded this decision as too important to be taken out of the hands of the states.

Such conservatism had an enduring effect on Johnson's policies, but at first it appeared that his old enmity toward the planters might produce a plan for radical changes in class relations among whites. As he appointed provisional governors in the South, Johnson also proposed rules that would keep the wealthy planter class out of power. He required every southern voter to swear an oath of loyalty as a condition of gaining amnesty or pardon. But some southerners would face special difficulties in regaining their rights.

Johnson barred certain classes of southerners from taking the oath and gaining amnesty. Former federal officials who had violated their oaths to support the United States and had aided the Confederacy could not take the oath. Nor could graduates of West Point or Annapolis who had resigned their commissions to fight for the South. The same was true for high-ranking Confederate officers and Confederate political leaders. To this list Johnson added another important group: all southerners who aided the rebellion and whose taxable property was worth more than $20,000. Such individuals had to apply personally to the president for pardon and restoration of political rights, or risk legal penalties, which included confiscation of their land.

Oaths of Amnesty and New State Governments

Thus it appeared that the South's old leadership class would be removed from power, for virtually all the rich and powerful whites of prewar days needed Johnson's special pardon. Many observers, South and North, sensed that the president meant to take his revenge on the haughty aristocrats whom he had always denounced and to raise up a new leadership of deserving yeomen.

Johnson's provisional governors began the Reconstruction process by calling constitutional conventions. The delegates chosen for these conventions had to draft new constitutions eliminating slavery and invalidating secession. After ratification of these constitutions, new governments could be elected, and the states would be restored to the Union with full congressional representation. But no southerners could participate in this process who had not taken the oath of amnesty or who had been ineligible to vote on the day the state seceded. Thus freedmen could not participate in the conventions. Although it was theoretically possible for the white delegates to enfranchise them, such action was at best unlikely.

If Johnson intended to end the power of the old elite, his plan did not work out as he had hoped. The old white leadership proved resilient and influential; prominent Confederates (a few with pardons, but many without) won elections and turned up in various appointive offices. Then, surprisingly, Johnson helped to subvert his own plan. He started pardoning aristocrats and chief rebels, who should not have been in office. By fall 1865 the clerks at the pardon office were straining under the burden, and additional staff had to be hired to churn out the necessary documents. These pardons, plus the return of planters' abandoned lands, put the old elite back in power.

Why did Johnson issue so many pardons? Perhaps vanity betrayed his judgment. Scores of gentlemen of the type who had previously scorned him now waited on him for an appointment. Too long a lonely outsider, Johnson may have succumbed to the attention and flattery of these pardon-seekers. Whether he did or not, he clearly had allowed himself too little time. It took months for the constitution-making and elections to run their course; by the time the process was complete and Confederate leaders had emerged in powerful positions, the reconvening of Congress was near. Johnson faced a choice between admitting failure and scrapping his entire effort or swallowing hard and supporting what had resulted. He decided to stand behind his new governments and declare Reconstruction completed. Thus in December 1865 many Confederate congressmen traveled to Washington to claim seats in the United States Congress, and Alexander Stephens, vice president of the Confederacy, returned to the capital as senator-elect.

Many northerners frowned on the election of such prominent rebels, and there were other results of Johnson's program that sparked negative comment in the North. Some of the state conventions were slow to repudiate secession; others only grudgingly admitted that slavery was dead. Two refused to take any action to repudiate the large Confederate debt. Northerners interpreted these actions as signs of defiance; subsequent legislation defining the status of freedmen confirmed their worst fears. Some legislatures merely revised large sections of the slave codes by substituting the word *freedman* for *slave,* and new laws written from scratch were also very restrictive. In these Black Codes, former slaves who were supposed to be free were compelled to carry passes, observe a curfew, live in housing provided by a landowner, and give up hope of entering many desirable occupations.

Black Codes

Finally, observers noted that the practice in state-supported institutions, such as schools and orphanages, was to exclude blacks altogether. To northerners, the South seemed intent on returning black people to a position of servility.

Thus it was not surprising that a majority of northern congressmen decided to take a close look at the results of Johnson's plan. On reconvening, they voted not to admit the newly elected southern representatives, whose credentials were subject under the Constitution to congressional scrutiny. The House and Senate established a joint committee to examine Johnson's policies and advise on new ones. Reconstruction had entered a second phase, one in which Congress would play a strong role.

THE CONGRESSIONAL RECONSTRUCTION PLAN

Northern congressmen disagreed on what to do, but they did not doubt their right to play a role in Reconstruction. The Constitution mentioned neither secession nor reunion, but it did assign a great many major responsibilities to Congress. Among them was the injunction to guarantee to each state a republican government. Under this provision, the legislators thought, they could devise policies for Reconstruction, just as Johnson had used his power to pardon for the same purpose.

They soon found that other constitutional questions had a direct bearing on the policies they followed. What, for example, had the fact of rebellion done to the relationship between southern states and the Union? Lincoln had always insisted that the Union remained unbroken, but not even Andrew Johnson could accept the southern view that the wartime state governments of the South could merely re-enter the nation. Johnson argued that the Union had endured, though individuals had erred; thus the use of his power to grant or withhold pardons. But congressmen who favored vigorous Reconstruction measures tended to argue that war *had* broken the Union. The southern

states had committed legal suicide and reverted to the status of territories, they argued, or the South was a conquered nation subject to the victor's will. Moderate congressmen held that the states had forfeited their rights through rebellion, and had thus come under congressional supervision.

These diverse theories mirrored the diversity of Congress itself. Northern legislators fell into four major categories: Democrats, conservative Republicans, moderate Republicans, and Radical Republicans. No one of these groups had decisive power. In terms of ideology the majority of congressmen were conservative. In terms of partisan politics the Republican party had a majority, but there was considerable distance between conservative Republicans, who desired a limited federal role in Reconstruction and were fairly happy with Johnson's actions, and the Radicals. These men, led by Thaddeus Stevens, Charles Sumner, and George Julian, were a minority within their party, but they had the advantage of a clearly defined goal. They believed that it was essential to democratize the South, establish public education, and ensure the rights of freedmen. They favored black suffrage, often supported land confiscation and redistribution, and were willing to exclude the South from the Union for several years if necessary to achieve their goals. Between these two factions lay the moderates, who held the balance of power.

The Radicals

One overwhelming political reality faced all the groups in Congress: the 1866 elections were approaching in the fall. Since Congress had questioned Johnson's program, its members had to develop some modification or alternative program before the elections. The northern public expected them to develop a new Reconstruction plan, and as politicians they knew better than to go before their constituents empty-handed. Thus they had to forge a majority coalition composed either of Democrats and Republicans or various elements of the Republican party. The kind of coalition that formed would determine the kind of plan that Congress developed.

Ironically, it was Johnson and the Democrats that pushed Congress toward Radical rather than conservative policies. The president and the Democrats in Congress refused to cooperate with conservative or moderate Republicans. They insisted, despite evidence of widespread concern, that Reconstruction was over, that the new state governments were legitimate, and that southern representatives should be admitted to Congress. These unrealistic, intransigent positions threw away the Democrats' potential influence and blasted any possibility of bipartisan compromise. Republicans found themselves all lumped together by Democrats; to form a new program, conservative Republicans had to work with the Radicals. Thus bargaining over changes in the Johnson program went on almost entirely within the party.

This development and subsequent events enhanced the influence of the Radicals. But in 1865, Republican congressmen were at first loath to break with the president; he was, for better or worse, the titular head of their party, so they made one last effort to work with him. Early in 1866 many lawmakers thought a compromise had been reached. Under its terms Johnson would agree to two modifications of his program. The life of the Freedmen's Bureau, which fed the hungry, negotiated labor contracts, and started schools, would be extended; and a civil rights bill would be passed to counteract the black codes. This bill, drawn up by a conservative Republican, was designed to force southern courts to recognize equality before the law by giving federal judges the power to remove cases in which blacks were treated unfairly. Its provisions applied to discrimination by private persons as well as government officials. As the first major bill to enforce the Thirteenth Amendment's abolition of slavery, it was a significant piece of legislation, and it became very important in the twentieth century (see page 948).

Congress Struggles for a Compromise

But in spring 1866, Johnson destroyed the compromise by vetoing both bills (they were later repassed). Denouncing any change in his program, the president condemned Congress's action in inflammatory language. In so doing he questioned the legitimacy of congressional involvement in policymaking and revealed his own racism. Because the Civil Rights Bill defined United States citizens as native-born persons who were taxed, Johnson pronounced it discriminatory toward "large numbers of intelligent, worthy, and patriotic foreigners . . . in favor of the negro." The bill, he said, would "operate in favor of the colored and against the white race."

All hope of working with the president was now gone. But Republican congressmen sensed that their constituents remained dissatisfied with the results of Reconstruction. Violence in the South—notably in Memphis and New Orleans, where police aided brutal raids on black citizens—also convinced Republicans, and the northern public, that more needed to be done. The Republican lawmakers therefore pushed on, and from bargaining among their various factions there emerged a plan. It took the form of a proposed amendment to the Constitution—the fourteenth—and it represented a compromise between radical and conservative elements of the party. The Fourteenth Amendment was Congress's alternative to Johnson's program of Reconstruction.

Of four points in the amendment, there was nearly universal agreement on one: the Confederate debt was declared null and void, the war debt of the United States guaranteed. Northerners uniformly rejected the notion of paying taxes to reimburse those who had financed a rebellion; and business groups agreed on the necessity of upholding the credit of the United States government. There was also fairly general support for altering the personnel of southern governments. In language that harkened back to Johnson's Amnesty Proclamation, the Fourteenth Amendment prohibited political power for prominent Confederates. Only at the discretion of Congress, by a two-thirds vote of each house, could these political penalties be removed.

Fourteenth Amendment

The section of the Fourteenth Amendment that would have by far the greatest legal significance in later years was the first (see Appendix). On its face, this section was an effort to strike down the black codes and guarantee basic rights to freedmen. It conferred citizenship on freedmen and prohibited states from abridging their constitutional "privileges and immunities." Similarly, the amendment barred any state from taking a person's life, liberty, or property "without due process of law" and from denying "equal protection of the laws." These clauses were phrased broadly enough to become in time powerful guarantees of black Americans' civil rights, indeed, of the rights of all citizens. They also took on added meaning with court rulings that corporations were legally "persons" (see page 487).

The second section of the amendment, which dealt with representation, clearly revealed the compromises and political motives that had produced the document. Northerners, in Congress and out, disagreed whether black citizens should have the right to vote. Commenting on the ambivalent nature of northern opinion, a citizen of Indiana wrote that there was strong feeling in favor of "humane and liberal laws for the government and protection of the colored population." But he admitted to a southern relative that there was prejudice, too. "Although there is a great deal [of] profession among us for the relief of the darkey yet I think much of it is far from being cincere. I guess we want to compell you to do right by them while we are not willing ourselves to do so."

Republican congressmen shied away from confronting this ambivalence, but political reality required them to do something. Under the Constitution, representation was based on population. During slavery each black slave had counted as three-fifths of a person for purposes of congressional representation. Republicans feared that emancipation, which made every former slave five-fifths of a person, might increase the South's power in Congress. If it did, and if blacks were not allowed to vote, the former secessionists would gain seats in Congress.

What a strange result that would seem to most northerners. They had never planned to reward the South for rebellion, and Republicans in Congress were determined not to hand over power to their political enemies. So they offered the South a choice. According to the second section of the Fourteenth Amendment, states did not have to give black men the right to vote. But if they did not do so, their representation would be reduced proportionally. If they did, it would be increased proportionally—but Republicans would be able to appeal to the new black voters. This compromise protected northern interests and gave Republicans a chance to compete if freedmen gained the ballot.

The Fourteenth Amendment dealt with the voting rights of black men but ignored female citizens, black and white. For this reason it elicited a strong reaction from the women's rights movement. Advocates of equal rights for women had worked with abolitionists for decades, often subordinating their cause to that of the slaves. During the drafting of the Fourteenth Amendment, however, female activists demanded to be heard. When legislators defined them as nonvoting citizens, prominent women's leaders such as Elizabeth

Cady Stanton and Susan B. Anthony decided that it was time to end their alliance with abolitionists. Thus the independent women's rights movement grew.

In 1866, however, the major question in Reconstruction politics was how the public would respond to the amendment. Would the northern public support Congress's plan or the president's?

Southern Rejection of the Fourteenth Amendment

Johnson did his best to block the Fourteenth Amendment and to convince northerners to reject it. Condemning Congress's plan and its refusal to seat southern representatives, the president urged state legislatures in the South to vote against ratification. Every southern legislature except Tennessee's rejected the amendment by a large margin. It did best in Alabama, where it failed by a vote of 69 to 8 in the assembly and 27 to 2 in the senate. In three states the amendment received no support at all.

To present his case to northerners, Johnson arranged a National Union convention to publicize his program. The chief executive also took to the stump himself. In an age when active personal campaigning was rare for a president, Johnson boarded a special train for a "swing around the circle" that carried his message far into the Midwest and then back to Washington. In cities such as Cleveland and St. Louis, Johnson castigated the Republicans in his old stump-speaker style. But increasingly audiences rejected his views and hooted and jeered at him.

The election was a resounding victory for Republicans in Congress. Men whom Johnson had denounced won re-election by large margins, and the Republican majority increased as some new candidates defeated incumbent Democrats. Everywhere Radical and moderate Republicans gained strength. The section of the country that had won the war had spoken clearly: Johnson's policies, people feared, were giving the advantage to rebels and traitors. Thus Republican congressional leaders received a mandate to continue with their Reconstruction plan.

But, thanks largely to Johnson, that plan had reached an impasse. All but one of the southern governments created by the president had turned their backs on the Fourteenth Amendment, determined to resist. Nothing could be accomplished as long as those governments existed and as long as the southern electorate was constituted as it was. The newly elected northern Republicans were not going to ignore their constituents' wishes and surrender to the South. To break the deadlock, Republicans had little choice but to form new governments and enfranchise the freedmen. They therefore decided to do both. The unavoidable logic of the situation had forced the majority toward the Radical plan.

The Radicals hoped Congress would do much more. Thaddeus Stevens, for example, argued that economic opportunity was essential to the freedmen. "If we do not furnish them with homesteads from forfeited and rebel property, and hedge them around with protective laws; if we leave them to the legislation of their late masters, we had better left them in bondage," Stevens declared. To provide that opportunity, Stevens drew up a plan for extensive confiscation and redistribution of land. Significantly, only one-tenth of the land affected by his plan was earmarked for freedmen, in 40-acre plots. All the rest was to be sold, to generate money for veterans' pensions, compensation to loyal citizens for damaged property, and payment of the federal debt. By these means Stevens hoped to win support for a basically unpopular measure. But he failed; and in general the Radicals were not able to command the support of the majority of the public. Northerners of that era were accustomed to a limited role for government, and the business community staunchly opposed any interference in private property.

As a result, the Military Reconstruction Act that was passed in 1867 incorporated only a small part of the Radical program. The act called for new governments in the South, with a return **Military Reconstruction Act of 1867** to military authority in the interim. It barred from political office those Confederate leaders listed in the Fourteenth Amendment. It guaranteed freedmen the right to vote in elections for state constitutional conventions and for subsequent state governments. In addition, each southern state was required to ratify the Fourteenth Amendment; to ratify its new constitution; and to submit the new constitution to Congress for approval. Thus black people gained an opportunity to fight for a better life through the political process. The only weapon put into their hands was the ballot, however. The law required no redistribution of land and guaranteed no basic changes in southern social structure. It also permitted an early return to the Union.

Congress's role as the architect of Reconstruction was not quite over, for its quarrels with Andrew Johnson grew more bitter. To restrict Johnson's influence and safeguard its plan, Congress passed a number of controversial laws. First it set the date for its own reconvening—an unprecedented act, since the president had traditionally summoned the legislature to Washington. Then it limited Johnson's power over the army by requiring the president to issue military orders through the General of the Army, Ulysses S. Grant, who could not be sent from Washington without the Senate's consent. Finally, Congress passed the Tenure of Office Act, which gave the Senate power to interfere with changes in the president's cabinet. Designed to protect Secretary of War Stanton, who sympathized with the Radicals, this law violated the tradition that a president controlled his own cabinet.

Johnson took several belligerent steps of his own. He issued orders to military commanders in the South limiting their powers and increasing the powers of the civil governments he had created in 1865. Then he removed army officers who conscientiously enforced Congress's new law, preferring commanders who allowed disqualified Confederates to vote. Finally, in August 1867 he tried to remove Secretary of War Stanton. With this act the confrontation reached its climax.

Twice before, the House Judiciary Committee had considered impeachment, rejecting the idea once and then recommending it by only a 5-to-4 vote. That recommendation had been decisively **Impeachment of President Johnson** defeated by the House. After Johnson's last action, however, a third attempt to impeach the president carried easily. In 1868, the angry House was so determined to indict Johnson that it voted before drawing up specific charges. The indictment concentrated on Johnson's violation of the Tenure of Office Act, though modern scholars regard his systematic efforts to impede enforcement of the Military Reconstruction Act as a far more serious offense.

Johnson's trial in the Senate lasted more than three months. The prosecution, led by such Radicals as Thaddeus Stevens and Benjamin Butler, argued that Johnson was guilty of "high crimes and misdemeanors." But they also advanced the novel idea

Chapter 15: RECONSTRUCTION BY TRIAL AND ERROR, 1865–1877

The confrontation between Congress and Andrew Johnson culminated in the president's impeachment. Here the Senate begins his trial, which ended in acquittal by a margin of one vote.   Library of Congress.

that impeachment was a political matter, not a judicial trial of guilt or innocence. The Senate ultimately rejected such reasoning, which would have transformed impeachment into a political weapon against any chief executive who disagreed with Congress. Though a majority of senators voted to convict Johnson, the prosecution fell one vote short of the necessary two-thirds majority. Johnson remained in office for the few months left in his term, and his acquittal established the precedent that only serious misdeeds merited removal from office.

In 1869, in an effort to write democratic principles and color-blindness into the Constitution, the Radicals succeeded in presenting the Fifteenth Amendment for ratification. This measure forbade states to deny the right to vote "on account of race, color, or previous condition of servitude." Ironically, the votes of four uncooperative southern states—

Fifteenth Amendment

required by Congress to approve the amendment as an added condition to rejoining the Union—proved necessary to impose this principle on parts of the North. Although several states outside the South refused to ratify, the Fifteenth Amendment became law in 1870.

RECONSTRUCTION POLITICS IN THE SOUTH

From the start, Reconstruction encountered the resistance of white southerners. Their opposition to change appeared in the black codes and other policies of the Johnson governments as well as in

Thomas Nast, in this 1868 cartoon, pictured the combination of forces—southern opposition and northern racism and indifference—that threatened the success of Reconstruction. *Library of Congress.*

their owners "didn't tell them it was freedom" or "wouldn't let [them] go." Agents of the Freedmen's Bureau in North Carolina agreed. One agent in Georgia concluded, "I find the old system of slavery working with even more rigor than formerly at a few miles distant from any point where U.S. troops are stationed." To hold onto their workers some landowners claimed control over black children and used guardianship and apprentice laws to bind black families to the plantation.

Whites also blocked blacks from acquiring land. Though a few planters divided up plots among their slaves, most condemned the idea of making blacks landowners. One planter in South Carolina refused to sell as little as an acre and a half to each family. Even a Georgian whose family was known for its concern for the slaves was outraged that two property owners planned to "rent their lands to the Negroes!" Such action was "injurious to the best interest of the community." The son of a free black landowner in Virginia who sold nearly two hundred acres to former slaves explained, "White folks wasn't lettin' Negroes have nothing."

Such adamant resistance by propertied whites soon manifested itself in other ways, including violence. In one North Carolina town a local magistrate clubbed a black man on a public street, and bands of "Regulators" terrorized blacks in parts of that state and Kentucky. Such incidents were predictable in a society in which many planters believed, as a South Carolinian put it, that blacks "can't be governed except with the whip."

After President Johnson encouraged the South to resist congressional Reconstruction, many white conservatives worked hard to capture the new state governments. Elsewhere, large numbers of whites boycotted the polls in an attempt to defeat Congress's plans. Since the new constitutions had to be approved by a majority of registered voters, registered whites could defeat them by sitting out the elections. This tactic was tried in North Carolina and succeeded in Alabama, forcing Congress to readjust and base ratification on a majority of those voting.

Very few black men stayed away from the polls. Enthusiastically and hopefully they seized the opportunity to participate in politics, voting solidly Republican. Most agreed with one man who felt that he should "stick to the end with the party that freed

private attitudes. Many whites set their faces against emancipation, and—as was true in

White Resistance

the British Caribbean—the former planter class proved especially unbending. In 1866 a Georgia newspaper frankly declared, "Most of the white citizens believe that the institution of slavery was right, and . . . they will believe that the condition, which comes nearest to slavery, that can now be established will be the best." Unwillingness to accept black freedom would have been a major problem in any circumstances; Andrew Johnson's encouragement of southern whites actively to resist Congress, only intensified the problem.

Fearing the end of their control over slaves, some planters attempted to postpone freedom by denying or misrepresenting events. Former slaves reported that

me." Illiteracy did not prohibit blacks (or uneducated whites) from making intelligent choices. Although William Henry could read only "a little," he testified that he and his friends had no difficulty selecting the Republican ballot. "We stood around and watched," he explained. "We saw D. Sledge vote; he owned half the county. We knowed he voted Democratic so we voted the other ticket so it would be Republican."

Zeal for voting spread through the entire black community. Women, who could not vote, encouraged their husbands and sons, and preachers exhorted their congregations to use the franchise. Such community spirit helped to counter white pressure tactics, and the freedmen's enthusiasm showed their hunger for equal rights.

With a large black turnout, and with prominent Confederates barred from politics under the Fourteenth Amendment, a new southern Republican party came to power in the constitutional conventions. Some blacks won seats as delegates, along with northerners who had moved to the South and some native southern whites. Together they brought the South's fundamental law into line with progressive reforms that had been adopted in the rest of the nation. The new constitutions were more democratic—they eliminated property qualifications for voting and holding office, and they made state and local offices elective that had been appointive. They provided for public schools and institutions to care for the mentally ill, the blind, the deaf, the destitute, and the orphaned, and they ended imprisonment for debt and barbarous punishments such as branding.

The conventions also broadened women's rights in possession of property and divorce. Usually, the main goal was not to make women equal but to provide relief to thousands of suffering debtors. In families left poverty-stricken by the war and weighed down by debts, the husband had usually contracted the debts. Thus, giving women legal control over their own property provided some protection to their families. There were some delegates, however, whose goal was to elevate women. Blacks in particular called for women's suffrage but were ignored by their white colleagues.

Under these new constitutions the southern states elected new governments. Again the Republican party triumphed, bringing new men into positions of power.

Triumph of Republican Governments The ranks of state legislators in 1868 included black southerners for the first time in history. Congress's second plan for Reconstruction was well under way. It remained to be seen what these new governments would do and how much change they would bring to society.

There was one possibility of radical change through these new governments. That possibility depended on the disfranchisement of substantial numbers of Confederate leaders. If the Republican regimes used their new power to exclude many whites from politics, as punishment for rebellion, they would have a solid electoral majority based on black voters and their white allies. Land reform and the assurance of racial equality would be possible. But none of the Republican governments did this, or even gave it serious consideration.

Why did the new legislators shut the door on the possibility of deep and thoroughgoing reform? First, they appreciated the realities of power and the depth of racial enmity. In most states whites were the majority, and former slaveowners controlled the best land and other sources of economic power. James Lynch, a leading black politician from Mississippi, candidly explained why Negroes shunned "the folly of" disfranchisement. Unlike northerners who "can leave when it becomes too uncomfortable," former slaves "must be in friendly relations with the great body of the whites in the state. Otherwise . . . peace can be maintained only by a standing army."

Second, blacks believed in the principle of universal suffrage and the Christian goal of reconciliation. Far from being vindictive toward the race that had enslaved them, they treated leading rebels with generosity and appealed to white southerners to adopt a spirit of fairness and cooperation. Henry McNeil Turner, like other Negro ministers, urged black Georgians to "love whites . . . soon their prejudice would melt away, and with God for our father, we will all be brothers." (Years later Turner criticized his own naiveté, saying that in the constitutional convention his motto had been, "Anything to please the white folks.") Therefore southern Republicans quickly (in come cases immediately) restored the voting rights of former Confederates, as Congress steadily released more individuals from the penalties of the Fourteenth Amendment.

Thus the South's Republican party committed itself

to a strategy of winning white support. To put the matter another way, the Republican party condemned itself to defeat if white voters would not cooperate. In a few short years Republicans were reduced to the embarrassment of making futile appeals to whites while ignoring the claims of their strongest supporters, blacks.

But for a time both Republicans and their opponents, who called themselves Conservatives or Democrats, moved to the center and appealed for support from a broad range of groups. Some propertied whites accepted congressional Reconstruction as a reality and declared that they would try to compete under the new rules. As these Democrats angled for some black votes, Republicans sought to attract more white voters. Both parties found an area of agreement in economic policies.

The Reconstruction governments devoted themselves to stimulating industry. This policy reflected northern ideals, of course, but it also sprang from a

**Industrial-
ization**

growing southern interest in industrialization. Confederates had learned how vital industry was, and many postwar southerners were eager to build up the manufacturing capacity of their region. Accordingly, Reconstruction legislatures designed many tempting inducements to investment. Loans, subsidies, and exemptions from taxation for periods up to ten years helped to bring new industries into the region. The southern railroad system was rebuilt and expanded, coal and iron mining laid the basis for Birmingham's steel plants, and the number of manufacturing establishments nearly doubled between 1860 and 1880. But this emphasis on big business interests also locked Republicans into a conservative strategy. They were appealing to elite whites who never responded, and the alternate possibility of making a strong, class-based appeal to poorer whites was lost.

Policies appealing to black voters never went beyond equality before the law. In fact, the whites who controlled the southern Republican party were reluctant to allow blacks a share of offices proportionate to their electoral strength. Black leaders, aware of

**Other
Republican
Policies**

their weakness, did not push for revolutionary economic or social change. In every southern state blacks led efforts to establish public

schools, but most did not press for integrated facilities. Having a school to attend was the most important thing at the time, for the Johnson governments had excluded blacks from schools and other state-supported institutions. As a result, virtually every public school organized during Reconstruction was racially segregated, and these separate schools established a precedent for segregation. By the 1870s segregation was becoming a common practice in theaters, trains, and other public accommodations in the South.

A few black politicians did fight for civil rights and integration. Most were mulattoes from cities such as New Orleans or Mobile, where large populations of light-skinned free blacks had existed before the war. Their experience in such communities had made them sensitive to issues of status, and they spoke out for open and equal public accommodations. But they were a minority. Most elected black officials sought instead to make more limited but essential gains in the face of enormous white hostility.

Economic progress was uppermost in the minds of many of the freed people, especially politicians from agricultural districts. Land above all else had the potential to benefit the former slave, but none of the black state legislators promoted confiscation; freedmen simply lacked the power to make that possible. South Carolina established a land commission, but its purpose was to assist in the purchase of land. Any widespread redistribution of land had to arise from Congress, which never supported such action.

Within a few years, as centrists in both parties met failure, the other side of white reaction to congressional Reconstruction began to dominate. Some conservatives had always favored fierce opposition to Reconstruction through pressure and racist propaganda. They put economic and social pressure on blacks: one black Republican complained that "my neighbors will not employ me, nor sell me a farthing's worth of anything." Charging that the South had been turned over to ignorant blacks, conservatives deplored "black domination." The cry of "Negro rule" now became constant.

Such attacks were gross distortions. Blacks participated in politics but did not dominate or control events. They were a minority in eight out of ten state conventions (northerners were a minority in nine out of ten). Of the state legislatures, only in

Chapter 15: RECONSTRUCTION BY TRIAL AND ERROR, 1865–1877

the lower house in South Carolina did blacks ever constitute a majority; generally their numbers among officials were far inferior to their proportion in the population. Sixteen blacks won seats in Congress before Reconstruction was over, but none was ever elected governor. Freedmen were participating in government, to be sure, but there was no justification for racist denunciations of "Ethiopian minstrelsy, Ham radicalism in all its glory."

Conservatives also stepped up their propaganda against the allies of black Republicans. "Carpetbagger" was a derisive name for whites who had come from the North. It suggested an evil and **Carpetbaggers** greedy northern politician, recently **and Scalawags** arrived with a carpetbag into which he planned to stuff ill-gotten gains before fleeing. The stranger's carpetbag, a popular travel bag whose frame was covered with heavy carpet material, was presumably deep enough to hold all the loot stolen from southern treasuries and filched from hapless, trusting former slaves. Immigrants from the north, who held the largest share of Republican offices, were all tarred with this brush.

In fact most northerners who settled in the South arrived before Congress gave blacks the right to vote. They came seeking business opportunities or a warmer climate, and most never entered politics. Those who did generally wanted to democratize the South and to introduce northern ways, such as industry, public education, and the spirit of enterprise. Hard times and ostracism by white southerners made many of these men dependent on officeholding for a living, a fact that increased Republican factionalism and damaged the party. And although carpetbaggers supported black suffrage and educational opportunities, most opposed social equality and integration.

Conservatives invented the term "scalawag" to stigmatize and discredit any native white southerner who cooperated with the Republicans. A substantial number of southerners did so, including some wealthy and prominent men. Most scalawags, however, were representatives of the yeoman class, men from mountain areas and small farming districts—average white southerners who saw that they could benefit from the education and opportunities promoted by Republicans. Banding together with freedmen, they pursued common class interests and hoped to make headway against the power of long-dominant planters.

A poster celebrating the election of blacks to Congress during Reconstruction. From left to right across the top can be seen portraits of Senator Hiram R. Revels, Representative Benjamin S. Turner, the Reverend Richard Allen, Frederick Douglass, Representatives Josiah T. Walls and Joseph H. Rainy, and the writer William Wells Brown. Library of Congress.

Yet this black-white coalition was always vulnerable to the issue of race, and scalawags shied away from support for racial equality. Except on issues of common interest, scalawags often deserted the other elements of the Republican party.

Besides propaganda, the conservatives had other weapons to use against Reconstruction. Financially the Republican governments, despite their achievements, were doomed to be unpopular. Republicans wanted to continue prewar services, repair war's destruction, and support such important new ventures as public schools. But the Civil War had destroyed much of the South's tax base. One category of valuable property—slaves—was entirely gone. Hundreds of thousands of citizens had lost much of the rest of their real and personal property—money, livestock, fences, and buildings—to the war. Thus an increase

With the rise of the Ku Klux Klan, terrorism against blacks became more organized and purposeful. Note the racist overtones even in this northern illustration of Klan violence. The Bettmann Archive.

in taxes was necessary even to maintain traditional services, and new ventures required much higher taxes.

Corruption was another powerful charge levied against the Republicans. Unfortunately, it was true. Many carpetbaggers and black politicians sold their votes, taking part in what scholars recognize was a nationwide surge of corruption (see page 526). Although white Democrats often shared in the guilt, and despite the efforts of some Republicans to stop it, Democrats convinced many voters that scandal was the inevitable result of a foolish Reconstruction program based on blacks and carpetbaggers.

All these problems damaged the Republicans, but in many southern states the deathblow came through

violence: the murders, whippings, and intimidation of the Ku Klux Klan. Terrorism **Ku Klux Klan** against blacks had occurred throughout Reconstruction, but after 1867 white violence became more organized and purposeful. The Ku Klux Klan rode to frustrate Reconstruction and keep the freedmen in subjection. Nighttime visits, whippings, beatings, and murder became common, and in some areas virtually open warfare developed despite the authorities' efforts to keep the peace.

Although the Klan persecuted blacks who stood up for their rights as laborers or people, its main purpose was political. Lawless nightriders made active Republicans the target of their attacks. Prominent white Republicans and black leaders were killed in several states. After blacks who worked for a South Carolina scalawag started voting, terrorists visited the plantation and "whipped every nigger man they could lay their hands on." Klansmen also attacked Union League Clubs (Republican organizations that mobilized the black vote) and schoolteachers who were aiding the freedmen.

Klan violence was not simply spontaneous; certain social forces gave direction to racism. In North Carolina, for example, Alamance and Caswell counties were the sites of the worst Klan violence. They were in the Piedmont, where slim Republican majorities rested on cooperation between black voters and whites of the yeoman class, particularly yeomen whose Unionism or discontent with the Confederacy had turned them against local Democratic officials. Together these black and white Republicans had ousted officials long entrenched in power. But the Republican majority was a small one, and it would fail if either whites or blacks faltered in their support.

In Alamance and Caswell counties the wealthy and powerful men who had lost their accustomed political control organized the campaign of terror. They brought it into being and used it for their purposes. They were the secret organization's county officers and local chieftains; they recruited members and planned atrocities. They used the Klan to regain political power: by whipping up racism or frightening enough Republicans, the Ku Klux Klan could split the Republican coalition and restore a Democratic majority.

Thus a combination of difficult fiscal problems, Republican mistakes, racial hostility, and terror brought down the Republican regimes, and in most southern states so-called Radical

Failure of Reconstruction

Reconstruction was over after only a few years. But the most lasting failure of Reconstruction governments was not political—it was social. The new governments failed to alter the southern social structure or its distribution of wealth and power. Exploited as slaves, freedmen remained vulnerable to exploitation during Reconstruction. Without land of their own, they were dependent on white landowners, who could use their economic power to compromise blacks' political freedom. Armed only with the ballot, southern blacks had little chance to effect major changes.

To reform the southern social order, Congress would have had to redistribute land; and never did a majority of congressmen favor such a plan. Radical Republicans like Albion Tourgée condemned Congress's timidity. Turning the freedman out on his own without advantages, said Tourgée, constituted "cheap philanthropy." Indeed, freedmen who had to live with the consequences of Reconstruction considered it a failure. The North should have "fixed some way for us," said former slaves, but instead it "threw all the Negroes on the world without any way of getting along."

Freedom had come, but blacks knew they "still had to depend on the southern white man for work, food, and clothing," and it was clear that most whites were hostile. Unless Congress exercised careful supervision over the South, the situation of the freedmen was sure to deteriorate. Whenever the North lost interest, Reconstruction would collapse.

THE SOCIAL AND ECONOMIC MEANING OF FREEDOM

Black southerners entered upon life after slavery hopefully, determinedly, but not naively. They had too much experience with white people to assume that all would be easy. As one man in Texas advised his son, even before the war was over, "our forever was going to be spent living among the Southerners, after they got licked." Expecting to meet with hostility, black people tried to gain as much as they could from their new circumstances. Often the most valued changes were personal ones—alterations in location, employer, or surroundings that could make an enormous difference to individuals or families.

One of the first decisions that many took was whether to leave the old plantation or remain. This meant making a judgment about where the chances of liberty and progress would be greatest. Former slaves drew upon their experiences in bondage to assess the whites with whom they had to deal. "Most all the Negroes that had good owners stayed with them," said one man, "but the others left." Not surprisingly, cruel slaveholders usually saw their former

Freed from slavery, blacks of all ages filled the schools to seek the education that had been denied them in bondage. Valentine Museum, Richmond, Virginia.

chattels walk off en masse. "And let me tell you," added one man who abandoned a harsh planter, "we sure cussed ole master out before we left there."

On new farms or old the newly freed men and women reached out for valuable things in life that had been denied them. One of these was education.

Education for Blacks

Whatever their age, blacks hungered for the knowledge in books that had been permitted only to whites. With freedom they filled the schools both day and night. On "log seats" or "a dirt floor," many freedmen studied their letters in old almanacs, discarded dictionaries, or whatever was available. Young children brought infants to school with them, and adults attended at night or after "the crops was laid by." Many a teacher had "to make herself heard over three other classes reciting in concert" in a small room, but the scholars kept coming. The desire to escape slavery's ignorance was so great that many blacks paid tuition, typically $1.00 or $1.50 a month, despite their poverty. This seemingly small amount

constituted one-tenth of many people's agricultural wage.

The federal government and northern reformers assisted this search for education. In its brief life the Freedmen's Bureau founded over four thousand schools, and idealistic men and women from the North established others and staffed them ably. The Yankee schoolmarm—dedicated, selfless, and religious—became an agent of progress in many southern communities. Thus, with the aid of religious and charitable organizations throughout the north, blacks began the nation's first assault on the problems created by slavery. The results included the beginnings of a public school system in each southern state and the enrollment of over 600,000 blacks in elementary school by 1877.

Blacks and their white allies also realized that higher education was essential—colleges and universities to train teachers and equip ministers and professionals for leadership. The American Missionary Association founded seven colleges, including Fisk and Atlanta universities, between 1866 and 1869. The Freedmen's Bureau helped to establish Howard University in Washington, D.C., and northern religious groups, such as Methodists, Baptists, and Congregationalists, supported dozens of seminaries, colleges, and teachers' colleges. By the late 1870s black churches had joined in the effort, founding numerous colleges despite their smaller financial resources. Though some of the new institutions did not survive, they brought knowledge to those who would educate others and laid a foundation for progress.

Even in Reconstruction blacks were choosing many highly educated individuals as leaders. Many blacks who won public office during Reconstruction came from the prewar elite of free people of color. This group had benefited from its association with wealthy whites, who were often blood relatives. Some planters had given their mulatto children outstanding educations. Francis Cardozo, who served in South Carolina's constitutional convention and was later that state's secretary of the treasury and secretary of state, had attended universities in Scotland and England. P. B. S. Pinchback, who became lieutenant governor of Louisiana, was the son of a planter who had sent him to school in Cincinnati at age nine. And the two black senators from Mississippi, Blanche K. Bruce and Hiram Revels, were both privileged in their educations. Bruce was the son of a planter who had provided tutoring on his plantation; Revels was the son of free North Carolina mulattoes who had sent him to Knox College in Illinois. These men and many self-educated former slaves brought experience as artisans, businessmen, lawyers, teachers, and preachers to political office.

While elected officials wrestled with the political tasks of Reconstruction, millions of former slaves concentrated on improving life at home, on their farms, and in their neighborhoods. A major goal of black men and women was to gain some living space for themselves and their families. Surrounded by an unfriendly white population, they sought to insulate themselves from white interference and to strengthen the bonds of their own community. Throughout the South they devoted themselves to reuniting their families, moving away from the slave quarters, and founding black churches. Given the eventual failure of Reconstruction, the practical gains that blacks made in their daily lives often proved the most enduring and significant changes of the period.

The search for long-lost family members was awe-inspiring. With only shreds of information to guide them, thousands of black people embarked on odysseys in search of a husband, wife, child, or parent. By relying on the black community for help and information, many succeeded in their quest, sometimes almost miraculously. Others walked through several states and never found their loved ones.

Reunification of Black Families

Husbands and wives who had belonged to different masters established homes together for the first time, and parents asserted the right to raise their own children. Saying "You took her away from me and didn' pay no mind to my cryin', so now I'm takin' her back home," one mother reclaimed a child whom the mistress had been raising in her own house. Another woman bristled when her old master claimed a right to whip her children, promptly informing him that "he warn't goin' to brush none of her chilluns no more." One girl recalled that her mistress had struck her soon after freedom. As if to clarify the new ground rules, this girl "grabbed her leg and would have broke her neck." The freedmen were too much at risk to act recklessly, but as one man put it, they were tired of punishment, and "they sure didn't take no more foolishment off of white folks."

Given the eventual failure of Reconstruction, many blacks, like this elderly couple, probably benefited most from small gains in their daily lives—greater freedom from white supervision, and more living space for themselves and their families. Valentine Museum, Richmond, Virginia.

Black people frequently wanted to minimize all contact with whites. "There is a prejudice against us . . . that will take years to get over," the Reverend Garrison Frazier told General Sherman in January 1865. To avoid contact with intrusive whites, who were used to supervising and controlling them, blacks abandoned the slave quarters and fanned out into distant corners of the land they worked. Some moved away to build new homes in the woods. "After the war my stepfather come," recalled Annie Young, "and got my mother and we moved out in the piney woods." Others described moving "across the creek to [themselves]" or building a "saplin house . . . back in the woods" or " 'way off in the woods." Some rural dwellers established small all-black settlements that still can be found today along the backroads of the South.

Even once-privileged slaves often shared this desire for independence and social separation. One man turned down the master's offer of the overseer's house as a residence and moved instead to a shack in "Free-town." He also declined to let the former owner grind his grain for free, because it "made him feel like a free man to pay for things just like anyone else." One couple, a carriage driver and trusted house servant during slavery, passed up the fine cooking of the "big house" so that they could move "in the colored settlement."

The other side of this distance from whites was closer communion within the black community. Freed from the restrictions and regulations of slavery, blacks could build their own institutions **Founding of** as they saw fit. The secret church **Black Churches** of slavery now came out into the open; in countless communities throughout the South, "some of the niggers started a brush arbor." A brush arbor was merely "a sort of . . . shelter with leaves for a roof," but the freedmen worshipped in it enthusiastically. "Preachin' and shouting sometimes lasted all day," ex-slaves recalled, for there were "glorious times then" when black people could worship together in freedom. Within a few years independent black branches of the Methodist and Baptist churches had attracted the great majority of black Christians in the South.

This desire to gain as much independence as possible carried over into the freedmen's economic arrangements. Since most former slaves lacked money to buy land, they preferred the next best thing—renting the land they worked. But many whites would not consider renting land to blacks; there was strong social pressure against it. And few blacks had the means to rent a farm. Therefore other alternatives had to be tried.

Northerners and officials of the Freedmen's Bureau favored contracts between owners and laborers. To northerners who believed in "free soil, free labor, free men," contracts and wages seemed the key to progress. For a few years the Freedmen's Bureau helped to draw up and enforce such contracts, but they proved unpopular with both blacks and whites. Owners often filled the contracts with detailed requirements that reminded blacks of their circumscribed lives under slavery. Disputes frequently arose over efficiency, lost time, and other matters. Besides, cash was not readily available in the early years of Reconstruction; times were hard and the failure of Confederate banks left the South with a shortage of credit facilities.

Black farmers and white landowners therefore turned to a system of sharecropping: in return for use of the land and "furnishing" (tools, mules, seed, a cabin, and food to last until harvest), the **Rise of the** farmer paid the landowner a share **Sharecropping** of his crop. The cost of food and **System** clothing was deducted from the crop before the owner took his share. Naturally, landowners tended to set their share at a high level, but blacks had some bargaining power. By holding out and refusing to make contracts at the end of the year, sharecroppers succeeded in lowering the owners' share to around one-half during Reconstruction.

The sharecropping system originated as a desirable compromise. It eased landowners' problems with cash and credit; blacks accepted it because it gave them a reasonable amount of freedom from daily supervision. Instead of working under a white overseer as in slavery, they were able to farm a plot of land on their own in family groups. But sharecropping later proved to be a disaster, both for blacks and for the South. Part of the problem lay in the fact that an unscrupulous owner in a discriminatory society had many opportunities to cheat a sharecropper. Owners and merchants frequently paid less for blacks' cotton than they paid for whites'. Greedy men could overcharge or manipulate records so that the sharecropper always stayed in debt. But the problem was even more fundamental than that.

Southern farmers were concentrating on cotton, a crop with a bright past and a dim future. During the Civil War, India, Brazil, and Egypt had begun to supply cotton to Britain; not until **Overdepen-** 1878 did the South recover its pre-**dence** war share of British cotton pur-**on Cotton** chases. This temporary loss of markets reduced per capita income, as did a decline in the amount of labor invested by the average southern farmer. Part of the exploitation of slavery had been the sending of black women and children into the fields. In freedom these people stayed at home, like their white counterparts, when possible. Black families valued human dignity more highly than the levels of production that had been achieved with the lash.

But even as southerners grew more cotton, matching and eventually surpassing prewar totals, their reward diminished. Cotton prices began a long decline whose causes merely coincided with the Civil War. From 1820 to 1860 world demand for cotton had grown at a rate of 5 percent per year; but from 1866 to 1895 the rate of growth was only 1.3 percent per year. By 1860 the English textile industry, world leader in production, had penetrated all the major new markets, and from that point on increases in demand were slight. As a result, when southern farmers planted more cotton they tended to depress the price.

In these circumstances overspecialization in cotton was a mistake. But most southern farmers had no choice. Landowners required sharecroppers to grow the prime cash crop, whose salability was sure. And due to the shortage of banks and credit in the South, white farmers often had to borrow from a local merchant, who insisted on cotton production to secure his loan. Thus southern agriculture slipped deeper and deeper into depression. Black sharecroppers struggled under a growing burden of debt that reduced their independence and bound them to landowners almost as oppressively as slavery had bound them to their masters. Many white farmers became debtors too and gradually lost their land. All these problems were serious, but few people in the North were paying attention.

THE END OF RECONSTRUCTION

The North's commitment to racial equality had never been total. And by the early 1870s it was evident that even its partial commitment was weakening. New issues were capturing people's attention, and soon voters began to look for reconciliation with southern whites. In the South Democrats won control of one state after another, and they threatened to defeat Republicans in the North as well. Before long the situation had returned to "normal" in the eyes of southern whites.

The Supreme Court, after first re-establishing its power, participated in the northern retreat from Reconstruction. During the Civil War the Court had been cautious and reluctant to assert itself. Reaction to the Dred Scott decision had been so violent, and the Union's wartime emergency so great, that the Court had refrained from blocking or interfering with government actions. The justices, for example, had breathed a collective sigh of relief when legal technicalities prevented them from reviewing the case of Clement Vallandigham, who had been convicted of aiding the enemy by a military court when regular civil courts were open (see page 407).

But in 1866 a similar case, *Ex parte Milligan,* reached the Court through proper channels. Lambdin P. Milligan of Indiana had participated in a plot to free Confederate prisoners of war and overthrow state governments; for these acts a military court had sentenced Milligan, a civilian, to death.

Supreme Court Decisions on Reconstruction

In sweeping language the Court declared that military trials were illegal when civil courts were open and functioning, thus indicating that it intended to reassert itself as a major force in national affairs. This decision could have led to a direct clash with Congress, which in 1867 established military districts and military courts in the initial phase of its Reconstruction program. But Congress altered part of the Court's jurisdiction; it was constitutionally empowered to do so, but had never taken such action before (or since). By altering the Court's jurisdiction, Congress protected its Reconstruction policy and avoided a confrontation.

In 1873, however, an important group of cases, the *Slaughter-House* cases, tested the scope and meaning of the Fourteenth Amendment. In 1869 the Louisiana legislature had granted one company a monopoly on the slaughtering of livestock in New Orleans. Rival butchers in the city promptly sued. Their attorney, former Supreme Court justice John A. Campbell, argued that the Fourteenth Amendment had revolutionized the constitutional system by bringing individual rights under federal protection. Campbell expressed what had been a major Radical goal: to nationalize civil rights and guard them from state interference. Over the years his argument would win acceptance, offering shelter from government regulation to corporate "persons" in the nineteenth century and providing protection for blacks and other minorities in the twentieth.

The Court did not go that far, however, in the *Slaughter-House* decision. In a blow to the hopes of blacks, it refused to accept Campbell's argument. Neither the "privileges and immunities" clause nor the "due process" clause of the amendment guaranteed the great basic rights of the Bill of Rights against state action, the justices said. State and national citizenship remained separate, with the former more important. National citizenship involved only such things as the right to travel freely from state to state and to use the navigable waters of the nation. Thus the Court limited severely the amendment's potential for securing the rights of black citizens.

In 1876 the Court regressed even further, emasculating the enforcement clause of the Fourteenth Amendment and interpreting the Fifteenth in a narrow and negative fashion. In *United States v. Cruikshank* the Court dealt with Louisiana whites who were indicted for attacking a meeting of blacks and conspiring to deprive them of their rights. The justices ruled that the Fourteenth Amendment did not extend federal power to cover the misdeeds of private individuals against other citizens; only flagrant state discrimination was covered. And in *United States v. Reese* the Court held that the Fifteenth Amendment did not guarantee a citizen's right to vote, but merely listed certain impermissible grounds for denying suffrage. Thus a path lay open for southern states to disfranchise blacks for supposedly nonracial reasons—lack of education, lack of property, or lack of descent from a grandfather qualified to vote before the Military Reconstruction Act. ("Grandfather clauses" became a way of excluding blacks from suffrage, since most blacks were slaves before Reconstruction and hence could not vote.)

The retreat from Reconstruction continued steadily in politics as well. In 1868 Ulysses S. Grant, running as a Republican, defeated Horatio Seymour, a Democrat of New York, in a presidential

Election of 1868

campaign that revived sectional divisions. Although he was not a Radical, Grant realized that Congress's program represented the wishes of northerners, and he supported a platform that praised congressional Reconstruction and endorsed Negro suffrage in the South. (The platform stopped short of endorsing black suffrage in the North.) The Democrats went in the opposite direction; their platform vigorously denounced Reconstruction. By associating themselves with rebellion and with Johnson's repudiated program, the Democrats went down to defeat in all but eight states, though the popular vote was fairly close.

In office Grant sometimes used force to support Reconstruction, but only when he had to. He hoped to avoid confrontation with the South, to erase the image of dictatorship that his military background summoned up. In fact, neither he nor Johnson had imposed anything approaching a military occupation on the South. Rapid demobilization had reduced a federal army of more than 1 million to 57,000 within a year of surrender. Thereafter the number of troops in the South continued to fall, until in 1874 there were only 4,082 in the southern states outside Texas. Throughout Reconstruction the strongest federal units were in Texas and the West, fighting Indians, not white southerners.

In 1870 and 1871 the violent campaigns of the Ku Klux Klan moved Congress to pass two Force Acts and an anti-Klan law. These acts (important precedents for the modern enforcement of civil rights) permitted martial law and suspension of the writ of habeas corpus to combat murders, beatings, and threats by the Klan. Federal troops and prosecutors used them vigorously but unsuccessfully, for a conspiracy of silence frustrated many prosecutions. Possible witnesses were frightened or unwilling to testify and juries unwilling to convict. Thereafter the Klan disbanded officially and went underground. Paramilitary organizations known as Rifle Clubs and Red Shirts often took the Klan's place.

In 1872 a revolt within the Republican ranks foreshadowed the end of Reconstruction. A group calling itself the Liberal Republicans bolted the party and

Liberal Republicans Revolt

nominated Horace Greeley, the well-known editor of the *New York Tribune,* for president. The Liberal Republicans were a varied group, including civil-service reformers, foes of corruption, and advocates of a lower tariff; they often spoke of a more lenient policy toward the South. That year the Democrats too gave their nomination to Greeley. Though the combination was not enough to defeat Grant, it reinforced his desire to avoid confrontation with white southerners. Grant used troops very sparingly thereafter, and in 1875 refused

Chapter 15: RECONSTRUCTION BY TRIAL AND ERROR, 1865–1877

President Grant with wife Julia and his youngest son Jessie. Photographed in 1872. Keystone-Mast Collection, University of California, Riverside.

a desperate request for troops from the governor of Mississippi.

The Liberal Republican challenge revealed the growing dissatisfaction with Grant's administration. Strong-willed but politically naive, Grant made a series of poor appointments. His secretary of war, his private secretary, and officials in the Treasury and Navy departments were all involved in bribery or tax-cheating scandals. Instead of exposing the corruption, Grant defended some of the culprits. As the clamor against dishonesty in government grew, Grant's popularity declined. So did his party's; in the 1874 elections Democrats recaptured the House of Representatives.

Congress's resolve on southern issues weakened steadily. By joint resolution it had already removed the political disabilities of the Fourteenth Amendment from many former Confederates. Then in 1872 it adopted a sweeping Amnesty Act, **Amnesty Act** which pardoned most of the re-

maining rebels and left only five hundred excluded from political participation. A Civil Rights Act passed in 1875 purported to guarantee black people equal accommodations in public places, like inns and theaters. But it was weak and contained no effective provisions for enforcement. (The law was later struck down by the Supreme Court; see page 474.)

Democrats regained power in the South rather quickly, winning four states before 1872 and a total of eight by the start of 1876 (see map, page 444). As they did so, northern Republicans worried about their opponents' stress on the failure and scandals of Reconstruction governments. Many Republicans sensed that their constituents were tiring of the same old issues. In fact, a variety of new concerns were catching the public's eye. The Panic of 1873, which threw 3 million people out of work, focused attention on economic and monetary problems. Businessmen were disturbed by the strikes and industrial violence that accompanied the panic; debtors and unemployed

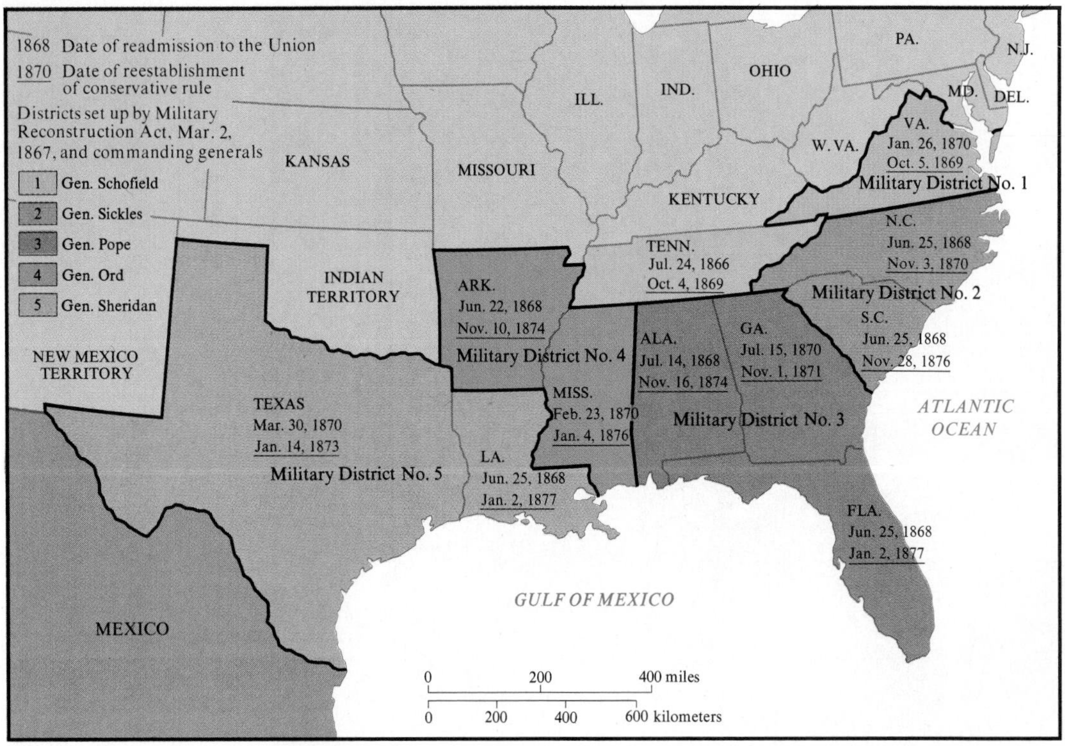
1868 Date of readmission to the Union
1870 Date of reestablishment of conservative rule
Districts set up by Military Reconstruction Act, Mar. 2, 1867, and commanding generals
1 Gen. Schofield
2 Gen. Sickles
3 Gen. Pope
4 Gen. Ord
5 Gen. Sheridan
PA.
N.J.
MD.
DEL.
OHIO
IND.
ILL.
KANSAS
MISSOURI
W. VA.
VA.
Jan. 26, 1870
Oct. 5, 1869
Military District No. 1
KENTUCKY
N.C.
Jun. 25, 1868
Nov. 3, 1870
TENN.
Jul. 24, 1866
Oct. 4, 1869
INDIAN TERRITORY
ARK.
Jun. 22, 1868
Nov. 10, 1874
Military District No. 2
S.C.
Jun. 25, 1868
Nov. 28, 1876
GA.
Jul. 15, 1870
Nov. 1, 1871
ALA.
Jul. 14, 1868
Nov. 16, 1874
Military District No. 4
NEW MEXICO TERRITORY
MISS.
Feb. 23, 1870
Jan. 4, 1876
TEXAS
Mar. 30, 1870
Jan. 14, 1873
Military District No. 3
ATLANTIC OCEAN
LA.
Jun. 25, 1868
Jan. 2, 1877
Military District No. 5
FLA.
Jun. 25, 1868
Jan. 2, 1877
GULF OF MEXICO
MEXICO
0 200 400 miles
0 200 400 600 kilometers

The Reconstruction

sought easy-money policies to spur economic expansion.

The monetary issue aroused strong controversy. Civil War greenbacks had the potential to expand the money supply and lift prices, if they were kept in circulation. In 1872 Democratic farmers and debtors had urged such a policy, but they were overruled by "sound money" men. Now the depression swelled the ranks of "greenbackers"—voters who favored greenbacks and easy money. In 1874 Congress voted to increase the number of greenbacks in circulation, but Grant vetoed the bill in deference to the opinions of financial leaders. The next year sound-money interests prevailed in Congress, winning passage of a law requiring that after 1878 greenbacks be convertible into gold. The law limited the inflationary impact of the greenbacks and aided creditors, not debtors.

Greenbacks Versus Sound Money

Indeed, the government's financial policies were almost perfectly tailored to revive and support industrial growth. Soon after the war Congress had shifted some of the government's tax revenues to pay off the interest-bearing war debt. The debt fell from $2.33 billion in 1866 to only $587 million in 1893, and every dollar repaid was a dollar injected into the economy for potential reinvestment. Thus approximately 1 percent of the gross national product was pumped back into the economy from 1866 to 1872, and only slightly less than that during the rest of the 1870s. Low taxes on investment and high tariffs on manufactured goods also aided industrialists. With such help the northern economy quickly recovered the rate of growth it had enjoyed just before the war.

Another issue that claimed new attention in the 1870s was immigration. After the war the number of immigrants entering the United States began to rise again, along with the ingrained suspicions and hostilities of native Americans. The Mormon question too—how Utah's growing Mormon community, which practiced polygamy, could be reconciled to American law—became prominent.

Renewed pressure for expansion revived interest in international affairs. Secretary of State William H. Seward accomplished the only major addition of territory during these years in 1867. Through ne-

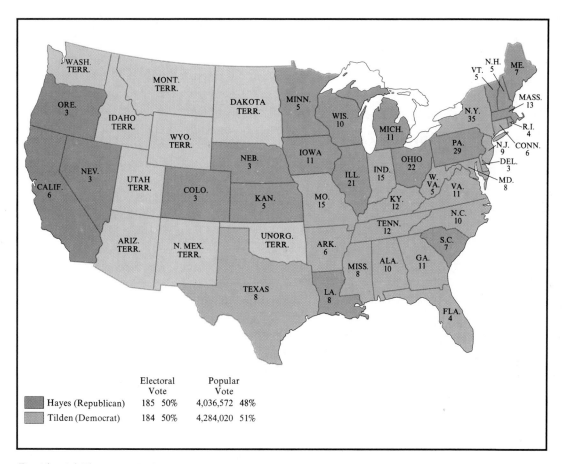

Presidential Election, 1876

	Electoral Vote		Popular Vote	
Hayes (Republican)	185	50%	4,036,572	48%
Tilden (Democrat)	184	50%	4,284,020	51%

gotiation with the Russian government, he arranged the purchase of Alaska for $7.2 million dollars. Opponents ridiculed Seward's venture, calling Alaska Frigidia, the Polar Bear Garden, or Walrussia. But Seward convinced important congressmen of Alaska's economic potential, and other lawmakers favored the dawning of friendship with Russia. In the same year the United States took control of the Midway Islands, a thousand miles from Hawaii, which were scarcely mentioned again until the Second World War. Though in 1870 President Grant tried to annex the Dominican Republic, Senator Charles Sumner blocked the attempt. Seward and his successor, Hamilton Fish, used diplomacy to arrange a financial settlement of claims against Britain for permitting the sale of the *Alabama* and other Confederate cruisers (see page 625).

By 1876 it was obvious to most political observers that the North was no longer willing to pursue the goals of Reconstruction. The results of a disputed

Election of 1876

presidential election confirmed this fact. Samuel J. Tilden, Democratic governor of New York, ran strongly in the South and took a commanding lead in both the popular vote and the electoral college over Rutherford B. Hayes, the Republican nominee. Tilden won 184 electoral votes and needed only one more for a majority. Nineteen votes from Louisiana, South Carolina, and Florida were disputed; both Democrats and Republicans claimed to have won in those states despite fraud on the part of their opponents. One vote from Oregon was undecided due to a technicality (see map).

To resolve this unprecedented situation, on which the Constitution gave no guidance, Congress established a fifteen-member electoral commission. In the interest of impartiality, membership on the commission was to be balanced between Democrats and Republicans. But one independent Republican, Supreme

All Colored People

THAT WANT TO

GO TO KANSAS,

On September 5th, 1877,

Can do so for $5.00

IMMIGRATION.

WHEREAS, We, the colored people of Lexington, Ky,. knowing that there is an abundance of choice lands now belonging to the Government, have assembled ourselves together for the purpose of locating on said lands. Therefore,

BE IT RESOLVED, That we do now organize ourselves into a Colony, as follows:— Any person wishing to become a member of this Colony can do so by paying the sum of one dollar ($1.00), and this money is to be paid by the first of September, 1877, in instalments of twenty-five cents at a time, or otherwise as may be desired.

RESOLVED, That this Colony has agreed to consolidate itself with the Nicodemus Towns, Solomon Valley, Graham County, Kansas, and can only do so by entering the vacant lands now in their midst, which costs $5.00.

RESOLVED, That this Colony shall consist of seven officers—President, Vice-President, Secretary, Treasurer, and three Trustees. President—M. M. Bell; Vice-President —Isaac Talbott; Secretary—W. J. Niles; Treasurer—Daniel Clarke; Trustees—Jerry Lee, William Jones, and Abner Webster.

RESOLVED, That this Colony shall have from one to two hundred militia, more or less, as the case may require, to keep peace and order, and any member failing to pay in his dues, as aforesaid, or failing to comply with the above rules in any particular, will not be recognized or protected by the Colony.

Exodusters, southern blacks dismayed by the failure of Reconstruction, left the South by the thousands for Kansas in 1877. This handbill advertised the establishment of a black colony in Graham County, Kansas. Kansas State Historical Society.

Court Justice David Davis, refused appointment in order to accept his election as a senator. A regular Republican took his place, and the Republican party prevailed 8 to 7 on every decision, a strict party vote. Hayes would then become the winner if Congress accepted the commission's findings.

Congressional acceptance, however, was not sure. Democrats controlled the House and had the power to filibuster to block action on the vote. Many citizens worried that the nation had entered a major constitutional crisis and was slipping once again into civil war. But the crisis was resolved when Democrats acquiesced in the election of Hayes. Scholars have found that negotiations went on between some of Hayes's supporters and southerners who were interested in federal aid to railroads, internal improvements, federal patronage, and removal of troops from southern states. But the most recent studies suggest that these negotiations did not have a deciding effect on the outcome. Neither party was well enough organized to implement and enforce a bargain between the sections. Northern and southern Democrats decided they could not win and failed to contest the election. Thus Hayes became president, and southerners looked forward to the withdrawal of federal troops from the South. Reconstruction was unmistakably over.

Southern Democrats rejoiced, but black Americans grieved over the betrayal of their hopes for equality. Tens of thousands of blacks pondered leaving the South, where freedom was no longer a real possibility. "[We asked] whether it was possible we could stay under a people who had held us in bondage," said Henry Adams, who led a migration to Kansas. "[We] appealed to the President . . . and to Congress . . . to protect us in our rights and privileges," but "in 1877 we lost all hopes." Thereafter many southern blacks "wanted to go to a territory by ourselves." In South Carolina, Louisiana, Mississippi, and other southern states, thousands gathered up their possessions and migrated to Kansas. They were known as Exodusters, disappointed people still searching for their share in the American dream. Even in Kansas they met disillusionment, as the welcome extended by the state's governor soon gave way to hostile public receptions.

Black Exodusters

Thus the nation ended over fifteen years of bloody civil war and controversial reconstruction without establishing full freedom for black Americans. Their status would continue to be one of the major issues facing the nation. A host of other issues would arise from industrialization. How would the country develop its immense resources in a growing and increasingly integrated national economy? How would farmers, industrial workers, immigrants, and capitalists fit into the new social system? Industrialization promised not just a higher standard of living but also a different lifestyle in both urban and rural areas. Moreover, it augmented the nation's power and laid the foundation for an increased American role in international affairs. Again Americans turned their thoughts to expansion and the conquest of new frontiers. As the United States entered its second hundred years of existence, it confronted these serious challenges. The experience of the 1860s and 1870s suggested that the solutions, if any, might not be clear or complete.

Chapter 15: RECONSTRUCTION BY TRIAL AND ERROR, 1865–1877

SUGGESTIONS FOR FURTHER READING

National Policy, Politics, and Constitutional Law

Richard H. Abbott, *The First Southern Strategy* (1986); Herman Belz, *Emancipation and Equal Rights* (1978); Herman Belz, *A New Birth of Freedom* (1976); Herman Belz, *Reconstructing the Union* (1969); Michael Les Benedict, *A Compromise of Principle* (1974); Michael Les Benedict, *The Impeachment and Trial of Andrew Johnson* (1973); Charles S. Campbell, *The Transformation of American Foreign Relations, 1865–1900* (1976); Adrian Cook, *The Alabama Claims* (1975); David Donald, *Charles Sumner and the Rights of Man* (1970); Harold M. Hyman, *A More Perfect Union* (1973); Ronald J. Jensen, *The Alaska Purchase and Russian-American Relations* (1975); William S. McFeely, *Grant* (1981); William S. McFeely, *Yankee Stepfather: General O. O. Howard and the Freedmen* (1968); Eric L. McKitrick, *Andrew Johnson and Reconstruction* (1966); James M. McPherson, *The Abolitionist Legacy* (1975); Kenneth M. Stampp, *Era of Reconstruction* (1965); Mark W. Summers, *Railroads, Reconstruction, and the Gospel of Prosperity* (1984); Glyndon C. Van Deusen, *William Henry Seward* (1967).

The Freed Slaves

Roberta Sue Alexander, *North Carolina Faces the Freedmen* (1985); Ira Berlin, ed., *Freedom* (1984); Edmund L. Drago, *Black Politicians and Reconstruction in Georgia* (1982); Paul D. Escott, *Slavery Remembered* (1979); Eric Foner, "Reconstruction and the Crisis of Free Labor," in *Politics and Ideology in the Age of the Civil War* (1980); Peter Kolchin, *First Freedom* (1972); Leon Litwack, *Been in the Storm So Long* (1979); Howard Rabinowitz, ed., *Southern Black Leaders in Reconstruction* (1982); C. Peter Ripley, *Slaves and Freedmen in Civil War Louisiana* (1976); Willie Lee Rose, *Rehearsal for Reconstruction* (1964); Emma Lou Thornbrough, ed., *Black Reconstructionists* (1972); Okon Uya, *From Slavery to Public Service* (1971); Clarence Walker, *A Rock in a Weary Land* (1982).

Politics and Reconstruction in the South

Jonathan Daniels, *Prince of Carpetbaggers* (1958); W. E. B. Du Bois, *Black Reconstruction* (1935); Paul D. Escott, *Many Excellent People* (1985); W. McKee Evans, *Ballots and Fence Rails* (1966); Eric Foner, *Nothing But Freedom* (1983); William C. Harris, *Day of the Carpetbagger* (1979); Thomas Holt, *Black over White* (1977); Robert Manson Myers, ed., *The Children of Pride* (1972); Elizabeth Studley Nathans, *Losing the Peace* (1968); Lillian A. Pereyra, *James Lusk Alcorn* (1966); Michael Perman, *The Road to Redemption* (1984); Michael Perman, *Reunion Without Compromise* (1973); Lawrence N. Powell, "The Politics of Livelihood," in J. Morgan Kousser and James M. McPherson, eds., *Region, Race and Reconstruction* (1982); Lawrence N. Powell, *New Masters* (1980); George C. Rable, *But There Was No Peace* (1984); James Roark, *Masters Without Slaves* (1977); James Sefton, *The United States Army and Reconstruction, 1865–1877* (1967); Mark W. Summers, *Railroads, Reconstruction, and the Gospel of Prosperity* (1984); J. Mills Thornton III, "Fiscal Policy and the Failure of Radical Reconstruction," in J. Morgan Kousser and James M. McPherson, eds., *Region, Race and Reconstruction* (1982); Albion W. Tourgée,

A Fool's Errand (1979); Allen Trelease, *White Terror* (1967); Ted Tunnell, *Crucible of Reconstruction* (1984); Sarah Woolfolk Wiggins, *The Scalawag in Alabama Politics, 1865–1881* (1977).

Women and Family History

Ellen Carol Dubois, *Feminism and Suffrage* (1978); Herbert G. Gutman, *The Black Family in Slavery & Freedom, 1750–1925* (1976); Elizabeth Jacoway, *Yankee Missionaries in the South* (1979); Jacqueline Jones, *Labor of Love, Labor of Sorrow* (1985); Jacqueline Jones, *Soldiers of Light and Love* (1980); Rebecca Scott, "The Battle over the Child," *Prologue*, 10, No. 2 (Summer 1978), 101–113.

The End of Reconstruction

Michael Les Benedict, "Southern Democrats in the Crisis of 1876–1877," *Journal of Southern History*, LXVI, No. 4 (November 1980), 489–524; William Gillette, *Retreat from Reconstruction, 1869–1879* (1980); William Gillette, *The Right to Vote* (1969); Keith Ian Polakoff, *The Politics of Inertia* (1973); C. Vann Woodward, *Reunion and Reaction* (1951).

Reconstruction's Legacy for the South

Robert G. Athearn, *In Search of Canaan* (1978); Norman L. Crockett, *The Black Towns* (1979); Stephen J. DeCanio, *Agriculture in the Postbellum South* (1974); Steven Hahn, *The Roots of Southern Populism* (1983); Susan Previant Lee and Peter Passell, *A New Economic View of American History* (1979); Jay R. Mandle, *The Roots of Black Poverty* (1978); Nell Irvin Painter, *Exodusters* (1976); Howard Rabinowitz, *Race Relations in the Urban South, 1865–1890* (1978); Roger L. Ransom and Richard Sutch, *One Kind of Freedom* (1977); Jonathan M. Wiener, *Social Origins of the New South* (1978); Joel Williamson, *After Slavery* (1966); C. Vann Woodward, *Origins of the New South* (1951).

APPENDIX

HISTORICAL REFERENCE BOOKS BY SUBJECT

Encyclopedias, Dictionaries, Atlases, Chronologies, and Statistics

General

Geoffrey Barraclough, ed., *The Times Atlas of World History* (1979); *Concise Dictionary of American Biography* (1980); *Concise Dictionary of American History* (1983); *Dictionary of American Biography* (1928–   ); *Dictionary of American History* (1976–1978); Robert H. Ferrell and John S. Bowman, eds., *The Twentieth Century: An Almanac* (1984); Edward W. Fox, *Atlas of American History* (1964); George H. Gallup, *The Gallup Poll: Public Opinion, 1935–1971* (1972) and *1972–1977* (1978); John A. Garraty, ed., *Encyclopedia of American Biography* (1974); Bernard Grun, *The Timetables of History* (1975); Stanley Hochman, *Yesterday and Today* (1979); *International Encyclopedia of the Social Sciences* (1968–   ); Kenneth T. Jackson and James T. Adams, *Atlas of American History* (1978); R. Alton Lee, ed., *Encyclopedia USA* (1983–   ); Michael Martin and Leonard Gelber, *Dictionary of American History* (1981); Richard B. Morris, *Encyclopedia of American History* (1982); *National Cyclopedia of American Biography* (1898–   ); Arthur M. Schlesinger, Jr., ed., *The Almanac of American History* (1983); *Scribner Desk Dictionary of American History* (1984); U.S. Bureau of the Census, *Historical Statistics of the United States* (1975); U.S. Department of the Interior, *National Atlas of the United States* (1970).

The American Revolution

Mark M. Boatner, III, *Encyclopedia of the American Revolution* (1974); Lester J. Cappon, ed., *Atlas of Early American History: The Revolutionary Era, 1760–1790* (1976); Douglas W. Marshall and Howard H. Peckham, *Campaigns of the American Revolution* (1976); Gregory Palmer, ed., *Biographical Sketches of Loyalists of the American Revolution* (1984); *Rand-McNally Atlas of the American Revolution* (1974).

Architecture

William D. Hunt, Jr., ed., *Encyclopedia of American Architecture* (1980).

Blacks

Peter M. Bergman, *The Chronological History of the Negro in America* (1969); Rayford W. Logan and Michael R. Winston, eds., *The Dictionary of American Negro Biography* (1983); W. A. Low and Virgil A. Clift, eds., *Encyclopedia of Black America* (1981); Harry A. Ploski and James Williams, eds., *The Negro Almanac* (1983); Erwin A. Salk, ed., *A Layman's Guide to Negro History* (1967); Mabel M. Smythe, ed., *The Black American Reference Book* (1976); Edgar A. Toppin, *A Biographical History of Blacks in America* (1971).

Cities and Towns

Charles Abrams, *The Language of Cities: A Glossary of Terms* (1971); John L. Androit, ed., *Township Atlas of the United States* (1979); Ory M. Nergal, ed., *The Encyclopedia of American Cities* (1980). *See also* "Politics and Government."

The Civil War

Mark M. Boatner, III, *The Civil War Dictionary* (1959); *The Civil War Almanac* (1983); E. B. Long, *The Civil War Day by Day* (1971); Mark E. Neely, Jr., *The Abraham Lincoln Encyclopedia* (1982); Craig L. Symonds, *A Battlefield Atlas of the Civil War* (1983); U.S. War Department, *The Official Atlas of the Civil War* (1958); Jon L. Wakelyn, ed., *Biographical Dictionary of the Confederacy* (1977); Ezra J. Warner and W. Buck Yearns, *Biographical Register of the Confederate Congress* (1975). *See also* "The South."

Conservation

Forest History Society, *Encyclopedia of American Forest and Conservation History* (1983).

The Constitution and Supreme Court

Congressional Quarterly, *Guide to the Supreme Court* (1979); Leon Friedman and Fred I. Israel, eds., *The Justices of the United States Supreme Court, 1789–1978* (1980); *Judges of the United States* (1980).

Crime

Sanford H. Kadish, ed., *Encyclopedia of Crime and Justice* (1983); Carl Sifakis, *The Encyclopedia of American Crime* (1982).

Culture and Folklore

M. Thomas Inge, ed., *Handbook of American Popular Culture* (1979–1981); Marjorie Tallman, *Dictionary of American Folklore* (1959); Justin Wintle, ed., *Makers of Nineteenth Century Culture, 1800–1914* (1982). *See also* "Entertainment," "Music," and "Sports."

The Economy and Business

Christine Ammer and Dean S. Ammer, *Dictionary of Business and Economics* (1983); Douglas Auld and Graham Bannock, *The American Dictionary of Economics* (1983); Douglas Greenwald, *Encyclopedia of Economics* (1982); John N. Ingham, *Biographical Dictionary of American Business Leaders* (1983); Glenn G. Munn, *Encyclopedia of Banking and Finance* (1973); David W. Pearce, *Dictionary of Modern Economics* (1983); Glenn Porter, *Encyclopedia of American Economic History* (1980).

Education

Lee C. Deighton, ed., *The Encyclopedia of Education* (1971); Joseph C. Kiger, ed., *Research Institutions and Learned Societies* (1982); John F. Ohles, ed., *Biographical Dictionary of American Educators* (1978).

Entertainment

Tim Brooks and Earle Marsh, *The Complete Directory to Prime Time Network TV Shows, 1946–present* (1979); Barbara N. Cohen-Stratyner, *Biographical Dictionary of Dance* (1982); John Dunning, *Tune in Yesterday* [radio] (1967); Stanley Green, *Encyclopedia of the Musical Film* (1981); *Notable Names in the American Theater* (1976); *New York Times Encyclopedia of Television* (1977); Andrew Sarris, *The American Cinema: Directors and Directions, 1929–1968* (1968); Evelyn M. Truitt, *Who Was Who on Screen* (1977). *See also* "Culture and Folklore," "Music," and "Sports."

Foreign Policy

Alexander DeConde, ed., *Encyclopedia of American Foreign Policy* (1978); John E. Findling, *Dictionary of American Diplomatic History* (1980); *International Geographic Encyclopedia and Atlas* (1979); Warren F. Kuehl, ed., *Biographical Dictionary of Internationalists* (1983); George T. Kurian, *Encyclopedia of the Third World* (1981); Richard B. Morris and Graham W. Irwin, eds., *Harper Encyclopedia of the Modern World* (1970); Jack C. Plano, ed., *The International Relations Dictionary* (1982); Jack E. Vincent, *A Handbook of International Relations* (1969).

Immigration and Ethnic Groups

American Jewish Biographies (1982); Stephanie Bernardo, *The Ethnic Almanac* (1981); Matt S. Meier and Feliciano Rivera, *Dictionary of Mexican American History* (1981); Stephan Thernstrom, ed., *Harvard Encyclopedia of American Ethnic Groups* (1980).

Indians

Frederick J. Dockstader, *Great North American Indians* (1977); *Handbook of North American Indians* (1978–   ); Barry Klein, ed., *Reference Encyclopedia of the American Indian* (1978).

Labor

Gary M. Fink, ed., *Biographical Dictionary of American Labor Leaders* (1974); Gary M. Fink, ed., *Labor Unions* (1977); Philip S. Foner, *First Facts of American Labor* (1984).

Literature

James T. Callow and Robert J. Reilly, *Guide to American Literature* (1976–1977); *Dictionary of Literary Biography* (1978–   ); Eugene Ehrlich and Gorton Carruth, *The Oxford Illustrated Literary Guide to the United States* (1982); Jon Tuska and Vicki Piekarski, *Encyclopedia of Frontier and Western Fiction* (1983). *See also* "Culture and Folklore," "The South," and "Women."

Medicine

Martin Kaufman, *et al.*, eds., *Dictionary of American Medical Biography* (1984).

Music

John Chilton, *Who's Who of Jazz* (1972); Edward Jablonski, *The Encyclopedia of American Music* (1981); Roger Lax and

Frederick Smith, *The Great Song Thesaurus* (1984). *See also* "Culture and Folklore" and "Entertainment."

Politics and Government: General and Elections

Congressional Quarterly, *Congress and the Nation, 1945–1976* (1965–1977); Congressional Quarterly, *Guide to U.S. Elections* (1975); Jack P. Greene, ed., *Encyclopedia of American Political History* (1984); Kenneth C. Martis, *The Historical Atlas of United States Congressional Districts, 1789–1983* (1982); Edwin V. Mitchell, *An Encyclopedia of American Politics* (1968); Svend Peterson, *A Statistical History of the American Presidential Elections* (1963); William Safire, *Safire's Political Dictionary* (1978); Richard M. Scammon, ed., *America at the Polls* (1965); Edward L. and Frederick H. Schapsmeier, eds., *Political Parties and Civic Action Groups* (1981); Arthur M. Schlesinger, Jr., and Fred I. Israel, eds., *History of American Presidential Elections, 1789–1968* (1971); Robert Scruton, *A Dictionary of Political Thought* (1982); Hans Sperber and Travis Trittschuh, *American Political Terms* (1962). *See also* "The Constitution and Supreme Court," "States and the West," and the following section.

Politics and Government: Leaders

Roy R. Glashan, comp., *American Governors and Gubernatorial Elections, 1775–1978* (1979); Otis L. Graham, Jr., and Meghan R. Wander, eds., *Franklin D. Roosevelt: His Life and Times* (1985); Melvin G. Holli and Peter d'A. Jones, eds., *Biographical Dictionary of American Mayors, 1820–1980: Big City Mayors* (1981); Joseph E. Kallenbach and Jessamine S. Kallenbach, *American State Governors, 1776–1976* (1977); Thomas A. McMullin and David Walker, *Biographical Directory of American Territorial Governors* (1984); *Political Profiles, Truman Years to . . .* (1978); John W. Raimo, ed., *Biographical Directory of American Colonial and Revolutionary Governors, 1607–1789* (1980); John W. Raimo, ed., *Biographical Directory of the Governors of the United States, 1789–1978* (1978); John W. Raimo, ed., *Biographical Directory of the Governors of the United States, 1978–1983* (1984); Robert Sobel, ed., *Biographical Directory of the United States Executive Branch, 1774–1977* (1977); U.S. Congress, Senate, *Biographical Directory of the American Congress, 1774–1971* (1971); Robert Vexler, *The Vice-Presidents and Cabinet Members* (1975). *See also* the previous section.

Religion

Henry Bowden, *Dictionary of American Religious Biography* (1977); John T. Ellis and Robert Trisco, *A Guide to American Catholic History* (1982); Edwin S. Gaustad, *Historical Atlas of Religion in America* (1976); Samuel S. Hill, Jr., ed., *Encyclopedia of Religion in the South* (1984); J. Gordon Melton, *The Encyclopedia of American Religions* (1978); Mark A. Noll and Nathan O. Hatch, eds., *Eerdmans Handbook to Christianity in America* (1983); Arthur C. Piepkorn, *Profiles in Brief: The Religious Bodies of the United States and Canada* (1977–1979).

Science

Charles C. Gillispie, ed., *Dictionary of Scientific Biography* (1970–); National Academy of Sciences, *Biographical Memoirs* (1877–).

Social Issues

Louis Filler, *A Dictionary of American Social Reform* (1963); Louis Filler, *Dictionary of American Social Change* (1982); Robert S. Fogarty, *Dictionary of American Communal and Utopian History* (1980); Mark E. Lender, *Dictionary of American Temperance Biography* (1984); Alvin J. Schmidt, *Fraternal Organizations* (1980). *See also* "Crime."

The South

Robert Bain, *et al.*, eds., *Southern Writers: A Biographical Dictionary* (1979); Kenneth Coleman and Charles S. Gurr, eds., *Dictionary of Georgia Biography* (1983); William C. Ferris and Charles R. Wilson, eds., *Encyclopedia of Southern Culture* (1986); David C. Roller and Robert W. Twyman, eds., *The Encyclopedia of Southern History* (1979); Walter P. Webb, *et al.*, eds., *The Handbook of Texas* (1952, 1976). *See also* "Politics and Government" and "States and the West."

Sports

Ralph Hickok, *New Encyclopedia of Sports* (1977); Ralph Hickok, *Who Was Who in American Sports* (1971); Zander Hollander, *The NBA's Official Encyclopedia of Pro Basketball* (1981); Frank G. Menke and Suzanne Treat, *The Encyclopedia of Sports* (1977); *The NFL's Official Encyclopedic History of Professional Football* (1977); Paul Soderberg, *et al.*, *The Big Book of Halls of Fame in the United States and Canada* (1977). *See also* "Culture and Folklore."

States and the West

John Clayton, ed., *The Illinois Fact Book and Historical Almanac, 1673–1968* (1970); Doris O. Dawdy, *Artists of the American West* (1974–1984); Howard R. Lamar, ed., *The Reader's Encyclopedia of the American West* (1977);

Mose Y. Sachs, ed., *The Worldmark Encyclopedia of the States* (1981). *See also* "Politics and Government" and "The South."

Wars and the Military

R. Ernest Dupuy and Trevor N. Dupuy, *The Encyclopedia of Military History* (1977); Holger H. Herwig and Neil M. Heyman, *Biographical Dictionary of World War I* (1982); Michael Kidrow and Dan Smith, *The War Atlas: Armed Conflict, Armed Peace* (1983); Roger J. Spiller and Joseph G. Dawson, III, eds., *Dictionary of American Military Biography* (1984); U.S. Military Academy, *The West Point Atlas of American Wars, 1689–1953* (1959); *Webster's American Military Biographies* (1978). *See also* "The American Revolution," "The Civil War," and "World War II."

Women

Edward T. James, *et al.*, *Notable American Women, 1607–1950* (1971); Lina Mainiero, ed., *American Women Writers* (1979–1982); Barbara Sicherman and Carol H. Green, eds., *Notable American Women, The Modern Period* (1980).

World War II

Marcel Baudot, *et al.*, eds., *The Historical Encyclopedia of World War II* (1980); Simon Goodenough, *War Maps: Great Land Battles of World War II* (1983); Robert Goralski, *World War II Almanac, 1931–1945* (1981); John Keegan, ed., *The Rand-McNally Encyclopedia of World War II* (1977); Thomas Parrish, ed., *The Simon and Schuster Encyclopedia of World War II* (1978); Louis L. Snyder, *Louis L. Snyder's Historical Guide to World War II* (1982); U.S. Military Academy, *Campaign Atlas to the Second World War: Europe and the Mediterranean* (1980); Peter Young, ed., *The World Almanac Book of World War II* (1981). *See also* "Wars and the Military."

DECLARATION OF INDEPENDENCE IN CONGRESS, JULY 4, 1776

The unanimous declaration of the thirteen United States of America

When, in the course of human events, it becomes necessary for one people to dissolve the political bonds which have connected them with another, and to assume, among the powers of the earth, the separate and equal station to which the laws of nature and of nature's God entitle them, a decent respect to the opinions of mankind requires that they should declare the causes which impel them to the separation.

We hold these truths to be self-evident: That all men are created equal; that they are endowed by their Creator with certain unalienable rights; that among these are life, liberty, and the pursuit of happiness; that, to secure these rights, governments are instituted among men, deriving their just powers from the consent of the governed; that whenever any form of government becomes destructive of these ends, it is the right of the people to alter or to abolish it, and to institute new government, laying its foundation on such principles, and organizing its powers in such form, as to them shall seem most likely to effect their safety and happiness. Prudence, indeed, will dictate that governments long established should not be changed for light and transient causes; and accordingly all experience hath shown that mankind are more disposed to suffer, while evils are sufferable, than to right themselves by abolishing the forms to which they are accustomed. But when a long train of abuses and usurpations, pursuing invariably the same object, evinces a design to reduce them under absolute despotism, it is their right, it is their duty, to throw off such government, and to provide new guards for their future security. Such has been the patient sufferance of these colonies; and such is now the necessity which constrains them to alter their former systems of government. The history of the present King of Great Britain is a history of repeated injuries and usurpations, all having in direct object the establishment of an absolute tyranny over these states. To prove this, let facts be submitted to a candid world.

He has refused his assent to laws, the most wholesome and necessary for the public good.

He has forbidden his governors to pass laws of immediate and pressing importance, unless suspended in their operation till his assent should be obtained; and, when so suspended, he has utterly neglected to attend to them.

He has refused to pass other laws for the accommodation of large districts of people, unless those people would relinquish the right of representation in the legislature, a right inestimable to them, and formidable to tyrants only.

He has called together legislative bodies at places unusual, uncomfortable, and distant from the depository of their public records, for the sole purpose of fatiguing them into compliance with his measures.

He has dissolved representative houses repeatedly, for opposing, with manly firmness, his invasions on the rights of the people.

He has refused for a long time, after such dissolutions, to cause others to be elected; whereby the legislative powers, incapable of annihilation, have returned to the people at large for their exercise; the state remaining, in the mean time, exposed to all the dangers of invasions from without and convulsions within.

He has endeavored to prevent the population of these states; for that purpose obstructing the laws for naturalization of foreigners; refusing to pass others to encourage their migration hither, and raising the conditions of new appropriations of lands.

He has obstructed the administration of justice, by refusing his assent to laws for establishing judiciary powers.

He has made judges dependent on his will alone, for the tenure of their offices, and the amount and payment of their salaries.

He has erected a multitude of new offices, and sent hither swarms of officers to harass our people and eat out their substance.

He has kept among us, in times of peace, standing armies, without the consent of our legislatures.

He has affected to render the military independent of, and superior to, the civil power.

He has combined with others to subject us to a jurisdiction foreign to our constitution, and unacknowledged by our laws, giving his assent to their acts of pretended legislation:

For quartering large bodies of armed troops among us;

For protecting them, by a mock trial, from punishment for any murders which they should commit on the inhabitants of these states;

For cutting off our trade with all parts of the world;

For imposing taxes on us without our consent;

For depriving us, in many cases, of the benefits of trial by jury;

For transporting us beyond seas, to be tried for pretended offenses;

For abolishing the free system of English laws in a neighboring province, establishing therein an arbitrary government, and enlarging its boundaries, so as to render it at once an example and fit instrument for introducing the same absolute rule into these colonies;

For taking away our charters, abolishing our most valuable laws, and altering fundamentally the forms of our governments;

For suspending our own legislatures, and declaring themselves invested with power to legislate for us in all cases whatsoever.

He has abdicated government here, by declaring us out of his protection and waging war against us.

He has plundered our seas, ravaged our coasts, burned our towns, and destroyed the lives of our people.

He is at this time transporting large armies of foreign mercenaries to complete the works of death, desolation, and tyranny already begun with circumstances of cruelty and perfidy scarcely paralleled in the most barbarous ages, and totally unworthy the head of a civilized nation.

He has constrained our fellow-citizens, taken captive on the high seas, to bear arms against their country, to become the executioners of their friends and brethren, or to fall themselves by their hands.

He has excited domestic insurrection among us, and has endeavored to bring on the inhabitants of our frontiers the merciless Indian savages, whose known rule of warfare is an undistinguished destruction of all ages, sexes, and conditions.

In every stage of these oppressions we have petitioned for redress in the most humble terms; our repeated petitions have been answered only by repeated injury. A prince, whose character is thus marked by every act which may define a tyrant, is unfit to be the ruler of a free people.

Nor have we been wanting in our attentions to our British brethren. We have warned them, from time to time, of attempts by their legislature to extend an unwarrantable jurisdiction over us. We have reminded them of the circumstances of our emigration and settlement here. We have appealed to their native justice and magnanimity; and we have conjured them, by the ties of our common kindred, to disavow these usurpations, which would inevitably interrupt our connections and correspondence. They, too, have been deaf to the voice of justice and of consanguinity. We must, therefore, acquiesce in the necessity which denounces our separation, and hold them, as we hold the rest of mankind, enemies in war, in peace friends.

We, therefore, the representatives of the United States of America, in General Congress assembled, appealing to the Supreme Judge of the world for the rectitude of our intentions, do, in the name and by the authority of the good people of these colonies, solemnly publish and declare, that these United Colonies are, and of right ought to be, FREE AND INDEPENDENT STATES; that they are absolved from all allegiance to the British crown, and that all political connection between them and the state of Great Britain is, and ought to be, totally dissolved; and that, as free and independent states, they have full power to levy war, conclude peace, contract alliances, establish commerce, and do all other acts and things which independent states may of right do. And for the support of this declaration, with a firm reliance on the protection of Divine Providence, we mutually pledge to each other our lives, our fortunes, and our sacred honor.

JOHN HANCOCK
and fifty-five others

Constitution of the United States of America and Amendments

Preamble

We the people of the United States, in order to form a more perfect union, establish justice, insure domestic tranquillity, provide for the common defense, promote the general welfare, and secure the blessings of liberty to ourselves and our posterity, do ordain and establish this Constitution for the United States of America.

Article I

Section 1 All legislative powers herein granted shall be vested in a Congress of the United States, which shall consist of a Senate and a House of Representatives.

Section 2 The House of Representatives shall be composed of members chosen every second year by the people of the several States, and the electors in each State shall have the qualifications requisite for electors of the most numerous branch of the State Legislature.

No person shall be a Representative who shall not have attained to the age of twenty-five years, and been seven years a citizen of the United States, and who shall not,

when elected, be an inhabitant of that State in which he shall be chosen.

Representatives and direct taxes shall be apportioned among the several States which may be included within this Union, according to their respective numbers, *which shall be determined by adding to the whole number of free persons, including those bound to service for a term of years and excluding Indians not taxed, three-fifths of all other persons.* The actual enumeration shall be made within three years after the first meeting of the Congress of the United States, and within every subsequent term of ten years, in such manner as they shall by law direct. The number of Representatives shall not exceed one for every thirty thousand, but each State shall have at least one Representative; *and until such enumeration shall be made, the State of New Hampshire shall be entitled to choose three, Massachusetts eight, Rhode Island and Providence Plantations one, Connecticut five, New York six, New Jersey four, Pennsylvania eight, Delaware one, Maryland six, Virginia ten, North Carolina five, South Carolina five, and Georgia three.*

When vacancies happen in the representation from any State, the Executive authority thereof shall issue writs of election to fill such vacancies.

The House of Representatives shall choose their Speaker and other officers; and shall have the sole power of impeachment.

Section 3 The Senate of the United States shall be composed of two Senators from each State, *chosen by the legislature thereof,* for six years; and each Senator shall have one vote.

Immediately after they shall be assembled in consequence of the first election, they shall be divided as equally as may be into three classes. The seats of the Senators of the first class shall be vacated at the expiration of the second year, of the second class at the expiration of the fourth year, and of the third class at the expiration of the sixth year, so that one-third may be chosen every second year; *and if vacancies happen by resignation or otherwise, during the recess of the legislature of any State, the Executive thereof may make temporary appointments until the next meeting of the legislature, which shall then fill such vacancies.*

No person shall be a Senator who shall not have attained to the age of thirty years, and been nine years a citizen of the United States, and who shall not, when elected, be an inhabitant of that State for which he shall be chosen.

The Vice-President of the United States shall be President of the Senate, but shall have no vote, unless they be equally divided.

The Senate shall choose their other officers, and also a President *pro tempore,* in the absence of the Vice-President, or when he shall exercise the office of President of the United States.

Passages no longer in effect are printed in italic type.

The Senate shall have the sole power to try all impeachments. When sitting for that purpose, they shall be on oath or affirmation. When the President of the United States is tried, the Chief Justice shall preside: and no person shall be convicted without the concurrence of two-thirds of the members present.

Judgment in cases of impeachment shall not extend further than to removal from the office, and disqualification to hold and enjoy any office of honor, trust or profit under the United States: but the party convicted shall nevertheless be liable and subject to indictment, trial, judgment and punishment, according to law.

Section 4 The times, places and manner of holding elections for Senators and Representatives shall be prescribed in each State by the legislature thereof; but the Congress may at any time by law make or alter such regulations, except as to the places of choosing Senators.

The Congress shall assemble at least once in every year, and such meeting *shall be on the first Monday in December, unless they shall by law appoint a different day.*

Section 5 Each house shall be the judge of the elections, returns and qualifications of its own members, and a majority of each shall constitute a quorum to do business; but a smaller number may adjourn from day to day, and may be authorized to compel the attendance of absent members, in such manner, and under such penalties, as each house may provide.

Each house may determine the rules of its proceedings, punish its members for disorderly behavior, and with the concurrence of two-thirds, expel a member.

Each house shall keep a journal of its proceedings, and from time to time publish the same, excepting such parts as may in their judgment require secrecy; and the yeas and nays of the members of either house on any question shall, at the desire of one-fifth of those present, be entered on the journal.

Neither house, during the session of Congress, shall, without the consent of the other, adjourn for more than three days, nor to any other place than that in which the two houses shall be sitting.

Section 6 The Senators and Representatives shall receive a compensation for their services, to be ascertained by law and paid out of the treasury of the United States. They shall in all cases except treason, felony and breach of the peace, be privileged from arrest during their attendance at the session of their respective houses, and in going to and returning from the same; and for any speech or debate in either house, they shall not be questioned in any other place.

No Senator or Representative shall, during the time for which he was elected, be appointed to any civil office under the authority of the United States, which shall have been created, or the emoluments whereof shall have been increased, during such time; and no person holding any office under the United States shall be a member of either house during his continuance in office.

Section 7 All bills for raising revenue shall originate in the House of Representatives; but the Senate may propose or concur with amendments as on other bills.

Every bill which shall have passed the House of Representatives and the Senate, shall, before it become a law, be presented to the President of the United States; if he approve he shall sign it, but if not he shall return it with objections to that house in which it originated, who shall enter the objections at large on their journal, and proceed to reconsider it. If after such reconsideration two-thirds of that house shall agree to pass the bill, it shall be sent, together with the objections, to the other house, by which it shall likewise be reconsidered, and, if approved by two-thirds of that house, it shall become a law. But in all such cases the votes of both houses shall be determined by yeas and nays, and the names of the persons voting for and against the bill shall be entered on the journal of each house respectively. If any bill shall not be returned by the President within ten days (Sundays excepted) after it shall have been presented to him, the same shall be a law, in like manner as if he had signed it, unless the Congress by their adjournment prevent its return, in which case it shall not be a law.

Every order, resolution, or vote to which the concurrence of the Senate and House of Representatives may be necessary (except on a question of adjournment) shall be presented to the President of the United States; and before the same shall take effect, shall be approved by him, or being disapproved by him, shall be repassed by two-thirds of the Senate and House of Representatives, according to the rules and limitations prescribed in the case of a bill.

Section 8 The Congress shall have power

To lay and collect taxes, duties, imposts, and excises, to pay the debts and provide for the common defense and general welfare of the United States; but all duties, imposts and excises shall be uniform throughout the United States;

To borrow money on the credit of the United States;

To regulate commerce with foreign nations, and among the several States, and with the Indian tribes;

To establish an uniform rule of naturalization, and uniform laws on the subject of bankruptcies throughout the United States;

To coin money, regulate the value thereof, and of foreign coin, and fix the standard of weights and measures;

To provide for the punishment of counterfeiting the securities and current coin of the United States;

To establish post offices and post roads;

To promote the progress of science and useful arts by securing for limited times to authors and inventors the exclusive right to their respective writings and discoveries;

To constitute tribunals inferior to the Supreme Court;

To define and punish piracies and felonies committed on the high seas and offenses against the law of nations;

To declare war, grant letters of marque and reprisal, and make rules concerning captures on land and water;

To raise and support armies, but no appropriation of money to that use shall be for a longer term than two years;

To provide and maintain a navy;

To make rules for the government and regulation of the land and naval forces;

To provide for calling forth the militia to execute the laws of the Union, suppress insurrections, and repel invasions;

To provide for organizing, arming, and disciplining the militia, and for governing such part of them as may be employed in the service of the United States, reserving to the States respectively the appointment of the officers, and the authority of training the militia according to the discipline prescribed by Congress;

To exercise exclusive legislation in all cases whatsoever, over such district (not exceeding ten miles square) as may, by cession of particular States, and the acceptance of Congress, become the seat of government of the United States, and to exercise like authority over all places purchased by the consent of the legislature of the State, in which the same shall be, for erection of forts, magazines, arsenals, dock-yards, and other needful buildings;—and

To make all laws which shall be necessary and proper for carrying into execution the foregoing powers, and all other powers vested by this Constitution in the government of the United States, or in any department or officer thereof.

Section 9 The migration or importation of such persons as any of the States now existing shall think proper to admit shall not be prohibited by the Congress prior to the year 1808; but a tax or duty may be imposed on such importation, not exceeding $10 for each person.

The privilege of the writ of habeas corpus shall not be suspended, unless when in cases of rebellion or invasion the public safety may require it.

No bill of attainder or ex post facto law shall be passed.

No capitation, or other direct, tax shall be laid, unless in proportion to the census or enumeration herein before directed to be taken.

No tax or duty shall be laid on articles exported from any State.

No preference shall be given by any regulation of commerce or revenue to the ports of one State over those of another; nor shall vessels bound to, or from, one State, be obliged to enter, clear, or pay duties in another.

No money shall be drawn from the treasury, but in consequence of appropriations made by law; and a regular statement and account of the receipts and expenditures of all public money shall be published from time to time.

No title of nobility shall be granted by the United States: and no person holding any office of profit or trust under them, shall, without the consent of the Congress, accept of any present, emolument, office, or title, of any kind whatever, from any king, prince, or foreign state.

Section 10 No State shall enter into any treaty, alliance, or confederation; grant letters of marque and reprisal; coin money; emit bills of credit; make anything but gold and silver coin a tender in payment of debts; pass any bill of attainder, ex post facto law, or law impairing the obligation of contracts, or grant any title of nobility.

No State shall, without the consent of Congress, lay any imposts or duties on imports or exports, except what may be absolutely necessary for executing its inspection laws: and the net produce of all duties and imposts, laid by any State on imports or exports, shall be for the use of the treasury of the United States; and all such laws shall be subject to the revision and control of the Congress.

No State shall, without the consent of Congress, lay any duty of tonnage, keep troops or ships of war in time of peace, enter into any agreement or compact with another State, or with a foreign power, or engage in war, unless actually invaded, or in such imminent danger as will not admit of delay.

Article II

Section 1 The executive power shall be vested in a President of the United States of America. He shall hold his office during the term of four years, and, together with the Vice-President, chosen for the same term, be elected as follows:

Each State shall appoint, in such manner as the legislature thereof may direct, a number of electors, equal to the whole number of Senators and Representatives to which the State may be entitled in the Congress; but no Senator or Representative, or person holding an office of trust or profit under the United States, shall be appointed an elector.

The electors shall meet in their respective States, and vote by ballot for two persons, of whom one at least shall not be an inhabitant of the same State with themselves. And they shall make a list of all the persons voted for, and of the number of votes for each; which list they shall sign and certify, and transmit sealed to the seat of government of the United States, directed to the President of the Senate. *The President of the Senate shall, in the presence of the Senate and House of Representatives, open all the certificates, and the votes shall then be counted. The person having the greatest number of votes shall be the President, if such number be a majority of the whole number of electors appointed; and if there be more than one who have such majority, and have an equal number of votes, then the House of Representatives shall immediately choose by ballot one of them for President; and if no person have a majority, then from the five highest on the list said house shall in like manner choose the President. But in choosing the President the votes shall be taken by States, the representation from each State having one vote; a quorum for this purpose shall consist of a member or members from two-thirds of the States, and a majority of all the States shall be necessary to a choice. In every case, after the choice of the President, the person having the greatest number of votes of the electors shall be the Vice-President. But if there should remain two or more who have equal votes, the Senate shall choose from them by ballot the Vice-President.*

The Congress may determine the time of choosing the electors and the day on which they shall give their votes; which day shall be the same throughout the United States.

No person except a natural-born citizen, *or a citizen of the United States at the time of the adoption of this Constitution,* shall be eligible to the office of President; neither shall any person be eligible to that office who shall not have attained to the age of thirty-five years, and been fourteen years a resident within the United States.

In case of the removal of the President from office or of his death, resignation, or inability to discharge the powers and duties of the said office, the same shall devolve on the Vice-President, and the Congress may by law provide for the case of removal, death, resignation, or inability, both of the President and Vice-President, declaring what officer shall then act as President, and such officer shall act accordingly, until the disability be removed, or a President shall be elected.

The President shall, at stated times, receive for his services a compensation, which shall neither be increased nor diminished during the period for which he shall have been elected, and he shall not receive within that period any other emolument from the United States, or any of them.

Before he enter on the execution of his office, he shall take the following oath or affirmation:—"I do solemnly swear (or affirm) that I will faithfully execute the office of the President of the United States, and will to the best of my ability preserve, protect and defend the Constitution of the United States."

Section 2 The President shall be commander in chief of the army and navy of the United States, and of the militia of the several States, when called into the actual service of the United States; he may require the opinion, in writing, of the principal officer in each of the executive departments, upon any subject relating to the duties of their respective offices, and he shall have power to grant reprieves and pardons for offenses against the United States, except in cases of impeachment.

He shall have power, by and with the advice and consent of the Senate, to make treaties, provided two-thirds of the Senators present concur; and he shall nominate, and by and with the advice and consent of the Senate, shall appoint ambassadors, other public ministers and consuls, judges of the Supreme Court, and all other officers of the United States, whose appointments are not herein otherwise provided for, and which shall be established by law: but Congress may by law vest the appointment of such inferior officers, as they think proper, in the President alone, in the courts of law, or in the heads of departments.

The President shall have power to fill up all vacancies that may happen during the recess of the Senate, by granting commissions which shall expire at the end of their next session.

Section 3 He shall from time to time give to the Congress information of the state of the Union, and recommend to their consideration such measures as he shall judge necessary and expedient; he may, on extraordinary occasions, convene both houses, or either of them, and in case of disagreement between them, with respect to the time of adjournment, he may adjourn them to such time as he shall think proper; he shall receive ambassadors and other public ministers; he shall take care that the laws be faithfully executed, and shall commission all the officers of the United States.

Section 4 The President, Vice-President and all civil officers of the United States shall be removed from office on impeachment for, and on conviction of, treason, bribery, or other high crimes and misdemeanors.

Article III

Section 1 The judicial power of the United States shall be vested in one Supreme Court, and in such inferior courts as the Congress may from time to time ordain and establish. The judges, both of the Supreme and inferior courts, shall hold their offices during good behavior, and shall, at stated times, receive for their services a compensation which shall not be diminished during their continuance in office.

Section 2 The judicial power shall extend to all cases, in law and equity, arising under this Constitution, the laws of the United States, and treaties made, or which shall be made, under their authority;—to all cases affecting ambassadors, other public ministers and consuls;—to all cases of admiralty and maritime jurisdiction;—to controversies to which the United States shall be a party;—to controversies between two or more States;—*between a State and citizens of another State;*—between citizens of different States;—between citizens of the same State claiming lands under grants of different States, and between a State, or the citizens thereof, and foreign states, citizens or subjects.

In all cases affecting ambassadors, other public ministers and consuls, and those in which a State shall be party, the Supreme Court shall have original jurisdiction. In all the other cases before mentioned, the Supreme Court shall have appellate jurisdiction, both as to law and fact, with such exceptions, and under such regulations, as the Congress shall make.

The trial of all crimes, except in cases of impeachment, shall be by jury; and such trial shall be held in the State where said crimes shall have been committed; but when not committed within any State, the trial shall be at such place or places as the Congress may by law have directed.

Section 3 Treason against the United States shall consist only in levying war against them, or in adhering to their enemies, giving them aid and comfort. No person shall be convicted of treason unless on the testimony of two witnesses to the same overt act, or on confession in open court.

The Congress shall have power to declare the punishment of treason, but no attainder of treason shall work corruption of blood, or forfeiture except during the life of the person attainted.

Article IV

Section 1 Full faith and credit shall be given in each State to the public acts, records, and judicial proceedings of every other State. And the Congress may by general laws prescribe the manner in which such acts, records, and proceedings shall be proved, and the effect thereof.

Section 2 The citizens of each State shall be entitled to all privileges and immunities of citizens in the several States.

A person charged in any State with treason, felony, or other crime, who shall flee from justice, and be found in another State, shall on demand of the executive authority of the State from which he fled, be delivered up, to be removed to the State having jurisdiction of the crime.

No person held to service or labor in one State, under the laws thereof, escaping into another, shall, in consequence of any law or regulation therein, be discharged from such service or labor, but shall be delivered up on claim of the party to whom such service or labor may be due.

Section 3 New States may be admitted by the Congress into this Union; but no new State shall be formed or erected within the jurisdiction of any other State; nor any State be formed by the junction of two or more States, or parts of States, without the consent of the legislatures of the States concerned as well as of the Congress.

The Congress shall have power to dispose of and make all needful rules and regulations respecting the territory or other property belonging to the United States; and nothing in this Constitution shall be so construed as to prejudice any claims of the United States, or of any particular State.

Section 4 The United States shall guarantee to every State in this Union a republican form of government, and shall protect each of them against invasion; and on application of the legislature, or of the executive (when the legislature cannot be convened), against domestic violence.

Article V

The Congress, whenever two-thirds of both houses shall deem it necessary, shall propose amendments to this Constitution, or, on the application of the legislatures of two-thirds of the several States, shall call a convention for proposing amendments, which, in either case, shall be valid to all intents and purposes, as part of this Constitution, when ratified by the legislatures of three-fourths of the several States, or by conventions in three-fourths thereof, as the one or the other mode of ratification may be proposed by the Congress; provided *that no amendments which may be made prior to the year one thousand eight hundred and eight shall in any manner affect the first and fourth clauses in the ninth section of the first article;* and that no State, without its consent, shall be deprived of its equal suffrage in the Senate.

Article VI

All debts contracted and engagements entered into, before the adoption of this Constitution, shall be as valid against the United States under this Constitution, as under the Confederation.

This Constitution, and the laws of the United States which shall be made in pursuance thereof; and all treaties made, or which shall be made, under the authority of the United States, shall be the supreme law of the land; and the judges in every State shall be bound thereby, anything in the Constitution or laws of any State to the contrary notwithstanding.

The Senators and Representatives before mentioned, and the members of the several State legislatures, and all executive and judicial officers, both of the United States and of the several States, shall be bound by oath or affirmation to support this Constitution; but no religious test shall ever be required as a qualification to any office or public trust under the United States.

Article VII

The ratification of the conventions of nine States shall be sufficient for the establishment of this Constitution between the States so ratifying the same.

Done in Convention by the unanimous consent of the States present, the seventeenth day of September in the year of our Lord one thousand seven hundred and eighty-seven and of the Independence of the United States of America the twelfth. In witness whereof we have hereunto subscribed our names.

GEORGE WASHINGTON
and thirty-seven others

*Amendments to the Constitution**

Amendment I

Congress shall make no law respecting an establishment of religion, or prohibiting the free exercise thereof; or abridging the freedom of speech, or of the press; or the right of the people peaceably to assemble, and to petition the government for a redress of grievances.

Amendment II

A well-regulated militia being necessary to the security of a free State, the right of the people to keep and bear arms shall not be infringed.

Amendment III

No soldier shall, in time of peace, be quartered in any house without the consent of the owner, nor in time of war, but in a manner to be prescribed by law.

Amendment IV

The right of the people to be secure in their persons, houses, papers, and effects, against unreasonable searches and seizures, shall not be violated, and no warrants shall issue but upon probable cause, supported by oath or affirmation, and particularly describing the place to be searched, and the persons or things to be seized.

---

*The first ten Amendments (the Bill of Rights) were adopted in 1791.

Amendment V

No person shall be held to answer for a capital, or otherwise infamous crime, unless on a presentment or indictment of a grand jury, except in cases arising in the land or naval forces, or in the militia, when in actual service in time of war or public danger; nor shall any person be subject for the same offense to be twice put in jeopardy of life or limb; nor shall be compelled in any criminal case to be a witness against himself, nor be deprived of life, liberty, or property, without due process of law; nor shall private property be taken for public use without just compensation.

Amendment VI

In all criminal prosecutions, the accused shall enjoy the right to a speedy and public trial, by an impartial jury of the State and district wherein the crime shall have been committed, which district shall have been previously ascertained by law, and to be informed of the nature and cause of the accusation; to be confronted with the witnesses against him; to have compulsory process for obtaining witnesses in his favor, and to have the assistance of counsel for his defense.

Amendment VII

In suits at common law, where the value in controversy shall exceed twenty dollars, the right of trial by jury shall be preserved, and no fact tried by a jury shall be otherwise reexamined in any court of the United States, than according to the rules of the common law.

Amendment VIII

Excessive bail shall not be required, nor excessive fines imposed, nor cruel and unusual punishments inflicted.

Amendment IX

The enumeration in the Constitution, of certain rights, shall not be construed to deny or disparage others retained by the people.

Amendment X

The powers not delegated to the United States by the Constitution, nor prohibited by it to the States, are reserved to the States respectively, or to the people.

Amendment XI
[Adopted 1798]

The judicial power of the United States shall not be construed to extend to any suit in law or equity, commenced or prosecuted against one of the United States by citizens of another State, or by citizens or subjects of any foreign state.

Amendment XII
[Adopted 1804]

The electors shall meet in their respective States, and vote by ballot for President and Vice-President, one of whom, at least, shall not be an inhabitant of the same State with themselves; they shall name in their ballots the person voted for as President, and in distinct ballots the person voted for as Vice-President, and they shall make distinct lists of all persons voted for as President, and of all persons voted for as Vice-President, and of the number of votes for each, which lists they shall sign and certify, and transmit sealed to the seat of government of the United States, directed to the President of the Senate;—the President of the Senate shall, in the presence of the Senate and House of Representatives, open all the certificates and the votes shall then be counted;—the person having the greatest number of votes for President shall be the President, if such number be a majority of the whole number of electors appointed; and if no person have such majority, then from the persons having the highest numbers not exceeding three on the list of those voted for as President, the House of Representatives shall choose immediately, by ballot, the President. But in choosing the President, the votes shall be taken by States, the representation from each State having one vote; a quorum for this purpose shall consist of a member or members from two-thirds of the States, and a majority of all the States shall be necessary to a choice. And if the House of Representatives shall not choose a President whenever the right of choice shall devolve upon them, before *the fourth day of March* next following, then the Vice-President shall act as President, as in the case of the death or other constitutional disability of the President.

The person having the greatest number of votes as Vice-President shall be the Vice-President, if such number be a majority of the whole number of electors appointed; and if no person have a majority, then from the two highest numbers on the list the Senate shall choose the Vice-President; a quorum for the purpose shall consist of two-thirds of the whole number of Senators, and a majority of the whole number shall be necessary to a choice. But no person constitutionally ineligible to the office of President shall be eligible to that of Vice-President of the United States.

Amendment XIII
[Adopted 1865]

Section 1 Neither slavery nor involuntary servitude, except as a punishment for crime whereof the party shall have been duly convicted, shall exist within the United States, or any place subject to their jurisdiction.

Section 2 Congress shall have power to enforce this article by appropriate legislation.

Amendment XIV
[Adopted 1868]

Section 1 All persons born or naturalized in the United States, and subject to the jurisdiction thereof, are citizens of the United States and of the State wherein they reside. No State shall make or enforce any law which shall abridge the privileges or immunities of citizens of the United States; nor shall any State deprive any person of life, liberty, or property, without due process of law; nor deny to any person within its jurisdiction the equal protection of the laws.

Section 2 Representatives shall be apportioned among the several States according to their respective numbers, counting the whole number of persons in each State, excluding Indians not taxed. But when the right to vote at any election for the choice of Electors for President and Vice-President of the United States, Representatives in Congress, the executive and judicial officers of a State, or the members of the legislature thereof, is denied to any of the male inhabitants of such State, being twenty-one years of age and citizens of the United States, or in any way abridged, except for participation in rebellion, or other crime, the basis of representation therein shall be reduced in the proportion which the number of such male citizens shall bear to the whole number of male citizens twenty-one years of age in such State.

Section 3 No person shall be a Senator or Representative in Congress, or Elector of President and Vice-President, or hold any office, civil or military, under the United States, or under any State, who, having previously taken an oath, as a member of Congress, or as an officer of the United States, or as a member of any State legislature, or as an executive or judicial officer of any State, to support the Constitution of the United States, shall have engaged in insurrection or rebellion against the same, or given aid or comfort to the enemies thereof. Congress may, by a vote of two-thirds of each house, remove such disability.

Section 4 The validity of the public debt of the United States, authorized by law, including debts incurred for payment of pensions and bounties for services in suppressing insurrection or rebellion, shall not be questioned. But neither the United States nor any State shall assume or pay any debt or obligation incurred in aid of insurrection or rebellion against the United States, or any claim for the loss of emancipation of any slave; but all such debts, obligations, and claims shall be held illegal and void.

Section 5   The Congress shall have power to enforce, by appropriate legislation, the provisions of this article.

Amendment XV
[Adopted 1870]

Section 1   The right of citizens of the United States to vote shall not be denied or abridged by the United States or by any State on account of race, color, or previous condition of servitude.

Section 2   The Congress shall have power to enforce this article by appropriate legislation.

Amendment XVI
[Adopted 1913]

The Congress shall have power to lay and collect taxes on incomes, from whatever source derived, without apportionment among the several States, and without regard to any census or enumeration.

Amendment XVII
[Adopted 1913]

Section 1   The Senate of the United States shall be composed of two Senators from each State, elected by the people thereof, for six years; and each Senator shall have one vote. The electors in each State shall have the qualifications requisite for electors of [voters for] the most numerous branch of the State legislatures.

Section 2   When vacancies happen in the representation of any State in the Senate, the executive authority of such State shall issue writs of election to fill such vacancies: Provided, that the Legislature of any State may empower the executive thereof to make temporary appointments until the people fill the vacancies by election as the Legislature may direct.

Section 3   This amendment shall not be so construed as to affect the election or term of any Senator chosen before it becomes valid as part of the Constitution.

Amendment XVIII
[Adopted 1919; Repealed 1933]

Section 1   After one year from the ratification of this article the manufacture, sale, or transportation of intoxicating liquors within, the importation thereof into, or the exportation thereof from the United States and all territory subject to the jurisdiction thereof, for beverage purposes, is hereby prohibited.

Section 2   The Congress and the several States shall have concurrent power to enforce this article by appropriate legislation.

Section 3   This article shall be inoperative unless it shall have been ratified as an amendment to the Constitution by the legislatures of the several States, as provided by the Constitution, within seven years from the date of the submission thereof to the States by the Congress.

Amendment XIX
[Adopted 1920]

Section 1   The right of citizens of the United States to vote shall not be denied or abridged by the United States or by any State on account of sex.

Section 2   The Congress shall have power to enforce this article by appropriate legislation.

Amendment XX
[Adopted 1933]

Section 1   The terms of the President and Vice-President shall end at noon on the 20th day of January, and the terms of Senators and Representatives at noon on the 3d day of January, of the years in which such terms would have ended if this article had not been ratified; and the terms of their successors shall then begin.

Section 2   The Congress shall assemble at least once in every year, and such meeting shall begin at noon on the 3d day of January, unless they shall by law appoint a different day.

Section 3   If, at the time fixed for the beginning of the term of the President, the President-elect shall have died, the Vice-President-elect shall become President. If a President shall not have been chosen before the time fixed for the beginning of his term, or if the President-elect shall have failed to qualify, then the Vice-President-elect shall act as President until a President shall have qualified; and the Congress may by law provide for the case wherein neither a President-elect nor a Vice-President-elect shall have qualified, declaring who shall then act as President, or the manner in which one who is to act shall be selected, and such persons shall act accordingly until a President or Vice-President shall have qualified.

Section 4   The Congress may by law provide for the case of the death of any of the persons from whom the House of Representatives may choose a President whenever the right of choice shall have devolved upon them, and for the case of the death of any of the persons from whom the Senate may choose a Vice-President whenever the right of choice shall have devolved upon them.

Section 5 Sections 1 and 2 shall take effect on the 15th day of October following the ratification of this article.

Section 6 This article shall be inoperative unless it shall have been ratified as an amendment to the Constitution by the Legislatures of three-fourths of the several States within seven years from the date of its submission.

Amendment XXI
[Adopted 1933]

Section 1 The eighteenth article of amendment to the Constitution of the United States is hereby repealed.

Section 2 The transportation or importation into any State, Territory, or Possession of the United States for delivery or use therein of intoxicating liquors, in violation of the laws thereof, is hereby prohibited.

Section 3 This article shall be inoperative unless it shall have been ratified as an amendment to the Constitution by conventions in the several States, as provided in the Constitution, within seven years from the date of submission thereof to the States by the Congress.

Amendment XXII
[Adopted 1951]

Section 1 No person shall be elected to the office of President more than twice, and no person who has held the office of President, or acted as President, for more than two years of a term to which some other person was elected President shall be elected to the office of President more than once. But this article shall not apply to any person holding the office of President when this article was proposed by the Congress, and shall not prevent any person who may be holding the office of President, or acting as President, during the term within which this article becomes operative from holding the office of President or acting as President during the remainder of such term.

Section 2 This article shall be inoperative unless it shall have been ratified as an amendment to the Constitution by the legislatures of three-fourths of the several States within seven years from the date of its submission to the States by the Congress.

Amendment XXIII
[Adopted 1961]

Section 1 The District constituting the seat of Government

of the United States shall appoint in such manner as the Congress may direct:

A number of electors of President and Vice-President equal to the whole number of Senators and Representatives in Congress to which the District would be entitled if it were a State, but in no event more than the least populous State; they shall be in addition to those appointed by the States, but they shall be considered for the purposes of the election of President and Vice-President, to be electors appointed by a State; and they shall meet in the District and perform such duties as provided by the twelfth article of amendment.

Section 2 The Congress shall have the power to enforce this article by appropriate legislation.

Amendment XXIV
[Adopted 1964]

Section 1 The right of citizens of the United States to vote in any primary or other election for President or Vice-President, for electors for President or Vice-President, or for Senator or Representative in Congress, shall not be denied or abridged by the United States or any State by reason of failure to pay any poll tax or other tax.

Section 2 The Congress shall have the power to enforce this article by appropriate legislation.

Amendment XXV
[Adopted 1967]

Section 1 In case of the removal of the President from office or of his death or resignation, the Vice President shall become President.

Section 2 Whenever there is a vacancy in the office of the Vice President, the President shall nominate a Vice President who shall take office upon confirmation by a majority vote of both Houses of Congress.

Section 3 Whenever the President transmits to the President pro tempore of the Senate and the Speaker of the House of Representatives his written declaration that he is unable to discharge the powers and duties of his office, and until he transmits to them a written declaration to the contrary, such powers and duties shall be discharged by the Vice President as Acting President.

Section 4 Whenever the Vice President and a majority of either the principal officers of the executive departments or of such other body as Congress may by law provide, transmit to the President pro tempore of the Senate and the Speaker of the House of Representatives their written declaration that the President is unable to discharge the powers and duties of his office, the Vice President shall immediately assume the powers and duties of the office as Acting President.

Thereafter, when the President transmits to the President pro tempore of the Senate and the Speaker of the House of Representatives his written declaration that no inability exists, he shall resume the powers and duties of his office unless the Vice President and a majority of either the principal officers of the executive department[s] or of such other body as Congress may by law provide, transmit within four days to the President pro tempore of the Senate and the Speaker of the House of Representatives their written declaration that the President is unable to discharge the powers and duties of his office. Thereupon Congress shall decide the issue, assembling within forty-eight hours for that purpose if not in session. If the Congress, within twenty-one days after receipt of the latter written declaration, or, if Congress is not in session, within twenty-one days after Congress is required to assemble, determines by two-thirds vote of both Houses that the President is unable to discharge the powers and duties of his office, the Vice President shall continue to discharge the same as Acting President; otherwise, the President shall resume the powers and duties of his office.

Amendment XXVI
[Adopted 1971]

Section 1   The right of citizens of the United States, who are eighteen years of age or older, to vote shall not be denied or abridged by the United States or by any State on account of age.

Section 2   The Congress shall have power to enforce this article by appropriate legislation.

THE AMERICAN PEOPLE AND NATION: A STATISTICAL PROFILE

Population of the United States

Year	Number of States	Population	Percent Increase	Population Per Square Mile	Percent Urban/ Rural	Percent Male/ Female	Percent White/ Nonwhite	Persons Per Household	Median Age
1790	13	3,929,214		4.5	5.1/94.9	NA/NA	80.7/19.3	5.79	NA
1800	16	5,308,483	35.1	6.1	6.1/93.9	NA/NA	81.1/18.9	NA	NA
1810	17	7,239,881	36.4	4.3	7.3/92.7	NA/NA	81.0/19.0	NA	NA
1820	23	9,638,453	33.1	5.5	7.2/92.8	50.8/49.2	81.6/18.4	NA	16.7
1830	24	12,866,020	33.5	7.4	8.8/91.2	50.8/49.2	81.9/18.1	NA	17.2
1840	26	17,069,453	32.7	9.8	10.8/89.2	50.9/49.1	83.2/16.8	NA	17.8
1850	31	23,191,876	35.9	7.9	15.3/84.7	51.0/49.0	84.3/15.7	5.55	18.9
1860	33	31,443,321	35.6	10.6	19.8/80.2	51.2/48.8	85.6/14.4	5.28	19.4
1870	37	39,818,449	26.6	13.4	25.7/74.3	50.6/49.4	86.2/13.8	5.09	20.2
1880	38	50,155,783	26.0	16.9	28.2/71.8	50.9/49.1	86.5/13.5	5.04	20.9
1890	44	62,947,714	25.5	21.2	35.1/64.9	51.2/48.8	87.5/12.5	4.93	22.0
1900	45	75,994,575	20.7	25.6	39.6/60.4	51.1/48.9	87.9/12.1	4.76	22.9
1910	46	91,972,266	21.0	31.0	45.6/54.4	51.5/48.5	88.9/11.1	4.54	24.1
1920	48	105,710,620	14.9	35.6	51.2/48.8	51.0/49.0	89.7/10.3	4.34	25.3
1930	48	122,775,046	16.1	41.2	56.1/43.9	50.6/49.4	89.8/10.2	4.11	26.4
1940	48	131,669,275	7.2	44.2	56.5/43.5	50.2/49.8	89.8/10.2	3.67	29.0
1950	48	150,697,361	14.5	50.7	64.0/36.0	49.7/50.3	89.5/10.5	3.37	30.2
1960	50	179,323,175	18.5	50.6	69.9/30.1	49.3/50.7	88.6/11.4	3.33	29.5
1970	50	203,302,031	13.4	57.4	73.5/26.5	48.7/51.3	87.6/12.4	3.14	28.0
1980	50	226,545,805	11.4	64.0	73.7/26.3	48.6/51.4	86.0/14.0	2.76	30.0
1983	50	236,600,000*	4.4	64.0	NA/NA	48.7/51.3	85.3/14.7	2.73	30.9

*1984 figure.
NA = Not available.

Vital Statistics

Year	Birth Rate*	Death Rate*	Life Expectancy in Years					Marriage Rate	Divorce Rate
			Total Population	White Females	Nonwhite Females	White Males	Nonwhite Males		
1790	NA	NA	NA	NA	NA	NA	NA	NA	NA
1800	55.0	NA	NA	NA	NA	NA	NA	NA	NA
1810	54.3	NA	NA	NA	NA	NA	NA	NA	NA
1820	55.2	NA	NA	NA	NA	NA	NA	NA	NA
1830	51.4	NA	NA	NA	NA	NA	NA	NA	NA
1840	51.8	NA	NA	NA	NA	NA	NA	NA	NA
1850	43.3	NA	NA	NA	NA	NA	NA	NA	NA
1860	44.3	NA	NA	NA	NA	NA	NA	NA	NA
1870	38.3	NA	NA	NA	NA	NA	NA	NA	NA
1880	39.8	NA	NA	NA	NA	NA	NA	NA	NA
1890	31.5	NA	NA	NA	NA	NA	NA	NA	NA
1900	32.3	17.2	47.3	48.7	33.5	46.6	32.5	NA	NA
1910	30.1	14.7	50.0	52.0	37.5	48.6	33.8	NA	NA
1920	27.7	13.0	54.1	55.6	45.2	54.4	45.5	12.0	1.6
1930	21.3	11.3	59.7	63.5	49.2	59.7	47.3	9.2	1.6
1940	19.4	10.8	62.9	66.6	54.9	62.1	51.5	12.1	2.0
1950	24.1	9.6	68.2	72.2	62.9	66.5	59.1	11.1	2.6
1960	23.7	9.5	69.7	74.1	66.3	67.4	61.1	8.5	2.2
1970	18.4	9.5	70.9	75.6	69.4	68.0	61.3	10.6	3.5
1980	15.9	8.8	73.7	78.1	73.6	70.7	65.3	10.6	5.2
1983	15.5	8.6	74.7	78.8	75.3	71.6	67.1	10.5	5.0

Data per one thousand for Birth, Death, Marriage, and Divorce rates.
NA = Not available.
*Data for 1800, 1810, 1830, 1850, 1870, and 1890 for whites only.

Immigration Totals by Decade

Years	Number	Years	Number
1820–1830	151,824	1911–1920	5,735,811
1831–1840	599,125	1921–1930	4,107,209
1841–1850	1,713,251	1931–1940	528,431
1851–1860	2,598,214	1941–1950	1,035,039
1861–1870	2,314,824	1951–1960	2,515,479
1871–1880	2,812,191	1961–1970	3,321,677
1881–1890	5,246,613	1971–1980	4,493,000
1891–1900	3,687,546	Total	49,655,620
1901–1910	8,795,386		

Source: U.S. Bureau of the Census, *Historical Statistics of the United States, Colonial Times to 1970* (1975), Part I, pp. 105–106; U.S. Bureau of the Census, *Statistical Abstract of the United States, 1984* (1983), p. 88.

Regional Origins of Immigrants (in percentages)

Period	Europe			Western Hemisphere	Asia	All Other
	Total Europe	North and West[a]	East and Central[b]	South and Other[c]		
1821–1830	69.2	67.1	—	2.1	8.4	—	22.4
1831–1840	82.8	81.8	—	1.0	5.5	—	11.7
1841–1850	93.3	92.9	0.1	0.3	3.6	—	3.1
1851–1860	94.4	93.6	0.1	0.8	2.9	1.6	1.1
1861–1870	89.2	87.8	0.5	0.9	7.2	2.8	0.8
1871–1880	80.8	73.6	4.5	2.7	14.4	4.4	0.4
1881–1890	90.3	72.0	11.9	6.3	8.1	1.3	0.3
1891–1900	96.5	44.5	32.8	19.1	1.1	1.9	0.5
1901–1910	92.5	21.7	44.5	26.3	4.1	2.8	0.6
1911–1920	76.3	17.4	33.4	25.5	19.9	3.4	0.4
1921–1930	60.3	31.7	14.4	14.3	36.9	2.4	0.4
1931–1940	65.9	38.8	11.0	16.1	30.3	2.8	0.9
1941–1950	60.1	47.5	4.6	7.9	34.3	3.1	2.5
1951–1960	52.8	17.7	24.3	10.8	39.6	6.0	1.6
1961–1970	33.8	11.7	9.4	12.9	51.7	12.9	1.7
1971–1979	18.4	4.8	4.4	9.2	44.9	34.1	2.6

Note: dash indicates less than 0.1 percent.

[a]Great Britain, Ireland, Norway, Sweden, Denmark, Iceland, Netherlands, Belgium, Luxembourg, Switzerland, France.

[b]Germany (Austria included, 1938–1945), Poland, Czechoslovakia (since 1920), Yugoslavia (since 1920), Hungary (since 1861), Austria (since 1861, except 1938–1945), U.S.S.R. (excludes Asian U.S.S.R. between 1931 and 1963), Latvia, Estonia, Lithuania, Finland, Romania, Bulgaria, Turkey (in Europe).

[c]Italy, Spain, Portugal, Greece, and other European countries not classified elsewhere.

Source: Stephan Thernstrom, ed., *Harvard Encyclopedia of American Ethnic Groups* (1980), p. 480; and U.S. Bureau of the Census, *Statistical Abstract of the United States, 1984* (1983), p. 9. Reprinted by permission of Harvard University Press.

Major Sources of Immigrants by Country (in thousands)

Period	Germany	Italy	Britain	Ireland	Austria-Hungary	Russia[a]	Canada	Denmark, Norway, Sweden[b]	Mexico	West Indies
1820–1830	8	—	27	54	—	—	2	—	5	4
1831–1840	152	2	76	207	—	—	14	2	7	12
1841–1850	435	2	267	781	—	—	42	14	3	14
1851–1860	952	9	424	914	—	—	59	25	3	11
1861–1870	787	12	607	436	8	3	154	126	2	9
1871–1880	718	56	548	437	73	39	384	243	5	14
1881–1890	1,453	307	807	655	354	213	393	656	2[c]	29
1891–1900	505	652	272	388	593	505	3	372	—	—[d]
1901–1910	341	2,046	526	339	2,145	1,597	179	505	50	108
1911–1920	144	1,110	341	146	896	922	742	203	219	123
1921–1930	412	455	330	221	64	89	925	198	459	75
1931–1940	114	68	29	13	11	7	109	11	22	16
1941–1950	227	58	132	28	28	4	172	27	61	50
1951–1960	478	185	192	57	104	6	378	57	300	123
1961–1970	191	214	206	40	26	7	413	43	454	470
1971–1979	68	124	122	11	15	31	156	13	584	668
Total	6,985	5,300	4,906	4,727	4,317	3,423	4,125	2,495	2,176	1,726

Notes: Numbers are rounded. Dash indicates less than one thousand.

[a]Includes Finland, Latvia, Estonia, and Lithuania.

[b]Includes Iceland.

[c]Figure for 1881–1885 only.

[d]Figure for 1894–1900 only.

Source: U.S. Bureau of the Census, *Historical Statistics of the United States: Colonial Times to 1970* (1975), Part I, pp. 105–108; U.S. Bureau of the Census, *Statistical Abstract of the United States, 1984* (1983), p. 91.

The American Farm

Year	Farm Population (in thousands)	Percent of Total Population	Number of Farms (in thousands)	Total Acres (in thousands)	Average Acreage Per Farm	Corn Production (millions of bushels)	Wheat Production (millions of bushels)
1850	NA	NA	1,449	293,561	203	592[a]	100[a]
1860	NA	NA	2,044	407,213	199	839[b]	173[b]
1870	NA	NA	2,660	407,735	153	1,125	254
1880	21,973	43.8	4,009	536,082	134	1,707	502
1890	24,771	42.3	4,565	623,219	137	1,650	449
1900	29,875	41.9	5,740	841,202	147	2,662	599
1910	32,077	34.9	6,366	881,431	139	2,853	625
1920	31,974	30.1	6,454	958,677	149	3,071	843
1930	30,529	24.9	6,295	990,112	157	2,080	887
1940	30,547	23.2	6,102	1,065,114	175	2,457	815
1950	23,048	15.3	5,388	1,161,420	216	3,075	1,019
1960	15,635	8.7	3,962	1,176,946	297	4,314	1,355
1970	9,712	4.8	2,949	1,102,769	374	4,200	1,370
1980	6,051	2.7	2,428	1,042,000	427	6,600	2,400
1983	5,787	2.5	2,370	1,024,000	432	4,200	2,400

[a]Figure for 1849.
[b]Figure for 1859.
NA = Not available.

The American Worker

Year	Total Number of Workers	Males as Percent of Total Workers	Females as Percent of Total Workers	Married Women as Percent of Female Workers	Female Workers as Percent of Female Population	Percent of Labor Force Unemployed	Percent of Workers in Labor Unions
1870	12,506,000	85	15	NA	NA	NA	NA
1880	17,392,000	85	15	NA	NA	NA	NA
1890	23,318,000	83	17	13.9	18.9	4 (1894 = 18%)	NA
1900	29,073,000	82	18	15.4	20.6	5	3
1910	38,167,000	79	21	24.7	25.4	6	6
1920	41,614,000	79	21	23.0	23.7	5 (1921 = 12%)	12
1930	48,830,000	78	22	28.9	24.8	9 (1933 = 25%)	7
1940	53,011,000	76	24	36.4	27.4	15 (1944 = 1%)	27
1950	59,643,000	72	28	52.1	31.4	5	25
1960	69,877,000	68	32	59.9	37.7	5.4	26
1970	82,049,000	63	37	63.4	43.3	4.8	25
1980	108,544,000	58	42	59.7	51.5	7.0	23
1983	113,226,000	57	43	58.9	52.9	9.5	19[a]

[a]1984 figure.
NA = Not available.

Year	Gross National Product (GNP) (in $ billions)	Steel Production (in short tons)	Automobiles Registered	New Housing Starts	Foreign Trade	
					Exports (in millions of dollars)	Imports
1790	NA	NA	NA	NA	20	23
1800	NA	NA	NA	NA	71	91
1810	NA	NA	NA	NA	67	85
1820	NA	NA	NA	NA	70	74
1830	NA	NA	NA	NA	74	71
1840	NA	NA	NA	NA	132	107
1850	NA	NA	NA	NA	152	178
1860	NA	13,000	NA	NA	400	362
1870	7.4[a]	77,000	NA	NA	451	462
1880	11.2[b]	1,397,000	NA	NA	853	761
1890	13.1	4,779,000	NA	328,000	910	823
1900	18.7	11,227,000	8,000	189,000	1,499	930
1910	35.3	28,330,000	458,300	387,000 (1918 = 118,000)	1,919	1,646
1920	91.5	46,183,000	8,131,500	247,000 (1925 = 937,000)	8,664	5,784
1930	90.7	44,591,000	23,034,700	330,000 (1933 = 93,000)	4,013	3,500
1940	100.0	66,983,000	27,465,800	603,000 (1944 = 142,000)	4,030	7,433
1950	286.5	96,836,000	40,339,000	1,952,000	10,816	9,125
1960	506.5	99,282,000	61,682,300	1,365,000	19,600	15,046
1970	992.7	131,514,000	89,279,800	1,469,000	42,700	40,189
1980	2,631.7	111,800,000	121,600,000	1,313,000	220,783	244,871
1983	3,304.8	84,600,000	125,382,000	1,712,000	200,538	258,048

[a]Figure is average for 1869–1878.
[b]Figure is average for 1879–1888.
NA = Not available.

Federal Spending and Debt

Year	Defense[a]	Interest on Public Debt[a]	Veterans Benefits and Services[a]	Income Security[ad]	Health[a]	Education and Manpower[a]	Federal Debt (dollars)
1790	14.9	55.0	4.1[b]	NA	NA	NA	75,463,000[c]
1800	55.7	31.3	.6	NA	NA	NA	82,976,000
1810	48.4 (1814 = 79.7)	34.9	1.0	NA	NA	NA	53,173,000
1820	38.4	28.1	17.6	NA	NA	NA	91,016,000
1830	52.9	12.6	9.0	NA	NA	NA	48,565,000
1840	54.3 (1847 = 80.7)	.7	10.7	NA	NA	NA	3,573,000
1850	43.8	1.0	4.7	NA	NA	NA	63,453,000
1860	44.2 (1865 = 88.9)	5.0	1.7	NA	NA	NA	64,844,000
1870	25.7	41.7	9.2	NA	NA	NA	2,436,453,000
1880	19.3	35.8	21.2	NA	NA	NA	2,090,909,000
1890	20.9 (1899 = 48.6)	11.4	33.6	NA	NA	NA	1,222,397,000
1900	36.6	7.7	27.0	NA	NA	NA	1,263,417,000
1910	45.1 (1919 = 59.5)	3.1	23.2	NA	NA	NA	1,146,940,000
1920	37.1	16.0	3.4	NA	NA	NA	24,299,321,000
1930	25.3	19.9	6.6	NA	NA	NA	16,185,310,000
1940	15.7 (1945 = 85.7)	10.9	6.5	15.2	.5	.8	42,967,531,000
1950	30.4 (1953 = 59.4)	13.3	20.5	10.9	.6	.5	257,357,352,000
1960	49.0	7.5	5.9	20.6	.9	1.1	286,330,761,000
1970	40.1	7.3	4.4	26.6	3.0	4.4	370,918,707,000
1980	23.6	9.1	3.7	41.1	4.0	5.3	914,300,000,000
1983	26.4	11.3	3.1	43.4	3.6	3.3	1,381,900,000,000

[a]Figures represent percentage of total federal spending for each category.
[b]1789–1791 figure.
[c]1791 figure.
[d]Includes Social Security and Medicare.
NA = Not available.

Territorial Expansion of the United States

Territory	Date Acquired	Square Miles	How Acquired
Original states and territories	1783	888,685	Treaty with Great Britain
Louisiana Purchase	1803	827,192	Purchase from France
Florida	1819	72,003	Treaty with Spain
Texas	1845	390,143	Annexation of independent nation
Oregon	1846	285,580	Treaty with Great Britain
Mexican Cession	1848	529,017	Conquest from Mexico
Gadsden Purchase	1853	29,640	Purchase from Mexico
Alaska	1867	589,757	Purchase from Russia
Hawaii	1898	6,450	Annexation of independent nation
The Philippines	1899	115,600	Conquest from Spain (granted independence in 1946)
Puerto Rico	1899	3,435	Conquest from Spain
Guam	1899	212	Conquest from Spain
American Samoa	1900	76	Treaty with Germany and Great Britain
Panama Canal Zone	1904	553	Treaty with Panama (returned to Panama by treaty in 1978)
Corn Islands	1914	4	Treaty with Nicaragua (returned to Nicaragua by treaty in 1971)
Virgin Islands	1917	133	Purchase from Denmark
Pacific Islands Trust (Micronesia)	1947	8,489	Trusteeship under United Nations (some granted independence)
All others (Midway, Wake, and other islands)		42	

Admission of States into the Union

State	Date of Admission	State	Date of Admission
1. Delaware	December 7, 1787	26. Michigan	January 26, 1837
2. Pennsylvania	December 12, 1787	27. Florida	March 3, 1845
3. New Jersey	December 18, 1787	28. Texas	December 29, 1845
4. Georgia	January 2, 1788	29. Iowa	December 28, 1846
5. Connecticut	January 9, 1788	30. Wisconsin	May 29, 1848
6. Massachusetts	February 6, 1788	31. California	September 9, 1850
7. Maryland	April 28, 1788	32. Minnesota	May 11, 1858
8. South Carolina	May 23, 1788	33. Oregon	February 14, 1859
9. New Hampshire	June 21, 1788	34. Kansas	January 29, 1861
10. Virginia	June 25, 1788	35. West Virginia	June 20, 1863
11. New York	July 26, 1788	36. Nevada	October 31, 1864
12. North Carolina	November 21, 1789	37. Nebraska	March 1, 1867
13. Rhode Island	May 29, 1790	38. Colorado	August 1, 1876
14. Vermont	March 4, 1791	39. North Dakota	November 2, 1889
15. Kentucky	June 1, 1792	40. South Dakota	November 2, 1889
16. Tennessee	June 1, 1796	41. Montana	November 8, 1889
17. Ohio	March 1, 1803	42. Washington	November 11, 1889
18. Louisiana	April 30, 1812	43. Idaho	July 3, 1890
19. Indiana	December 11, 1816	44. Wyoming	July 10, 1890
20. Mississippi	December 10, 1817	45. Utah	January 4, 1896
21. Illinois	December 3, 1818	46. Oklahoma	November 16, 1907
22. Alabama	December 14, 1819	47. New Mexico	January 6, 1912
23. Maine	March 15, 1820	48. Arizona	February 14, 1912
24. Missouri	August 10, 1821	49. Alaska	January 3, 1959
25. Arkansas	June 15, 1836	50. Hawaii	August 21, 1959

PRESIDENTIAL ELECTIONS

Year	Number of States	Candidates	Parties	Popular Vote	% of Popular Vote	Electoral Vote	% Voter Participation[b]
1789	11	**George Washington**	No party			69	
		John Adams	designations			34	
		Other candidates				35	
1792	15	**George Washington**	No party			132	
		John Adams	designations			77	
		George Clinton				50	
		Other candidates				5	
1796	16	**John Adams**	Federalist			71	
		Thomas Jefferson	Democratic-Republican			68	
		Thomas Pinckney	Federalist			59	
		Aaron Burr	Democratic-Republican			30	
		Other candidates				48	
1800	16	**Thomas Jefferson**	Democratic-Republican			73	
		Aaron Burr	Democratic-Republican			73	
		John Adams	Federalist			65	
		Charles C. Pinckney	Federalist			64	
		John Jay	Federalist			1	
1804	17	**Thomas Jefferson**	Democratic-Republican			162	
		Charles C. Pinckney	Federalist			14	
1808	17	**James Madison**	Democratic-Republican			122	
		Charles C. Pinckney	Federalist			47	
		George Clinton	Democratic-Republican			6	
1812	18	**James Madison**	Democratic-Republican			128	
		DeWitt Clinton	Federalist			89	
1816	19	**James Monroe**	Democratic-Republican			183	
		Rufus King	Federalist			34	
1820	24	**James Monroe**	Democratic-Republican			231	
		John Quincy Adams	Independent Republican			1	

Year	Number of States	Candidates	Parties	Popular Vote	% of Popular Vote	Electoral Vote	% Voter Participation[b]
1824	24	**John Quincy Adams**	Democratic-Republican	108,740	30.5	84	26.9
		Andrew Jackson	Democratic-Republican	153,544	43.1	99	
		Henry Clay	Democratic-Republican	47,136	13.2	37	
		William H. Crawford	Democratic-Republican	46,618	13.1	41	
1828	24	**Andrew Jackson**	Democratic	647,286	56.0	178	57.6
		John Quincy Adams	National Republican	508,064	44.0	83	
1832	24	**Andrew Jackson**	Democratic	688,242	54.5	219	55.4
		Henry Clay	National Republican	473,462	37.5	49	
		William Wirt	Anti-Masonic	101,051	8.0	7	
		John Floyd	Democratic			11	
1836	26	**Martin Van Buren**	Democratic	765,483	50.9	170	57.8
		William H. Harrison	Whig			73	
		Hugh L. White	Whig	739,795	49.1	26	
		Daniel Webster	Whig			14	
		W. P. Mangum	Whig			11	
1840	26	**William H. Harrison**	Whig	1,274,624	53.1	234	80.2
		Martin Van Buren	Democratic	1,127,781	46.9	60	
1844	26	**James K. Polk**	Democratic	1,338,464	49.6	170	78.9
		Henry Clay	Whig	1,300,097	48.1	105	
		James G. Birney	Liberty	62,300	2.3		
1848	30	**Zachary Taylor**	Whig	1,360,967	47.4	163	72.7
		Lewis Cass	Democratic	1,222,342	42.5	127	
		Martin Van Buren	Free Soil	291,263	10.1		
1852	31	**Franklin Pierce**	Democratic	1,601,117	50.9	254	69.6
		Winfield Scott	Whig	1,385,453	44.1	42	
		John P. Hale	Free Soil	155,825	5.0		
1856	31	**James Buchanan**	Democratic	1,832,955	45.3	174	78.9
		John C. Frémont	Republican	1,339,932	33.1	114	
		Millard Fillmore	American	871,731	21.6	8	
1860	33	**Abraham Lincoln**	Republican	1,865,593	39.8	180	81.2
		Stephen A. Douglas	Democratic	1,382,713	29.5	12	
		John C. Breckinridge	Democratic	848,356	18.1	72	
		John Bell	Constitutional Union	592,906	12.6	39	
1864	36	**Abraham Lincoln**	Republican	2,206,938	55.0	212	73.8
		George B. McClellan	Democratic	1,803,787	45.0	21	
1868	37	**Ulysses S. Grant**	Republican	3,013,421	52.7	214	78.1
		Horatio Seymour	Democratic	2,706,829	47.3	80	
1872	37	**Ulysses S. Grant**	Republican	3,596,745	55.6	286	71.3
		Horace Greeley	Democratic	2,843,446	43.9	a	
1876	38	**Rutherford B. Hayes**	Republican	4,036,572	48.0	185	81.8
		Samuel J. Tilden	Democratic	4,284,020	51.0	184	

Year	Number of States	Candidates	Parties	Popular Vote	% of Popular Vote	Electoral Vote	% Voter Participation[b]
1880	38	**James A. Garfield**	Republican	4,453,295	48.5	214	79.4
		Winfield S. Hancock	Democratic	4,414,082	48.1	155	
		James B. Weaver	Greenback-Labor	308,578	3.4		
1884	38	**Grover Cleveland**	Democratic	4,879,507	48.5	219	77.5
		James G. Blaine	Republican	4,850,293	48.2	182	
		Benjamin F. Butler	Greenback-Labor	175,370	1.8		
		John P. St. John	Prohibition	150,369	1.5		
1888	38	**Benjamin Harrison**	Republican	5,477,129	47.9	233	79.3
		Grover Cleveland	Democratic	5,537,857	48.6	168	
		Clinton B. Fisk	Prohibition	249,506	2.2		
		Anson J. Streeter	Union Labor	146,935	1.3		
1892	44	**Grover Cleveland**	Democratic	5,555,426	46.1	277	74.7
		Benjamin Harrison	Republican	5,182,690	43.0	145	
		James B. Weaver	People's	1,029,846	8.5	22	
		John Bidwell	Prohibition	264,133	2.2		
1896	45	**William McKinley**	Republican	7,102,246	51.1	271	79.3
		William J. Bryan	Democratic	6,492,559	47.7	176	
1900	45	**William McKinley**	Republican	7,218,491	51.7	292	73.2
		William J. Bryan	Democratic; Populist	6,356,734	45.5	155	
		John C. Wooley	Prohibition	208,914	1.5		
1904	45	**Theodore Roosevelt**	Republican	7,628,461	57.4	336	65.2
		Alton B. Parker	Democratic	5,084,223	37.6	140	
		Eugene V. Debs	Socialist	402,283	3.0		
		Silas C. Swallow	Prohibition	258,536	1.9		
1908	46	**William H. Taft**	Republican	7,675,320	51.6	321	65.4
		William J. Bryan	Democratic	6,412,294	43.1	162	
		Eugene V. Debs	Socialist	420,793	2.8		
		Eugene W. Chafin	Prohibition	253,840	1.7		
1912	48	**Woodrow Wilson**	Democratic	6,296,547	41.9	435	58.8
		Theodore Roosevelt	Progressive	4,118,571	27.4	88	
		William H. Taft	Republican	3,486,720	23.2	8	
		Eugene V. Debs	Socialist	900,672	6.0		
		Eugene W. Chafin	Prohibition	206,275	1.4		
1916	48	**Woodrow Wilson**	Democratic	9,127,695	49.4	277	61.6
		Charles E. Hughes	Republican	8,533,507	46.2	254	
		A. L. Benson	Socialist	585,113	3.2		
		J. Frank Hanly	Prohibition	220,506	1.2		
1920	48	**Warren G. Harding**	Republican	16,143,407	60.4	404	49.2
		James M. Cox	Democratic	9,130,328	34.2	127	
		Eugene V. Debs	Socialist	919,799	3.4		
		P. P. Christensen	Farmer-Labor	265,411	1.0		
1924	48	**Calvin Coolidge**	Republican	15,718,211	54.0	382	48.9
		John W. Davis	Democratic	8,385,283	28.8	136	
		Robert M. La Follette	Progressive	4,831,289	16.6	13	

Year	Number of States	Candidates	Parties	Popular Vote	% of Popular Vote	Electoral Vote	% Voter Participation[b]
1928	48	**Herbert C. Hoover**	Republican	21,391,993	58.2	444	56.9
		Alfred E. Smith	Democratic	15,016,169	40.9	87	
1932	48	**Franklin D. Roosevelt**	Democratic	22,809,638	57.4	472	56.9
		Herbert C. Hoover	Republican	15,758,901	39.7	59	
		Norman Thomas	Socialist	881,951	2.2		
1936	48	**Franklin D. Roosevelt**	Democratic	27,752,869	60.8	523	61.0
		Alfred M. Landon	Republican	16,674,665	36.5	8	
		William Lemke	Union	882,479	1.9		
1940	48	**Franklin D. Roosevelt**	Democratic	27,307,819	54.8	449	62.5
		Wendell L. Wilkie	Republican	22,321,018	44.8	82	
1944	48	**Franklin D. Roosevelt**	Democratic	25,606,585	53.5	432	55.9
		Thomas E. Dewey	Republican	22,014,745	46.0	99	
1948	48	**Harry S Truman**	Democratic	24,179,345	49.6	303	53.0
		Thomas E. Dewey	Republican	21,991,291	45.1	189	
		J. Strom Thurmond	States' Rights	1,176,125	2.4	39	
		Henry A. Wallace	Progressive	1,157,326	2.4		
1952	48	**Dwight D. Eisenhower**	Republican	33,936,234	55.1	442	63.3
		Adlai E. Stevenson	Democratic	27,314,992	44.4	89	
1956	48	**Dwight D. Eisenhower**	Republican	35,590,472	57.6	457	60.6
		Adlai E. Stevenson	Democratic	26,022,752	42.1	73	
1960	50	**John F. Kennedy**	Democratic	34,226,731	49.7	303	62.8
		Richard M. Nixon	Republican	34,108,157	49.5	219	
1964	50	**Lyndon B. Johnson**	Democratic	43,129,566	61.1	486	61.7
		Barry M. Goldwater	Republican	27,178,188	38.5	52	
1968	50	**Richard M. Nixon**	Republican	31,785,480	43.4	301	60.6
		Hubert H. Humphrey	Democratic	31,275,166	42.7	191	
		George C. Wallace	American Independent	9,906,473	13.5	46	
1972	50	**Richard M. Nixon**	Republican	47,169,911	60.7	520	55.2
		George S. McGovern	Democratic	29,170,383	37.5	17	
		John G. Schmitz	American	1,099,482	1.4		
1976	50	**Jimmy Carter**	Democratic	40,830,763	50.1	297	53.5
		Gerald R. Ford	Republican	39,147,793	48.0	240	
1980	50	**Ronald Reagan**	Republican	43,899,248	50.8	489	52.6
		Jimmy Carter	Democratic	35,481,432	41.0	49	
		John B. Anderson	Independent	5,719,437	6.6	0	
		Ed Clark	Libertarian	920,859	1.1	0	
1984	50	**Ronald Reagan**	Republican	54,451,521	58.8	525	53.3
		Walter Mondale	Democratic	37,565,334	40.5	13	

Candidates receiving less than 1 percent of the popular vote have been omitted. Thus the percentage of popular vote given for any election year may not total 100 percent.

Before the passage of the Twelfth Amendment in 1804, the Electoral College voted for two presidential candidates; the runner-up became vice president.

Before 1824, most presidential electors were chosen by state legislatures, not by popular vote.

[a]Greeley died shortly after the election; the electors supporting him then divided their votes among minor candidates.

[b]Percent of voting-age population casting ballots.

PRESIDENTS, VICE PRESIDENTS, AND CABINET MEMBERS

The Washington Administration

President	George Washington	1789–1797
Vice President	John Adams	1789–1797
Secretary of State	Thomas Jefferson	1789–1793
	Edmund Randolph	1794–1795
	Timothy Pickering	1795–1797
Secretary of Treasury	Alexander Hamilton	1789–1795
	Oliver Wolcott	1795–1797
Secretary of War	Henry Knox	1789–1794
	Timothy Pickering	1795–1796
	James McHenry	1796–1797
Attorney General	Edmund Randolph	1789–1793
	William Bradford	1794–1795
	Charles Lee	1795–1797
Postmaster General	Samuel Osgood	1789–1791
	Timothy Pickering	1791–1794
	Joseph Habersham	1795–1797

The John Adams Administration

President	John Adams	1797–1801
Vice President	Thomas Jefferson	1797–1801
Secretary of State	Timothy Pickering	1797–1800
	John Marshall	1800–1801
Secretary of Treasury	Oliver Wolcott	1797–1800
	Samuel Dexter	1800–1801
Secretary of War	James McHenry	1797–1800
	Samuel Dexter	1800–1801
Attorney General	Charles Lee	1797–1801
Postmaster General	Joseph Habersham	1797–1801
Secretary of Navy	Benjamin Stoddert	1798–1801

The Jefferson Administration

President	Thomas Jefferson	1801–1809
Vice President	Aaron Burr	1801–1805
	George Clinton	1805–1809
Secretary of State	James Madison	1801–1809
Secretary of Treasury	Samuel Dexter	1801
	Albert Gallatin	1801–1809
Secretary of War	Henry Dearborn	1801–1809
Attorney General	Levi Lincoln	1801–1805
	Robert Smith	1805
	John Breckinridge	1805–1806
	Caesar Rodney	1807–1809

Postmaster General	Joseph Habersham	1801
	Gideon Granger	1801–1809
Secretary of Navy	Robert Smith	1801–1809

The Madison Administration

President	James Madison	1809–1817
Vice President	George Clinton	1809–1813
	Elbridge Gerry	1813–1817
Secretary of State	Robert Smith	1809–1811
	James Monroe	1811–1817
Secretary of Treasury	Albert Gallatin	1809–1813
	George Campbell	1814
	Alexander Dallas	1814–1816
	William Crawford	1816–1817
Secretary of War	William Eustis	1809–1812
	John Armstrong	1813–1814
	James Monroe	1814–1815
	William Crawford	1815–1817
Attorney General	Caesar Rodney	1809–1811
	William Pinkney	1811–1814
	Richard Rush	1814–1817
Postmaster General	Gideon Granger	1809–1814
	Return Meigs	1814–1817
Secretary of Navy	Paul Hamilton	1809–1813
	William Jones	1813–1814
	Benjamin Crowninshield	1814–1817

The Monroe Administration

President	James Monroe	1817–1825
Vice President	Daniel Tompkins	1817–1825
Secretary of State	John Quincy Adams	1817–1825
Secretary of Treasury	William Crawford	1817–1825
Secretary of War	George Graham	1817
	John C. Calhoun	1817–1825
Attorney General	Richard Rush	1817
	William Wirt	1817–1825
Postmaster General	Return Meigs	1817–1823
	John McLean	1823–1825
Secretary of Navy	Benjamin Crowninshield	1817–1818
	Smith Thompson	1818–1823
	Samuel Southard	1823–1825

The John Quincy Adams Administration

President	John Quincy Adams	1825–1829
Vice President	John C. Calhoun	1825–1829
Secretary of State	Henry Clay	1825–1829
Secretary of Treasury	Richard Rush	1825–1829
Secretary of War	James Barbour	1825–1828
	Peter Porter	1828–1829
Attorney General	William Wirt	1825–1829
Postmaster General	John McLean	1825–1829
Secretary of Navy	Samuel Southard	1825–1829

The Jackson Administration

President	Andrew Jackson	1829–1837
Vice President	John C. Calhoun	1829–1833
	Martin Van Buren	1833–1837
Secretary of State	Martin Van Buren	1829–1831
	Edward Livingston	1831–1833
	Louis McLane	1833–1834
	John Forsyth	1834–1837
Secretary of Treasury	Samuel Ingham	1829–1831
	Louis McLane	1831–1833
	William Duane	1833
	Roger B. Taney	1833–1834
	Levi Woodbury	1834–1837
Secretary of War	John H. Eaton	1829–1831
	Lewis Cass	1831–1837
	Benjamin Butler	1837
Attorney General	John M. Berrien	1829–1831
	Roger B. Taney	1831–1833
	Benjamin Butler	1833–1837
Postmaster General	William Barry	1829–1835
	Amos Kendall	1835–1837
Secretary of Navy	John Branch	1829–1831
	Levi Woodbury	1831–1834
	Mahlon Dickerson	1834–1837

The Van Buren Administration

President	Martin Van Buren	1837–1841
Vice President	Richard M. Johnson	1837–1841
Secretary of State	John Forsyth	1837–1841
Secretary of Treasury	Levi Woodbury	1837–1841
Secretary of War	Joel Poinsett	1837–1841
Attorney General	Benjamin Butler	1837–1838
	Felix Grundy	1838–1840
	Henry D. Gilpin	1840–1841
Postmaster General	Amos Kendall	1837–1840'
	John M. Niles	1840–1841
Secretary of Navy	Mahlon Dickerson	1837–1838
	James Paulding	1838–1841

The William Harrison Administration

President	William H. Harrison	1841
Vice President	John Tyler	1841
Secretary of State	Daniel Webster	1841
Secretary of Treasury	Thomas Ewing	1841
Secretary of War	John Bell	1841
Attorney General	John J. Crittenden	1841
Postmaster General	Francis Granger	1841
Secretary of Navy	George Badger	1841

The Tyler Administration

President	John Tyler	1841–1845
Vice President	None	
Secretary of State	Daniel Webster	1841–1843
	Hugh S. Legaré	1843
	Abel P. Upshur	1843–1844
	John C. Calhoun	1844–1845
Secretary of Treasury	Thomas Ewing	1841
	Walter Forward	1841–1843
	John C. Spencer	1843–1844
	George Bibb	1844–1845
Secretary of War	John Bell	1841
	John C. Spencer	1841–1843
	James M. Porter	1843–1844
	William Wilkins	1844–1845
Attorney General	John J. Crittenden	1841
	Hugh S. Legaré	1841–1843
	John Nelson	1843–1845
Postmaster General	Francis Granger	1841
	Charles Wickliffe	1841
Secretary of Navy	George Badger	1841
	Abel P. Upshur	1841
	David Henshaw	1843–1844
	Thomas Gilmer	1844
	John Y. Mason	1844–1845

The Polk Administration

President	James K. Polk	1845–1849
Vice President	George M. Dallas	1845–1849
Secretary of State	James Buchanan	1845–1849
Secretary of Treasury	Robert J. Walker	1845–1849
Secretary of War	William L. Marcy	1845–1849
Attorney General	John Y. Mason	1845–1846
	Nathan Clifford	1846–1848
	Isaac Toucey	1848–1849
Postmaster General	Cave Johnson	1845–1849
Secretary of Navy	George Bancroft	1845–1846
	John Y. Mason	1846–1849

The Taylor Administration

President	Zachary Taylor	1849–1850
Vice President	Millard Fillmore	1849–1850
Secretary of State	John M. Clayton	1849–1850
Secretary of Treasury	William Meredith	1849–1850
Secretary of War	George Crawford	1849–1850
Attorney General	Reverdy Johnson	1849–1850
Postmaster General	Jacob Collamer	1849–1850
Secretary of Navy	William Preston	1849–1850
Secretary of Interior	Thomas Ewing	1849–1850

The Fillmore Administration

President	Millard Fillmore	1850–1853
Vice President	None	
Secretary of State	Daniel Webster	1850–1852
	Edward Everett	1852–1853
Secretary of Treasury	Thomas Corwin	1850–1853
Secretary of War	Charles Conrad	1850–1853
Attorney General	John J. Crittenden	1850–1853
Postmaster General	Nathan Hall	1850–1852
	Sam D. Hubbard	1852–1853
Secretary of Navy	William A. Graham	1850–1852
	John P. Kennedy	1852–1853
Secretary of Interior	Thomas McKennan	1850
	Alexander Stuart	1850–1853

The Pierce Administration

President	Franklin Pierce	1853–1857
Vice President	William R. King	1853–1857
Secretary of State	William L. Marcy	1853–1857
Secretary of Treasury	James Guthrie	1853–1857
Secretary of War	Jefferson Davis	1853–1857
Attorney General	Caleb Cushing	1853–1857
Postmaster General	James Campbell	1853–1857
Secretary of Navy	James C. Dobbin	1853–1857
Secretary of Interior	Robert McClelland	1853–1857

The Buchanan Administration

President	James Buchanan	1857–1861
Vice President	John C. Breckinridge	1857–1861
Secretary of State	Lewis Cass	1857–1860
	Jeremiah S. Black	1860–1861
Secretary of Treasury	Howell Cobb	1857–1860
	Philip Thomas	1860–1861
	John A. Dix	1861
Secretary of War	John B. Floyd	1857–1861
	Joseph Holt	1861
Attorney General	Jeremiah S. Black	1857–1860
	Edwin M. Stanton	1860–1861
Postmaster General	Aaron V. Brown	1857–1859
	Joseph Holt	1859–1861
	Horatio King	1861
Secretary of Navy	Isaac Toucey	1857–1861
Secretary of Interior	Jacob Thompson	1857–1861

The Lincoln Administration

President	Abraham Lincoln	1861–1865
Vice President	Hannibal Hamlin	1861–1865
	Andrew Johnson	1865
Secretary of State	William H. Seward	1861–1865
Secretary of Treasury	Samuel P. Chase	1861–1864
	William P. Fessenden	1864–1865
	Hugh McCulloch	1865
Secretary of War	Simon Cameron	1861–1862
	Edwin M. Stanton	1862–1865
Attorney General	Edward Bates	1861–1864
	James Speed	1864–1865

Postmaster General	Horatio King	1861
	Montgomery Blair	1861–1864
	William Dennison	1864–1865
Secretary of Navy	Gideon Welles	1861–1865
Secretary of Interior	Caleb B. Smith	1861–1863
	John P. Usher	1863–1865

The Andrew Johnson Administration

President	Andrew Johnson	1865–1869
Vice President	None	
Secretary of State	William H. Seward	1865–1869
Secretary of Treasury	Hugh McCulloch	1865–1869
Secretary of War	Edwin M. Stanton	1865–1867
	Ulysses S. Grant	1867–1868
	Lorenzo Thomas	1868
	John M. Schofield	1868–1869
Attorney General	James Speed	1865–1866
	Henry Stanbery	1866–1868
	William M. Evarts	1868–1869
Postmaster General	William Dennison	1865–1866
	Alexander Randall	1866–1869
Secretary of Navy	Gideon Welles	1865–1869
Secretary of Interior	John P. Usher	1865
	James Harlan	1865–1866
	Orville H. Browning	1866–1869

The Grant Administration

President	Ulysses S. Grant	1869–1877
Vice President	Schuyler Colfax	1869–1873
	Henry Wilson	1873–1877
Secretary of State	Elihu B. Washburne	1869
	Hamilton Fish	1869–1877
Secretary of Treasury	George S. Boutwell	1869–1873
	William Richardson	1873–1874
	Benjamin Bristow	1874–1876
	Lot M. Morrill	1876–1877
Secretary of War	John A. Rawlins	1869
	William T. Sherman	1869
	William W. Belknap	1869–1876
	Alphonso Taft	1876
	James D. Cameron	1876–1877
Attorney General	Ebenezer Hoar	1869–1870
	Amos T. Ackerman	1870–1871
	G. H. Williams	1871–1875
	Edwards Pierrepont	1875–1876
	Alphonso Taft	1876–1877

Postmaster General	John A. J. Creswell	1869–1874
	James W. Marshall	1874
	Marshall Jewell	1874–1876
	James N. Tyner	1876–1877
Secretary of Navy	Adolph E. Borie	1869
	George M. Robeson	1869–1877
Secretary of Interior	Jacob D. Cox	1869–1870
	Columbus Delano	1870–1875
	Zachariah Chandler	1875–1877

The Hayes Administration

President	Rutherford B. Hayes	1877–1881
Vice President	William A. Wheeler	1877–1881
Secretary of State	William B. Evarts	1877–1881
Secretary of Treasury	John Sherman	1877–1881
Secretary of War	George W. McCrary	1877–1879
	Alex Ramsey	1879–1881
Attorney General	Charles Devens	1877–1881
Postmaster General	David M. Key	1877–1880
	Horace Maynard	1880–1881
Secretary of Navy	Richard W. Thompson	1877–1880
	Nathan Goff, Jr.	1881
Secretary of Interior	Carl Schurz	1877–1881

The Garfield Administration

President	James A. Garfield	1881
Vice President	Chester A. Arthur	1881
Secretary of State	James G. Blaine	1881
Secretary of Treasury	William Windom	1881
Secretary of War	Robert T. Lincoln	1881
Attorney General	Wayne MacVeagh	1881
Postmaster General	Thomas L. James	1881
Secretary of Navy	William H. Hunt	1881
Secretary of Interior	Samuel J. Kirkwood	1881

The Arthur Administration

President	Chester A. Arthur	1881–1885
Vice President	None	
Secretary of State	F. T. Frelinghuysen	1881–1885

Secretary of Treasury	Charles J. Folger	1881–1884
	Walter Q. Gresham	1884
	Hugh McCulloch	1884–1885
Secretary of War	Robert T. Lincoln	1881–1885
Attorney General	Benjamin H. Brewster	1881–1885
Postmaster General	Timothy O. Howe	1881–1883
	Walter Q. Gresham	1883–1884
	Frank Hatton	1884–1885
Secretary of Navy	William H. Hunt	1881–1882
	William E. Chandler	1882–1885
Secretary of Interior	Samuel J. Kirkwood	1881–1882
	Henry M. Teller	1882–1885

The Cleveland Administration

President	Grover Cleveland	1885–1889
Vice President	Thomas A. Hendricks	1885–1889
Secretary of State	Thomas F. Bayard	1885–1889
Secretary of Treasury	Daniel Manning	1885–1887
	Charles S. Fairchild	1887–1889
Secretary of War	William C. Endicott	1885–1889
Attorney General	Augustus H. Garland	1885–1889
Postmaster General	William F. Vilas	1885–1888
	Don M. Dickinson	1888–1889
Secretary of Navy	William C. Whitney	1885–1889
Secretary of Interior	Lucius Q. C. Lamar	1885–1888
	William F. Vilas	1888–1889
Secretary of Agriculture	Norman J. Colman	1889

The Benjamin Harrison Administration

President	Benjamin Harrison	1889–1893
Vice President	Levi P. Morton	1889–1893
Secretary of State	James G. Blaine	1889–1892
	John W. Foster	1892–1893
Secretary of Treasury	William Windom	1889–1891
	Charles Foster	1891–1893
Secretary of War	Redfield Proctor	1889–1891
	Stephen B. Elkins	1891–1893
Attorney General	William H. H. Miller	1889–1891
Postmaster General	John Wanamaker	1889–1893
Secretary of Navy	Benjamin F. Tracy	1889–1893
Secretary of Interior	John W. Noble	1889–1893
Secretary of Agriculture	Jeremiah M. Rusk	1889–1893

The Cleveland Administration

President	Grover Cleveland	1893–1897
Vice President	Adlai E. Stevenson	1893–1897
Secretary of State	Walter Q. Gresham	1893–1895
	Richard Olney	1895–1897
Secretary of Treasury	John G. Carlisle	1893–1897
Secretary of War	Daniel S. Lamont	1893–1897
Attorney General	Richard Olney	1893–1895
	James Harmon	1895–1897
Postmaster General	Wilson S. Bissell	1893–1895
	William L. Wilson	1895–1897
Secretary of Navy	Hilary A. Herbert	1893–1897
Secretary of Interior	Hoke Smith	1893–1896
	David R. Francis	1896–1897
Secretary of Agriculture	Julius S. Morton	1893–1897

The McKinley Administration

President	William McKinley	1897–1901
Vice President	Garret A. Hobart	1897–1901
	Theodore Roosevelt	1901
Secretary of State	John Sherman	1897–1898
	William R. Day	1898
	John Hay	1898–1901
Secretary of Treasury	Lyman J. Gage	1897–1901
Secretary of War	Russell A. Alger	1897–1899
	Elihu Root	1899–1901
Attorney General	Joseph McKenna	1897–1898
	John W. Griggs	1898–1901
	Philander C. Knox	1901
Postmaster General	James A. Gary	1897–1898
	Charles E. Smith	1898–1901
Secretary of Navy	John D. Long	1897–1901
Secretary of Interior	Cornelius N. Bliss	1897–1899
	Ethan A. Hitchcock	1899–1901
Secretary of Agriculture	James Wilson	1897–1901

The Theodore Roosevelt Administration

President	Theodore Roosevelt	1901–1909
Vice President	Charles Fairbanks	1905–1909
Secretary of State	John Hay	1901–1905
	Elihu Root	1905–1909
	Robert Bacon	1909

Secretary of Treasury	Lyman J. Gage	1901–1902
	Leslie M. Shaw	1902–1907
	George B. Cortelyou	1907–1909
Secretary of War	Elihu Root	1901–1904
	William H. Taft	1904–1908
	Luke E. Wright	1908–1909
Attorney General	Philander C. Knox	1901–1904
	William H. Moody	1904–1906
	Charles J. Bonaparte	1906–1909
Postmaster General	Charles E. Smith	1901–1902
	Henry C. Payne	1902–1904
	Robert J. Wynne	1904–1905
	George B. Cortelyou	1905–1907
	George von L. Meyer	1907–1909
Secretary of Navy	John D. Long	1901–1902
	William H. Moody	1902–1904
	Paul Morton	1904–1905
	Charles J. Bonaparte	1905–1906
	Victor H. Metcalf	1906–1908
	Truman H. Newberry	1908–1909
Secretary of Interior	Ethan A. Hitchcock	1901–1907
	James R. Garfield	1907–1909
Secretary of Agriculture	James Wilson	1901–1909
Secretary of Labor and Commerce	George B. Cortelyou	1903–1904
	Victor H. Metcalf	1904–1906
	Oscar S. Straus	1906–1909
	Charles Nagel	1909

The Taft Administration

President	William H. Taft	1909–1913
Vice President	James S. Sherman	1909–1913
Secretary of State	Philander C. Knox	1909–1913
Secretary of Treasury	Franklin MacVeagh	1909–1913
Secretary of War	Jacob M. Dickinson	1909–1911
	Henry L. Stimson	1911–1913
Attorney General	George W. Wickersham	1909–1913
Postmaster General	Frank H. Hitchcock	1909–1913
Secretary of Navy	George von L. Meyer	1909–1913
Secretary of Interior	Richard A. Ballinger	1909–1911
	Walter L. Fisher	1911–1913
Secretary of Agriculture	James Wilson	1909–1913
Secretary of Labor and Commerce	Charles Nagel	1909–1913

The Wilson Administration

President	Woodrow Wilson	1913–1921
Vice President	Thomas R. Marshall	1913–1921
Secretary of State	William J. Bryan	1913–1915
	Robert Lansing	1915–1920
	Bainbridge Colby	1920–1921
Secretary of Treasury	William G. McAdoo	1913–1918
	Carter Glass	1918–1920
	David F. Houston	1920–1921
Secretary of War	Lindley M. Garrison	1913–1916
	Newton D. Baker	1916–1921
Attorney General	James C. McReynolds	1913–1914
	Thomas W. Gregory	1914–1919
	A. Mitchell Palmer	1919–1921
Postmaster General	Albert S. Burleson	1913–1921
Secretary of Navy	Josephus Daniels	1913–1921
Secretary of Interior	Franklin K. Lane	1913–1920
	John B. Payne	1920–1921
Secretary of Agriculture	David F. Houston	1913–1920
	Edwin T. Meredith	1920–1921
Secretary of Commerce	William C. Redfield	1913–1919
	Joshua W. Alexander	1919–1921
Secretary of Labor	William B. Wilson	1913–1921

The Harding Administration

President	Warren G. Harding	1921–1923
Vice President	Calvin Coolidge	1921–1923
Secretary of State	Charles E. Hughes	1921–1923
Secretary of Treasury	Andrew Mellon	1921–1923
Secretary of War	John W. Weeks	1921–1923
Attorney General	Harry M. Daugherty	1921–1923
Postmaster General	Will H. Hays	1921–1922
	Hubert Work	1922–1923
	Harry S. New	1923
Secretary of Navy	Edwin Denby	1921–1923
Secretary of Interior	Albert B. Fall	1921–1923
	Hubert Work	1923
Secretary of Agriculture	Henry C. Wallace	1921–1923
Secretary of Commerce	Herbert C. Hoover	1921–1923
Secretary of Labor	James J. Davis	1921–1923

The Coolidge Administration

President	Calvin Coolidge	1923–1929
Vice President	Charles G. Dawes	1925–1929
Secretary of State	Charles E. Hughes	1923–1925
	Frank B. Kellogg	1925–1929
Secretary of Treasury	Andrew Mellon	1923–1929
Secretary of War	John W. Weeks	1923–1925
	Dwight F. Davis	1925–1929
Attorney General	Henry M. Daugherty	1923–1924
	Harlan F. Stone	1924–1925
	John G. Sargent	1925–1929
Postmaster General	Harry S. New	1923–1929
Secretary of Navy	Edwin Derby	1923–1924
	Curtis D. Wilbur	1924–1929
Secretary of Interior	Hubert Work	1923–1928
	Roy O. West	1928–1929
Secretary of Agriculture	Henry C. Wallace	1923–1924
	Howard M. Gore	1924–1925
	William M. Jardine	1925–1929
Secretary of Commerce	Herbert C. Hoover	1923–1928
	William F. Whiting	1928–1929
Secretary of Labor	James J. Davis	1923–1929

The Hoover Administration

President	Herbert C. Hoover	1929–1933
Vice President	Charles Curtis	1929–1933
Secretary of State	Henry L. Stimson	1929–1933
Secretary of Treasury	Andrew Mellon	1929–1932
	Ogden L. Mills	1932–1933
Secretary of War	James W. Good	1929
	Patrick J. Hurley	1929–1933
Attorney General	William D. Mitchell	1929–1933
Postmaster General	Walter F. Brown	1929–1933
Secretary of Navy	Charles F. Adams	1929–1933
Secretary of Interior	Ray L. Wilbur	1929–1933
Secretary of Agriculture	Arthur M. Hyde	1929–1933
Secretary of Commerce	Robert P. Lamont	1929–1932
	Roy D. Chapin	1932–1933
Secretary of Labor	James J. Davis	1929–1930
	William N. Doak	1930–1933

The Franklin D. Roosevelt Administration

President	Franklin D. Roosevelt	1933–1945
Vice President	John Nance Garner	1933–1941
	Henry A. Wallace	1941–1945
	Harry S Truman	1945
Secretary of State	Cordell Hull	1933–1944
	Edward R. Stettinius, Jr.	1944–1945
Secretary of Treasury	William H. Woodin	1933–1934
	Henry Morgenthau, Jr.	1934–1945
Secretary of War	George H. Dern	1933–1936
	Henry A. Woodring	1936–1940
	Henry L. Stimson	1940–1945
Attorney General	Homer S. Cummings	1933–1939
	Frank Murphy	1939–1940
	Robert H. Jackson	1940–1941
	Francis Biddle	1941–1945
Postmaster General	James A. Farley	1933–1940
	Frank C. Walker	1940–1945
Secretary of Navy	Claude A. Swanson	1933–1940
	Charles Edison	1940
	Frank Knox	1940–1944
	James V. Forrestal	1944–1945
Secretary of Interior	Harold L. Ickes	1933–1945
Secretary of Agriculture	Henry A. Wallace	1933–1940
	Claude R. Wickard	1940–1945
Secretary of Commerce	Daniel C. Roper	1933–1939
	Harry L. Hopkins	1939–1940
	Jesse Jones	1940–1945
	Henry A. Wallace	1945
Secretary of Labor	Frances Perkins	1933–1945

The Truman Administration

President	Harry S Truman	1945–1953
Vice President	Alben W. Barkley	1949–1953
Secretary of State	Edward R. Stettinius, Jr.	1945
	James F. Byrnes	1945–1947
	George C. Marshall	1947–1949
	Dean G. Acheson	1949–1953
Secretary of Treasury	Fred M. Vinson	1945–1946
	John W. Snyder	1946–1953
Secretary of War	Robert P. Patterson	1945–1947
	Kenneth C. Royall	1947
Attorney General	Tom C. Clark	1945–1949
	J. Howard McGrath	1949–1952
	James P. McGranery	1952–1953

Postmaster General	Frank C. Walker	1945
	Robert E. Hannegan	1945–1947
	Jesse M. Donaldson	1947–1953
Secretary of Navy	James V. Forrestal	1945–1947
Secretary of Interior	Harold L. Ickes	1945–1946
	Julius A. Krug	1946–1949
	Oscar L. Chapman	1949–1953
Secretary of Agriculture	Clinton P. Anderson	1945–1948
	Charles F. Brannan	1948–1953
Secretary of Commerce	Henry A. Wallace	1945–1946
	W. Averell Harriman	1946–1948
	Charles W. Sawyer	1948–1953
Secretary of Labor	Lewis B. Schwellenbach	1945–1948
	Maurice J. Tobin	1948–1953
Secretary of Defense	James V. Forrestal	1947–1949
	Louis A. Johnson	1949–1950
	George C. Marshall	1950–1951
	Robert A. Lovett	1951–1953

The Eisenhower Administration

President	Dwight D. Eisenhower	1953–1961
Vice President	Richard M. Nixon	1953–1961
Secretary of State	John Foster Dulles	1953–1959
	Christian A. Herter	1959–1961
Secretary of Treasury	George M. Humphrey	1953–1957
	Robert B. Anderson	1957–1961
Attorney General	Herbert Brownell, Jr.	1953–1958
	William P. Rogers	1958–1961
Postmaster General	Arthur E. Summerfield	1953–1961
Secretary of Interior	Douglas McKay	1953–1956
	Fred A. Seaton	1956–1961
Secretary of Agriculture	Ezra T. Benson	1953–1961
Secretary of Commerce	Sinclair Weeks	1953–1958
	Lewis L. Strauss	1958–1959
	Frederick H. Mueller	1959–1961
Secretary of Labor	Martin P. Durkin	1953
	James P. Mitchell	1953–1961
Secretary of Defense	Charles E. Wilson	1953–1957
	Neil H. McElroy	1957–1959
	Thomas S. Gates, Jr.	1959–1961
Secretary of Health, Education, and Welfare	Oveta Culp Hobby	1953–1955
	Marion B. Folsom	1955–1958
	Arthur S. Flemming	1958–1961

The Kennedy Administration

President	John F. Kennedy	1961–1963
Vice President	Lyndon B. Johnson	1961–1963
Secretary of State	Dean Rusk	1961–1963
Secretary of Treasury	C. Douglas Dillon	1961–1963
Attorney General	Robert F. Kennedy	1961–1963
Postmaster General	J. Edward Day	1961–1963
	John A. Gronouski	1963
Secretary of Interior	Stewart L. Udall	1961–1963
Secretary of Agriculture	Orville L. Freeman	1961–1963
Secretary of Commerce	Luther H. Hodges	1961–1963
Secretary of Labor	Arthur J. Goldberg	1961–1962
	W. Willard Wirtz	1962–1963
Secretary of Defense	Robert S. McNamara	1961–1963
Secretary of Health, Education, and Welfare	Abraham A. Ribicoff	1961–1962
	Anthony J. Celebrezze	1962–1963

The Lyndon Johnson Administration

President	Lyndon B. Johnson	1963–1969
Vice President	Hubert H. Humphrey	1965–1969
Secretary of State	Dean Rusk	1963–1969
Secretary of Treasury	C. Douglas Dillon	1963–1965
	Henry H. Fowler	1965–1969
Attorney General	Robert F. Kennedy	1963–1964
	Nicholas Katzenbach	1965–1966
	Ramsey Clark	1967–1969
Postmaster General	John A. Gronouski	1963–1965
	Lawrence F. O'Brien	1965–1968
	Marvin Watson	1968–1969
Secretary of Interior	Stewart L. Udall	1963–1969
Secretary of Agriculture	Orville L. Freeman	1963–1969
Secretary of Commerce	Luther H. Hodges	1963–1964
	John T. Connor	1964–1967
	Alexander B. Trowbridge	1967–1968
	Cyrus R. Smith	1968–1969
Secretary of Labor	W. Willard Wirtz	1963–1969
Secretary of Defense	Robert F. McNamara	1963–1968
	Clark Clifford	1968–1969

Secretary of Health, Education, and Welfare	Anthony J. Celebrezze	1963–1965
	John W. Gardner	1965–1968
	Wilbur J. Cohen	1968–1969
Secretary of Housing and Urban Development	Robert C. Weaver	1966–1969
	Robert C. Wood	1969
Secretary of Transportation	Alan S. Boyd	1967–1969

The Nixon Administration

President	Richard M. Nixon	1969–1974
Vice President	Spiro T. Agnew	1969–1973
	Gerald R. Ford	1973–1974
Secretary of State	William P. Rogers	1969–1973
	Henry A. Kissinger	1973–1974
Secretary of Treasury	David M. Kennedy	1969–1970
	John B. Connally	1971–1972
	George P. Shultz	1972–1974
	William E. Simon	1974
Attorney General	John N. Mitchell	1969–1972
	Richard G. Kleindienst	1972–1973
	Elliot L. Richardson	1973
	William B. Saxbe	1973–1974
Postmaster General	Winton M. Blount	1969–1971
Secretary of Interior	Walter J. Hickel	1969–1970
	Rogers Morton	1971–1974
Secretary of Agriculture	Clifford M. Hardin	1969–1971
	Earl L. Butz	1971–1974
Secretary of Commerce	Maurice H. Stans	1969–1972
	Peter G. Peterson	1972–1973
	Frederick B. Dent	1973–1974
Secretary of Labor	George P. Shultz	1969–1970
	James D. Hodgson	1970–1973
	Peter J. Brennan	1973–1974
Secretary of Defense	Melvin R. Laird	1969–1973
	Elliot L. Richardson	1973
	James R. Schlesinger	1973–1974
Secretary of Health, Education, and Welfare	Robert H. Finch	1969–1970
	Elliot L. Richardson	1970–1973
	Casper W. Weinberger	1973–1974
Secretary of Housing and Urban Development	George Romney	1969–1973
	James T. Lynn	1973–1974

Secretary of Transportation	John A. Volpe	1969–1973
	Claude S. Brinegar	1973–1974

The Ford Administration

President	Gerald R. Ford	1974–1977
Vice President	Nelson A. Rockefeller	1974–1977
Secretary of State	Henry A. Kissinger	1974–1977
Secretary of Treasury	William E. Simon	1974–1977
Attorney General	William Saxbe	1974–1975
	Edward Levi	1975–1977
Secretary of Interior	Rogers Morton	1974–1975
	Stanley K. Hathaway	1975
	Thomas Kleppe	1975–1977
Secretary of Agriculture	Earl L. Butz	1974–1976
	John A. Knebel	1976–1977
Secretary of Commerce	Frederick B. Dent	1974–1975
	Rogers Morton	1975–1976
	Elliot L. Richardson	1976–1977
Secretary of Labor	Peter J. Brennan	1974–1975
	John T. Dunlop	1975–1976
	W. J. Usery	1976–1977
Secretary of Defense	James R. Schlesinger	1974–1975
	Donald Rumsfeld	1975–1977
Secretary of Health, Education, and Welfare	Casper Weinberger	1974–1975
	Forrest D. Mathews	1975–1977
Secretary of Housing and Urban Development	James T. Lynn	1974–1975
	Carla A. Hills	1975–1977
Secretary of Transportation	Claude Brinegar	1974–1975
	William T. Coleman	1975–1977

The Carter Administration

President	Jimmy Carter	1977–1981
Vice President	Walter F. Mondale	1977–1981
Secretary of State	Cyrus R. Vance	1977–1980
	Edmund Muskie	1980–1981
Secretary of Treasury	W. Michael Blumenthal	1977–1979
	G. William Miller	1979–1981
Attorney General	Griffin Bell	1977–1979
	Benjamin R. Civiletti	1979–1981
Secretary of Interior	Cecil D. Andrus	1977–1981

Secretary of Agriculture	Robert Bergland	1977–1981	Secretary of Treasury	Donald Regan	1981–1985	
				James A. Baker, III	1985–	
Secretary of Commerce	Juanita M. Kreps	1977–1979	Attorney General	William F. Smith	1981–1985	
	Philip M. Klutznick	1979–1981		Edwin A. Meese, III	1985–	
Secretary of Labor	F. Ray Marshall	1977–1981	Secretary of Interior	James Watt	1981–1983	
Secretary of Defense	Harold Brown	1977–1981		William P. Clark, Jr.	1983–1985	
				Donald P. Hodel	1985–	
Secretary of Health, Education, and Welfare	Joseph A. Califano	1977–1979	Secretary of Agriculture	John Block	1981–	
	Patricia R. Harris	1979				
Secretary of Commerce				Malcolm Baldrige	1981–	
Secretary of Health and Human Services	Patricia R. Harris	1979–1981	Secretary of Labor	Raymond Donovan	1981–1985	
				William E. Brock	1985–	
			Secretary of Defense	Casper Weinberger	1981–	
Secretary of Education	Shirley M. Hufstedler	1979–1981				
Secretary of Housing and Urban Development	Patricia R. Harris	1977–1979	Secretary of Health and Human Services	Richard Schweiker	1981–1983	
	Moon Landrieu	1979–1981		Margaret Heckler	1983–1985	
			Secretary of Education	Terrel H. Bell	1981–1985	
				William J. Bennett	1985–	
Secretary of Transportation	Brock Adams	1977–1979	Secretary of Housing and Urban Development	Samuel Pierce	1981–	
	Neil E. Goldschmidt	1979–1981				
Secretary of Energy	James R. Schlesinger	1977–1979				
	Charles W. Duncan	1979–1981				
			Secretary of Transportation	Drew Lewis	1981–1983	
				Elizabeth Dole	1983–	

The Reagan Administration

			Secretary of Energy	James Edwards	1981–1982	
President	Ronald Reagan	1981–		Donald P. Hodel	1982–1985	
Vice President	George Bush	1981–		John S. Herrington	1985–	
Secretary of State	Alexander M. Haig	1981–1982				
	George P. Shultz	1982–				

PARTY STRENGTH IN CONGRESS

Period	Congress	House					Senate					Party of President
		Majority Party		Minority Party		Others	Majority Party		Minority Party		Others	
1789–91	1st	Ad	38	Op	26		Ad	17	Op	9	F	Washington
1791–93	2nd	F	37	DR	33		F	16	DR	13	F	Washington
1793–95	3rd	DR	57	F	48		F	17	DR	13	F	Washington
1795–97	4th	F	54	DR	52		F	19	DR	13	F	Washington
1797–99	5th	F	58	DR	48		F	20	DR	12	F	J. Adams
1799–1801	6th	F	64	DR	42		F	19	DR	13	F	J. Adams
1801–03	7th	DR	69	F	36		DR	18	F	13	DR	Jefferson

Period	Congress	House Majority Party		House Minority Party		Others	Senate Majority Party		Senate Minority Party		Others	Party of President	
1803–05	8th	DR	102	F	39		DR	25	F	9		DR	Jefferson
1805–07	9th	DR	116	F	25		DR	27	F	7		DR	Jefferson
1807–09	10th	DR	118	F	24		DR	28	F	6		DR	Jefferson
1809–11	11th	DR	94	F	48		DR	28	F	6		DR	Madison
1811–13	12th	DR	108	F	36		DR	30	F	6		DR	Madison
1813–15	13th	DR	112	F	68		DR	27	F	9		DR	Madison
1815–17	14th	DR	117	F	65		DR	25	F	11		DR	Madison
1817–19	15th	DR	141	F	42		DR	34	F	10		DR	Monroe
1819–21	16th	DR	156	F	27		DR	35	F	7		DR	Monroe
1821–23	17th	DR	158	F	25		DR	44	F	4		DR	Monroe
1823–25	18th	DR	187	F	26		DR	44	F	4		DR	Monroe
1825–27	19th	Ad	105	J	97		Ad	26	J	20		C	J. Q. Adams
1827–29	20th	J	119	Ad	94		J	28	Ad	20		C	J. Q. Adams
1829–31	21st	D	139	NR	74		D	26	NR	22		D	Jackson
1831–33	22nd	D	141	NR	58	14	D	25	NR	21	2	D	Jackson
1833–35	23rd	D	147	AM	53	60	D	20	NR	20	8	D	Jackson
1835–37	24th	D	145	W	98		D	27	W	25		D	Jackson
1837–39	25th	D	108	W	107	24	D	30	W	18	4	D	Van Buren
1839–41	26th	D	124	W	118		D	28	W	22		D	Van Buren
1841–43	27th	W	133	D	102	6	W	28	D	22	2	W	W. Harrison
												W	Tyler
1843–45	28th	D	142	W	79	1	W	28	D	25	1	W	Tyler
1845–47	29th	D	143	W	77	6	D	31	W	25		D	Polk
1847–49	30th	W	115	D	108	4	D	36	W	21	1	D	Polk
1849–51	31st	D	112	W	109	9	D	35	W	25	2	W	Taylor
												W	Fillmore
1851–53	32nd	D	140	W	88	5	D	35	W	24	3	W	Fillmore
1853–55	33rd	D	159	W	71	4	D	38	W	22	2	D	Pierce
1855–57	34th	R	108	D	83	43	D	40	R	15	5	D	Pierce
1857–59	35th	D	118	R	92	26	D	36	R	20	8	D	Buchanan
1859–61	36th	R	114	D	92	31	D	36	R	26	4	D	Buchanan
1861–63	37th	R	105	D	43	30	R	31	D	10	8	R	Lincoln
1863–65	38th	R	102	D	75	9	R	36	D	9	5	R	Lincoln
1865–67	39th	U	149	D	42		U	42	D	10		R	Lincoln
												R	Johnson
1867–69	40th	R	143	D	49		R	42	D	11		R	Johnson
1869–71	41st	R	149	D	63		R	56	D	11		R	Grant
1871–73	42nd	R	134	D	104	5	R	52	D	17	5	R	Grant
1873–75	43rd	R	194	D	92	14	R	49	D	19	5	R	Grant
1875–77	44th	D	169	R	109	14	R	45	D	29	2	R	Grant
1877–79	45th	D	153	R	140		R	39	D	36	1	R	Hayes
1879–81	46th	D	149	R	130	14	D	42	R	33	1	R	Hayes

Period	Congress	House Majority Party		House Minority Party		Others	Senate Majority Party		Senate Minority Party		Others	Party of President	
1881–83	47th	D	147	R	135	11	R	37	D	37	1	R	Garfield
												R	Arthur
1883–85	48th	D	197	R	118	10	R	38	D	36	2	R	Arthur
1885–87	49th	D	183	R	140	2	R	43	D	34		D	Cleveland
1887–89	50th	D	169	R	152	4	R	39	D	37		D	Cleveland
1889–91	51st	R	166	D	159		R	39	D	37		R	B. Harrison
1891–93	52nd	D	235	R	88	9	R	47	D	39	2	R	B. Harrison
1893–95	53rd	D	218	R	127	11	D	44	R	38	3	D	Cleveland
1895–97	54th	R	244	D	105	7	R	43	D	39	6	D	Cleveland
1897–99	55th	R	204	D	113	40	R	47	D	34	7	R	McKinley
1899–1901	56th	R	185	D	163	9	R	53	D	26	8	R	McKinley
1901–03	57th	R	197	D	151	9	R	55	D	31	4	R	McKinley
												R	T. Roosevelt
1903–05	58th	R	208	D	178		R	57	D	33		R	T. Roosevelt
1905–07	59th	R	250	D	136		R	57	D	33		R	T. Roosevelt
1907–09	60th	R	222	D	164		R	61	D	31		R	T. Roosevelt
1909–11	61st	R	219	D	172		R	61	D	32		R	Taft
1911–13	62nd	D	228	R	161	1	R	51	D	41		R	Taft
1913–15	63rd	D	291	R	127	17	D	51	R	44	1	D	Wilson
1915–17	64th	D	230	R	196	9	D	56	R	40		D	Wilson
1917–19	65th	D	216	R	210	6	D	53	R	42		D	Wilson
1919–21	66th	R	240	D	190	3	R	49	D	47		D	Wilson
1921–23	67th	R	301	D	131	1	R	59	D	37		R	Harding
1923–25	68th	R	225	D	205	5	R	51	D	43	2	R	Coolidge
1925–27	69th	R	247	D	183	4	R	56	D	39	1	R	Coolidge
1927–29	70th	R	237	D	195	3	R	49	D	46	1	R	Coolidge
1929–31	71st	R	267	D	167	1	R	56	D	39	1	R	Hoover
1931–33	72nd	D	220	R	214	1	R	48	D	47	1	R	Hoover
1933–35	73rd	D	310	R	117	5	D	60	R	35	1	D	F. Roosevelt
1935–37	74th	D	319	R	103	10	D	69	R	25	2	D	F. Roosevelt
1937–39	75th	D	331	R	89	13	D	76	R	16	4	D	F. Roosevelt
1939–41	76th	D	261	R	164	4	D	69	R	23	4	D	F. Roosevelt
1941–43	77th	D	268	R	162	5	D	66	R	28	2	D	F. Roosevelt
1943–45	78th	D	218	R	208	4	D	58	R	37	1	D	F. Roosevelt
1945–47	79th	D	242	R	190	2	D	56	R	38	1	D	Truman
1947–49	80th	R	245	D	188	1	R	51	D	45		D	Truman
1949–51	81st	D	263	R	171	1	D	54	R	42		D	Truman
1951–53	82nd	D	234	R	199	1	D	49	R	47		D	Truman
1953–55	83rd	R	221	D	211	1	R	48	D	47	1	R	Eisenhower
1955–57	84th	D	232	R	203		D	48	R	47	1	R	Eisenhower
1957–59	85th	D	233	R	200		D	49	R	47		R	Eisenhower

Period	Congress	House Majority Party		House Minority Party		Others	Senate Majority Party		Senate Minority Party		Others	Party of President
1959–61	86th	D	284	R	153		D	65	R	35		R	Eisenhower
1961–63	87th	D	263	R	174		D	65	R	35		D	Kennedy
1963–65	88th	D	258	R	177		D	67	R	33		D	Kennedy
												D	Johnson
1965–67	89th	D	295	R	140		D	68	R	32		D	Johnson
1967–69	90th	D	246	R	187		D	64	R	36		D	Johnson
1969–71	91st	D	245	R	189		D	57	R	43		R	Nixon
1971–73	92nd	D	254	R	180		D	54	R	44	2	R	Nixon
1973–75	93rd	D	239	R	192	1	D	56	R	42	2	R	Nixon
1975–77	94th	D	291	R	144		D	60	R	37	3	R	Ford
1977–79	95th	D	292	R	143		D	61	R	38	1	D	Carter
1979–81	96th	D	276	R	157		D	58	R	41	1	D	Carter
1981–83	97th	D	243	R	192		R	53	D	46	1	R	Reagan
1983–85	98th	D	267	R	168		R	55	D	45		R	Reagan
1985–87	99th	D	253	R	182		R	53	D	47		R	Reagan

AD = Administration; AM = Anti-Masonic; C = Coalition; D = Democratic; DR = Democratic-Republican; F = Federalist; J = Jacksonian; NR = National Republican; Op = Opposition; R = Republican; U = Unionist; W = Whig. Figures are for the beginning of first session of each Congress, except the 93rd, which are for the beginning of the second session.

JUSTICES OF THE SUPREME COURT

	Term of Service	Years of Service	Life Span		Term of Service	Years of Service	Life Span
John Jay	1789–1795	5	1745–1829	Henry B. Brown	1890–1906	16	1836–1913
John Rutledge	1789–1791	1	1739–1800	George Shiras, Jr.	1892–1903	10	1832–1924
William Cushing	1789–1810	20	1732–1810	Howell E. Jackson	1893–1895	2	1832–1895
James Wilson	1789–1798	8	1742–1798	Edward D. White	1894–1910	16	1845–1921
John Blair	1789–1796	6	1732–1800	Rufus W. Peckham	1895–1909	14	1838–1909
Robert H. Harrison	1789–1790	—	1745–1790	Joseph McKenna	1898–1925	26	1843–1926
James Iredell	1790–1799	9	1751–1799	Oliver W. Holmes	1902–1932	30	1841–1935
Thomas Johnson	1791–1793	1	1732–1819	William R. Day	1903–1922	19	1849–1923
William Paterson	1793–1806	13	1745–1806	William H. Moody	1906–1910	3	1853–1917
John Rutledge•	1795	—	1739–1800	Horace H. Lurton	1910–1914	4	1844–1914
Samuel Chase	1796–1811	15	1741–1811	Charles E. Hughes	1910–1916	5	1862–1948
Oliver Ellsworth	1796–1800	4	1745–1807	Willis Van Devanter	1911–1937	26	1859–1941
Bushrod Washington	1798–1829	31	1762–1829	Joseph R. Lamar	1911–1916	5	1857–1916

	Term of Service	Years of Service	Life Span		Term of Service	Years of Service	Life Span
Alfred Moore	1799–1804	4	1755–1810	*Edward D. White*	1910–1921	11	1845–1921
John Marshall	1801–1835	34	1755–1835	Mahlon Pitney	1912–1922	10	1858–1924
William Johnson	1804–1834	30	1771–1834	James C. McReynolds	1914–1941	26	1862–1946
H. Brockholst				Louis D. Brandeis	1916–1939	22	1856–1941
Livingston	1806–1823	16	1757–1823	John H. Clarke	1916–1922	6	1857–1945
Thomas Todd	1807–1826	18	1765–1826	William H. Taft	1921–1930	8	1857–1930
Joseph Story	1811–1845	33	1779–1845	George Sutherland	1922–1938	15	1862–1942
Gabriel Duval	1811–1835	24	1752–1844	Pierce Butler	1922–1939	16	1866–1939
Smith Thompson	1823–1843	20	1768–1843	Edward T. Sanford	1923–1930	7	1865–1930
Robert Trimble	1826–1828	2	1777–1828	Harlan F. Stone	1925–1941	16	1872–1946
John McLean	1829–1861	32	1785–1861	*Charles E. Hughes*	1930–1941	11	1862–1948
Henry Baldwin	1830–1844	14	1780–1844	Owen J. Roberts	1930–1945	15	1875–1955
James M. Wayne	1835–1867	32	1790–1867	Benjamin N. Cardozo	1932–1938	6	1870–1938
Roger B. Taney	1836–1864	28	1777–1864	Hugo L. Black	1937–1971	34	1886–1971
Philip P. Barbour	1836–1841	4	1783–1841	Stanley F. Reed	1938–1957	19	1884–1980
John Catron	1837–1865	28	1786–1865	Felix Frankfurter	1939–1962	23	1882–1965
John McKinley	1837–1852	15	1780–1852	William O. Douglas	1939–1975	36	1898–1980
Peter V. Daniel	1841–1860	19	1784–1860	Frank Murphy	1940–1949	9	1890–1949
Samuel Nelson	1845–1872	27	1792–1873	*Harlan F. Stone*	1941–1946	5	1872–1946
Levi Woodbury	1845–1851	5	1789–1851	James F. Byrnes	1941–1942	1	1879–1972
Robert C. Grier	1846–1870	23	1794–1870	Robert H. Jackson	1941–1954	13	1892–1954
Benjamin R. Curtis	1851–1857	6	1809–1874	Wiley B. Rutledge	1943–1949	6	1894–1949
John A. Campbell	1853–1861	8	1811–1889	Harold H. Burton	1945–1958	13	1888–1964
Nathan Clifford	1858–1881	23	1803–1881	*Fred M. Vinson*	1946–1953	7	1890–1953
Noah H. Swayne	1862–1881	18	1804–1884	Tom C. Clark	1949–1967	18	1899–1977
Samuel F. Miller	1862–1890	28	1816–1890	Sherman Minton	1949–1956	7	1890–1965
David Davis	1862–1877	14	1815–1886	*Earl Warren*	1953–1969	16	1891–1974
Stephen J. Field	1863–1897	34	1816–1899	John Marshall Harlan	1955–1971	16	1899–1971
Salmon P. Chase	1864–1873	8	1808–1873	William J. Brennan, Jr.	1956–	—	1906–
William Strong	1870–1880	10	1808–1895	Charles E. Whittaker	1957–1962	5	1901–1973
Joseph P. Bradley	1870–1892	22	1813–1892	Potter Stewart	1958–1981	23	1915–
Ward Hunt	1873–1882	9	1810–1886	Byron R. White	1962–	—	1917–
Morrison R. Waite	1874–1888	14	1816–1888	Arthur J. Goldberg	1962–1965	3	1908–
John M. Harlan	1877–1911	34	1833–1911	Abe Fortas	1965–1969	4	1910–
William B. Woods	1880–1887	7	1824–1887	Thurgood Marshall	1967–	—	1908–
Stanley Matthews	1881–1889	7	1824–1889	*Warren C. Burger*	1969–	—	1907–
Horace Gray	1882–1902	20	1828–1902	Harry A. Blackmun	1970–	—	1908–
Samuel Blatchford	1882–1893	11	1820–1893	Lewis F. Powell, Jr.	1971–	—	1907–
Lucius Q. C. Lamar	1888–1893	5	1825–1893	William H. Rehnquist	1971–	—	1924–
Melville W. Fuller	1888–1910	21	1833–1910	John P. Stevens, III	1975–	—	1920–
David J. Brewer	1890–1910	20	1837–1910	Sandra Day O'Connor	1981–	—	1930–

*Appointed and served one term, but not confirmed by the Senate.

Note: Chief justices are in italics.

Chapter Opener Credits

Chapter 1

Columbus on the island of Hispaniola. Etching. Spanish. The Granger Collection.

Chapter 2

Mrs. Elizabeth Freake and Baby Mary. Unknown artist, ca. 1674. Oil on canvas, 42 ½″ × 36 ¾″. Worcester Art Museum, Massachusetts/The Granger Collection.

Chapter 3

Wedding needlepoint, 1756. American Antiquarian Society, Worcester, Massachusetts.

Chapter 4

Tory Stamp agents being tarred and feathered. J. Trumbull. The Granger Collection.

Chapter 5

The Battle of Bunker's Hill (detail). John Trumbull. Oil on canvas, 1786. Copyright Yale University Art Gallery.

Chapter 6

Mr. and Mrs. Thomas Mifflin (Sarah Morris). J. Singleton Copley, 1773. Oil on canvas, 60 ½″ × 48″. Historical Society of Pennsylvania, Philadelphia/The Granger Collection.

Chapter 7

Arrival of George Washington at the Battery, New York City, for his inauguration. The Granger Collection.

Chapter 8

Andrew Jackson at the Battle of New Orleans. The Granger Collection.

Chapter 9

Powerloom weaving at textile mill. The Granger Collection.

Chapter 10

American Farm Scene by Currier & Ives. J. Martin/Scala/Art Resource.

Chapter 11

Slave coffle passing unfinished Capitol Building, Washington, D.C., ca. 1820. The Granger Collection.

Chapter 12

Stump Speaking. George Caleb Bingham. Oil, 1854. From the Collection of the Boatman's National Bank of St. Louis.

Chapter 13

American troops storming the palace of Chapultepec, 1847. The Granger Collection.

Chapter 14

General Stonewall Jackson at the Battle of First Bull Run, 21 July 1861. The Granger Collection.

Chapter 15

The First Vote. Colored engraving, 1867. The Granger Collection.

INDEX

Democratic party (*cont.*)
  construction/black rights, 423, 427,
  441, 442, 443
Democratic-Republican societies, 191–
  192, 216
Demographic factors, A-16–A-17
  AGE: of colonists, 71–72
  BIRTHS AND BIRTH RATE: colonies, 28,
    34, 71; decline in, 278–279; south-
    ern women, 309; birth control,
    268, 279, 309; abortion, 279
  DIVORCE: in colonies, 84; post–Revo-
    lutionary War, 160
  LIFE EXPECTANCY: in colonies, 28, 34
  MARRIAGE: in colonies, 27–28, 34,
    71; among slaves, 315–316; post–
    Revolutionary War, 159–160; in
    frontier areas, 201; 19th-century,
    308–309. *See also* DIVORCE, *above*;
    Family life
  MORTALITY RATE: in Chesapeake colo-
    nies, 26–27; among slaves, 52,
    311. *See also* Health factors
  See also Immigrants; Migration;
    Population
Deposit Act (1836), 341
Depression/recession, *see* Economic con-
  ditions, DEPRESSION
de Soto, Hernando, 16
Detroit, Michigan, 106, 223, 264, 271
Dew, Thomas, 309
Dial (transcendentalist journal), 329
Dias, Bartholomew, 15
Dickinson, John, 116, 129, 156, 175;
  Letters from a Farmer . . . , 115,
  130
Diet, *see* Health factors, DIET AND
  NUTRITION
Dinwiddie, Robert, 103–104
Discrimination, *see* Blacks; Racism;
  Women
Disease, *see* Health factors, DISEASE
District of Columbia, *see* Washington,
  D.C.
Divine right of kings, 21
Divorce, *see* Demographic factors,
  DIVORCE
Dixon, Archibald, 364
Doeg tribe, 56. *See also* Indians
Domesticity, cult of, 277, 279, 294, 327
Dominican Republic, 445
Dominion of New England, 63
Donelson, Fort, capture of, 384
Douglas, Stephen A., 354, 359–360,
  363–364, 371, 372–373, 374
Douglass, Frederick, 290, 291, 292,
  332, 398, 423, 435
Down, John, 282
Draft, the, *see* Conscription and
  recruitment
Dragging Canoe, Chief, 136, 148
Dred Scott case, 371–372, 373, 374, 441
Duane, James, 130
Duels, 318
Duke's Laws (1665), 44
Dulany, Daniel, 116; . . . *Imposing
  Taxes on the British Colonies*, 111
Dun & Bradstreet, 253
Duniway, Abigail Scott, 262

Dunmore, Lord, 134, 147–148
Durfee, Amos, 345
Dutch, the, *see* Netherlands
Dutch West India Company, 43–44
Dyer, Mary, 45

East India Company, 121–122
Economic conditions: colonial, 58, 60,
  71, 75–81, 85–86, 87, 90, 109;
  Revolutionary War and, 172; pub-
  lic/national debt, 187–188, 212,
  413, 414, 428, 444; growth, 238–
  239; transportation and technology
  and, 239, 242, 244–245; of yeomen, 303, 305; economic expansionism, 343; American economy,
  A-21
  CAPITALISM: and specialization, 238;
    rise of and faith in, 396
  DEPRESSION (Panic)/recession: postwar,
    171; *1807*, 221; British, 222; of
    1819–23, 231, 240, 337, 339, 341;
    of *1837*, 253; of *1839–43*, 240,
    344; of *1857*, 240, 256; in south-
    ern cotton economy, 441; of *1873–
    78*, 443
  GOVERNMENT INVOLVEMENT WITH,
    242–243; exploration, 241–242; by
    state government, 243–244; and
    Jacksonians, 338; by Confederacy,
    388. *See also* Business, AND
    GOVERNMENT
  INFLATION, 16, 21; *1779–80*, 167;
    Civil War, 383, 390, 394
  MARKET ECONOMY, 239; agriculture in,
    239–240, 257–258, 262, 366; de-
    velopment of, 239–240, 298;
    boom-or-bust in, 240–241; and
    wage workers, 256; consumerism,
    248; and yeomen, 303, 319
  POVERTY: in colonies, 76–77; and so-
    cial conflict, 268, 274–275; urban,
    274, 283, 327; Civil War and, 389
  WEALTH, DISTRIBUTION OF: *1830s–
    50s*, 273–274, 275–276; in the
    South, 302, 319. *See also* Social
    class
  See also Banking and finance; Labor;
    Lifestyle; Trade
Edenton Ladies Tea Party, 117, 118
Edmondston, Catherine Devereux, 308
Education: religion in, 331
  AND BLACKS: after Revolution, 162;
    during Reconstruction, 434, 438
  COLLEGE AND UNIVERSITY: colonial,
    89, 90
  AND WOMEN: and republicanism, 154;
    Murray on, 158–159; as teachers,
    277–278; among upper-class south-
    erners, 308
Edwards, Jonathan, 94–95
Egypt, 409, 440
Elderly, *see* Demographic factors, AGE
Elections, congressional: of *1788*, 184;
  of *1834–40s*, 343; of *1854*, 364–
  365; of *1862*, *1863*, 406, 407; of
  1865, 426, 427; of *1866*, 427, 429;
  of *1874*, 443

Elections, presidential, of *1789*, 185–
  186; of *1792*, 190; of *1796*, 194–
  195; of *1800*, 198–199, 218;
  peaceful transition of power in,
  233; of *1804*, 216; of *1808*, 221; of
  1812, 226; of *1816*, 228; of *1820*,
  231, 263, 336; of *1824*, 233, 336–
  337, 336 (map), 343; caucus system ends, 336–337; of *1828*, 335,
  337; of *1832*, 341; of *1836*, 344;
  voting participation increase, 343;
  of *1840*, 343, 344–345; of *1844*,
  348–349, 354; foreign policy issue
  arises, 348; of *1848*, 357–358; of
  1852, 363; of *1856*, 370; *1860*,
  354–355, 374, 375; of *1864*, 410;
  of *1868*, 442; of *1872*, 442; of
  1876, 445 (map), 445–446
Eleventh Amendment, 185
Eliot, John, 32
Elizabeth I, queen of England, 13, 19,
  20
Ellsworth, Oliver, 173, 185
Emancipation, *see* Slavery, EMANCIPA-
  TION FROM
Emancipation Proclamation, 399–400
Embargo Act, 219, 221
Emerson, Ralph Waldo, 329, 373
Energy, *see* Technology
England: pre-1400 unimportance of, 13;
  Reformation in, 20–21; social dis-
  ruption in, 21, 26; ethnocentrism
  of, 47; slave trade by, 51–52; and
  French Revolution, 191; and Amer-
  ican manufacturing system, 247–
  248. *See also* Revolutionary War
  AND COLONIES, 16, 19–25; as trading
    with Indians, 53, 54; and French
    and Indian War, 100–101; Ameri-
    can virtue contrasted with, 156.
    See also Colonies, English
  U.S. RELATIONS WITH: Jay Treaty,
    192–193; impressment by, 219;
    events leading to War of *1812*,
    219–222; continued conflict with,
    226; and Monroe Doctrine, 230–
    231; and cotton trade, 299, 440;
    1830s tensions, 345; and Republic
    of Texas, 348, 349; and Oregon,
    355; and Civil War, 409–410; and
    Alabama dispute, 410, 445
English Civil War, 41, 43
Enlightenment, the, 71, 87, 89–90, 91,
  94, 203, 334
Entertainment: and republican virtue,
  157
  THEATER: 268
  See also Arts; Lifestyle, SOCIAL LIFE
    AND RECREATION
Equality: and republicanism, 156; of opportunity, 156, 278; and women,
  160 (*see also* Feminism; Women);
  and racism, 163, 164 (*see also* Civil
  rights; Racism); and Second Awakening, 204; Tocqueville on, 273;
  among whites, 369. *See also* Economic conditions, WEALTH, DISTRI-
  BUTION OF
Equiano, Olaudah, 40–41, 47, 51, 53

Era of Good Feelings, 229
Erie Canal, 238, 245, 251, 258, 262, 269, 326
Ethnicity: in politics, 194; and Whigs vs. Democrats, 343. See also Immigrants; Racism
Europe: social organization of, 13; political and technological change in, 14; American virtue contrasted with, 156; Napoleonic Wars in, 218; American disengagement from, 226
European exploration and expansion, 4, 14–17, 22 (map); cultural contact through, 5; motives for, 15; disease spread by, 17–18; plant/animal exchange through, 18–19; impact of, 36
Evangelism, see Religion, EVANGELICAL
Executive branch: and separation of powers, 175, 430; and executive privilege, 193; and Jackson, 339; and veto, 342; and Civil War, 383, 392, 396. See also Government, federal; Presidency
Exodusters, 446
Exogamy, and European social organization, 13
Expansion and expansionism, 199–201, 206, 210–211, 214, 354; and War of 1812, 222; and Adams, 229; and slavery, 232, 234, 363; commercial and industrial, 238–239; Indian resistance to, 285; economic, 343. See also Foreign affairs; Westward expansion
Ex parte Milligan, 441
Extended family, 86

Factors, Scots, 79–80
Factory Girl, 255
Factory Girl's Garland, 255
Fairbanks House, Dedham, Massachusetts, 33
Fallen Timbers, battle of, 170, 171
Fall River, Massachusetts, 241
Family life: slavery and, 86, 201, 315, 439; extended family, 86; of yeomen, 303, 305
  CHANGE IN, 277, 279
  CHILDREN: slum, 274–275
  IN COLONIES, 27–28, 34, 81–83; patriarchal system, 13
  See also Demographic factors; Women
Farming, see Agriculture; Lifestyle, RURAL
Farragut, Adm. David, 383–384
Federal government, see Government, federal
Federalist, The (political essays), 178, 187
Federalist party, 190, 193–195, 210, 211, 221, 226–227, 229, 336, 337; and Supreme Court, 212, 213; and Younger Federalists, 216–217, 218, 221, 226
Female Moral Reform Society, 327
Feminism: of Abigail Adams, 154; of Murray, 158–159; and mother's

role, 160; Seneca Falls meeting, 280; and antiprostitution movement, 327; and Shakers, 328; rise of, 331; of the Grimkés, 331–332; and abolitionism, 331–332, 429; female suffrage, 433. See also Civil rights; Women
Ferdinand, king of Spain, 14
Fifteenth Amendment, 421, 431, 442, 447
"Fifty-four Forty or Fight," 348
Fillmore, Millard, 357, 370
Finance, see Banking and finance
Finney, Charles G., 326–327
Fish, Hamilton, 445
Fisher, Sidney George, 240
Fisk University, 438
Fitzhugh, George, 362–363
Five Nations, see Iroquois/Iroquois Confederacy
Five Points, N.Y., 274, 275, 281
Fleming, Samuel, 318
Fletcher, Benjamin, 94
Fletcher v. Peck, 229
Flintoff, John F., 303–305
Florida: Spanish, 53, 54, 105, 150, 224, 229–230, 289, 319; Indians in, 54; negotiations for and purchase of, 259, 346; secedes, 376
Floyd, John, 341
Food riots, 403
Forbes, John M., 396
Force Act(s), 340, 442
Foreign affairs: president given charge of, 175; and Washington's Farewell Address, 194; "Quasi-War" with France, 195–196, 198; in Civil War, 409–410
  POLICIES: neutrality between British and French, 191
  See also specific nations, presidents, treaties, and wars
Forrest, Edwin, 268
Forrest, Gen. Nathan Bedford, 389
Fort Christina, 16
Fort Dearborn, 223
Fort Donelson, 384
Fort Duquesne, 104, 106
Forten, James, 293
Fort Henry, 384
Fort Necessity, 104
Fort Orange, 17, 55
Fort Pitt, 106
Fort Stanwix: treaty of, 135, 169; battle at, 145
Fort Washington, 142
Fort Wayne, treaty of, 285
Foster, Augustus John, 210
Fourier, Charles, 329
Fourteenth Amendment, 421, 428–429, 430, 433, 441–442, 443, 447
France, 13; explorations and colonization by, 16, 36, 53, 54, 55; Revolution in (1789), 191; Spain and, 214, 230
  -BRITAIN RELATIONS: battle for North America, 78, 100, 101–103; Napoleonic wars, 218–219, 222, 224, 280

  -COLONIAL/U.S. RELATIONS: in American Revolution, 146, 147; and trade restrictions, 168, 221; and "Quasi-War," 195–196, 198; and Louisiana Purchase, 214; and Civil War, 409–410
Franklin, Benjamin, 90–91, 113, 157, 334; on population growth, 72; and education, 91; on electricity, 91; and Stamp Act mob, 114; in Paris, 128, 146, 150; and Declaration of Independence, 140; at Constitutional Convention, 173, 178
Franklin, James, 90
Franklin, Sally, 113
Frazier, Rev. Garrison, 399, 439
Fredericksburg, battle at, 387
Free banking, 253
Freedmen's Bureau, 428, 432, 438, 440
Freedom: Jefferson on, 241; slaves' gain-
Freedom's Journal, 293
Freemasonry, 334–335
Freeport Doctrine, 373
Free-Soil party and free-soilers, 358, 363, 364, 366, 369, 372, 374, 375
Frémont, Capt. John C., 242, 261, 357, 370, 373
French and Indian War, 100–101, 103–105; depression following, 109
Friends, Society of, see Quakers
Frontier: as set by Proclamation of 1763, 107; at Ohio River, 171; across Appalachians, 183, 201; ideal vs. reality of, 259; advance of, 259, 264, 268, 269; and fur trade, 259–261; farming, 262; cities of, 264; in Alabama, 301; values of, 318; and southern class tensions, 319
Fugitive Slave Law, 293, 360, 361, 364
Fugitive slaves, 292–293, 332, 359
Fulkes, Minnie, 312
Fuller, Margaret, 158, 329
Fulton, Robert, 242, 247
Fundamental Constitutions of Carolina, 46
Fundamental Orders of Connecticut (1639), 31
Fur trade, 17, 53, 54, 55, 58, 259–261

Gabriel's Rebellion, 205, 291, 316
Gadsden Purchase, 259
Gage, Gen. Thomas, 134, 136
Gag rule, 333, 356
Gallatin, Albert, 212
Galloway, Joseph, 129, 130, 142, 144; . . . Claims of Great Britain and the Colonies, 132
Gama, Vasco da, 15
Garlic, Delia, 312
Garnet, Rev. Henry Highland, 293, 332
Garrison, William Lloyd, 332–333, 334
Gaspée incident, 120
Gates, Gen. Horatio, 145, 147
Gaugin, Michael, 282–283
Genet, Edmond, 191, 215
Geographic mobility, see Migration; Mobility
George I, king of England, 74

Recruitment, *see* Conscription and recruitment
Red Shirts, 442
Red Strings, 406
Reform: 19th-century, 256; "age of reform," 326; and Reconstruction, 421
  TYPES OF: political, 256, 319, 324, 334, 335, 338–339, 343; antislavery as, 322, 334, 346; temperance, 329–330; asylum reform, 330–331; educational, 331
Reformation, English, 20–21
Regionalization, 354; and slavery, 50, 233, 356, 369, 370; in political system, 175; and War of 1812 vote, 222; and sectional differences, 234; and Mexican War, 357; and 1848 election, 358; and Compromise of *1850*, 361; and Democrats, 363; and political parties, 365, 368–369. *See also* Reconstruction
"Regulator" movement, 94
Relief programs, *see* Public welfare and relief
Religion: of Indians, 8, 11; of West Africa, 11, 12; in founding of New England, 28; and New England life, 34; black churches, 163, 440; civic, 203; in Sarah Ripley Stearns' life, 280; and anti-Catholicism, 283; and Indians' education, 287; of yeomen, 303, 304, 305, 318; slave, 314; and education, 331; north-south split in, 374; of freed blacks, 440
  EVANGELICAL: and Great Awakening, 94–96, 201 (*see also* Great Awakening); and Second Great Awakening, 201–203 (*see also* Second Great Awakening); of yeomen, 318; in abolitionism, 333
  AND POLITICS AND GOVERNMENT: in colonies, 34, 62; disestablishment of, 203; and Whigs vs. Democrats, 343, 344
  See also Churches; Civil rights, FREEDOM, of religion; *individual denominations and sects*
Removal Act (1830), 289
Renaissance, 13
Representative government, *see* Self-government
Republicanism, 154–155, 156, 160, 165; and virtue, 154, 156–157, 210, 256, 326, 339, 349; threats to, 173, 182; and U.S. Constitution, 178; Hamilton vs. Jefferson and, 187, 190, 206; and French Revolution, 191; and faction, 192; and economic growth, 241; and market economy, 256; and women's role, 277; and nullification, 340; and westward expansion, 346; and Republican party, 366; southern version of, 369
Republican party (original), 190, 193–195, 210; and XYZ affair, 196; and judiciary, 212–213, 214; in 1804

election, 216; and coercive federal power, 221; and 1824 election, 233
Republican party (newer), 364–365, 398; as antislavery, 368; ideology of, 378; conventions of, 400; in Reconstruction, 421, 427, 433–434, 435–436, 437, 441, 442, 443; and blacks, 423, 432–433; Liberal group in, 442
Revels, Hiram, 435, 438–439
Revere, Paul, 116, 119, 122, 136
Revolutionary War, 128–129; loyalists in, 74, 132–133, 133–134, 141, 142, 144, 147, 148, 149; and Enlightenment, 87; events leading to, 100, 109–124; beginning of (Lexington and Concord, Bunker Hill), 128, 136–137; active patriots in, 133; Indians and blacks in, 134–136, 143, 145, 147–148, 149–150; in the North, 141–146, 145 (map); peace commission, 146; France in, 146, 147; in the South, 147–150, 147 (map); social and economic impact of, 154, 159, 160–161, 203, 204, 241
Rhett, R. B., 402
Rhode Island: as colony, 34, 36, 62, 63, 131; and slavery and free blacks, 161, 291, 364; under Articles of Confederation, 168; and Constitution, 178; industrialization in, 253
Rice, 49, 58, 61, 80, 299
Rice Coast, 11, 49
Richmond, Virginia, 205, 302, 386, 388, 403, 413
Rifle Clubs, 442
Riots, *see* Violence
Roads and highways, *see* Transportation, ROADS AND HIGHWAYS
Roanoke colony, 19. *See also* Virginia
Roanoke Island, 383
Rochambeau, Count, 149
Rockefeller, John D., 396
Rockingham, Lord, 114
Rock Island railroad, 238
Rolfe, John, 23, 24
Romantic movement, 313
Royal African Company, 51, 51–52, 53
Royal Society, 90
Rural life, *see* Lifestyle, RURAL
Rush, Dr. Benjamin, 156, 160–161
Rush-Bagot Treaty, 229, 230
Russell, Lord, 400
Russia, tsarist, 230; and Alaska, 444–445
Rutgers University, 89
Rutledge, John, 173

Sacajawea, 215
Sacramento, California, 394
St. Augustine, Florida, 53
St. Clair, General Arthur, 171
Saint Domingue (Haiti), 204
St. Joseph, Missouri, 246
St. Leger, Col. Barry, 145
St. Louis, Missouri, 251, 264, 282

St. Mary's Mutual Benevolent Total Abstinence Society, 330
Salem, Massachusetts, 31
Salem Village, witchcraft in, 64–66
Sampson, Deborah, 144
San Antonio, Texas, 348
San Francisco, California, 262, 271, 282; population of, 264
Santa Anna, Gen. Antonio López de, 348
Santa Fe, New Mexico, 53
Santa Fe Trail, 215, 262
Saratoga, Burgoyne's surrender at, 145, 146
Savannah, Georgia, 281–282, 383
Scalawags, 435
Scandinavian immigrants, 282
Schenectady, New York, 64
Schoolcraft, Henry Rowe, 242
Schuyler, Elizabeth, 186
Science: and Enlightenment, 90; Franklin on electricity, 91; proslavery theories from, 162
Scotch and Scotch-Irish immigrants, 74, 79–80, 94, 133, 194, 283, 303
Scott, Gen. Winfield, 346, 357, 358, 363
Sea Islands, 383
Sea-island blacks, 420, 424
Secession: New England, New York plans for, 221, 226–227; Southern, 376–378; opposition to and rejection of, 376–377
Second Great Awakening, 201–205, 232, 287, 324, 326–327, 331–332
Sectionalism, *see* Regionalization
Seddon, James, 404
Sedgwick, Catharine Maria and Elizabeth Dwight, 298
Sedition Act(s), *see* Alien and Sedition Acts
Segregation, *see* Education; Racism, AND SEGREGATION AND DESEGREGATION
Self-government: House of Burgesses as, 25; in the Chesapeake, 28; in Massachusetts Bay, 31; in New York, 44; in New Jersey, 45; in Pennsylvania, 45; as established in colonies, 62–63; strengthening of, 92; American vs. English definitions of, 108; colonists' pre-Revolutionary assumption of, 132; and republicanism, 366. *See also* Democracy; Vote
Selma, Alabama, 388
Seminoles and Seminole War, 230, 285, 287, 289, 290, 338. *See also* Indians
Seneca Falls Convention, 280, 332
Senecas, 55, 107, 145. *See also* Indians
Separation of powers, 175–176. *See also* Government, federal
Separatism, 29
Sergeant, John, 341
Seven Days' battles, 386
Seven Years' War, *see* French and Indian War
Seward, William H., 398, 400, 401, 410, 444–445
Sewing bee, 270

Sex roles, *see* Lifestyle, SEX ROLES

Sexual division of labor: as common to all civilization, 5; among Indians, 7, 8; in West Africa, 12, 13, 50; in Europe, 13, 14; and English-Algonkian conflict, 23; in colonial families, 81; and childrearing, 84; among blacks, 85; and Revolutionary War, 159–160; Iroquois shift in, 205–206. *See also* Lifestyle, SEX ROLES

Seymour, Horatio, 442

Shaker sect, 327–328. *See also* Religion

Sharecropping, 440

Shaw, Lemuel, 257

Shawnees, 46, 103, 106, 107, 136, 169, 171, 201, 222, 224, 226, 285, 286. *See also* Indians

Shays, Daniel, and Shays' Rebellion, 172–173, 189, 274

Shelburne, Lord, 150

Shenandoah Valley, 386

Sherman, Roger, 129, 140, 173, 175

Sherman, Gen. William Tecumseh, 410–412, 420, 423, 439

Shiloh, battle of, 386

Shoshoni (Shoshone) Indians, 7

Silk Road, 11

Silver, Spanish, 16

Sioux tribe, 8. *See also* Indians

Slater, Samuel, 249

Slaughter-House cases, 441

Slave Coast, 11

Slave Power, 356, 357, 364, 372, 398

Slavery, 310–316, 378; in the Chesapeake, 26; bases of, 47; establishment of, 47–48, 49–50; in South Carolina, 48, 52; culture of, 48, 313–316; in northern colonies, 50; and Georgia colony, 54; natural increase in, 79, 311; and plantation economy, 84–85, 298; artisans vs. field hands, 85; colonial escape attempts, 85; master-slave relations, 87, 312, 316, 439; and colonial patriots' fears, 120; and Revolutionary War, 134–135, 147–148; and Jay Treaty, 192; slave codes strengthened, 206; and Missouri Compromise, 232, 233, 234; and wage labor, 255, 362–363; as investment, 302, 311, 312, 317; size of holdings, 306; Quakers oppose, 309; and urban artisans, 319–320; and Republican party, 368; Lincoln on, 372, 378, 398, 399; and Civil War, 378, 383, 384, 415; blacks as freed from, 421–422, 432–433, 437–440 (*see also* Blacks, FREE)
CONDITIONS UNDER: family life, 86, 201, 315; paternalism, 307–308; working conditions, 310–311; punishments, 311–312
EMANCIPATION FROM: in North, 161; southern resistance to, 161; vs. equality, 162–163; turning away from, 206; and Missouri admit-

tance, 232; southern prohibition of, 291; owners' motives for, 292; and Civil War, 398–401, 407, 409
AND IDEOLOGY: republicanism, 155; revolutionary ideology, 160–161; U.S. Constitution, 175; states' rights, 369
REBELLIONS AGAINST: in colonial times, 85; Stono Rebellion, 93–94; and Stamp Act protest, 114; and Revolution, 204; Gabriel's Rebellion, 205, 316; free blacks as incentive in, 316; difficulties in, 316; by Denmark Vesey, 316; Nat Turner's, 316, 317, 319; whites' safeguards against, 317
AND SOUTHERN SOCIETY: economy, 298; southern women, 309; social system, 317–320, 377, 398; debate on, 319; criticism of, 320
AND WESTWARD EXPANSION, 232, 378; and slave families, 201; and Adams, 229; and Missouri Compromise, 232, 233, 234, 334; and antislavery movement, 324; and Texas, 348, 349; and Slave Power, 356, 372; in California, 358–360; in proslavery arguments, 362; and Kansas-Nebraska Act, 363–364; Bleeding Kansas, 369–370; and Dred Scott case, 371–372, 373, 374, 441; and practicality of slavery, 373
See also Abolitionism

Slavery, in Spanish colonies, 16, 47

Slavery, in West Africa, 40

Slave trade, 4, 51–53; African sources for, 11, 12–13; beginning of, 26; Equiano's account of, 40–41; colonial impact of, 41; into New Netherland, 43–44; magnitude of, 50; West Africa impact of, 50–51; slave ship conditions, 52–53; Indian slaves in, 54; closing of, 175, 231–232

Slave trade, into Europe, 15

Slave trade, trans-Saharan, 11

Smallpox, 4, 17, 35, 83, 90, 135

Smith, Adam, 241

Smith, Janie, 389

Smith, Capt. John, 23

Smith, Joseph, 329

Smith, Gen. Kirby, 386

Smith, Margaret B., 210

Smith, William, 70

Smuggling: by English colonists, 61, 63, 118, 121; after Embargo Act, 221

Social class: and Winthrop's vision, 30; and New England land distribution, 31; and slavery impact in the Chesapeake, 48; and Great Awakening, 95; and natural aristocracy, 156; and theater, 268; and public transportation, 271, 273; among slaves, 314–315; and southern tensions, 319–320; and Masonry, 335; and Whigs vs. Democrats, 343; and secession vote, 377; and Confederate war effort, 383, 391; and Civil

War conscription, 391, 407; and Reconstruction strategy, 434, 435, 437
CLASSES: "street rats," 274–275; urban elite, 275–276; middle class, 276; yeomen, 303–305; southern planters, 306
IN COLONIAL ERA, 70, 71; and colonial economic growth, 76; and church attendance, 88; and education, 89, 90; and government, 92; in anti-Stamp Act protests, 113, 114, 117; and Boston Tea Party, 123

Social mobility, *see* Mobility

Society of the Cincinnati, 158

Society of Friends, *see* Quakers

Sojourner Truth, 292–293, 332

Sons of Liberty, 114, 116, 119–120, 191–192

South: plantation life in, 79, 84–85, 298, 306–320; and partisan politics, 194; in War of *1812*, 226; economic development in, 234, 299–301, 302; transportation and regionalization in, 244; Indian removal from, 287–290, 299; free blacks in, 291, 292, 305–306; as slave society, 298, 317–320 (*see also* Slavery); and cotton, 299–301 (*see also* Cotton growing and industry); population distribution in, 301–302; wealth and income distribution in, 302; yeomen in, 303–305, 318–319 (*see also* Yeomen farmers); and national slavery debate, 348, 354, 356, 359, 360, 361; Democratic party in, 368–369, 374; secession of, 373, 376–377; in Civil War, 382, 383, 386, 387–391, 401–404, 405–406; Reconstruction in, 431–437
ATTITUDES AND VALUES IN: and North-South differences, 298, 354, 367; paternalism, 307–308, 311, 363; toward slavery, 319–320, 361–363, 398; from Civil War, 389; and Davis' ideology, 398

South Carolina: and Charles II reign, 43; founding of, 47; and West Africa, 48; slavery in, 52, 73, 86; blacks in, 48–49, 52, 84, 162; Indian slaves in, 54; Indian trade in, 54; and Yamasee War, 54; colonial government of, 63, 92; Indian-black antagonism in, 75; depression in, 80; Stono Rebellion in, 93–94; Regulators in, 94; and resistance against England, 134, 135; Revolutionary War in, 147–148; war debts of, 187; rice and sugar in, 299; urban population in, 302; and democratic reforms, 319; abolitionist literature burned in, 333; and federal power, 339; nullification, 339–340; electors in, 341; secession of, 376; Sherman in, 412; in Reconstruction, 434–435. *See also* Carolinas; Charleston, South Carolina

Whitefield, George, 95
Whitman, Walt, 397
Whitmarsh, T.S., 248
Whitney, Eli, 248, 299
Wilderness, battle of the, 412
Wilderness Road, 201
Wilkes, John, 116, 120
Wilkinson, General James, 218
William III (of Orange), king of England, 63, 64
William and Mary, College of, 89, 140, 173
Williams, Roger, 34, 36
Wilmot, David, and Wilmot Proviso, 356, 371
Wilson, James, 173, 175, 176
Wine Islands, 58
Winthrop, Hannah, 128
Winthrop, John, 30–31, 35, 36, 64, 91
Wisconsin, 364, 407, 423; settlement of, 282
Wistar, Richard, 117
Witchcraft trials, 64–66
Wolfe, James, 104
Women: Indian, 8, 12, 32–33, 55; in West Africa, 12–13, 48; in Europe, 13; in colonies, 27–28, 48, 70, 77, 84, 85, 88, 89; among Puritans, 36, 58; as colonial patriots, 116–117, 118; in Revolutionary War, 143, 147, 159; and republican virtue, 154; and Second Awakening, 203–204, 327; on California frontier, 262; purity of, 279; and birth control, 279 (see also Birth control); on southern plantation, 308–309; slave, 311, 315; in Confederacy, 388–389; during Civil War, 394, 397; and Reconstruction, 433
BLACK: freed, 162, 277, 280; in Reconstruction, 433, 440–441
EDUCATION FOR: and republicanism, 154, 158–159; as teachers, 277–278; for upper-class southerners, 308
ROLES FOR: home role, 160; and charitable enterprise, 204; clothing made, 248, 249, 250; nurturing, 278, 294; public roles, 327. See also Lifestyle, SEX ROLES
WORKING: in textile mills, 250, 254, 256, 277, 291; wage-work for, 277, 280, 309; as teachers, 277–278, 280, 331, 389, 438; as nurses, 389, 397
See also Feminism

Woodbury, Levi, 342
Woodmason, Rev. Charles, 82–83
Woolman, John: . . . on the Keeping of Negroes, 87
Worcester v. Georgia, 288–289
Worth, Jonathan, 421
Wright, Lucy, 328
Wyoming, 355
Wythe, George, 140

XYZ Affair, 195–196

Yale College/University, 89, 173
Yamasees, 54. See also Indians
Yancey, William L., 373, 374
Yellow fever, 83, 85
Yeoman farmers, 201, 303–305, 318, 338, 369, 377, 389, 426, 435, 437
York Peninsula, 386
Yorktown, surrender at, 148–149
Young, Annie, 439
Young, Brigham, 329

Zenger, John Peter, 92
Zimbabwe (Bantu capital), 11